**Better Homes and Gardens®**

# COMPLETE GUIDE TO HOME REPAIR MAINTENANCE & IMPROVEMENT

## BETTER HOMES AND GARDENS® BOOKS

Editor in Chief: James A. Autry
Editorial Director: Neil Kuehnl
Executive Art Director: William J. Yates

Editor: Gerald M. Knox
Art Director: Ernest Shelton
Associate Art Directors: Randall Yontz,
  Neoma Alt West
Copy and Production Editors: David Kirchner,
  Lamont Olson, David A. Walsh
Assistant Art Director: Harijs Priekulis
Senior Graphic Designer: Faith Berven
Graphic Designers: Linda Ford,
  Richard Lewis, Sheryl Veenschoten,
  Thomas Wegner
Building and Remodeling Editor: Noel Seney
Building Books Editor: Larry Clayton

**Complete Guide to Home Repair,
Maintenance, and Improvement**
Project Editors: Larry Clayton, Noel Seney
Copy and Production Editor: David Kirchner
Graphic Designer: Richard Lewis
Illustrations: Graphic Center

**Research and Writing: James A. Hufnagel**
with valuable assistance from
  Robert L. Brightman, David Chase,
  David Haupert, and Richard V. Nunn

© 1980 by Meredith Corporation, Des Moines, Iowa
All Rights Reserved.
Printed in the United States of America.
First Edition. Third Printing, 1981.
Library of Congress Catalog Card Number: 77-74600
ISBN: 0-696-00050-4

# ACKNOWLEDGMENTS

Our appreciation goes to the following companies and agencies for their assistance in preparing this book:

Abitibi Corporation
Adhesive and Sealant Council
Air-Conditioning and Refrigeration Institute
American Gas Association
American Home Lighting Institute
American Olean Tile Company, a division of National Gypsum Company
American Plywood Association
American Standard, Inc.
American Wood Preservers Institute
Andersen Corporation
Arkla Industries
Armstrong Cork Company
Arno Adhesive Tapes
Asphalt Roofing Manufacturers Association
Azrock Floor Products, a division of Uvdale Rock Asphalt Company
The Bilco Company
Blaine Window Hardware, Inc.
Bostich, a division of Textron
Bradley Corporation
Brammer Manufacturing Company
Broan Manufacturing Company, Inc.
Burnham Corporation
Cadillac Plastic and Chemical Company
California Redwood Association
Carpet and Rug Institute
Carrier Corporation
The Celotex Corporation
Chamberlain Manufacturing Corporation
Charmglow Products
Chas. W. Goering, Plumbing-Heating-Cooling
Chicago Specialty Manufacturing Company
Closet Maid Corporation
Connor Kitchen Cabinets
Consolidated Edison Company
Culligan, Inc.
Duo-Fast Corporation
Elco Industries, Inc.
Evans Products Company
Fedders Corporation
Flintkote Building Products Group
Fluidmaster, Inc.
Formco, Inc.
Frank Paxton Lumber Company
Frigidaire, a division of General Motors Corporation
GAF Corporation
General Electric Company
Georgia-Pacific Corporation
Graber Company
Grant Hardware Company

H.B. Smith Company, Inc.
Homasote Company
Honeywell, Inc.
Hotpoint Division, General Electric Company
Hydronics Institute
In-Sink-Erator Division, Emerson Electric Co.
International Association of Wall and Ceiling Gypsum Drywall Contractors
Iowa Paint Mfg. Co. Inc.
Iowa Power and Light Company
IXL, a Triangle Pacific Company
Jacuzzi Research, Inc.
Johns-Manville Sales Corporation
Kaiser Aluminum and Chemical Corporation
Kemper, a Tappan Division
Kirsch Company
Kohler Company
Kwikset, a division of Enhart Industries, Inc.
Lennox Industries, Inc.
Leslie-Locke Co.
Lighting Corporation of America
Lightolier, Inc.
Magic Chef, Inc.
The Majestic Company
The Malta Company, a division of Philips Industries, Inc.
Marshall Manufacturing Company, Inc.
Masonite Corporation
Master Lock Company
The Maytag Company
Miami-Carey
Midwest Sales and Service
Minnesota Mining and Manufacturing Company
Montgomery Ward and Company
National Association of Home Builders
National Fire Protection Association
National Forest Products Association
National Gypsum Company
National Home Improvement Council, Inc.
National Kitchen Cabinet Association
National Paint and Coatings Association
National Retail Hardware Association
E.A. Nord Sales Company
NuTone Division, Scovill Housing Products Group
Oneida Heater Company, Inc.
Owens-Corning Fiberglas Corporation
Peachtree Doors, Inc.
Pease Company, Ever-Strait Division
Peerless Faucet Company
Plaskolite, Inc.
Portland Cement Association
PPG Industries, Inc.
Pratt & Lambert
Preway, Inc.
Progress Division, Lighting Corporation of America

QuickSet, a division of Spartek, Inc.
Red Cedar Shingle & Handsplit Shake Bureau
Reichhold Chemicals, Inc.
Resilient Floor Covering Institute
Reynolds Metals Company
Riviera Products, a division of Evans Products Company
Rockwell International, Building Components Division
Rohm and Haas Co.
Ronson, Consumer Products Division
Rust-Oleum Corporation
Sears, Roebuck and Company
Senco Products, Inc.
Sierra Marketing, Inc.
Standard Dry Wall Products
The Stanley Works
Steelcraft, an American Standard Company
Steel Window Institute
Superior Fireplace Company, a division of Mobex Corporation
Sylvania, a GT&E Subsidiary
Thermador Wasteking Division of Norris Industries
Thomas Industries, Inc.
Tile Council of America, Inc.
Trine Manufacturing, a Square D Company
Tub Master Corporation
United States Department of Agriculture
United States Department of Energy
United States Department of Housing and Urban Development
United States Gypsum Company
Universal-Rundle
Vega Industries, Inc.
Vistron Corporation
Weiser Lock, a division of Norris Industries
Wessel Hardware Corporation, a subsidiary of Shelburne Industries, Inc.
Western Wood Products Association
Weyerhaeuser Company
Whirlpool Corporation

Our sincere thanks also go to the following people who have played significant roles in the development and production of this book: Don Dooley, Duane Gregg, Ann Levine, Douglas Lidster, Stephen Mead, Chris Neubauer, William C. Schuster, Linda Smith, Hugh Stirts.

**About the writer:** James A. Hufnagel is a New York City free-lance writer and editor. Formerly he was senior writer for *Better Homes and Gardens Magazine*, contributing editor to *Apartment Life Magazine*, and *Building Ideas*. We greatly appreciate his efforts on this book.

# ABOUT THIS BOOK

The early 1950s saw a fundamental change in the way America lives. During that time period, families were buying homes at a rate never equalled before or since. Budgets often were tight and skilled help hard to find, so many an accountant, barber, or salesman found himself serving as a weekend handyman as well.

To help unhandy men become handy, the editors of Better Homes and Gardens introduced a looseleaf, thumb-indexed guide to hundreds of around-the-house repair and improvement jobs—the *Handyman's Book*, first published in 1951. In the decades since then, more than 3½ million people have looked to and received assistance from this homeowner's classic.

Subsequent revisions kept the original *Handyman's Book* current for the families of the '60s and '70s. But as the '80s approached, Better Homes and Gardens' editors began to see changes not only in America's homes, but also in their owners. For instance, the recent increase in

single-parent households means that not all would-be handymen are necessarily men. Materials have come a long way, too, since the days of linoleum floors and galvanized steel plumbing systems. And energy, which once was cheap and plentiful, now must be carefully conserved.

To meet the needs of today's new generation of homes and homeowners, the editors decided it was time to replace the *Handyman's Book* with an all-new version—a monumental task that required more than four years of painstaking planning, researching, illustrating, writing, editing, and checking.

The result of their efforts is before you now. With more than 2,700 illustrations and nearly 600 different topics, it delves into just about every single one of your home's myriad components—telling how each works, how you can maintain and repair it, and ways you can make it look or function better.

Better Homes and Gardens' new *Complete Guide to Home Repair, Maintenance, and* improvement is divided into four broad sections—"Inside Your Home," "Outside Your Home," "Your Home's Systems," and "Basics You Should Know." Each opens with a page-by-page listing that enables you to find exactly what you want to know about a particular subject without hunting through page after page of unrelated material.

The sections then break down into a series of chapters, each dealing in depth with one of the book's major subject areas. Again, each chapter is carefully organized to help you quickly locate the information you need.

Most of the chapters that make up the first three sections open with cutaway drawings that show you just what's under a floor, behind a wall, or on top of a roof. Study these before you tackle a job to get a good idea of what's in store for you. Next, step-by-step drawings depict cures to virtually all the ills that can afflict a house—from a damp basement to a crumbling chimney top. Consult these

pages—identified by finder heads in their outer margins—to solve any repair or maintenance problem.

Be warned, though, that success at a few fix-it projects may very well entice you to try some of the home improvements covered in the latter part of each chapter. Here's where you'll learn—to give just a few examples—how to lay new flooring, put up (or take down) an interior wall, install a fireplace, increase the energy efficiency of heating and cooling equipment, or build a patio, deck, or even an entire garage.

Keep this organization in mind—cutaway drawings, problem-solving helps, and improvement projects—and you'll soon know your way around your home's interior, exterior, and various systems.

Finally, whenever you have questions about a particular tool, technique, material, or finish coating, turn to the final "Basics" section. You'll find a wealth of valuable reference material, also organized to give you answers in a hurry.

# CONTENTS

## SECTION 1

# INSIDE YOUR HOME

## SECTION 2

# OUTSIDE YOUR HOME

# INSIDE YOUR HOME

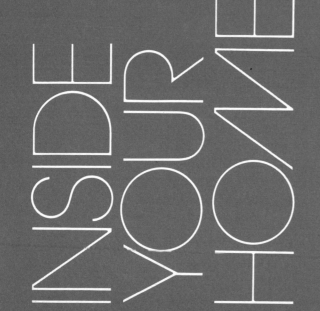

Squeaky hinges, cracks inching across a ceiling, windows that won't budge—you don't have to look hard to find at least a few things that need tending to inside your home.

And it's inside that most homeowners are first bitten by the improvement bug. You get to thinking about how a few shelves could help organize a room, and pretty soon you're on your way to the lumberyard.

"Inside Your Home" shows how you can keep interior repair and maintenance problems at bay—and takes you step by step through just about any indoor home improvement project you might contemplate. In fact, the only inside items not covered here are painting and wallpapering (see pages 488–509), and plumbing, electricity, and your home's other systems (turn to Section 3).

# FLOORS AND STAIRS

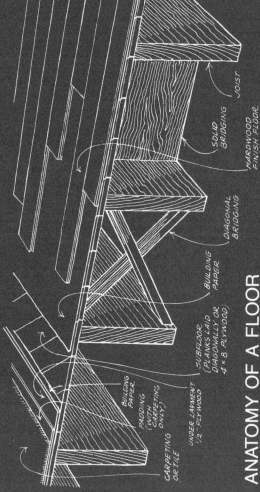

Labels on the anatomy diagram:

- JOIST
- SOLID BRIDGING
- HARDWOOD FINISH FLOOR
- DIAGONAL BRIDGING
- BUILDING PAPER
- SUBFLOOR (PLANKS LAID DIAGONALLY OR 4 x 8 PLYWOOD)
- UNDERLAYMENT ½" PLYWOOD
- PADDING (WITH CARPETING ONLY)
- BUILDING PAPER
- CARPETING OR TILE

## ANATOMY OF A FLOOR

## SOLVING FLOOR PROBLEMS

### SILENCING SQUEAKS FROM ABOVE

Most hardwood floors will develop squeaks at some time or another. Study the section view above and you can see why. The 2x8-, 10-, or 12-inch *joists* stretch from exterior wall to exterior wall; *bridging* stiffens the joists and keeps them from twisting; and the *subfloor* adds still more rigidity to the joists. *Building paper* quiets floors by separating the subfloor and the underlayment or the finish floor. And the *underlayment* strengthens floors, and provides a smooth base for the *finish floor*.

Changes in humidity cause these various wood members to swell and shrink at different rates. The result: squeaks wherever boards rub against each other or against nails. If joists below the squeaks are exposed, start with the techniques on the opposite page. If they're concealed, you'll have to work from above.

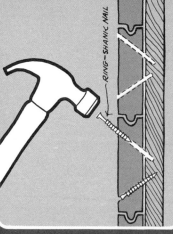

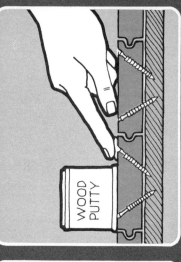

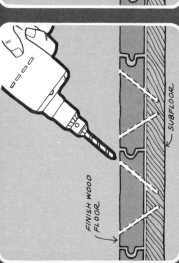

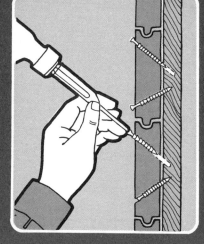

To quiet a loose board from above, nail it to the subfloor. Drill pilot holes so the wood won't split, angling them as shown.

Labels: FINISH WOOD FLOOR, SUBFLOOR, RING-SHANK NAIL

Now drive ring-shank or cement-coated flooring nails. Both have excellent holding power. Smooth nails might work loose.

Using a nail set, countersink the nail heads about ⅛ inch below the surface. Then test the board for squeaking.

WOOD PUTTY

Finally, conceal the nail heads by filling the holes with wood putty. Mound it slightly, then sand flush when it's dry.

# SILENCING SQUEAKS FROM BELOW

If your basement ceiling isn't finished off, you can readily diagnose and treat squeaks from below. Watch from there while someone walks over the noisy spot. Does the subfloor move, or do the joists themselves twist slightly? No movement at all may indicate that the finish floor has pulled loose.

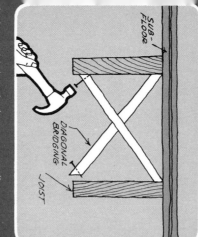

If the bridging isn't snug, pull loose nails and drive larger ones at an angle. If squeaks persist, add bridging as shown at right.

Use a tapered shim to tighten up of the loose subfloor boards. Dip the tip of the shim in glue and tap until the wedge is snug.

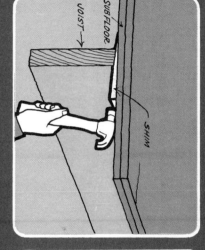

To quiet squeaks between joists, add solid bridging. Toenail it to the subfloor first, then end-nail through joists.

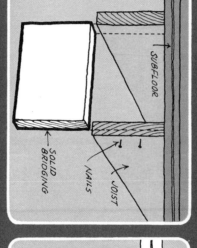

To tighten up a series of loose boards, force pieces of 2x4 up against the subfloor. Then secure the 2x4s to the joists with nails.

Pull down loose finish floor boards by driving 1- or 1¼-inch round-head screws. Drill pilot holes; fit the screws with washers.

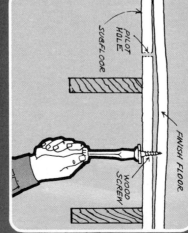

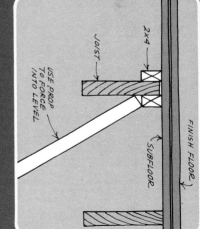

---

## LIFTING A SAGGING FLOOR

Weak or improperly spaced joists will cause a floor to sag. To solve the problem once and for all, install an adjustable jack post. First, open the basement floor and pour a 24x24-inch concrete pad for the post to sit on. Turn the jack until it's snug against joists, then raise a quarter turn more. Wait a week or so and make another quarter turn, if needed. Follow the same schedule until the floor is level. Don't lift faster or you may cause structural damage.

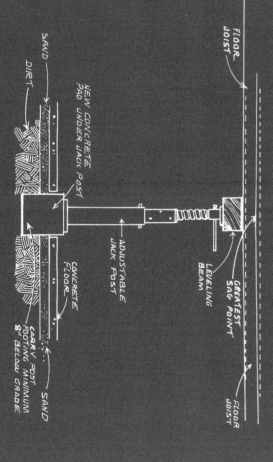

## PATCHING WOOD FLOORS

Warped, splintered, or curled floor boards not only look unsightly, they can be dangerous underfoot. But how can you

pull up and replace a section of a floor that's totally interlocked with tongues and grooves? Actually the job's not difficult; you can split off the bottom edge of a groove and drop a new board into place.

To replace a damaged board or series of boards, use the technique shown

below. You'll need to square off the area around the damage, make cuts with a circular saw and chisel beyond each end of the area, pry out the board(s), then slip new ones into place.

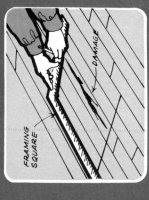

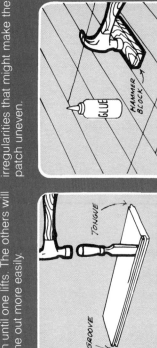

Use a framing square to accurately mark the outline of the patch. Align it with the edges of the nearest sound boards.

Now make a "pocket cut" (see page 410). Use an old blade (or a nail-cutting blade); you'll probably encounter some nails.

Pull any old nails remaining in the subfloor. And check for any other irregularities that might make the patch uneven.

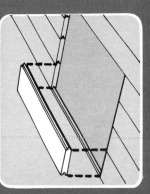

Carefully cut the new boards for a snug fit. Then fit the groove of each new piece to the tongue of the adjacent board.

Blind-nail each board at a 50-degree angle through its tongue. The next board's groove will conceal the nail heads.

When you get to the last board, turn it over and chisel away the lower part of its groove. Note how the boards will interlock.

Slip or drive a pry bar between two boards and work it back and forth until one lifts. The others will come out more easily.

Apply glue to the subfloor, tongue, and half-groove, then tap the piece into place. Use a hammer block to protect the surface.

## REMOVING SCRATCHES

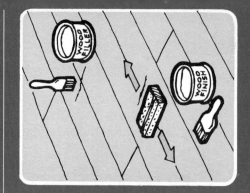

Erase surface cuts (left) with steel wool and a solvent, such as cleaning fluid. Rub with the grain, rinse, and refinish.

Sand deeper cuts (right), then work in wood filler with a brush. Let the filler set overnight, sand with the grain, and refinish.

12

# REFINISHING WOOD FLOORS

Rent the proper equipment and you can strip any floor down to smooth, bare wood in a single day. The equipment

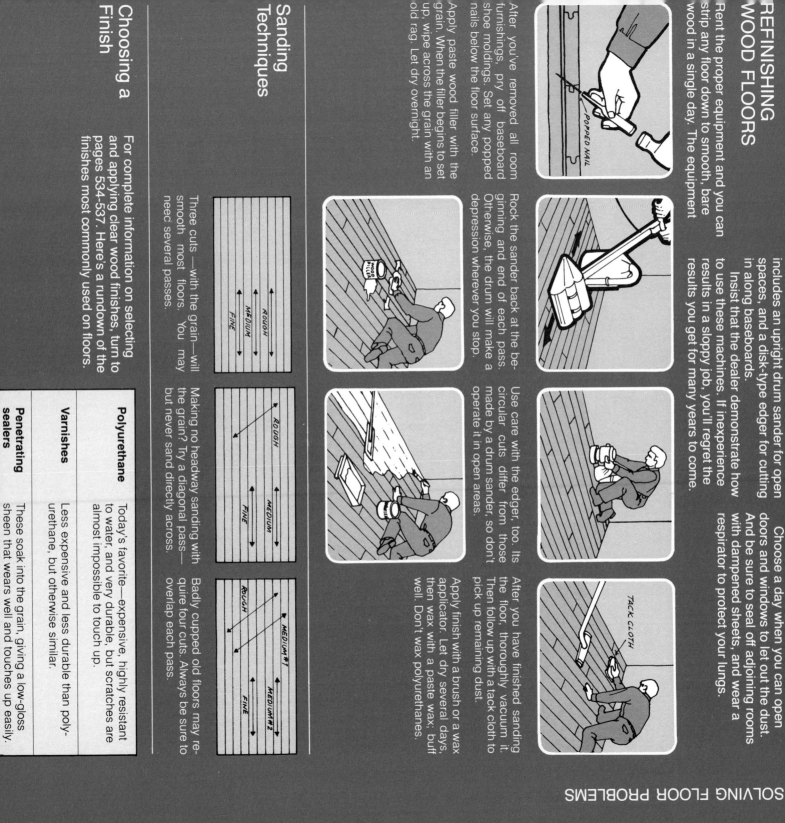

POPPED NAIL

TACK CLOTH

FILLER

ROUGH
MEDIUM
FINE

ROUGH
MEDIUM
FINE

MEDIUM #1
MEDIUM #2
ROUGH
FINE

includes an upright drum sander for open spaces, and a disk-type edger for cutting in along baseboards.

Insist that the dealer demonstrate how to use these machines. If inexperience results in a sloppy job, you'll regret the results you get for many years to come.

Choose a day when you can open doors and windows to let out the dust. And be sure to seal off adjoining rooms with dampened sheets, and wear a respirator to protect your lungs.

Rock the sander back at the beginning and end of each pass. Otherwise, the drum will make a depression wherever you stop.

Use care with the edger, too. Its circular cuts differ from those made by a drum sander, so don't operate it in open areas.

After you have finished sanding the floor, thoroughly vacuum it. Then follow up with a tack cloth to pick up remaining dust.

Apply finish with a brush or a wax applicator. Let dry several days, then wax with a paste wax; buff well. Don't wax polyurethanes.

## Sanding Techniques

After you've removed all room furnishings, pry off baseboard shoe moldings. Set any popped nails below the floor surface.

Apply paste wood filler with the grain. When the filler begins to set up, wipe across the grain with an old rag. Let dry overnight.

Three cuts —with the grain—will smooth most floors. You may neec several passes.

Making no headway sanding with the grain? Try a diagonal pass—but never sand directly across.

Badly cupped old floors may require four cuts. Always be sure to overlap each pass.

## Choosing a Finish

For complete information on selecting and applying clear wood finishes, turn to pages 534-537. Here's a rundown of the finishes most commonly used on floors.

| Polyurethane | Today's favorite—expensive, highly resistant to water, and very durable, but scratches are almost impossible to touch up. |
| --- | --- |
| Varnishes | Less expensive and less durable than polyurethane, but otherwise similar. |
| Penetrating sealers | These soak into the grain, giving a low-gloss sheen that wears well and touches up easily. |

13

## PATCHING TILE FLOORING

Most resilient tiles lift out easily once you apply some heat to soften the adhesive underneath them. To do this, use a heat lamp or an electric iron, working carefully

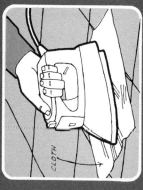

to make sure that you don't mar the adjacent tiles.

If you can't raise a corner, use a chisel, working out from the center to the edges. Once the tile is removed, scrape all old adhesive off floor so new tile will lie flat.

Different types of tile require different adhesives. To save yourself some

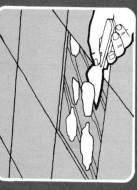

confusion, follow the recommendation of the salesperson from whom you make the purchase.

To make the new tile look less conspicuous, rub off the gloss with fine steel wool or a solvent such as spot remover or lighter fluid.

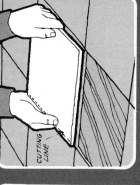

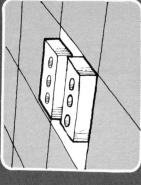

Check to see if the new tile will fit and lie perfectly flat. If not, mark as shown. Pay attention to pattern matches, too.

SoftEn the tile by working a medium-hot iron over its entire surface. Be careful not to overlap onto adjoining tiles.

Slip the blade of a putty knife under one corner and lift as shown. Don't pry against the edges of surrounding tiles.

Scrape away as much of the old adhesive as possible. You may need sandpaper to remove it from the edges of adjoining tiles.

Again, use an iron to make the new tile pliable . . . or heat it in the oven. Protect the tile's surface with a pressing cloth.

If the new tile is just a little too large, sand the edges. If you must cut, use a sharp knife and a straightedge as shown.

Apply a thin coat of adhesive with a serrated spreader (available from tile dealers). Some adhesives simply brush on.

Don't slide the new tile into place. Stand it on edge against an adjoining tile, then drop it into position. Weight well.

## SOLVING OTHER TILE PROBLEMS

Generally, heat is also the answer for tiles that have come partially unglued. Exceptions to this are asphalt and vinyl asbestos tiles, which you'll have to remove by chipping from the center out with a chisel. Work an iron (protected by a pressing cloth) back and forth until you can peel up the curled corner, then remove as much of the old adhesive from the tile as possible. The more adhesive you can remove, the better the repair you can make.

If the tile has cooled, be sure to heat it again, then apply a thin, even coat of adhesive to the tile. Stand on the corner

of the tile to press it into place, wipe off any excess adhesive with a damp cloth, then weight down the tile with a heavy object of some sort.

Often, you can remove stains by scrubbing them with a mild detergent solution. However, if that doesn't work, try a white appliance wax. As a last resort, scour the stains with very fine steel wool and a household cleanser.

Scouring—plus some careful scraping with a sharp knife—will also remove shallow burns. For scratches, use the techniques that are explained on the opposite page.

14

# PATCHING SHEET FLOORING

Most sheet flooring is fastened to the floor with a bed of adhesive, but some of the newer types, designed especially or do-it-yourself installation, require

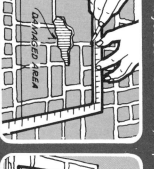

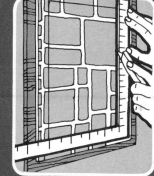

adhesive only at seams and edges, or no adhesive at all (see page 27).

If the entire floor has been laid in adhesive, you can usually work a putty knife underneath a piece and peel it up for replacement. But first, it may be necessary to apply heat. To make the patch as inconspicuous as possible, take

the time to carefully match its pattern to the surrounding area.

To patch the newer types of sheet flooring, simply cut around the damaged area, lift out a section, and cement a new one in its place.

Use a framing square to mark and cut around the damaged area's perimeter. Slice through flooring with a linoleum or utility knife.

Now lay the cutout atop a piece of matching material and carefully trace around it. Accuracy is essential for a good fit.

Scrape or clean the underlayment well, then test the patch for fit. If it's too snug, sand the edges slightly.

Apply adhesive with a serrated spreader, align one edge (match the pattern, too), and lower the new section into place.

Guide your cuts with the square or other straightedge. A scrap of plywood helps prevent scoring the surface underneath.

Wipe off any adhesive that might have oozed up around the edges, then weight the patch evenly for at least 24 hours.

# SOLVING OTHER SHEET FLOORING PROBLEMS

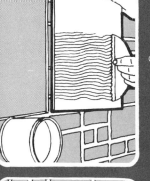

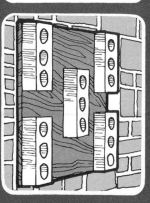

Many resilient floorings tend to heal themselves. In fact, if you fill shallow scratches with floor wax, they'll probably disappear in time. For deeper cuts, try compressing the edges by dragging a worn coin along them.

If the material has torn all the way through, lift the wound's edges, scrape away any old adhesive, apply fresh adhesive, and stick them down again. For the repair to lie flat, you may need to sand one edge.

If a blister develops in your flooring, flatten it by making a clean cut through its center. Press down on one of the cut edges, work adhesive underneath, and apply weight.

Filling small holes in vinyl floorings is a more hefty assignment, but one that's accomplishable nonetheless. The best

and quickest way is to fill the void with a special seam-welding product offered by the manufacturer of the covering. This product actually dissolves the vinyl then sets up again to complete the repair.

Or, scrape flakes from a piece of scrap and grind them into a powder. Next, mix the powder with clear lacquer or nail polish to make a putty-like paste. Work the paste into the hole, packing it well and mounding slightly to compensate for shrinkage. After the paste dries, sand the repaired area and wax.

# SOLVING STAIR PROBLEMS

Examine these drawings and you'll see that your home's staircase has many parts . . . all of them interlocked with sophisticated joinery that's usually concealed from view.

The basics are simple enough: a pair of *stringers* slopes from one level to the next. The composite illustration at right shows both "open-" and "closed-stringer" staircases.

The stringers support a series of steps called *treads*. A very simple staircase—such as you might have to the basement or a deck—consists of little more than stringers and treads.

Complications begin when *risers* are added to fill the gaps between treads. Finally, a *balustrade*—including the *handrail, balusters,* and a *newel post*—provides safety.

You can treat most of the ills that afflict staircases with patience and a few hand tools, as shown on the opposite page. If you'd like to build a basic, open-riser staircase, see page 170.

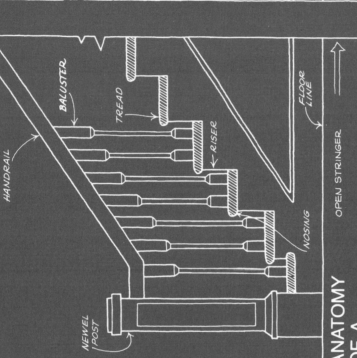

## ANATOMY OF A STAIRCASE

**Labels in illustration:** STRINGER, CLOSED STRINGER, FLOOR LINE, OPEN STRINGER, HANDRAIL, BALUSTER, TREAD, RISER, NOSING, NEWEL POST

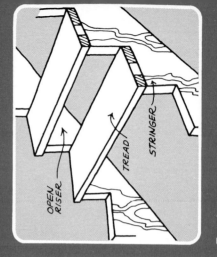

Treads on open-riser staircases usually are just nailed to the stringers. Note that this staircase also has open stringers.

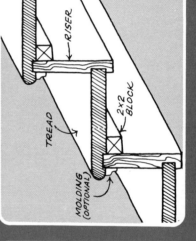

Treads and risers usually fit together with dado joints. Wood blocks underneath (optional) provide additional reinforcement.

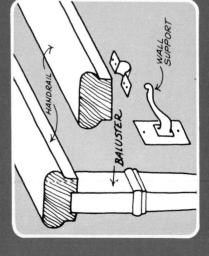

Some balusters fit into holes in the handrail and treads. Others are toenailed and glued. Brackets support wall-mounted rails.

16

# SILENCING SQUEAKS FROM ABOVE

Most stairway squeaks are the result of a tread rubbing against the top or bottom of a riser, or against a stringer. To pinpoint

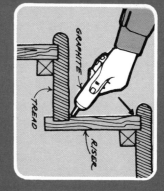

the source of the problem, rock your weight back and forth on each tread. If the tread moves, it's time for you to take corrective action—a loose tread can cause a dangerous spill.

Work from below if you can get at the underside of the stairs. Otherwise, you

have little choice but to attack the situation from above. A few well-placed nails, screws, or hardwood wedges should solve this problem.

# SILENCING SQUEAKS FROM BELOW

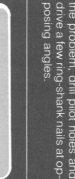

Lubricating stairway squeaks with powdered graphite may quiet them temporarily—but eventually the noise will return.

For a more permanent solution to the problem, drill pilot holes and drive a few ring-shank nails at opposing angles.

Or, drive wedges as shown. Coat wedges with glue, gently tap them into place, and let dry. Then cut off protruding ends.

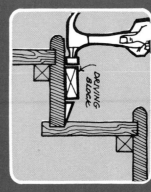

If your stairs aren't carpeted, you can tighten loose joints with molding. Nail into the riser as well as the stair tread.

Small wood blocks will tighten up tread-riser joints. Glue them to both surfaces, then secure with screws in each direction.

If the entire tread seems loose, use metal angles or a full-width cleat to make the repair. Wide steps may require three angles.

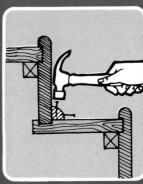

Wedges also are excellent for tightening up joints from below. If any existing wedges are loose, remove, reglue, and tap gently.

# TIGHTENING RAILS AND BALUSTERS

Wobbly handrails call for some detective work. Are the rails working loose from the balusters, or are the balusters parting company with the treads? You can cure either problem as shown here. If the rail is pulling away from a newel post, adapt these techniques. Loose newel posts require a pro's help.

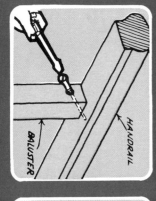

Drill at an angle through the baluster and into the rail or tread, then drive a long wood screw to tighten up the joint.

Or, work glue into the loose joint and drive nails through the railing's side. First drill pilot holes for the nails.

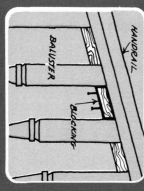

If the entire railing is loose, add blocking to its underside. Carefully cut angles for a snug fit, glue, and nail.

# LAYING NEW FLOOR MATERIALS

## CHOOSING AND BUYING WOOD FLOORING

Wood flooring comes in strips, planks, and blocks. Strip flooring, by far the most common, typically measures 2¼ inches wide. Plank flooring is wider—3 to 8 inches—and often is installed as a combination of several different "random" widths. Most block (or parquet) flooring consists of strips that have been glued together into squares or rectangles.

You can purchase all of these types finished or unfinished. Prefinished flooring costs more, and you must install

it with extreme care lest you mar the surface; unfinished flooring, on the other hand, must be sanded (see page 13) to smooth minor surface irregularities.

Flooring grades vary somewhat, depending on the kind of wood, but *clear* is generally the best, followed by *select, No. 1 common, No. 2 common,* and *1½-foot shorts,* which are remnants from the other grades.

Before you lay flooring, let the wood acclimate to the conditions at your house. Have it delivered at least 72 hours in advance and spread it out in the room where it's to be laid.

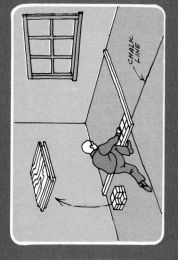

## LAYING A WOOD BLOCK FLOOR

One reason for the popularity of wood block flooring is that it's fairly easy to install, regardless of whether you're laying it in a basement or on-grade. You don't even need to use nails; adhesive will work just as well. On concrete, it's best to lay down a layer of polyethylene film, sleepers positioned 16 inches on center, and a subfloor material (see opposite page) before laying the flooring.

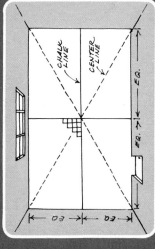

Plan the installation by squaring off the room with chalk lines and checking out what will happen at borders, as shown on page 26.

Lay a pair of 1x2s along the chalk lines and you'll get off to a square start. Tongue-and-groove edges keep later courses true.

## USING A POWER NAILER

Almost all wood flooring interlocks in tongue-and-groove fashion. To fasten it to your old floor or subfloor, blind-nail at a 45- to 50-degree angle through the tongue along the length of each board, then set the nail so that the groove of the next board will fit over the tongue of the one you've just nailed.

A power nailer—available from flooring and tool rental dealers—speeds the job and saves your back. Clips of special nails load much like staples into a stapler. Using a heavy flooring hammer, simply whap the machine's piston drive mechanism to set each nail. With one of these tools, you can lay several hundred square feet of flooring a day.

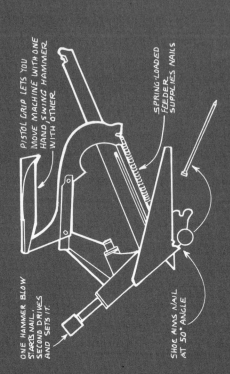

PISTOL GRIP LETS YOU MOVE MACHINE WITH ONE HAND; SWING HAMMER WITH OTHER.

SPRING-LOADED FEEDER SUPPLIES NAILS

ONE HAMMER BLOW STARTS NAIL— SECOND DRIVES AND SETS IT.

SHOE AIMS NAIL AT 50° ANGLE

18

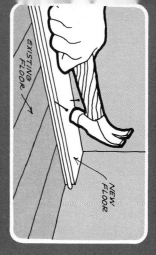

Always lay strip and plank flooring across the grain of existing floor boards. But if you're nailing directly to floor boards, the direction of the finished floor should be perpendicular to joists.

Start by sweeping the old floor well, setting popped nails, and removing baseboard moldings. Level bad dips by pulling up the old flooring, nailing shims to the joists, and re-nailing the old boards. You can smooth minor irregularities by laying heavy building paper before you begin (see page 25). Since wood swells and shrinks with humidity changes, leave a ⅜-inch gap between the floor and wall around the room's perimeter.

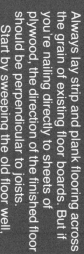

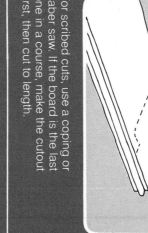

Place the groove of the first board ⅜-inch away from the walls. Blind-nail through the tongue at 12- to 15-inch intervals.

To keep the courses parallel, tap boards together before nailing. Protect the tongues from damage by using a wood scrap.

For scribed cuts, use a coping or saber saw. If the board is the last one in a course, make the cutout first, then cut to length.

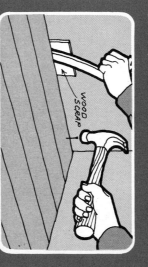

Measure carefully before cutting the last piece in each course—and don't cut off the tongue or groove you'll need at one end.

Pull the last few courses tight with a pry bar, protecting the wall with a wood scrap. You'll need to face-nail the last course.

To fit around irregularities, scribe a piece that's longer than you need with a compass (see page 402), or use a contour gauge.

## LAYING WOOD FLOORING OVER CONCRETE

Unlike parquet tiles, strip and plank flooring can't be cemented directly to concrete. If you don't want to build a subfloor, lay a polyethylene vapor barrier, fasten down 2x4 sleepers, then nail flooring to the sleepers. First, be sure the concrete is properly sealed against moisture (see page 102). And if the floor is cold, lay rigid foam insulation between the sleepers.

Attach sleepers to the floor every 16 inches. Secure them with adhesive or masonry nails (see pages 45 and 426).

Lay the flooring, cutting the strips or planks so joints are centered over sleepers—a must for sound floor construction.

## CHOOSING AND BUYING CARPETING

Carpeting offers a far wider variety of colors, patterns, and textures than anything else you can put underfoot. When considering the many options, first decide what fiber you want (see the chart below).

Next, ask about the *density* of the fiber or pile. Generally, the more fibers per square inch, the longer the carpeting will wear. The *height* and *texture* of the pile you select depends on personal preference.

Most carpeting is sold by the square yard in widths of 9, 12, and 15 feet. To compute roughly how many square yards you'll need, measure the room (in feet) at its widest and longest points. Then, multiply these two numbers and divide by 9. Now take your room's measurements to a carpeting salesperson who can figure the exact yardage requirements.

Be sure not to skimp on padding. A quality cushion prolongs the life of the carpeting, makes it more comfortable, and insulates against noise and cold. Here you can choose between felt and sponge-rubber types. Don't use a felt pad in high-humidity areas, or rubber over radiant-heated floors.

Integral-pad carpeting is bonded to its own cushioned backing. It's skid-proof, ravel-proof, and mildew-proof, which means you can lay it directly over a concrete basement floor. Installation is easy (see page 23).

Indoor/outdoor carpeting also can be laid without a pad. Its waterproof backing makes it a good choice for basements as well as for most outdoor locations.

Take a look, too, at the wide range of colors and fibers now available in carpet tiles. Most of these 12x12-inch squares come with a paper-protected self-stick backing that requires no adhesive. Lay them exactly as you would resilient tiles (see page 26).

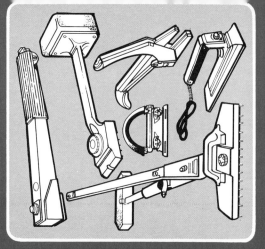

### COMPARING CARPET FIBERS

| Fiber | Properties | Relative Cost |
|---|---|---|
| Wool | The traditional standard against which other fibers are compared. Durable, resilient, and abrasion-resistant. Needs mothproofing. Fairly easy to clean. | Expensive |
| Acrylic | Closest to wool of all man-made fibers. Resists abrasion, mildew, insects, and crushing. Wide choice of colors. Some tendency to pill (form fuzz balls). Sheds dirt. | Moderate |
| Nylon | Strongest man-made fiber. Very durable and resistant to abrasion, mildew, and moths. Should be treated for static electricity. Hides dirt. | Wide price range |
| Polyester | Bright, clear colors. Cool to the touch. Resists mildew and moisture. Can be used anywhere. Susceptible to oil-based stains. Resists soiling. | Moderate |
| Polypropylene olefin | A key fiber in most indoor/outdoor carpeting. Extremely durable, moisture-resistant, and non-absorbent. Lower-priced versions tend to crush. Most stain-resistant of all. | Wide price range |

## TOOLS FOR LAYING CARPETING

No matter what job you're trying to accomplish, things go much more smoothly if you have the right tools for the job—and carpet laying is no exception. You probably already have on hand some of the tools you need: a utility knife, tape measure, metal cutter, straightedge, chalk line, and an awl. But if you plan to stretch in jute-back carpeting, you'll need to rent several items.

*Strip cutters* make quick work of cutting tackless strip, which fits around the perimeter of a room. A *staple hammer* does the same for fastening padding to wood floors. (You'll need pad adhesive if the floor is concrete.) Join pieces of carpeting using seam tape and a *seaming iron*. A *knee kicker* and a *power stretcher*, both of which have rake-like teeth, help you pull the carpeting taut. A dial on the knee kicker lets you adjust the depth of the kicker's bite according to the depth of your carpeting's pile. And a *carpet trimmer* neatly shears excess goods along walls.

With integral-pad carpeting (see page 23), you can get by without all the rented gear.

By installing carpeting yourself—a fairly difficult job—you can save a few dollars a square yard. But prepare yourself for some back-straining work, not the least of which is maneuvering the room-size pieces of heavy goods.

Prepare the room by removing all furniture, baseboard shoe moldings, doors (optional), and so on. Plane down any high spots on the floor, and fill wide cracks or dips with floor leveling compound. For badly worn floors, lay an *underlayment* (see page 25).

Now unroll the goods and check to make sure you have the correct carpeting in the amount ordered. Also check for defects.

## Installing Tackless Strip and Padding

By securing tackless strip to the floor, you create the framework over which carpeting is stretched and held in position.

When laying out the strip, make sure the pins face the wall or opening they're next to. Position them from ⅜ to ½ inch out from the wall. Then nail them in place.

If you're carpeting an area that joins a room with a floor covering other than carpeting, nail a special metal strip with gripper pins to the floor. In situations where the room adjoins another carpeted area, don't use tackless strip. Later, you'll seam the two pieces of carpeting together.

Next, lay the padding within the framework and cut it to size with a utility knife. One side of the padding will have a slick membrane covering it. Make sure this side faces up. Staple the padding in place, paying special attention to seam lines and edges. If the floor is concrete, roll back a section of padding at a time and spread pad adhesive. Lay the padding back in place.

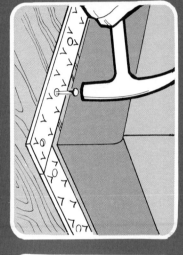

With pins facing the wall, nail the tackless strip to the floor. On concrete floors, you also can use adhesive.

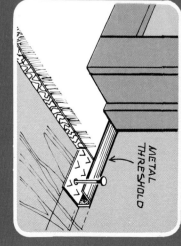

At openings onto wood, resilient, or hard-surface floors, use metal thresholds. Flatten the lip with a hammer to grip carpeting.

METAL THRESHOLD

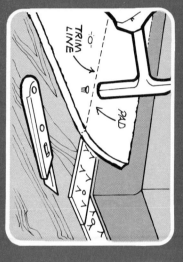

TRIM LINE
PAD

Nail or staple padding to wood floors. Glue it to concrete floors. Make sure padding doesn't overlap the tackless strip.

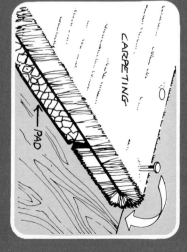

CARPETING
PAD

Another way to finish an edge is to fold the carpeting as shown. If you go this way, be sure to stop the padding short.

## Seaming Techniques

You once needed a heavy-duty needle, thread, and lots of patience to join two pieces of carpeting. Now most pros bond a special heat-setting tape to the backing, as shown at right.

First trim edges straight and butt them carefully. Now fold back both and lay tape along the floor where the seam will fall. Then move the heated iron slowly along the tape. As the adhesive melts, press the edges of the carpeting into it with your other hand.

Weight down the seam with a toolbox or other heavy object for a few minutes after joining the carpeting.

## Stretching and Trimming Techniques

Start by making a stretch with the power stretcher from the doorway to the opposite side of the room—1. (See the

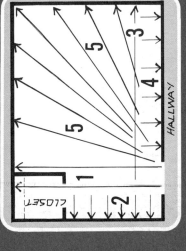

typical bedroom below.) A 2x4 straddling the doorway will give you a surface to stretch against. Then with your knee kicker, secure the goods to the wall adjacent to your stretch—2. Next, make another power-stretch away from the wall you've just kicked into—3. Kick the carpeting into the wall adjacent to your last stretch—4. Finish by power-

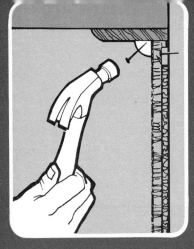

stretching the carpeting toward the far corner of the room working your first two stretch locations—5.

Trimming comes last. Start anywhere you want, and work your way around the perimeter of the room, using a utility knife or a special carpet trimmer. The trimmer will give better results. Replace base shoe molding, if desired.

Knee kickers and power stretchers force the carpeting's backing onto the tackless strip's pins. See copy above for how-to.

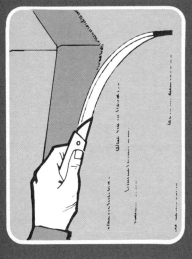

Trim off the excess, leaving ¼ inch to tuck between strips and the baseboard. Do the tucking with a wide-blade masonry chisel.

Finish off the job by replacing shoe moldings. Nail them to the baseboard, not the floor, as explained on page 38.

## Carpeting a Stairway

When carpeting stairs, you can use a strip left over from carpeting in an adjoining room, or purchase a runner. If you opt for a carpeting strip, use tackless strips to anchor it. If you decide on a runner, the best way to secure it is with stair rods.

To install carpeting with rods, first lay padding in one continuous strip from top to bottom. Tack it only at the top.

Next, spread the runner the entire length of the stairway. Starting at the bottom, fold under enough carpeting to cover one tread. Tack the excess against the bottom of the first tread or against the first riser, stretch the carpeting over the next step, and tack it temporarily at the back of the tread.

Screw an eye to each side of the riser—¼ inch above the tread and ½ inch from carpeting edges—slip a rod over the

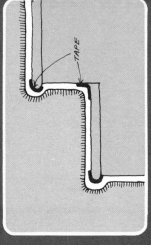

carpeting and through the eyes, and proceed to the next step. At the top, stretch the runner up against the last rise and tack it just under the nosing.

Because it involves tricky cutting and seaming techniques, carpeting stairs that turn or curve is something that's best left to professionals.

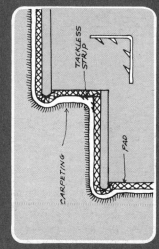

Instead of stair rods, you can use special tackless strips to secure carpeting. Lay the pad first, then install the strips.

Double-face tape works well for padless installations. Stick it to each nosing as well as to tread-riser joints.

22

# LAYING INTEGRAL-PAD CARPETING

Integral-pad carpeting is the easiest of all to install. You don't need tackless strips, a kicker, or separate padding. In fact, in small spaces such as baths, closets, laundries, or studies, you can cut the carpeting to fit and loose-lay it if you wish.

Edges do have a tendency to curl in time, though, so it's best to anchor bigger pieces of carpeting with double-face tape.

You can also lay the carpeting in adhesive (not shown), but with this type installation, the carpeting can't be taken up again without ruining it.

Prepare the room as you would for any other type of carpeting (see page 21). Also, be sure to clean the floor thoroughly before you begin the job. The tape won't adhere properly to a dirty surface.

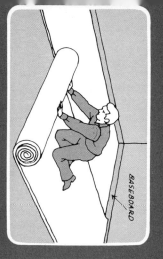

First, dry-fit the carpeting. If you must seam, make sure piles fall in the same direction. Allow about an inch extra all around.

To seam two pieces, fold back one piece and draw a line along the other.

Center double-face tape on the line and stick it to the floor. Double-check the seam before peeling off the tape's paper.

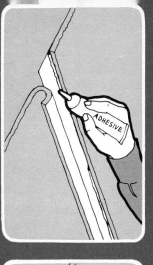

Press one piece of carpeting into place and apply a thin bead of seam adhesive along its edge to cement the backings together.

Smooth the seam with a rolling pin, pressing the carpeting firmly against the tape. Brush the pile lightly for an invisible seam.

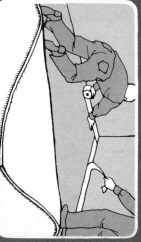

Now fold back the carpeting and make a border of tape around the room. Smooth the tape well before pulling off its paper.

Pull the carpeting taut, then drop it onto the tape. Smooth edges with your hands so the adhesive gets a good grip.

Finally, trim off excess around the edges with a sharp knife and tamp edges down. The pile will hide minor irregularities.

## CHOOSING AND BUYING RESILIENT FLOORING

Resilient flooring—so-called because it's softer underfoot than anything but carpeting—includes tiles and sheet goods. Tiles have been a popular do-it-yourself item since World War II, though they've changed considerably since that time in size (from 9 to 12 inches square), appearance (from dull, streaked greens and beiges to vivid colors and patterns), and composition (from asphalt to varying blends of vinyl).

Sheet goods have been around awhile, too, but because they come in bulky rolls up to 12 feet wide, installation is best left to a flooring contractor. An exception to this is cushioned vinyl, which you can lay according to the instructions on page 27.

Whether you choose to install tiles or sheet vinyl depends to some extent upon the use your new floor will get. Cushioned vinyl is soft underfoot, has a

minimum of dirt-catching seams, and does a decent soundproofing job. Tiles, on the other hand, are less expensive, easier to install (for how-to, see page 26), and more resistant to dents from items such as chair legs and pointed heels. For more comparisons, see the chart below.

Consider also whether you want a smooth or textured surface on your resilient floor. Smooth tiles and sheet goods mop up easily, show dirt more readily, and inevitably collect a few scuffs and dents that won't come out.

And before you buy the goods, be sure you're clear about the manufacturer's installation recommendations. Most of today's resilient floorings can be installed on any grade. A few, though, shouldn't be laid on concrete in contact with soil. Most shouldn't be applied over an existing resilient floor, either.

If an old wood floor is in good condition and has a subfloor underneath, you can successfully lay resilient materials directly over it. Otherwise, you'll have to put down an underlayment first (see

opposite page).

Since all but a few of today's tiles are one foot square, determining how many you'll need requires only simple computations.

Estimating the amount of sheet flooring needed is trickier, especially if there's a pattern involved and you have to seam somewhere. It's best to make an accurate plan of the room on graph paper and take it to the flooring dealer.

### COMPARING RESILIENT FLOORINGS

| Material | Properties | Cost |
|---|---|---|
| Sheet vinyl | Solid vinyl. Several grades are available. Must be laid by a professional. Vulnerable to burns, but quite durable otherwise. | Moderately expensive |
| Cushioned sheet vinyl | Several grades of this material available—from moderately durable to very durable. Resistant to abrasion and discoloration. Durability ranges from that of vinyl asbestos tile to approximately one-half as durable. Vulnerable to burns. This product usually contains a vinyl foam layer. | Wide price range |
| Roto sheet vinyl | Design is printed on a cellulose felt or mineral fiber backing, then coated with a thin film of vinyl. Easy to lay loose or with tape. Mineral-backed grade can be used from basement to bedroom. Cellulose-backed can be used only above grade. Less durable than other types listed. Vulnerable to burns and tears. This product usually contains a vinyl foam layer. | Wide price range |
| Solid vinyl tile | Basically the same composition and characteristics as sheet vinyl. Vulnerable to burns. | Moderately expensive |
| Vinyl asbestos tile | The most popular of today's tiles. It ranks just a notch below solid vinyl tile in durability. Good resistance to burns, impact, scuffing, dents, oil, and grease. Easy to install, especially if you choose adhesive-backed versions. | Moderately priced |
| Asphalt tile | A pioneer among resilient floor coverings. Durable but difficult to maintain; grease will soften it; poor recovery from indentation. Brittle composition makes it difficult to cut. | Inexpensive. |

## Installing Underlayment

Smooth badly worn wood floors with underlayment before you install resilient tiles or sheet goods. But make sure that the material you choose is suitable for use as underlayment (¼-inch or thicker hardboard or plywood will work well). If possible, buy 4x4-foot squares, as they're easier to work with than standard 4x8-foot panels. And it's also a very good idea to acclimate the panels to the room in which you plan to lay them. Accomplish this by standing them on edge for a couple of days.

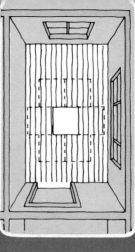

To secure the underlayment, you'll need lots of ring-shank flooring nails. Drive one every four inches across the face of each panel. Stagger the panels, and space them about 1/64 inch apart—approximately the thickness of a matchbook cover.

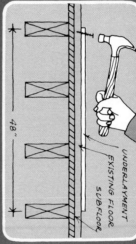

UNDERLAYMENT
EXISTING FLOOR
SUBFLOOR
48"

At edges, slide a full sheet against the wall, overlapping it with previously nailed panels and squaring it up with them.

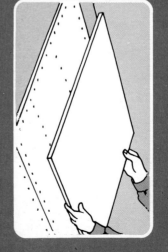

Begin at the approximate center of the room, and arrange the panels so you'll never have four corners converging at one point.

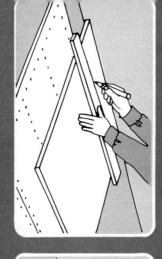

Tap with a hammer to locate a floor joist, then center one edge of the first panel over it and nail through the subfloor.

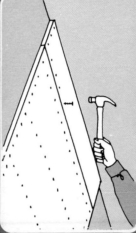

Next, using a scrap piece of underlayment as a guide, draw a line along the entire length of the border piece. Cut along line.

Lay the piece into place. Don't worry if it doesn't fit exactly—the base shoe will cover irregularities. Nail the border in place.

## Laying Building Paper

A blanket of building paper quiets wood floors and smooths out minor irregularities in both wood and resilient floors. Cut the paper in strips that will stretch from wall to wall. Lay it at right angles across old floor boards, or in any direction across underlayment.

Apply adhesive with a serrated trowel and unroll the paper. Butt edges of adjacent strips; don't overlap.

WATERPROOF ADHESIVE

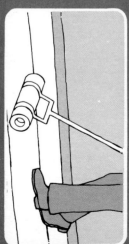

Smooth out bubbles with a flooring roller, which you can rent from a tile dealer. Or use an ordinary rolling pin.

# LAYING RESILIENT TILES

Self-sticking, adhesive-backed tiles make tiling a room easier than ever. To lay them, you simply peel off a paper backing, place the tile carefully, and kneel on it. If the brand you choose doesn't have an adhesive backing, buy a brush-on adhesive, not the trowel type used by professionals.

Most tiles come with instructions written for do-it-yourselfers. Pay particular attention to the way you must prepare your old floor or subfloor. (For wood floors, see page 25; for concrete, see pages 19 and 102.)

Start with a dry run, as shown below, so you'll end up with even margins at the room's edges. If borders will measure less than half a tile, shift the layout 6 inches for 12-inch tiles, and 4½ inches for 9-inch sizes. Put down the first tile with one corner at the center point.

Locate midpoints on opposite walls and snap the chalk lines as shown. Adjust, if necessary, so the lines make a right angle.

APPROX. CENTER

CHALK LINES

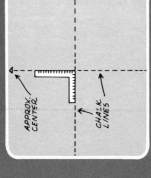

At edges, lay one tile squarely atop the last full one in that row. Place another flush against the wall, and mark as shown.

Dry-lay tiles in an L from center to two walls to get proper spacing. If necessary, shift the L half a tile, and snap new chalk lines.

BAD BORDER SPACING

PROPER BORDER SPACING

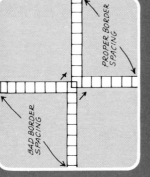

You can cut most tiles with a utility or linoleum knife. If you have difficulty doing this, simply warm the tile in an oven first.

To lay out a diagonal pattern, locate the exact center of the room and snap chalk lines to the walls at 45-degree angles.

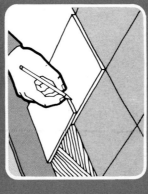

Now begin applying the tiles, starting with the L and building a pyramid. Be certain to keep tiles square with chalk lines.

Don't slide tiles into position. But edges against adjacent ones, lay in place, and press firmly. Pay attention to pattern matches.

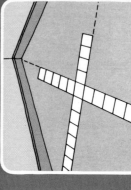

Inside or outside corners are also easy to cut. First, mark from one of the walls just as you would for a border tile.

Next, shift the two tiles to the other wall (but don't turn them) and mark again. Put an X on the section to be cut out.

For door frames and other shapes, mark as you would for a corner, then scribe details with a compass (see page 402).

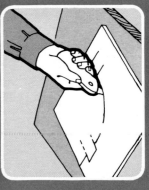

Dry-lay tiles along the lines, and adjust them for good border spacings. At the walls, you'll need to cut triangular pieces.

For a really interesting look, stop diagonals short of the walls and border the field with a course of conventionally laid tiles.

26

# LAYING CUSHIONED SHEET FLOORING

Though trickier than tiling, installing sheet vinyl is a manageable, one-day job—providing you choose the cushioned type that's designed specifically for loose laying.

The problem with laying sheet goods is that you must first roll out the material in a space that's bigger than the room you'll be flooring, then painstakingly transfer measurements from the room to the material. Or make a pattern first. If the temperature's about the same outdoors, you might want to consider doing this on a patio or driveway.

First, orient one edge of the vinyl to the longest and straightest wall, then make all measurements from this "starting edge." Allow a couple of inches extra at the other edges, and trim them off later. This margin lets you compensate for errors and corners that aren't square.

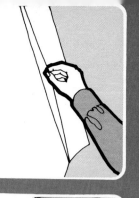

Make sure the starting edge of your material is perfectly true. If it isn't, snap a chalk line on the rolled-out vinyl and cut.

Cut the vinyl with a pair of heavy shears. Or, protect the floor underneath and use a straightedge and linoleum knife.

Double-check all measurements before cutting. In complicated situations, make a precisely scaled plan on graph paper.

When you move the material, roll it up so that the starting edge is outside. Position it against the starting wall.

As you unroll the vinyl, you may have to trim off the margin here and there before you can continue. Cut others to fit later.

Make tricky contour cuts after the material is in place. Mark them with a compass or a scriber (see page 402).

If you have to seam two pieces of sheet goods, overlap them, matching the pattern, and draw a line along the lower piece.

*DRAW LINE HERE*

Make a few marks, too, to help you align the two pieces of goods later. Tape the pieces together and continue measuring.

*ALIGNMENT MARKS*

For seams, overlap the edges and align your markings, then using a straightedge as a guide, cut through both thicknesses.

Clear seam of scraps and check that edges butt perfectly. Roll them back, apply a wide swath of adhesive, and press edges into it.

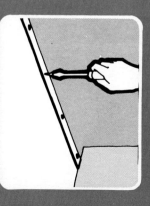

Secure goods around the room's perimeter by brushing on adhesive, then pressing on goods. Further secure with base shoe.

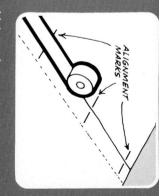

At doorways, protect raw edges with metal threshold strips. Put screws directly into the floor, not through the vinyl.

*STARTING EDGE*

## CHOOSING AND BUYING HARD-SURFACE FLOORS

Hard-surface floor materials—ceramic, mosaic, slate, and quarry tiles—come in myriad sizes, shapes, and colors. They're easy to maintain but some are difficult to install.

Bear in mind that floor tiles are heavier than wall tiles, and those with mirror-like glazes will be slippery when wet.

### COMPARING HARD-SURFACE TILES

| Material | Description | Installation |
|---|---|---|
| Glazed ceramic tile | Sizes range from 1x1 inch to 12 inches square. Most common size is 4¼ inches square by ⁵⁄₁₆ inch thick. Wide selection of colors, glazes, patterns, and shapes. | Moderately easy |
| Ceramic mosaic tile | Available in 1- and 2-inch squares and 1x2-inch rectangles, ¼ inch thick. These are mounted to sheets of paper or mesh. Very popular with do-it-yourselfers. | Easy |
| Pre-grouted tile | Individual or mosaic-sized units also bonded to big sheets, but with flexible, pre-grouted joints. Quick installation, but relatively expensive. Limited selection. | Easiest |
| Quarry and paver tile | Made from natural clays in large sizes, 6- to 8-inch squares, and 4x8-inch rectangles. Normally ½ inch thick (some paver tile is available in ⅜-inch thickness). Earthen colors in reds, browns, and buffs; also available in a variety of irregular shapes suitable for both indoor and outdoor use. | Fairly difficult. |
| Special-purpose tile | Usually larger than 7 inches, with sizes up to 1 foot square, ½ inch thick. Widest selection of colors, glazes, patterns, designs, and shapes. | Difficult |

## PREPARING YOUR FLOOR FOR HARD-SURFACE FLOORING

Because hard-surface materials are brittle and inflexible, they can only be laid over a surface that's absolutely smooth and rigid.

Over wood floors, you must lay down an underlayment (½-inch exterior plywood concrete board) to prevent movement that could crack the grout between tiles. Install underlayment as explained on page 25.

Concrete also makes an excellent tile base. But check the floor carefully with a straightedge to locate any low spots, fill them with latex or vinyl cement, then sand smooth. Also, be sure to clean the floor thoroughly to ensure a good bond between flooring and base. A special dry-set mortar does a good job of bonding tiles to concrete, but don't use it over underlayment.

Next, lay out the job so you'll have full tiles at the doorway, as shown at right.

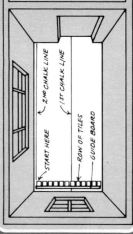

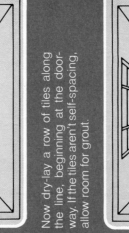

Now dry-lay a row of tiles along the line, beginning at the doorway. If the tiles aren't self-spacing, allow room for grout.

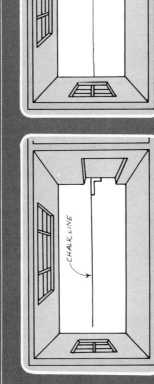

First, snap a chalk line from the doorway to the opposite wall. Note that this line must be perpendicular to the door.

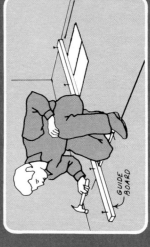

Adjust this row for even borders (see page 26). Snap a second line from the point where the border begins. Start laying here.

Nail a guide board perpendicular to the chalk line at the point where the last full tile will be. Dry-lay along the board.

28

Ask your dealer to recommend an adhesive and grouting material for the tiles you've chosen. Unlike wall tiles, floor tiles have no spacer lugs to set them the proper distance apart, so make your own spacers in the width required for the grouting you'll be using. Lay the tiles as shown here, then grout them as you would wall tiles (see page 43).

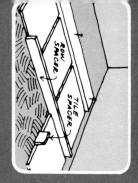

Use tile and row spacers to set each tile apart from its neighbors. Make them from strips of wood or scrap tile.

Fit borders last. Mark pieces as you would with resilient tiles (see page 26), then trim them with a tile cutter (see page 42).

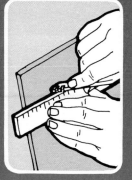

You also can trim tiles with a glass cutter and straightedge. First, score the tile as shown. Try for one deep, even cut.

With a serrated trowel, spread out about two square feet of adhesive. Its ridges should be full, valleys almost bare.

Drop, don't slide, tiles into position, then twist slightly for even adhesion. Level them by laying down a board and pounding.

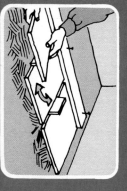

Now place the tile, scored side up, at the edge of a board and snap it with a downward motion. Smooth the cut edge with a file.

## LAYING MOSAIC TILES

Mounted on 1x1- or 1x2-foot sheets (and faced with paper or backed by non-removable mesh), mosaics go down much faster than individual tiles. And you needn't worry about equalizing borders. Square up the room with guide boards (see opposite page) and begin laying from a corner. Use spacers so gaps will be the same.

Mark for border cuts on the underside. Cut sheets between tiles by snipping the paper with a sharp knife or scissors.

Cut tiles themselves by nibbling at them with tile nippers. To make a hole, cut a tile in half, nibble notches in either side.

Align edges of the sheets carefully, lay in place, and twist slightly. Peel back paper to check that tiles line up.

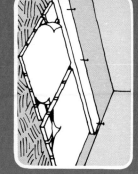

After you've laid several sheets, tamp them into the adhesive by pounding on a piece of plywood. Wipe off any excess mastic.

After the adhesive sets up, soak the paper thoroughly with warm water and, starting in a corner, peel it off.

A squeegee simplifies grouting floor tiles. Pack grout into each joint, then scrape off excess. More about grouting on page 43.

# INTERIOR WALLS

Unless you take on a major remodeling project, you may never have occasion to break into an interior wall. Often, though, you need to know what's inside—and where—before you can even hang a heavy picture.

All wood-frame walls begin with a *sole plate* nailed to the subfloor. The plate supports vertical *studs*, which are in turn nailed to a *top plate*.

Around any opening, the studs are "doubled up" for extra rigidity, and topped off with a *header*, usually a pair of 2x4s or 2x6s installed on edge. Some walls also include horizontal *fire blocking*, usually at the four-foot level.

Finally comes the wall's *surface*, the only element you actually see. This might be gypsum-board drywall, as shown here; plaster, as illustrated on the opposite page; or paneling, as shown on pages 37 and 44-47.

## ANATOMY OF A DRYWALL PARTITION

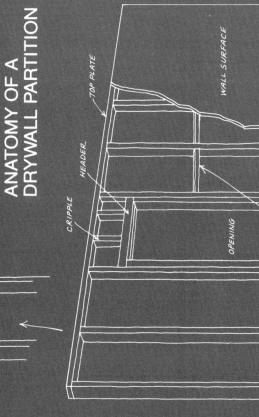

USUALLY DOUBLE TOP PLATE FOR BEARING WALL

TOP PLATE

HEADER

CRIPPLE

OPENING

WALL SURFACE

SOLE PLATE

FIRE BLOCKING (OPTIONAL)

STUD

## HOW TO IDENTIFY A BEARING WALL

Carpenters say all walls divide into two structural categories—*bearing* walls, which help support the entire house, and *nonbearing* walls, which support only themselves. Remove or make a big opening in a bearing wall and you could literally bring down the house.

To determine whether a wall is bearing or not, you'll have to do some sleuthing in the basement or attic—wherever there are exposed joists or rafters. If these run *parallel* to the wall in question, you can be sure it's *not* a bearing type. If, however, they're *perpendicular* to the wall (as shown at right), you can be fairly sure it *is* bearing a load.

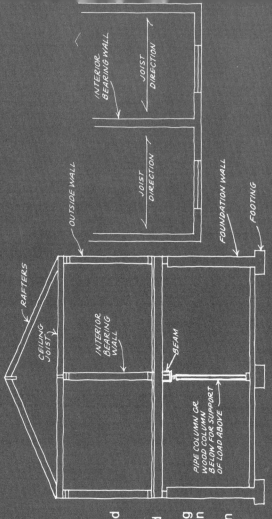

INTERIOR BEARING WALL

JOIST DIRECTION

JOIST DIRECTION

OUTSIDE WALL

FOUNDATION WALL

FOOTING

RAFTERS

CEILING JOIST

INTERIOR BEARING WALL

BEAM

PIPE COLUMN OR WOOD COLUMN BELOW FOR SUPPORT OF LOAD ABOVE

30

# ANATOMY OF A PLASTER WALL

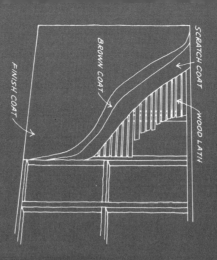

Most plaster or "wet" walls begin with *lath*—formerly narrow strips of wood, but more recently a heavy mesh called expanded metal lath or strips of drywall known as *rock lath* (not shown). The lath then gets three layers of plaster.

The first of these, the *scratch coat*, grips the lath. The second, or *brown coat*, smooths out the surface. Finally, a finish coat gives any texture from rough to glassy smooth.

First the studs must be covered with lath. But the same three coats might be applied directly to the masonry, as shown below.

Though a standard wall surface for many centuries, plaster has all but disappeared from modern-day homes. The reason: application is slow, highly skilled work—and even a good job is prone to cracks as the structure settles.

If your home has solid stone, brick, or block walls, the same three coats might be applied directly to the masonry, as shown below.

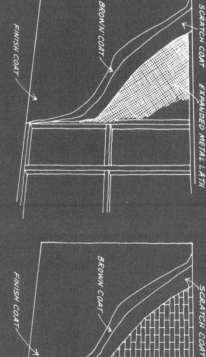

# HOW TO FIND STUDS

Almost anything you attach to a wall will be more secure if you can fasten it to one or more of the studs underneath. How, though, can you locate them without ripping open the drywall or plaster?

No one technique works for every situation, but all are based on the same principle—that most of the studs in a wall are spaced at regular intervals. This means that after you've found one or two, you generally can plot the others with a few measurements.

The drawings at right show four common ways to find that first stud. Begin your search toward the wall's center, not at the ends, where spacing might be irregular. Also ignore the studs on either side of a door or window opening.

Once you've pinpointed a stud, measure 16 inches—the most common spacing—in one direction or the other. If you can't find a second stud there, try 24 inches, a spacing now being used in some newer houses.

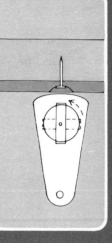 

Usually, you can "sound out" a wall by rapping along it with your knuckles. A solid *thunk* indicates you've found a stud.

If rapping doesn't tell you anything, look along the baseboard for any nails. They're usually driven in at stud intervals.

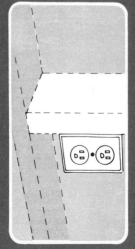

Or use a special magnetic finding device that homes in on nails or screws holding the wall surface to the studs.

Or take the face plate off of a receptacle located somewhere along the wall. Wall boxes almost always are nailed to a stud.

# SOLVING WALL PROBLEMS

## TEN WAYS TO HANG THINGS
### Light Objects

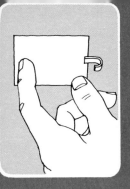

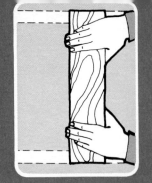

Ordinary picture hooks hold items up to about 20 pounds. With plaster walls, nail through masking tape to prevent crumbling.

Gummed hooks also do light-duty hanging. To remove these, moisten with warm water, peel off, then wipe away any adhesive.

### Medium-Weight Objects

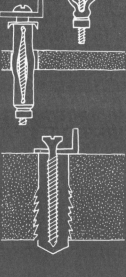

Plastic anchors grip the wall by expanding as you drive screws into them. Drill the proper size hole for a snug fit.

Hollow-wall anchors open up behind the wall's surface for an installation that can't pull loose. They work only in hollow walls.

Toggle bolts screw into spring-loaded wings that pop open inside the wall. Assemble with the fixture before inserting.

### Heavy Objects

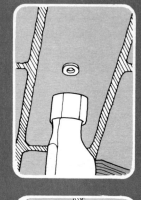

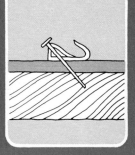

Nail or screw directly to the studs to provide excellent security for mirrors and the like. To locate studs, see page 31.

Better yet, bridge two or more studs with a piece of 1x4 or 1x6 lumber. You gain strength and aren't limited by stud spacings.

### Attaching to Masonry Walls

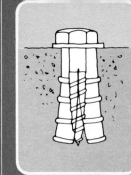

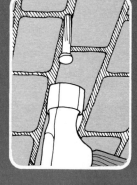

For more holding power, use a lead expansion shield and lag screw. The screw cuts its own threads as it goes in.

Or drill a hole and tap a fiber or lead anchor into it. These expand and grip as you drive screws into them.

Drive specially hardened masonry nails into concrete block or mortar joints. Use a heavy hammer and wear safety goggles.

Drywall—also known as *gypsum board* and *plasterboard*—consists of big sheets of pressed gypsum faced with heavy paper on both sides. After the panels have been nailed, screwed, or glued to the studs, the joints between them are covered with a perforated paper tape, then smoothed over with *joint compound* to create the appearance of a continuous surface.

Most repairs are easy once you get the knack of working with these unique materials. Besides ordinary hand tools, you'll need a can of premixed compound, a roll of tape, and a broad taping knife. More about working with drywall on pages 51-53.

## Filling Dents

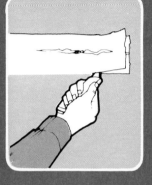

Sand the depression to roughen its surface, then pack with compound. If the patch shrinks as it dries, apply a second coat.

To blend in the repair with its surroundings, sand it very lightly —or smooth it out by wiping with a dampened sponge.

Joint compounds, being relatively porous, must be primed before you paint them. Some paints also serve as primers.

## Mending Split Tape

Begin by carefully pulling away the loose tape. Use a sharp knife at edges or you may pull off material from either side as well.

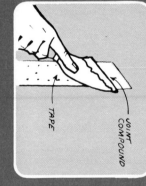

Apply compound to the wall, position the new tape, then smooth out any bubbles with light, vertical knife strokes.

While the compound is still wet, apply a second coat. Let it dry, then lightly coat again, feather out the edges, and sand or sponge.

## Setting Popped Nails

Press the panel against the stud, then drive new nails above and below the old one. Ring-shank types have better holding power.

"Dimple" each nail below the surface with your last hammer blow. Pull the popped nail and fill dimples with compound.

After the compound dries, apply a second thin coat, feathering it out at the edges. Wait a day, then sponge, prime, and paint.

# Patching Small Holes

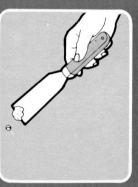

For very small holes, simply apply some patching compound to the void with a putty knife. After letting it dry, sand smooth.

Or try this technique. First cut a piece of perforated hardboard that's slightly larger than the hole. Tie fine wire to it.

Smear some compound on the hardboard, then slip it into the wall and pull the wire taut. This patch clings to the back of the wall.

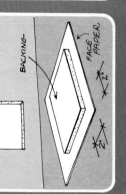

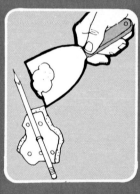

Tie the wire to a pencil and twist tight. After the patch dries, cut away the wire and pencil, then fill the recess.

To minimize shrinkage and cracking, fill with two or three thin coats, then lightly sand and sponge to blend in the repair.

# Patching Large Holes

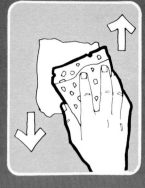

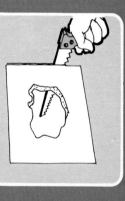

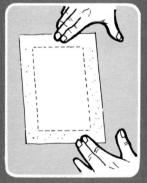

With holes up to about 8 inches wide, mark a rectangle around the damage, then cut it out with a keyhole saw.

Using a piece of scrap drywall, cut another rectangle two inches larger all around. Then cut as shown to make a plug.

Spread joint compound around the damaged area's perimeter. Also butter its edges. This will serve as an adhesive.

Press the patch into place, smooth the perimeter, and hold in place for a few minutes. Blend in by feathering with compound.

With larger holes, cut back to the centers of the nearest studs; toenail 2x2s top and bottom so you'll have wood to nail to.

Then nail in your patch, and tape and smooth the repair as shown on page 53. You'll need three coats for a really slick job.

SOLVING WALL PROBLEMS

# REPAIRING PLASTER WALLS

If your home has plaster walls, you may as well resign yourself to patching before every paint job. Certain harmless cracks—especially diagonals from a corner, door, or window—will return with annoying regularity no matter how many times you fill them.

Watch, though, for loose or crumbly cracks, holes, and bulges; these often mean there's a leak somewhere. (More about water-damaged plaster on the following page.)

Too much or too little water in the original mix also weakens plaster. That's why it makes sense to use premixed materials for smaller repairs.

*Drywall joint compound,* a synthetic-based formula, works easily into all but the finest cracks, smooths bumpy surfaces, and fills even fairly deep holes in a couple of applications.

*Spackle,* available in powder, paste, and aerosol forms, fills hairline cracks, holes left by picture hooks, and other small blemishes.

*Patching plaster* must be mixed with water, but it's stronger than joint compound or spackle. Select it for broad cracks and big holes.

## Spackling Hairline Cracks

Wipe the crack with a finger-full of spackle, pressing it into the fissure. You may need to repeat this in an hour or so.

Always seal patches with primer before painting; otherwise, the repair might "bleed" through the finish coat.

## Patching Large Cracks

Widen the crack to about ⅛ inch and blow out any loose plaster. For a stronger repair, dig about an inch past each end.

Mix patching plaster in small batches, following the manufacturer's recipe. Skip this step if using premixed joint compound.

If you're working with plaster, thoroughly wet the crack just before patching to make a good bond between old and new.

Undercut wide cracks to make them broader at the bottom than on the surface. This helps lock in the filler material.

Pack patching plaster or joint compound into the crack with a putty knife or—better—a wider-bladed taping knife.

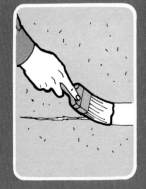

Wait about 24 hours, then level off the repair with a second application. If you're using plaster, wet the area first.

After the second coat has dried, smooth it with fine sandpaper or a damp sponge, then seal with primer before painting.

## Patching Holes

Before you attack a big hole or bulge, find out what caused the plaster to fail in the first place. For example, roof leaks often follow mysterious paths and cause trouble where you'd least expect it.

Water stains and damp plaster are sure tip-offs—but since leakage usually attacks walls from behind, you may have to do some probing to find the real source of trouble. To learn about tracking down and repairing leaks, see pages 110-117.

Whether you're dealing with a hole or a bulge, always cut back to sound plaster before beginning the repair; you won't get a good bond with crumbling edges. If a hole has no lath behind it, make a backing as shown on page 34.

Fill medium-size holes with patching plaster, and larger ones with ready-mix—the same material used for plastering new walls. Don't use spackle or joint compound—they shrink too much.

Use the techniques shown here for damage up to about a foot across. With larger areas, piece in drywall, then blend it in with tape and joint compound (see pages 34 and 53).

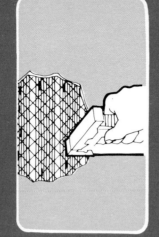

Dig back several inches from the core of the damage, or until you encounter sound plaster. Brush or blow away remaining debris.

Thoroughly dampen the hole's edges and backing. Dry surfaces will absorb water from the plaster and weaken the patch.

You can sand after 24 hours, but don't prime or paint until the plaster sets up. High humidity slows the curing process.

Though not as important with holes as it is with cracks, undercutting at the edges makes a stronger, smoother repair.

Fill the hole's edges first, then work toward the center. Apply two or three thin coats. Allow time to dry between coats.

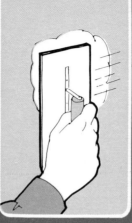

If there's wood lath behind the hole, staple wire mesh to it. This gives the patching material a much better grip.

For a slick finish, run a wet brush across the patch, followed by the trowel's edge. Make two or three passes for a good sheen.

# REPAIRING PANELING

Properly applied plywood and hardboard paneling stands up well even under tough conditions. And if you happen to scratch or mar the surface, you can usually make the needed repair in a few minutes; a quick rub with paste wax, the meat of an oily nut, or a crayon-like touch-up stick should do the trick. Don't try to spot-sand and refinish prefinished paneling, though; you risk doing more harm than good.

If a panel has suffered a puncture wound or some other serious damage, no matter how small, you'll have to replace an entire 4x8-foot section. Follow the steps shown here and you can do the job in a few hours provided you find an exact match among the myriad styles and finishes offered by manufacturers.

Before you begin, consider what's behind the wall. Is your paneling fastened to studs or furring strips, or was it cemented to drywall or masonry? If there's something solid back there, carefully adjust your saw's cutting depth so you won't damage the blade—or make your cuts with a chisel.

For more about choosing and working with paneling, see pages 44-47.

Carefully pry off the baseboard and top moldings by inserting a putty knife, and then a pry bar. Pull nails with pliers.

Mark lines about 3 inches in from each of the panel's edges, then make pocket cuts with a circular saw (see page 410).

Begin pulling the panel off of the wall. Start at the bottom, where there's usually no adhesive. Pull nails as they pop.

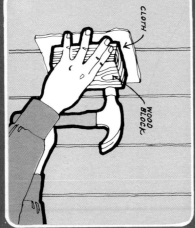

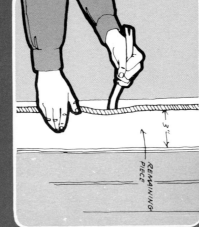

With the center section out of the way, you can easily get at the remaining margins on either side. Again, pry with care.

Use a scraper or cold chisel to remove old adhesive from studs, furring strips, or the wall. Apply new adhesive as shown.

Fit the new panel and install as illustrated on page 46. Fix it to the adhesive by tapping on a cloth-padded block, as shown.

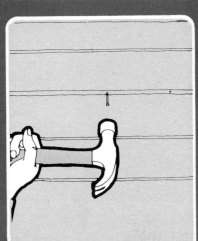

If you prefer to nail, drive and countersink paneling nails every 6 inches along vertical edges, 16 inches in intermediate studs.

37

# REPAIRING BASEBOARDS

Like most other trim work, fitting a new baseboard is trickier than you might imagine. So don't be overly dismayed if you miscut a miter on your first effort; it takes concentration to keep track of which way those angles should go.

Also, check the anatomy drawing at right and note that baseboards are always nailed to the wall studs or sole plate, never to the floor. This lets the flooring expand and contract with humidity changes.

*Baseboard moldings,* sometimes called base moldings, come in a wide variety of sizes and styles, so take along a piece of your old one when you shop for a replacement. In an older home, you may discover the baseboard actually consists of several different moldings fastened together. If so, you might be able to fabricate a convincing-from-a-distance facsimile with modern-day millwork.

*Base shoe molding* not only protects the baseboard from scuffing, it's also flexible enough to rise and fall with uneven flooring. So instead of scribing and painstakingly fitting your new baseboard to the floor, you might prefer to hide any gaps with a base shoe. Nail it to either the baseboard or the floor, but never to both.

Finally, to save yourself some frustration when cutting miters, bring your miter box to the job and set it up beside the angle you're cutting. This lets you orient the miter in the box to the one on the wall.

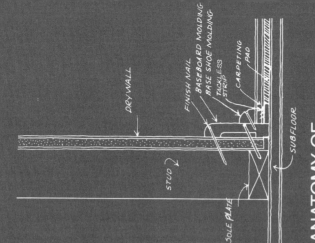

## ANATOMY OF A BASEBOARD

DRYWALL
FINISH NAIL
BASEBOARD MOLDING
BASE SHOE MOLDING
TACKLESS STRIP
CARPETING
PAD
SUBFLOOR
SOLE PLATE
STUD

# Replacing a Damaged Baseboard

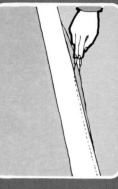

Measure carefully, taking miters into account. Some carpenters add ⅛ inch to long runs and spring the molding into place.

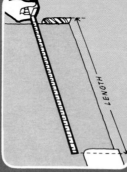

"Scribe" a molding to fit an uneven floor by drawing a compass along it as shown. Let the point follow the floor's contour.

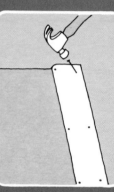

Two pry bars do a more efficient job with the baseboard itself. On longer stretches, wedge it from the wall as you go.

Protect sound baseboard with a scrap of wood as you pry away the shoe. As soon as a few nails pop, move on and pry again.

PRY BAR
BASEBOARD MOLDING
BASE SHOE MOLDING

With narrower molding, drive one finishing nail into each stud at an angle; use two for wider types. Glue outside corners.

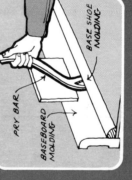

You can do most baseboard and other trim jobs with an inexpensive wood miter box and a backsaw or 12-point crosscut saw.

NEW BASEBOARD

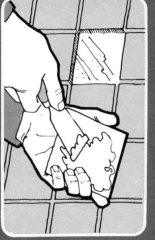

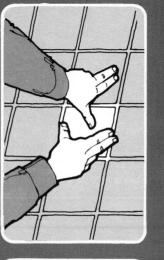

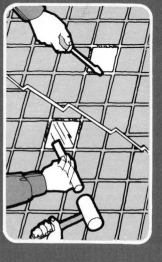

# REPLACING CERAMIC TILES

What do you do about a leaking pipe sealed inside a ceramic tile wall? You've got to go in after it, of course, but in the process you'll create a secondary problem—a sizable wall opening.

When confronted with this situation, work carefully and try to plan the opening so it straddles two studs. Doing this makes it easier to patch the drywall or plaster behind the tiles. Don't bother trying to salvage the tiles themselves, though; most will break anyway.

When you shop for replacement tiles, also pick up a small can of adhesive and some grout mix for the joints between the tiles. And when you buy drywall for the patch, be sure to ask for the water-resistant type designed for wet locations.

The drawings here show how to replace a single tile. Adapt the same technique for larger areas, but apply adhesive to the wall, not the tiles, as illustrated on pages 42 and 43.

Isolate the tiles you want to remove by chipping away the grout, then smash them one at a time and knock out the pieces.

Press the tile into place, adjusting the grout spacing all around, then pound with your fist to fix the adhesive.

Immediately wipe any excess adhesive from the surface. Clean out the grout spaces, too, then grout as shown on page 43.

Scrape any old adhesive from the wall, then butter the back of each new tile. Strive for a thin, even coat across the entire surface.

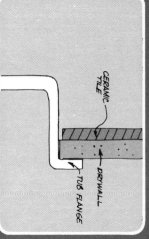

CERAMIC TILE

DRYWALL

TUB FLANGE

## SEALING AROUND A TUB

You can't see them, but bathtubs have their ups and downs—caused by filling and emptying hundreds of pounds of

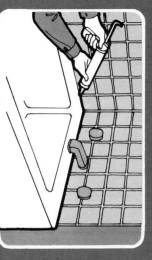

water. Grout, a rigid mortar compound, just can't withstand this flexing. The result: cracks where the tub meets the walls.

Fill these potential troublemakers with vinyl- or silicone-based caulking

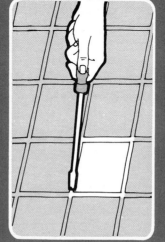

compounds especially formulated to ride out rises and falls. And while you're at it, also seal off openings where plumbing comes through the wall. More about working with caulking materials on pages 131 and 132.

Chip away old grout or caulk and you'll find a narrow space between the bottom of the wall and the top of the tub.

Run an even bead of caulk along the joint. You can buy either the cartridge-type caulk shown here or smaller squeeze-tubes.

To seal under a spout, unscrew it first, with faucets and shower heads, you often need to remove only the decorative covers.

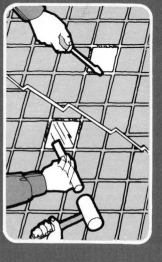

39

# PUTTING UP NEW WALLS

## CHOOSING AND BUYING CERAMIC TILE

Made of clay fired in high-temperature kilns, ceramic tiles are relatively brittle. But once you've cemented them to a solid backing and *grouted* the joints with special mortar, you have an exceptionally sturdy wall.

In shopping, you'll discover an enormous range of tile colors, shapes, sizes, and textures. Specialty items— especially vivid colors—can cost two or three times as much as standard tiles. Note, too, that wall tiles are thinner and slicker than floor tiles.

To piece together a smooth installation, you'll need two different types of tiles. *Field tiles* (4¼- and 6-inch squares are typical sizes) cover most of the surface; *trim tiles* (a few are shown below) round off edges and get around corners. Don't get carried away with a low per-square-

foot price for field tiles until you've checked out what the trim tiles will cost. Sold by the lineal foot, these can add quite a bit to the final bill.

Smaller *mosaic tiles* (see page 29) come bonded to pieces of 1x1- or 1x2-foot paper or fabric mesh; they go up a little faster, but require more grouting.

*Pre-grouted tile sheets* include 4¼-inch tiles and flexible synthetic grouting; you cement the sheets to the wall, then seal edges with a caulking gun. These are the easiest to put up, but you find only a limited selection of colors and styles to choose from.

Many pros still prefer to "mud-set" ceramic tiles in cement-based mortar—a tricky masonry process. Fortunately, you can now choose from a number of mastic-like adhesives especially developed for amateurs. Ask your dealer for his recommendation.

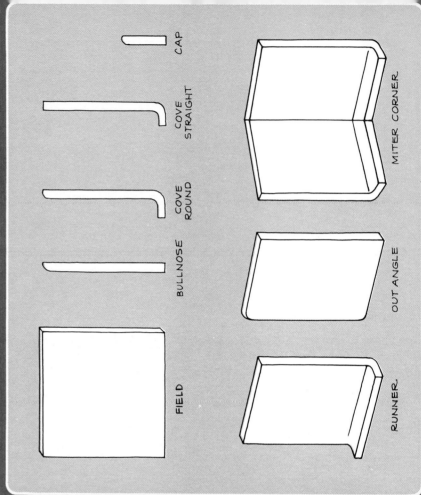

FIELD

BULLNOSE

COVE ROUND

COVE STRAIGHT

CAP

RUNNER

OUT ANGLE

MITER CORNER

## FIGURING TILE NEEDS

To compute how many field tiles you'll need for an entire bathroom or other complex installation, draw each wall on graph paper, count the squares, and add about 5 percent for waste. Or simply calculate the square footage and let your dealer do the figuring; most outlets give credit for returned tiles.

In a shower, plan to take the tiles to a height of at least six inches above the showerhead; other bathroom walls usually are tiled to the four-foot level; kitchen walls, to the bottoms of the wall cabinets.

Estimate trim tiles such as bullnoses, caps, and coves by the lineal foot; order mitered corners, angles, and other specialty items by the piece.

For adhesive, choose an organic "Type I" for tub-shower areas and other wet locations, and "Type II" for lightly wetted surfaces. One gallon covers about 50 square feet.

Dry-mix grout usually comes in five-pound bags. One bag will grout 100 square feet of 4¼-inch tiles, or about 15 square feet of mosaics.

40

# TOOLS FOR TILE WORK

Many tile dealers rent some of the specialized equipment shown at right on a per-day basis. But since a good job can take a surprising amount of time, plan to first set all the tiles that don't have to be cut, then rent the cutter and nippers you'll need for trimming around the edges.

A *tile cutter* cuts quick, accurate, straight lines. Ask your dealer for a demonstration—and expect to ruin a few tiles before you get the hang of it. You can also trim with a *glass cutter* (see page 42), but the work goes more slowly. *Nippers* nibble out curved cuts.

The serrated edges on the *notched trowel* let you spread adhesive to just the right thickness; a *notched spreader* gets into tight spots.

A *rubber float* facilitates grouting, but you can also get by with an ordinary window washer's squeegee.

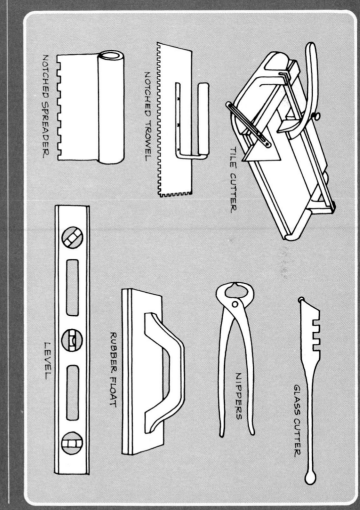

NOTCHED SPREADER

NOTCHED TROWEL

TILE CUTTER

LEVEL

RUBBER FLOAT

NIPPERS

GLASS CUTTER

# PREPARING WALLS FOR TILE

You can apply ceramic tiles to any drywall, plaster, or plywood surface that's smooth, sound, and firm. With existing walls, strip off flexible coverings such as wallpaper and scrape away loose paint. Knock the sheen off glossy finishes with a light sanding.

Don't bother taping and smoothing joints in new drywall. Seal it first, though,

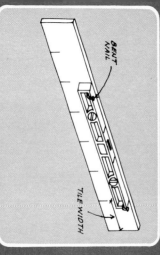

BENT NAIL

TILE WIDTH

with a thin coat of adhesive, taking care to pack any openings where pipes come through. In a shower or other high-moisture location, use special water-resistant drywall or exterior-grade plywood.

Pay particular attention to the point where tile will meet the top of a tub or shower base. Chip away any old material here and leave a ¼-inch space. After tiling, caulk as shown on page 39.

Now you're ready to begin laying out the job. The drawings below show how to

establish guidelines for an installation that starts in the center of a wall and proceeds toward the edges. This method gives you equally sized cut tiles at each corner.

If that's not important to you, go ahead and start in a corner. But check it for plumb first; you'll probably have to trim some tiles to compensate.

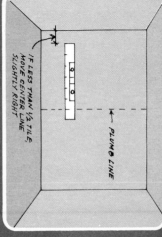

PLUMB LINE

IF LESS THAN ½ TILE, MOVE CENTER LINE SLIGHTLY RIGHT

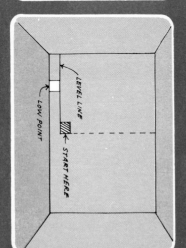

LEVEL LINE

LOW POINT

START HERE

Improvise a layout tool by fastening a level to a board you know is straight. Then mark off tile widths, including ⅟₁₆-inch grouting.

Mark a plumb line at the wall's midpoint. Now use your guide to see what will happen at edges. Shift the field if necessary.

Finally, find the wall's lowest point. Mark a level line one tile width above it. Begin setting full tiles above this line.

# INSTALLING CERAMIC TILE

Of all the things you can do with a wall, veneering it with ceramic tile makes the most lasting, water-resistant, and easily cleanable improvement. It's also one of the most expensive—and though only a medium-difficult project, setting tiles calls for slow and sometimes exacting work.

The field tiles that cover the body of your new wall go up relatively quickly. Set all of them before turning to the more tedious tasks of trimming and fitting around edges, pipes, and fixtures.

Begin by establishing guidelines, as shown on page 41. You may want to tack up a 1x2 along the bottom to support the weight of the tiles—especially if they're the heavier type with lugs at the edges.

Apply the adhesive in two- to three-square-foot sections at first; you can increase the coverage after you get a feel for setting the tiles. Caution: most adhesives give off toxic and flammable fumes, so provide good ventilation, especially in confined locations such as a shower stall.

After all the field tiles are up (be sure to leave space for soap dishes and other accessories), you're ready to begin filling in the edges. Expect slow going here—especially at first when you have to master the knack of fracturing tiles (illustrated below).

Grouting—the final stage in any tile job—goes fairly quickly. Some types of tile require special grout mixes, so check with your dealer before you buy. With conventional cement-mix grout, you can speed the curing process by misting the grout with water for three or four days. And after the grout has thoroughly cured—about two weeks—you can coat it with a special sealer designed to ward off dirt and mildew.

To learn about laying ceramic floor tiles, see page 29. For outdoor tile work, turn to page 197.

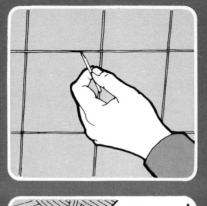

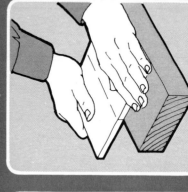

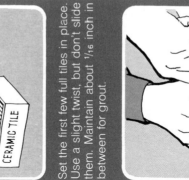

Spread adhesive with the trowel's notched edge, combing it out in beaded lines. Spaces between the lines should be almost bare.

Set the first few full tiles in place. Use a slight twist, but don't slide them. Maintain about 1/16 inch in between for grout.

After you've checked that a tile is square with its neighbors and is properly spaced, press it firmly into the adhesive.

If adhesive oozes from under the tile, you're applying too much. Use a toothpick to clean out excess adhesive before it dries.

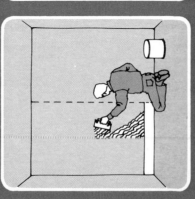

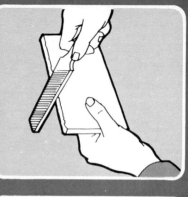

To trim with a tile cutter, bear down fairly heavily and score a single, even line. Then snap with a flick of the handle.

If you score tiles with a glass cutter, use a square as a guide. Don't go back over the score or you'll get a crumbly break.

Place the score over an edge, hold the tile firmly, and snap downward. With practice, tiles will snap right where you want.

Smooth cut edges with an ordinary wood file or abrasive stone. A file also will cut shallow notches and enlarge bored holes.

42

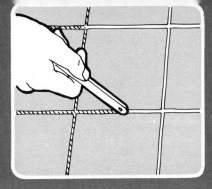

Scribe-fit tiles to a tub or other fixture with a compass, as shown. Let the steel point follow the contour. Mark with a pen.

SET COMPASS TO THIS WIDTH

Make curved cuts with nippers. To avoid breaking the tile, start at the edge and bite out only tiny chunks at a time.

Install soap dishes and other ceramic accessories last. Cement them in place with adhesive or two-part epoxy putty.

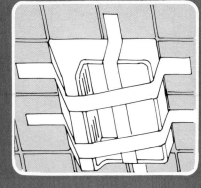

Use masking tape to hold accessories until the adhesive or putty dries. Don't apply pressure to them for a week or so.

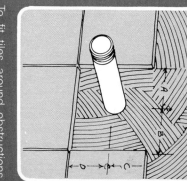

To fit tiles around obstructions, crack the glaze and drill through with a masonry bit, or piece in by measuring as shown.

After measuring, cut the tile in two, then fit the pieces around the pipe. After grouting, seal with caulking compound.

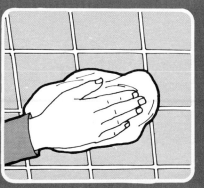

After 10 to 15 minutes, tool the joints with a rounded object such as the handle of a toothbrush. This further compacts the grout.

Now wash all grout off the tiles' surfaces with a wet sponge. Expect to do a lot of scrubbing, but don't damage joints.

Finally, polish the tiles with a soft, dry cloth. Don't use a newly tiled shower during the curing period —about two weeks.

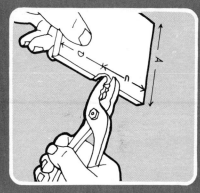

Smooth the notches with a file, along the pipe's center axis and nibble out semicircular notches from each piece.

Mix grout to the consistency of a thick paste and apply it with diagonal passes of a rubber float, taking care to pack all joints.

## CHOOSING AND BUYING PANELING

The secret to paneling's popularity with do-it-yourselfers lies in those vertical grooves scored down every panel's face. Though they may seem to be randomly located, you'll always find one every 16 and 24 inches—the most typical stud spacing. This lets you hide any nails in the grooves, and disguises joints between panels as well.

What's more, you don't need many nails for most applications; instead, put up the lightweight sheets with special panel adhesives that bond to studs, furring strips, drywall, or almost any existing wall.

In shopping for sheet paneling, you'll find dozens upon dozens of styles, textures, and wood tones to select from—but all can be divided into three categories.

*Plywoods faced with genuine hard- and softwoods* give the most natural look; often, no two panels are exactly the same. The more exotic the veneer, the more you'll pay.

*Embossed, color-toned, or simulated wood-grain plywoods* look convincingly like wood, except that the patterns repeat every so often along the wall.

*Hardboards faced with textured or printed overlays* have come a long way from the flimsy, obvious fakes you may

remember. In fact, many can't be distinguished from plywood.

And despite the popularity of sheet materials, solid-board paneling—with or without interlocking edges—still offers the greatest design versatility. You can nail up boards vertically, horizontally, diagonally, and even in herringbone patterns.

### COMPARING PANELING MATERIALS

| Material | Features | Relative Cost |
|---|---|---|
| Plywood | Three-ply construction, usually with a tough, prefinished face. Though normally ¼ inch thick, you also can buy 5/32-, 3/16-, and 7/16-inch sizes. Easy to install. | Moderate to expensive |
| Hardboard | Compressed wood fibers with durable vinyl or paper overlays. Good resistance to moisture. Thicknesses range from 1/8 to ¼ inch. Installation is al- most the same as for plywood. | Low to moderate |
| Solid boards | Includes everything from rose- wood to barn siding. Edges may be plain, tongue-and-groove, or shiplapped. Thicknesses range from 3/8 to ¾ inch. Installation is slower and requires more carpentry skills than applying sheet goods. | Moderate to very expensive |

## FIGURING YOUR PANELING NEEDS

A successful paneling project calls for more head than hand work. Careful planning, based on accurate measurements, assures that you don't waste costly materials.

First assess what you expect the paneling to do. If you simply want to dress up drab or deteriorating walls, you can probably cement most materials directly to the old surfaces. They must be even, though; molehills sometimes turn into mountains under paneling.

Before you can panel a basement wall, or any uneven surface, you'll need to put up furring strips, as shown opposite. And

if you want to panel a new partition, plan to put up drywall first; paneling simply isn't designed to retard noise or fire.

Next, draw up the job on graph paper, as shown opposite. Counting squares will help you compute exactly how many 4x8-foot sheets you'll need.

Now make elevation drawings of each wall individually, accurately locating all windows, doors, offsets, pipes, and electrical outlets. Tailor 4x8-square graph-paper cutouts to these detailed plans and you'll have a cutting diagram for each panel. Just be sure to double-check all measurements before picking up a saw.

44

How flat are your walls? To find out, select a long, straight 2x4 and hold it on edge against the surface you want to cover. Move it around, trying out horizontal, vertical, and diagonal positions. If you can see hollows under the 2x4, or if it rocks at points, you need

to even up the wall with furring before applying paneling or drywall.

Also plan to fur out any masonry wall, and some wood shingles for shimming the strips.

In a basement, you might prefer to build a 2x4 stud framework instead (see pages 48-50). This makes more space for pipes, insulation, and electrical outlets. Make sure, too, that your foundation walls have been properly sealed against moisture (see pages 101-105).

For furring materials, choose

inexpensive 1x2s or 1x3s. You'll also need several tubes of panel adhesive, and some wood shingles for shimming the strips.

When putting up furring strips, be sure to use standard 16-inch center-to-center spacing. This lets you put up standard, four-foot-wide materials without a lot of trimming.

To learn about insulating basement walls, turn to page 373.

Begin by gluing up a strip at one corner. With all verticals, leave 2-inch space at the bottom to facilitate installation.

Now lay wavy beads of adhesive along the lines, press strips against them, remove the strips, and reapply after 10 minutes.

Set the first panel in place, plumb it, and check the fit at the corner. Trim if necessary, then mark for the first joint.

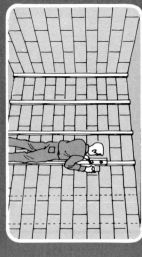

Take all future measurements from that joint line, not from the corner. Remember to maintain the correct center-to-center spacing.

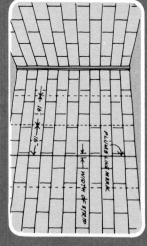

Plumb each furring strip carefully before you permanently fix it to the wall. Double-check the 16-inch spacings, too.

Next nail 1x2s or 1x3s across the verticals. Insert shingles behind these horizontals wherever you need to shim.

With uneven walls, use 2x3s or 2x4s on 24-inch centers for vertical furring. If you plan to insulate the wall, do it now.

If the wall was even to begin with, just glue up short horizontals top and bottom and your furring job is complete.

Then fill in spaces between the horizontals with short lengths of furring. Shim low spots here, too, if necessary.

45

# INSTALLING PANELING

Once you've done the preparation work—which, granted, is considerable —paneling with plywood or hardboard goes more quickly and easily than wallpapering the same space. The reason: instead of cumbersome rolled goods, you're working with lightweight, semirigid sheets, each of which covers a lot of wall territory.

Paneling and paper do have several things in common, though. Both, for example, are wall *coverings*, meant to be applied to a firm backing. Just as you wouldn't stretch paper over a gaping hole, neither should you expect paneling to bridge wide spans without buckling.

Also like wallpaper, paneling often tends to play up irregularities in its backing. Nail sheets directly to studs and you could end up with an undulating wall as the lumber shrinks, swells, and warps. Instead, put up a layer of drywall first (see pages 51 and 52), then laminate your paneling to the drywall with adhesive.

Even-up irregular and masonry walls with furring, as shown on page 45. In checking out your furring job, make sure that all panels will be well supported at their edges and every 16 or 24 inches horizontally and vertically.

If an existing non-masonry wall is true, just blend in any rough spots with sandpaper, then find and mark the studs' locations (see page 31).

Next, figure out where panels will join and spray-paint wide black swaths down the backing or furring strips. These stripes provide reference points as you work, and if a panel shrinks later, the gap won't be conspicuous.

Acclimate panels to your home by buying them several days in advance of application and stacking them in the room where they'll go up.

Before you begin, measure the exact ceiling height at several different points. When cutting the panels, allow for a ½-inch clearance between the paneling and the floor. This makes it easier to fit the panels into place and compensates for settlement.

Cut plywood or hardboard with a fine-tooth power or handsaw—faceup for a hand or table saw, facedown for a portable circular or saber saw. To avoid costly mistakes, make a cutting diagram for each piece as explained on page 44, then double-check each measurement before you cut. Support long cuts with sawhorses and a helper; otherwise, the relatively thin material might snap.

Pry off baseboard molding and remove covers from receptacles and anything else that might get in the panels' way.

Apply adhesive—for one panel at a time—to furring strips or at 16-inch intervals along an existing wall surface.

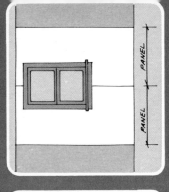

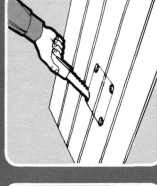

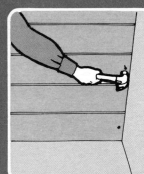

Now pull the bottom of the pane away from the wall about eight inches and prop it there until the adhesive gets tacky.

Place a panel and secure by partially driving nails along the top. You may have to scribe-cut a panel to fit a corner (see page 43).

To fit around a receptacle, mark its edges with chalk, press the panel against it, bore holes at the corners, then make a cutout.

Around larger openings, try to piece together panels as shown. It's much easier than trying to make one big cutout.

Then drive the top nails home and space four more along the bottom edge. These will be concealed by moldings.

Pull out the prop, press the panel to the wall, and embed it in the adhesive by tapping the surface with a padded block.

46

Finish off your paneling project by trimming with dimension lumber and millwork, stained to match—or use prefinished moldings available from paneling manufacturers.

You can make most cuts with an inexpensive wood miter box and a backsaw, fine-tooth crosscut saw, or even a hacksaw. You also may need a coping saw for fitting "coped" joints in curved moldings.

The only really tricky part of trim work comes at first, when you have to accurately measure for mitered or coped joints and get the miters angled in the proper directions. For help in mastering these rather specialized techniques, see pages 38 and 460.

Secure the moldings with special color-matched nails, or use ordinary four- or six-penny casing nails. Countersink both types.

To conceal nails, you can daub them with touch-up stick putty from paneling manufacturers—or, for a really smooth look, try the technique shown at the bottom of the page.

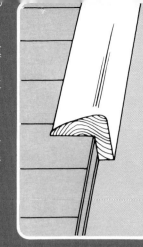

BASEBOARD MOLDING

BASE SHOE MOLDING

*Casing molding* trims around door and window frames. Most prefinished moldings look like those illustrated here.

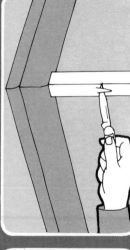

*Baseboard molding* protects walls from scuffing and hides gaps at the floor line. You may want to add a base shoe as well.

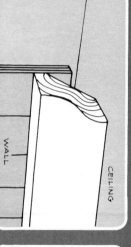

*Outside-corner molding* not only hides panel edges, it also protects against damage. Be sure to nail it to both surfaces.

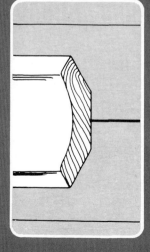

You may or may not need *inside-corner moldings*, depending up-on how neatly your paneling butts together in corners.

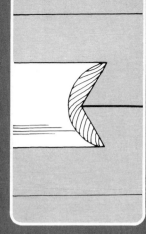

WALL

CEILING

To simplify fitting, cut the paneling ½ inch short, then conceal the gap with crown or *cove molding* at the top of the wall.

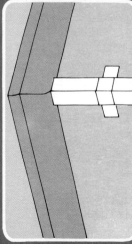

*Cap molding* trims panels that stop short of the ceiling. Use it for wainscoting and other partial-wall installations.

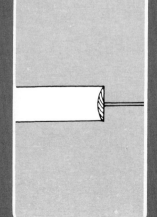

*Seam molding,* sometimes called a *batten,* hides joints between panels. You don't usually need it with grooved styles.

To completely hide molding nails, cut with a sharp knife to lift silvers of wood, then drive and counter-sink the nails.

Now press the silvers down again using dabs of glue, tape until dry, then smooth off by rubbing lightly with sandpaper.

## FRAMING A PARTITION

"Roughing in" the studs for a new wall calls for a different carpentry orientation than you may be used to. With framing, appearances don't count much. What does matter is that you keep everything plumb, square, and structurally sound.

Start by figuring out how you're going to tie a new partition into your home's structure. How do the ceiling joists run in relation to your proposed wall? In a basement with an exposed-ceiling situation, that's easy to determine; for closed-ceiling situations, see pages 30 and 56.

If the new wall will cross the joists, simply pinpoint exactly where you want

the wall and nail the top plate to the joists at those points. If, however, it will run *parallel* to the joists, you may have to shift the wall's location a few inches so you can nail directly to a joist.

Next, check cut the walls you'll be attaching to. Fasten to masonry with adhesive and/or expansion shields and lag screws. In a hollow-wall situation, you may be lucky enough to find a stud back there. If not, secure the new wall's first and last studs with toggle bolts.

After you know exactly where everything is, mark chalk lines for the top and sole plates. If you're not proficient with a plumb bob, tape your level to a straight 2x4 and use it to take vertical readings.

The drawings here and on the opposite page show two different framing techniques. Preassembly (below) makes sense for relatively short walls on relatively level floors. You build the entire partition flat on the floor, making it 1½ inches shorter than the ceiling height, then lift it into place atop a second sole plate.

Toenailing studs (opposite page) saves you the lumber for the extra plate, and better accommodates uneven terrain. But it takes some practice before you can squarely toenail the studs to the top and sole plates.

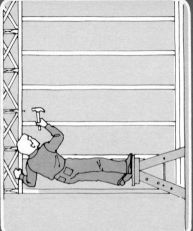

Cut the top and sole plates, lay them side by side, and mark off stud spacings as shown. Begin ¾ inch from one end.

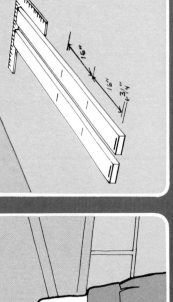

Next, measure the ceiling height at several points. Tailor your partition to fit the shortest floor-to-ceiling dimension.

You'll probably need help to lift the partition into place. Once it's up, plumb carefully, then nail the top and bottom plates.

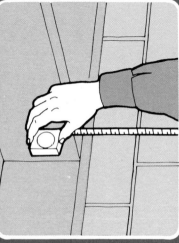

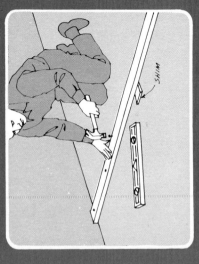

Lay out your new wall with chalk lines, as explained above, then level a 2x4 with shingle shims and nail or screw to the floor.

If your new wall will include a doorway, now's the time to add trimmers. Cut out opening's sole-plate after positioning wall.

Then cut the studs, allowing for the plates' thicknesses. Assemble the framework by nailing through the plates.

48

# Toenailing Studs

Installing the top and sole plates first, then custom-cutting the studs one at a time assures you of a tight-fitting wall—and you needn't bother with shimming anything.

You will encounter two problems, though. The first comes when you attach the top plate—a four-handed job that requires you to hold a heavy length of lumber against the ceiling, then nail up through it to the joist.

Make this job easier by starting the nails first, then asking a helper to force the plate against the ceiling with another length of lumber or hand pressure while you nail. Or use the metal-track tech-

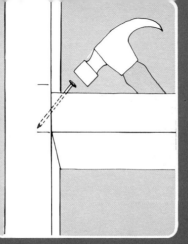

nique shown on page 50. Either way, wear goggles and keep your mouth closed while you hammer; you'll probably create a shower of dust and debris with each blow.

Expect frustration, too, the first time you try to toenail at an angle through the stud into the plates. With each hammer blow, the stud will move a little.

To minimize this, cut each stud about 1/8 inch longer than necessary and tap it into place for a force fit. Next, make a 14½-inch-long block—the space between two studs—lay it against the plate, and nail as shown below. After you get the knack of hitting the nail, not the stud, you can dispense with the block.

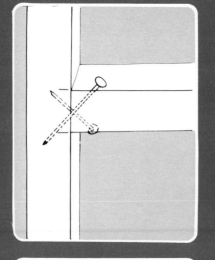

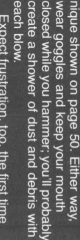

To toenail, drive one nail at a 45-degree angle as shown. Don't be surprised to see the stud move from its mark.

Now drive a second nail from the other side. With practice, you'll be able to knock the stud back into its original position.

Until you get the hang of toenailing, use a spacer to temporarily brace each stud against the previous one.

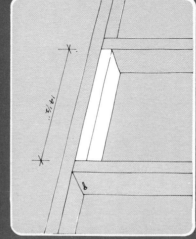

With a helper, secure the top and sole plates and the partition's end studs. Then toenail the wall's intermediate studs into place.

# Two Ways to Turn a Corner

At corners, you have to provide nailing surfaces for all drywall or paneling edges. So, fit in an extra stud, as shown at left.

Or, locate the third stud about 1½ inches from the one at the end (right). With 2x3 studs, cut this distance to ¾ inch.

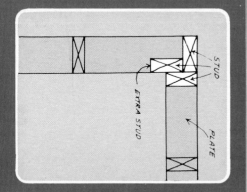

STUD
PLATE
EXTRA STUD

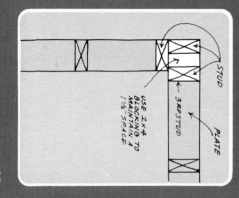

STUD
PLATE
3RD STUD
USE 2x4 BLOCKING TO MAINTAIN A 1½" SPACE

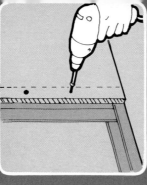

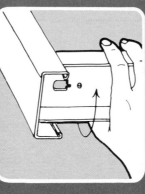

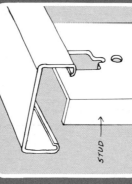

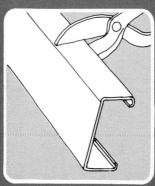

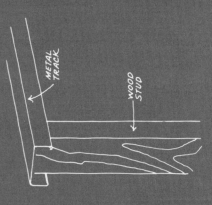

## FRAMING WITH METAL

Sheet-metal studs—a standard framing material in commercial construction —have a lot to offer amateur carpenters as well. You can lift several with one hand, cut them with tin snips, and simply snap and screw each into place.

A metal-stud partition seems flimsy and unsubstantial only until you lock it together with ⅝-inch drywall and special self-tapping sheet-metal screws. Then you have a system with as much lateral strength as a wood-frame wall. It'll probably be a lot straighter, too, since metal can't warp the way wood does.

The only big disadvantage with metal framing is that it doesn't have much compression strength, which means you can't use it for bearing walls or load it with heavy shelving.

You'll especially appreciate the convenience of working with metal at the outset, when it's time to install the *tracks*, which serve as plates at top and bottom. Instead of hefting a heavy 2x4 up a ladder and then trying to nail it to the ceiling from an upside-down position, you just hold the track up there and secure it by driving a few wood screws with an electric drill.

Once the tracks are in place, snip studs to the lengths you need—they can be as much as ¼ inch short—then slip them into position and twist, as illustrated below. Finally, check to be sure everything is located on 16-inch centers, secure the studs with screws, then begin drywalling.

To trim track or studs, snip the sides first, then bend back and ¼ inch short. Hold each one cut across the face. Wear gloves to protect against sharp edges.

For an easier fit, cut the studs ⅛ to ¼ inch short. Hold each one sideways when you slip it into the tracks top and bottom.

Then twist the stud to snap it into place. This will hold the studs in position until you lock them in place at top and bottom.

To fasten drywall to metal studs use an electric drill and a Phillips-head screwdriver bit. Ease off when the screws "bite."

## FRAMING WITH WOOD AND METAL

Building a partition with sheet-metal components doesn't have to be an either-or proposition. If you prefer solid-wood studs—or need their compression strength to support heavy cabinets or other wall-mounted loads —you can still save time, trouble, and toenailing by substituting metal tracks for the usual lumber plates.

You'll find metal studs (and the tracks they fit into) sized almost the same as their wooden ancestors—1½x3⅝ inches for "2x4s," and 1½x2½ inches for "2x3s." (To fit a 3½-inch stud into a 3⅝-inch track, just pinch the track's sides.)

As with metal studs, you simply cut a length of wood slip it between the tracks, and twist. Then you get a chance to step back and examine whether the wood has any curvature. Does this stud "belly out" or "bow" away from you? Align all those bows and bellies for a wall that looks even from either side. Then secure studs with screws.

FASTENING SCREW
TRACK
WIRING CHASE
STUD

STUD

STUD

METAL TRACK
WOOD STUD

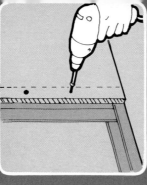

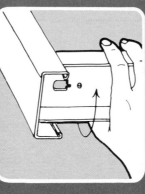

50

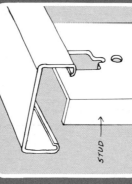

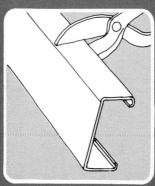

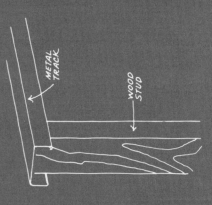

# INSTALLING DRYWALL

If you've never worked with drywall before, prepare yourself for some surprises. The first will come when you pick up a sheet of this basic building material. Drywall is heavy—thanks to its rocklike gypsum core—yet if you mishandle a panel, it will bend and snap under its own weight.

Think of drywall as a cross between plywood and plaster. Like plywood, it comes in layered, uniformly sized sheets; it's dense, non-combustible, noise-retarding, and prone to crumbling once you break through its paper face. That fragility makes drywall easy to work with, though. Cut it with a utility knife and straightedge, as shown below, or use a keyhole saw, as illustrated on page 52. Power tools kick up too much dust.

And though you can chop a hole through drywall with almost any pointed implement, don't dismiss it as a weak covering material. Nailed, glued, or screwed to studs, it becomes an integral part of the wall's structure. Use it as a base for paint, paper, plaster, ceramic tile, or paneling; laminate double layers for superior fire or sound control.

Drywall typically comes in 4x8-foot panels that are 3/8, 1/2, or 5/8 inch thick, but you can order other lengths ranging from six to 16 feet. Check building codes before you buy. Most specify 1/2-inch drywall for home construction, but some require 5/8-inch material. A few even call for "Type X," which has a core that's even more fire- and sound-resistant. Use 3/8-inch drywall only for double-layer applications, or over an existing wall.

Nail up 3/8- and 1/2-inch panels with 1 5/8-inch ring-shank drywall nails; for 5/8-inch panels, use 1 7/8-inch nails. Buy about 5 1/2 pounds of nails for every 1,000 square feet of wall surface.

If you're attaching to metal studs, you'll need to drive drywall screws with an electric drill. Some pros also prefer screws for wood-stud applications; though more expensive, they can't pop loose, as nails sometimes do. Fasten 1/2-inch drywall to metal studs with 7/8-inch screws; use 1-inch lengths for 5/8-inch material. With wood studs, you'll need 1 1/4-inch screws, regardless of the drywall thickness.

For a really strong installation, combine nails with special drywall adhesive. For each 1,000 square feet of drywall, you'll need about eight tubes of adhesive.

## Cutting Drywall

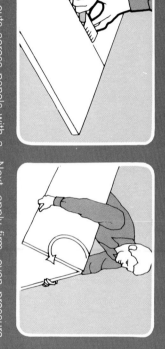

Make cuts across panels with a metal straightedge and utility knife. First, you score completely through the paper face.

Next, apply firm, even pressure and snap the board downward. This breaks through the gypsum core along the line you've scored.

Finally, slice through the paper backing with a utility knife, then smooth any rough edges with a medium-tooth wood file.

## Nailing Drywall

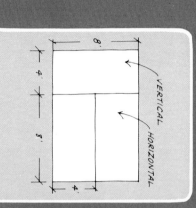

Install panels either parallel to the studs or perpendicular to them, whichever arrangement will result in fewer joints.

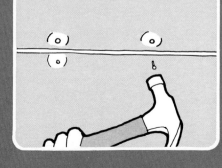

Locate nails or screws every eight inches. "Dimple" nails below the surface, but be sure not to break the paper.

51

PUTTING UP NEW WALLS

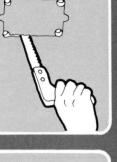
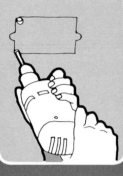

## Making Openings in Drywall

Measure carefully, and transfer dimensions to the panel's face. For receptacles, trace an outline around a spare electrical box.

Then bore holes at each corner—or try simply poking the pointed end of a keyhole or drywall saw through the drywall.

Most saws slice through drywall like a knife through bread. Protect your floors; gypsum dust is difficult to clean up.

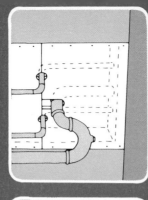
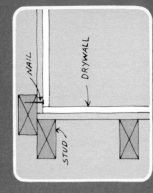
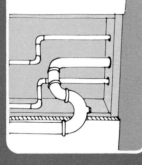

## Fitting Around Pipes

Rather than going to the trouble of disconnecting a plumbing fixture, drywall just to the middle of the studs flanking the pipes.

Next, cut a piece to fit the opening, measure and mark the location of the pipes, bore holes, and connect them with cuts.

Finally, piece your puzzle back together and nail to the studs. Cement small pieces in place with joint compound.

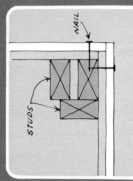

## Laminating Drywall

To beef up a wall's sound and fire resistance, glue one layer of ½- or ⅜-inch drywall to another—or use this same technique to bond a new surface to an existing wall. For either job, you'll need drywall cement and joint compound, plus some 8-penny common nails to tack the top layer until the adhesive sets.

First, find all wall studs and mark their locations on the floor and ceiling. Then laminate as shown below. Partially drive a few nails through the top layer into each stud to temporarily hold panels in place. Then, after the adhesive has set, pull them. Or, countersink nails and cover the heads with compound when you tape the joints.

Apply cement to the wall surface according to directions on the tube. Or use dabs of joint compound spaced eight inches apart.

Fit the panel, then, with a hammer and a scrap of lumber, go over its surface, firmly tapping to embed it in the adhesive or compound.

Plan to stagger the panel joints so one never falls atop another. At the outside corners, laminate layers as shown here.

At inside corners, nail only the overlapping board of the first layer. For corner-taping techniques, see the opposite page.

The trickiest part of a drywalling project comes when you finish off the joints and nailheads. For this multi-step process, you'll need about three gallons of premixed joint compound and 250 feet of paper "tape" for each 500 square feet of surface.

Invest, too, in a pair of 4- and 10-inch-wide finishing knives. And budget plenty of time for the first coat. Get the tape up smoothly and you'll be spared headaches later.

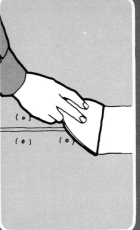

Starting with the four-inch knife, apply a full, uniform swath of compound to the tapered trough between the two panels.

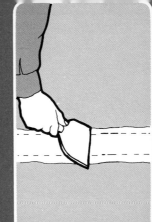

Now immediately begin to unroll the tape, using the knife to embed it in the compound. Saturate the tape; smooth out wrinkles.

Fill nail dimples and other imperfections at this time, too. Pack in a dab of compound, then level with the surface.

Give your "bedding" coat about 24 hours to dry, then apply compound again, feathering out edges about six inches.

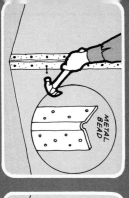

After it's dry, smooth the second coat by lightly sanding or wiping with a damp sponge. Don't sand the paper surface.

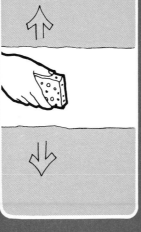

Finally, apply a skim coat with the 10-inch knife or a trowel; spreading edges to about 12 inches. Sand or sponge if needed.

## Taping Corners

Inside and outside corners call for slightly different taping techniques. Reinforce outside corners with strips of lightweight perforated metal angle. Use ordinary joint tape for inside corners, but cut it to length first, then crease it vertically down the middle before applying.

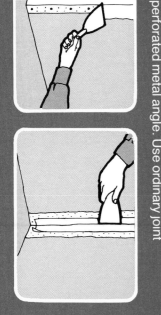

Install metal "corner bead" by nailing through drywall to framing every five inches. Be careful not to dent the metal.

METAL BEAD

Apply two or three coats of compound as explained above. Feather it out about four inches on each wall surface.

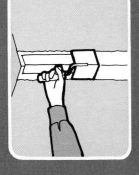

For inside corners, spread compound down both walls, cut the tape, and fold it down the middle before embedding it.

Apply later coats with this inside-corner tool—or use a taping knife on one wall, let the compound dry, then do the other.

## REMOVING A PARTITION

Armed with a hefty wrecking bar, you can knock out an average-size nonbearing wall in a couple of hours. The hard work comes afterward, when you have to cart out several hundred pounds of debris, then patch in around the perimeter.

Before you begin, make absolutely sure that the wall you want to get rid of isn't supporting part of your home's structure (see page 30). If you have doubts, consult an expert. Also find out in advance whether the wall includes any wiring, plumbing, or heating lines. These can be relocated later, but you'll want to shut off the systems while you work.

Cover all furnishings within range with heavy drop cloths; plaster and gypsum dust make a terrible mess. Protect yourself, too, by wearing a hard hat,

goggles, heavy shirt, and face mask while the chips fly.

After the partition goes, patch the walls and ceiling as shown on pages 34-38. Wood flooring that runs parallel to the former wall also can be smoothly repaired (see page 12). If it runs the other way, consider tiling or carpeting the entire combined space.

Door casings, baseboards, and other trim go first. You might want to salvage these for patching in the gaps later on.

Forget about recycling plaster, lath, or drywall. Just whack to loosen the surface, then peel it off with a wrecking bar.

With a hammer and wrecking bar, you can make short work of most studs. Sawing takes more time, but minimizes potential damage.

Take care when you pry off the plates and end studs. Pull all nails, and try to reuse most of the framing lumber.

Once the wall is stripped to its studs, remove any wiring. Toss out all old cable, but save the boxes and fittings.

## EXPOSING BRICK WALLS

Before you remove plaster veneer from a solid masonry wall, chip away a small section and decide whether the brick or stone is worth the effort.

If you like what you see, prepare for a dusty and laborious but visually rewarding task. In some cases, the plaster may have been applied directly to the masonry; with others, it clings to a lath-and-furring-strip framework. The

drawing at right illustrates what you'll encounter in each situation.

Either way, attack first with a sledgehammer and wrecking bar. Next, wire-brush the surface to get rid of solid residue, then go over it again with a mild muriatic acid solution. Do this an area at a time, wear a respirator and protective clothing, and rinse each section well.

After you've finished, seal the wall by brushing or spraying it with polyurethane. Otherwise, more dust will periodically work its way out of the mortar joints.

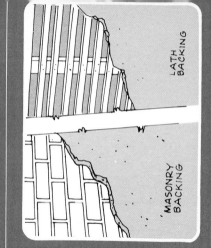

MASONRY BACKING

LATH BACKING

54

# CONTROLLING NOISE

Most wood-stud interior walls make poor sound insulators. First of all, they leak a surprising amount of airborne noise through tiny cracks under baseboards, around electrical receptacles, and so on. Secondly, their solid, drum-like construction transmits sound waves through the studs themselves.

The best time to attack both problems happens before you build a wall. The anatomy drawing at right illustrates one engineered system.

*Acoustic caulking* under the plates, at the tops and bottoms of all drywall panels, and around all receptacles stops airborne noise. And *insulation* between the studs soaks up sound that might penetrate wall cavities.

Most importantly, special metal *resilient channels* "decouple" the wall's surfaces, cutting off acoustic pathways through the studs. A second layer of drywall on the decoupled side further muffles sound.

*Caution:* get design help before you build a "quiet" wall; many small points make a big acoustic difference.

## Hushing an Existing Wall

If you need a *totally* soundproof room, line its walls and ceiling with lead-core drywall developed for recording studios and X-ray facilities—and expect to pay dearly for your acoustic privacy. Otherwise, follow the series of

## ANATOMY OF A QUIET WALL

less-expensive steps outlined below and stop when you get the din down to an acceptable level.

Consider first the origin of the unwanted noise. If most of it comes from a single place—an appliance, for example—try to muffle the sound at its source. Use carpeting, heavy draperies, and "acoustical" or cork tiles to help cut clatter within a room—but don't expect them to block transmission from one space to another.

If you decide to caulk, buy non-hardening acoustic sealant. And be thorough—miss just one small crack and most of your work will be in vain.

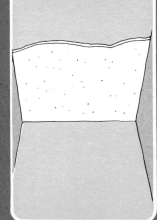

Replace hollow-core doors with solid types (see page 74), then weather-strip around the entire perimeter (see pages 364-365).

Remove baseboards, any ceiling moldings, and receptacle and switch covers, then carefully seal all gaps with acoustic sealant.

As a last resort, laminate on another layer of drywall. Or better yet, use the resilient channel system shown above.

*Labels on anatomy drawing:* 2ND LAYER · CAULKING AT RECEPTACLES · ACOUSTIC CAULK · DRYWALL · FIBER-GLASS INSULATION · STUD · RESILIENT CHANNEL

55

# CEILINGS

Combine the framing of a floor with the covering materials used for walls, and you get the anatomy of a typical home ceiling shown here.

It begins with the same *joists* that support the *subfloor* above. Next, the builder may level off the joists' bottom edges with *furring strips*, or—if the lumber is even to begin with—he may fasten drywall or plaster lath directly to the joists. Finally, he finishes off the ceiling with plaster, or joint tape and compound.

You'll find several obvious exceptions to this construction cutaway, though. Sloping top-floor ceilings, for example, usually are attached to the roof framing and, in properly built homes, have insulation above them (see page 369). You also may encounter lightweight tiles suspended below the joists of an old ceiling, as shown on page 62. And open-beam ceilings consist of nothing more than the underside of the roof decking above.

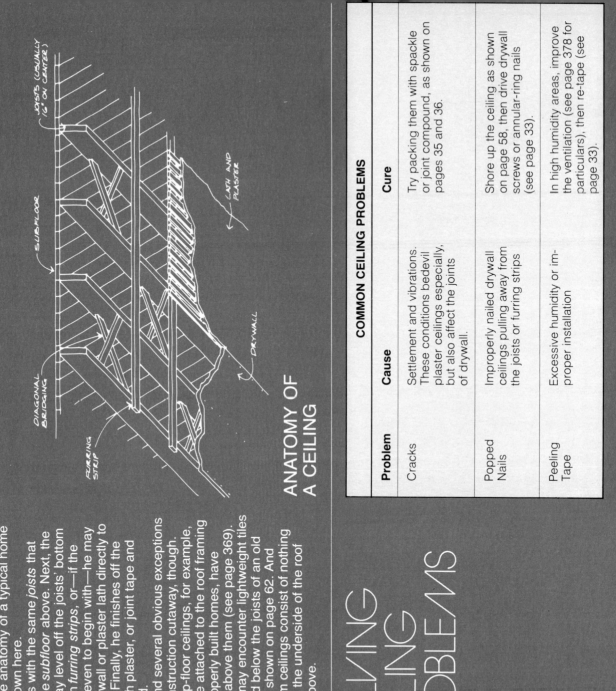

ANATOMY OF
A CEILING

# SOLVING CEILING PROBLEMS

## COMMON CEILING PROBLEMS

| Problem | Cause | Cure |
|---|---|---|
| Cracks | Settlement and vibrations. These conditions bedevil plaster ceilings especially, but also affect the joints of drywall. | Try packing them with spackle or joint compound, as shown on pages 35 and 36. |
| Popped Nails | Improperly nailed drywall ceilings pulling away from the joists or furring strips | Shore up the ceiling as shown on page 58, then drive drywall screws or annular-ring nails (see page 33). |
| Peeling Tape | Excessive humidity or improper installation | In high humidity areas, improve the ventilation (see page 378 for particulars), then re-tape (see page 33). |

# REPAIRING LARGE HOLES

Though plaster and drywall ceilings resemble walls in many ways, they're more difficult to patch. First of all, you have to tackle the repair from an uncomfortable position. Second, the patch must cling to the ceiling more securely than is necessary with a wall.

That's why you may as well forget about trying to re-plaster a broken-out section yourself. Either hire a professional, or piece-in drywall as shown below.

If you choose to do the drywalling, use annular-ring nails or, better yet, self-tapping drywall screws (these hold better than nails, are easier to drive into ceilings, and make less mess). And protect yourself against dust and debris with

goggles, a hard hat, and a painter's mask.

For a smooth repair, measure the exact thickness of your ceiling, then either buy drywall that size, or purchase thinner material and shim it.

## Plaster Ceilings

Small holes and cracks can be filled with compound, but when the hole is larger, patching is easier. The patching technique shown here works well for repairs when the lath above is in fairly good condition. If the lath is as much of a problem as the ceiling plaster, you'll want to consider redoing the whole thing.

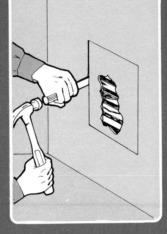

Locate sound plaster around the damaged area, then carefully square off a section and chip it out with a hammer and cold chisel.

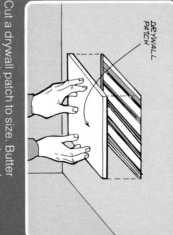

Cut a drywall patch to size. Butter edges with joint compound and press in place. Drive nails or screws into lath above.

DRYWALL PATCH

## Drywall Ceilings

The technique shown above will mend a drywall ceiling, too. But because the drywall's backing is as regular as its face, you'll get an even smoother repair with the technique at right.

Begin by squaring off around the hole, then bore holes at the corners and cut out the section with a keyhole saw. Then, cut a piece of ½-inch plywood that's about two inches longer and two inches narrower than the opening. Make sure the plywood will clear the joists on either side, then slip it into place and secure it and the drywall patch with screws as shown.

Tape a ceiling repair as you would any drywall joint (see page 53). But when you apply the second and third coats of compound, feather them out more than you would on a wall. To check your progress, beam a strong light at the ceiling, stand back, and note where you need to do more work. Especially on ceilings, imperfections in taping don't become obvious until you paint.

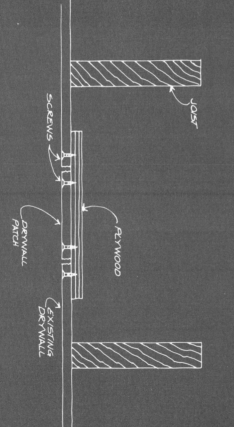

JOIST

SCREWS

PLYWOOD

DRYWALL PATCH

EXISTING DRYWALL

**57**

## RAISING A SAGGING CEILING

Check the inset at right and you'll see that a plaster ceiling is *keyed* into its lath support system. Sometimes humidity, vibration, or old age breaks off several of those keys and lets the ceiling down. More rarely, the lath itself begins to pull away from the joists.

If big expanses are descending on you, resign yourself to the arduous task of ripping them out and either piecing in drywall, as shown on page 57, or redoing the entire ceiling (see the opposite page for how-to).

For lesser sags, try anchoring the plaster with screws and nickel-size washers as illustrated here. Make a T-shaped brace about ½ inch taller than your ceiling's height, then wedge it in place to raise the sag. Space the anchors about four inches apart, drilling pilot holes first and gouging out shallow depressions for the washers and screw heads. Wherever you encounter a joist, drive several longer screws for additional support.

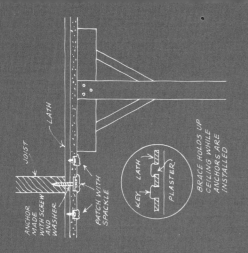

JOIST

LATH

ANCHOR MADE WITH SCREW AND WASHER

PATCH WITH SPACKLE

KEY LATH

PLASTER

BRACE HOLDS UP CEILING WHILE ANCHORS ARE INSTALLED

## REPLACING A DAMAGED CEILING TILE

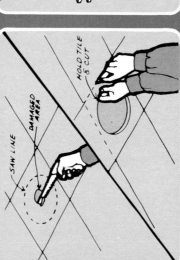

SAW LINE

DAMAGED AREA

HOLD TILE & CUT

Completely cut away the damage first so you can get a grip on the tile, then work in a knife and slice the edges free.

FURRING STRIP

Clear away any old adhesive or staples from furring strips and the other tiles, then apply fresh adhesive to them.

Trim the appropriate edges from a new tile, guiding your cuts with a metal straightedge. Lift tile into position to check for a snug fit.

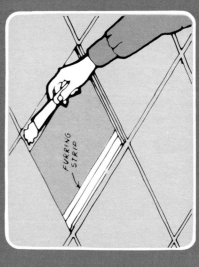

RABBET JOINT

Fit one edge first, then press the tile firmly into position and hold for a few minutes until the adhesive grabs.

58

## DRYWALLING A CEILING

The hardest part of this project comes when you have to wrestle those big drywall panels into place. If you have someone to help you, try donning soft hats and supporting each sheet with your heads while fastening it to the joists or furring strips.

If that proves cumbersome, rig up bracing as shown here. For bigger ceiling jobs, you can rent a jack designed for ceiling work.

To determine whether or not you need furring strips, stretch level, diagonal strings ½ inch below the old ceiling or joists. If the surface rises or falls more than ¼ inch, fur it down with 1x3s.

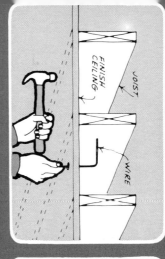

To locate hidden joists, drill a hole, insert a bent wire, and rotate. Double-check the joist's location by tapping with a hammer.

Next, measure carefully to find the ceiling's exact center, then nail strips across the joists, spaced 16 inches apart.

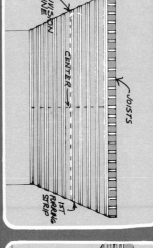

Start drywalling at the center and work toward the edges. Use two braces to hold the panels while you drive nails or screws.

## CHOOSING AND BUYING CEILING TILES

Compared to installing drywall, putting up ceiling tiles or panels is a breeze. Instead of handling awkward, 4x8-foot sheets, you work with lightweight materials and modular installation techniques tailor-made for do-it-yourselfers. And once your new ceiling is up, just wipe off any fingerprints and forget about it—there's no need to mess around with drywall joint compound or painting.

Before choosing from among the dazzling array of materials available today, ask yourself a couple of questions. First, how's the headroom? If you have space to drop the new surface a minimum of 3 inches—and especially if you want to cover a network of pipes, wiring, and ducts—consider suspending panels from a grid system, as shown on page 62.

If, however, a dropped ceiling would cut the room's overall height to less than 7½ feet, you'll have to apply interlocking tiles to the old ceiling or to a network of furring strips as illustrated on pages 60 and 61. You can cement or staple tiles directly to a sound, even ceiling; with uneven surfaces or exposed joists, you must put up furring first.

Also ask yourself what you expect the tiles or panels to do. Some—but by no means all—have acoustical properties that help to reduce the racket within a room. But don't expect them to completely muffle sound transmission from one space to another.

Finally, compute your ceiling's square footage by multiplying the length of the room by its width. Then figure in several extra tiles to allow for cutting and waste.

Before going shopping for the tiles, study the chart below. It summarizes the various types available, their characteristics, and relative cost.

### COMPARING CEILING TILES AND PANELS

| Material | Properties/Costs | Sizes/Application |
| --- | --- | --- |
| Wood-Fiber Tiles | The oldest and least expensive type. Some are treated for fire resistance. | 1x1-, 1x2-, and 2x2-foot tiles. Cement to existing plaster; cement or staple to drywall or furring. |
| Mineral-Fiber Tiles and Panels | Most expensive and durable. Non-combustible. Many are acoustically quieting. | 1x1- and 2x2-foot tiles; 2x4-foot panels. The panels fit into suspended grid systems. |
| Fiber Glass Panels | Some are fire-resistant and acoustically quieting. Thicker versions also provide thermal insulation. Medium-priced. | 2x2-, 2x4-, and 2x8-foot panels for grid systems. You can also buy 4-foot-wide panels in lengths to 16 feet for beamed ceilings. |

**59**

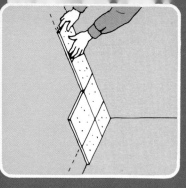

## ATTACHING TILES TO AN OLD CEILING

Make a to-scale drawing of the room, then lay a tracing-paper grid over it. Shift until the partial border tiles are equal.

With a chalk line, transfer measurements from the grid to the ceiling. Mark starter lines and cut the border tiles to fit.

Begin tiling in a corner. Apply tile adhesive according to the manufacturer's directions, or staple as explained below.

## ATTACHING TILES TO FURRING STRIPS

Even up an irregular ceiling or exposed joists with wood furring strips (shimmed) spaced to suit the size of the tiles you've chosen. One tile company also offers a metal furring system similar to a suspended-ceiling grid, except that all supporting elements are hidden from view. This method requires a minimum two-inch drop from the existing ceiling line.

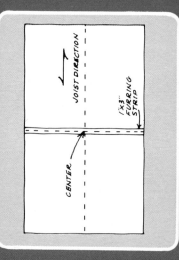

Locate the room's exact center and put up the first strip there. Furring should always run perpendicular to the joists.

Space the subsequent strips with centers a tile's-width apart, then nail up a spacer wherever two tiles will interlock.

Drive two staples—one atop the other—into each exposed tile corner. The first staple flares the legs of the second.

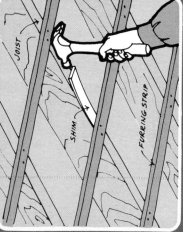

Shims level minor irregularities. With a very bumpy ceiling, use the double-furring technique shown on the opposite page.

Begin in a corner, cutting the border tiles first. Chalk lines on the furring will help you align the first full tiles.

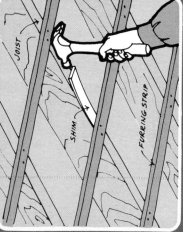

# Concealing Obstructions

Heating ducts, wiring, beams, and plumbing lines usually need hiding when you finish off a room. If the obstruction is small, you may be able to tuck it against the joists and add double-furring as shown at right.

Chances are, though, you'll need to do some boxing-in. If you do, bear in mind that ceilings do only light duty, so use lightweight materials—1x2s, 1x3s, and 2x2s for framing, and ½- or even ¼-inch plywood or hardboard coverings.

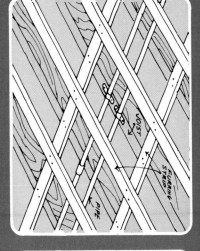

Double-furring often lowers a ceiling line just enough to get below electrical conduit and plumbing supply lines.

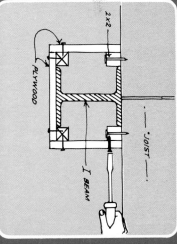

To cover a support beam, nail up 2x2s along either side, then build a three-sided plywood box. Attach it as shown.

# Installing Recessed Lighting

For even, unobtrusive lighting, you can buy incandescent fixtures that fit into the ceiling-tile furring grid. Start by routing electrical wires to the places where you'll install the lights (see pages 232-243), then build the furring network.

Begin tiling in a corner as shown on the opposite page, set in each fixture as you come to it, then continue on your way.

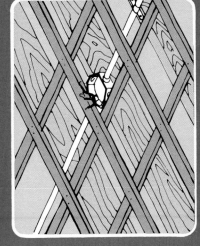

Often, you can tap power from an existing ceiling box—but first check to make sure the circuit isn't heavily loaded.

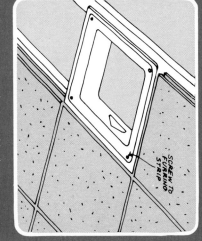

Align the fixture's frame with the tiles on either side, then drive screws into the furring at all four corners.

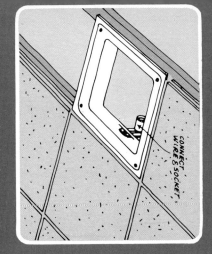

Shut off the power and make the electrical connections next. Many lamps come prewired, with their own junction boxes.

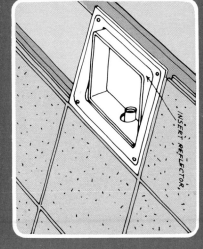

Now assemble the reflector system. Read the manufacturer's instructions carefully before installing any fixture.

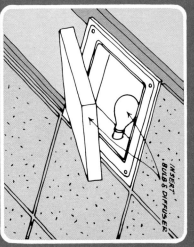

Finally, screw in a bulb no brighter than the wattage specified on the socket, and snap the plastic diffuser into place.

PUTTING UP NEW CEILING MATERIALS

## INSTALLING A SUSPENDED CEILING

Finishing an exposed-joist ceiling isn't the tedious, labor-intensive job it used to be. Today you can crown any room with a suspended ceiling in a day or so—without much sweat at all. The secret lies with the components—lightweight steel or aluminum channels that you

hang from wires and snap together into a grid, then flesh out by simply setting the ceiling panels into place.

Systems differ somewhat, but here are the major items you'll need:

*Wall angles* extend around the room's edges at finished-ceiling height.

*Main tees* run perpendicular to the ceiling joists and are suspended from wires. They come in 10-foot lengths, which you can cut or splice.

*Cross tees* measure two or four feet long, depending on the size of your ceiling panels and the direction you want them to run. Clip them to the main tees at each intersection.

One joy of a suspended ceiling installation is that you need to do almost no preparation work. Just mark the locations of any concealed joists and establish a height for your new ceiling.

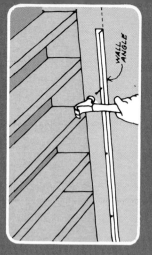

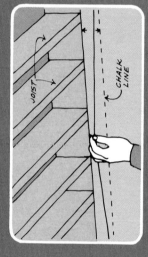

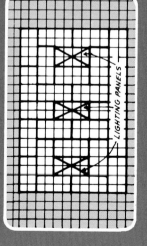

Make careful measurements on a scaled layout to plot sizes for the border tiles and locations of lighting panels.

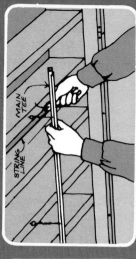

Next, determine the height necessary for clearance above the grid, then snap chalk lines along the walls at this level.

To guide you in hanging the main tees, stretch strings across the room at several points. These must be perfectly level.

Attach the wall angles, aligning their bottom edges with the chalk line. If you're fastening to concrete, use adhesive.

Starting a border tile's distance from the wall, drive screw eyes into every other joist at 4-foot intervals. Hang and twist wire.

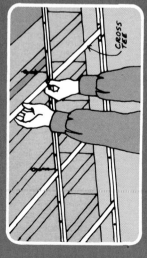

Install the cross tees now. Cut them to length wherever this is necessary and rest their ends on the main tees.

Loop the wire through holes in the main tees, level them, then twist the wire tight. Make minor adjustments with the screw eyes.

Trim the border panels with a knife and straightedge, set them in place, then fill in the rest of the grid with uncut panels.

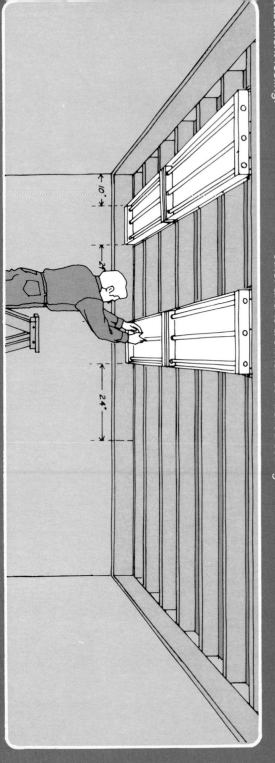

## Installing Lighting

Suspended ceilings lend themselves to a variety of different lighting arrangements. You can surface-mount almost any incandescent light, recess fluorescent fixtures that are sized to exactly fit your grid's modules, or even illuminate the entire ceiling, as illustrated below.

So you'll have room to work, install all fixtures first. With this type, a pair of mounting brackets clamps to the main tees.

A tab-and-slot system lets you adjust the distance between a fixture's tubes and its plastic diffuser panel.

## Installing a Luminous Ceiling

The moment you flip the switch for a luminous ceiling system, you bathe the entire room in even, glare-free light that instantly dispels any down-in-the-basement feeling.

Begin your installation by painting all surfaces above the new ceiling with a couple of coats of flat white paint. Next, fasten rows of ordinary fluorescent fixtures end to end across the joists. Space them 24 inches apart and about 10 inches from all walls, as shown. After you connect the lights to each other and to a switch-controlled ceiling

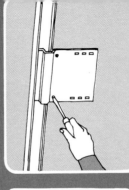

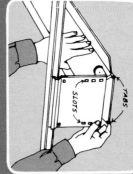

For incandescent fixtures, first determine where you want to locate the light, position the panel involved, and cut a hole for the junction box. Then, cut a 2x4 long enough to straddle two main tees, attach a junction box to it, then rest the 2x4 atop the main tees and lash it to them with wire.

One type of fluorescent fixture substitutes for a ceiling panel. You simply drop it into place, then make the electrical

Make the electrical connections now, then fit the fixture's reflector panels in place and install fluorescent tubes.

box (in a bigger room, you may want two or more switches), you're ready to start on the ceiling grid. For more about fluorescent fixtures, see page 258.

hookups. Another type stands up on brackets above the grid. Install it as shown here.

Whichever way you decide to go, bear in mind that fixtures put additional stress on the main tees—so be sure to add extra hanger wires to carry the load.

For the diffusers, you can select clear, translucent white, or egg-crate styles. They rest on the grid like any other panel.

# WINDOWS

*Wind eye*—the original meaning of the word *window*—pretty well describes the dual function of these important home components. Not only do they provide light and views of the outside world, they also control the flow of air throughout your home's interior spaces.

Not all windows are openable, of course. *Fixed lights* in the center of picture windows, at the sides of entry doors, or high on walls, have no mechanical parts. Most windows, however, include one or more *movable sashes*. Keeping these—and their related shades, blinds, and draperies—in good operating order is the main focus of this chapter.

Note first a few things you *won't* find here. These include replacing broken glass, repairing and installing screens and storm windows, and putting in an entirely new window or sliding glass door—all outside jobs covered on pages 144-151.

Windows also play a vital role in the way your home gains and loses heat. To learn about sealing them with weatherstripping, see pages 360-363.

## GETTING TO KNOW YOUR WINDOWS

Often, there's more to a window than meets the eye. That's especially the case with the *double-hung* type shown here. Its secrets include heavy *sash weights* concealed behind the frame's *side jambs*. Connected via a rope-and-pulley system, the weights provide a counterbalance that not only makes the sashes easier to open, but also holds them in any vertical position you choose.

A series of *stops* fitted to the jambs provides channels in which the sashes slide. Check the top view and note that though the outside *blind stop* is more or less permanently affixed, the *parting stop* and *inside stop* can be pried loose if you want to remove the sashes.

Newer double-hung windows replace the weight-and-pulley mechanisms with a pair of the *spring lift* devices illustrated on pages 66 and 67.

With both types, the lower sash comes to rest behind a flat *stool*; its outside counterpart, the *sill*, slopes so water can run off. Trim—called *casing* at the sides and top, and an *apron* below—covers any gaps between the jambs and the wall material.

## ANATOMY OF A DOUBLE-HUNG WINDOW

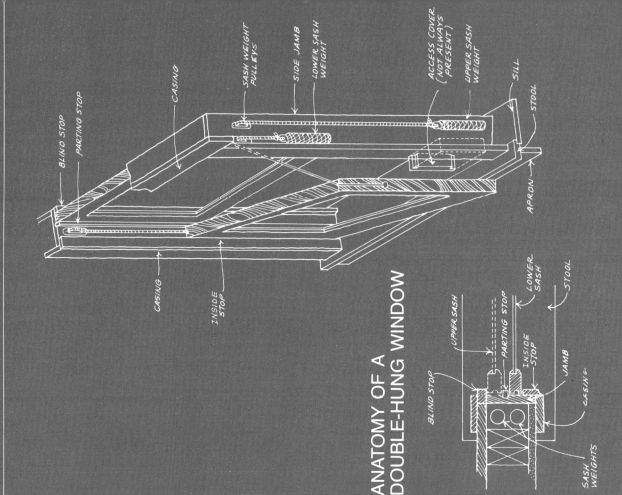

BLIND STOP
PARTING STOP
CASING
SASH WEIGHT PULLEYS
SIDE JAMB
LOWER SASH WEIGHT
ACCESS COVER (NOT ALWAYS PRESENT)
UPPER SASH WEIGHT
SILL
STOOL
APRON
INSIDE STOP
CASING

UPPER SASH
LOWER SASH
PARTING STOP
INSIDE STOP
BLIND STOP
JAMB
CASING
STOOL
SASH WEIGHTS

# ANATOMY OF A CASEMENT WINDOW

Casement windows open and close door-fashion, usually with the help of a crank-type *operator*. In the version at right, *muntins* separate the panes. With some double-glazed casements, though, the muntins snap to the inside of the window to facilitate cleaning, or are absent altogether.

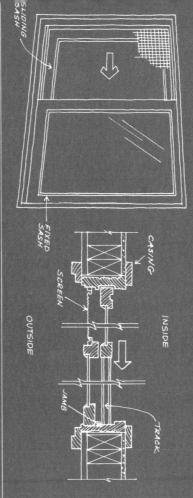

SLIDING SASH

FIXED SASH

CASING

SCREEN

OUTSIDE

INSIDE

JAMB

TRACK

MUNTIN

SASH

CASING

STOOL

SILL

SCREEN

OPERATOR

# ANATOMY OF AN AWNING WINDOW

Awning sashes tilt outward, under the direction of a *scissors-* or *hinge-*type cranking system. Some awnings slide downward as they tilt, so you can open them to an almost horizontal position for maximum air flow. Sometimes, awning units serve as the only operable elements in a big bank of windows.

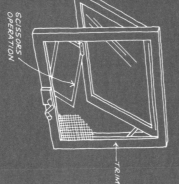

SCISSORS OPERATION

TRIM

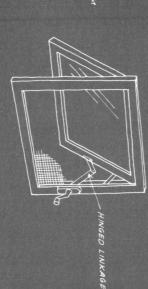

HINGED LINKAGE

# ANATOMY OF A SLIDING WINDOW

As with double-hungs, sliding sashes open up only 50 percent of the total window area for ventilation. Some have one *fixed* and one *sliding* sash, as shown here, with others, both sashes slide along continuous *tracks*. Sliding windows may have wood or metal construction.

# ANATOMY OF A JALOUSIE WINDOW

Jalousie windows also let in lots of air —and each turn of the crank pivots a series of glass slats for maximum flow control. The *frames* here consist of short metal channels at either end of the slats. Those glass-to-glass joints tend to leak air, so you usually find jalousies only in breezeways, porches, and other zones normally not heated.

PIVOT

GLASS SLATS

METAL FRAME

# SOLVING WINDOW PROBLEMS

When a window binds or refuses to budge, don't try to force it—you risk damaging the sash, the frame, or both. Instead, take a look around the sash's perimeter, both inside and out. Chances are, you'll find that paint has sealed the window shut, or that a stop molding has warped. Both difficulties usually respond to the gentle prying techniques shown below.

With double-hung windows, the culprit also could be a faulty spring lift or a broken sash cord. Replacing these involves dismantling the window, a not-too-tricky job illustrated on the opposite page.

## REPAIRING DOUBLE-HUNG WINDOWS

### Freeing a Balky Sash

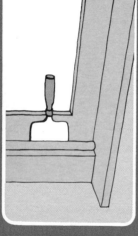

To break a paint seal, tap a broad-blade putty knife between the sash and stop, then work it back and forth.

If a sash is binding between its stops, you can often separate them slightly by tapping along their length with a wooden block.

Or try prying from outside with a wide-bladed tool such as a pry bar. Work around the window's perimeter until the sash pops free.

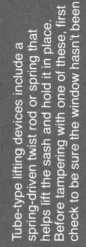

Once you get the window moving again, lightly sand its jambs, then lubricate with paste wax, paraffin, or bar soap.

## Adjusting Spring Lifts

Get a good grip on the tube before you remove the screw holding it to the jamb. Otherwise, the spring will unwind in a hurry.

Tube-type lifting devices include a spring-driven twist rod or spring that helps lift the sash and hold it in place. Before tampering with one of these, first check to be sure the window hasn't been painted shut. If that's the case, follow the procedures explained above. But if the device doesn't seem to be working at all, it's probably broken and needs to be replaced, as shown on the opposite page.

If the window sails up and down too easily, hang on to the screw and let the spring turn a couple of revolutions.

If the window is hard to move, tighten the spring by turning it clockwise. You may need to adjust both lifts.

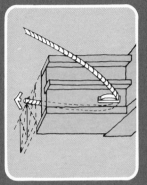

To remove the sash, pull off the inside stop at one side. Using a swing one side clear from the putty knife, pry at several points to frame. It will still be connected to avoid breaking it.

Now just lift the sash slightly and the cords, of course.

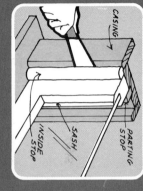

Hang on to the weighted cord when you unhook it, then slip a nail through the knotted end so it won't be pulled inside the jamb.

An access cover at the base of the jamb lets you get at the weight. With some windows, you may have to pry off the jamb.

Feeding new sash cords over pulleys can be tricky. Bend the cord before inserting. You may as well replace both cords.

To replace the cords on an upper sash, you first have to remove the lower one, then one or both of the parting stops.

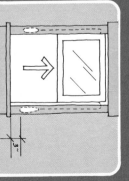

Now tie weights to the cords and set them back into their pockets. Knot the other ends and fit them into grooves in the sashes.

Weights should hang about three inches above their channel bottoms when the lower sash is in its fully open position.

When you replace the stops, partially drive new, longer nails, then raise and lower the sash to check positioning.

---

## Replacing Spring Lifts

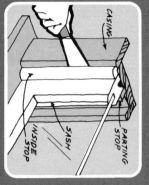

Begin by removing the inside stop from one side of the window. This should make room enough to remove the sash.

Next, remove the screw that secures the tube, let the spring unwind, then pull out the sash. You may need to pry a little.

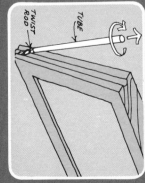

Remove the twist rod/tube unit and replace with a new one. Then reinstall the sash and adjust as shown on the opposite page.

## REPAIRING CASEMENT WINDOWS

Heavy accumulations of paint, grease, or dirt cause most casement window difficulties. If you have one that's malfunctioning, open it wide and check all sash and frame edges. Usually, a few

minutes with a wire brush, scraper, or some sandpaper will remove the rub. If not, partially close the sash and check its fit. Wood casements sometimes suffer the same warping, swelling, and out-of-square problems that bedevil doors. Solve these by adapting the door-fitting and planing techniques illustrated on pages 75 and 76.

Finally, examine the unit's mechanical components. You'll probably need only a screwdriver and the right lubricant to set things right again.

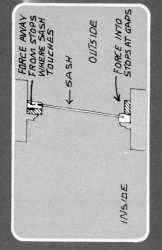

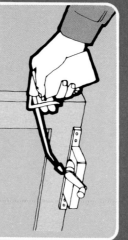

FORCE AWAY FROM STOPS WHERE SASH TOUCHES

← SASH

OUTSIDE

FORCE INTO STOPS AT GAPS

INSIDE

Bent, sagging, or loose hinges throw a sash out of kilter. Replace, shim, or tighten them up as shown on page 75.

Tighten loose latch screws. If a handle won't pull its sash snug, shim under it, or—with lipped windows—add weatherstripping.

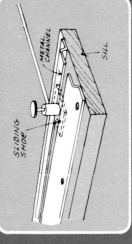

If a wood sash has warped, try counter-warping it with wood strips, as shown. Leave them in place for a couple weeks.

## Servicing Operators

Operator mechanisms differ, but most consist of a sliding- or scissor-arm arrangement that may or may not be driven by a geared cranking device.

If a sash isn't opening and closing smoothly, check its arm first. Look for loose screws, bent metal, rust, and caked grease or paint that might be interfering with the action.

Next, turn your attention to the cranking system. You may have to remove it for servicing.

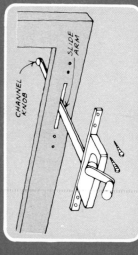

CHANNEL KNOB

SLIDE ARM

To dismantle an operator, first disconnect its arm from the sash, then remove the screws that hold it to the frame.

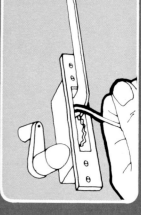

To keep crank assemblies turning freely, apply a few drops of light oil. With some, you may need to take off the handle first.

METAL CHANNEL

SILL

SLIDING SHOE

Sill-mounted sliding shoe devices trap dirt. Unscrew the channel, clean it and the sill, then lube both with paste wax.

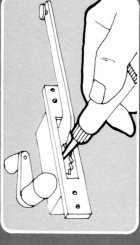

Sometimes you can free jammed gears with coat-hanger wire. If they're stripped or badly worn, replace the entire assembly.

If the gears are encrusted with old grease, soak the unit in a solvent, then repack with a multipurpose lubricant.

**68**

## REPAIRING SLIDING WINDOWS

To keep sliding sashes moving smoothly, clear any paint or debris from their tracks and lubricate with paste wax, paraffin, or silicone lube. When a slider jams, binds, or jumps loose, you'll usually find that something's lodged in the lower track, or that the track itself is bent.

If all seems clear and straight, lift out the sash and check its grooved edges. Clean and wax these, too, if necessary.

Bigger windows and sliding glass doors roll on sets of nylon wheels called sheaves, which are self-lubricating and rarely need attention. If a sheave has been mangled, remove the assembly and replace it.

To remove a sliding sash for repair, unlock and partially open the window, then just lift it and flip its lower edge toward you.

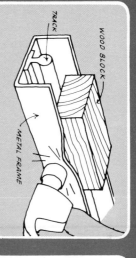

To straighten a bent track, cut a wooden block that just fits in the channel, then carefully tap the soft metal against it.

"Catch-and-dog" window latches sometimes get bent out of shape. Adjust them so that the dog's "hind leg" hits against the catch.

## REPAIRING AWNING WINDOWS

Awning windows—and their inverted cousins, called *hoppers*—operate much like casements, and require the same repair procedures (see opposite page).

Keep latches, hinges, and operators moving freely. If you neglect an arm assembly that's too stiff, it could pull screws loose, or even force the sash points apart. Clean off any rust with steel wool, and lubricate with paraffin or graphite; never use oil—it attracts dust.

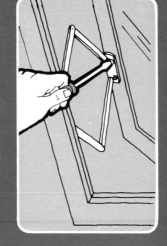

To remove an awning sash, first open it as far as you can, then disconnect the operator's side or scissors arm.

Now tilt the sash to a horizontal position, disengage its sliding hinges, and pull the window free from its frame.

## REPAIRING JALOUSIE WINDOWS

Jalousie windows resemble venetian blinds, except that instead of cords and tapes (see page 71), their mechanisms depend on a series of gears and levers that may be partly or entirely concealed in the jambs. This makes jalousies relatively difficult to repair; often you have to dismantle the entire window to get at its vertical arms. If your unit jams, try freeing it with graphite or another non-oil lubricant, as shown at far right.

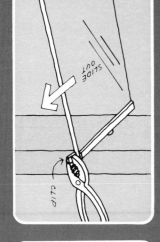

Simple tab-like clips hold jalousie slats in place. To remove one, just bend open the tab and slide out the pane.

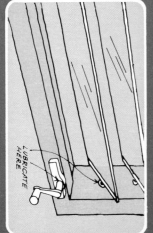

Don't force a balky mechanism. Instead, lubricate the crank shaft and all pivot points, then work the handle back and forth.

69

## REPAIRING WINDOW SHADES

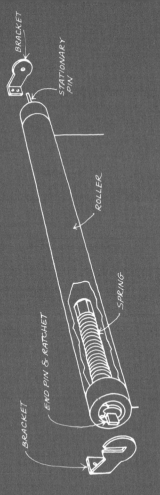
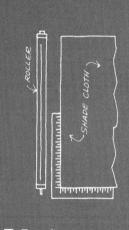

The business end of a shade consists of a hollow *roller* with a coiled *spring* inside. Drawing the shade puts tension on the spring; a *ratchet* and *flat pin* at one end hold this tension until you release it. A *stationary pin* at the other end turns freely in its *bracket.* You also can buy brackets for mounting the shade inside a window casing.

### TROUBLESHOOTING WINDOW SHADES

| Problem | Cause | Solution |
|---|---|---|
| Goes up with a bang | Too much tension on the spring | Take down the shade, unroll a few inches, and replace it. |
| Goes up too slowly | Not enough tension | Increase tension by rerolling. |
| Won't catch | Bent or worn brackets; ratchet not holding | Straighten or replace brackets; if it's the ratchet, replace roller. |
| Binds | Not enough clearance from brackets | Separate the brackets by bending them apart, or shorten the stationary pin. |
| Falls | Too much clearance at the brackets; broken spring | Bend or relocate the brackets; if spring is shot, replace roller. |
| Wobbles | Bent pin | Straighten the pin. |

## Replacing Shade Cloth

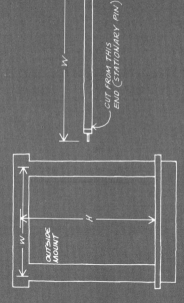

If you take down an old shade and unroll it, you'll see that its shade material (often plastic or vinyl) has been stapled to the roller. To attach new material, first square off its top edge. Then, carefully align this edge with the guideline on the roller before you drive the new staples.

## Measuring and Cutting Shades

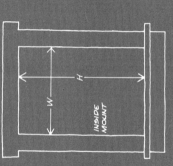

Most stores will custom-cut shades to your dimensions, but you can easily fit them yourself. For inside mounting, measure from jamb to jamb, then subtract about 1/8 inch so the pins will clear; add 8 to 12 inches to the height. Now remove the cloth, saw the roller to length, reinsert the stationary pin, cut the cloth to size, and replace it.

Inside the *head box* of a venetian blind is a puzzling assortment of parts. A *tilt tube* supports a pair of *tape ladders* on which the blind's slats rest. To open or close the slats, you pull one end of a *tilt cord* wrapped around the pulley of a *worm gear*. This gear rotates the tube and changes the slats' pitch. A *lift cord*, strung over a series of pulleys, raises and lowers the blind.

When the tilting mechanism balks, look for dirt or cord threads in the worm gear. If the blind refuses to go up or down, the lift cord has either broken or jumped a pulley.

Most likely you'll find a frayed or broken cord. If so, you may as well replace the other cord and maybe the ladders, too.

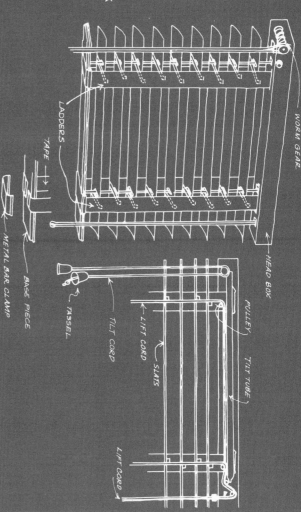

LADDERS

TAPE

METAL BAR CLAMP

BASE PIECE

WORM GEAR

HEAD BOX

PULLEY

TILT TUBE

SLATS

LIFT CORD

TILT CORD

TASSEL

LIFT CORD

## Replacing Tapes (Ladders) and Cords

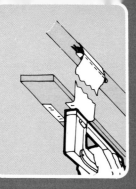

WOOD

STAPLES

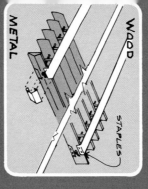

METAL

First pull off the clamps holding the tapes to the bottom slat. On wood blinds, you'll find the tapes secured with staples.

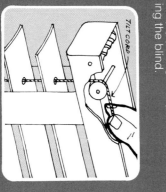

TILT CORD

Next, untie or snip off the lift cord at either side, then withdraw it by simply pulling as if you were raising the blind.

Now you can easily slide the slats from the ladders. If you're replacing only the cords, leave the slats in position.

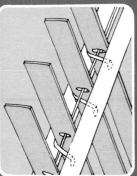

Up top, you'll find a hairpin-like clip holding each tape to the tilt tube. Remove these to completely free the tapes.

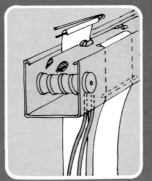

WORM GEAR

PULLEY

HEAD BOX

Finally, snip the tassels from the old tilt cord, thread a new cord over the gear pulley, and replace the tassels.

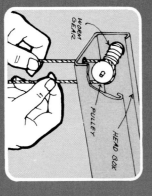

Attach the new tapes to the tilt tube and base piece, then extend the ladders and slide the other slats into place.

Thread the lift cord from the base piece on the left side, up, over the pulleys, and back down the right side, as shown above.

Note that the ladders' "rungs" are offset from each other. Be sure to weave the cord on alternate sides of these rungs.

71

# CONTROLLING HEAT GAINS AND LOSSES

Stand in front of an undraped window on a chilly evening and it seems to radiate cold. Actually, you're feeling indoor warmth rushing out through the glass —a phenomenon called *heat loss*.

Now try the same spot on a sunny day. Regardless of the temperature outside, the area will feel hotter than its surroundings; this is *heat gain*. Learn to modulate window gains and losses and you can substantially reduce the amount of energy you need to heat and cool your home.

First, make sure your windows are snugly weatherstripped (see pages

361-363). Any air leaks around sashes or frames can completely negate whatever gain-loss strategy you might attempt.

Next, analyze your windows' insulation value. By itself, a single thickness of glass has almost none. Add a second layer—either with storm windows or insulating glass—and you can cut heat losses considerably. The improvement comes not so much from the extra glass as from the blanket of air entrapped between the sashes. A third layer of glass—called *triple glazing*—reduces heat losses even further. A well-insulated window pulls sunlight into a room, then traps its heat—often gaining far more than it loses.

The window treatment you choose to use with your windows has some bearing on insulation value, too. Here again, the

idea is to hold a layer of air against the glass, as with thickly lined draperies. The tighter the fit, the less heat you'll lose.

Window treatments play an even greater role, though, when it comes to controlling heat gains. Opening draperies, blinds, or shades on a sunny winter day takes a big load off the furnace; conversely, closing them on hot days reflects solar rays, making less work for your air conditioning system.

Look for substantial heat gains at south-facing windows first, and then at eastern and western exposures. Also consider beefing up the insulation value of north-facing sashes. The chart below—based on data compiled by the Federal Energy Administration—compares the relative effectiveness of different gain-loss tactics.

Double-glazing uses air—a good insulator—to block heat losses through glass, which is an excellent conductor.

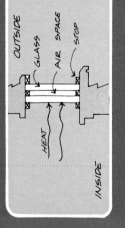

Shades cut heat gains by reflecting solar rays. Awnings, eaves, and trees do this even better than window treatments.

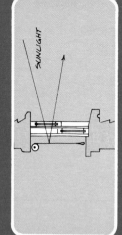

## HOW THRIFTY ARE YOUR WINDOWS?

| Treatment | Description | Reflective Efficiency | Heat-Loss Efficiency |
|---|---|---|---|
| Venetian Blinds | White or polished metal | Fairly effective reflectors, even when their slats are adjusted to a 45-degree angle. | Can reduce losses by only a few percentage points. |
| Draperies | Tightly woven white or white-lined material | Also fairly effective sunlight reflectors | Slightly better than venetian blinds; for better insulation, fit linings inside casings. |
| Window Shades | White shade cloth; for decorative appeal, you can laminate fabric to inner faces. | Excellent reflectors | Can reduce losses by as much as 25 percent—provided they fit snugly inside their casings so entrapped air can't escape. |
| Double Glazing | Either insulating glass or a conventional sash with storm windows inside or out. Wood sashes make better insulators than metal sashes, which readily conduct heat. | Poor reflectors | Cuts losses by 50 percent or more compared to single glazing; storms are comparable to insulating glass in terms of efficiency. |
| Triple Glazing | Storm windows inside and out or one set plus insulating glass add yet another air space. | Poor reflectors | Reduces losses by as much as two-thirds, compared to single glazing. |

72

# INSTALLING INTERIOR STORM SASHES

Fitting another sash on the inner side of an existing window offers a quick way to get the insulation benefits of double or triple glazing—without the expense of replacing the windows themselves or buying exterior storms. In fact, with some out-swinging windows, you may have no other choice.

The biggest problem with an inside sash is the most obvious—you have to remove it for ventilation. Also, since clear acrylic plastic makes better sense here than glass, you have to remember to avoid conventional window cleaning products, which might scratch or chemically discolor the soft surface. Wash plastic only with mild liquid detergent and lots of water or a cleaner specified by the manufacturer.

Install kit-form sashes as shown below. Or adapt the idea and fabricate your own from ⅛-inch acrylic held in place with wood picture frame molding. Use self-adhesive foam weatherstripping around all edges, and fasten the molding to window casings with screws so you can easily remove the pane.

For more about working with acrylic, see pages 474 and 476. If you're also considering exterior combination windows, turn to page 149.

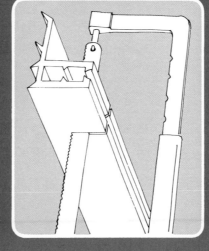

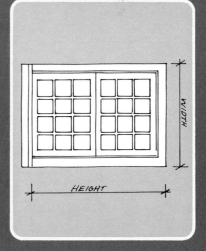

Measure to the outside of the casings, then subtract enough to allow for trim at the sides, top, and sill, if any.

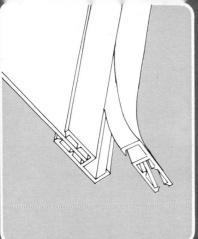

To trim the pane, draw a sharp knife along a straightedge several times, place the scored line along a table edge, and snap it.

You can cut the sill trim with almost any hand saw. When you measure, be sure to allow for the strips at the sides.

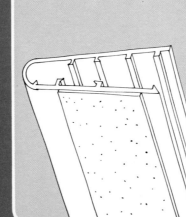

The side and top trim snap open and have an adhesive backing that sticks to the casings. Apply it around the pane's perimeter.

After you've assembled the entire unit, lift it into place, secure the sill trim, then the sides and top. Make sure there are no air gaps.

To remove the pane for cleaning or ventilation, you just snap open the side and top trim and lift out the plastic.

You can also buy special joiner strips and splice together several plastic sheets for really big windows or patio doors.

73

SOLVING WINDOW PROBLEMS

# INTERIOR DOORS

Ever been vexed by a sticking door? Usually you need spend only a few minutes with a screwdriver, some sandpaper, or a plane to get it swinging freely again. Finding the bind can be the trickiest part of the job.

Master the basics in this chapter and you can repair or hang almost any door—inside or out. Exterior, screen, and storm doors have a few unique features, though. To learn about these, see pages 144-151.

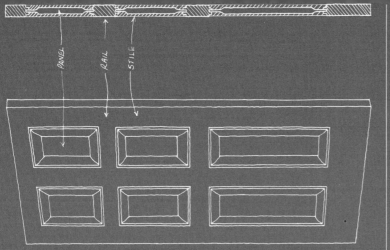

## DOOR TYPES

### ANATOMY OF A PANEL DOOR

Almost every modern door has a vertical *stile* and horizontal *rail* framework. This construction helps counteract wood's tendency to shrink, swell, and warp with humidity changes.

With a *panel* door (right), you can see the framing. Spaces between frame members can be paneled with wood, louvered slats, or glass.

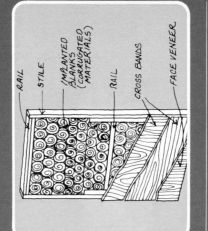

### ANATOMY OF A FLUSH DOOR

Flush doors hide their framing beneath two or three layers of veneer. Alternating the veneers' directions—called *banding*—minimizes warping.

A *solid-core* flush door has a dense center of hardwood blocks or particleboard; a *hollow-core* door uses lighter material, such as corrugated cardboard.

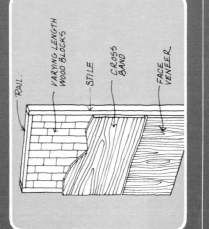

### ANATOMY OF A BYPASS DOOR

Bypass doors come in pairs. Panel or flush, solid or hollow-core, they roll along an overhead track and are guided by metal or nylon angles screwed to the floor.

### ANATOMY OF A FOLDING DOOR

Folding doors—sometimes called *bifolds*—are hinged together. One pivots on fixed pins; the other slides along a track. More about folding and bypass doors on page 77.

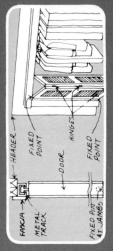

# SOLVING DOOR PROBLEMS

## REPAIRING A HINGED DOOR

When a hinged door gives you trouble, don't be too quick to take it down and begin planing its edges. Many difficulties call more for analysis than for work—and they're better dealt with by making minor adjustments while the door is in place.

Almost all problems result from one or more of these causes—improperly aligned or loose hinges, an improperly aligned strike plate, warping of the door itself, or a frame that's out-of-square.

DOOR
HEAD JAMB
CASING
STOP
HINGE JAMB
JAMB
STOP
CASING
LATCH JAMB

### Where's the Rub?

If a door sticks or refuses to fit into its frame, close it as best you can and sight carefully around its perimeter. Look for an uneven gap along the hinge jamb; this means the hinges need attention. If the door seems too big for its frame—or out of square with it—mark the tight spots, then sand or plane them.

## Freeing a Binding Door

Loose hinge screws cause sags. To tighten, first open the door wide and support it by slipping a wedge under the latch edge.

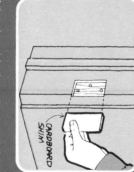

WOOD DOWEL

Remove loose screws, fold back hinge, and plug their holes with glue-coated scrap wood or dowel. Drive screws into the dowels.

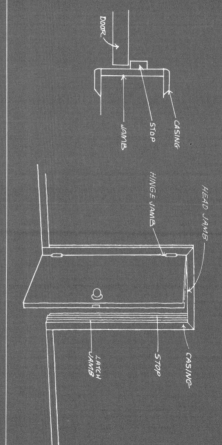

CARDBOARD SHIM

SHIM

If the door binds at the top or bottom, use cardboard shims. Shim the bottom hinge for a bottom bind, top for top bind.

For doors that are difficult to close, even though they don't bind, insert shims under each of the hinges.

HINGE PIN

Plane or sand a door if it's too high or wide for its opening. You usually can trim the top edge without removing the door.

To trim a too-wide door, first mark high spots, then tap out the hinge pins as shown. Take out the bottom pin first.

Brace the door for planing as shown (always plane the hinge side). Work toward the middle to avoid splintering the door.

75

## Curing Strike Problems

When a door won't latch, or rattles when it's latched, examine the strike plate attached to the jamb. A minor adjustment here will probably solve the problem for you.

First, take a close look at what happens when the door closes. Is the latch engaging the strike? If not, determine if the latch is too far from the strike, or if it's hitting the strike but missing the hole. Often, scratches on the plate will give you a good idea of how far it's out of alignment.

A door that doesn't fit snugly against its stop molding will almost certainly rattle. To silence it, either move the strike plate or reposition the stop (see below).

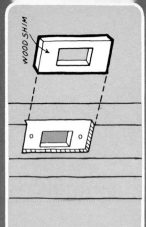

WOOD SHIM

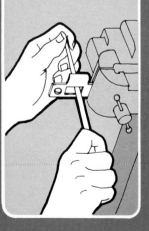

If the strike plate is off only an ⅛ inch or so, enlarge the opening with a file. You may need to chisel away some wood, too.

Accommodate a bigger disparity by relocating the strike. You'll need to extend the mortise. (For cutting mortises, see page 78.)

Use thick cardboard or thin wood to shim out a strike that's too far away to engage the latch. Resetting hinges can cause this.

## What To Do About Warping

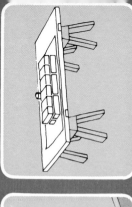

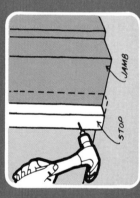

JAMB

STOP

For latch-side door warpage, pry off the stop, close the door, and draw a line along its inside edge. Renail stop on this line.

You may be able to straighten a warped door by weighting it. To prevent new doors from warping, seal all edges and surfaces.

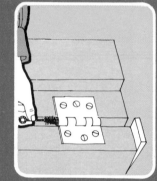

For a hinge-edge warp, add another hinge to the center of the door. Force the door into line before screwing down.

## Silencing Squeaky Hinges

Rusty hinges wear rapidly. If oiling doesn't quiet them, prop the door, then dismantle and clean one hinge at a time.

Scour rust from pins with steel wool. Poke out the leaves with a wire-brush pipe cleaner—or twist in rolled-up emery cloth.

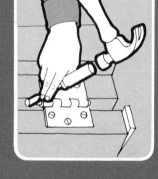

Finally, coat all moving parts with light oil. When you replace the pins, don't drive them tight; leave a little space for prying.

76

## REPAIRING BYPASS DOORS

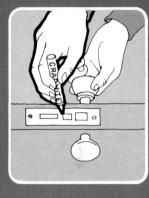

Turn handle to retract the latch, then puff powdered graphite into the works. Lubricate collars of lock body. Never use oil—it will gum the mechanism.

Lubricate a thumb-operated latch lever by puffing graphite into the door. Correct other alignment difficulties as shown in the sketches below.

A few bypass doors—most notably sliding glass patio versions—roll on wheels along a bottom track. Adjust and maintain these as you would a sliding window (see page 69 for particulars).

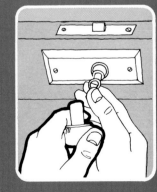

Latch assemblies aren't terribly expensive, so if you find that lubricating won't free one, replace it as illustrated on page 81.

Compared to swinging doors, bypass units rarely malfunction—and when they do, a few turns of a screwdriver will usually put them right again. Maintenance is practically nil, too, since almost all of them roll on self-lubricating nylon wheels.

If a bypass jams or jumps its track, suspect alignment problems. Check first to see that the door hasn't warped. You may be able to compensate for minor warping by shifting the guides slightly; otherwise, you might as well replace the door.

ROLLER

"KEY" OPENING

TRACK

With others, you can only free the door when its wheels are adjacent to a "key" opening. This arrangement prevents track jumping.

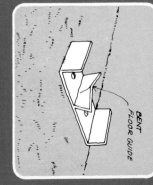

PLATE OUT OF ALIGNMENT

The plates holding bypass doors in position can work loose and slip out of alignment. Realign and tighten screws.

UP

OUT

To remove a bypass door, lift it and tilt slightly. With some designs, wheels will lift off at any point along the top track.

## REPAIRING FOLDING DOORS

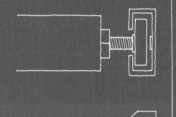

Use a wrench to raise or lower folding doors. A screw-and-slot on the lower pivot bracket helps you get them plumb, too. Don't lubricate the top assembly glides, as most of them are self-lubricating.

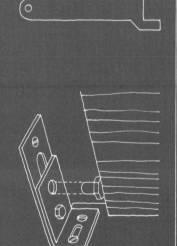

BENT FLOOR GUIDE

Fix or replace floor guides that are broken, bent, or out of line. The doors should clear the floor by at least ⅜ inch.

# INSTALLING NEW DOORS

## HANGING A DOOR

Replacing a door—or hanging a new one in an existing opening—makes a satisfying carpentry project . . . provided you keep everything square, measure and cut carefully, and visually check your work at every step.

Most doors measure 80 inches high. If you have to alter the size of one, allow ⅛ inch for clearance at top and sides, and at least ⅜ inch at bottom—more if it must clear carpeting. Never cut more than ¾ inch from either end.

Once you've hung a door, install stop moldings on the jamb so the door can't swing against its hinges. To mark for stops, just close the door and draw a line on the jambs along the door's inside edge.

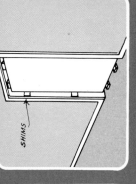

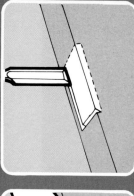

Check to see if the frame is square, measure its height on both sides, then trim the door to fit. See above for clearances.

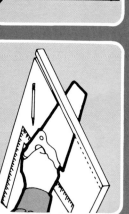

Now measure the frame's width, checking it at several points. If you have to plane, work toward the center of the door's edge.

Unless the frame already has stops, you'll need help to prop the door in its opening. Square it up with shims at all edges.

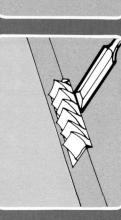

Measure for hinge locations and mark with a pencil on door and jamb. Solid-core doors should have three hinges.

Position top hinges no less than six inches from the top, bottom hinges at least nine inches from the floor. Mark as shown.

Begin a mortise cut by scoring around marked edges. Take care you don't cut deeper than the thickness of the hinge leaf.

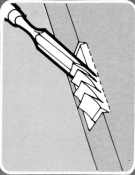

Next, make a series of parallel cuts across the grain. Hold the chisel as shown. For more about mortises, see page 413.

Work from the side to knock out chips, then lay in the hinge leaf. You may need to shave away more wood for it to lie flush.

Finally, screw the leaves to the mortises, set the door in place, and insert pins. To install a latch, see page 81.

## CUTTING IN A DOORWAY

If you've done little or no basic framing work, opening up an interior wall for a new doorway provides a great introduction. Just be sure to measure carefully and keep everything plumb and square.

Plot a location that won't involve moving heating or plumbing lines. You may encounter wiring, but it's fairly easy to relocate.

Size the opening to accurately fit your new door and frame. Page 80 tells how to install a pre-hung assembly. Most require about ½-inch clearance all around.

Use a hammer and chisel to break open a plaster wall. Cut wood lath with a saw; use snips on metal lath. A saber or keyhole saw makes short work of cutting through drywall.

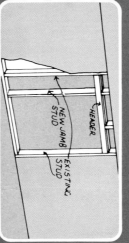

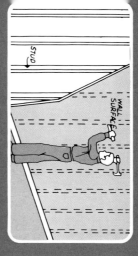

Begin by marking stud locations (see page 31). Open up the wall to the ceiling and nearest stud on either side of the new opening.

Before removing studs from the opening, measure down the appropriate distance from the ceiling. Make cuts along this line.

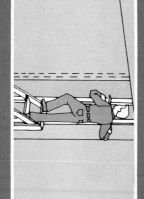

Build a header by nailing ½-inch material between two pieces of 2x material. Nail it to studs on either side. Toenail to cripples above.

Note that these instructions apply only to interior walls. To learn about making openings in exterior walls, see pages 150 and 151. Pages 48-53 tell how walls are constructed and how to finish off the surface around your new doorway once you've cut it in.

## CLOSING UP A DOORWAY

To save lumber, locate one side of the opening against an existing stud. Leave an additional three inches for trimmers.

Now cut trimmers for either side of the opening. These add support for the header and make the doorway much more rigid.

Cut the sole plate last. You may need a chisel and hammer to pry it out. Patch the floor or install a saddle (see page 146).

Pry off moldings on either side of the door, then slip a hacksaw blade between the frame and studs to cut the nails.

Once the nails are cut, you can remove the frame in one piece and reuse it. If the assembly sticks, tap lightly to free it.

Nail 2x4s to the top, sides, and bottom of opening, then toenail a stud in the center. Apply drywall as shown on pages 51-53.

## INSTALLING A PRE-HUNG DOOR

Once you've made an opening for a new door, you have two options: cut, fit, and assemble a 12-piece frame, then hang the door; or slip in a pre-hung door-frame assembly: shim, and nail it into place.

Custom building saves money, but takes time—and you risk botching the job. A pre-hung unit costs more, but you get everything you need—door, hinges, jamb, stop and casing moldings, even a latch if you want it—all in one accurately made component.

Pre-hung units come in standard 80x24-, 30-, and 32-inch sizes, with a

limited choice of casing moldings. Some lumberyards will order other sizes and styles.

Before you buy a pre-hung door, measure the thickness of the wall in which you'll be installing it; plaster and drywall surfaces call for different jamb widths.

The procedure shown here applies to door assemblies with a removable casing on one side. With another type, both casings are permanently attached, but side and head jambs are split down the middle. You plug half the unit into one side of the wall, then install the other half from the opposite side.

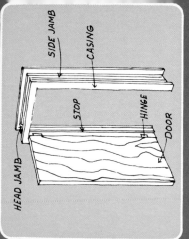

STUD GOES HERE
JAMB GOES HERE

Align a unit in its opening with wood shims—or use these metal versions. Some manufacturers include them with the door kit.

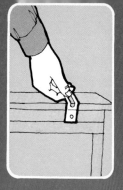

Pre-hung doors arrive like this, though they also include several braces you remove after shimming and nailing the unit in place.

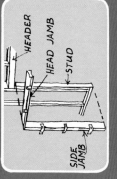

HEADER
HEAD JAMB
STUD
SIDE JAMB

Clip metal shims onto the jambs after the door, jamb, and one casing are in place. Then use a level to plumb side jambs.

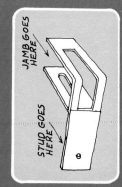

Check to be sure that the head jamb is square. In the likely event that it isn't, shim wherever necessary before nailing.

Now drive nails through the jambs into the studs, then break off the shims' tabs. Finally, install casing molding.

---

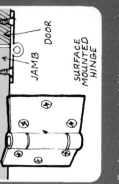

HEAD JAMB
SIDE JAMB
CASING
STOP
HINGE
DOOR

## CHOOSING AND BUYING HINGES

Most full-size doors hang on *butt* hinges. The drawings below depict three uses of this classic; other special-purpose butts close themselves, carry heavy loads on ball bearings, even lift a door in mid-swing to clear carpeting.

If you're replacing a butt hinge, replace its mate, too. To order, measure the old

hinge, noting first its height, then its width when open. With some types, you'll also need to know whether yours is a right- or left-hand door (see below).

Generally, it's best to get loose-pin hinges, as they permit you to remove the door more easily than the fixed-pin type.

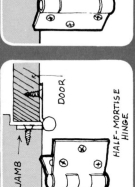

SURFACE MOUNTED HINGE
JAMB
DOOR

Surface-mounted hinges require no gains at all. This arrangement works only on doors that are flush with their casings.

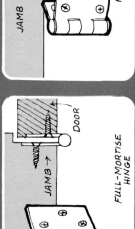

HALF-MORTISE HINGE
JAMB
DOOR

For a half-mortise hinge, you cut a gain only in the jamb. You can fasten the hinge to the door with bolts for extra strength.

FULL-MORTISE HINGE
JAMB
DOOR

Full-mortise hinges—the most common type—require "gains" in both jamb and door edge. They make a neat installation.

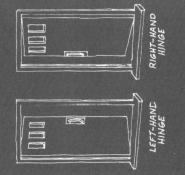

LEFT-HAND HINGE
RIGHT-HAND HINGE

A hinge's "hand" refers to the side of the door it is installed on. To check this, stand opposite the door's swing.

# INSTALLING A KNOB SET

Interior knob-and-latch sets differ surprisingly little in overall design, though you can choose from different styles and quality levels. Most modern doors have the cylinder-type knob-and-latch set shown here, or a slight variation called the tubular lock.

Older *mortise* knob sets aren't used on interior doors any more, but you can easily replace one with a cylinder or tubular unit (see below). Large-size escutcheons hide holes left by the old knob-and-keyhole arrangement.

Measure the door's thickness before buying a knob set. Some units fit both 1 3/8- and 1 3/4-inch doors; others, only one.

If you're installing a knob set in a new door, you'll need a hole saw or an

expansive bit and a spade bit in a size specified by the manufacturer. Most companies also provide fairly complete instructions, plus a template for locating the holes you must bore.

Be warned, too, that a cylinder set provides little protection for exterior doors or other points of entry to your home. To learn about more secure locks, see pages 385-387.

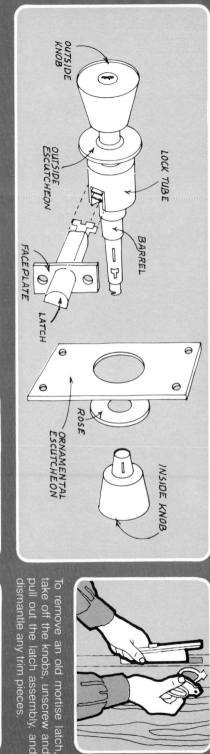

OUTSIDE KNOB

OUTSIDE ESCUTCHEON

LOCK TUBE

BARREL

FACEPLATE

LATCH

ROSE

ORNAMENTAL ESCUTCHEON

INSIDE KNOB

To remove an old mortise latch, take off the knobs, unscrew and pull out the latch assembly, and dismantle any trim pieces.

Now carefully position the new latch assembly as shown and mark where you must bore a hole through the door.

To avoid splintering, bore halfway through from one side, half from the other. Keep bit perpendicular to the door's surface.

Slip in the latch assembly and fasten it with screws top and bottom. On new doors, locate knob sets 36 inches from floor.

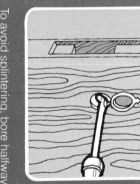

You'll probably need to rework the mortise to accommodate the new unit. Make adjustments with a file or chisel.

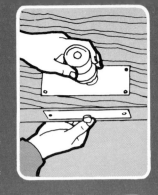

Now close the door, carefully locate the strike plate, then open and mark its position on the jamb bottom. For more information about mortises, see page 78.

You'll probably need to enlarge the original mortise both top and bottom. For more information about mortises, see page 78.

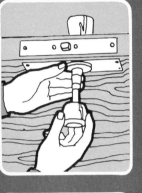

Complete the door work by securing the rose, then the inside knob. Before tightening, check to be sure the latch works freely.

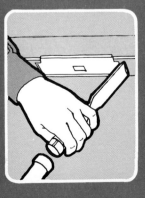

Install the escutcheons, then slip in the outside knob assembly. Most latches can be set for left- or right-hand operation.

81

# STORAGE

Solving all of a family's storage problems is a bit like painting the Golden Gate Bridge—by the time you're finished, it's time to start over again. With proper planning, though, you can clear most of your existing clutter, and anticipate future crunches as well.

Begin by asking yourself whether you really need *more* places to put things, or just better organization of what you have. Often, the simple space-engineering techniques shown on the next three pages can do wonders for a closet's capacity. And remember that you can rotate seasonal gear. Try letting things such as the charcoal grill and snow shovel trade places.

Next, decide *where* to locate any new units. Keep everyday items at or near their points of use, and once-a-year specials such as holiday decorations in more remote spots.

It might help to survey your entire home, noting and measuring all sites with potential for development, then indicating

them on a graph paper floor plan. The overview below points out the most likely spots to check. If you have several options, concentrate on first-floor storage first—it's handier and will probably add more to your home's resale value.

Finally, select the type of storage you need. Open shelves (see pages 86-87) are relatively inexpensive and easy to install; they also invite dust. Cabinets (see pages 88-89) provide more protection for stored items, and are available in sizes to fit almost any space you have. New closets (see page 90) offer the most permanent and least obtrusive storage. Also available is an impressive array of ready-made storage units (see page 91).

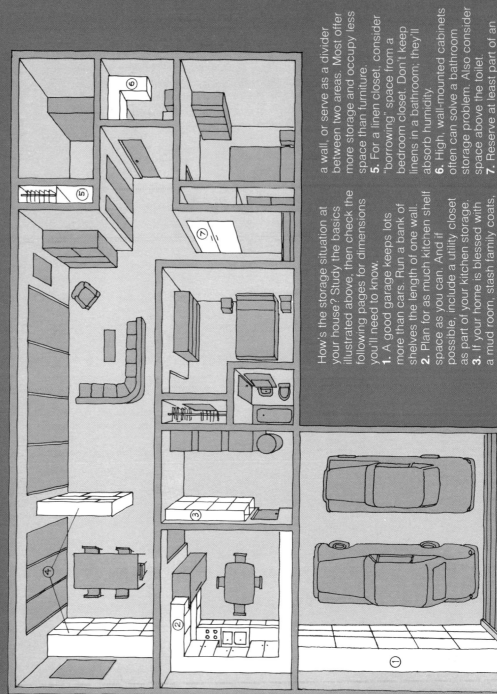

How's the storage situation at your house? Study the basics illustrated above, then check the following pages for dimensions you'll need to know.

**1.** A good garage keeps lots more than cars. Run a bank of shelves the length of one wall.

**2.** Plan for as much kitchen shelf space as you can. And if possible, include a utility closet as part of your kitchen storage.

**3.** If your home is blessed with a mud room, stash family coats, boots, umbrellas, and other everyday outerwear here.

**4.** Shelves or cabinets can span

a wall, or serve as a divider between two areas. Most offer more storage and occupy less space than furniture.

**5.** For a linen closet, consider "borrowing" space from a bedroom closet. Don't keep linens in a bathroom; they'll absorb humidity.

**6.** High, wall-mounted cabinets often can solve a bathroom storage problem. Also consider space above the toilet.

**7.** Reserve at least part of an entry closet for guests' coats. Hooks on the inside of doors hold hats, handbags, and whatnot.

# ORGANIZING EXISTING STORAGE

Tailored storage not only makes everything easier to get at, it also increases the capacity of a closet or cabinet by as much as a third. This means that modifying three closets could give you a fourth—without the trouble of building it.

The drawings below and on the next two pages show how. Study them, inventory the things you want to make places for, then adapt the designs to suit your particular needs.

Plan spacings carefully. Tables on the following pages give typical sizes for many household items. And be sure to allow for the thickness of shelves and dividers.

Don't over-engineer, though. You'll need a few inches of free space for getting contents in and out . . . and enough flexibility to accommodate changes later on.

## GETTING MORE INTO A SHALLOW CLOSET

Shallow bedroom closets—typically 24 inches deep by 5 to 8 feet wide—offer lots of room for improvement. With most, you get a single pole, plus a shelf above it, and a pair of sliding bypass doors.

Start your analysis of a closet's efficiency with the doors. Do you find yourself opening one, then rolling them both to the other side (and maybe back again) every morning? If so, consider replacing these awkward panels with a set of bifold units (see pages 74, 77).

Next, study how space is utilized inside. Chances are, you'll notice that a few dressers, robes, and coats fill most of the vertical space between the rod and the floor, while the bulk of your clothing hangs down only a little more than half-way. Group garments by size and you'll "discover" a sizable empty space under the shorter items.

Both of the designs shown here put the space inside shallow closets to better use. The one at top, which works with either bypass or bifold doors, includes a drawer case, taking pressure off freestanding storage elsewhere. The closet below features two rods on one side to accommodate shorter clothes, creating more hanging space. With it, you need bifolds.

In adapting these designs, keep in mind that the spaces allowed for hanging clothes are minimums. For a table of typical clothing sizes, see page 84.

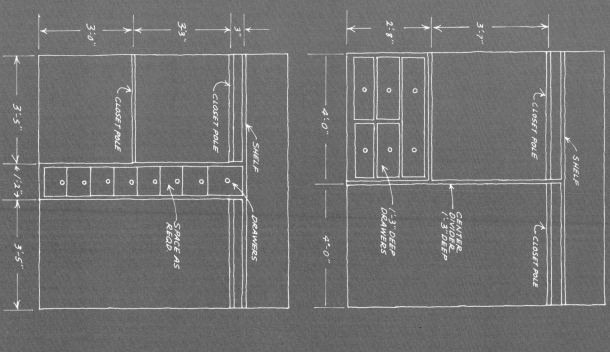

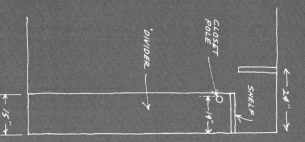

## GETTING MORE INTO A WALK-IN CLOSET

Walk-in closets, though usually larger than their shallow cousins (see page 83), actually provide less storage per square foot. Subtract the minimal 2-foot-wide corridor needed for access and you can see why. If a walk-in measures just 4 to 5 feet deep and access isn't a problem, you might be storage ahead to convert it into two shallow closets located back to back.

Otherwise, install closet poles along the longer wall or walls, as illustrated. Double-tier poles for suits, skirts, and other shorter items can give you half again as much hanging space.

Shelves—either at the back or along one wall—often will hold all of your folded clothes. It's best to space them about 7 inches apart to minimize rummaging.

And don't neglect shelf possibilities above the closet poles. Though you may have to stretch to reach them, boxes stored here can hold seasonal or seldom-worn clothing. Install a second shelf approximately 12 inches above the existing one and you won't have to stack the boxes on top of each other.

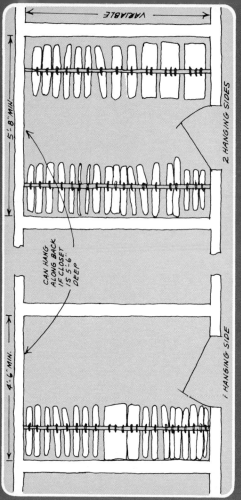

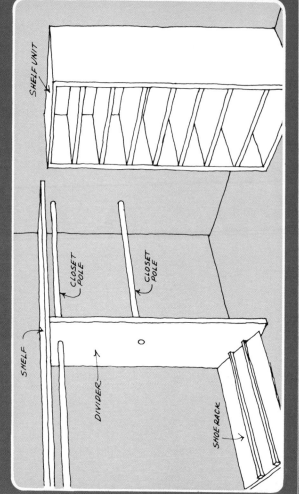

## Dimensions You Need to Know

You'll be wise to familiarize yourself with a few basic measurements before you take on a closet reorganization. A wood coat hanger with a heavily padded jacket on it occupies a space about 20 inches deep. Closet poles are normally hung 12 to 14 inches from the wall, but in a tight situation you could cut this distance to 10 inches. The table shown at right lists other typical dimensions. Use them as an aid in allocating space in your remodeled closet.

### CLOTHES CLOSET PARAPHERNALIA

| Women's Items | | Men's Items | | Accessories | |
|---|---|---|---|---|---|
| Long dresses | 69" | Topcoats | 50" | Garment bags | 57" |
| Robes | 52" | Suits | 38" | Hanging shoe bags | 36" |
| Skirts | 35" | Travel bags | 41" | Umbrellas | 36" |
| Dresses | 45" | Trousers (cuff-hung) | 44" | Canes | 36" |
| Dress bags | 48" | Trousers | | | |
| Blouses | 28" | (double-hung) | 20" | | |
| Coats | 52" | Ties | 27" | | |
| Suits | 29" | Shirts | 28" | | |
| Suit bags | 41" | | | | |

# GETTING MORE INTO A LINEN CLOSET

The trouble with tall stacks of folded sheets or towels is that you have to be a magician to get out the lower ones without rumpling the rest . . . and maybe toppling adjacent stacks as well. The solution: compartmentalize.

Check the drawing at right to see one scheme for putting foldables in their places. Bulky blankets go up top, then bath towels, sheets, hand towels, and so on. Drawers and a cabinet add concealed storage below.

Plan your divisions according to the things you have, leaving a few inches of clearance for getting them in and out. And keep your arrangement flexible—home fashions change.

# GETTING MORE INTO A CLEANING CLOSET

Here again, compartments can help organize the jumble of awkward shapes that utility storage must handle. The closet at right garages an upright vacuum, provides shelves for an assortment of cleaning products, and secures a mop and broom so they won't fall out every time you open the door. Note, too, how a slanting compartment near the bottom of the closet cuts the clutter of stored paper bags.

For even more storage, look to the inside of the closet door. Lipped shelves and/or a cloth caddy for vacuum attachments put this bonus space to good use. And if space in a cleaning or linen closet is really tight, consider outfitting it with perforated metal shelving rather than wood shelving. You'll gain storage space and improve air circulation as well.

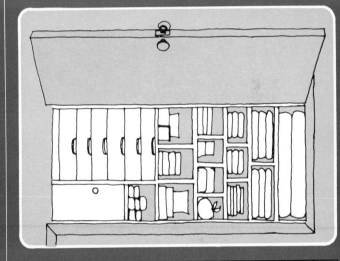

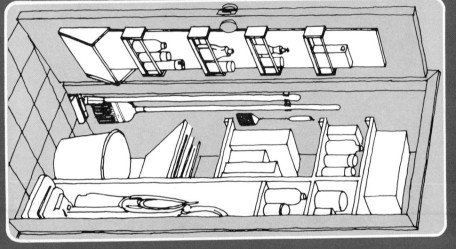

## LINEN CLOSET ITEMS

| (Maximum Space Requirements—Folded) | |
|---|---|
| Pillowcases | 7x15'' |
| Blankets | 27x22½'' |
| Sheets | |
| Flat | 13½x15'' |
| Fitted | 18x10½'' |
| Washcloths | 7x7'' |
| Hand Towels | 6x10'' |
| Bath Towels | 14x13'' |
| Bath Mats | 10x9'' |
| Dish Towels | 10x16'' |

## CLEANING EQUIPMENT

| | |
|---|---|
| Canister vacuum | 14x17'' |
| Floor polisher | 12x45'' |
| Upright vacuum | 14x48'' |
| Carpet sweeper | 16x54'' |
| Broom | 10 x up to 60'' |
| Whisk broom | 6x10'' |
| Dust pan | 11x9'' |
| Push broom | 14 x up to 54'' |
| Dry mop | 13½x66'' |
| Wet mop | 12x48'' |
| Scrub bucket | 10½x12'' |
| Cleansers | 8-10x6-14'' |

# ADDING
# NEW
# STORAGE

The answer to a storage shortage may be as simple as a few coat hooks at the front entry—or as complex as an entire wall of custom living room built-ins. Most solutions fall somewhere in between, with open shelving leading the list. If you select the right hardware (below) and master a few basics (opposite), you'll never again be floored by a shelf project. Pages 88-89 show another way to go—prefabricated kitchen cabinets.

Available in a wide variety of styles and finishes, they make sense for almost any room.

As a last resort, consider building a new closet or closets (see page 90). Before you begin, though, consider the almost-instant alternatives offered by storage you can buy (see page 91).

## CHOOSING SHELF HARDWARE

The success of any shelving project rests—quite literally—upon its support system. So ask yourself these questions before making your choice. What weights and spans must the hardware hold (see opposite below)? Can shelves be supported at the ends, or must they be rear-mounted? Do you want fixed or adjustable brackets? How will you attach the shelves to the wall (see opposite above and page 32)? Do you really need hardware at all? Cleats (at right) and dadoing (see page 459) offer two alternatives.

Once you've answered the mechanical questions, consider appearance. Styling ranges from strictly utilitarian to hardwood wall furniture. You'll discover that price is a relevant factor, too—the hardware sometimes costs more than the lumber for the shelves.

The chart at right illustrates the eight most commonly used support systems, but there are dozens of variations. With standards and brackets, for instance, you can choose painted or plated finishes, different bracket shapes and locking mechanisms, and even specialties such as angled supports that serve as magazine racks.

And while you're selecting hardware, give some thought to buying prefinished shelving as well. Though considerably more expensive than ordinary lumber or plywood, it saves a lot of tedious work.

| Item | Application |
|------|-------------|
| | Rigid pressed-steel angle brackets hold medium-weight loads. Always mount them with the longer leg against the wall. For heavier duty, choose types reinforced with triangular gussets between the legs (not shown). |
| | Brackets clip into slotted standards, allowing you to adjust the spacing between shelves. Choose 8-, 10-, or 12-inch brackets. Properly installed (see opposite above), this system supports surprisingly heavy loads. |
| | The simplest (and least expensive) way to hold shelves inside closets, bookcases, or cabinets is to install cleats at each end. For longer spans, attach a third strip to the unit's back to support the rear of the shelves. |
| | For a dresser look, mount shelves by popping pin-type clips into pre-drilled holes. Relatively inexpensive, they'll support heavy loads on ¾-inch-thick boards up to about 30 inches long. |
| | Or make end-mounted shelves adjustable with standards and clips such as these. Again, limit spans to about 30 inches. For a flush installation, you can dado the the standards into the cabinet's sides. |
| | So-called "tension" poles—actually they work by expansion—wedge between floor and ceiling in situations where you can't or don't want to make holes in the walls. They're relatively expensive. |
| | Folding brackets let you drop a shelf out of the way when you're not using it. You can buy a variation of these for spring-loaded typewriter-style installations (not shown); the shelf pops up when you pull it from a cabinet. |
| | Light-duty wire brackets like this one are among the many accessories you can mount on perforated hardboard. Measure the board's thickness before you buy: ¼- and ⅛-inch sizes require different devices. |

# PUTTING UP SHELF STRIPS

Bracket shelving seems to concentrate a lot of weight on the few small fasteners that secure the strips. But those fasteners don't actually bear the load—they simply clamp the strips to the wall. This means that the strength of a shelving system actually depends more

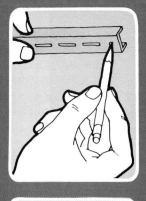

on the fasteners' holding power than it does on their size.

Use plastic anchors only for light-duty installations. Wood screws driven directly into studs hold much better—but with them you must adjust your design according to the way the wall was framed. Hollow-wall fasteners such as toggle and expansion bolts (see page 433) let you put strips exactly where you want them.

Armed with the proper fasteners and a screwdriver, drill, and level, you can hang the strips in an hour or so. Generally, it's best to plumb the strips so they'll be perfectly vertical. However, if you have walls that are out of square, you may have to measure from floor or ceiling to make the shelving aesthetically acceptable.

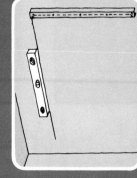

Before hanging the first strip, note whether it has a definite top and bottom. Mark and drill for the top hole only.

Insert a bolt, but don't tighten it until you've plumbed the strip, drilled remaining holes, and installed the lower bolt or bolts.

Draw a level line from the strip's top or bottom to locate the last strip. See note above if you have out-of-square walls.

Position the intermediate strips, using the line you've drawn as a guide. Maintain equal spacing between them.

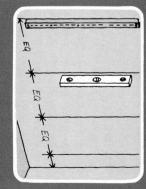

# FIGURING SHELF SPACINGS AND SPANS

Plot any shelf layout carefully, using graph paper and the dimensions at right to minimize any "surprises" later. The span table gives the maximum distance you should allow between supports. It assumes a full load of books or records, which are the heaviest items you're likely to put on shelves. Don't allow the unsupported ends of shelves to extend more than half the span distance beyond the last support or they may begin to bow on you.

With adjustable shelving, you can save space and cut down dusting by tailoring vertical spacings to accommodate your possessions exactly. Just be sure to leave an extra inch or two so you can easily tip out a book or record (allow a little more leeway if you decide on fixed shelves).

Before determining your final shelving layout, consult the lower table at right for the spacing required between shelves for several often-shelved items.

## SHELVING SPANS

| Material Used | Maximum Span | Material Used | Maximum Span |
|---|---|---|---|
| 3/4-inch plywood | 36" | 2x10 or 2x12 lumber | 48-56" |
| 3/4-inch particleboard | 28" | 1/2-inch acrylic | 22" |
| 1x12 lumber | 24" | 1/2-inch glass | 18" |

(Assumes shelves fully loaded with books)

## SHELF SPACING GUIDE

| Item | Space Required | Item | Space Required |
|---|---|---|---|
| Paperback books | 8" | Record albums | 13 1/4" |
| Hardback books | 11" | 8-track tapes | 6 1/4" |
| Oversize hardbacks | 15" | Cassette tapes | 5" |
| Catalog-format books | 15 1/2" | Circular slide trays | 9 3/4" |

## COMPARING CABINET MATERIALS

| Cabinet Material | Features | Relative Cost |
|---|---|---|
| Particleboard | The better units have wood or plastic veneers, but some lacquered or photographed finishes work well, too. | Low to moderate |
| Hardboard | Often used for doors, backs, and sides on wooden frames. | Moderate |
| Hardwood | Usually veneered plywood with hardwood frames. Sturdy construction, easy-care finishes. | Moderate to high |
| Steel | Baked enamel finishes. Some are noisy, prone to rusting. Not much demand for them. | Low to high |

## CHOOSING AND BUYING KITCHEN CABINETS

Quality control and a broad range of styling options make today's mass-produced cabinets competitive with all but the most costly custom-made units. You can order stock cabinets *knocked down,* then assemble and finish them; purchase units *in the white,* which require only finishing; or select *prefinished* versions ready for installation. Also keep in mind that most manufacturers offer several lines, each constructed of slightly different materials and priced accordingly.

Judge construction by taking a close look at how joints are fitted and the way insides and backs have been finished. Check hardware, too. Quality cabinets have doors that swing freely and latch securely, and drawers that roll on metal tracks. Look, too, for a NKCA (National Kitchen Cabinet Association) certification label. This group sets minimum standards for the cabinet industry.

## MEASURING FOR NEW CABINETS

Standardized dimensions and modular designs greatly simplify the job of tailoring cabinets to your kitchen. Just measure the space available, order a series of units that comes close to fitting it, then make up the difference with *fillers* between cabinets.

First, carefully plot your kitchen on graph paper, making both floor plan and elevation drawings. For base cabinets, measure at countertop height as well as along baseboards and note any variations. Be sure to include door swings, heating outlets, window casings, pipes, appliance sizes, and any other features that could cause an unpleasant surprise.

Now fill in the layout you want, using the information at right as a guide. Height measurements shown accommodate the reach of an average-height person and are accepted as standards throughout the kitchen and appliance industries.

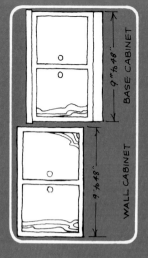

WALL CABINET

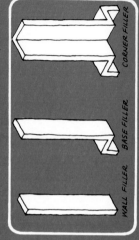

BASE CABINET

Manufacturers offer plenty of choices when it comes to cabinet widths. Purchase them from 9 to 48 inches wide.

WALL FILLER   BASE FILLER   CORNER FILLER

Fillers fit between units, letting you adjust a bank of cabinets to the space available. Rip them to the width you need.

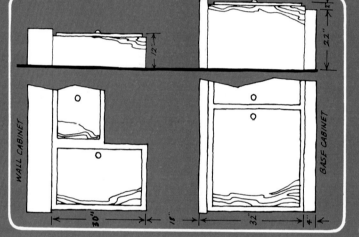

WALL CABINET

BASE CABINET

Base cabinets typically measure 36 inches high by 24 inches deep. Wall cabinets are 12 to 30 inches high, 12 inches deep.

# INSTALLING KITCHEN CABINETS

Achieving a built-in look with prefabricated cabinets might seem to call for some tricky carpentry. Not so! Examine a unit and you'll see that the manufacturer has done most of the work, providing you with perfectly square modules that you can interlock with screws or dowels. Assembly consists of carefully leveling and plumbing each cabinet, then fastening it to the wall studs and to its neighbors.

Level base cabinets as shown below. You'll probably need to use shims to accomplish this. Use the screw sizes specified by the manufacturer; drive screws through frames, not the thinner back and side panels. And never install cabinets with nails—they don't have the holding power of screws, and they might split the wood.

If a baseboard, door or window casing gets in the way, remove it and trim to fit after the cabinets are in place.

Cap off base cabinets with a countertop from a lumberyard or a kitchen or building supplier. Most will cut one to size and even make a cutout for the sink if you supply a pattern. (Measure carefully, though—mistakes cost.) You can also make your own countertop by veneering exterior-grade plywood with plastic laminate (see page 475).

Install the countertop by screwing angle brackets to the counter's underside and to the cabinet frame.

To hang wall cabinets, first build a movable support you can set on the counter. Next, rest a unit on the support, shim behind to plumb the cabinet, then screw through the frame to the wall studs.

Finish off the job by installing molding to cover any gaps between the cabinets and wall or floor.

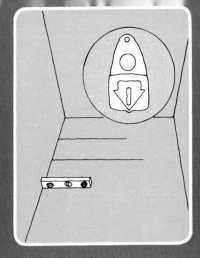

Begin the installation by marking the locations of the wall studs. Find them with a stud finder as shown in the inset.

Set a cabinet into place, then level it by tapping shims underneath. Level from front to back as well as from side to side.

Now drill pilot holes and drive screws into the studs. A screwdriver attachment on an electric drill speeds this job along.

Once a unit has been leveled and secured, chisel away any shims that protrude. Now you're ready to install the next cabinet.

Sometimes a thin shim between cabinets will compensate for minor irregularities. Face edges must butt tightly, though.

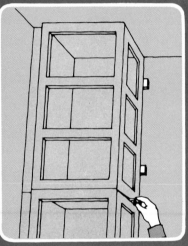

Fasten units together by drilling holes and driving screws as shown. Countersink the screws' heads about ½ inch.

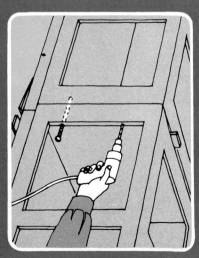

## BUILDING A CLOSET

Before you leap into a closet-building project, look at your overall storage situation. Are you making the best use of existing facilities? The organizing techniques shown on pages 83-85 might help create enough space in your existing closets.

Next, give some thought to how big a unit you'll need. Pages 83-84 give minimum dimensions for shallow and walk-in closets; a little bigger would be a lot better in both cases.

Now, consider the best location for a new storage unit. If at all possible, locate it near the point of use for the items you'll be keeping. But all too often,

rooms that lack storage don't have floor space to spare, either. So instead of further cramping a bedroom, for instance, you might want to take a look at under-utilized areas of the basement, attic, or garage; a large closet in one of these spots might just be able to handle all of your excess gear. (For more storage location possibilities, see the overview on page 82.)

Finally, ask yourself if a new unit could help you solve another problem as well. A new closet by the front door, for example, might also provide much-needed separation between the entry and living room. Or treat a child to a loft bed and tuck drawers underneath.

Innovative closet ideas abound. Familiarize yourself with the two basic

designs illustrated below, then adapt one to your own needs. The conventionally framed unit at lower left goes together just as your existing closets did: use it for a generous walk-in that looks as if it came with the house. Because it doesn't require framing, a closet made from panels (below right) provides more storage per square inch of floor space. Units like this can be as compact and dressy as a bookcase.

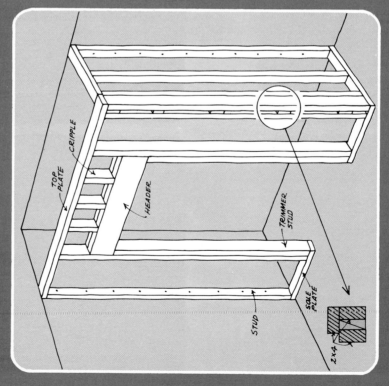

The conventionally framed closet above fits nicely into a corner, along the narrowest wall of a room, or at the end of a hallway. Learn the elements of building partitions (see pages 48-50) and you can construct its framing in a single day.

For the studs, choose 2x4s, as illustrated—or save space with

2x3s. Either way, you'll need a pair of 2x4s or 2x6s for the header. You also have a choice of finishing materials: cover the unit with drywall (see pages 51-52), then tape the joints (see page 53) and paint; or sheathe with paneling (see page 46).

Finish off your new closet with shelves, rods, and a door.

The closet above goes together with 3/4-inch-thick panels like a huge box (see page 470).

Cut its components from plywood or particleboard. Which you select depends largely upon your budget and the finish you want. *Medium-density overlay* plywood (see page 466) lends itself to a smooth, painted look.

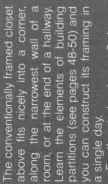

You can also paint particleboard or cover it with plastic laminate (see page 475).

Once you have applied the finish, set the unit directly on the floor in the desired location. Or, i you'd rather, rest it on a base made with 2x4s.

# STORAGE YOU CAN BUY

Sometimes it makes sense for even an ardent do-it-yourselfer to buy storage units rather than build them. Why spend several evenings cutting and joining the lumber for a simple bookcase, for example, when you can purchase a similar unfinished piece for just a few dollars more than it would cost to buy the materials?

You don't have to settle for a utilitarian look, either. You can dress up unfinished or drab units with paint, stain, or fabric coverings. To learn about wood finishes, see pages 528-537; for metal-finishing techniques, turn to page 522.

The chart below shows some of the more common modular, knocked-down, and unfinished units. For additional possibilities, check out paint stores, lumberyards, department stores, and do-it-yourself centers.

| STORAGE UNIT | APPLICATIONS | HOW TO CHOOSE |
| --- | --- | --- |
| | **Unfinished bookcases** come in modular sizes ideal for lining up or stacking anywhere you need open-shelf storage. Get steel bookcases from office suppliers. | The better quality wood units have rabbeted backs and dadoed shelves; surfaces should need only light sanding. |
| | **Wardrobes** may be wood, metal, or hardboard; they come knocked-down or assembled. For an entire wall of storage, flank a desk with a pair of them. | Better wood and hardboard versions have hardwood frames. Avoid flimsy construction and metal cabinets with sharp edges. |
| | **Open-frame steel shelving** stands on its own, making it handy for use as a divider as well as against the wall. Shelves run as deep as 24 inches. | Sturdy posts and nut-and-bolt locking systems minimize swaying. Big units may need cross-bracing or fastening to a wall. |
| | **Drawer cases** stack to any height. Some have open sides for built-in situations. For a desk, lay a door across two stacks. Note this compact study. | Good ones have rabbeted fronts and move easily on metal or hardwood guides. (More about drawer construction on page 471.) |
| | **Plastic trays and bins** make inexpensive drawers. To construct a case for them, build a large plywood box with cleats inside to support the trays' lips. | Clear acrylic trays let you see contents at a glance. Rubberized types, available in a variety of colors, hold heavier loads. |
| | **Cubes and boxes** stack any which way for modular storage. Choose wood, plastic laminate, or solid plastic versions. Some interlock with each other. | Well-made wood cubes have reinforced corners all around. If particleboard is used, be sure to surface it with plastic laminate. |
| | **Freestanding cabinets** made of wood, metal, or hardboard provide storage and a counter. Typically, they're 30 or 36 inches high and 20 to 36 inches wide. Keep tools and other bulky gear in file cabinets. Legal-size drawers measure 11 inches high, 24 to 28 inches deep, 15 inches wide (inside); letter-size are 12 inches wide. | For a quick test of a cabinet's quality, try to pick it up; sturdy ones are heavier. Look, too, for tight, well-fitting joints and seams. |

# FIREPLACES

As you can see here, there's a lot more to a good fireplace than just a cheery glow. Efficient modern-day versions keep logs burning for hours at a time—and send all but a few whiffs of smoke up the chimney.

Most of the action takes place in the *firebox.* Its splayed sides help funnel air across the *hearth* to the base of the fire. The firebox's sloping rear wall then deflects heat back into the room.

Above, a *throat* pulls the smoke up the chimney. Here there's usually a *damper* so you can control the draft. Note, too, that the *lintel,* the firebox's top front edge, helps direct smoke up the chimney.

Above the damper-throat assembly, a *smoke chamber* stops cold air coming down the chimney and diverts it back up the *flue;* were it not for this feature, outside air could drop straight into the fire

and push the smoke directly back into the living area.

An *ash door* in the hearth, plus an *ash pit* and *clean-out* door mean you don't have to haul dusty debris through the house. And in some fireplaces, a *ven...* in the ash pit helps create a better draft.

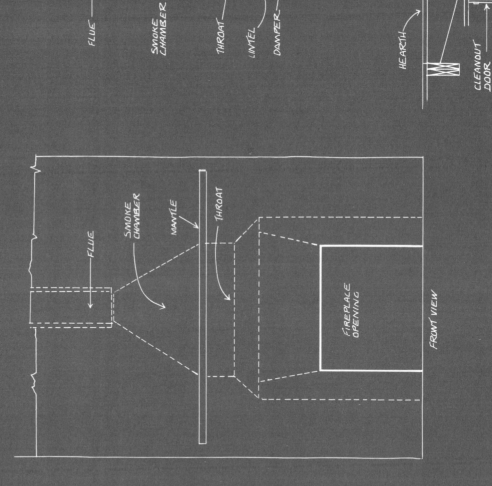

FLUE

SMOKE CHAMBER

MANTLE

THROAT

FIREPLACE OPENING

FRONT VIEW

FLUE

SMOKE CHAMBER

THROAT

LINTEL

DAMPER

FIREBOX

HEARTH

ASH DROP

VENT

ASHPIT

CLEANOUT DOOR

SECTION VIEW

ANATOMY OF
A FIREPLACE

92

With building codes and centuries of development behind them, today's fireplaces need little tending to. Chimney fires still happen, though—often because someone neglected a quick inspection before lighting the first logs of the season. Besides the indoor jobs detailed below, look over your chimney from basement to attic to roof. If you see any major, settlement-related cracks, call in a masonry contractor.

## CHECK THESE EVERY FALL

| | |
|---|---|
| **Flue** | Open the damper and peer up the flue. If you can't see light, check the flue with a mirror and flashlight to determine what the blockage is. Clean a chimney flue every few years, as shown on page 118. Repair any masonry cracks (see pages 134 and 135). |
| **Damper** | A damper has to seal tightly, or you'll lose heated house air through it. If yours won't close securely, feel around its edges; sometimes small bits of mortar lodge there. Ensure that the hinges and handle work smoothly so you can make necessary draft adjustments. |
| **Firebox** | For safety, most fireboxes are lined with high-temperature firebricks. Check to see if any have broken or come loose. If so, repair as shown on page 94. Clean soot off masonry with a mild solution of muriatic acid and water; wear rubber gloves. |
| **Ash pit** | Usually this needs attention only every other year, depending on your fire-building habits. If the ashes seem soggy and hard to remove, suspect leakage. With outside clean-out doors, seal any gaps that might admit cold air. |

## BUILDING A FIRE THAT LIGHTS AND LASTS

When you can't get a good blaze going, don't be too quick to blame the fireplace or fuel. A fire also consumes a surprising amount of air—and in a tightly weather-stripped house, you just might not have enough of it for a strong updraft.

Test this when you open the damper by wetting a finger and sticking it into the firebox. If you feel air coming from above, there's a downdraft that will either kill your fire or smoke up the house.

To increase the amount of inside air available, shut off any exhaust fans that may be running; even a small bathroom ventilator can evacuate a lot of air. Crack open a window near the fireplace. As last resorts, try the experiments shown on page 94.

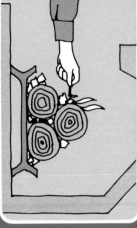

For a fast start, place a couple pieces of crumpled paper between the andirons, and then crisscross kindling on top.

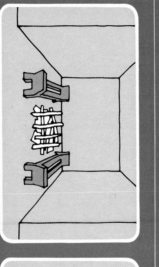

You need at least three loosely laid logs for any fire. Note how the draft rises around them and feeds on their inner surfaces.

Before lighting the kindling, set a match to a crumpled paper laid on top. This warms the flue for a positive draft.

After your fire is burning well, try throttling down the damper. With it partially closed, you won't lose so much heat.

# SOLVING FIREPLACE PROBLEMS

## REPLACING FIREBRICKS

Any break in a firebox's lining poses a safety hazard, so make all needed repairs before lighting that first fire of the season. If any of the mortar joints have deteriorated, restore them with the repointing techniques illustrated on page 134—but mix your mortar with special fireclay cement rather than the ordinary type.

You'll need fireclay mortar for replacement jobs, too. If you have to install a few new bricks, measure the old ones first; sizes vary.

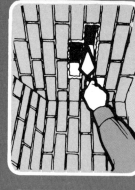

Chop out loose or broken bricks by chipping away mortar with a heavy hammer and bricklayer's chisel. Protect your eyes.

Butter the bricks, too, before you slip them into place. If the fit is tight, tap them with the handle of your trowel.

Once the bricks are out, remove any remaining mortar, then clear debris from the cavity with a vacuum cleaner.

Thoroughly dampen the cavity before applying fresh mortar. Dry bricks draw water from the mortar and weaken the bond.

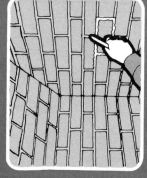

Butter all surfaces of surrounding bricks with a 1:3 mix of fireclay cement and sand, and enough water to make a paste.

Scrape away any excess mortar, let the repair set for 10 minutes, then shape the joints with a pipe or joint strike.

## CURING A FAULTY DRAW

If your fireplace chronically smokes, first make sure it's getting an adequate supply of oxygen, as explained at the bottom of page 93. If those strategies don't clear the air, experiment with the more drastic remedies illustrated here.

Loose-laying firebricks lets you adjust the firebox's size and proportions. If that does the job, mortar them as shown above.

Check out the situation on the roof, too. For a proper draw, a chimney must extend at least two feet higher than any nearby structure. A new home in the neighborhood, or even a sizable tree may be causing your problem.

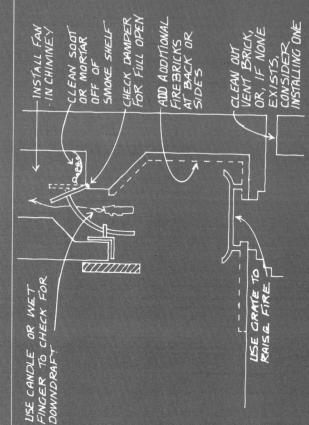

USE CANDLE OR WET FINGER TO CHECK FOR DOWNDRAFT

INSTALL FAN IN CHIMNEY

CLEAN SOOT OR MORTAR OFF OF SMOKE SHELF

CHECK DAMPER FOR FULL OPEN

ADD ADDITIONAL FIREBRICKS AT BACK OR SIDES

CLEAN OUT VENT BRICK, OR, IF NONE EXISTS, CONSIDER INSTALLING ONE

USE GRATE TO RAISE FIRE

# TRACKING DOWN FLUE PROBLEMS

Your home's chimney probably includes several different flues—one for each fireplace, plus separate venting for a furnace and water heater.

This makes a defective flue doubly dangerous. It could, of course, set the house afire. But more subtly, a flue leak or downdraft problem could poison your atmosphere with deadly, odorless carbon monoxide.

To protect against both of these hazards, modern-day chimneys are lined with firebricks or flue tiles that rarely leak.

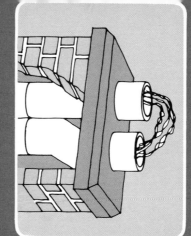

If a fireplace smokes even when there's no fire in it, suspect either a flue-to-flue leak or a downdraft problem.

(If yours is an older home, don't put an unused fireplace back into action until a professional has examined its flue.)

When a flue does give trouble, the problem usually involves loose joints between tiles, or downdrafts that pull smoke from one flue to another at the chimney top. For solutions to either problem, call in a chimney contractor.

You can easily test for leaks yourself, though. Wait for a day warm enough to open doors and windows, then build a fire. After it gets going, cover the flue with wet burlap, then dump wet leaves on the fire. You'll soon see any leaks.

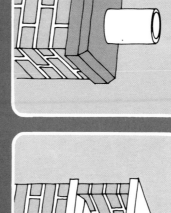

Staggering the heights of adjacent flues eliminates downdrafts from one to the other. This is a job for a mason.

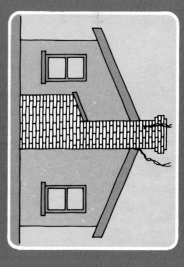

If you have a leaky flue, you'll be able to see smoke oozing from the chimney's exterior mortar joints. Check in the attic, too.

Another answer to downdrafts involves increasing the chimney's height, separating the flues, and capping them with a hood.

# INSTALLING GAS LOGS AND STARTERS

If wood is scarce in your area—or if you just don't like cleaning up the mess after a solid-fuel fire—consider warming your hearth with a set of ceramic logs fired by natural or LP gas. With many, you don't need a match, and a few also include thermostatic controls.

Install gas log sets only in a wood-burning fireplace, and operate them only with the damper open. You may need a plumber to route a gas line to the firebox. Installation involves a simple hookup.

A gas log lighter fires conventional logs quickly without kindling. You just touch a match under the fire basket, wait a few minutes until the wood is thoroughly

ignited, then shut off the starter and let the logs burn normally. Again, of course, you'll have to get gas to the fireplace.

If you run the gas line yourself, use pipe tape or the sealer specified by the manufacturer of the unit at all pipe joints. And when you fill the line, check all of the joints for leaks. To do this, mix a solution of household detergent and water and dab some on each joint. Bubbles will form at the joint if you have a leak. (More about gas systems on pages 308-315.)

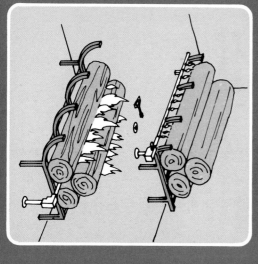

# INSTALLING A NEW FIREPLACE

Thinking about treating yourself to the warmth and crackling aroma of a new fireplace? If so, you have lots of choices and decisions to make.

Unless you're building a new home or addition, you'll probably rule out an all-masonry type right away. Pouring deep footings and making structural alterations is just too expensive compared to the cost of installing kit-form prefab units.

What's more, many prefabs burn more efficiently than all-masonry fireplaces. Some old-timers, built before energy became a major expense, lose as much as 90 percent of their heat up the chimney. Worse yet, they pull heated air from your home for combustion, which means that your furnace might actually work harder to heat rooms not warmed by the fire.

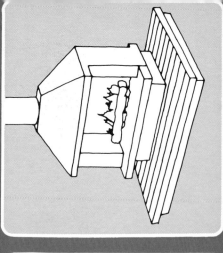

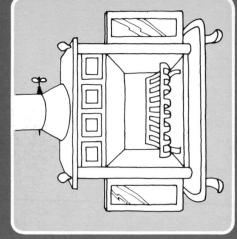

Freestanding fireplaces usually occupy less space and offer more design flexibility. Just set one in place and hook up a chimney.

## CHOOSING AND BUYING A PREFAB FIREPLACE

In shopping for a prefabricated unit, you have to first decide whether you prefer a built-in or freestanding model (see the drawings at right).

Built-ins, which can be fairly difficult to install, look quite like traditional masonry fireplaces. Freestanding units come in myriad shapes, sizes, colors, and styles, and most have a contemporary look.

Both vent through insulated metal chimney components that you can run through walls, ceilings, and roofs. Not only are these metal flues easy to assemble—some also feature a "positive draft" that guarantees a smokeless fire.

You can veneer built-in prefabs with masonry or even—in some cases—build conventional wood-frame walls around them.

## ENERGY SAVERS

If you plan to use your new fireplace as a source of primary or auxiliary heat, look for one designed to get the most from every log you put into it.

*Heat-circulating types* include built-in ducting that directs warmed air back into the room or to adjacent rooms. Add electric blowers and you have a wood-burning furnace.

*Fresh-air-feed fireplaces* don't rob heat from your home while they burn. Instead, they pull in combustion air from outdoors via a dampered duct. Not only that, but they also throw a surprising amount of heat back out into the room.

For an even more efficient solid-fuel heat source, check out the airtight stove shown on page 349.

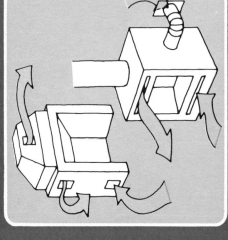

Both heat-circulating (left) and fresh-air-feed fireplaces create convection currents that supplement the firebox's radiant heat.

The old-fashioned Franklin stove is still a fairly thrifty design. Closing the doors greatly improves its efficiency.

96

# INSTALLING A FREESTANDING UNIT

Lightweight construction and easily assembled components make installing a freestanding fireplace a feasible project

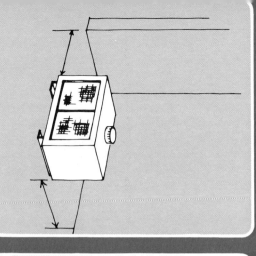

for any do-it-yourselfer willing to tackle the slightly tricky task of getting a chimney through the roof (see page 99).

Be sure, though, to check building codes before you buy any prefab—not all makes are widely approved. You may need a building permit, too.

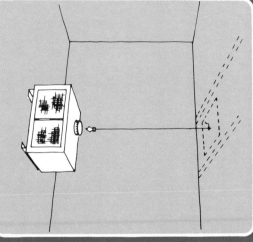

If the fireplace you've selected requires a noncombustible base, construct this first. You can pour a thin concrete slab, mortar bricks or tiles together, or even fill a wood frame with loose gravel.

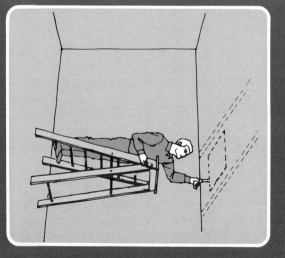

---

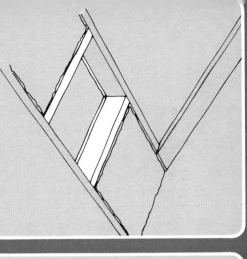

check codes and the manufacturer's data for minimum clearances from combustible and noncombustible wall surfaces.

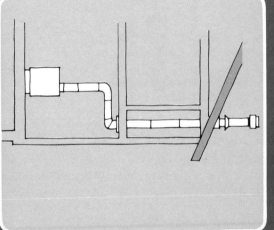

Drop a plumb line to find where you must cut into the ceiling. You may have to shift the unit slightly to pass between joists.

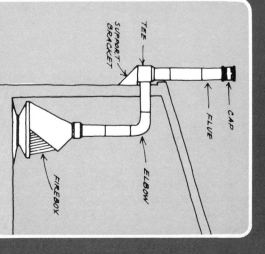

To make the ceiling opening, bore holes at each corner, then cut with a keyhole saw. Do the same with any floor above.

---

...enail 2x6 headers between the ...ists in the ceiling opening, then ...stall a chimney base, as shown ...n page 99.

If there's a room upstairs, you may have to box-in the chimney—or route it through a closet. Offsets provide some flexibility.

As an alternative, consider an installation that goes up an outside wall. Watch roof clearances, though (see page 99).

CAP
FLUE
TEE
SUPPORT BRACKET
ELBOW
FIREBOX

## INSTALLING A
## BUILT-IN FIREPLACE

Face a prefabricated fireplace assembly with brick or stone, and no one need ever

know you didn't build the whole thing yourself. You'll have to master a few masonry techniques, of course—and provide a concrete footing.

Or choose a double-wall unit designed for "zero clearance" from combustible

materials. These can be enclosed with wood-stud walls, as shown here.

With either type, you first locate the fireplace and install a chimney (see pages 97 and opposite), then construct the enclosure.

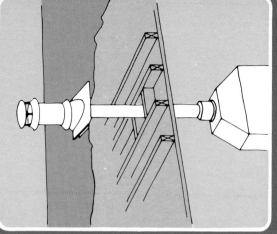

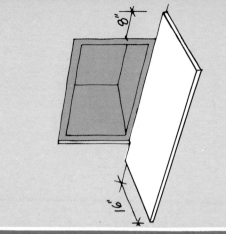

You have a choice when it comes to topping off your prefabricated unit. The housing style here is called a contemporary cap.

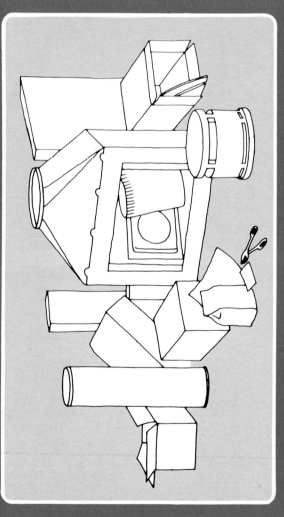

When you unpack your fireplace, read the instructions closely. Codes require that you follow them to the letter.

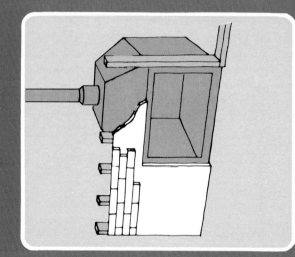

To create a masonry look indoors, cover the framing with plywood, then mortar up an artificial brick or stone facing.

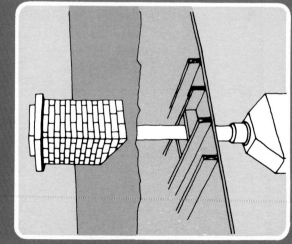

If you don't like the appearance of a metal stack, conceal it in a simulated brick housing. These come in a range of colors.

Most codes specify a noncombustible hearth at least 16 inches wider than the fireplace opening and 16 inches deep.

98

# INSTALLING A PREFAB CHIMNEY

Whether you've chosen a built-in or freestanding fireplace, preassembled metal chimney components get you through the roof at a fraction of what it would cost for masonry work. And because the flue sections are insulated, you need maintain only a small distance between them and combustible materials that are adjacent.

Before you order chimney components, measure the height you'll need—including any spaces between floors and enough up top to reach a point at least two feet higher than any portion of the roof within 10 feet.

Besides the sections, you'll need special flashing to seal against roof leaks, sheet metal fire-stop spacers for each floor or ceiling the chimney penetrates, a terminal cap or chimney housing, and, if you're venting a freestanding unit, a chimney base support.

Lay in all the parts you'll need, make any in-the-house openings beforehand, and you can finish off your chimney-building project in a day or less.

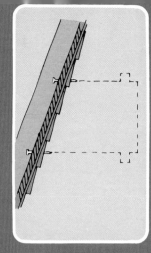

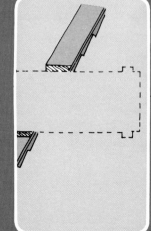

After you know exactly where the chimney will exit, mark for the opening, then drive four long nails up through the roofing.

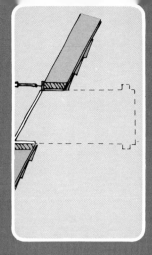

Slice away composition roofing with a sharp knife, then cut completely through the sheathing with a keyhole or saber saw.

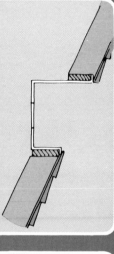

Frame the opening with the same size members as the rafters. This frame allows for attaching a fire-stop or a support box.

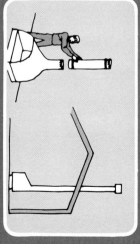

Slip the fire-stop spacer up into the opening and secure it by nailing or screwing through the flanges into the frame.

For freestanding units, insert the chimney support box in the opening, make flaps of its edges, and nail to headers.

Stack the flue sections atop the firebox, snapping, twisting, or screwing them together until you penetrate the roof.

Secure the flue housing, slip sections, and housing top (or round lashing, collar, and cap) to the roof. Cement housing/roof joint.

Up on the roof, slip the flashing under the roofing on the upper side, as shown on page 116. Seal lower edge with roofing cement.

# BASEMENTS AND FOUNDATIONS

Your home's foundation has several heavy-duty assignments. First, of course, it has to support an entire house. Second, it acts as a series of retaining walls and must have enough lateral strength to hold back the earth around its edges. Finally, it also may shelter a *basement*—the main subject of this chapter.

Basement/foundation walls begin with a concrete *footing* designed to spread out the thousands-of-pounds-per-square-foot loads down there. Note that the footing also supports the much thinner slab used for most basement floors; in some cases a flexible *expansion joint* around the perimeter of the floor accommodates any minor shifts in the walls or floor. Your home's footings may or may not be protected by *drain tile* laid in sand or gravel to divert water.

The walls themselves can be almost any material—concrete block, cinder block, poured concrete, clay tile, brick, or stone. Some newer homes even boast specially treated wood underpinnings. Regardless of a foundation's construction, though, its exterior face should be waterproofed before the soil is replaced.

Up top, the walls support a wood *sill plate* on which carpenters lay *joists* for the *subfloor* and *finish floor* above. More about sill plates and floors on pages 10 and 128.

The following pages discuss basements and foundations from the inside out—beginning indoors where you're likely to first notice any basement problems, then moving out to their exterior foundation sides if all interior remedies fail.

Note that some foundations differ from the one shown here. If your home has only a crawl space underneath, it either sits atop shorter versions of these supporting walls, or it's held up by a series of piers. To learn about crawl-space problems and their solutions, see pages 370 and 377.

Alternatively, your house may have no space under it at all. If this is the case, the structure rests on a slab similar to those used for patios (see pages 154 and 160-166)—but much thicker, of course.

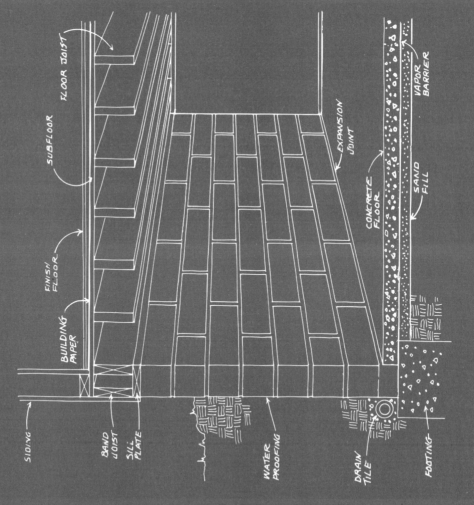

SIDING
BAND JOIST
SILL PLATE
BUILDING PAPER
FINISH FLOOR
SUBFLOOR
FLOOR JOIST
EXPANSION JOINT
WATER PROOFING
DRAIN TILE
CONCRETE FLOOR
VAPOR BARRIER
SAND FILL
FOOTING

## ANATOMY OF A BASEMENT

Basements suffer many of the same ills that afflict other spaces inside your home, plus a special one of their own—moisture. Differences between the temperature below ground (usually a constant 55 degrees F.) and that of the air upstairs or outside often make a slight mustiness inevitable, especially in rainy or muggy weather.

But if the floor or walls down there chronically sweat, or—worse yet—if puddles of water collect on the floor, it's time to take action. A wet basement not only wastes much potential for living or storage, it also could eventually undermine your home's footings and foundation walls.

The chart below contrasts the four possible sources of below-ground moisture problems. Simple tests help you distinguish one from the other and direct you to their remedies. In tracking down the water's origin, don't neglect the possibility that it may result from a combination of factors—condensation coupled with seepage, for instance.

If you're planning to finish your basement's walls and floor, you'll want to permanently dry them out first, of course. That may require the more costly exterior waterproofing methods shown on pages 104 and 105. But don't worry about mild condensation; putting up insulation and a vapor barrier (see page 373) usually will eliminate this. If you're not sure this alone will work in your situation, apply two coats of interior sealant.

To learn about finishing basement walls, see pages 44-53; for floors, check out pages 19 and 24-27; for ceilings, turn to pages 59-63.

## WHERE'S THE WATER COMING FROM?

| Problem | Symptom/Test | Cause | Solution |
|---|---|---|---|
| Condensation | Damp walls, dripping pipes, rusty hardware, mildew. To identify condensation, tape a mirror in the dampest spot and wait 24 hours. If it's foggy or beaded with water, suspect condensation. | Excess humidity in the air—usually from an internal source such as a basement shower, washing machine, or unvented dryer—or a significant temperature difference between the wall and the inside air. | Install a dehumidifier, improve ventilation, or seal the interior walls. |
| Seepage | General dampness on the floor or a particular wall, especially down near floor level. As with condensation, tape a mirror to the wall. If moisture condenses behind it, seepage is the culprit. | Surface water is forcing its way through pores in the foundation or an expansion joint. The source may be poor roof drainage (see pages 120-123) or a leaky window well. | Improve surface drainage. If you have a relatively minor problem with seepage, an interior sealer may work. If not, waterproof the foundation from outside. |
| Leaks | Localized wetness that seems to be oozing or even trickling from a foundation wall or floor. Check the damp area carefully, paying particular attention to mortar joints between blocks. | Cracks that may result from normal settling, or an abnormal condition such as faulty roof drainage or a grade that slopes toward the wall. | You may be able to plug a single hole from inside. Otherwise, you'll have to dig down and work from outside. If leaking is widespread, waterproof the entire foundation wall and install drain tile. |
| Subterranean Water | A thin, barely noticeable film of water on the basement floor could be the first sign. Test by laying down vinyl sheet goods or plastic for two or three days; if moisture is penetrating, it will dampen the concrete underneath. | Usually a spring or high water table is forcing water up from below under high pressure, turning your basement into a well. This may happen only in rainy periods. | Drain tiles around the perimeter of the foundation or floor may help, but only if they can direct water to a lower spot or a storm sewer. You may need a sump pump (see page 105). |

## WRAPPING PIPES

Exposed cold water lines sweat or collect moisture even under ideal humidity conditions. Insulating them solves this problem. While you're at it, wrap hot water pipes, too—you'll save energy that's normally wasted during cool weather.

Adhesive-backed insulating tape just winds around the pipes. Cover all fittings, too—but leave the valve handles exposed.

Pre-slit sleeve-type insulation makes a thick jacket for longer pipe runs. More about installing these on page 372.

## SEALING INTERIOR WALLS

Waterproofing compounds designed especially for basement walls and other masonry surfaces effectively stop the kind of seepage that feels clammy to the touch. But don't expect them to solve a severe moisture problem.

If you can see a film of water on the wall, it's probably coming in under pressure—and that force will simply push any sealer aside. In this situation, you need to seal from outside, as shown on pages 104 and 105.

Waterproofing formulations come as either a powder or a liquid. The powder type, which includes cement, must be mixed with water and applied to an already damp surface. The liquids, on the other hand, are ready to use after stirring—but the wall must be dry for them to adhere.

Both require that you first clean away any dirt, grease, or powder. Wash dirty walls with a strong household cleaner and wire brush; remove grease with a degreaser or solvent.

If a wall has any visible holes or cracks, plug them as illustrated on the opposite page, then let the repairs thoroughly cure before applying a sealer. And prepare yourself for some hard work when you apply these heavy coatings.

Pay special attention to packing the mortar joints. The first coat will require lots of time and sealing compound.

Apply these paste-like sealers with a stiff, coarse-bristle brush. Take care to fill every single pore in the blocks.

If you don't like the color of your waterproofed wall, you can paint over it. Wait until it's thoroughly cured, though.

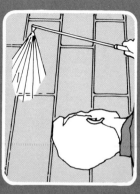

Mix both liquid and powder compounds thoroughly. The liquids are thick and require a heavy-duty stirrer to blend them.

Prepare walls for a cement-base sealer by thoroughly wetting them with a fine mist from a garden hose or portable sprayer.

For a tight seal, you'll need two applications. The second goes on more easily—but again, strive for complete coverage.

With cement-base sealants, you want to prevent too-rapid drying. To do this, keep the base coat moist for several days.

# PLUGGING HOLES AND CRACKS

Before you attempt to patch any break in a basement wall or floor, watch it over a period of time. Most cracks come from normal settling and soon stabilize. However, they can be the first sign of a major structural fault. For these you'll need professional help.

Next, determine if water is leaking through the opening. If so, fill it with a quick-hardening expansive cement or epoxy compound; this remedy works even if the water is coming in under pressure at the time you're making the repair. You can patch dry spots with a mortar mix of one part cement, two parts sand, and just enough water to make a doughy consistency. Add the water slowly and stir it in well.

Use a cold chisel to enlarge the hole slightly and undercut its edges. This "keys" the plug so it can't pop loose.

Now mix plugging cement and work it into a stopper shape. Its fatter end should be slightly larger than the hole's diameter.

Turn the mortar with a trowel several times, then pack the crack. Use the trowel's tip to work the mix in well.

The moment the cement begins to stiffen, pop it into place like a cork and hold it there for three or four minutes.

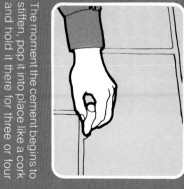

Cracks also must be cut back to sound material and their edges beveled. If you're using ordinary mortar, moisten cracks well first.

After the mortar begins to harden, pack it again, then shave off any excess with a wet trowel, pointing tool, or putty knife.

After your repair hardens, check it and its surroundings from time to time. You may find that the plug holds, but that a new leak springs up somewhere nearby. This could mean that water is backing up against the exterior side of the foundation or underneath the floor—cases for the more drastic remedies illustrated on pages 104 and 105.

# REPAIRING WINDOW WELLS

Water stains or seepage in the wall under a basement window usually indicate that the well outside is flooding. Often a faulty downspout or clogged gutter turns out to be the culprit, so check your roof drainage first (see pages 120 and 121).

If the well doesn't seem to be getting more water than it can handle, clean out any debris and flush with a hose to see if it's draining properly. The drawings at right show the types of construction you'll most likely encounter.

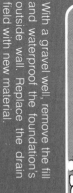

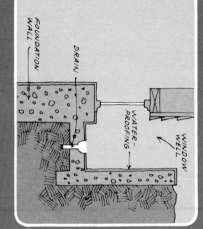

With concrete wells, try inserting a hose in the drain and blowing out any obstructions. If it's clear, waterproof as shown opposite.

With a gravel well, remove the fill and waterproof the foundation's outside wall. Replace the drain field with new material.

# SOLVING FOUNDATION PROBLEMS

## IMPROVING DRAINAGE

A good drainage system catches water and sends it elsewhere before it reaches your foundation. One that's often overlooked consists of the plantings in your yard. Shallow-rooted shrubs and trees can drink up a surprising quantity of moisture. Check with a nursery for the best species to plant and their optimum locations.

Also make sure that downspouts and gutters aren't dumping water alongside foundation walls. Spouts should empty onto concrete splash blocks, connect to underground pipes, or drain into a catch basin or dry well, such as the one depicted on page 121.

Most of the systems illustrated here use perforated or solid tiles to collect and carry off water. Realize, though, that they depend upon gravity and must discharge water to a lower area of your property or into a storm sewer.

If you decide to install tiles alongside your foundation, you may as well waterproof it, too, as shown on the opposite page. This way the time, money, and inconvenience of excavating pay off in double protection.

Think of the earth around your home as a gigantic sponge that soaks up rainfall, then gradually releases it into the water table below. Water that this sponge can't absorb flows downhill until it meets resistance—a foundation wall, for instance. There, a reservoir fills up, pressure increases, and the wall turns into a natural dam.

Just as you can't repair a dam from its downstream side, neither can you stop severe seepage from inside your basement. Instead, you have to either divert the flow or totally waterproof the wall—both outside projects that usually entail a lot of excavation.

Beware of waterproofing "specialists" who promise to do the job without digging. These outfits inject a chemical into the ground under pressure, much the same way exterminators eradicate termites (see page 137). The processes use different chemicals, of course—and they greatly differ in effectiveness; soil injection works well against termites, but it won't waterproof a foundation wall or floor.

Before you begin tearing up the yard, ask your local water department about the level of your water table. If it's only slightly below your basement floor, you might be better off to install a sump pump, as shown on the opposite page.

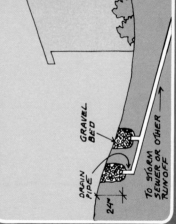

8" MIN.

24" MIN.

DRAIN PIPE

GRAVEL BED

TO STORM SEWER OR OTHER RUNOFF

24"

A grade that slopes away from the foundation will deter water. Build up the earth at least eight inches and level it out as shown.

If you're getting flooding from a higher elevation, consider a "curtain drain." Two trenches span the width of your house.

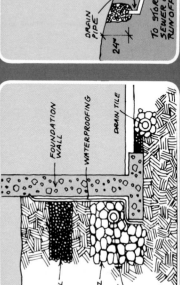

FOUNDATION WALL

WATERPROOFING

DRAIN TILE

GRAVEL

GRAVEL

DRAIN TILE

If water is coming up through your basement floor, install tiles inside the footing. This means breaking open the floor.

VAPOR BARRIER

EXCAVATION LINE

GRAVEL

DRAIN TILE

In more severe cases, you should dig down to the footing, lay drain tiles, apply waterproofing, then backfill with gravel and earth.

# WATERPROOFING A FOUNDATION

If sealing basement walls and regrading around the foundation fail to stem your water problem, resign yourself to some arduous ditch digging. Narrowing down the leaks to one or two walls can, of course, save you or your contractor a lot of work. And if the leaks show up only near the top of basement walls, you may be able to get by with sealing only partway down, as shown below.

Otherwise, you'll have to excavate to the footings. This also gives you an opportunity to install drain tiles, as illustrated on the opposite page.

Call in a ditching contractor and have him backhoe a trench that is wide enough to provide you with ample working space.

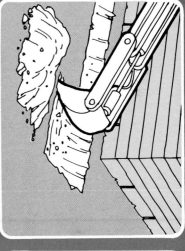

When he gets down near the footing, shore the ditch's sides with heavy lumber to prevent sliding or a cave-in.

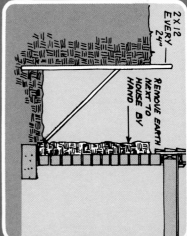

Scrub the surface clean, patch any cracks wider than ⅛ inch (see page 155), then coat the wall with asphalt compound.

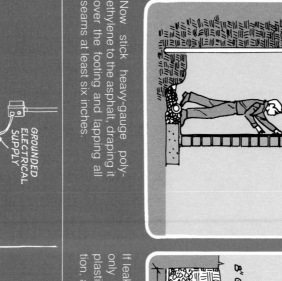

Now stick heavy-gauge polyethylene to the asphalt, draping it over the footing and lapping all seams at least six inches.

If leaking is near the surface, dig only two feet down, extend the plastic four feet from the foundation, and fill as shown.

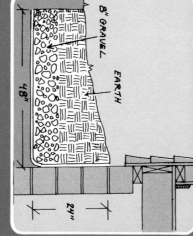

## INSTALLING A SUMP PUMP

If you can't keep moisture out of a basement—and if subterranean water is welling up from below, you may not be able to—*pump* it out. First you must dig a *sump pit* at the floor's lowest point, then install a pump as shown.

As water rises in the sump, it lifts a *float*, activating a motor that expels the water. A one-way *check valve* prevents backups. Make sure any sump system will handle the largest flow you might receive; you'll also need a warning device to tell when the pump isn't working.

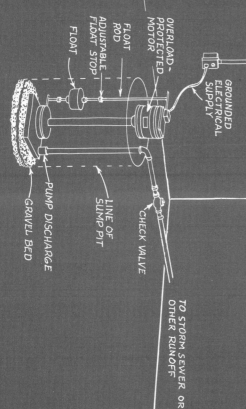

- FLOAT
- ADJUSTABLE FLOAT STOP
- FLOAT ROD
- OVERLOAD-PROTECTED MOTOR
- GROUNDED ELECTRICAL SUPPLY
- CHECK VALVE
- LINE OF SUMP PIT
- PUMP DISCHARGE
- GRAVEL BED
- TO STORM SEWER OR OTHER RUNOFF

**SECTION 2**

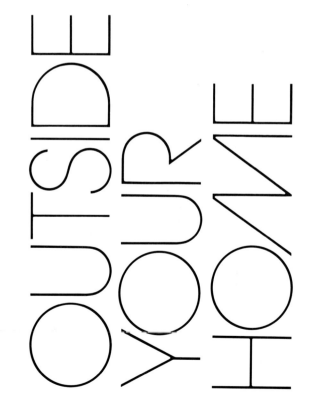

# OUTSIDE YOUR HOME

This section talks a lot about the weather—how rain, snow, ice, wind, and even sunshine subject a home's exterior to a terrific beating, and how you can keep its skin tight. Outside especially, an ounce of preventive maintenance can be worth pounds of costly repairs. That's why we've put special emphasis on annual and semiannual inspections that will enable you to head off exterior problems—such as leaks—before they become interior problems as well.

But "Outside Your Home" doesn't stop there. The latter part of each chapter presents improvement projects—everything from laying a bricks-in-sand patio to building a new garage—that add to your home's comfort now, and to its value when you decide to sell it.

# ROOFS

A pitched roof sheds water much the same way a duck does. *Courses* of roofing material—most often some variation of the *shingles* shown below— lay one atop the other, like a bird's feathers. Any shingle roof's "feathers" go at least two deep, with *exposures* that are slightly narrower than their *coverages*. Up top, an extra layer straddles the *ridge*.

*Valleys* wherever two slopes meet help direct runoff into *gutters*, which in turn drain through *downspouts*. For additional protection against leaking, metal or composition *flashings*, feathered in under the shingles, beef up a roof at its most vulnerable points. You'll find them in valleys and around chimneys, plumbing vents, dormers, and anything else that penetrates the roof's surface.

Underneath this plumage lies the most complex part of your home's structure. *Rafters* rise from the wall's *top plate* to the *ridge board*, defining the roof's pitch. *Collar beams* in the attic help keep the rafters from spreading; *headers* box-in any openings.

Next, carpenters nail on the board or plywood *sheathing* (sometimes called *decking*) that gives the roof rigidity, then they seal it against moisture with a layer of *building felt*. Finally, they trim off rafter ends at the eaves with a *fascia board*, and usually add *rake boards* to the roof's edges, as well.

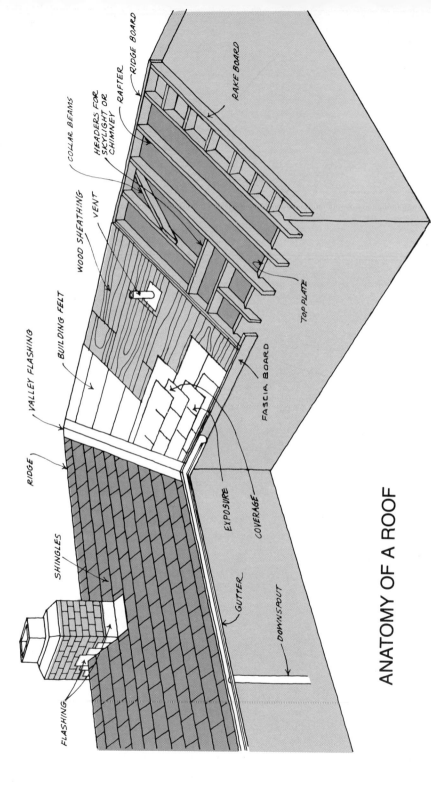

**ANATOMY OF A ROOF**

RAKE BOARD
RIDGE BOARD
COLLAR BEAMS
HEADERS FOR SKYLIGHT OR CHIMNEY
RAFTER
WOOD SHEATHING
VENT
TOP PLATE
BUILDING FELT
FASCIA BOARD
VALLEY FLASHING
RIDGE
EXPOSURE
COVERAGE
GUTTER
SHINGLES
DOWNSPOUT
FLASHING

# GETTING TO KNOW YOUR ROOF

You may already know what's up on your roof—but do you know how long it will last, and how to maintain it?

The chart below answers these questions for the materials most commonly used in the United States during the past 50 years. Consult it when selecting a new roof, too.

Note that the first five categories are all the water-shedding type explained on the opposite page. These work well on pitched roofs, but they won't protect you from water standing on a flat or only slightly sloping surface. Here you'll need a watertight membrane system—either metal or built-up roofing.

## COMPARING ROOFING MATERIALS

| Material | Features | Maintenance | Life Span |
|---|---|---|---|
| Asphalt Shingles | By far the most popular and least expensive, they're made of roofing felt saturated with asphalt and coated with mineral granules. Some newer ones have a fiber glass base for greatly improved weather- and fire-resistance. | These require very little at first, but over the years, some shingles begin to curl, crack, and lose their surface coatings. Older types lift in high winds, but newer versions interlock or cement themselves down. Repairs are fairly easy (see page 113). | 15 to 30 years under temperate weather conditions. Better-quality asphalt shingles carry 25-year guarantees. |
| Wood Shingles and Shakes | Shingles have a uniform, machine-made appearance; shakes, a rustic, hand-split look. Both have a poor fire rating unless specially treated. Both shakes and shingles are quite expensive. | Unsealed types sometimes tend to rot, warp, and split—and also soon weather to a soft gray. Like asphalt shingles, they're not difficult to repair or replace (see page 112). | 20 years or more for shingles; up to 50 years for shakes if maintained well. |
| Asbestos Cement Shingles | Made of Portland cement reinforced with asbestos and often coated with plastic, this highly fire-resistant material costs more than wood. | Brittle composition makes them vulnerable to tree limbs and foul balls. Use wood-shingle repair and replacement techniques (see page 112). | 25 to 50 years, but you can expect them to darken as they age. |
| Slate, Clay Tiles | Both are heavy, expensive, and absolutely fireproof. Tiles are more commonly used in the southwest, and slate in the east, where the quarries are located. | An occasional cracked or chipped tile can present you with a tricky repair project (see page 114). Slate is somewhat easier to repair (see page 113). | The life of your house, provided you make repairs before the underlayment is damaged. |
| Roll Roofing | This is similar to asphalt shingles, but comes in wide strips that are lapped horizontally across the roof's surface. Generally used on shallow slopes. | Lightweight, single-layer installations fail frequently—but repairs are very easy (see page 115). | From 5 to 15 years. With short-term warranties, ask if the company will come back for patching. |
| Metal Roofing | Although usually aluminum these days, older ones may be terne—a tin-steel alloy—or even copper. Modern-day styles include corrugated or ribbed panels and shingle strips. A good, non-combustible heat reflector, some types are suitable on flat roofs. | If aluminum comes in contact with any other metal, electrolytic action will cause deterioration. May need periodic painting (for repairs, see page 114). | Aluminum lasts up to 35 years; copper and terne are even more durable. |
| Built-Up Roofing | Unlike shingles, shakes, slate, and tiles, built-up roofs must be absolutely waterproof, a quality you need only in flat or very low-pitched situations. It's usually fabricated on the job by laminating layers of felt with asphalt or coal tar, then topping with gravel. | Leaks from a poor job can plague you through the life of the roof. Fortunately, repairs aren't too difficult (see page 115). | From 5 to 20 years. Generally, the more layers, the longer life you can expect. |

## GIVING YOUR ROOF A CHECKUP

To keep a tight roof overhead, examine it every spring and fall. You needn't haul out that awkward extension ladder and risk life and limb getting up on the roof, either. Just scan it from all sides through a pair of field glasses, paying particular attention to the points illustrated below.

If you do decide to climb up for a closer look, exercise caution. Also bear in mind that sun does more damage than wind and rain combined, so you may want to focus most of your effort on sunny slopes.

If a number of shingles are broken, blistered, or balding, and most seem to have lost their luster, prepare yourself for a re-roofing job.

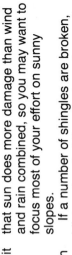
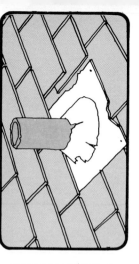

Ridge shingles often fail first. Look for cracks and wind damage. A leak here could show up almost anywhere in the house.

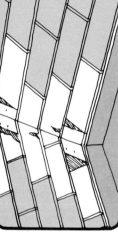

Valleys are another place where deterioration soon causes problems. If there's flashing here, make sure it's still sound.

Any loose, curled-up, or missing shingle will admit moisture that could weaken sheathing and harm walls and ceilings below.

Check all other flashings, too. They should be tight, rust-free, and sealed with pliable caulking or roofing cement.

A large accumulation of granules in the gutter means your roof is losing its coating. You can expect problems soon.

Wait for a heavy rain to find out if gutters and spouts are clean and free-flowing. Flooding can work up under lower shingle courses.

## PINPOINTING LEAKS

Any water that gets through your roof may follow a meandering, brook-like course—along sheathing, a rafter, even electrical cable—before it shows up as a damp spot on a ceiling or wall.

If you have an attic, you may be able to trace the stream to its source from up there. Look for water stains on framing, sheathing, and insulation, bearing in mind that any leak will originate higher than the area where it first appeared.

On a sunny day, a leak may show up as a tiny pinhole of light. If you find one of these, push a wire up through it as shown at right. This marks the spot on the roof itself; it may also guide the water to a bucket until you have time to make repairs. If there's no hole, but dampness indicates that you've found a leak, drive a nail up through the sheathing.

If your attic is finished, you'll have to do your sleuthing on the roof itself, carefully examining the critical points shown above. Wait for a dry, mild day, wear sneakers or other rubber-soled shoes, and don't walk on the roof any more than you have to—you could cause further damage.

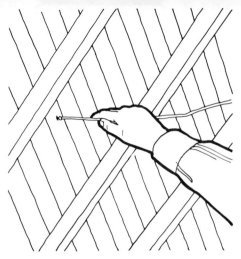

# CHOOSING AND USING EXTENSION LADDERS

If you've never scaled an extension ladder before, borrow or rent one and ask someone to steady it from below while you make your first few climbs. Most of us soon gain confidence.

For strength and rigidity, select a Type I- or Type II-class ladder (see page 494).

To set up a ladder, place its feet firmly against the foundation. You can extend it now, or wait until it's vertical.

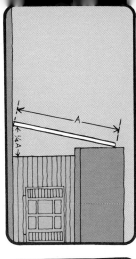

It should be long enough to extend three feet above your home's highest eave. To this distance add another foot to make up for the propping angle. Remember, too, that a ladder's extended height will measure about three feet less than the total of its sections.

Set up and use a ladder as shown below—and observe these precautions.

● Stay away from power lines. Even a wet wood ladder can conduct electricity.

● Never allow more than one person on a ladder at a time.
● Don't use ladders on windy days.
● Never paint a wooden ladder. You could be hiding future defects.
● Always store ladders indoors, away from moisture and would-be second-story burglars.

For stability, position the ladder so that the distance from its base to the wall is about one-fourth of its extended length.

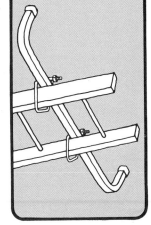

Now "walk" the ladder up, hand over hand, keeping your arms fairly straight. It will seem to get lighter as it rises.

To lengthen a ladder, brace one rail with your foot, lift from the house, then pull the rope. Make sure both locks catch.

To maintain your balance, keep your hips between the rails and don't overreach; erect ladders aren't difficult to move.

For stability, position the ladder so that the distance from its base to the wall is about one-fourth of its extended length.

Make sure the feet rest on firm ground. Don't try to shim them with bricks or boards; instead, extend one leg as shown.

Always use two hands when you climb. And instead of loading yourself down with tools, put them in a bucket and hoist them.

This accessory improves a ladder's stability, protects siding, spans obstacles, and keeps the ladder away from the house.

For roof work, hook a stabilizer over the ridge. Or secure the ladder with ropes tied to a tree on the other side.

# SOLVING ROOF PROBLEMS

If you're queasy about scrambling around on high places—and especially if your roof is slippery or steeply pitched—hire a professional for even minor fix-it jobs.

If you can conquer your fears, though, you'll find most repairs relatively simple Saturday-afternoon projects. Often, the biggest challenges come when you have to figure out how to hoist tools and materials up there, and how to get around on the roof itself.

On gentle slopes, just wear shoes with slip-resistant soles—and wait until the sun burns any dew off the roof's surface. Climb steeper pitches by hooking or tying an ordinary ladder over the ridge of the roof. Or make a "chicken ladder" by nailing 1x2 cleats across a 1x10-inch board. Both of these distribute your weight more evenly across materials not meant to be walked on; neither relies on relatively insubstantial gutters.

Of course, don't put off repairs too long, and try to do them on a medium-warm day. Some materials—especially those with an asphalt base—turn brittle in cold weather, but become too soft to handle when hot. Wood shingles and shakes aren't notably temperature-sensitive, but they are affected by humidity. A good soaking makes them much more pliable; dry shingles will split when you try to drive nails in them.

You'll need only a few supplies for repair work—roofing cement, butyl caulk, galvanized roofing nails, and probably a few shingles, slates, or sections of roll goods that match your present roofing.

Patch any cracks, minor splits, and holes with roofing cement. Then drive home any popped nails and seal them or the shingles that cover them. Also make sure all shingles lie flat; if any are even slightly curled, fasten them down with dabs of cement. And don't be stingy with roofing cement or caulking around flashings.

The following pages show how to replace various roofing materials and components. If you find that substantial sections are failing, it might be time to get estimates on a new roof.

## REPAIRING WOOD SHINGLES

For holes, drive a sheet of aluminum or galvanized steel under the shingle. Be sure it extends well above the leak.

Finally, drive a couple of rust-resistant roofing nails just below the lap line for the next course. Seal with roofing cement.

Mend splits by drilling pilot holes and nailing, then seal the gap with roofing cement. Some can be applied like caulk.

Next, drive a new shingle into place as shown. Be sure to leave about a ¼-inch space at either side to accommodate swelling.

Remove a decayed shingle by splitting it along the grain, then use a hacksaw blade to cut out nails under the course above.

## REPAIRING ASPHALT SHINGLES

Asphalt's flexibility makes this type of shingle especially easy to repair. Seal minor cracks and holes, and glue down curled shingles with roofing cement.

If the damage is more extensive, replace all or part of the shingle strip as shown here. If you have the option, wait for a moderately warm day to make the repair—asphalt materials are easiest to work with then.

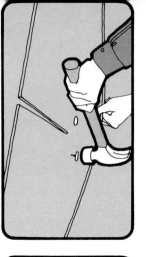

First loosen nails in the shingle above by slipping a flat shovel underneath. Then pull the nails and remove the bad shingle.

After measuring for a snug fit, cut a new piece and slip it into place under the shingle above. Align with adjacent shingles.

Now coat the nailheads with roofing cement, then press the upper course firmly back into place. Weight it down if necessary.

You can also back up a mutilated shingle with a piece of metal flashing. Secure it with cement and nails under the shingle.

Try to drive new nails through the holes left by the old ones. If you can't, carefully seal the old openings with cement.

## REPAIRING SLATE SHINGLES

To remove a broken slate shingle, slip a hacksaw blade underneath and cut the two nails concealed under the course above.

Liberally coat both the under-course and concealed parts of the new tile with roofing cement before you slip it into place.

To cut slate, deeply score both sides with a screwdriver or cold chisel. Align the score with a table edge and snap downward.

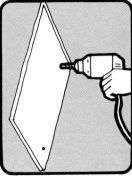

Use a masonry bit to drill two nail holes. Locate them about 3/4 inch below the bottom edge of the course above.

Slate is fragile, so drive the nails carefully and use a nail-set for the final blows. Seal the heads with roofing cement.

## REPAIRING TILE ROOFS

Some ceramic clay tiles weigh as much as 15 pounds apiece, and on a roof, they must be maneuvered on a fragile, slippery surface that may shift underfoot. For your own safety, hire a mason for replacement and major repair jobs—or for any work on a steep pitch. If you do venture onto your tile roof, always spread your weight over at least two tiles.

You can seal small cracks and flashings with roofing cement. Bigger gaps, and especially cap tiles at the ridge, must be professionally mortared.

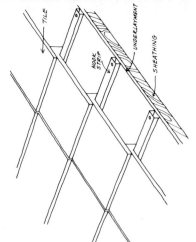

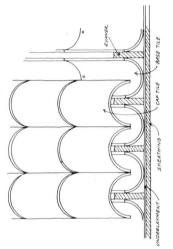

Mission tiles are laid two-deep, supported by runners. Some other curved styles have interlocking flanges along their edges.

Shingle tiles hook onto wood or metal strips nailed horizontally across the roof. These are easier to replace than mission tiles.

## REPAIRING METAL ROOFS

Master a few simple soldering skills (see page 482), and you can easily mend any roofing metal except aluminum. Each, however, calls for a slightly different approach.

Solder terne with rosin flux, then coat the repair with red-lead primer and paint to match the rest of your roof. Terned stainless steel needn't be primed or painted.

Galvanized steel also requires rosin flux, but needn't be primed and painted until its zinc coating begins to wear off. Then prime with zinc-oxide or a specially formulated zinc-enriched finish paint.

You must use acid flux in soldering copper. It doesn't require paint.

Aluminum needn't be painted, either —and you can't solder it. Seal any cracks with caulk, as shown at right, and patch bigger damage with fiber glass (see page 477).

And remember that when dissimilar metals come in contact, you risk an electrolytic reaction that greatly accelerates corrosion. This means that terne roofs must be patched with terne, copper with copper, and so forth. Don't let any different metal, even a TV mast, directly touch your roof.

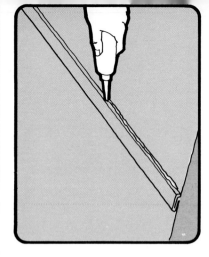

Aluminized caulk seals aluminum roofing. With other metals, other caulks offer a less-durable alternative to soldering.

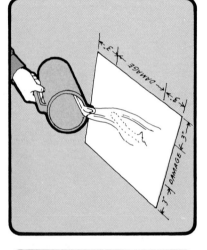

Any patch should lap sound metal by at least three inches. To test the repair, pour water over the area, then check below for leaks.

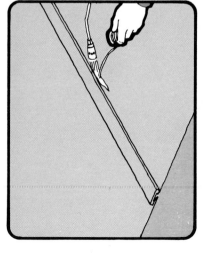

Solder roofing only with a torch or non-electric iron. Properly clean, flux, and heat a seam so solder will flow into it.

114

Mineral-clad roll roofing and surfaces built up from alternating layers of felt and tar differ considerably in cost and durability—but you can patch them in exactly the same way.

Since both are usually applied only to flat or nearly flat roofs, you can get at any damage much more easily. What's more, leaks almost always show up near their point of origin, so you needn't spend a lot of time and energy tracking them down. Watch, though, when you repair the

blisters these roofs are prone to. After you've excised one, as shown here, look inside for any traces of moisture. These mean water has seeped under the roofing, usually from a defective flashing nearby. Flashing repairs are illustrated on pages 116 and 117.

Asphalt-aluminum roof paint offers a way to add a few years to the life of deteriorated flashings or roofing. Apply the mastic-like fibered type to fill small holes and cracks, especially in flashings. For bigger expanses, brush on the non-fibered version.

As with any roof, don't walk around up there any more than necessary, and don't go up at all in extremely hot or cold weather.

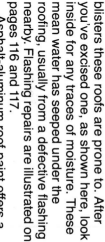

If your roof is topped with gravel or crushed stones, carefully brush them away from any damage with a whisk broom.

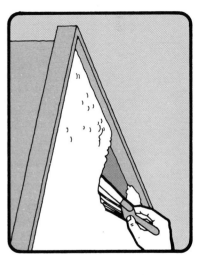

Clean out any small cracks, pack them with roofing cement, then feather out more cement for about three inches on either side.

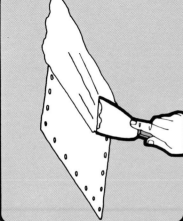

Slice open blisters, work cement inside, then fasten them down by driving roofing nails along each side of the incision.

Top off the repair with a building paper patch much larger than the damaged area. Cement it, nail, and apply more cement.

Replace extensively blistered or buckling sections. First cut out the old roofing and scrape away the old cement.

Trim a new piece of roofing for a snug fit, then nail and cement it in place. Apply enough cement to lap all sides by three inches.

Press a second, larger patch into the cement; nail and seal it, too. Double-patching makes a strong, watertight repair.

## REPAIRING AND REPLACING FLASHINGS

Think of flashings as special-purpose shingles. Like shingles, they lap one another and interweave with other roofing materials, shedding water the same way a bird's feathers do.

Most flashings, however, are made of thin-gauge metal that can be easily bent and formed to fit joints where two or more surfaces come together. Because these intersections are more vulnerable to leaking, flashings deserve even closer scrutiny than the rest of your roof.

When you inspect flashings, look for pieces that have pulled away from the adjoining surfaces, and for existing roofing cement or caulk that has dried up. Leaks here are sometimes almost microscopic, so when in doubt, apply new cement or caulk.

Badly rusted, cracked, or corroded flashings around chimneys, dormers, and plumbing vents will last a few more years if you trowel on a coat of fibered asphalt-aluminum roof paint. Widespread deterioration or valley-flashing failure means you should call in a roofer or sheet-metal specialist to replace them entirely.

Often, though, the shields around vents and chimneys go first. These you can replace yourself if you're handy at snipping and shaping lightweight materials. (For more about working with metals, see pages 480-485.)

Flashing materials include copper, aluminum, galvanized steel, roll roofing, and even plastic and rubber. For durability at a reasonable price, choose aluminum—but first note the caution about metal roofing on page 114. Vent flashings come as a single molded piece of metal or plastic that you simply fit over the pipe and cover with roofing on the uphill side, as shown below. Fabricate other types from rolls, strips, and sheets, as illustrated on the opposite page.

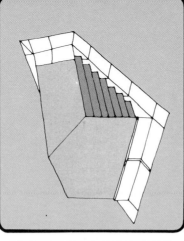

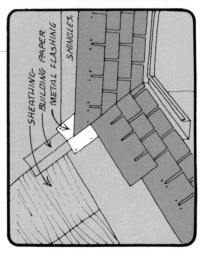

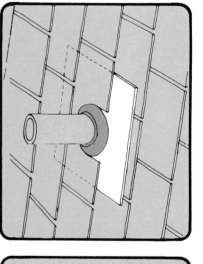

Dormer flashings tuck up under lap siding or are capped with counterflashing, as illustrated on the opposite page.

Closed-valley flashings hide beneath the roofing. In some cases, shingles are interlaced atop, making them impossible to check.

Because they're visible, open-valley flashings are easy to inspect. Cement down any shingle that's even slightly curled.

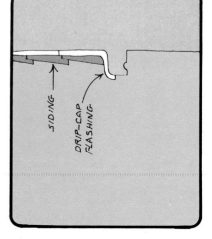

Don't bother repairing a faulty vent flashing. To install a new one, you need to remove and replace only a few shingles.

Over windows and doors, drip-cap flashings keep water from seeping under the frames. Check them periodically for damage.

116

# Flashing a Chimney

Most chimneys have a two-part flashing system designed to ride out minor structural shifting. *Base* or *roof flashing* fits under shingles at the sides and "up roof" from the chimney, and lays on top of those below. Then *counterflashing*, mortared or cemented to the chimney, caps off the joint (see sketch at right).

Replacing this seal is a medium-to-tricky task that calls for time and patience, but no special tools or skills. Use copper here for a more durable seal. You also can expect to find counterflashing anywhere your roof meets a wall.

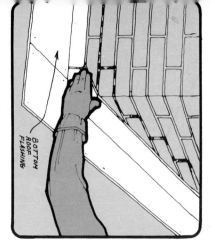

Install the bottom flashing first, then work up, always lapping higher courses over lower ones. Cement and nail in place.

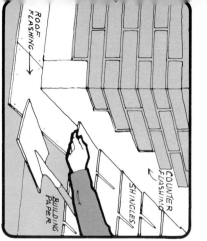

Begin by removing all shingles that overlap the roof flashing. Work carefully and you can reuse most of them.

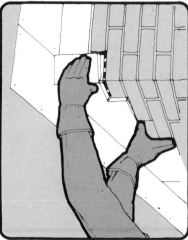

After you cut the counterflashing, bend tabs to fit into the brick joints, then pack them with mortar (see page 134).

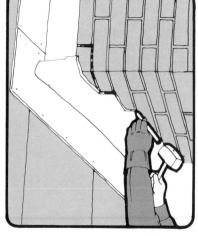

Counterflashing is usually mortared into the joints of brick chimneys. Chip the metal loose and save it for patterns.

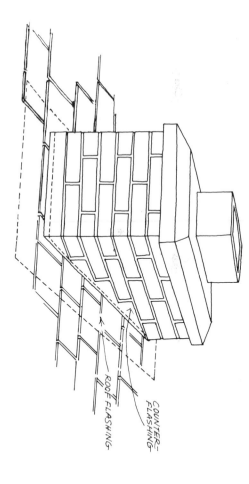

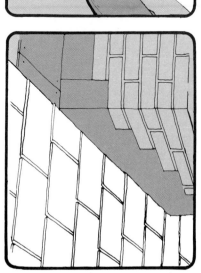

Use roofing cement to fasten the shingles to the base flashing. Weight down the shingles to achieve a tight seal.

A spade makes it easier to salvage roof flashings. If these are in good shape, you might not need to replace them.

# REPAIRING AND CLEANING FIREPLACE CHIMNEYS

Chimneys have two formidable enemies—heat and water. That crackling fire you enjoy on winter evenings subjects masonry to temperature extremes that can chip out mortar, especially up top where the *flue* penetrates the *cap* (see the cutaway at right). Seepage here can eventually weaken the chimney's structure or crack a flue lining.

In examining your chimney, you may notice quite a few differences from the sketch shown here. Some are all brick—several tiers thick—and a few use firebrick instead of a ceramic tile flue liner. Many also include a cap of some sort to keep out rain, nesting birds, and downdrafts.

Regardless of how your chimney was constructed, it pays to check out its upper reaches periodically. Don't stop there, though. Inspect every surface you can

see—including any in-the-attic portions—looking for cracks and deteriorated mortar. Repair these as shown below and on page 134.

Every once in a while, test for hot spots by feeling reachable areas with your hand. These may mean a broken flue—a definite fire hazard that a mason should attend to before you use the fireplace again.

How often a chimney needs cleaning depends on how often you use it and the sort of wood you burn. Pine and a few other sap-laden species send up creosote, which cakes the flue and constricts the opening. The result: smoking and possibly fire in the chimney wall itself. Hire a pro to "sweep" your chimney, or do the job yourself as shown below.

Note, too, that other conditions, including downdrafts and faulty firebox design, can cause smoking. To learn about cures for these, see pages 92-95.

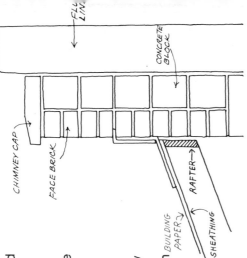

FLUE LINING
CHIMNEY CAP
CONCRETE BLOCK
FACE BRICK
RAFTER
BUILDING PAPER
SHEATHING

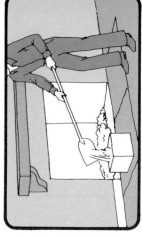

To clean a chimney, first open the damper, then seal your fireplace opening with a wet sheet, canvas, or polyethylene.

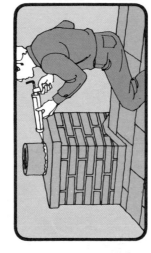

Pack mortar around the flue, too. Better yet, caulk for a flexible seal that rides out heat-produced expansion and contraction.

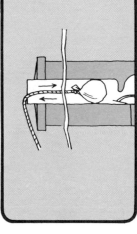

To minimize dust problems, wet down the soot before you clean out the firebox. Vacuum around the damper before closing it.

Wind-driven rain often erodes mortar joints. Chip away any loose material, then repoint as explained on page 134.

To dislodge soot, work the rope up and down vigorously. Lower your weighted sack all the way down to damper level.

Now wrap chains or broken bricks in canvas, tie it all to a rope, and lower your "sweep" down the chimney. It should just fit.

**118**

# PREVENTING ATTIC CONDENSATION

An attic that can't breathe properly has lots of problems winter and summer. In hot weather, temperatures up there can hit 150 degrees or more, adding a big load to your cooling system. In cold spells, temperature differences between the attic and heated spaces below

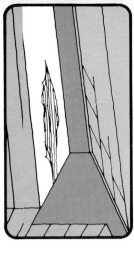

condense moisture, which can lower the R-value of insulation, rot framing and sheathing, and shorten your roof's life.

The solution to both problems is to provide adequate air flow through inlets at the eaves or soffits, then up and out via vents near the ridge.

Exactly how much ventilation your attic needs depends on whether or not its insulation includes a vapor barrier (see pages 367-369). If it does, you should

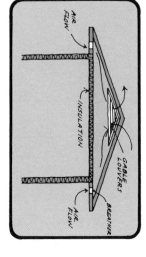

have one square foot of venting for each 300 square feet of attic floor space. If there's no vapor barrier, double this figure.

The drawings below show the most commonly used "passive" ventilation systems and their components. To learn about buying and installing powered units, see pages 378-380.

---

Paint peeling from soffits is a sign that your attic needs better ventilation. Also check insulation for dampness.

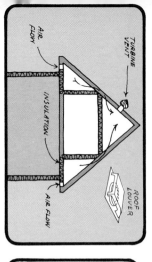

Icicles sometimes form on roofing nails that penetrate the sheathing. To prevent dripping, just clip off the nails.

In an unfinished attic, you might get by with gable louvers at each end. For more air flow, install vents or breathers in the soffits.

---

Finished attics *definitely* need both soffit vents and roof louvers. Inlets and outlets should be about equal in coverage.

Insulated flat roofs need ventilation, too. Strip-style soffit vents might be the answer here. Size them as explained above.

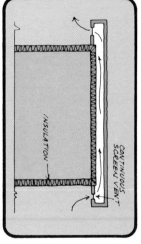

You can find ventilation components for almost any roof/attic situation. Aluminum *breathers* are the easiest to install, but you'd need a bunch of them to provide much ventilation. *Strip-style vents* provide greater air flow; *perforated* metal or vinyl *soffits* (not shown), even more.

Up top, you can choose *gable* or *roof-mounted louvers* (shown above). A *ridge vent* offers another unobtrusive answer. Or add design interest with a *cupola*. *Penthouse louvers* work especially well on big, flat roofs.

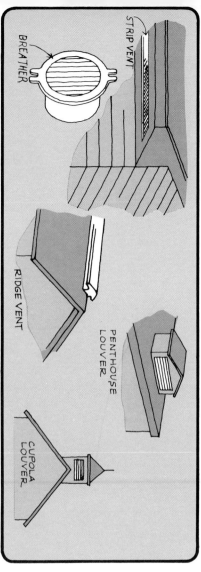

## REPAIRING AND MAINTAINING GUTTERS AND DOWNSPOUTS

Once you consider that your roof's drainage system annually diverts thousands of gallons of water from exterior and foundation walls, you can see why it merits a semiannual inspection.

First, familiarize yourself with the system's key elements, illustrated below, left. *Hangers* include any of three different devices—a *strap* nailed to the roof sheathing, a *fascia bracket* attached to the fascia, or a *spike and ferrule* driven through the gutter into rafter ends.

All gutters must slope slightly toward their *outlets*. From there, an *elbow* connects with a *leader*, then another elbow, the downspout, and finally, a third elbow that directs the spout outlet away from the wall.

Try to check out your gutters and downspouts every spring, before the heavy rains begin, and again late in the fall, after most of the leaves are down. Remove any debris clogging the system, and be especially vigilant for low spots where water may be standing.

Since standing water causes most gutter problems, make sure that all gutters slope toward their outlets. To check this, pour some water into the gutter and watch what happens. Eliminate gutter sags by lifting the gutter section slightly. Usually you can do this by bending the hanger with a pair of pliers. If this doesn't do the trick, install an additional hanger.

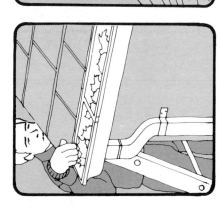

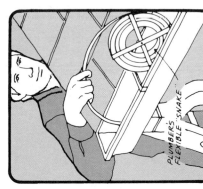

To extend your reach, fasten an angle to the end of a long pole or board, then use it to rake debris toward you.

If the insides of your gutters are beginning to rust, scrape and wire-brush them, then apply a thin coat of roofing cement.

Mud and rotting leaves not only clog up gutters and downspouts, they also hold moisture that causes rust, rot, and corrosion.

Sometimes you can blast out a spout blockage with hose pressure. If not, break up the jam with a plumber's snake.

Now hose your gutters clean. Begin at the high end of each run—or in the middle of runs with spouts at both ends.

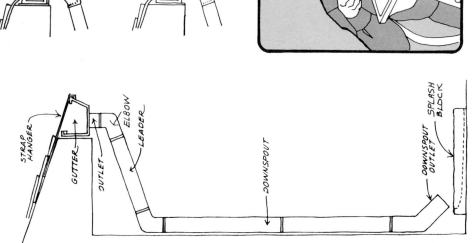

FASCIA BRACKET

FERRULE — SPIKE

STRAP HANGER — GUTTER — OUTLET — ELBOW — LEADER — DOWNSPOUT — DOWNSPOUT OUTLET — SPLASH BLOCK

METAL ANGLE — 1 x 2

ROOF CEMENT

PLUMBER'S FLEXIBLE "SNAKE"

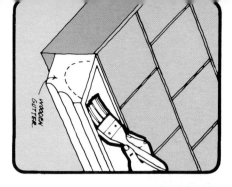
WOODEN GUTTER

To renew wooden gutters, sand them down to bare wood, apply linseed oil, let dry, then apply two coats of roofing cement.

STRAP HANGER

Don't nail strap hangers through shingles. Instead, lift one, fasten them to the sheathing, then seal the nail heads with roof cement.

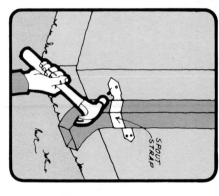
SPOUT STRAP

Before you nail a spout strap, pull it from the wall and coat the underside with roof cement. This seals the nails.

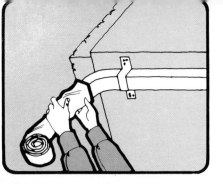

Or install a perforated roll-up hose such as this one. When the water comes down, it extends like a New Year's Eve noisemaker.

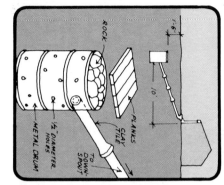
ROCK — PLANKS — CLAY TILE — TO DOWN-SPOUT — METAL DRUM — ½" DIAMETER HOLES — 1'-6" — 10'

To solve a serious runoff problem, you may have to provide a dry well. Here's one commonly used do-it-yourself type.

SCREEN GUARD

Vinyl-clad screens keep leaves out of gutters. Just slip them under the first course of shingles and fasten with roofing nails.

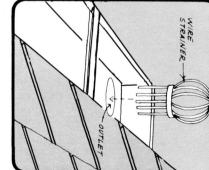
WIRE STRAINER — OUTLET

Special wire strainers eliminate downspout clogging. You still have to clear debris from around the cages, of course.

Cut gutters or downspouts with a fine-tooth hacksaw. Mark a line around the circumference first so the edges will be square.

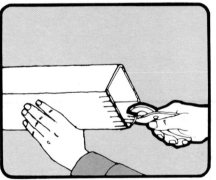

In joining two pieces of spout, crimp the end of one so it will slip into the other. The upper section always goes inside.

Patch a rusted-out gutter with lightweight metal or heavy roofing paper. Cement the patch in place, then coat with more cement.

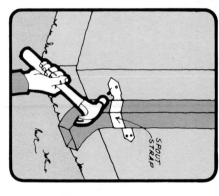
CONCRETE SPLASH BLOCK

To work properly, splash blocks must be pitched away from foundation walls. Raise and shim underneath with gravel or sand.

# INSTALLING NEW ROOF PRODUCTS

No one, especially a professional roofer, likes to spend a lot of time aboard ladders or scrambling around on steep surfaces. Knowing this, the manufacturers of most roofing components have designed their products so they are relatively lightweight and easy to install.

You'll need assistance, though, especially in hoisting materials up there. And if you'll be working on the roof itself, consider investing in a pair of roof brackets. These simple devices support a level plank or two on which you can rest materials. To install one, you just lift a shingle, drive a nail, then hook the bracket on it.

Remember to always wear sneakers or other slip-resistant shoes when working on roofs. And don't burden yourself with a belt-load of tools that could throw you off balance or injure you in a fall. Keep them in a bucket instead.

## CHOOSING GUTTERS AND SPOUTS

Today's rain-carrying systems consist of a series of modular pieces that you simply assemble to suit your situation.

Before you order, make a list of the components shown below, then circle your house and write down how many of each you'll need.

Most gutters come in 10-foot lengths, and require a spout every 35 feet. Longer runs should be pitched toward an outlet at either end. Also note that they should always be pitched away from valleys and toward corners.

If you're replacing only parts of a system, be sure you don't mix metals; copper, steel, and aluminum aren't compatible with each other.

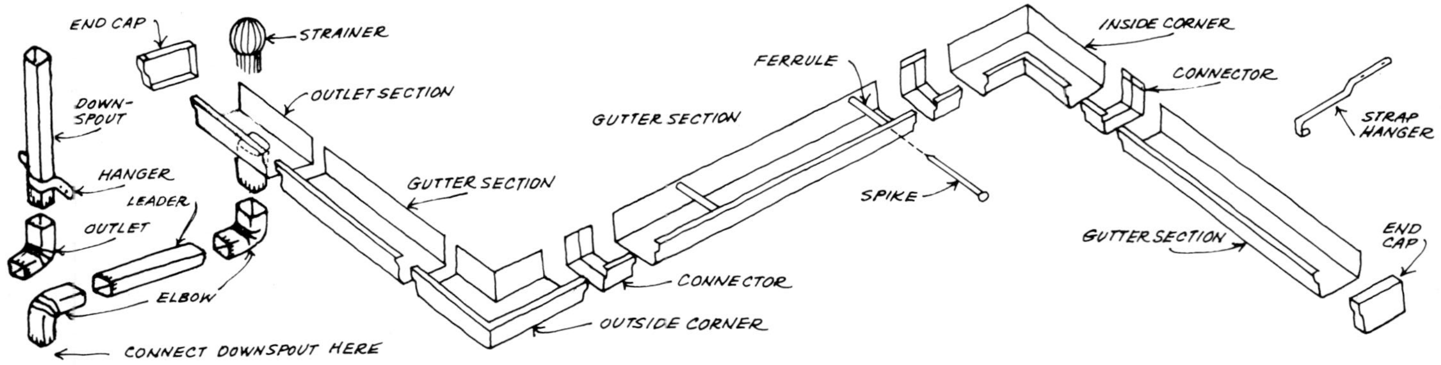

STRAP HANGER
END CAP
CONNECTOR
INSIDE CORNER
GUTTER SECTION
FERRULE
SPIKE
CONNECTOR
OUTSIDE CORNER
GUTTER SECTION
GUTTER SECTION
GUTTER SECTION
OUTLET SECTION
STRAINER
CONNECT DOWNSPOUT HERE
END CAP
DOWN-SPOUT
HANGER
LEADER
OUTLET
ELBOW

## GUTTER MATERIALS SELECTION GUIDE

| Material | Features | Maintenance | Life Span/Cost |
|---|---|---|---|
| Steel | Available with enamel or raw galvanized finishes. | Prone to rusting. Must be repainted periodically. | Relatively short. Inexpensive. |
| Aluminum | The most popular. Enamel or plastic-clad finish. Easily handled, but not as strong as steel. | Highly resistant to corrosion, but eventually may need repainting. | Often warranted for 15-20 years. Moderately priced. |
| Vinyl | Sturdy and durable, but slightly tricky to install. Usually available only in white. | Sold vinyl can't rot, blister, or rust. You can't paint it, either. | Some carry lifetime warranties. Expensive. |
| Copper | Very durable but not widely used on homes. Joints must be soldered. | Won't rust or corrode, but you may have to re-solder leaking joints. | 50 years or more. Very expensive. |
| Wood | Vulnerability to rot makes them unpopular. They're also heavy. | Require frequent waterproofing and repainting. Watch for warping, too. | 10-15 years. Moderate price. |

# PUTTING UP NEW GUTTERS AND SPOUTS

Installing new metal or plastic gutters and downspouts calls for two ladders and an extra pair of hands, but preformed components make it basically a cutting, assembling, and hanging job.

When you remove the old system, try to dismantle it as little as possible so you can use it to take measurements for the new parts. If your home's fascia boards have deteriorated, now's the time to scrape, prime, and repaint them—or

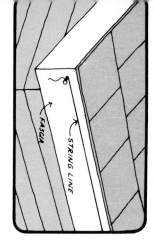

STRING LINE
FASCIA

install one of the prefinished fascias offered by gutter manufacturers.

Usually you can cut aluminum and steel gutters with metal shears. For heavier-gauge metal or vinyl, use the hacksaw technique depicted here.

Be sure to caulk all joints, nail heads, etc., then assemble the sections with the slip connector shown, or use a pop riveter (see page 434). With some materials—especially vinyl—expansion and contraction can be a problem, so follow the manufacturer's joining instructions carefully. And never use anything but aluminum nails, screws, and

rivets with aluminum; use rust-resistant steel fasteners with steel gutters and downspouts.

Check the drawings here and on page 120, and you'll see you have a choice of different hangers. Strap hangers work only with flexible roof materials such as asphalt shingles. If your roof has rigid wood shingles or slate, use fascia brackets or spike-and-ferrule hangers. Spikes are the easiest of all to install, but they're more likely to sag under loads of heavy ice and snow.

---

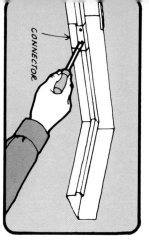

CONNECTOR

Gutters must always slope toward their spouts. Check the manufacturer's recommendations, then pick up a string for a guide.

Most end caps simply snap onto gutter sections. First apply a bead of caulk or joint sealer to prevent leaking.

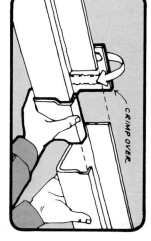

CAULK

If you have to saw gutter sections, insert a 2x4 to keep them rigid. Always file cut edges to knock off any burrs.

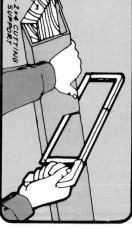

2x4 CUTTING SUPPORT

Assemble each gutter run on the ground first, caulking and screwing or riveting all joints except those at corners.

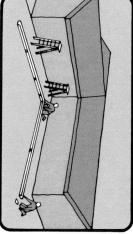

STRAP

SPIKE & FERRULE

---

After you've installed two runs, connect them with corner sections. Caulk, then fasten with rivets or sheet-metal screws.

Be sure to caulk slip-joint connectors between sections, too. These important components are the most susceptible to leaking.

CRIMP OVER

Space hangers 24 or 32 inches apart. Spikes should go into the rafters; drill their holes before lifting the run into position.

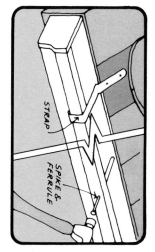

Cut leaders long enough to fit within three inches of the side of the house, then attach a second elbow and hang the spout.

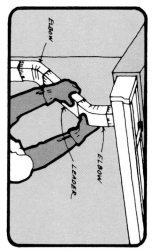

ELBOW
ELBOW
LEADER

**123**

# INSTALLING NEW SHINGLES

Roofing materials tend to wear out at a uniform rate. So when aging shingles develop a few problems, you can anticipate more of the same in the seasons to come.

Unless your home already has slate or tile shingles, you can rule out these heavyweights right away; ordinary framing usually can't bear the load.

Wood shingles and shakes offer high insulation value, superior durability, and classic good looks. However, they require a relatively steep roof pitch, and fire codes prohibit them in some communities. For more about wood shakes and shingles, see the opposite page and page 140.

The asphalt shingles that cover most American roofs come in a broad array of colors, shapes, textures, and quality levels. Like all shingles, they're sold by the *square*, which is the amount of material needed to cover 100 square feet. Conventional asphalt shingles often are rated by their weight per square—the heavier the better (and more expensive).

In comparing weights, though, don't try to rate asphalt shingles from one *class* against those from another. Class C shingles—which have an organic felt base—offer only moderate resistance to fire; Class A shingles—those backed by

noncombustible glass or asbestos fibers—are highly fire-resistant. Premium-quality Class A shingles shouldn't rot, blister, curl, or absorb water, either. A few of the most expensive resemble wood shingles and shakes.

If mildew or algae are a problem in your area, consider buying specially treated wood or asphalt roofing. These contain a chemical designed to wash away very gradually. As rain releases the chemical, it destroys the algae.

Generally, you can apply new shingles and shakes—either asphalt or wood—over any existing roofing except shakes. This saves the trouble and expense of tearing off the old roof.

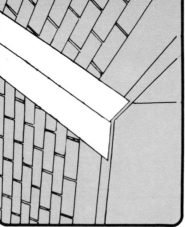

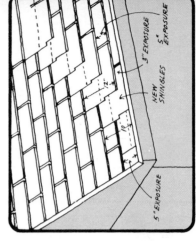

To flash valleys, use either roll roofing or sheet metal. Flashings here should project an inch or so beyond the eaves.

Build later courses stair-step fashion. The first course will have only a three-inch exposure, but the gutter will conceal this.

## Asphalt Shingles

Establish a *starter course* at the eaves, use your old shingles as guides, and you'll find re-shingling goes about as fast as you can nail them down.

Before you begin, though, go over the old surface, nail all loose or curled shingles, and replace any that are missing. Reset popped nails, too.

Most shingles measure 1x3 feet, with five-inch-deep cutouts that divide the bottom into three *tabs*. Assuming the old courses are straight, you simply butt each new shingle against the bottom edge of an old one, staggering the tabs from course to course.

Check drip-edge flashings at the eaves and rakes. If they're failing, replace as you would any other flashing (see page 116).

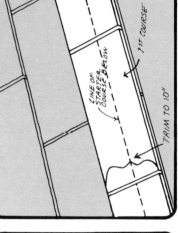

Now completely lap the starter course with the first course. (Always stagger end joints from one course to the next.)

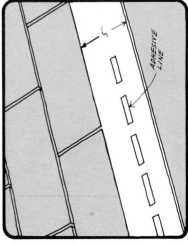

For the starter course, trim off tabs to make strips as wide as the old exposure—usually five inches. Fit them as shown.

**124**

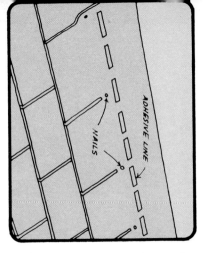

Each shingle gets four nails, driven about ½ inch above the cutouts. Don't sink the nailheads into the shingle's surface.

A cant strip at the base of vertical surfaces improves runoff. For more about chimney flashings, see page 117.

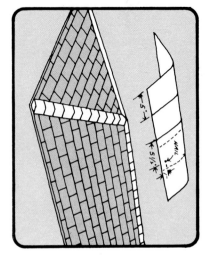

Cover the ridge with special shingles or cut ordinary ones to fit. Start at the end opposite prevailing winds.

## Wood Shingles and Shakes

To lay up wood shingles and shakes, you use the same basic techniques illustrated above and opposite—but you'll need a couple more tools and a little more preparation work.

The additional tools include a multipurpose shingler's hatchet for nailing, trimming, and gauging courses, and a lightweight portable power saw for more precise cutting.

For the prep work, buy lengths of 1x6 cedar, redwood, or pressure-treated lumber and a few pieces of beveled siding, then install these at eaves, rakes, and ridges, as shown here.

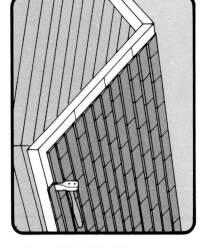

The hatchet makes short work of cutting back old roofing. If yours is asphalt, you could do this job with a sharp knife.

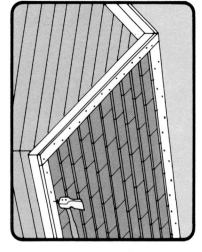

Nail 1-inch lumber at the eaves and gables, and beveled siding at the ridge. Nails must penetrate ½ inch into sheathing.

At each valley, install 1-inch lumber to separate the old metal from the new. Flash as explained on the opposite page.

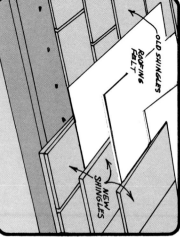

With shakes—but not shingles —you must interlay courses with strips of heavy roofing felt. These seal against the elements.

Precut ridge units save time at the top. Some come as a continuous strip; others are coursed like ordinary shingles.

125

## INSTALLING A SKYLIGHT

A skylight brightens interior rooms in a way no artificial source can match. Even on cloudy days, you get a surprising amount of solar illumination—and the operating cost is nil.

Prefabricated kits—available in different domed, rectangular, and square shapes—include an acrylic "light" and a metal frame flanged so you can nail it to your roof deck.

Getting through the roof (see the opposite page) calls for only modest framing and flashing expertise. However,

keep in mind that you'll also need to construct a light shaft through your attic unless your home has a flat roof or integral roof-ceiling deck.

Work from the inside out, framing the ceiling opening and building the shaft before you cut into the roof. Most skylights are designed to span two or three rafters on typical 24-inch spacings, so it's often necessary to cut and tie off rafters and ceiling joists to accommodate the shaft. Caution: be sure that you shore up the ceiling with T-braces (see page 151) before doing this operation. (For more information about ceiling framing,

see page 56.)

The drawings below show three shafts for different situations. Regardless of the one you choose, construct a sleeve with ½-inch plywood, check it for fit, then paint its inside white to ensure maximum reflective value.

For a flat-roof installation, just frame the opening, paint the rafters and headers around it, then install the skylight. Note that you may also need to raise the unit with nailers, as shown opposite.

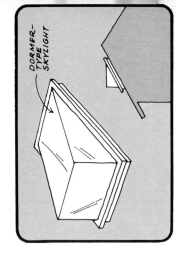

DOMED-TYPE SKYLIGHT

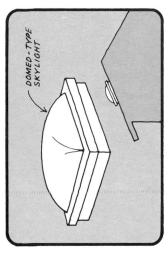

DORMER-TYPE SKYLIGHT

Domed skylights make sense only for pitched roofs. Good skylights are double-glazed, with an air space to cut heat loss.

Dormer skylights suit either flat or pitched roofs. Some also include a cranking system so you can open them for ventilation.

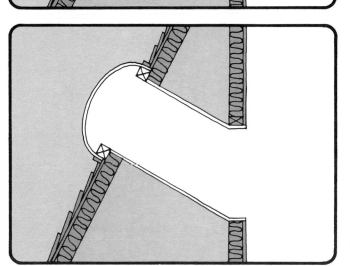

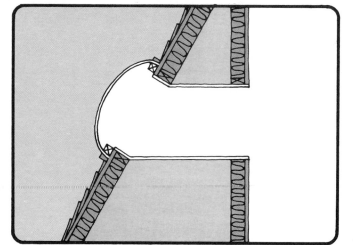

Locate your skylight directly above the ceiling opening and you can get by with a straight shaft—the easiest to build.

A tilted shaft lets you offset the roof and ceiling openings somewhat. These are trickier to construct, of course.

You can make the ceiling opening bigger than the skylight, too. A splayed shaft disperses daylight over a broader area.

# Getting Through the Roof

Once you've built a shaft, topping it off with a prefab skylight takes a day or less. First you must cut and tie off the rafters with headers, as you did with the ceiling joists.

Locate the opening by sliding the shaft into position and marking around its perimeter. Before cutting into the rafters, be sure to set up some type of temporary bracing.

When you set the unit in place, fit its flange under roofing at the top and sides, but let it overlap shingles on the down-roof side.

Double-check all measurements before cutting into roof framing. And install headers before you open up the sheathing.

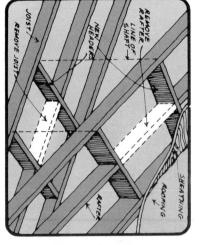

To mark for the opening, drive long nails through the roof at each corner, then go topside and chalk an outline.

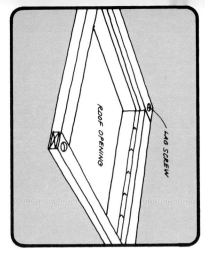

ROOF OPENING

LAG SCREW

On a flat roof, you may need to shim around the opening with nailers. Otherwise, any standing water could overflow the frame.

Slice away shingles and building felt with a utility knife. When you saw the sheathing, don't let it fall into the room below.

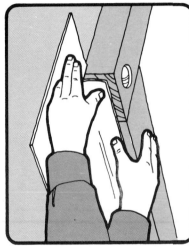

Now slide the shaft up from below and nail it to the framing. If your attic floor is insulated, insulate the shaft, too.

Seal under the flange before you nail it, then cement the shingles to it with more roofing cement for a watertight joint.

Seal under the nailer with roofing cement, then slip metal flashing under the roofing and up the sides of the nailer.

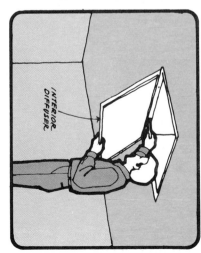

INTERIOR DIFFUSER

If you want to add a light diffuser, just screw its frame to the inside of the shaft. Wipe the shaft clean first.

**127**

# EXTERIOR WALLS, WINDOWS, AND DOORS

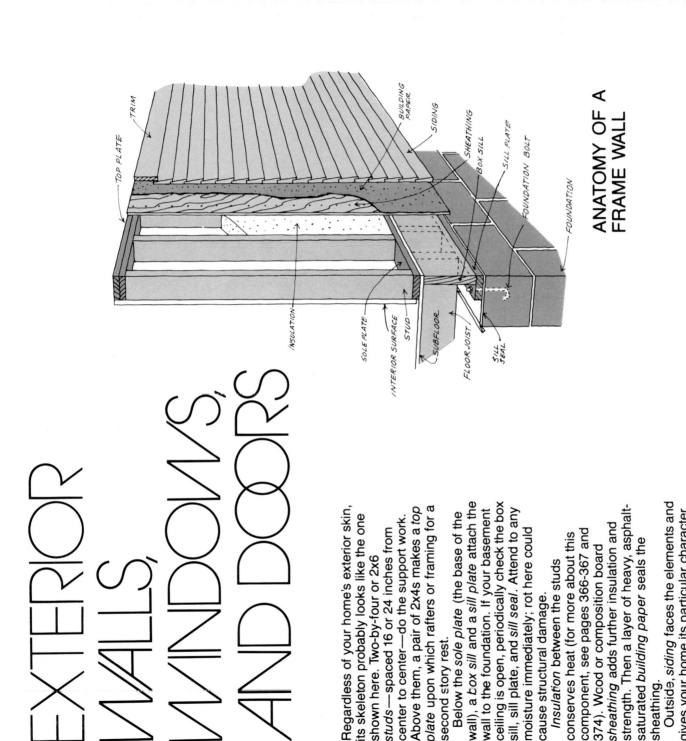

Labels (diagram): TRIM, TOP PLATE, BUILDING PAPER, SIDING, SHEATHING, BOX SILL, SILL PLATE, FOUNDATION BOLT, FOUNDATION, INSULATION, SOLE PLATE, INTERIOR SURFACE, STUD, SUBFLOOR, FLOOR JOIST, SILL SEAL

## ANATOMY OF A FRAME WALL

Regardless of your home's exterior skin, its skeleton probably looks like the one shown here. Two-by-four or 2x6 *studs*—spaced 16 or 24 inches from center to center—do the support work. Above them, a pair of 2x4s makes a *top plate* upon which rafters or framing for a second story rest.

Below the *sole plate* (the base of the wall), a *box sill* and a *sill plate* attach the wall to the foundation. If your basement ceiling is open, periodically check the box sill, sill plate, and *sill seal*. Attend to any moisture immediately; rot here could cause structural damage.

*Insulation* between the studs conserves heat (for more about this component, see pages 366-367 and 374). Wood or composition board *sheathing* adds further insulation and strength. Then a layer of heavy, asphalt-saturated *building paper* seals the sheathing.

Outside, *siding* faces the elements and gives your home its particular character. Shown here is lap siding, so-called because the boards overlap each other. Don't assume, however, that what looks like a board or shingle is actually made of wood. A variety of manufactured materials (see pages 138-143) give the appearance of wood without its relatively high maintenance requirements.

Regardless of its composition, siding deserves a careful, semiannual inspection. Scan its surface system-atically, using field glasses for closeups of high places, if necessary. Look for cracks, splits, peeling paint, and any evidence of rot or insect damage. Any breaks in your home's skin—no matter how small—will eventually admit water into wall cavities. Neglect the repairs explained on pages 130-133 and on pages 137, and moisture could wreck insulation framing, even interior wall surfaces.

If a new paint job seems imminent, see pages 510-521. And to learn about basic wall building techniques, turn to pages 48-50 and 209-210.

Most so-called brick or stone houses built in this century don't actually have solid masonry walls. Instead, builders face conventional framing with a masonry veneer—combining the strength and weather resistance of brick or stone with the lighter weight and superior insulating qualities of wood stud construction.

Check the section view at right and note that in most respects its skeleton is identical to the wood-sided wall shown on page 128. Studs, not bricks, bear the load. Outside, a single tier of brick connects to the studs with short metal strips called *ties*. Between the brick and sheathing is an air space, which improves insulation and drains away any moisture that might have penetrated the exterior surface.

One big difference between masonry and frame walls occurs at the foundation. With masonry-veneer construction, a home's foundation must support the heavy masonry skin as well as the framing system. Such foundations must be engineered to support this load at the time they're built. For this reason, it's simply not feasible to veneer an existing frame wall with conventional masonry materials.

Masonry-veneered walls are relatively impervious to the ravages of weather and time. Inspect them periodically, though, paying particular attention to mortar joints, which may need to be repointed (see page 134). Watch, too, for long vertical cracks in masonry walls (see page 135). In a new house, these may be due to shrinkage of the mortar. Or more seriously, the foundation upon which the wall rests may be shifting or settling.

Solid masonry walls—usually used today only for garages, garden walls, and commercial structures—may consist of several tiers of brick or stone, or they may be concrete blocks that have been veneered. To learn more about both, see pages 181-191.

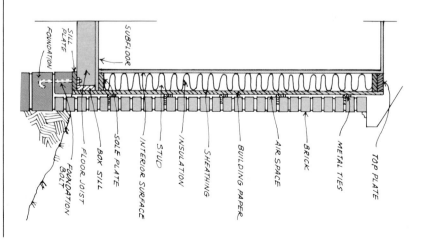

Labels: TOP PLATE, METAL TIES, BRICK, AIR SPACE, BUILDING PAPER, SHEATHING, INSULATION, STUD, INTERIOR SURFACE, SOLE PLATE, BOX SILL, FLOOR JOIST, FOUNDATION BOLT, FOUNDATION, SILL PLATE, SUBFLOOR

## ANATOMY OF A STUCCO WALL

Stucco walls also usually begin with wood-stud framing, though you can apply stucco directly to masonry surfaces, if desired. As the drawing at right shows, *spacer strips* are nailed to the sheathing and a *ground* of wood or metal lath is attached to the spacers. Then, stucco—a cement-based plaster—is troweled onto the ground.

As with interior plaster work, it takes three layers to build up a smooth surface. The first application, called the *scratch coat*, oozes through the ground for a good grip; the second or *brown coat* smooths out major irregularities in the surface; a final *finish coat* completes the job. Newer, vinyl-based materials are sprayed on.

Stucco lends itself to a wide variety of surface effects. As with concrete (see page 166), you can trowel, scrape, stipple, and spatter textures ranging from glassy smooth to rugged rustic. And you

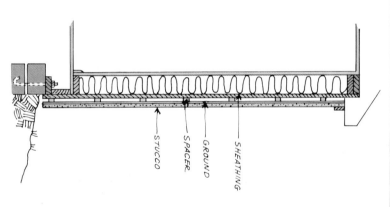

Labels: STUCCO, SPACER, GROUND, SHEATHING

can add coloring pigments to the finish coat of both cement and vinyl stucco for an exterior that will never need painting.

Note that a stucco skin hangs from the framing, just as conventional siding materials do. This means that you could opt to re-side with stucco, but it would be a costly job.

Properly applied, stucco lasts for decades with little attention. Watch, though, for cracks that may develop around windows, doors, and chimneys. If not remedied, these can admit moisture that could eventually rot away framing. And as with masonry-veneered walls, keep your eye on long, running cracks that might indicate settlement.

For information about patching cracks and holes, see pages 130-136. If you're planning to paint stucco, be sure to use a coating formulated for concrete, as explained on page 519.

# SOLVING WALL PROBLEMS

Preventive maintenance is the key to keeping wall problems at bay. With just a bucket of tools, a few tubes of caulk, a garden hose, and a ladder to get at high places, you can probably tone up your walls in a single day.

Start by giving wood siding and trim a good scrubbing. As dirt washes away, watch for mildew, popped nails, and minor cracks that need caulking. You can

deal with most of these problems during the course of your home's semiannual bath, as illustrated below.

Bigger difficulties—split siding or shingles, or brickwork or stucco in need of repair—are best treated in a separate session (see pages 133-136).

## CLEANING AND MAINTAINING EXTERIOR WALLS

Wash down wood surfaces with a light detergent solution, then rinse well. Pay particular attention to areas under eaves, porches, and other sheltered places. The reason: house paints are designed to *chalk*, or gradually wear away with exposure to rain—a sort of self-cleaning action that doesn't occur in protected zones.

If you encounter dark, rash-like spots that won't wash off, suspect mildew. This fungus thrives in areas with high humidity and little sunlight. Masonry surfaces sometimes suffer from another type of blemish called *efflorescence*. It shows up as a white, powdery residue that resists scrubbing. Both mildew and efflorescence are easily treated, as explained below.

Include nails and screws in your tool bucket so you can also make minor repairs as you go along. Choose screw-type or annular ring nails for better

holding power—and drill pilot holes so you don't risk splitting the wood. Be sure to use rust-resistant galvanized, aluminum, or brass nails and screws; otherwise, they'll eventually stain the paint around them.

With masonry walls, watch for cracks that might indicate settling and apply the test shown below. Any movement will happen slowly over a period of several months.

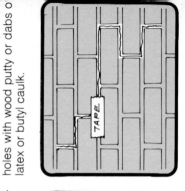

Using a nail set, drive all popped nails beneath the surface; fill the holes with wood putty or dabs of latex or butyl caulk.

To learn if cracked masonry is settling, bridge the crack with a piece of tape. A split or twist in the tape indicates movement.

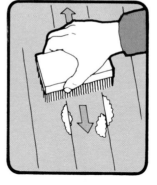

If mildew has already damaged the paint, strip to bare wood, bleach with oxalic acid, then refinish with mildewcide paint.

Undercut cracks in stucco as shown on page 36. Pack with patching cement, then smooth with a putty knife or trowel.

To remove mildew, scrub with a trisodium phosphate solution, or use special mildew remover available at paint stores.

Scour efflorescence with a mild (1 to 10) solution of muriatic acid and water. Clean small areas at a time and rinse well.

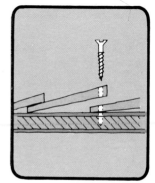

Using a long-handled car washing brush for extra reach, wash the siding. Pay special attention to the lower edges of lap siding.

Warped boards sometimes resist nailing. Drill pilot holes, secure with rustproof screws (countersink them), caulk screw heads.

130

# SEALING WITH CAULK

Different building materials swell and shrink at different rates, resulting in cracks where siding meets the foundation, for instance, or where flashing comes in contact with roofing. Ignore these cracks and they'll widen with each passing season, admitting air, water, and insects. Your best weapon

against them is a caulking gun charged with the proper sealant.

Caulking compounds differ in formulation and intended use (see chart below), but all set up to a chewing gum consistency that rides out expansion and contraction around them. Use caulk wherever unlike materials meet. Illustration below shows typical applications.

Caulk indoors, too, in basements, bathrooms, kitchens—wherever you need a water- or airtight seal. And bear in mind that no caulk lasts forever, though some newer types come close. Test old caulk by poking it with a screwdriver or nail. If it cracks, scrape out the brittle material and recaulk, as shown on page 132.

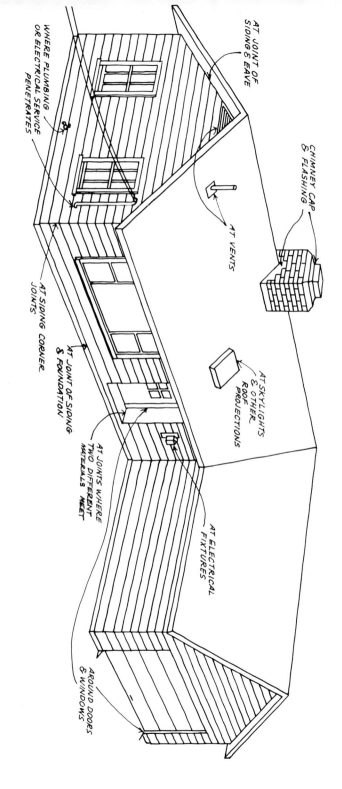

CHIMNEY CAP & FLASHING

AT JOINT OF SIDING & EAVE

AT VENTS

WHERE PLUMBING OR ELECTRICAL SERVICE PENETRATES

AT SIDING CORNER JOINTS

AT JOINT OF SIDING & FOUNDATION

AT SKYLIGHTS & OTHER ROOF PROJECTIONS

AT JOINTS WHERE TWO DIFFERENT MATERIALS MEET

AT ELECTRICAL FIXTURES

AROUND DOORS & WINDOWS

## Choosing the Right Sealant

Caulk falls into three broad categories —traditional oil- or resin-based compounds; rubber-derived formulations such as latex and butyl; and synthetic-based materials originally developed for the aerospace program's high-performance requirements. Which type you select depends largely upon the job you want it to do and the amount you need.

Before buying, read product data to learn about surface preparation requirements, which materials the caulk will adhere to, and how long it must cure before you can paint over it. The chart at right compares the most commonly available sealants.

### SURVEY OF COMMON SEALANTS

| Type | Where to Use | Cost |
|---|---|---|
| Oil-base | Although it bonds to most surfaces if they're clean and dry, oil-base caulk is falling into disfavor; there are now better products available. | Inexpensive |
| Acrylic Latex | A good general-purpose sealant that is fast-drying. Ideal for filling small cracks and joints, patching plaster walls, and sealing around baseboards and window trim. Can be painted. | Moderately expensive |
| Vinyl Latex | Highly adhesive as well as water- and weatherproof, this type is excellent for use around wet areas such as tubs and showers. | Moderately expensive |
| Butyl | Exceptionally good for sealing seams in gutters and around roof flashings, storm windows, and air conditioners. Great, too, for joints between metal and masonry and for filling cracks or joints. Remains flexible after setup; can be painted. | Moderately expensive |
| Silicone | Save for small jobs where exceptional adhesion and long-lasting elasticity are necessary. Great for sealing around tubs, showers, and outdoor outlets and fixtures. Paints won't adhere well to most. | Very expensive |

131

SOLVING WALL PROBLEMS

## Using Caulk

If you haven't worked with caulk before, start in an inconspicuous area. Some types, especially butyl, seem to stick more readily to fingers and tools than to the surfaces they're sealing . . . and it takes practice to learn how hard to squeeze and how fast to move the nozzle for a smooth, unbroken bead. After just a

tube or two, though, you'll get the knack.

For most jobs, use an inexpensive half-barrel gun. Its squeeze-action handle pushes a ratchet-activated plunger against the bottom of a disposable cartridge, forcing caulk through the nozzle.

To apply caulk, first scrape out old, cracked caulk and flaked paint, then blow out or wipe the crevice to be sure it's clean and dry. Hold the gun at a

45-degree angle and pull it toward you in a smooth, steady stroke, maintaining an even pressure on the trigger. In general, it's better to apply too much caulk than too little. You can always remove the excess and smooth out irregularities with a moist fingertip or putty knife. Note: don't caulk at temperatures below 50 degrees.

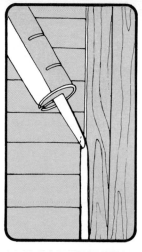

If you have a lot of caulking to do, save money by buying a full-barrel gun and loading it with compound sold in bulk.

Between perpendicular surfaces, bisect the angle with the gun's nozzle to make a smooth, coved bead that sheds moisture.

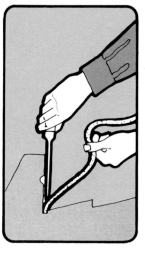

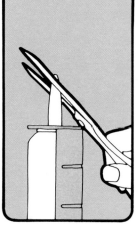

Pack ¾-inch or wider gaps with oakum—an asphalt-impregnated fibrous material—then complete the seal by caulking.

Snip off the nozzle's tip. The closer to the tip you cut, the narrower the bead will be. Puncture inside seal with a nail.

Save partial tubes for future use by sealing them with a nail. Or invert the cut-off tip and stuff it into the opening.

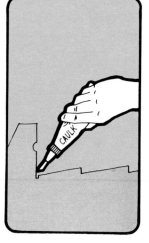

Toothpaste-style squeeze tubes are handy for minor touch-up jobs, but very costly if you have much caulking to do.

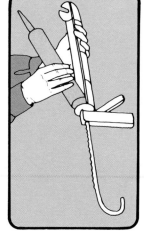

To load a half-barrel gun, invert its plunger handle, pull all the way back, and slip in a cartridge of caulk.

At the end of a stroke, lift off the gun with a twisting motion to catch any caulk oozing from the nozzle, then pull back plunger.

Between flat surfaces, straddle the joint with the nozzle and pack it so that the caulk bulges out rather than dips in.

# REPAIRING WOOD SIDING AND SHINGLES

Any wounds in your home's skin let moisture enter exterior walls and rot away their framing. Clearly, it pays to make repairs as soon as you spot damage. Pack small cracks and splits with latex or butyl caulk; do the same with open seams between board ends and at corners. If more than just a few boards or shingles are failing, however, consider re-siding the entire wall (see pages 138-143).

You may be able to repair badly split pieces with waterproof glue. To do this, coat both sides of the split, then force them together and secure with nails or screws.

If glue won't do the job, you'll have to replace the damaged board or shingle—an operation that requires careful but not skilled carpentry. The problem is that each course of lapped siding is held in place by nails driven through the course above it. The drawings below show how to repair lapped wood siding. Use the same basic techniques to replace wood shingles, but don't try to pry the nails. Instead, cut them with a hacksaw from beneath, or split the shingle vertically.

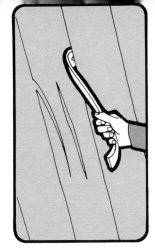

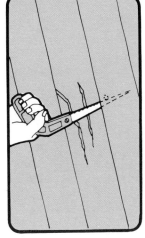

To remove an entire length of siding, work a wide chisel under the upper course, then switch to a pry bar.

If the nails begin to come out with the board, tap the board down and pull nails as shown. A block protects siding.

If the nails aren't accessible from the surface, slip a hacksaw blade underneath and cut them. Do the same on the lower edges.

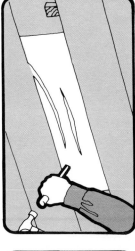

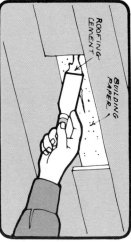

In an isolated damaged area, tap wedges under the upper course and use a square to mark the saw cuts. Cut along each mark.

Split damaged area along the grain and remove a piece at a time. Be sure to remove the siding below the board above.

If you've punctured the building paper underneath, it's essential that you seal it with a liberal coat of roofing cement.

*ROOFING CEMENT*

*BUILDING PAPER*

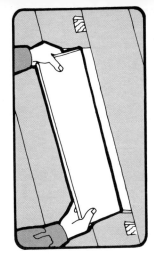

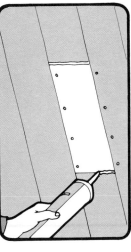

Cut the replacement for a tight fit, then slide it under the board above, tap into place, and remove the wedges.

Finally, nail the new board top and bottom, fill nail holes and the vertical seams with caulk, prime, and paint.

# REPAIRING BRICKWORK

Though far more permanent than wood siding or shingles, brick walls require occasional attention, too. Their most common malady: crumbling mortar. You can repair deteriorated joints by tucking mortar into them with the point of a trowel—a process masons call *pointing* or *tuck pointing.*

To do the job, you'll need a couple of specialized tools. One is a *pointing trowel,* which is slightly smaller than an ordinary masonry trowel. The other is a

*hawk,* which you can buy or improvise by screwing a short length of dowel or broom handle to a square of plywood.

Pack the joints with mortar mixed with a liquid latex binder. You also can use conventional mortar mix (see page 184) or vinyl patching cement, which is easier to apply but doesn't look like mortar.

After you have filled and smoothed the joints, *strike* or shape them to match existing joints. (For typical mortar treatments, see page 189.)

You also can point long vertical cracks whether they involve the joints or the bricks themselves. But a better solution is

to *grout* them as shown opposite, above. Don't overlook a broken brick, either (opposite, below); the freezing and thawing of any water it admits could cause more extensive damage.

With any masonry repair, it's important to keep the mortar damp for several days—rapid drying weakens the bond. Mist the repair with a hose, or cover with wet burlap.

## Repointing Bricks

Clean out all loose mortar to a depth of about ¾ inch, making sure that what's left is tight. Take care not to chip the brick.

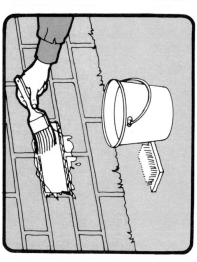

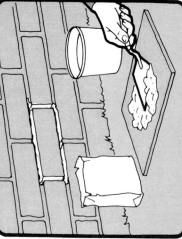

Mix mortar to a consistency that will slide slowly off your trowel. Pick up by slicing off a hunk and slipping trowel under.

Pack mortar into the joint with the trowel's tip, then slice off the excess. A hawk lets you bring mortar right to the work.

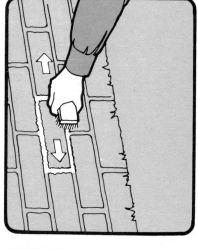

Brush the joints with a wire or scrub brush, then wet them down so the bricks won't draw water from the mortar.

Strike the joints with the appropriate tool (see page 189). Dampen periodically for the next two or three days.

After pointing 8 to 10 bricks, go back and scrub the joints with a soft, wet brush. This further compacts the mortar.

# Grouting Long Cracks

Before filling a vertical crack like the one at right, first apply the test on page 130 to determine if the wall is settling. If you're satisfied that it's not, follow this procedure: loosen any clinging material with a knife or small screwdriver, then remove all debris from the crack with a vacuum.

With this done, force grout into the crack with a pointing trowel. Use a vinyl-based grout, as this type has the elasticity necessary to ride out expansion and contraction. Finish by striking grout.

# Replacing a Damaged Brick

If yours is an older home, the most difficult part of this job will be finding a brick that harmonizes with its neighbors. Match colors by chipping out a piece and taking it to a dealer who specializes in used brick. Note the dimensions of your bricks, too; sizes vary.

For the work, you'll need mortar, a broad bricklayer's chisel, a heavy hammer or mallet, trowel, and a tool for striking joints (see page 189). When working with the hammer and chisel, protect your eyes with goggles and your chisel hand with a leather work glove—misses hurt.

The illustrations at right show how to replace a full brick. (If you must cut one, see page 188.) Coat porous bricks with masonry sealer to minimize future repairs.

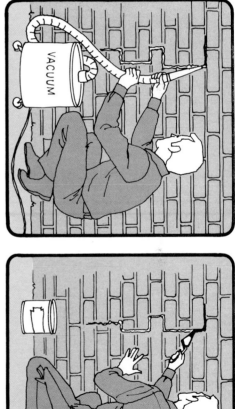

Chip out the damaged brick a piece at a time. Remove the old mortar, too, and thoroughly clean dust and debris from the cavity.

Dampen the surrounding bricks to retard evaporation, then lay fresh mortar on the cavity's bottom and sides.

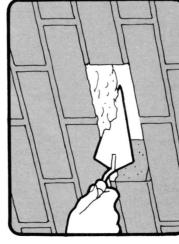

Wet the new brick, slide it into place, and pack mortar into the joints. Scrape off any excess and scrub with a wet brush.

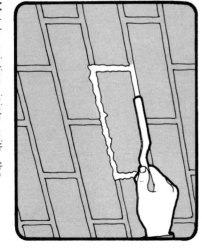

Match existing joints with the proper striking technique (see page 189). Use a mason's strike or a piece of pipe.

**135**

# REPAIRING STUCCO

Of all wall materials, stucco is one of the most difficult to patch. Small cracks are easily filled, as explained on pages 35-36 and 130. But if the damage is more extensive, you must chip away old material down to the lath or masonry underneath, then build up a new surface in two or three layers.

Areas larger than about 4 feet square usually require that the entire wall be restuccoed—a job for a masonry contractor experienced in this sort of work. Plan smaller patching for mild weather when there's no danger of freezing, and figure the project will take at

least three days, with two days to a week between them for curing.

To begin the job, first repair any tears in the building paper with asphalt roofing cement. Replace defective wood or metal lath with metal lath, being sure to leave a ¼-inch space behind it so the first coat will grip well.

You can repair stucco with ordinary patching cement. If the existing stucco is white all the way through, mix one part white cement with 2½ to 3 parts white sand. Add water gradually, bringing the batch to a putty-like consistency.

Remember that stucco—and all cement-based compounds—gain strength from a slow cure. Retard this process by keeping repairs damp for 2 to

3 days. Wait at least six weeks before painting, then prime and finish with a concrete coating (see page 519).

Colored stucco can be difficult to match. Experiment with mortar pigments, keeping in mind that colors will fade as much as 70 percent during the drying process. Never let the pigments exceed 3 percent of the batch's total volume.

To blend the patch's final surface with surrounding areas, use one of the concrete finishing techniques described on page 166.

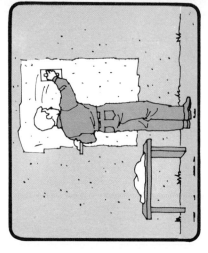

Apply the first coat of stucco to within approximately ¼ inch of the surface. Press with the trowel to embed it firmly in the lath.

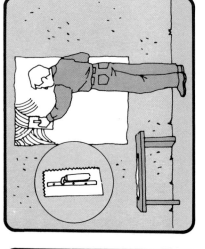

When the stucco begins to firm up, scratch it with an improvised rake made by driving nails through a piece of wood.

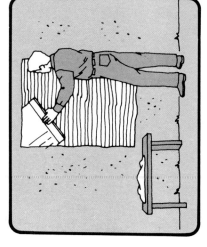

Mist the "scratch" coat with fine spray, keeping it damp for two days. In windy or sunny weather, repeat several times daily.

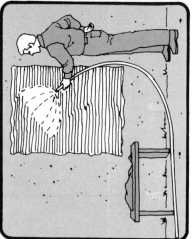

Apply the second "brown" coat to within about ⅛ inch of the surface and level it off with a metal straightedge as shown.

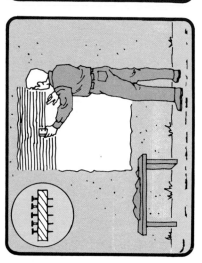

Now "float" the brown coat by working it with a trowel until water comes to the surface. More about floating on page 165.

Mist the brown coat for two days, wait a week, moisten again, and smooth on the finish coat. Texture it within a half-hour.

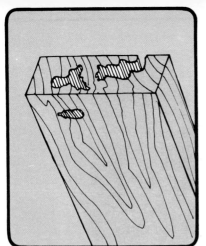

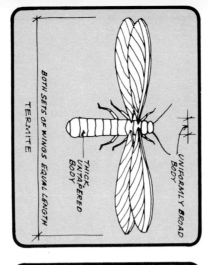

BOTH SETS OF WINGS EQUAL LENGTH
TERMITE
UNIFORMLY BROAD BODY
THICK UNTAPERED BODY

# WARDING OFF TERMITES

Watch for evidence of these devastating insects in early spring and fall. During these times, reproductive members of termite colonies sprout wings, take off on mating flights, discard the wings, and establish nesting places. If you find a pile of wings, suspect a colony nearby.

Termites can be classified into two categories—*subterranean* (those that eat wood but nest underground) and *non-subterranean* (those that live in the wood itself). Subterranean termites are more widespread and destructive. Each day, workers leave the nest, climb above ground, and procure the colony's cellulose food supply.

Non-subterranean wood-boring insects—including powder-post beetles and carpenter ants as well as several termite species—remain above ground. Sometimes you can spot their entrance holes in the wood's surface; a pile of sawdust pellets is another tell-tale sign.

If you suspect termites, call a licensed exterminator (many offer free inspections). And don't panic—though these pests can demolish a house, it would take years.

To eliminate subterranean termites, exterminators surround the house with what amounts to an underground moat of insecticide—usually injecting chemicals into the soil with special equipment. Isolated from the earth, workers in the house soon die of thirst; the remainder of the colony starves or moves on.

Non-subterranean termites confine their activities to limited areas such as the inside of a porch column, a window, or a door frame. If the wood hasn't been structurally weakened, extermination consists of boring holes into it and injecting a liquid or powdered chemical; if the damage is more extensive, it must be cut away and replaced with treated lumber (see page 177).

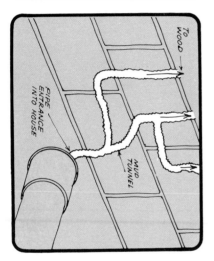

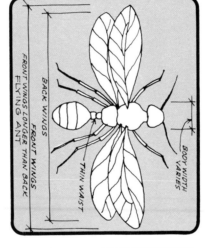

BACK WINGS
FRONT WINGS LONGER THAN BACK
FLYING ANT
THIN WAIST
BODY WIDTH VARIES

Termites look similar to ants, but have thick waistlines and—in their reproductive forms—two pairs of equal-length wings.

In contrast, flying ants have very thin waists, with one pair of wings shorter than the other. They don't attack wood.

Non-subterranean termites dig across the grain, hollowing out tunnels. Occasionally they break through the surface.

To get to wood, termites often bridge foundations, pipes, and even air spaces with flattened mud shelter tubes like these.

TO WOOD
PIPE ENTRANCE INTO HOUSE
MUD TUNNEL

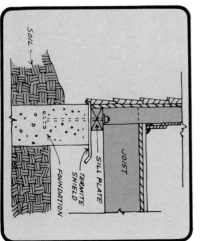

SOIL
JOIST
SILL PLATE
TERMITE SHIELD
FOUNDATION

A metal termite shield, installed during construction, helps protect wood above ground—but watch for shelter tubes anyway.

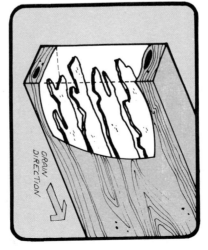

GRAIN DIRECTION

Subterranean termites bore along the grain of wood. They avoid exposure, and often leave nothing but a shell behind.

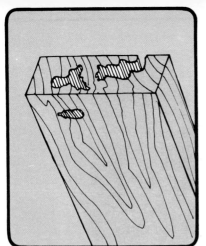

137

# INSTALLING NEW SIDING MATERIALS

No other single improvement can do as much for your home's appearance and livability as a new exterior covering. Re-side to create an entirely different appearance. Or duplicate the old look—but with a low-maintenance product that won't need painting for decades, if ever.

The range of materials and styles (below and opposite) is almost staggering. But before you choose a siding for your house, examine what's underneath. Tightly interlocked new siding will greatly reduce air infiltration through exterior walls, but it won't make up for lack of insulation and sheathing.

In some cases you might be energy-dollars ahead to strip walls to their sheathing or studs and upgrade their "R" values first (see pages 366-367). Or maybe the answer is to beef-up existing insulation with a polystyrene backing that's available with some manufactured sidings (see page 143).

## SIDING ALTERNATIVES

| Siding Material | Appearance | Features/Price | Durability |
|---|---|---|---|
| Wood, Plywood | Widest range of styles, textures, and finishes. Available pre-primed, pre-sealed, or vinyl-clad. | Difficult to apply over existing siding. Prices vary from low (yellow pine, fir) to high (redwood, cedar, plywoods). | Depends upon species and pretreatment. |
| Hardboard | Lap and vertical panel styles with a variety of textures and prefinished colors. Also available pre-primed. | No problems with grain, splitting, or knots. Large panels mean fewer joints for easier installation and greater weather-resistance. Limited color selection. Moderate price. | Vinyl-clad types carry guarantees to 30 years; pre-primed types must be repainted periodically. |
| Mineral fiber | Shingles, shakes, and a few lap designs; usually textured. | Of some insulation value. Resistant to fire and termites. Prone to splitting. Low price. | Guarantees to 20 years. Needn't be painted. |
| Composition | Panels that simulate lap siding. Dated look. | Fair insulation value. Temperature extremes cause deterioration. No longer used widely. Low price. | Guarantees to 20 years, but appearance deteriorates. |
| Aluminum | Wide range of lap, vertical, shingle, and shake styles; broad selection of prefinished colors. | Most popular, next to wood. Choice of baked enamel or plastic finishes at prices ranging from moderate to high. Lightweight, unaffected by fire and termites. Drawbacks: dents easily, noisy, conducts electricity. | Guarantees to 35 years for plastic-clad types. Easily cleaned; needn't be repainted. |
| Steel | Limited selection of lap or vertical styles and colors. | Most of the same properties as aluminum but heavier and more resistant to denting. Higher-priced than aluminum. | Several makers offer lifetime guarantees. |
| Vinyl | Limited choice of lap and vertical styles. Handful of colors. | Impervious to most perils. Color is impregnated all the way through. Higher rate of expansion and contraction makes application critical. Most costly. | Lifetime guarantees. Cannot be repainted. |

138

# CHOOSING AND BUYING SIDING

Wood—once the only practical choice for non-masonry walls—has now become the standard against which other materials are compared. Its competitors include hardboard, mineral fiber (usually asbestos), composition (typically asphalt-saturated felt), aluminum, steel, and solid vinyl. Properties of these materials are summarized in the chart on the opposite page.

What type you select depends largely upon the appearance you want, local availability, and how much you're willing to invest against maintenance savings later on. All simulate wood styles (see below) with varying degrees of success. If you like the look of painted boards or

shingles, any manufactured siding will come close; imitations of natural wood finishes and textures are less convincing.

Most of wood's alternatives eliminate its susceptibility to splitting, warping, rot, and termites. And most—including wood—are available with factory finishes that needn't be repainted. Vinyl formulations, the best of these coatings, protect surfaces from deterioration for up to 35 years. Solid vinyl siding is so tough that it's often guaranteed for the life of your house.

Manufactured sidings have made giant strides since the early days of "Insul-Brick" and raw aluminum, but wood still remains the most popular. Redwood and cedar heartwoods naturally resist rot and insects and never need painting. Stain them or let weather bleach the boards to a silvery gray. Less expensive

woods are available pre-sealed for a low-maintenance, natural appearance. If you decide against prepainted wood or hardboard siding, you can also buy these materials *pre-primed* with an undercoat, which will increase the life of the final finishes.

Though more expensive than board sidings, plywood types offer several advantages. The 4x8-, 9-, or 10-foot panels go up faster and seal tighter than individual boards or shingles. In certain instances, you may not need sheathing underneath. More about plywood siding on page 142.

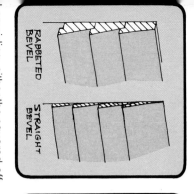

RABBETED BEVEL

STRAIGHT BEVEL

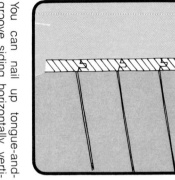

Lap siding, either the squared-off or beveled type, is always applied horizontally, with boards lapped about 1 inch.

You can nail up tongue-and-groove siding horizontally, vertically, even diagonally. Widths may be uniform or random.

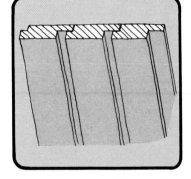

Shiplap or channel-groove siding uses rabbeted edges to interlock boards. Install them horizontally or vertically.

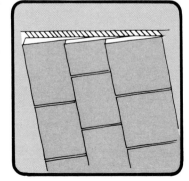

Shingles have a regular appearance, and adapt readily to misshapen walls, and are one of the easiest sidings to apply.

Shakes go up like shingles, but have tapered tops and an irregular, hand-split look. They're more expensive than shingles.

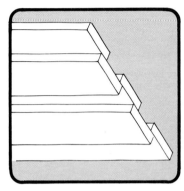

Board-on-board siding is always applied vertically, with boards lapped about 1 inch. Widths may be random or regular.

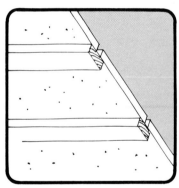

Board-and-batten siding also goes up vertically. With *reverse* board and batten, the battens are applied first, then the boards.

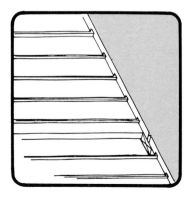

Grooves give hardboard and plywood sheets the appearance of boards. Joints may be ship-lapped or covered with battens.

## APPLYING WOOD SHINGLES AND SHAKES

Of all siding materials, shingles and shakes are the easiest to install. The job is repetitive, but calls for no special tools or skills. Nail up a batten for each row or course, fit each piece ⅛ inch from its neighbor, and drive two or three nails. You can apply shingles and shakes directly over old wood siding. If your home has wood or plywood sheathing, you can opt to remove the old siding, repair any defects, and put up new building paper first. Use the techniques shown here for wood shingles and shakes; mineral fiber or composition types go up in the same manner, but check manufacturer's data. (More about composition shingles on page 124.)

Shingle grades run from 1 to 4, in a variety of sizes and textures. Choose Nos. 1 or 2 for exterior walls. Nos. 3 and 4 also are suitable for outside use, but only where appearance is not a factor, such as in the first layer in a double-course application.

To apply double-course shingles, nail up two layers, one on top of the other (see below). This lets you expose more of the shingles' surfaces and creates a deeper shadow line between courses. Expose slightly less than half with single coursing, about ⅔ with double-course applications.

For the neat, uniform look of typical shingle jobs, carefully plot exposures so they'll line up with window tops and sills, then hold courses to dead level lines. For more design interest, nail them up randomly.

Shingles up to 8 inches wide need two rustproof shingle nails each; with wider ones, drive a third nail in the center. If you're double-coursing shakes, nail their bottom or *butt* edges, too.

Before you begin, soak bundles for several hours. Otherwise, the wood might begin to expand and pull away in the first heavy rain.

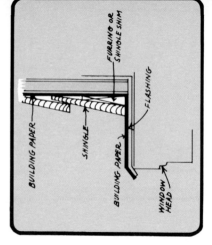

To keep butts perfectly level, nail up a batten strip as shown. Always stagger edge joints from course to course.

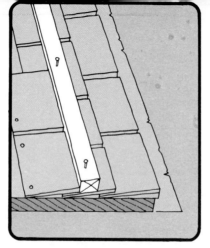

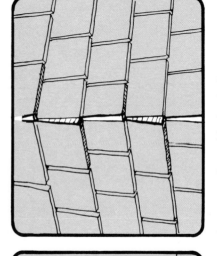

Drive nails about ¾ inch from each edge and at least an inch above where the butt edges of the next course will fall.

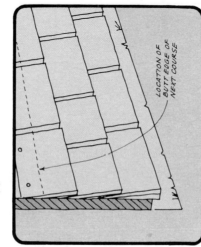

Carefully fit building paper and shingles over flashing atop windows. Shim with partial shingles to shed rain.

At corners, lace shingles by butting each course alternately, mitering edges or covering them with wood or metal molding.

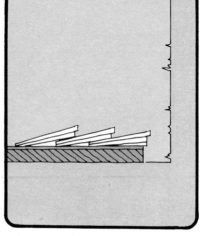

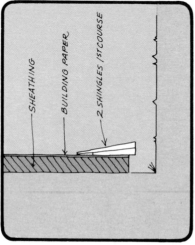

Use two shingles for the first course, three if you'll be double-coursing. Overlap the foundation about 1 inch.

For double-coursing, you'll need longer nails. The butt edges of the outer course should be about ½ inch below the undercourse.

140

# APPLYING BOARD SIDINGS

Horizontal wood sidings go up in much the same way as wood shingles and shakes (opposite). The work calls for much more precise calculations, though, and may require extensive carpentry as well.

First, you must decide whether to retain the existing siding as a nailing base or to rip it off and start over again. Old coverings such as tongue-and-groove boards present a flat surface to which you can nail directly. The new siding will make your walls about ¾ inch thicker, so be sure to keep in mind that you'll have to fur-out door and window frames by that amount.

With lap siding, you must fur-out walls first (see below). The ¾-inch air space between new and old sidings adds valuable insulation, but it means door and window openings may be recessed as much as 1½ inches.

Next, ensure that boards will remain perfectly level from course to course, and that they'll properly line up with door and window frames. Carpenters typically calculate locations for lap joints in advance with the aid of a *story pole* (see page 185). Then they mark the laps on frames and on walls around the corner from the one they're working on. Plan to overlap boards at least an inch; increase this slightly if necessary for a proper fit around openings and at the eaves.

Vertical applications—especially random-width boards—require fewer painstaking calculations. Consider openings and corners before you get to them, though—and be sure to plumb each board. Handle all siding lumber carefully, especially prefinished and pre-primed types. These relatively soft woods often split when you nail near an edge. To keep this from happening, drill pilot holes first, or try special pre-blunted siding nails.

To apply horizontal siding over clapboard, first nail up 1x3s as shown. Drive nails through old siding into studs underneath.

Horizontal and vertical channel-groove sidings get two nails across the width of each board. Nail about 1 inch from edges.

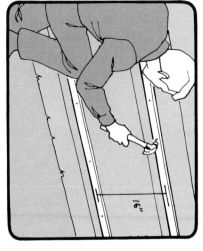

Nailing strips for vertical siding must run horizontally. Space them uniformly, usually 16 inches from center to center.

Tongue-and-groove sidings are blind-nailed through the tongue of each course. Wide boards may need an additional nail.

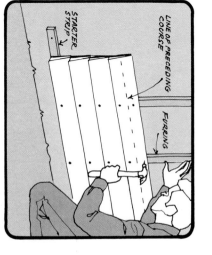

Siding up to 10 inches wide requires two nails driven into each of the studs. Wider versions will need three nails.

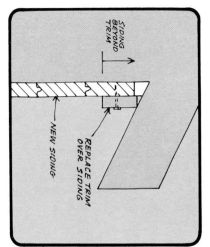

At eaves, siding must extend up under any trim boards concealing rafter ends. Pry trim loose, or remove and replace it.

## APPLYING PANEL SIDING

Big hardboard and plywood panels cover a wall rapidly—and with types as slender as 7/16 inch thick, they minimize trim problems around doors and windows. To install them yourself, though, you'll need a good grounding in basic carpentry techniques, plus an assistant to help handle sheets.

Some panels come with rabbeted edges that interlock to make a vertical *shiplap* joint; others simply butt together, their seams covered by a batten strip or special T-shaped molding (both are shown below).

Nail to studs, spacing nails 6 inches apart on edges and 12 inches apart on intermediate studs. Use rust-resistant annular-ring nails or color-matching types available from the manufacturers of prefinished siding materials. Never drive two panels tightly together; compensate for expansion by leaving a 1/16-inch space and filling with caulk.

Cut with the panel's good face down if you're using a saber or portable circular saw, and good face up with a hand or stationary power saw. An inaccurate cut can spoil an entire panel, so plot dimensions on graph paper and double-check them before sawing. And remember to seal cuts in pre-primed and prefinished panels before installation

(check the manufacturer's specifications for the appropriate sealer).

Metal accessories similar to the ones shown on the opposite page simplify fitting panels together at corners and around doors and windows. Or, if you'd rather, fabricate your own corner treatments as shown below. (For more about working with plywood and hardboard, see pages 467-471 and 473).

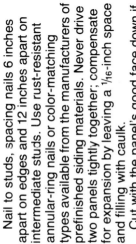

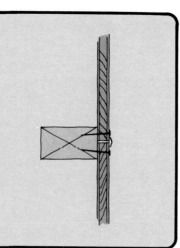

To make shiplap joints, nail up one sheet, caulk, then install the next. Don't try to drive one nail through both edges.

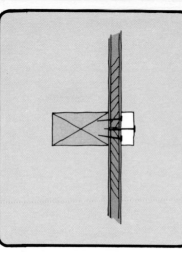

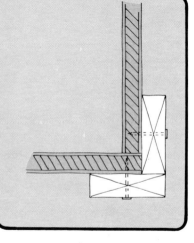

Metal moldings offer an inconspicuous way to finish-off butt joints. Some prefinished types simply snap into place.

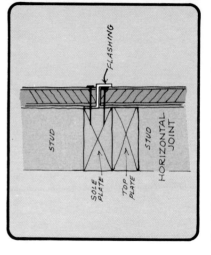

Or, cover butt joints with wood battens. For a board-and-batten effect (see page 139), also space strips across the panel's width.

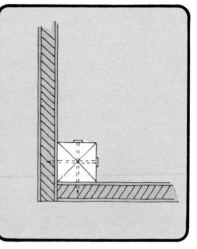

Complete inside corners with 2x2 trim, as shown. You can also select from a variety of cove moldings milled for this purpose.

At outside corners, lap a pair of 1x3s or 1x4s. To accommodate expansion, nail them to the siding, not to each other.

On taller walls, you'll have horizontal joints. Nail bottom panel in place, caulk, lay flashing in place, and nail top panel.

142

# APPLYING MANUFACTURED SIDING

Aluminum, steel, hardboard, mineral fiber, and vinyl sidings are designed especially for re-siding applications and are relatively easy to install. Check the warranty, however, to see if you risk voiding it by doing the work yourself. If not, follow the manufacturer's instructions closely.

Aluminum, steel, and vinyl sidings have lips top and bottom. You nail one course through pre-punched holes, then interlock its top edge with the bottom of the next. Lay-up mineral fiber, plywood, and hardboard types as you would conventional lumber (see page 141), or attach them to metal channel moldings between courses.

All manufactured sidings utilize standardized, lightweight components that go up fast and fit snugly, with none of the warping and splitting problems natural materials are prone to. Vinyl sometimes turns brittle at low temperatures, though, and may lose shape with exposure to very strong sunlight. Hardboard can absorb condensation from within walls, so don't use it unless your home has a vapor barrier in the exterior walls. And since metal sidings conduct electricity, they must be grounded.

Also note that aluminum and vinyl expand and contract considerably with temperature changes. That's why they come with slots instead of holes for nailing. Locate nails near the center of these slots—and don't drive the nails so tightly that they'll impede this inevitable movement.

Finally, beware of companies whose salespeople approach you with hard-sell presentations and too-good-to-be-true financing arrangements. The vast majority of siding contractors are reputable tradesmen, but there are still a few fast-buck operators in this field.

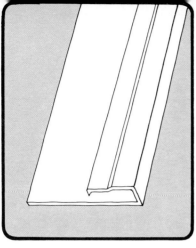

Since manufactured sidings are fairly thin, they present few problems around openings. This channel fits under windowsills.

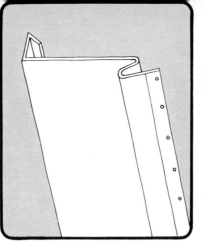

Aluminum, steel, and vinyl sidings consist of extruded strips with interlocking flanges for tight joints between courses.

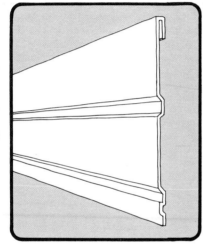

With manufactured soffits, you can extend a new siding job up under the eaves, avoiding a chronic maintenance problem.

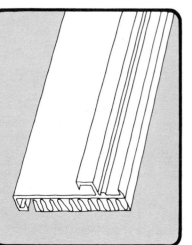

Insulation-backed sidings do a good job of muffling noise—a problem with metal sidings. Thermal resistance is only fair.

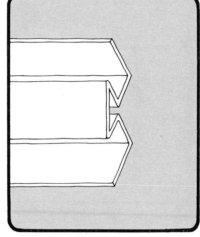

Inside corner posts usually are installed first, carefully caulked, then plumbed so each course will be level.

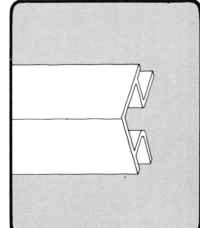

Cover outside corners with continuous strips (shown) or put individual caps over each course. Caps go up last.

143

# SOLVING WINDOW AND DOOR PROBLEMS

Few are the homes that don't occasionally suffer shattered glass, a torn screen, or other minor damage to windows and doors. And because few repairmen find it worth their while to make house calls for these simple ailments, finding someone to do the work can be a big problem. If you'll take the time to learn the techniques on the following pages, though, you needn't be at anyone's mercy.

Note that this chapter covers only the *exterior* parts of windows and doors, or parts such as glass that are normally repaired from the outside. Inside jobs are explained on pages 64-73; to learn about weather-stripping, see pages 361-365.

## REPLACING BROKEN GLASS

Faced with a broken window, you have three choices: 1) remove the sash and take it to a hardware store or glass shop for reglazing; 2) buy a new pane cut to size and install it yourself; or 3) cut the glass yourself from standard-size sheets kept on hand for such emergencies.

Dismantling a window (see page 67) can be far more work than simply replacing the glass; cutting glass (opposite) isn't difficult, but you might break a pane or two before acquiring the knack. If you opt for the middle course, you can make the repair yourself in under an hour.

Before buying glass, measure carefully as shown below. Check the thickness, too (most panes are ⅛-inch). You'll need

glazier's points—or spring clips if the frame is metal—and a can of glazing compound. Try to get the push-in type of point shown on the opposite page; they're easier to insert.

Caution: always wear heavy gloves when handling broken glass. Take care with the sharp edges and corners of new panes, too.

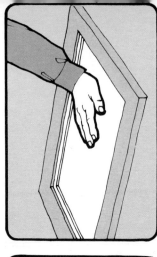

Sashes aren't always perfectly square, so measure at several points, then subtract ⅛ inch from each dimension.

Line up one edge of the pane in the sash, gently lower it into place, and press gently with your palm or fingertips to seal it.

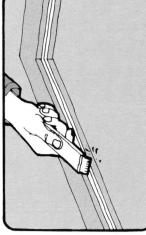

Scrape away the rest of the old compound, then roughen the groove with a scraper so new compound will adhere properly.

Before you insert the new pane, apply a ⅛-inch-thick bead of glazing compound. This helps seal and cushion the glass.

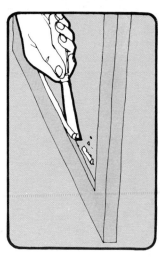

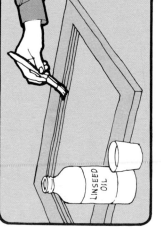

Chipping off old compound can be the hardest part of the job. Use a putty knife or old chisel, or soften with a soldering iron.

Prime the groove with linseed oil, turpentine, or oil-base paint. Untreated wood will draw oil from the glazing compound.

**144**

Tools include glass cutter, ¼x3-inch strip of wood, brush and oil to wipe the cut, square, and measur-ing tape.

Tools include glass cutter, ¼x3-inch strip of wood, brush and oil to wipe the cut, square, and measur-ing tape.

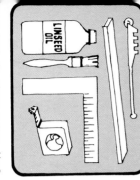

# CUTTING GLASS

In cutting glass, you take advantage of its inherent brittleness. Scoring it with a cutting wheel focuses all its breaking tendencies along a single line. A smooth, even score lets you snap glass with

ease. The trick is to make the right score in a single stroke. Exert too little pressure on the glass and the cutting wheel will skip; too much and the edges will crack or chip.

Working on a flat surface, use a glass-cutting jig like the one shown below—or guide the cutter with a strip of hard-

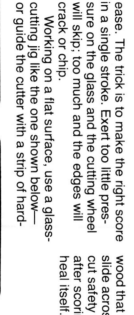

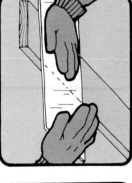

Fasten the strip to a workbench and line up the square, lubricate the line, then draw cutter along it in one smooth stroke.

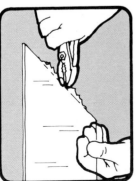

Make the break by laying glass scored-side-up over a board, hold-ing the good side with one hand and slapping down the other.

If you get an uneven break, nip away irregularities with pliers. Teeth in the cutting tool are also designed for this purpose.

wood that has been dampened so it won't slide across the surface. Don't attempt to cut safety glass, and don't wait too long after scoring to snap glass—it tends to heal itself.

Let the compound dry a week be-fore painting. Paint should over-lap the glass about 1/16 inch for a tight weather seal.

Spring clips substitute for glazier's points in steel sashes. Install as shown. Metal windows needn't be primed.

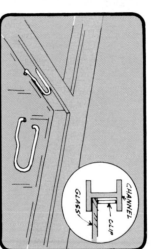

CHANNEL — CLIP — GLASS

Aluminum storm windows need no compound. A rubber gasket, which you force into place with a putty knife, holds the glass.

Now secure the pane by pressing points into the sash with a putty knife. Don't push too hard or you may crack the glass.

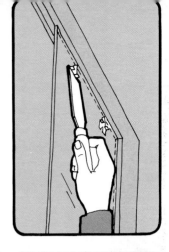

Roll glazing compound to make a ¼-inch rope, then press into place, making sure it sticks to both glass and wood.

Dress-off the compound by bevel-ing it with a putty knife. If com-pound sticks to the knife, wet it with turpentine.

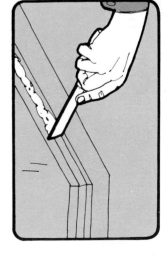

## REPLACING SILLS AND SADDLES

Windowsills take a terrific beating. Rain not only hits them directly, but also cascades onto them from windows and siding. Angled as they are, windowsills catch plenty of sunlight as well. Alternate soaking and baking eventually make them veritable sponges that can't hold paint for very long periods.

The best preventative is a couple coats of paint applied annually. If a sill at your house is too far gone for that, there are two alternatives. The first is to rebuild it with a fiber glass-type product made especially for the purpose. The second

is to install a new sill. Door sills—called saddles or thresholds—also fail in time. Replace either with the procedures illustrated here.

First, determine if the sill or saddle fits under the jambs on either side, measure, and buy a new piece. The drawings below show how to install a new piece of wood in either situation—but you might opt to replace a saddle with a preformed, predrilled metal or plastic unit.

Next, remove the old saddle or sill. This will probably be the most difficult part of the job. Use a chisel or old screwdriver to hunt for any nails that may be holding the piece in place. In the end, you may decide simply to saw out a

section, as shown below, or to demolish by splitting along the grain with a hammer and chisel, then pulling out the splintered remains.

If you can manage to get the old one out intact, use it as a template for marking the replacement. If not, you'll have to measure carefully. Strive for a snug fit.

Prime all sides and edges of a new si before installing it. For more about how windows and doors are put together, see pages 64-65 and 74. To learn about weather-stripping-type saddles, see page 365.

Gently tap the new sill or saddle into place. Don't force. If it resists, remove and sand the ends, bevel-ing them slightly.

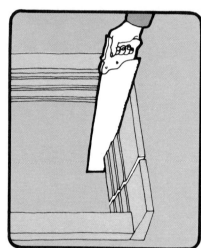

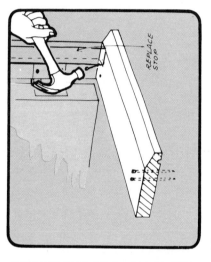

You may have to saw out a section from the center of the sill, then drive the ends inward. Use these as patterns for new piece.

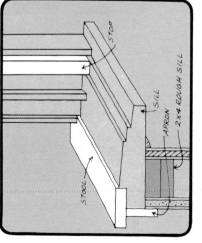

Note that you'll probably have to remove the apron, stool, and stop molding to get a sill out. Pry these carefully.

Nail a saddle at both ends and in the middle. Countersink and hide nailheads with putty. Be sure also to caulk the ends.

Using rust-resistant nails, secure the sill from underneath. Counter-sink the nails, then caulk the nailheads and the ends of the sill.

146

# REPAIRING AND MAINTAINING SCREENS AND STORMS

Rustproof screen materials (see page 148) and combination screen/storm sashes (see page 149) have taken the semiannual drudgery out of securing a home against drafts and insects. But even low-maintenance types require occasional attention. Check caulking around the frames of combination units; vacuum dirt from screening; and clean oxidized aluminum with car polish. Also, mend any punctured screening with a dab of quick-drying household cement. Try darning a tear in metal screens with

fine wire, but patch larger holes as shown below. If you have plastic or fiber glass screens, you're better off replacing the entire screen.

Wood-frame screens and storms are more bothersome, but careful monitoring and diligent maintenance can minimize the hassle. Check each as you take it down, set aside those that need help, and repair them at your leisure.

Consider, too, how many windows you actually open during the summer. Leaving a storm window in place not only saves you some work, it also helps keep a room cooler.

Adjust or replace screen/storm door closers as soon as they begin malfunctioning—doors that slam or flap

in the breeze don't last long. Adjustments vary widely. Look for a knurled knob, screw, or ratchet at one end of the pneumatic tube. On some types, the tube itself rotates.

Finally, paint wood frames whenever they need it. Shrinkage and warping greatly undercut their weather-stripping value. (For information about weather-stripping storm windows and doors, see pages 362-365.)

Paint steel screens with a pad. To unclog holes, turn screen over and scrub with a dry pad. Let dry; paint other side.

To patch metal screens, cut a section larger than the opening; unravel a few strands. Fit over hole; bend strands back.

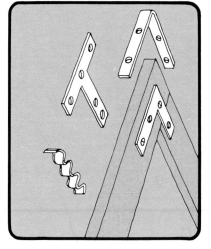

Reinforce loose corner joints with mending plates. Corrugated fasteners work especially well for mitered joints.

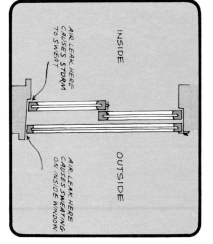

INSIDE

OUTSIDE

AIR LEAK HERE CAUSES STORM TO SWEAT

AIR LEAK HERE CAUSES SWEATING ON INSIDE WINDOW

Air leaks in either an interior or an exterior sash cause sweating. Condensation forms on the sash that's *not* leaking.

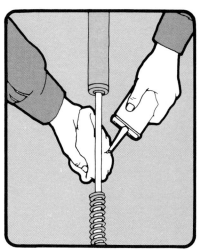

Lubricate door closers every fall by wiping the shaft with light oil. Check the adjustment for proper operation, too.

Clean screens by blasting them with water from a hose, then scrubbing with a stiff brush. Don't forget the frame's edges.

# REPLACING SCREENING

You install screening in much the same way an artist stretches a canvas—fasten it at one end of the frame, pull the material taut, then secure at the sides and other end. The drawings below show how to improvise a "stretcher" with a couple of 1x2s and a pair of wood wedges. A spline-and-channel arrangement built into aluminum frames does the same thing.

When removing moldings from wood frames, begin with the middle rail and spring the molding loose with a chisel or putty knife. Always work from the center to the ends, applying pressure near brads. If a molding breaks, you can find a reasonable facsimile at a lumberyard. Ask for screen molding. To learn about fitting moldings, see page 47.

For the mesh, choose aluminum, plastic, fiber glass, copper, or bronze. Let appearance and upkeep be your guides. Aluminum is inconspicuous, but is subject to staining; plastic and fiber glass won't stain, but their filaments are thicker, which affects visibility; copper and bronze must be coated with spar varnish periodically to prevent staining. Buy 18/14 mesh or finer.

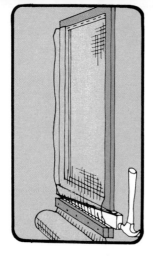

Now insert a wedge between the cleats and frame on either side. Gently tap the wedges until the screening is tight.

To stretch, nail a strip of wood to the bench or floor, roll mesh over it, and nail another strip on top of the first.

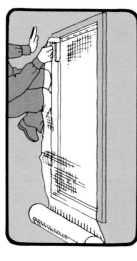

With a knife or shears, cut a screen that's slightly wider and at least a foot longer than the frame, then staple top edge.

To remove mesh from an aluminum frame, first pry out the spline around edges. You may need to buy new splining.

Trim off the excess, then refit the moldings with small brads. Countersink brads and fill holes with plastic wood.

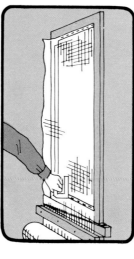

Staple screening to the bottom edge next, then to the sides. If the frame has a center rail, fasten screening to it last.

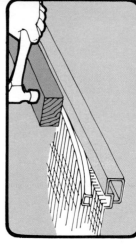

Now drive splining into the channel with a hammer and block as shown. As the spline goes in, it will pull the screening taut.

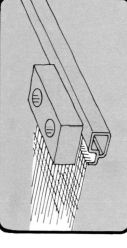

Bend the mesh's edges and force them into the channel with a putty knife. Weigh with a brick to hold it in place.

Carefully square-up the frame, lay new screening over it, and cut to the same dimensions as the frame's outside measurements.

148

# INSTALLING NEW WINDOWS AND DOORS

## CHOOSING AND BUYING COMBINATION UNITS

Combination windows and doors can soon pay for themselves with savings on your heating and cooling bills. Beware of shoddy ones, though—poorly made or fitted units leak air, are difficult to operate, and turn into eyesores after several seasons.

What are the considerations? Appearance is one. If you can live with aluminum's plain-Jane look, you'll save a few dollars. Insist that it be anodized, however; ordinary mill-finish aluminum oxidizes rapidly. Next, check the corners of the frames. Lapped joints are stronger and tighter than mitered ones; if you can see light through the joints, you can be sure that they'll admit air.

Many suppliers offer a choice between double- and triple-track designs.

Triple-track units are self-storing—you don't have to remove the sash you're not using. Generally speaking, the deeper the tracks are, the better a unit's insulation value will be.

Watch a new house go together and you'll notice that its doors and windows arrive preassembled, with doors or sashes already hung in their frames. Carpenters simply build "rough" openings, tip the units into place, and add trim around the edges. Knowing this takes most of the mystery (and work) out of adding a new window or door.

Combination screen/storm windows and doors are also factory assembled—

After combinations have been installed, make sure each window and door is well-caulked, operates smoothly, and seals tightly.

but since the openings they must fit into aren't rough, combinations usually are made to order. Though installation is commonly included in the sales price, you can sometimes save 10 to 15 percent by installing them yourself (see below).

Pre-hung exterior doors are installed in the same way as their interior counterparts (see page 80).

### COMBINATION UNIT CHOICES

| Material | Features | Relative Cost |
|---|---|---|
| Aluminum | Most widely used. Available with plain or baked-enamel finish. Plain aluminum should be anodized. Beware of flimsy, "bargain-priced" units. | Low to moderate |
| Steel | Sturdy construction. Baked-enamel finish, often with guarantees of 10 years or more. | Moderate to high |

## INSTALLING COMBINATION UNITS

Combination units include a frame designed to overlap your window's or door's exterior frame. Accurate measurements are critical for a tight fit and proper operation; let the supplier do this job.

After the units arrive, check to see if windows have two or three ¼-inch ventilation holes through their bottom frame members. These let moisture run off. If there are no holes, drill them yourself when the windows are in place.

Run two beads of butyl caulk around the frame's top and sides; lay one on its inside edge, the other along the jamb's edge.

Set the unit in place, press for a tight seal, drive rustproof screws through the flanges, then caulk the bottom edge.

**149**

# INSTALLING NEW WINDOWS

Don't undertake this project unless you have had some experience with basic framing techniques. To make an accurate rough opening for a new window, you should understand how walls go together (see pages 48-50) and how to keep everything plumb, level, and square.

Before cutting into the wall, plan carefully. Determine where you want the window. Will you run into any plumbing, heating, or electrical lines? It's relatively easy to relocate wiring, but difficult to move pipes or ducts.

Next, ask your supplier for the rough-in dimensions of the window you purchase. The exterior opening will need to be only slightly larger. Inside, you'll want to remove the wall surface (from ceiling to

floor) to the inner edge of the first stud past either side of the rough-in measurement.

Work from the inside out, cutting the exterior sheathing and siding just before you insert the window.

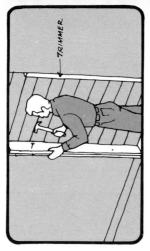

Mark the interior opening and cut from ceiling to floor; leave sole plate intact. Begin with a chisel, then switch to a keyhole saw.

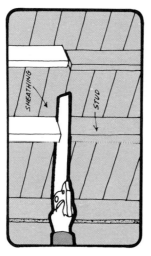

Remove studs that will be interrupted by the window. Cut in the center and pry them carefully away from the sheathing.

Nail a 2x4 trimmer piece to the exposed stud at either side of the opening. These trimmers will support the window's header.

Build a header with two 2x6s sandwiching a scrap of ½-inch plywood. Make sure the header's bottom edge is level and square.

Construct 2x4 sill. Support it with cripple studs. If necessary, nail two pairs of 2x4s between header and sill to frame side jambs.

Cut the exterior wall from inside or out, whichever is easier. If you cut from outside, first drill pilot holes to mark corners.

Set the unit in place, then insert shims between it and the framing so the window will be level and plumb.

After nailing the window to the framing, fit insulation into any gaps around its edges. Use strips of fiber glass insulation.

Finish-off the interior wall (see page 34). Finally, attach the inside casing; caulk around the exterior.

**150**

# INSTALLING A SLIDING GLASS DOOR

The procedure shown opposite tells how you can make rough openings to accommodate doors and windows up to 7½ feet wide. For broader openings, you'll need larger headers—2x8 for up to 4 feet, 2x10 to 6½ feet, and 2x12 to 8 feet.

Also, since many exterior walls bear the weight of upper floors and roof framing, you must devise a temporary support system to carry the load while you modify the walls. Install braces as illustrated below, and protect good flooring with sections of plank or plywood under the vertical supports.

Replacing an existing window with a bigger one or with sliding glass doors that open to an outdoor living area can entirely change a home's character. So before you settle on a location, consider all the factors—privacy, light, ventilation, and even basic traffic patterns may be altered.

And don't forget that big expanses of glass lose heat rapidly at night, and gain rapidly on sunny days. Minimize energy losses by choosing doors or windows away from prevailing winds, or by protecting them with walls or fences around your outdoor living area (see pages 172-191).

Sliding glass doors are sold both with and without glass, and are framed in aluminum, steel, or wood. Standard sizes are 5, 6, and 8 feet wide by 80 inches high. Unglazed types aren't difficult for two people to handle; pre-glazed units usually are installed by the supplier after you provide a rough opening.

Be relatively sure you can count on good weather the day you cut through the exterior of the house. (Because it's easier to remove framing from a wide opening if you first pull off the sheathing and siding, your home's interior will be exposed throughout most of the project.) And be sure to have a friend there to help you lift the header into position.

If your sliding glass doors will replace an existing window, you can remove the old unit intact—sash and all. Wait until the studs are exposed on both sides, then pry them away from the window's frame.

Making an opening in a brick-veneer wall calls for quite a bit more work, and you might want to hire a mason for some of it. First, score the bricks with a circular saw and carbide masonry blade, then chop them out with a hammer and chisel. Next, install an angle iron or I-beam lintel to support the bricks above. Finally, split a number of bricks and mortar them into place to trim off the opening's sides.

...ark opening, then cut away wall surface flush with the first stud face. Install header flush with the ... at either side of rough-in width. ...ough-in jamb studs if needed.

Set up bracing. You'll need one person to hold a 2x4 against the ceiling while you wedge in the vertical members.

...ut trimmers to support header at ends. Use them to wedge ...eader into position. Nail trim-...ers and toenail header.

Cut siding and sheathing at the top and at each side. When you get to the floor, saw through the 2x4 sole plate, too.

With an 8-foot-high ceiling, you probably won't need to cut studs for "cripples" above the door. Pry out the old studs intact.

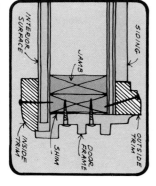

Carry the frame carefully to avoid twisting it out of shape, insert, then secure by partially driving screws into studs and header.

Level and plumb the door by inserting shims wherever required. Tighten screws. Insulate between the frame and the opening.

Outside, use molding to bridge any gap between frame and siding. Inside, patch the wall and trim with casing molding.

# PORCHES, PATIOS, AND DECKS

## ANATOMY OF A PORCH

Wooden porches vary considerably in appearance, but underneath, most have the basic construction illustrated here. It begins with *piers* or *footings* on which

wood or masonry *posts* rest. The posts, a *ledger* attached to the house, and one or more *beams* support *joists*.

*Decking,* usually tongue-and-groove or shiplap boards, is nailed directly to the joists. *Columns* extend the piers and posts to support the roof and railings.

*Face boards* above and below and a *skirt* underneath conceal various structural elements from view.

Up top, porches have virtually the same system of rafters, sheathing, and roofing shown on page 108.

Sooner or later, weather takes its toll on outdoor living areas—porches especially, but also patios and decks. The following pages show how to undo the damage and prevent its recurrence.

But the biggest problem with outdoor living at most homes is that there's just not enough of it—so we've devoted the bulk of this chapter to ways you can remedy that situation.

Here's where you'll learn how to lay a simple bricks-in-sand patio, pour a concrete slab, or get a sturdy deck project off the ground—improvements that can do wonders for the summertime scene around your house.

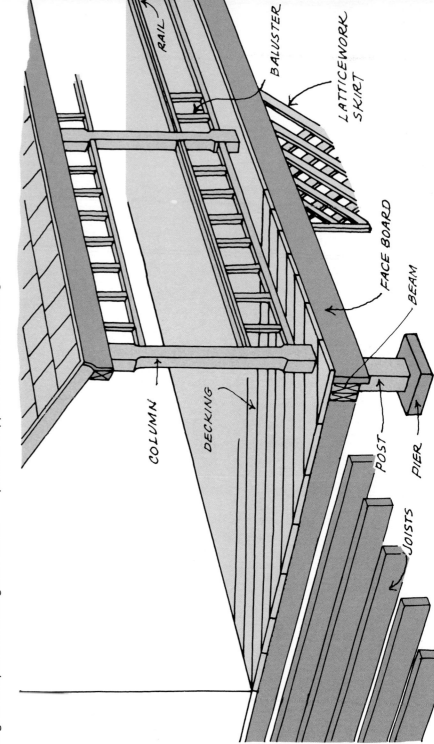

RAIL

BALUSTER

LATTICEWORK SKIRT

FACE BOARD

BEAM

COLUMN

DECKING

POST

PIER

JOISTS

# SOLVING PORCH PROBLEMS

One of the unhappy side effects of exposure to weather extremes—and the one that will cause you the most trouble—is rot. And whether your porch is suffering from prolonged exposure to water, or fungi working away at seasoned wood, the cures are the same: you need to repair or, if the damage is severe, replace the rotten members. The sketches below show how to repair and replace porch columns, the most difficult element to deal with.

Porches are susceptible to other maladies, too—pier or footing settlement, damaged decking, roof leaks, and damage to porch steps and railings. Inspect your porch annually, and if any of these difficulties pop up, deal with them early. See pages 116, 120, and 121 for help with repairing roof flashing and gutters.

## REPAIRING ROTTED COLUMNS

When you notice column damage (or, for that matter, damage to any other porch member), your first step is to determine its extent. To do this, take a pocketknife blade and probe into the wood. If the blade readily sinks into the wood and crumbles the wood on its way, order a new column and prepare to replace the old. If the damage is confined to the surface only, you can fairly easily repair it.

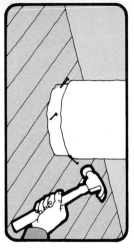

Before you do, though, try to ascertain what caused the problem. If only the surface seems rotted, chances are good that weather is the culprit. If water seems to be getting inside somehow, you'll need to find and seal the leak. And if you suspect termites, see page 137.

*Before attempting to remove a column, be certain to brace the porch roof.* Either improvise bracing with 4x4 timbers, as shown below, or rent metal jackposts to do the job.

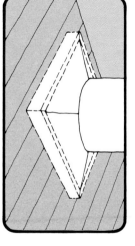

To conceal the repair, build a form around the column, pour in concrete, taper the top as shown, and paint the concrete.

If only the outer edges have rotted, saw or chisel away the damage. But don't remove any more than absolutely necessary.

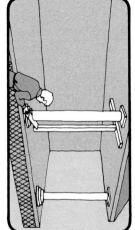

If the column is beyond repair, brace the roof and remove the column. You can saw completely through it and pry out the pieces.

Coat the bare, solid wood with pentachlorophenol (penta), then toenail some large nails through the column and into the floor.

Toenail the column to the new base. Nail the base to the floor. Caulk around the perimeters of both the base and the column.

Fashion a new base to match the others on the porch. Be sure to bevel the edges of the base so that it will shed water.

You may be able to duplicate ornamental trim by laminating scrap boards. You'll need a coping saw or router to make inside cuts.

# SOLVING PATIO PROBLEMS

All things considered, brick, concrete, stone, and other patio-surfacing materials stand up remarkably well to the rigors to which they are subjected. But even these super-tough materials find it difficult to cope with the damaging effects of the elements.

Frost creates most patio surface problems. When it leaves the ground each spring, it has a heaving effect that puts your surface to the test. If it can ride out the expansion, fine; if it can't, it's repair time. Extremely warm temperatures have a similar effect, but, except for concrete, don't usually cause as much damage.

If your patio falls prey to the elements or to accidental damage of any other type—such as dropping a heavy object on it, or staining it—make needed repairs as directed on these two pages.

## ANATOMY OF A PATIO

Regardless of the patio's surface— usually *concrete, brick,* or *flagstone*— it usually rests on a *sand base.* Large expanses of concrete paving require *expansion strips* between them and other structures (house foundations, for example) and *control joints* to help keep any possible cracking in check. Concrete also usually requires *reinforcing mesh* or *rods* for strength and to prevent cracking. Brick and stone units "float" on the sand base or rest in a bed of mortar.

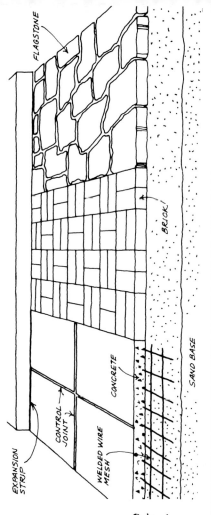

FLAGSTONE

BRICK

CONCRETE

SAND BASE

WELDED WIRE MESH

CONTROL JOINT

EXPANSION STRIP

## PATIO SURFACE STAIN REMOVAL GUIDE

| Type of Stain | Remedy |
|---|---|
| Food, grease, oil, lipstick | Mix dishwashing detergent in warm water. Work the mixture into the stain with a stiff scrub brush or broom. Don't skimp. Rinse with clean water. If this doesn't work, add ammonia to the detergent and water mixture, following the same rinsing procedures mentioned above. Or scrub well with mineral spirits. |
| Paint and candle wax | Remove all the paint or wax you can with a knife or a putty knife. Then scrub the area with metal-bristled brush and cold water. If this fails, apply mineral spirits to the area. If the stain is on concrete and these treatments don't work, try aluminum oxide abrasive or an abrasive brick. |
| Blood, coffee, juice, animal waste | Use dishwashing detergent in cold water. Remove the stain as soon as possible. Work with a stiff scrub brush or broom, and flood the area with the detergent mixture. Rinse with cold clean water. |
| Tar and heel marks | First try dishwashing detergent in warm water. If you're not successful, scour the area with a stiff-bristled brush and mineral spirits; don't use a scouring pad. If some residue remains, flood the area with mineral spirits and blot it up with a soft absorbent cloth. This may take several applications. |
| Efflorescence | Go over the area with a wire brush. This should remove the white stain, which is caused by salts in the masonry mixture. If this doesn't work, you can buy a commercial mixture that will remove the stain. It contains an acid, so be sure to wear gloves and safety glasses when using it. |
| Dirt and grime | Hose down the surface with water and scrub it with a stiff broom. If this doesn't work, mix dish-washing detergent or trisodium phosphate with warm water and go over the area with a stiff brush or broom. |
| Soot | Apply detergent and water. If this doesn't work, apply a mixture of one quart of muriatic acid and one quart of water. Wear gloves. |

# REPAIRING PATIO SURFACES

Though it may hurt a bit to think of it this way, you repair a patio surface in much the same way as a dentist fills a tooth: you clean away the old debris, prepare the cavity, and fill the void.

Don't, however, try to fill cavities in concrete with concrete; you won't get a good bond with the old surface. Instead, choose one of the commercial patching materials listed in the chart at right. (You'll find them handy for other masonry repair jobs, too.)

For stone and brick surfaces, you simply lever out the damaged unit, replace it with a new one, then pack around it with mortar. For more about repairing brick and stone, turn to pages 134 and 135.

Practice the "dentistry" illustrated below and your patio will look new again in no time—and with surprisingly little effort.

## CONCRETE PATCH SELECTOR

| Type | Uses | Description/Mixing Instructions |
|---|---|---|
| Latex patch Vinyl patch Epoxy patch | General-purpose repair jobs such as filling hairline cracks, small breaks and patches, and tuckpointing. Latex and epoxy are best for patio surfaces. | Sold in powdered form with or without a liquid binder. Mix with the appropriate binder, usually a sticky white liquid, to a whipped-cream consistency. |
| Hydraulic cement | To plug water leaks in masonry walls and floor surfaces. This fast-drying formulation allows you to make the repair even while the water is leaking in. | Available in powdered form. Mix a small amount with water or a commercial binder, then work quickly. |
| Dry pre-mixed concrete | Wherever whole sections of concrete are being repaired. | Mix this product with water. The thicker the consistency, the faster it will set up. |

Note: Mixing a synthetic binder with the patch material strengthens the repair and enables the patch to adhere more securely to the old surface.

When the patch begins to set up, smooth it with a trowel or straightedge. Cover the patch and let it cure for one week.

Chip away all cracked or crumbling material to solid concrete. Use a wire brush to clean any loose materials from crevices.

Undercut the edges of the damaged area to provide a "key," which will lock-in the patch. Remove all loose materials.

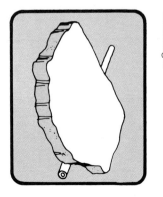

Remove damaged or misfitting stones or bricks. If the joints are mortar and have been damaged, use a latex or epoxy patch.

Dampen the area to be patched with water. Some patches call for priming the area with a water/portland cement mixture.

Tamp in the patching compound. Be sure to pack it firmly and try to mound it a bit to compensate for shrinkage.

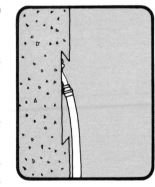

Level the cavity with sand or mortar. Tamp the area well before replacing the brick or stone, and tap it level. Then remortar.

To move slabs or large flagstones, roll them on a length of pipe. And when lifting chunks of masonry, use your legs, not your back.

# SOLVING DECK PROBLEMS

Especially if neglected, but even if well cared for, decks develop many of the same problems that plague porches—rot, plus a host of structural maladies.

Posts, beams, and joists are particularly prone to rot, as they're often near ground level and covered by decking. Steps and railings work loose through normal use, and finishes, no matter how tough, give way to weather. A twice-yearly inspection is your best protection against letting your deck's condition decline. If problems develop, tend to them quickly. The chart below describes the course of action to follow for several common ailments.

## ANATOMY OF A DECK

Like a porch, a deck is simple post-and-beam construction. The *decking* rests on *joists* and *beams*, which gain support from *posts* and *piers* or *footings*. And unless it's freestanding, the deck is tied to the house structure by a *ledger*. Joists sit on edge on the ledger. House joists also can be extended past the foundation wall (cantilevered) to form a support for the decking. On some decks, the posts extend up through the decking to function as part of the railing. On others, *balusters* fasten to joists or beams. A *cap rail* stabilizes and protects the other railing members.

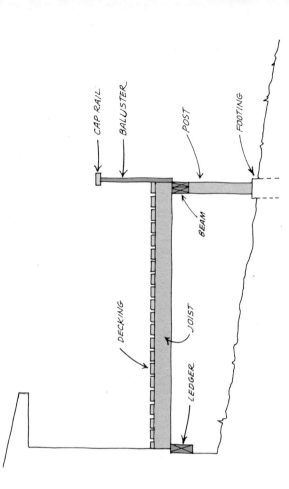

CAP RAIL
BALUSTER
POST
BEAM
FOOTING
DECKING
JOIST
LEDGER

## SOLVING DECK PROBLEMS

| Problem | Solution | Problem | Solution |
| --- | --- | --- | --- |
| Dirt, grime, grease, everyday stains | Wash the area thoroughly with mild household detergent. Rinse. See the stain removal chart on page 154. | Sap stains, finish bleed-throughs, finish failure | On unfinished wood, remove sap with mineral spirits. Prime bleeds and finish failures with clear shellac; refinish. |
| Mildew | Scrub the area with a mixture of water and household bleach, or use a commercial mildewcide. | Damaged decking and other deck components | Replacement parts are the best solution. See pages 168-171 for particulars on how decks are constructed (or reconstructed). |

## APPLYING STAINS AND PRESERVATIVES

As noted above, the finish protecting your deck will eventually succumb to the ravages of time and weather. Not even redwood, cedar, or pressure-treated wood will stand up forever.

Stains are by far the best dressings for a deck, so wherever possible use them. However, if your deck has been painted before, you'll have to settle for a fresh coat of paint after a thorough scraping.

If you opt for stain, be sure to ask for one formulated for exterior use, preferably one of the penetrating oil stains. These go beneath the wood's surface to give long-lasting protection and good looks. If you want the wood's grain to show through, use a clear or semi-transparent stain. Or if you prefer a painted look, buy a solid-color stain. For painted surfaces, choose an exterior latex- or alkyd-base floor paint.

Generally, it's best not to apply a clear finish such as varnish or polyurethane. These don't stand up well against moisture and sunlight.

# ADDING OUTDOOR LIVING AREAS

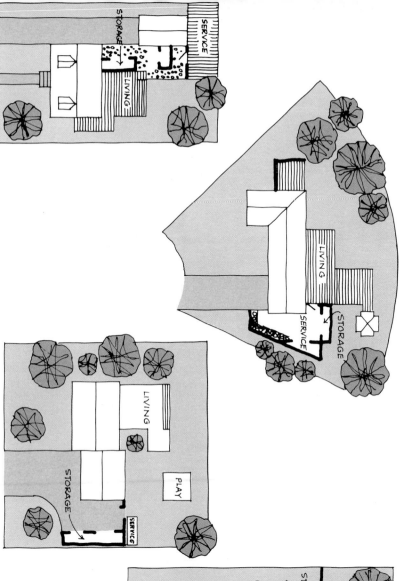

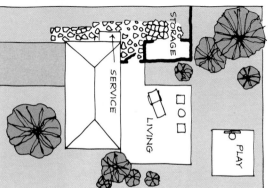

Your family's fair-weather life-style will get a big boost with the addition of a patio or deck. You'll find a well-planned outdoor living area can depressurize the interior spaces, just by adding alternative spots for cooking, eating, and relaxing.

Thoughtful up-front planning is well worth a little time; a long-range master plan will preclude later regrets. The four drawings below show excellent solutions for typical lots. Each has the big three ingredients you should include in your planning: an outdoor living area, outside storage facilities, and a service area. Add a play area if you have small children.

Start with the outdoor living facility first. The slope or flatness of your lot will help you decide whether to plan a deck or patio. Flat lots give you a complete choice from brick-in-sand patios to an on-grade deck. If you have a slope to work around, you may find an elevated deck the only practical alternative.

Then study the area's relationship to the interior floor plan. You'll need access for convenience's sake, so take advantage of existing doors, or consider installing a sliding glass door (see page 151). With these generalities in mind, next plan the location and size of the storage units you'll want.

The third step is to work out a spot for the service area. Make it large enough to handle garbage cans, a stack of firewood, potting benches, or whatever your family requires.

You may want to use graph paper and sketch in these things to scale, or you may find it easiest to stake out the areas on a trial-and-error basis. At this point you also should check for lot restrictions.

Many zoning regulations require outbuildings and decks to be a specified distance from your lot lines. Be sure you don't build on a part of your lot on which there's an easement—nor over an underground utility, such as a septic system.

All that's left in your planning is the privacy and screening you'll need. Consider the plantings you have and will add as well as fences you might want to build (see pages 174 to 180).

With your long-range goals established, you're ready to work out the exact size of your deck or patio and gather prices for the materials. And with the know-how that follows, doing it yourself will yield three very worthwhile results—convenience, comfort for years to come, and more money in your pocket.

157

# LAYING A PATIO IN SAND

If you've decided that you can't get along any longer without a patio, yet you don't really care for the look of concrete, why not consider laying bricks, flagstones, slate, paving blocks, or precast patio blocks in sand. The procedures involved are relatively simple, and you won't need many special tools—a mason's hammer, brick chisel, shovel, nail hammer, garden hose, broom, and a level will see you through.

In addition to the surfacing material of your choice, you'll also need a goodly amount of sand to serve as a base. The amount required for your project depends on the site, which should be fairly level. For a 10x20-foot patio, you'll need about 12 cubic yards of sand to provide a four-inch base; in a well-drained area, you could get by with a two-inch base—and only half as much sand.

The sketch below gives you a good idea of the looks you can achieve with a brick patio. Note, too, that bricks set any one of several ways can serve as permanent borders for your patio.

## Choosing and Buying Bricks

If you decide on bricks as the right patio surface for you, take a trip to one or more brick suppliers in your area. You'll be amazed by the selection. Not only will you find a huge number of standard-size bricks in many colors and textures, but you'll also encounter jumbo and irregular-shaped ones as well.

Once you make your selection, ask the supplier to estimate your needs (have the dimensions of the patio handy). For a 10x20-foot patio, you'll need approximately 920 standard-size bricks, including an allowance for breakage. And since bricks generally are sold in multiples of 500, you'll need two pallets of them.

The cost of bricks varies considerably, but for argument's sake, figure on each one costing from 15 to 25 cents. Delivery to the job site will cost you an additional amount.

Note: If you're a used-brick fan, be sure that the ones you purchase are hard; some will crumble when you crack them with a hammer. Also make certain that not too much mortar is sticking to them; mortar-encrusted bricks take a lot of work to clean.

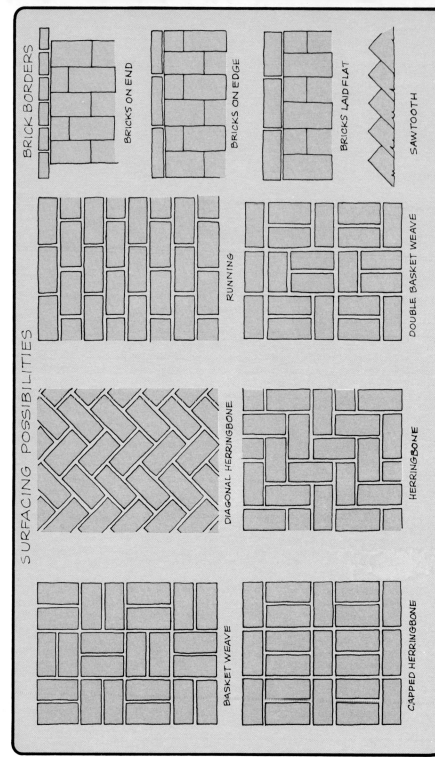

# Laying Bricks in Sand

Because the sand joints between bricks absorb water, eliminating drainage problems, you needn't do a lot of site preparation for a brick-in-sand patio. However, the area should be fairly level, which may require some digging on your part. If you have large amounts of dirt to move, hire a grading contractor to solve

the problem. As you shovel or grade, keep in mind that the bricks are laid over a two- to four-inch base of sand.

Consider brick thickness, too. Both can affect the grade depth.

Setting up forms to define the patio's perimeter makes good sense even when setting bricks. Whether or not you want to use internal forms is a design consideration. See page 161 for help on setting up forms. If you plan to remove

the forms after you complete the project, use economy-grade 1x6 or 1x8 boards. But if they'll be part of the design, be sure to use cedar, redwood, or pressure-treated wood, fastened together with galvanized nails.

If your project will be a weekend affair, order all the materials at once. But if you plan to take your time with the job, it's easy to work in sections.

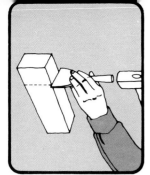

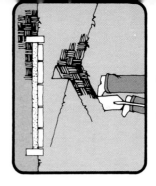

Stake out the area and level the surface. For patios with borders of bricks on end, also dig a trench along the perimeter.

Spray the ground with weed killer. Then cover the area with dark 4-mil polyethylene film. This will prevent most plant growth.

Now install the edging. Set bricks on end, edge, or flat. If you're using wood forms, stake them every 2½ feet.

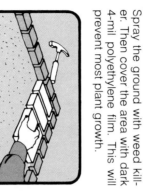

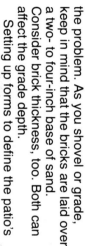

Spread coarse sand to a depth of two to four inches. Level it as best you can with a shovel. Then sprinkle the area with water.

Work in sections about three feet square. Screed the sand using a 2x4 with the ends notched to fit over the edging.

Lay the bricks in the screeded area. Set them in position as carefully as possible, being careful not to disturb the sand.

To help you lay the bricks level, stretch a mason's line. Also periodically check the units for level.

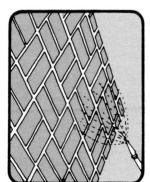
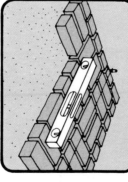
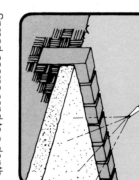

Cut the bricks with a brick chisel. Put the brick on a firm surface, score the break line with the chisel, and tap with a sledge.

After all bricks are set, spread shovelfuls of damp sand across the surface. Let it dry several hours, then sweep it into joints.

Wet the area thoroughly so the sand will settle into the joints. Use a fine spray to avoid forcing the sand from the joints.

If you find a low brick, lift it out and sprinkle more sand underneath. If it's too high, remove the brick and some sand.

You will have to repeat sanding and watering several times. After the cracks are full, let the surface dry and sweep it again.

# WORKING WITH CONCRETE

If you haven't already played with what masons call "mud," prepare to encounter a new world of products, processes, and terminology. Start by getting the terminology straight.

First comes the mud itself. If, like most people, you've been calling it "cement," now's the time to change your vocabulary. *Cement* is a dry, powdery substance. Mix it with sand and water and you get *mortar*, the stuff used to bind brick, block, and stone walls together. (More about this on pages 184-191.) Adding gravel to a mortar mix makes *concrete*—a basic paving and structural material.

Any concrete-working project calls for a series of strenuous jobs. Usually you have to level off the area you'll be surfacing. Then you have to build temporary or permanent *forms* to hold the concrete while it sets. Next you have

to *place* the concrete—heavy work that also has to be done quickly, before the mix sets. Finally, you have to level (*screed*) the surface, *float* it to work out any irregularities, and *finish* it—again while the mud is still wet.

The following pages take you step by step through each of these stages. Because of the work involved, you may as well forget about tackling a huge project such as a driveway or king-size patio.

Start by checking community building codes. Many require a building permit —especially for a sidewalk or patio that will be attached to your home. If your project requires one, you'll be asked for information such as the size of the project, its location, approximate cost, and so on. There's often a small permit fee, too.

Also as part of the planning stage of your project, ask yourself the following questions.

Does a concrete truck have access to the job site? If not, have a couple of

wheelbarrows and some help on hand.

Must any electric or telephone lines be disconnected so a concrete truck can gain access to the site? If so, notify the utilities in advance.

Does the site require any special drainage? Usually, sloping or crowning the area can provide adequate water drainage. But problem drainage areas may require regular drain tile beneath the concrete.

Does the project require special grading? If so, check with utilities to make sure there are no buried utility cables or lines where you're digging.

Is special concrete reinforcement such as welded wire mesh or reinforcing rods needed? Driveways and walkways over which cars and trucks will be driven, and some patios attached to house foundations, require reinforcement. Generally, you should reinforce all concrete projects—even if traffic over them is light. Reinforcement helps protect the concrete from cracks, breaks and other weather-induced problems.

## Tools for Concrete Work

For most new concrete projects and many repair and maintenance jobs, you'll need the equipment illustrated here.

A *mason's hammer* will help drive form and alignment stakes; break stone, block, and brick; and chip away crumbling concrete. Lay out concrete-, brick-, and block-laying jobs with a *50-foot tape, mason's line,* and *line level*. For smoothing and finishing concrete, you'll need a *darby,* a *float* or a *bull float,* and a *finish trowel*. And to mix and distribute concrete, have a *hoe* and *shovel* on hand.

To help you distribute your weight over the fresh concrete so you don't sink into it, make a *knee board* from lumber or plywood. Use a *jointing tool* to divide and smooth concrete, such as the lines dividing a sidewalk into sections. An *edger* smooths and finishes the edges of concrete; use it while the forms are still in position. Quality concrete tools are affordable, so buy the best.

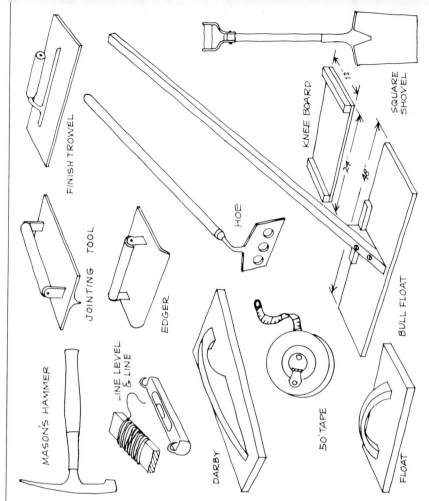

FINISH TROWEL

JOINTING TOOL

EDGER

HOE

KNEE BOARD

12"

24"

48"

SQUARE SHOVEL

MASON'S HAMMER

LINE LEVEL & LINE

DARBY

50' TAPE

BULL FLOAT

FLOAT

**160**

Don't look at the task of building forms as finish carpentry project. It's not. Here, strength is more important than good looks, so spend your extra effort on secure bracing. Concrete places a good amount of stress on forms, and having one or more of them give way while you're pouring is one of those disasters that happen all too often to do-it-yourself concrete workers.

The material used for forms varies, depending on the job. Economy-grade 2x4s work well for straight runs. For curves, use ¼-inch exterior plywood or tempered hardboard. A light coat of used motor oil applied to wood forms prevents them from sticking to the concrete and lets you recycle the lumber.

Most often, you'll want to disassemble and remove the forms after the concrete sets. To make this job easier and less time-consuming, secure the forms with double-headed nails. Allow the concrete to set a day or two before removing the forms (as it sets, it will change color— from a dark gray to its characteristic light gray color).

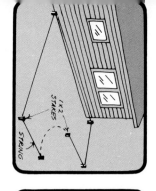

Locate the patio, adding two inches all around to accommodate forms. Stake off the outline, checking corners for square.

Transfer the outline to the ground by pouring sand over the mason's line. Carefully remove the stakes and the line guides.

Remove vegetation and excavate to allow for the sand bed and the slab. Excavate about one foot wider than the outline.

Level and tamp the excavated area, digging out rocks and roots and filling depressions. Wet the area to further compact the base.

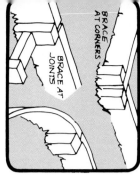

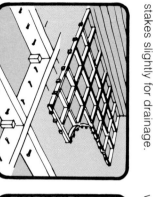

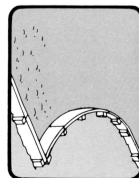

Using a short length of forming to space the stakes, drive one every 24 to 30 inches. Scrap boards make good stakes.

Establish grade by stretching a mason's line from the first to the last stake in each row. Pitch stakes slightly for drainage.

Secure the forms to the stakes with double-headed nails as shown. The stakes must be flush with or below the forms.

For curves, stake hardboard or plywood every 18 to 24 inches. You can outline the contour with a length of rope or garden hose.

Brace the forms at each corner and at any weak spots. Stakes should be about 24 inches long and well set.

If you divide the patio into grids, stake the permanent inner forms as shown. Drive nails into forms to help hold the concrete.

Cedar, redwood, or pressure-treated boards make excellent permanent forms. Add reinforcing rods or mesh, if desired.

BRACE AT CORNERS

BRACE AT JOINTS

1×2 STAKES

STRING

**161**

## BUYING CONCRETE

Knowing what's available and the type suited to a particular job is the secret to concrete buymanship. Here's a brief rundown.

*Ready-mix concrete.* To order concrete, simply call one of the many concrete companies in your area, telling the personnel what you want the concrete to do, and the area of your project. It's as simple as that. But before you make that call, be sure you have prepared the site completely. Don't expect the delivery man to sit around and watch you rebuild forms, place reinforcement mesh, or hunt for tools. Usually, excess time spent at a job results in an additional charge. Make sure, too, that the truck either has access to the site or that you have wheelbarrows on hand to transport the mix. Most ready-mix companies won't deliver less than one cubic yard of concrete, so keep this in mind when placing an order.

*Premixed concrete.* This product comes in bags. You simply add water and stir. Use this type for small jobs and repairs.

*You-mix-it concrete.* For large jobs, you should rent a concrete mixer; for small jobs and repairs, mix the material in a bucket or mortar box. The cost is fairly inexpensive, but you may have a cement gravel, and sand storage problem.

### CONCRETE ESTIMATOR
Expressed in both cubic feet and (cubic yards)

| Thick- ness | Surface Area of Job In Square Feet | | | | |
|---|---|---|---|---|---|
| | 20 | 50 | 100 | 200 | |
| 2 in. | 3.3 (.1) | 8.3 (.3) | 16.7 (.6) | 33.3 (1.2) | 83.3 (3.1) |
| 4 in. | 6.7 (.2) | 16.7 (.6) | 33.3 (1.2) | 66.7 (2.5) | 166.7 (6.2) |
| 6 in. | 10 (.4) | 25 (.9) | 50 (1.9) | 100 (3.7) | 250 (9.3) |

Note: If the ground over which you'll pour the concrete is sloped and the finished work will be level, you must take into consideration the thickness of the concrete from the top of the slope to the bottom of it.

## Estimating How Much You Need

Figuring your concrete needs is one of those jobs that's much easier than most people imagine. Just apply a little mathematics.

If your project is rectangular or square, multiply the width by the length by the thickness of the job *in feet*. This gives you *cubic feet*. If you're purchasing ready-mix, then divide the result by 27, the number of cubic feet in a *cubic yard*, which is the unit in which concrete is sold.

To determine the area (in square feet) of a circle, multiply the square of the radius by 3.1416. Then, refer to the formula above to determine cubic measurements. And for triangular projects, multiply the length of the base by the perpendicular height, and divide the result by two.

For all irregular shapes, it's best to draw the project to scale on graph paper. Let each square represent one square foot. This way, you can count the full, half, and quarter squares and determine approximately how many square feet your project covers.

When dealing with ready-mix concrete companies, you probably will find that the salesman will want to know the area and the thickness of the concrete project—even if you furnish him with your estimate. Since mixing procedures vary somewhat, take the salesman's estimate—unless it's vastly out of agreement with your figures.

## Choosing a Mix

The type of project you're undertaking determines the strength or "mix" of concrete you should blend or have mixed. Patios and sidewalks, for example, don't need the strength a footing or driveway does. And a thicker slab requires less cement proportionally than does a thinner one because of its greater mass.

For most home maintenance and improvement projects under normal conditions, the regular mix of three parts gravel mix to two parts sand to one part cement will give you the desired results. When mixed with water, this mixture contains enough cement powder to coat each particle of sand and gravel, and thereby create the bond that gives concrete its strength.

The amount of water added to the mixture is vitally important—use only enough to make the mixture workable. For more on this important aspect, see the opposite page. If you're mixing your own concrete, move the mixing container as close to your project as possible. Doing this allows you to keep the mixture thick and strong, yet workable.

If you're ordering ready-mix, specify a minimum bearing capacity of 3,500 psi (pounds per square inch) at 28 days' cure.

During inclement weather, it's advisable to add or ask for additives that speed curing times. These lessen the concrete's vulnerability to freezing, which weakens it.

# MIXING CONCRETE

Mixing concrete is much like mixing cake batter: you have to follow the recipe (or adapt it slightly) to obtain the very best results. Just as you can ruin a cake by adding too much liquid, so too can you weaken concrete if you add too much water in proportion to the other materials. On the other hand, too little makes the concrete very difficult to pour and finish properly.

The amount of water needed depends largely on the condition of the sand you're using. You'll need to add less water to a mix made with wet sand than to one that uses drier sand.

Test the sand by balling some in your hand. If water runs out, the sand is very wet. If the ball compacts, like moist clay, the sand is perfect. And if the ball crumbles, the sand is too dry.

As you're mixing the concrete, add only very small amounts of water at a time. At the outset, the concrete may crumble, but as you add more water, it will begin to flow together like thick mud. When it becomes one color—a medium gray—and has a shiny, plastic-like sheen, it's ready to use.

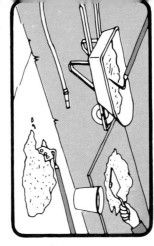

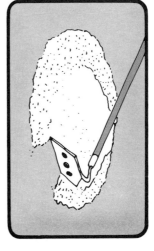

Mix batches of concrete in a wheelbarrow, on a piece of plywood, or on any flat, water-proof surface you can hose off.

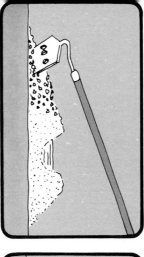

Make a well in the center of the pile and pour in water gradually, mixing the components to a thick, muddy consistency.

Measure the ingredients by the bucketful, leveling off the material with your shovel. Proper amounts are very important here.

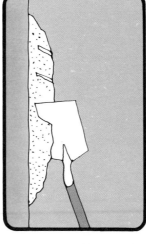

Test the batch first by smacking it with the back of a shovel. Then jab it lightly to make a series of grooves, as illustrated.

Use a concrete hoe or a shovel to thoroughly mix the right proportions of cement, sand, and gravel. Roll one into the other.

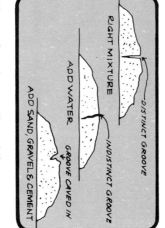

If the surface is smooth and the grooves maintain their separation, the mix is right. If not, add water, or add more material.

RIGHT MIXTURE
DISTINCT GROOVE
ADD WATER
INDISTINCT GROOVE
ADD SAND, GRAVEL & CEMENT
GROOVE CAVED IN

## Using a Power Mixer

If you need to mix lots of concrete, you should rent an electric- or gasoline-powered concrete mixer. These save many hours of hard labor.

To use a mixer, first add all of the gravel and some water, and switch on the mixer. Then add the sand, the cement, and finally, more water. Mix three minutes, gradually adding water until the mix achieves a uniform color. Stop the mixer often to test the batch, as shown above.

## GETTING READY FOR A POUR

There's no better way to ensure a successful pour than to have everything ready when the concrete is. Conversely, few things can cause more aggravation than a hasty setup. So start a couple days early; do all of the preparation work listed and shown here.

- Make sure all forms are in the correct position, and drive all stakes flush with or below the top edge of the forms. If in doubt about the stability of the forms, add more stakes.
- Install expansion joints along the edges of foundations, other slabs, and other structural members. These expansion joints allow for daily movement of the concrete due to changes in temperature and humidity.
- Have utility companies remove any necessary wire or cable obstructions. Also make firm arrangements for having these reconnected.
- Assemble all necessary concrete tools—shovels, hoes, floats, trowels.
- Recruit several helpers, if the project calls for a large amount of concrete.

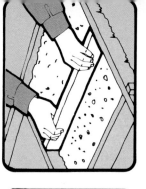

Screed the base material to level the surface. Then tamp the base lightly so it's well compacted and completely level.

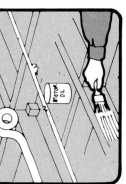

Make a bed for the concrete by spreading sand, cinders, or gravel. Generally, a couple inches of any of these will do.

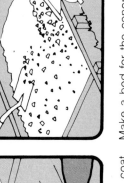

If you plan to reuse the forms, coat them with oil or shellac. If the forms will remain in place, protect the edges with masking tape.

Lay the mesh into each grid and prop it up with rocks to about midway up the forms. Avoid walking on the mesh.

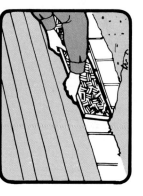

Fit expansion joints between the slab and any abutting structure, such as your foundation, and every 8 to 10 feet in slabs.

Use a heavy welded-wire mesh for reinforcement. Have a helper stand on one end, then unroll the mesh and cut it. Wear gloves.

If working with grids, cut the mesh to fit, then flatten it out by walking on it. Heavy bolt cutters make easy work of the cutting.

## GETTING READY FOR READY-MIX

A concrete truck weighs tons, and can ruin any walk or lawn over which it passes. If possible, have wheelbarrows ready to move the concrete or, if the project is within 18 to 20 feet of the street, have the truck park at curbside and chute the material to you. If necessary, you can spread out the weight of the truck by laying down planks.

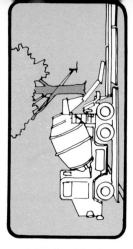

If the truck must roll over your lawn, make a road for it with 2-inch-thick lumber. Allow about 12 feet of overhead clearance.

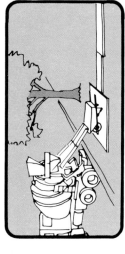

Lay plywood or 1-inch-thick boards for wheelbarrow runs. Select a smooth route and have plenty of help on hand.

Wet down the area the day before pouring the concrete. Sprinkle again just before pouring to slow the drying time.

**164**

# PLACING CONCRETE

For all its strength, concrete is a delicate building material. You have to baby it before and after it's placed.

More than anything else, concrete needs sufficient time to cure. If you pour concrete over frozen ground, it will break up when the ground thaws. Pouring it over extremely dry ground is almost as

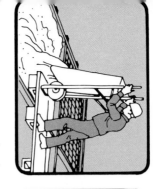

bad—the water in the concrete mixture will be absorbed by the ground, "starving" the mix and setting it before you have a chance to finish it.

After the concrete has been poured, you'll notice a thin layer of water forming over the top of it. You may be tempted to remove the water with a broom or start troweling the concrete surface. Don't! The cement and aggregate in concrete are suspended by water. As gravity

settles these "hard" materials, the water rises to the top of the mixture. If you trowel the surface now, it will "craze" and flake after the concrete has cured.

The proper sequence is to pour the concrete, strike or screed it, float it, and then trowel it. Do all of this quickly; if your project is a large one, have a couple of helpers available.

Begin pouring concrete in the least accessible area. Build a bridge, if you're wheelbarrowing the mixture.

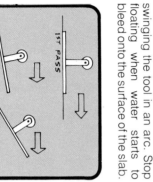

Spread the concrete with a shovel or concrete hoe. Tamp the mixture so it's only a bit higher than the top edges of the forms.

Dump succeeding loads against the first one, not on top of it or separated from it. Pull up reinforcing mesh with rake tines.

Strike off the surface with a straight 2x4 after the concrete has been poured. See-saw the 2x4, fill low spots.

Floating further levels the surface and pushes aggregate beneath it. The float will produce a rough but level finish.

Float small areas with a darby, swinging the tool in an arc. Stop floating when water starts to bleed onto the surface of the slab.

When the surface appears "dry," test it by scraping it with a steel trowel. If wetness appears, don't finish the slab yet.

Sandwich a trowel blade between the form and concrete to separate them, then run an edging trowel along the form's edge.

Make control joints by laying a 2-inch board across the slab. Then run a jointing tool across the slab, using the board as a guide.

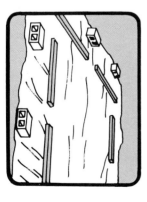

For a slick finish, trowel the surface three times. Move your arm in a wide arc and apply medium downward pressure to the tool.

A wooden trowel or float produces a rough, skidproof surface. It works like a steel trowel, but needs only one or two passes.

Cover the surface with sheets of polyethylene to hold moisture in the concrete. Or sprinkle it with water daily for one week.

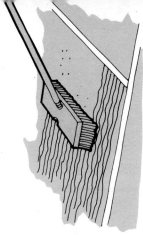

Ready-mix companies will add coloring—usually red, brown, green, and black—for an additional charge. If you're mixing your own, purchase a coloring powder and mix it with the other ingredients as specified on the label.

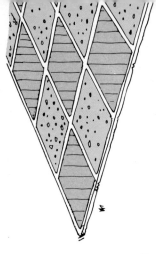

*Brooming.* For even more texture, treat the surface to a broom treatment after the concrete has been floated and has hardened somewhat. For a light texture, use a soft-bristled broom; for coarser effects, use a broom with heavy straw or steel bristles. You can create similar special effects with a bamboo lawn rake and a lawn rake with either close-set or wide-set tines. Use light pressure on the rake handle. It's smart, too, to test the design before total commitment. You can always re-trowel the surface and try something else.

*Combination effects.* Don't rule out the possibility of combining two or more designs to come up with other unique surfaces. The one depicted above successfully combines exposed aggregates and a smooth troweled look. It's best to sketch out your ideas ahead of time so you're not taken by surprise when you start finishing the surface. Often, you can adapt or duplicate ideas found in magazines, outside public buildings, or on a neighbor's patio.

# CUSTOM-FINISHING CONCRETE

There's a little bit of the artist in us all, and there's no better time to vent some of that artistic energy than when surface-finishing your concrete project.

Duplicate one of the designs shown below or, if you're really feeling creative, dream up a design of your own. Decide on the surface you want in advance, though. You'll need all the time you can get to execute the design.

You might also consider coloring your concrete to achieve a special look.

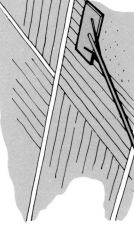

*Checkerboard.* This texture requires relatively little work. In fact, the less trowel work you do, the more interesting and skid-proof the final effect will be. Though especially attractive with a patio laid out in grids, checkerboarding will work on large expanses as well. Use a bull float, darby, or wood hand float as shown above. You also can buy floats with a sponge-like surface attached to them, which will create a more pronounced texture effect.

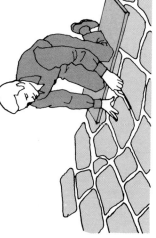

*Geometric.* Actually, any series of lines meeting at random points would fall into this category of design. The sample shown here resembles the effect you'd get if you laid flagstones. A joint strike makes a perfect tool for embedding this design into the concrete. Use a light hand with it, though, as deep recesses in the surface readily collect dirt and other matter. Work the design after the surface has set long enough to support you on a knee board.

*Swirl design.* By working the trowel across the surface as shown above, you can produce this subtle, yet intriguing look. Using the edge of a steel trowel, lightly work the concrete, making sure that you don't dig the edges of the trowel into it. The swirls should be random; don't try to establish any particular pattern. Just "freewheel" the trowel, forming a series of interconnecting arcs. Texture the surface at control joints and edges, too, so they match the swirled texture, or leave the controls as is and let them define separate sections.

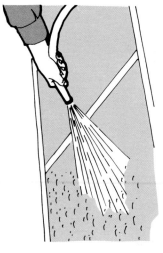

*Exposed aggregate.* Press the aggregate into the concrete with a wooden float, darby, or wide board until the pebbles are no longer visible. After the concrete begins to set, hose and scrub the surface with a stiff broom till you see the tops of the pebbles. Go easy, though; too much scrubbing will dislodge the pebbles. Let the concrete set for about three to four days, then wash the surface with a 1:5 solution of muriatic acid and water. Wear protective clothing, and rinse the area afterward.

**166**

# BUILDING A DECK

Most people would be scared stiff if faced with the prospect of building a deck. The reason: decks, especially well-constructed ones, look difficult to erect. A few are truly complex creations that require super-skilled hands to build, but most are well within reach of the average do-it-yourselfer. And that's the purpose of the next few pages—to make this entirely possible building project possible for you.

## Getting Started

With a tape measure and six or eight 1x2 stakes, go out into the yard where you plan to build the deck. Determine the width and length of the structure, measuring these distances and staking them out. Also determine the height of the deck by measuring up the side of the house and marking where you want the top of the decking. These initial procedures visually tell you whether or

not the deck site and the size are suitable for your needs. If you decide they aren't, shift the location, alter the size, or both.

Next, roughly design the deck on paper, using the actual staked-out measurements. Once you're happy with it, obtain any necessary building permits for the project.

Then, lay out the job. Mark the intended location of the ledger strip, which will support the joists at the house (not needed for freestanding decks). Build *batter boards* at the corners, using

Using the right materials and providing adequate support are the two most important aspects of deck building. If the deck can't withstand the impact of weather, or if it's so shaky that no one feels comfortable on it, your hard work and money will go to waste.

Use only woods specially intended for outdoor use, and even then take special pains to protect them (see page 156 for information on applying protective coatings). And to ensure that the deck you raise is structurally sound, build it in compliance with the span tables at right and the building basics that follow.

a mason's line to determine the height and squareness of the deck. To check the corners for square, measure three feet along the ledger strip mark and four feet down the mason's line. The distance between these two end points should be five feet, as the drawing shows. Also determine the location of all posts, using the chart above as a guide.

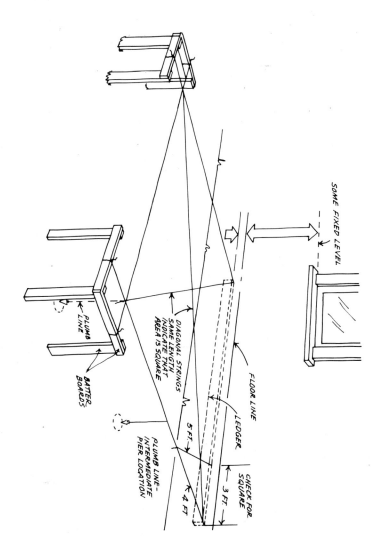

SOME FIXED LEVEL

PLUMB LINE

BATTER BOARDS

DIAGONAL STRINGS SAME LENGTH INDICATE THAT AREA IS SQUARE

FLOOR LINE

LEDGER

5 FT.

4 FT

3 FT.

CHECK FOR SQUARE

PLUMB LINE- INTERMEDIATE PIER LOCATION

## BEAM AND JOIST SPAN TABLE

| Beam Size | Maximum Distance Between Posts |
|---|---|
| 4x6 | 6 ft. |
| 4x8 | 8 ft. |
| 4x10 | 10 ft. |
| 4x12 | 12 ft. |

| Joist Size | Span at Different Spacings | | |
|---|---|---|---|
| | 16 in. | 24 in. | 32 in. |
| 2x6 | 8 ft. | 6 ft. | 5 ft. |
| 2x8 | 10 ft. | 8 ft. | 7 ft. |
| 2x10 | 13 ft. | 10 ft. | 8 ft. |

## Setting Posts

Though you could find dozens of examples to the contrary, posts, unless pressure-treated wood, should be set directly in concrete or (preferably) on top of a concrete footing. Otherwise, they won't hold up for long.

If you set them in concrete, first pour a footing that is several inches larger than the post and that extends below the frost line (check with contractors in your area for proper depth). Unless the project is an unusually large one, you should be able to get by with using premixed bagged concrete rather than ordering ready-mix. While the concrete is still wet, set and level the post. Attach outrigger stakes to steady the post until the concrete sets.

To set posts on concrete, first pour the footing and position any one of the

anchoring devices shown below in the still-workable concrete.

For most deck projects, 4x4 posts will provide adequate structural support. Just be sure you get them plumb (check each twice, taking readings on sides at right angles to each other) and in perfect alignment with each other. For more about erecting posts, turn to pages 176-178.

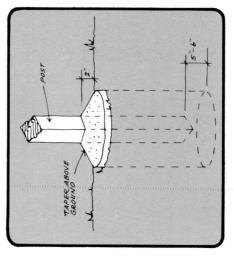

Set posts in concrete as shown above. Tapering the concrete at ground level helps shed water, which otherwise collects here.

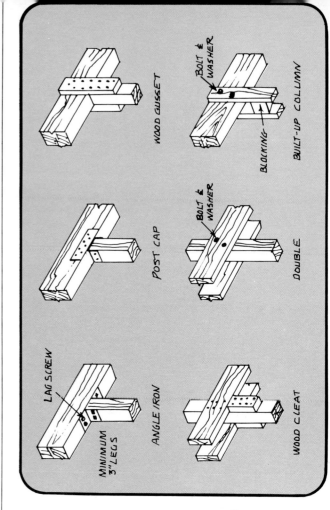

Any one of the above anchoring devices will serve as a stable post anchor. Also available are adjustable post bases that fit over machine or carriage bolts that have been set in the concrete footing or slab. These allow for making minor lateral adjustments.

## Attaching the Beams

As you can see from the sketch at right, you have several alternatives for attaching beams. If you plan to run the posts up through the decking to serve as supports for the deck's railing, fashion the beams of two lengths of 2x material and sandwich the posts between them.

If your deck is an on-grade type, in which case you won't need a railing, you'll want to cut the posts to the correct height and fasten the beams atop them.

For maximum strength, it's best to use bolts or large wood screws to anchor the beams. The movement so characteristic of decks works nails loose too easily.

**168**

Unless your deck is freestanding and depends on posts as its primary source of support, you must somehow fasten a ledger strip—usually a 2x8 or 2x10—to your house. The first three sketches below show your fastening options.

Regardless of which you choose, bear in mind that all vertical measurements must allow for the thickness of the decking you'll be using.

Before drilling the holes for the fasteners, decide whether you want the joists to rest atop the ledger or flush with it as would be the case if you're using joist hangers. For joist hangers, make certain that when positioned, the bottom of the ledger is level with the top of the beams toward the outer edges of the

deck. Double-check the ledger's intended position by running a string with a line level from the top of the beam to the house. With your measurements thus confirmed, attach the ledger, making sure that it's level.

The joists come next. The size you need for your project depends on the spans involved, but 2x6s, 2x8s, and 2x10s are most common. If you're using joist hangers, nail them along the ledger, usually at 16-inch intervals. Then position the joists on the beams and in the hangers and secure them. If you're setting the joists on the beams and ledger, toenail them into position with galvanized nails.

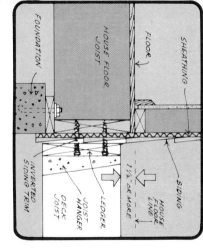

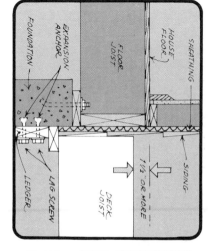

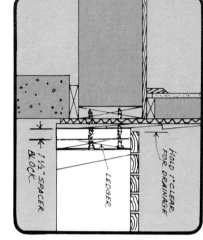

To attach a ledger strip to the house framing, use lag screws. If the house has lap siding, invert a piece for a shim.

To fasten ledgers to a foundation, use lag screws and expansion anchors. The joists rest on top of the ledger strip unit.

You'll need to install flashing to protect the ledger. Or, space the ledger 1½ inches from the house so water can run through.

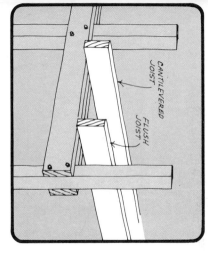

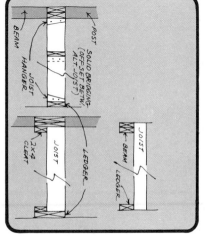

To attach a ledger strip to the house framing, use lag screws. If the house has lap siding, invert a piece for a shim.

Joists can be cantilevered over the beam, or flushed. You might prefer the cantilevered effect if you don't skirt the deck.

Rest joists on top of the ledger and beam, then toenail them. Or make them flush by butt-joining, or cleating and toenailing.

## Constructing Stairs

Laying out a stairway is one of the most challenging of all carpentry jobs. Not only do you have to accurately compute angles, you must also maintain equal riser and tread spacing from top to bottom.

Building an open-riser/open-stringer stairway such as the one illustrated here provides an excellent, relatively easy introduction to this advanced task.

Start by thinking of stairs as a means of dividing a difference of elevation into a series of equal steps. Then, measure this distance (the *total rise*) as well as the distance from your deck to where you want the stairs to end (the *total run*).

Generally, each step has a rise of about seven inches and a run of 10 or 11 inches. Divide these figures into the total rise and run to find out if they give you an even number of steps. Chances are, they won't. If so, adjust the individual rise and run measurements until you do come out even. Don't forget to include the thickness of the tread material you'll be using in your rise computations.

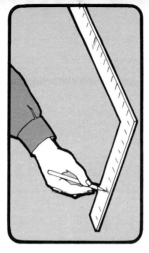

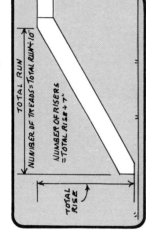

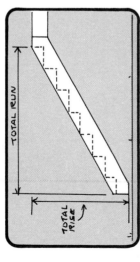

To determine total rise and run, measure height from the top of the deck to the ground, and from the deck to where stairs will end.

Take these figures and divide them by the standard rise and run figures given above to determine the number of steps required.

Next, mark off the riser height on one leg of a framing square and the depth of the tread on the other leg of the square.

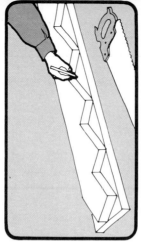

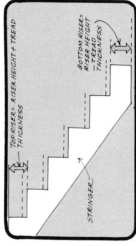

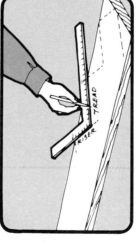

Lay the square against a 2x10 or 2x12, then scribe the marked points onto the lumber as illustrated here.

Tread thickness affects the height of the first and last steps. Subtract this thickness from the bottom; add it to the top.

Use the first cut stringer as a template for the second and/or third stringer. Be sure that you allow for the saw kerf here.

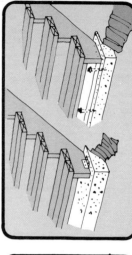

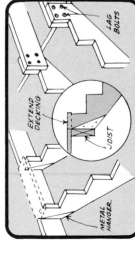

Fasten the stringers to the sides of a joist or header using a metal hanger. Or you can bolt the steps to the joists.

Next, nail on the treads, using large galvanized finishing nails. Cut tread material flush with the stringer or let it overlap.

Set the bottom of the steps on a concrete footing and fasten it with expansion anchors and lag screws or angle irons.

**170**

# ...aying Decking

It's when you nail the decking material to the joists that you'll begin to see what an attractive outdoor living area you've been erecting. And since the decking is one of the most visible of your deck's elements, it's very important that you lay it correctly.

Most people run the decking in one direction (across the joists), as it not only yields an attractive look, but also is the easiest design to lay. But with a little more work, you also can create a number of special-effect surfaces. You might, for example, want to fashion a parquet block design or run the decking diago-

nally. Just keep in mind that you'll need adequate joist support beneath.

As for the materials to use, choose 2x2s, 2x4s, or 2x6s. Most people go with 2x4s. Use galvanized nails to secure the decking to the joists.

When laying that first piece (start at the house and work outward), make certain that it's square to the house. This first piece serves as the all-important guide for the rest of the decking. Use ¼-inch spacers to separate all subsequent pieces, and after laying every three or four strips, double-check for square by running a line from the house to both ends of the same piece of decking. Butt the ends of the decking pieces together for a snug fit.

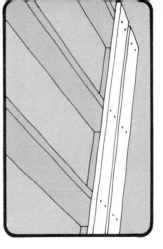

Always check the end grain of each board before you nail it. You'll notice that the tree rings hump toward one side of the board—called the *bark side*. Nail all decking bark-side-up to minimize cupping.

If the lumber you're using is slightly warped, nail one end of it to a joist, then "pull" the loose end into position and nail it, working from joist to joist.

Should you notice the decking splitting as you're nailing it, try blunting the nail points slightly with a hammer. Or drill pilot holes for the nails, especially at the ends of the lumber where splitting usually occurs.

---

Drive two nails into the decking at every joist. And don't worry about cutting the decking to the exact length yet.

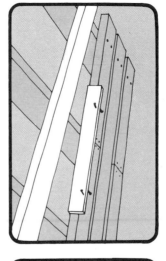

Maintain proper spacing between decking with a ¼-inch spacer strip. Stagger the end joints as you go across the deck.

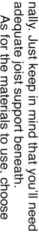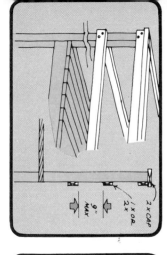

After all the boards are nailed, snap a chalk line along the edges and trim them with a saw. Nail on a board as a guide strip.

---

# Building Railings

Deck railings can be almost any design you want—as long as the design relates in scale to the deck and the structure adjoining it. But keep in mind that a railing's primary purpose is to provide

safe passage from the deck to the ground. So build it strong, and if children will frequent the deck, position the rails close together.

The sketches below show three typical railing options. Duplicate one of them or, if you'd rather, dream up a one-of-a-kind treatment.

Secure all railing posts to the decking superstructure with lag screws or carriage bolts. Nails don't provide the needed holding power. And tie the railing in with the structure's posts, beams, or joists; don't rely on the decking strips to properly hold it in place.

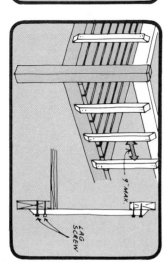

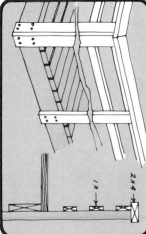

171

# FENCES AND GARDEN WALLS

Examine the anatomy drawing below and you'll see a skeleton common to almost any non-masonry fence. *Posts*—at ends, corners, gates and "along the line"— support *rails* top, bottom, and sometimes in the center.

Individuality comes when you add *screening* (pickets are shown here, but there are dozens of other possibilities, too). To learn about the many shapes a fence can take and how to build one, see pages 174-180.

Build a masonry fence and you've got what's known as a *screen wall*; position it to hold back a slope, and it's a *retaining wall*. More about both beginning on page 181.

## ANATOMY OF A FENCE

CORNER POST

SCREENING

TOP RAIL

LINE POST

BOTTOM RAIL

RAIL CAP

## SOLVING FENCE PROBLEMS

### REPAIRING DAMAGED RAILS

Rot—a fence's worst enemy—typically attacks bottom-rail joints first. Catch decay early and you can saturate the damaged spot with a preservative (see page 177), then mend it as shown below. If the rail has broken away, you'll have to replace it with treated wood.

To minimize rot around your fences, cut back surrounding vegetation; plants often serve as a poultice that holds moisture in the wood.

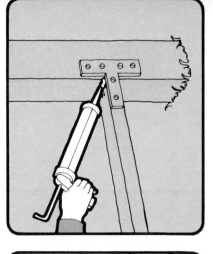

Apply a liberal amount of butyl caulk at the rail/post joint. It will remain flexible to deter rot for several years.

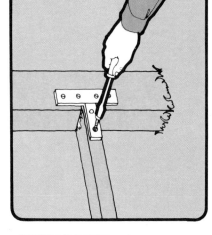

Or secure rails to posts with steel T-braces. Drill pilot holes for screws, and paint the brace to match the fence.

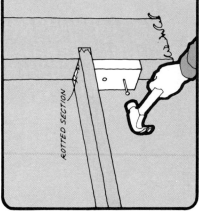

ROTTED SECTION

Shore up rotted rails with a short length of 2x4. Butt it tightly against the rail and fasten to post with galvanized nails.

172

# SHORING UP (OR REPLACING) A WOBBLY POST

Usually, fence posts wobble either because they weren't properly set or treated to begin with, or because moisture, freezing, and thawing have loosened their buried ends.

If the posts are still in fairly good condition, you often can steady a wobble with stakes or splints, as shown in the sketches below.

If the posts have rotted away at ground level, you'll have to replace them—a big job since the rails and screening usually have to be dismantled and reassembled.

To remove posts, your best bet is to rent a post puller. Or, if you're willing to work harder, try inching them out of the ground with a long wrecking bar, using a piece of 4x4 for more leverage. Digging away the earth around the posts with a

spade will make the prying and pulling job easier.

Install replacements as you would new posts (see pages 176-178). If possible, use pressure-treated lumber, clear all-heart redwood, or cedar. Failing this, treat the bottom of the posts with a preservative before setting them in the ground. Also double-check your measurements. Enlarging the holes may have put spacings slightly off.

To repair rusted-out pipe posts, cut near ground level. Replace with new pipe, using a pipe collar and bolts to secure joint.

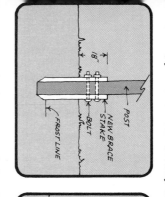

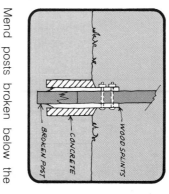

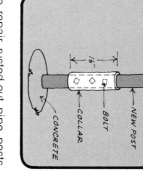

An easy way to shore up posts is with 2x4 stakes. Bevel driving ends; apply a preservative. Drive stakes; bolt together.

Concrete makes a more permanent repair. Enlarge postholes; pour concrete; tamp it. Braces keep posts plumb while you work.

Mend posts broken below the ground with aluminum or wood splints. Enlarge hole; position and bolt splints; pour concrete.

# LIFTING A SAGGING GATE

Kids swinging on a garden gate can make it sag, but so can wobbly gate or line posts, loose hinges, or an out-of-square gate frame.

Sometimes excessive moisture can make a wooden gate swell, forcing it out of alignment. The tendency then is to jam the gate to open or close it, which

loosens the hinges and causes the gate to sag when the moisture finally leaves the wood.

Metal gates sag because the posts are wobbly, or the pins that hold the gate to the post are bent.

Troubleshoot sagging gate problems by first checking gate posts to make sure they're firmly anchored in the ground and are plumb. If they're not, shore them up with one of the methods illustrated above.

If the posts are straight but the gate is binding, examine the hinges. Chances are, they're loose, worn, bent, or aren't heavy enough to support the weight of the gate. If so, replace them; don't attempt a repair.

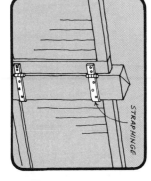

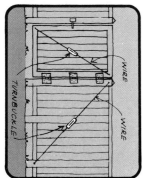

If the gate is hung on a masonry wall or post, remove hinges and shim them as shown. If the latch side binds, plane it.

If hinges are loose, remove screws and fill holes with dowel plugs. Replace hinges using longer screws or carriage bolts.

Replace worn hinges with larger ones. To make a strap hinge even stronger, bend its tip around a corner of the post.

True-up out-of-square gate frames with heavy-duty turnbuckles and wire. Attach wire to screw eyes in the gate or fence framework.

**173**

# BUILDING NEW FENCES

Thinking about putting up a new fence? If so, you have a satisfying project in store. But don't underestimate the amount of time and effort involved in building it—it's hard work!

Luckily, though, erecting a fence isn't complex. If you are reasonably handy and if you heed the advice given on the next few pages, you won't have much difficulty. No special skills are involved.

## PLANNING A FENCE

As with so many other home improvement projects, the building of your fence is only one part of the project.

The up-front time involved in planning is equally important.

One of the first things you need to do is to check the building codes in your community. Many ordinances specify the maximum height a fence may be, distances you can build from property lines and the street, even materials you can and can't use.

Learn, too, whether you'll be required to have a building permit. (If the fence will protect a swimming pool, for example, you almost certainly will.) To apply for a permit, you'll have to submit a plan for authorities' approval. Pick up the forms and relevant regulations from your local building department.

If your new fence will abut neighbors' properties or affect their views, discuss your plans with them as well. Double-check property lines (hire a surveyor if you're uncertain where they are), and clarify who will maintain the fence.

As you develop a design, consider what you want your fence to do. Must it mask trash cans or a work area? Provide

privacy or security? Define a garden or patio? Screen the sun or buffer wind? A well-planned fence often can do several of these jobs at once.

Try, too, to visualize your design in context with present or future landscaping and outdoor living areas. Will you need a gate? As an alternative, consider building a series of freestanding fence panels staggered in such a way that they provide privacy yet let people walk through easily.

Choose materials and styling that will complement your home's appearance. If a new fence will be visible from the street, it also should harmonize with your neighborhood's character.

Proper scale is important, too. A too-tall fence, for instance, will visually overwhelm a low ranch house. You'll have a scale problem with a squatty fence beside a tall house.

## BUFFERING WIND

Fences—like airplanes, bridges, and automobiles—are subject to some surprising principles of aerodynamics. It might seem, for instance, that a solid fence would make an excellent windbreak. But as you can see from the sketches below, solid construction could

actually aggravate a wind problem. What's more, a severe storm might flatten the entire fence.

If the winds in your area blow strong and often, slow them down with open-work screening such as slats, latticework, or bamboo. Louvers not only reduce the air's velocity considerably, they redirect it as well. Trees and shrubbery help control wind, too.

Before you orient a windbreak, check with the local weather bureau for the direction and severities of prevailing currents. If you happen to live in a rural area, ask your local extension service personnel for advice.

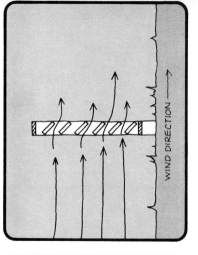

An open-work fence won't totally block the wind, but most types slow its velocity to a more comfortable level.

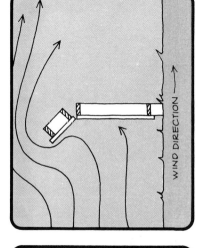

By adding a 45-degree baffle or cap at the top of the fence, you can greatly increase the wind-protected area on the other side.

Wind that strikes a solid fence tends to "hop" over it, creating a vacuum on the lee side that pulls the air down again.

# COPING WITH A SLOPE

...et the fence follow the land's ...ontour on a gentle slope. Open ...nce styles are better suited to ...is than solid ones.

Don't let a sloping or an up-and-down site discourage you from building a fence. In fact, building on uneven terrain often makes a fence more interesting visually than if it were straight-out level.

The drawings below show two ways to go, depending largely upon the slope's severity. For the first one, you'll have to

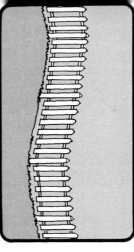

"rack" the rails as you install them. Here's how that's done.

First sink the end posts, stretch a line between them, and lay out the rails to locate positions for the line posts, as illustrated on pages 176 and 178. Now dig a hole for the first line post and sink it; make this one several inches taller than the fence will be.

Next, fasten the rails to the end post and pull them up or push them down until they're parallel to the ground. Fasten them to the line post. Repeat this procedure down the line.

After you've put up all the rails, go back and trim off the post tops to the proper height. Cut them at an angle so that rain and snow will not have a chance to collect there.

For steeper grades or fencing with solid screening, step the fence. Construct one section at a time—one post to the next.

# CHOOSING A STYLE

Let function and personal preference guide you in your selection of a fence style. Chances are, you have some general style in mind now, but it might be worthwhile to look around to see how other people have handled their fencing needs. And don't overlook the ideas that abound in books and magazines, one of which you might like to duplicate or modify somewhat.

You may also find that lumberyard or home center personnel will be able to help you choose a style. They usually have a good idea of what styles of fences will work well in various situations.

In addition, study the typical styles that are shown below. Many of them are sold in prefab form, which saves a lot of cutting and fitting.

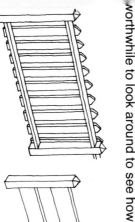

PICKET FENCE

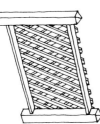

ALTERNATE BOARD

RAIL FENCE

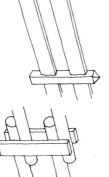

STAKE/STOCKADE

LATTICE WORK

BASKETWEAVE

HORIZONTAL SLATS

PLYWOOD PANELS

VERTICAL LOUVER

CHAIN LINK

**175**

# LAYING OUT A FENCE

Take plenty of time for this phase of your fence-building project. The reason: a measurement that's just an inch off at the outset can compound itself into feet down the line.

Start by establishing positions for end and corner posts, then stretch lines between them. Now step back and look at your layout from several angles. If it looks good, sink end posts, then locate positions for the line posts.

Make measurements with a 50-foot tape. For stakes, use 1x2s or 2x2s that have been pointed with a hatchet.

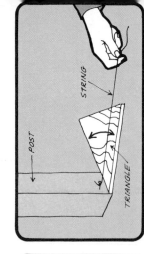

Locate the terminal posts (corners and ends). Mark them with stakes. Then locate gate posts, and stake their positions.

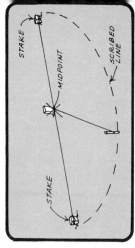

If a corner won't be 90 degrees, compute angle on graph paper and cut it from plywood scrap. Stretch lines on legs of angle.

Square the corners, using the 3-4-5 method. The square of the hypotenuse must equal the sum of the squares of the sides.

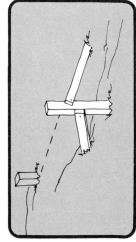

For a curved fence, stake ends. Stretch a line between them and find midpoint. Then trace circle with a line-and-stick compass.

Locate the line posts by laying rails on the ground along the chalk line. Then drive the stakes where the rail ends butt.

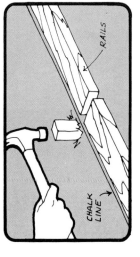

For a stepped fence, plumb lower post in two directions. Use a tape measure to pinpoint stakes for line posts.

# DIGGING POSTHOLES

Generally speaking, if you set fence posts from 24 to 30 inches into the ground, they'll provide all the strength the fence will need. Of course, it's best to go below the frost line, but this usually isn't practical.

Sink terminal and gate posts slightly deeper than line posts. And to give yourself some leeway for getting everything plumb, make holes considerably larger than the posts.

Always set terminal and gate posts first. Then dig a hole for the first line post, set it, and move on to the next. Space six to eight feet apart.

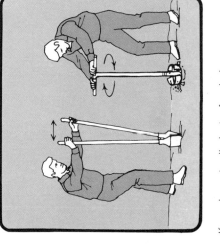

If you have to dig just a few holes in rock-free earth, rent an auger (right) or clamshell-type digger for the job.

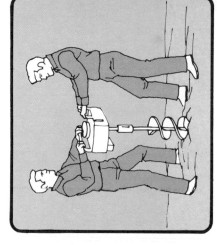

If you have a lot of holes to dig, rent a power-driven auger. These generate lots of torque, so you'll need a helper.

# WARDING OFF DECAY

Rot will eventually destroy any wood fence, but you can retard decay for years by using redwood or cedar for any part that will be below ground. Or buy

pressure-treated lumber that has been saturated with preservatives. A third, less desirable possibility is treating untreated lumber yourself (see below). Above-ground elements of the fence must be treated, too—but here applying a couple coats of paint or stain generally will get you by.

Setting posts in concrete slows down the decay process, but treat them anyway. Coat metal fences with rust-preventing primer and paint (for particulars, see pages 522 and 523).

If you choose to use a material such as canvas for screening, figure on replacing it every few years.

## COMPARING PRESERVATIVES

| Preservative | Use/Application | Cost |
|---|---|---|
| Creosote | For buried wood. Has a strong, medicinal smell and can't be painted over. Apply by dipping; provide plenty of ventilation. | Inexpensive |
| Pentachlorophenol | For buried wood. Can be painted. Harmful to plants until thoroughly dry. Paint two coats or dip. | Inexpensive |
| Copper naphthenate | Good for buried and above-ground lumber. Odorless, non-toxic. Gives wood a greenish look. Paint two coats or dip. | Moderate |
| Asphalt roofing compound | For buried wood. Paint three coats, allowing plenty of drying time between them. | Inexpensive |
| Exterior paints and stains | Ok above ground, but almost useless below. Stains can be dipped. | Moderate |

# APPLYING PRESERVATIVES

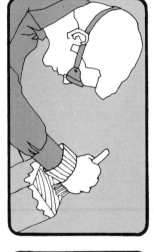

With a nail or punch, poke a series of holes around the post at grade level. This allows more preservative to soak into wood.

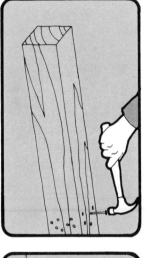

If dipping many components, pour preservative into a drum. Soak enough of the post to extend 6 inches above grade.

Be sure to give special attention to post tops and areas where you've made cuts. Wear protective clothing while applying.

After you've assembled all of the posts and rails, give them another coat. Also treat any newly exposed wood.

Or soak material in a shallow trench lined with a protective layer of polyethylene. Soak three days to ensure absorption.

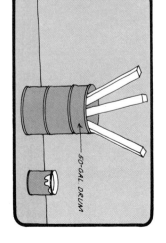

PLASTIC SHEETING

50-GAL. DRUM

**177**

## SETTING FENCE POSTS

For strength and long life, set terminal posts (at ends, corners, and gates) in concrete. You can anchor line posts in soil unless the fence will be extremely tall, heavy, or subjected to strong winds (see page 176 for posthole-digging help). Since the posts are set one at a time, consider buying premixed concrete for the job. The premixed material already has the proper amount of sand and gravel added to the cement; all you need to do is add water and mix.

The other choice is to buy the cement in bags, order sand and gravel, and stir up the mixture yourself (see pages 162 and 163). Although premixed concrete is more expensive than cement, sand, and gravel (be sure to order some extra gravel for the bottom of the postholes), the convenience usually is well worth the extra money spent.

Tools required for the job include a wheelbarrow or mixing box for concrete, spade, chalk line, line level, shovel, and steel trowel.

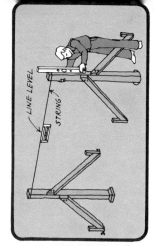

Shovel 2 to 3 inches of gravel in hole for first post. Set post in place; plumb it in two directions, bracing with outriggers.

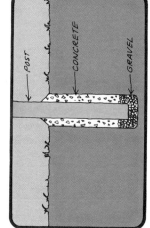

Add gravel around post. With a shovel, pour concrete, tamping each shovelful with a pipe to remove air bubbles in the mix.

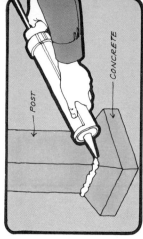

Set next terminal post. Plumb and brace it. Stretch line between posts to ensure equal heights. Then add concrete.

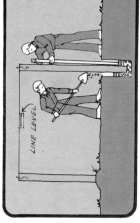

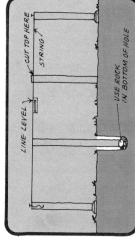

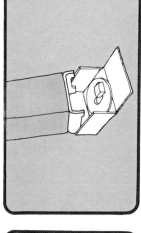

To set posts in soil, first lay down a gravel base, then have a helper shovel dirt into the hole while you tamp. Mound earth.

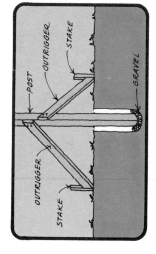

To square gate openings, measure between the posts at top and bottom. Equal measurements mean a square opening.

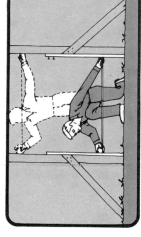

If you've accidentally dug a posthole too deep, use a rock as a filler. Dig shallow holes deeper or saw off post top later.

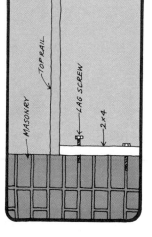

To fasten posts to a concrete slab, use metal post anchors, held in place with expansion anchors and lag screws.

To attach a fence to a masonry wall, use lead expansion anchors and lag screws. A star drill punches holes for the anchors.

For a watertight seal around posts set in concrete, wait until a dry spell and apply butyl caulk where concrete meets post.

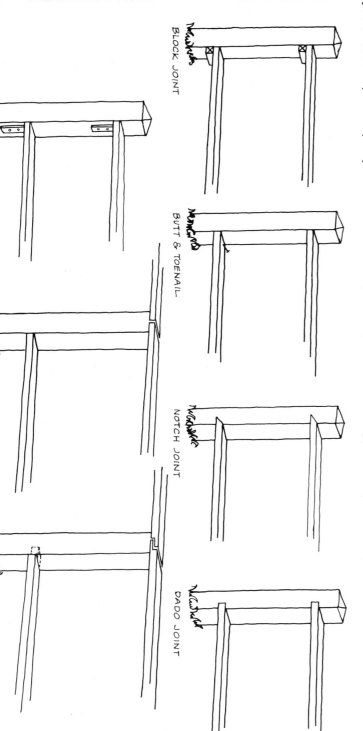

## APPLYING FINISHES

Remember Tom Sawyer and his white-washing project? He quickly discovered that it takes a lot of time to work a brush into all of a fence's nooks and crannies . . . and since you have to coat both sides and most of the edges of all components, even a short fence can soak up a surprisingly large quantity of paint or stain.

Unless you're like Tom and have some gullible friends, your best bet is to finish a fence *before* you assemble it. After the

posts are set, cut the rails and screening. Then lay them out on sawhorses or some other type of support system and apply the finish of your choice with a roller or a paintbrush.

Use any good exterior paint or stain (see page 511). Both wood and metal should be primed first; this properly seals the surface so that the top coating will hold up longer under exposure to severe weather.

Spraying (see pages 524–526) goes even faster, but the overspray wastes a lot of finish and may kill nearby vegetation if you're not careful. You also

take the risk of getting wind-blown paint on houses and cars that are in the area.

Once a prefinished fence is assembled, you'll have to go back and touch up spots that have been marred by hammer tracks, saw cuts, and other knocks and dings. Just to be on the safe side, apply a third coat to the tops of the posts and to the joints between the rails and the posts.

## PUTTING UP RAILS

Fastening rails to posts calls for only very simple joinery techniques. Once the posts are plumb and aligned, you simply cut each rail squarely, fasten it to one post, then level and attach it to the next.

The illustrations below show seven different ways to secure rails. Which one you choose depends upon your tools and

skills. It's tough, for instance, to cut dadoes, notches, and mortise-and-tenons without power equipment. On the other hand, butt joints supported by blocks or metal angles call for only regular hand tools and little nailing know-how. Toenailed joints are easy, too, once you've mastered the knack of making them (see page 49).

For fasteners, always use galvanized nails, screws, or bolts. Other types will

stain the finish.

Space bottom rails at least six inches above the ground—far enough away so that vegetation doesn't transfer moisture to wood or metal parts. You may want to put them a little higher to make mowing easier. And taller fences may need a third rail spaced equally between top and bottom members.

BLOCK JOINT

BUTT USING METAL ANGLE

BUTT & TOENAIL

BUTT CAP, BUTT RAIL

NOTCH JOINT

DADO JOINT

LAPPED CAP, MORTISE & TENON RAIL

**179**

screening must be custom made: you have to cut, fit, and fasten on the pieces—an easy but repetitious job. For a custom fence, adapt the basic screening techniques shown below.

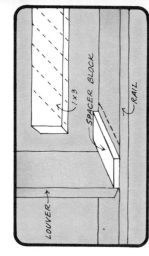

For a louvered fence, cut dozens of spacer blocks from 1x3 boards. Cut at 45-degree angles so each louver fits perfectly.

## PUTTING UP SCREENING

Now comes the fun part of building a fence—fleshing it out with screening material. As with any carpentry project, you must keep the parts square and level, so take your time putting them all together.

You can buy precut fence screening such as pickets, slats, wooden panels, metal mesh panels, and gates. Other types of

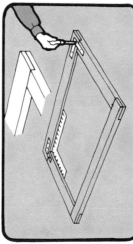

Nail screening to the sides of posts and rails. Sandwich it between molding strips, or fit it into dadoes in the rails.

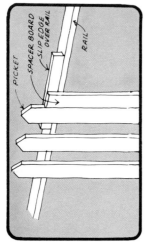

To space pickets, slats, and boards, rip a strip to the right width and nail a cleat to one end. Hang cleat on top rail.

## BUILDING A GATE

A gate that is strong and true will give you years of trouble-free service; a poorly constructed one will cause all kinds of grief. Hang the gate before attaching screening so you can correct an out-of-square opening.

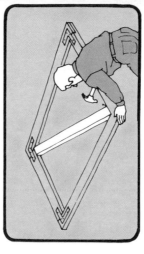

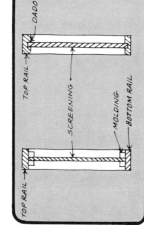

Square opening (see page 178). Make the frame ½ inch narrower than the opening. For very heavy gates, allow ¾ inch.

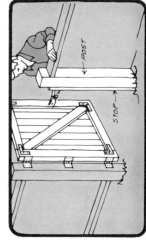

Brace the frame with a diagonal piece of wood that runs from the hinge side (top) to the latch side (bottom). Add screening.

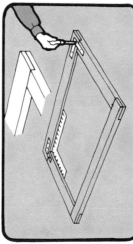

Use butt or lapped joints at corners of frame. Metal angle plates add strength at corners. Check square when assembling.

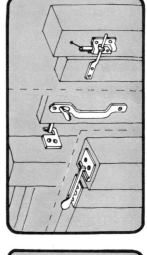

You can mount latches on the top or side of the gate. Three types are shown here. The thumb latch (center) requires boring to install.

With the gate closed, mark its inside edge on the latch post, then nail up a strip of wood to serve as a stop for the gate.

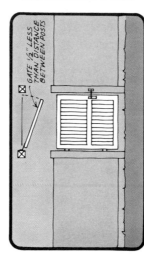

Screw or bolt the hinges to the gate and prop gate in the opening. Fasten hinges to the post and add the latch hardware.

## ANATOMY OF A SCREEN WALL

Garden walls fall into two broad categories: *screen walls*, which are really little more than masonry fences, and *retaining walls*, which hold back a slope and prevent erosion.

Both usually stand on concrete *footings*, and consist of successive *courses* of bricks, block, stone, or other material. Usually, *mortar*—a mixture of cement, sand, and water—binds the courses together. An exception is drywall construction, shown on page 183. Brick walls, such as the one shown in the sketch at left, ordinarily have two or more *tiers*, interlocked periodically with metal *wall ties*.

Many walls are topped with a concrete or stone *cap*. Below, there may be a drainage system to carry off water.

Freezing and thawing water can heave footings, crumble mortar joints, and topple caps. So, check masonry walls twice a year. Pay particular attention to the situation at ground level.

Maintain and repair garden walls as you would any exterior masonry (see pages 134 and 135).

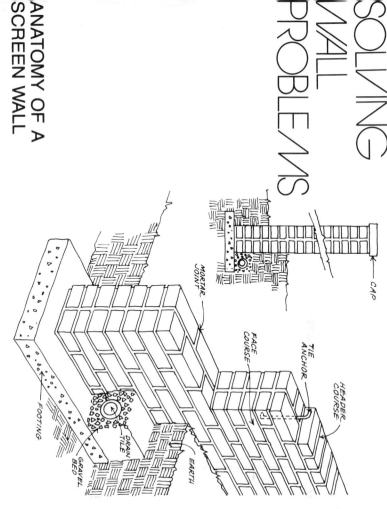

## ANATOMY OF A RETAINING WALL

Retaining walls include the same basic elements as screen walls, plus a few additional features. *Reinforcing rods*, in addition to being used to strengthen the wall itself, also help tie the wall to the earth it retains. And *weep holes* provide a place for excess water to escape, keeping pressure off the wall.

Water is a retaining wall's mortal enemy, so do whatever's necessary to make sure the wall can shed it. Inspect your walls twice yearly. Trouble points include blocked drainage tiles and weep holes, erosion along the hill or slope, and erosion directly in back of the retaining wall where it meets the earth. Plantings and additional buried drainage tile will help stop erosion.

Keep mortar joints in masonry walls in repair by tuck-pointing them; patch damaged wall caps; and if the wall is wood, replace any rotting wood members with specially treated lumber.

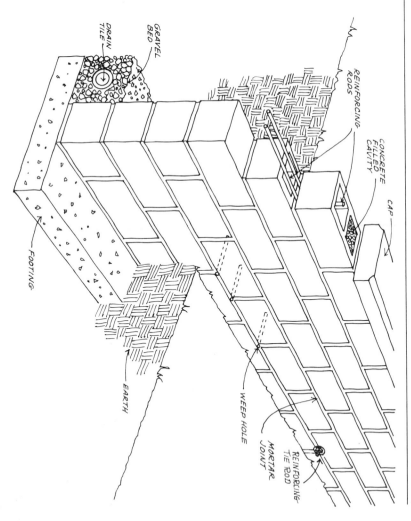

# BUILDING NEW WALLS

Admittedly, building a garden wall isn't the easiest around-the-house project you could tackle, but it's by no means impossible. If you've had a fair amount of do-it-yourself experience, the project should be well within your skills.

*Dry walls* (those without mortar) go up in a hurry because you're just piling layer upon layer of stone against the earth behind. *Wet walls* require more skill to build, as they use mortar for strength.

Before erecting a garden wall, plan its placement for maximum effect—visual and practical. And check to make sure that local codes don't restrict building in the location you've chosen.

## DRY WALLS

Rubble-stone walls go together like three-dimensional jigsaw puzzles. You simply stack them up against a bank of earth.

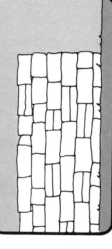

Ashlar stone is cut on four sides, so it's fairly easy to stack. You'll still have to do some final cutting and matching, though.

Railroad ties make terrific walls. Stack and nail them together, or anchor them in the ground with steel rods.

## WET WALLS

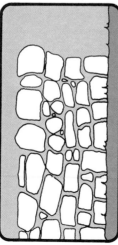

You can hurry your wall-building project along by dry-laying blocks then bonding them with fiberglass-reinforced mortar.

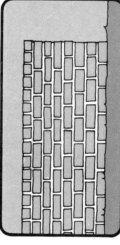

Brick walls, which require footings, gain their strength from mortar. (To learn about building them, see pages 188-191.)

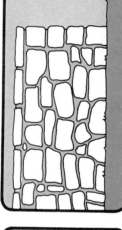

Field stone must be cut and fitted. You can use a heavier hand with the mortar than if you were working with brick or block.

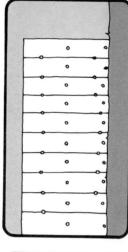

Like brick, mortared concrete block requires footings—but it goes up considerably faster. (See pages 186 and 187 for details.)

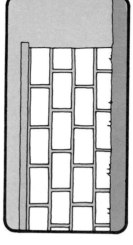

Poured concrete walls require forms, which you build or rent. These sturdy walls have footings and are reinforced with rods.

# LAYING UP A DRY STONE WALL

Stacking stone is the oldest and easiest way to build a wall. Excellent for use in retaining walls, stone also makes nifty-looking decorative walls. A dry stone wall usually won't work as a screening wall, though, since you can't effectively stack the stones high enough to achieve the screening effect—four feet is usually considered tops.

Generally, you won't need to lay footings when erecting a dry stone wall. The wall will ride out frost heaves, and if damage does occur, you can repair it quickly.

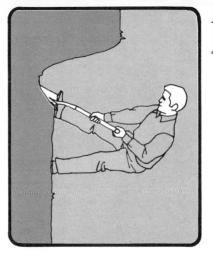

If the wall will stand on its own and is for decorative purposes only, you should level the ground with a shovel before stacking the stone. This especially applies to ashlar stone (see opposite page). A fairly level base will let you lay it up like bricks.

If desired, you can "mortar" with earth, which makes the stone-fitting job easier. If you use earth, dampen the soil so it balls in your hand. But don't let it get too wet, as it's supposed to form a "pad" between the stone units.

If you're given the opportunity to pick and choose when you purchase stone for your wall, select medium to large stones instead of the smaller ones—they fill up space faster. For your smaller stone

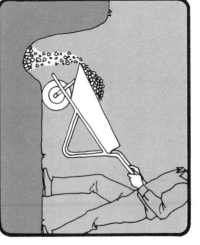

requirements, break the stones with a mason's hammer. If you're stuck with a potpourri of sizes, use the larger stones as the base for the wall and lay the smaller ones atop.

Tools you'll need include a mason's hammer, brick chisel, shovel, small garden potting shovel, wooden stakes, and chalk line. If you plan on using earth mortar, you'll need a piece of hardboard or plywood to serve as a mixing surface and a hoe for blending the dirt and water to the proper consistency.

---

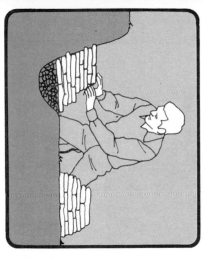

Lay out the wall, using stakes and a chalk line. Then dig a trench 6 to 12 inches deep and about 1 foot wider than the wall.

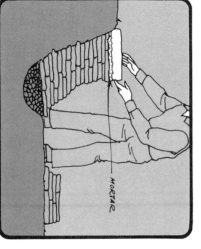

Fill the trench to within an inch of grade with pea gravel or small rocks. This base provides drainage and serves as a footing.

Begin the wall with stones that are large enough to span the gravel bed. Save the smaller ones for the top courses.

---

For the second and succeeding courses, make sure you stagger joints for greater strength. Tilt courses into the embankment.

For a tight cap, spread two inches of mortar along next-to-last course. Press in flat stones, filling gaps with small ones.

**183**

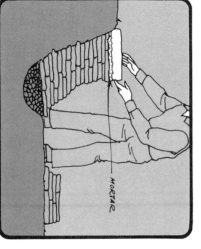
MORTAR

# WORKING WITH MORTAR

Mortar is such a strong compound, some people may think it contains some mysterious ingredients that only masons can mix. Not so! It just contains cement, sand, and water, and anyone can mix it to perfection. For convenience, most people prefer to buy premixed mortar, even though it costs a bit more than purchasing the ingredients separately.

If you decide to mix your own, a good formula for retaining and screen walls is one part masonry cement to three parts sand. Use new masonry cement, and be sure the sand is clean.

You'll need a mortar box or the bed of a large wheelbarrow to mix the mortar, as well as a hoe to blend the cement, sand, and water.

Plan about four bags of masonry cement and 12 cubic feet of sand for a brick wall four inches thick and measuring 100 square feet in surface area. If that same wall is to be eight inches thick, buy eight bags of masonry cement and double the amount of sand. In estimating brick needs, figure seven bricks per square foot.

Store the unmixed cement in a dry place, and have the delivery truck dump the sand near the job site to save you time and effort in the mixing operation. Also keep the sand covered with plastic film at night and especially during any rain. The sand should ball in your hand without crumbling or leaking water, so make sure it's slightly damp before mixing it with the cement and water.

To mix mortar, combine the cement and the sand and blend it together with a hoe until its color is consistent throughout. Then add water, a little at a time, stirring the mixture with the hoe until it becomes smooth like thick mud. Test its consistency with a trowel as illustrated below. Mix small amounts of mortar at a time; it sets quickly and becomes useless after an hour or so—even faster in hot weather.

## Using a Trowel

Practice makes perfect when it comes to working with mortar. So before attempting the finished project, build a test wall, then tear it down. You can reclaim the bricks or blocks, so your only "education expense"—and it's a minor one—is the mortar.

A trowel is used to place and trim mortar on bricks and blocks. It's also handy for making repairs in masonry walls (see pages 134 and 135). A lightweight trowel is the best for a beginning bricklayer. Buy a good one right from the start and it should last a lifetime.

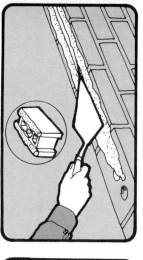

Mix the mortar so it slumps slightly on the trowel. Slice off a section of "mud" and pick it up with a twist of your wrist.

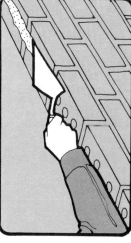

Flick your wrist as you would flip a pancake, *throwing* the mortar in a smooth, lengthwise movement along the bricks or blocks.

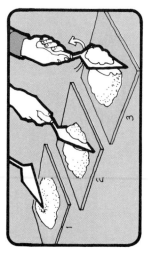

Press a dampened brick or a dry block firmly on the mortar. *Butter* one end of the next one and set it down (don't slide it).

*Furrow* the mortar, running your trowel down the center of the bricks. The procedure for blocks varies somewhat (see inset).

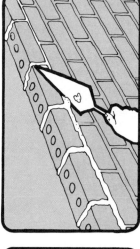

Use the edge of your trowel to slice off mortar that oozes out. Use this excess to butter the next brick end.

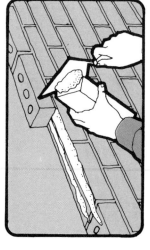

Using a joint strike or piece of pipe, smooth mortar joints when they begin to stiffen (see pages 187, 189).

184

# CHOOSING OTHER MASONRY TOOLS

For brick and block walls, you'll need a long *mason's level*, *mason's hammer*, *cape chisel*, and *line blocks* (or nails) and *mason's line* to align the blocks or bricks in each course. Fabricate your own *hawk* and *mortar board* from ¾-inch exterior-grade plywood and pieces of 2x2. Additional tools handy to have include a *brick chisel*, *sledge*, and a *story pole* to align bricks or blocks as the courses are laid. Make the story pole with a straight 1x3 that's the same height as the wall.

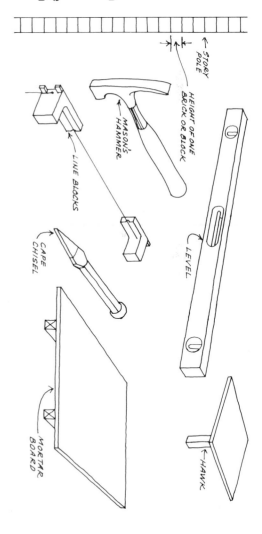

## POURING FOOTINGS

Whether it's a brick, block, or stone wall you're constructing—except dry walls—you'll need to pour a footing. And as

with all footings, those for walls should be below the frost line to avoid the ravages of cold weather. If you're unsure how deep the frost line is in your area, check with your community's building department or a local contractor.

Since footings usually require lots of concrete, it's best to buy premixed material and have it trucked in. This will save you time and plenty of back-breaking work.

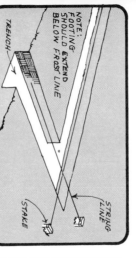

NOTE: FOOTING SHOULD EXTEND BELOW FROST LINE

TRENCH

STRING LINE

STAKE

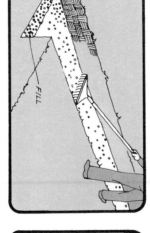

Place six inches of rock or gravel in the trench for drainage. Then level the material by pulling a garden rake across the top of it.

FILL

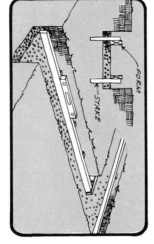

Stake the forms securely, making sure that they are perfectly level and square. Drive stakes on the outside of the forms.

FORM

STAKE

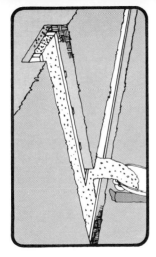

TRENCH

Stake out lines for the wall, then dig a trench twice the width of the footing. First courses will be below grade level.

Strike off excess concrete, seesawing a 2x4 screed along top edges of forms. Have a friend shovel away the excess.

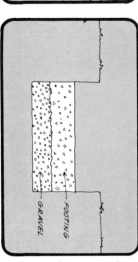

Coat sides of forms with old motor oil for easy removal later. Pour concrete, and jab with a shovel to compact it.

If ground is hard, you can place concrete without forms. Dig a straight-sided trench the width of the footing, as shown.

GRAVEL

FOOTING

**185**

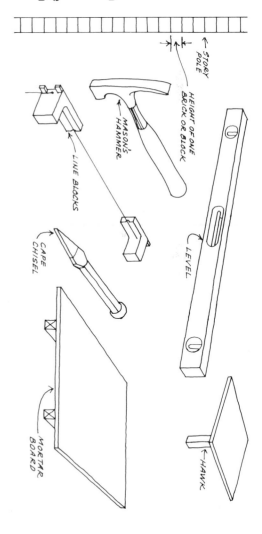
STORY POLE

HEIGHT OF ONE BRICK OR BLOCK

MASON'S HAMMER

LINE BLOCKS

LEVEL

CAPE CHISEL

MORTAR BOARD

HAWK

## WORKING WITH CONCRETE BLOCK

Mustering the strength to maneuver the blocks into position is the main difficulty you'll have in laying up a block wall. Even the lighter-weight aggregate blocks aren't exactly light, especially after you've lifted a few.

As when building brick walls, use a mortar mix consisting of one part cement to three parts sand. Don't use as much water, though, or the heavy blocks will compact the mixture. Mix small batches of mortar at a time; it sets quickly.

Lay out your block wall in multiples of eight inches. This will save you plenty of work cutting the units to fit. (Standard blocks measure 8x8x16 inches including the joints. Determine the number of blocks you need from this standard measurement.) The sketch below shows various types of blocks along with their actual sizes. Some blocks are sized to accommodate a ½-inch mortar joint.

Block walls need footings, which should be below the frost line. Ask a contractor how deep the frost line is in your area. For information on how to pour footings, see the previous page.

To some people, concrete blocks aren't as aesthetically pleasing as bricks, stone, lumber, and other materials. Solve this problem by using decorative screen blocks, which are manufactured in a variety of patterns and some special shapes. You can paint the blocks with masonry-type finishes, if desired.

Unlike bricks, which must be dampened with water before they're laid, concrete blocks should be bone-dry as they're mortared and set. Keep them under cover before you use them.

Tools you'll need for working with concrete blocks include a trowel, mason's hammer, brick chisel, joint strike, level, carpenter's square, line blocks and mason's line, and a story pole.

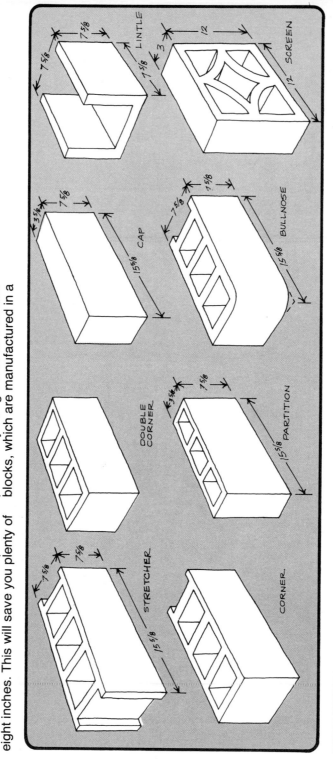

LINTLE

12 SCREEN

CAP

BULLNOSE

DOUBLE CORNER

PARTITION

STRETCHER

CORNER

## Cutting Concrete Blocks

Mark a line around the perimeter of block. Then, with a chisel and hammer, tap along line. The block will crack at the line.

## Reinforcing Block Walls

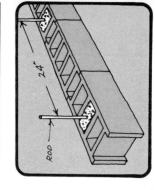

ROD

24"

For walls higher than four feet, sink metal reinforcing rods into the wet footing. Slip block over rods and fill cores with concrete.

"Start even and square; finish even and square" is an old adage that's especially true when you lay blocks or bricks; the units must be level, plumb, and square. If you're off an inch or so at the start, the error compounds itself as each block is set into position. You also must align properly along courses.

Set the ends and corners first—never begin in the center of the wall. And double-check all measurements to make sure the first blocks are level and square.

Next, to ensure that you lay the blocks level and plumb, stretch a mason's line between line blocks (or nails) at either end of the wall. Move the line blocks up

remember to keep the mortar joints consistent in width, or the blocks won't align properly along courses.

after each course is completed. Don't rely on the line blocks alone, though. Use a story pole to guide you (see page 185), and check each three blocks with a level as you lay them. If you spot an error, remove the guilty blocks immediately and start again.

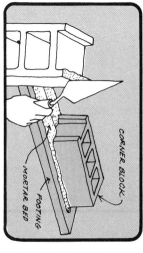

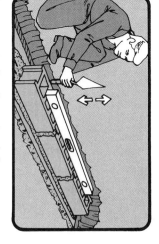

---

Before mixing mortar, lay blocks along footing to check fit. Use plywood strips for joint spacing. Mark spacings on footing.

Throw down 2-inch-deep lines of mortar and set end block. Butter and set second block. Smaller holes in blocks face down.

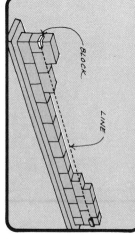

Set three blocks, then check for level and plumb. Make minor adjustments by tapping blocks with trowel handle. Reset if needed.

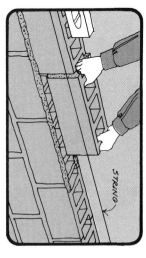

---

Build corners or ends when first course is laid. Check again with level and story pole. If they're off, pull blocks and start again.

When corners or ends are three or four courses high, stretch a line between them. Mason's line blocks (or nails) hold it taut.

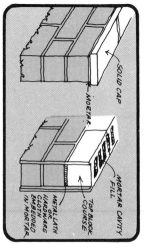

Lay blocks between corners, using the line for a level. Lift blocks into position; don't slide them—you'll foul the mortar.

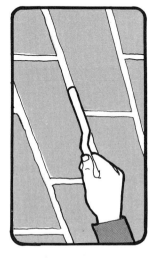

---

Butter both ends of last block in each course and ends of blocks that fit against last block. Carefully slip block into position.

Use solid caps to close the wall. Or, sandwich mesh in last mortar joint and then fill the cores in the top block with mortar.

Use a joint strike or a pipe to smooth mortar. Finish job by wiping joints with burlap; remove mortar from block faces.

187

# WORKING WITH BRICK

Laying up a brick wall is one of those projects that's more time-consuming than difficult. The reason: for every square foot of wall, you'll need to place approximately seven bricks. So, even a short wall translates into much work.

Many of the same tools and techniques that are used for raising block walls work equally well for brick walls. So before you undertake your project, refer to pages 184 and 185 for information on tools you'll need, pouring footings, estimating material needs, and working with mortar.

When shopping for bricks, you have three options: *SW (severe-weathering) brick*, used mainly in cold climates; *MW (moderate-weathering) brick*, for areas with moderate temperatures year-round; and *NW (no-weathering) brick*, for use in mild climates and interior construction such as fireplaces. For exterior retaining walls, purchase SW brick, since it withstands frost better below grade.

You also can choose between standard-size bricks or jumbo or irregular sizes. This is pretty much a matter of personal preference.

For strength, brick screen and retaining walls should be of two-tier rather than one-tier construction. This will

double the number of bricks you need for the project, so figure it in your estimates when you lay out the wall. You'll also have to order more cement and sand for the mortar. To be on the safe side, overestimate your needs so that you won't be caught short of material.

Plan a route for the delivery truck, bearing in mind that your driveway may not withstand the load. For small quantities, you may be better off to wheelbarrow the bricks from the curb to the site where you'll be building. Store bricks up off the ground on a wooden platform, and cover them with polyethylene so they don't absorb water.

## Fitting Bricks Together

Although bricks are all rectangular in shape, you can fit and lay them in a surprising number of ways that not only add strength to the wall but also give it a

distinct character of its own. On the facing page are some of the more popular bonds.

To get the design you want, you'll have to cut some of the bricks to fit. The tools needed to do this include a marking pencil, hammer, and brick chisel. First

mark all four sides of the brick where you want to cut it. Then score the brick along the line with a brick chisel, tapping the chisel gently with a hammer. The brick should break cleanly at this point.

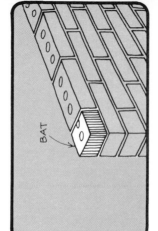

*Bats* are half-bricks. Use them on ends of walls and as closure units for header courses. Split full bricks to make bats.

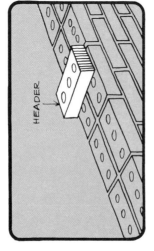

*Headers* laid every few courses (or at the top of a wall) add strength. Headers run at right angles to stretchers.

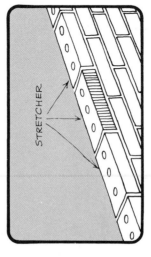

*Stretchers*, laid flat and with face outward, are an integral part of every brick wall, regardless of the bond you choose.

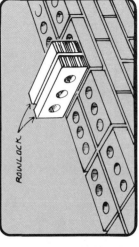

*Rowlock headers* are set across stretchers, but with their edges up. Rowlocks are quite often used to cap-off a wall.

Set bricks on their ends, face outward, and you have *soldiers*. Soldiers add design variation but little strength.

## Choosing a Bond

The pattern in which you set your bricks is called a "bond." As the bricks are laid, they're staggered so that vertical joints are never in alignment (except for a stacked bond). Staggered joints give the wall lots of additional strength.

You also can give more strength to two-tiered walls by using metal wall ties between the tiers. The ties, which are positioned at various intervals along the wall, lay across the bricks.

Before you make a decision on the type of wall bond you want, it's a good idea to buy a hundred or so bricks and build a test wall without mortar. Try several different bonds, then make your commitment.

In a *running bond*, all bricks are laid as stretchers. Use this popular bond for low walls—four feet high or less.

In *common bond*, headers every sixth course strengthen the wall. You'll still need bats to get the correct joint arrangement.

*English bond* alternates courses of headers and stretchers. Bricks that are split lengthwise stagger the vertical joints.

*Garden wall bond* features trios of stretchers separated by one header. It's stronger than common bond, weaker than English.

*Stack bond* is weak, but you can gain additional strength with a two-tiered wall. Keep it short—four feet or under.

Use *Flemish bond* whenever an exceptionally strong wall is desired. Alternate stretchers and headers in each course.

## Choosing a Mortar Joint

Pointing or striking a mortar joint helps make the joint watertight by sealing off tiny hairline cracks in the mortar. It also gives the wall a professionally finished appearance.

If your home has a brick veneer, you may want to finish your wall's joints to match. Use a piece of pipe, a tire iron, or even an old spoon for a pointing tool—or buy an inexpensive joint strike.

Make a *struck joint* with the edge of a trowel. Point joints before the mortar starts to harden. Test this with a finger—the mortar should be pliable to the touch. Stop work to point after every two courses.

The reverse of a struck joint, a *weathered joint* also is made with the edge of a trowel. Keep the bottom of the mortar line flush against the bricks below, carefully controlling trowel so the pointed end doesn't "dig" mortar.

To form a *flush joint*, simply cut excess mortar from the face of bricks. You can make this joint at the same time you lay the bricks. Go back after every two courses, though, and check to see if joints are tight.

Form *concave joints* with a pipe or joint strike. This very common finishing technique does a good job of letting water drain from the joints. Point the vertical joints first, then the horizontal ones.

Make a *raked joint* with a piece of wooden molding that's been trimmed on one end to match the width of the mortar joint. Keep the end of the molding wet with water to keep the mortar from sticking to the strip.

Cut a *vee joint* with a brick jointer. Or, if you'd rather, use a length of aluminum or steel angle. The trick is to strike the joint fairly quickly after the brick has been laid. Otherwise, the mortar will bunch up.

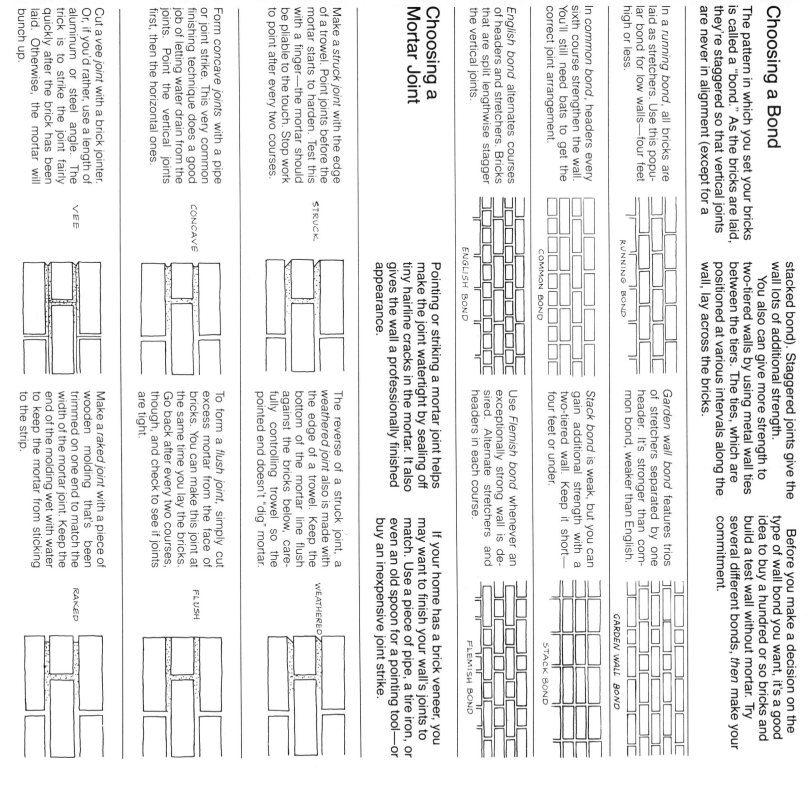

RUNNING BOND

COMMON BOND

ENGLISH BOND

GARDEN WALL BOND

STACK BOND

FLEMISH BOND

STRUCK

CONCAVE

VEE

WEATHERED

FLUSH

RAKED

# LAYING A BRICK WALL

As with concrete block walls, you should begin building brick walls from the ends or corners, then fill in to the middle of the wall.

String loose bricks along the length of the footings so they're in easy reach as you build the wall. The bricks should be wet when laid; sprinkle them with a hose before you start and keep them wet in a bucket as you work. If at all possible, have a friend mix the mortar for you as you lay the bricks. This will speed the job and keep the mortar fresh as well.

The starter or first *course* of brick must be absolutely level and square on the footing. If it's not, remove the bricks from the footing, clean away the mortar on both the footing and the bricks, and start again.

Continue with the next brick units and courses, double- and triple-checking each one with a level, square, and story pole (see pages 185 and 187).

## Building-Up Corners

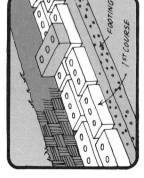

Dry-lay the first course, spacing each exactly ½ inch apart. Check spacing between tiers by laying a brick across them.

Start at an end or corner. Pick up three or four dry-laid bricks, and throw and furrow mortar line. Then lay the bricks; check level.

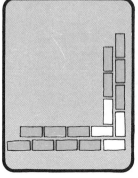

Soak the bricks thoroughly before laying them. Dry bricks absorb water from the mortar and as a result weaken the wall.

Positioning at the corners is crucial, so check your arrangement carefully. Note that joints between bricks are staggered.

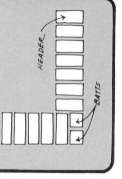

Build up corners, ends, and a section every 10 feet in long walls. Use a story pole to check for alignment with the rest of the wall.

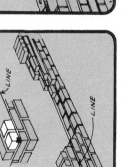

Check bricks carefully for alignment, as well as level and plumb. If a brick is slightly out, tap it gently into place.

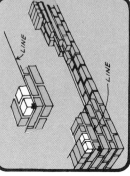

To ensure that all bricks in each course are correctly positioned, use a length of mason's line stretched between line blocks.

Turn headers around corners as illustrated. You'll have to cut a few bats from full bricks to form the proper corner bond.

Lay headers every sixth course on common-bond walls. But first trowel mortar between the tiers—this makes for a stronger wall.

Align intervening bricks with string line, raising it after each course. If a brick is out of line, remove it and start again.

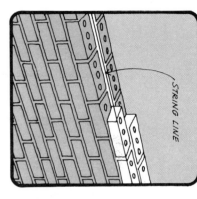

STRING LINE

To lay a closure brick, butter mortar on both ends and on ends of bricks in place. Gently place it between the other bricks.

A level makes an excellent straightedge. Check your work by holding it diagonally as well as horizontally and vertically.

Strike joints after every few courses—verticals first, then horizontals. (For different striking techniques, see page 189.)

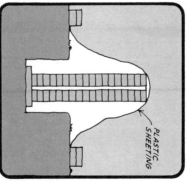

PLASTIC SHEETING

When you finish for the day, scrub the bricks to remove loose mortar. Then wet down the wall and cover it with polyethylene.

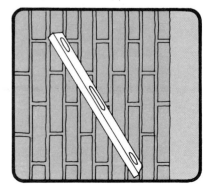

After three weeks or so, scrub the bricks with a mild solution of muriatic acid. This removes any mortar that remains on them.

## Capping Off a Brick Wall

When it's possible, top a wall with coping—bricks, stone, tiles, or precast concrete—to keep the water away from the bricks below. The coping should slope just enough to shed water, and if possible, project about ½ inch from the face of the wall so water won't run down the wall.

You can pitch the cap by building the mortar bed higher on one side of the wall. To add more strength to the entire unit, stagger coping joints with the vertical joints in the wall.

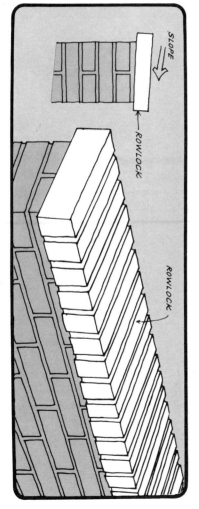

SLOPE

ROWLOCK

ROWLOCK

A course of rowlocks is the simplest way to top a wall. Choose bricks at least one inch longer than wall width.

# WALKS, STEPS, AND DRIVES

*Paving* encompasses everything from a series of stepping-stones to an interstate highway. Materials commonly used include concrete, brick, stone, asphalt, and even wood and gravel.

This chapter covers only those aspects of home paving not treated elsewhere in the book. For more about laying concrete surfaces, see pages 155 and 160-166; to learn about setting bricks or stones in sand, see page 159.

Paving of any type depends on proper drainage to protect it against damage from freezing and thawing. Underneath,

a porous base—usually sand or gravel—drains away water before it can do any harm to the surface.

Ignore a paving problem and it will only get worse. The repairs that are shown below and on the following three pages call for only a modest expenditure of time and money.

Laying new paving materials is a bigger job, of course, but you can easily master the basics (see pages 196-199). And since even a large paving project usually can be broken down into a series of smaller ones, the work needn't be overwhelming.

## SOLVING PAVING PROBLEMS

Frost, settlement, de-icing compounds, and tree roots all take their toll on even the best-laid paving. Fortunately, all you need for most repairs is a few dollars' worth of patching materials and simple hand tools.

Before you attack a problem, though, first find out what caused it. In chronic situations—usually the result of an inadequate base—you may be better off to rip up the old paving and start over.

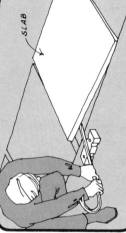
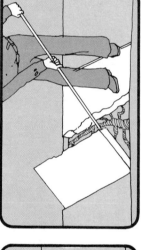

Fill underneath with equal parts sand, sifted dirt, and cement. Tamp, if possible, or overfill to allow for settling.

Level the section, then cement the pieces together. Or, fill the crack with asphalt. Put sand on asphalt to prevent tracking.

### LEVELING WALKS

To even-up a heaved or sunken walk, pry up the out-of-keel piece and add to or remove what's underneath. Flagstones, bricks, and small pieces of concrete lift out with little persuasion. Bigger slabs may demand a pick, wrecking bar, or pipe. Chop away any roots you encounter with a hatchet or ax.

Work a pick or wrecking bar under the settled section, lift it high enough to get underneath, then prop it up with a 2x4.

When a piece breaks free, pry and block it up, then chop out roots or add fill. If section is high, remove dirt.

If a heaved or sunken section is too large to lift, score near center and break slab with a chisel and hammer. Wear goggles.

# REPAIRING DAMAGED STEPS

Cracked, chipped, sunken, or heaved steps pose a serious safety hazard—and if you neglect repairs, you could end up having to replace the entire structure someday. Clearly, it pays to keep an eye out for problems and attend to them right away.

Steps differ considerably. Some have a brick superstructure and concrete treads. Others are all brick; still others are solid concrete. With brick-and-concrete construction, you have to guard against moisture getting in the bricks' mortar joints.

Repoint any crumbling material as shown on page 134. Patch the treads as you would any concrete surface (see below and page 155).

If your steps are constructed entirely of brick, look for mortar damage in the treads, where the treads meet the risers, and in joints between the steps and house or walk. Again, repoint if this is necessary.

To replace a broken brick, chisel out the mortar around it, chop out the pieces, and replace (see page 135). If you need more room to maneuver, remove and replace bricks on either side of the broken one, too.

Repair all-concrete steps as illustrated below. Note that it's important to

"undercut" old concrete so that the patch can get a secure hold. Use a cold chisel or brick chisel for this operation, then thoroughly flush away debris with a hose. Keep the crack damp until you fill it.

For patching material, mix one part cement with three parts sand and just enough water to make it doughy. Or purchase one of the special premixed patching compounds available in cartridges. Trowel this mixture into the damaged area, packing with the trowel's tip and smoothing with its edge.

To repair chips, spalled sections, and other damage that can't be undercut, use special epoxy patching cement mixed with sand according to the manufacturer's specifications.

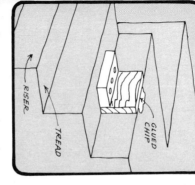

Sometimes, you can glue pieces back in place with epoxy cement. Clean area, press piece in place, and "clamp" as shown.

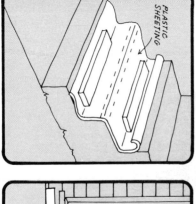

To make the patch stronger, keep damp for about a week. Cover the repair with polyethylene and weight it down with scrap lumber.

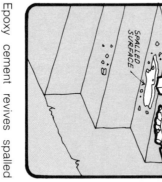

Epoxy cement revives spalled surfaces, too. Clean away loose concrete, then trowel on mix, feathering edges.

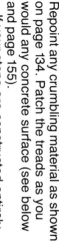

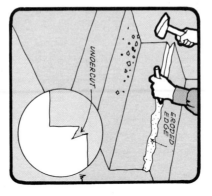

If an entire edge is broken, cut concrete back to make a V-groove. Groove helps hold the patch in place. Clean the area.

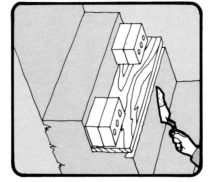

Press a board against the edge of the patch to serve as a form. Apply concrete, packing the groove full. Level top of patch.

Level a settled stoop as you would a slab (opposite). You may need a helper for the job and maybe a second wrecking bar.

Fill joint between foundation and stoop or steps with concrete joint filler, latex caulk, oakum, or an asphalt expansion strip.

193

# PATCHING ASPHALT

Asphalt—a sort of "soft concrete" made from gravel and petroleum extracts—has enough plasticity to ride out minor heaves and settling. And when a crack or chuckhole does appear, you can easily patch it with a ready-to-use mix sold in bags, or with a "mortar" you can mix by combining asphalt sealer and sand.

If possible, put off patching jobs until the temperature is 70 degrees or higher. Asphalt becomes pliable when warm, brittle when cold. If you must work in cool weather, store the compound indoors in a warm place. Break up any lumps by laying the bag on a hard surface and walking on it before opening.

Asphalt paving needs sealing every two years or so—whenever the surface becomes checked with hairline cracks or dries out. To do the job, buy five-gallon buckets of sealer and apply as shown in the sketches below.

Beware of door-to-door promoters who offer to seal your drive for a cut-rate price just because they "happen to be working in the neighborhood"; their sealers usually disappear as fast as they do.

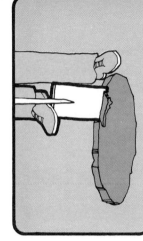

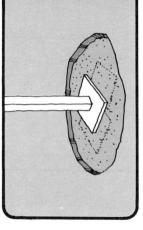

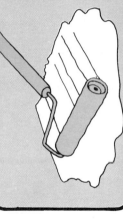

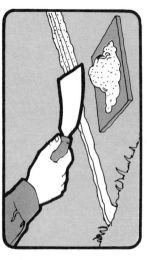

To fill chuckholes, dig out dirt and loose debris down to solid material. Cut edges vertical and tamp around top of hole.

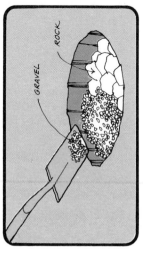

When the mix is within an inch of the top, pack it with an improvised tamper made from a 2x2 and a scrap of plywood.

Seal asphalt by pouring out big puddles of sealer, working it into the surface with a broom or paint roller. Apply two coats.

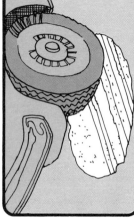

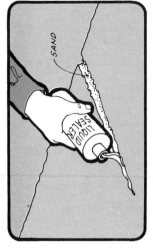

SAND

Partially fill small cracks with sand. Then pour in liquid sealer. Use this technique for cracks up to about ⅛ inch wide.

For larger cracks, mix sand with sealer, making a paste. Pack this mixture into the crack with a garden trowel or scraper.

ASPHALT MIX.

Now add asphalt mix, slicing it with a trowel or spade from time to time to open any air pockets and compact the mix.

ROCK
GRAVEL

In deep chuckholes, add several stones to conserve patching material. Fill with gravel to 4 inches from top.

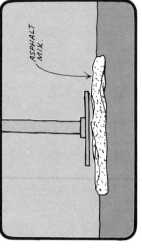

Sprinkle the patch with sand to prevent tracking. Then further compact it by driving a car back and forth over the repair.

LIQUID SEALER

ASPHALT MIX.

Add more patching material, mounding it slightly above the surface. Now, tamp the patch as firmly as possible.

**194**

Loose-fill materials such as gravel, pebbles, crushed rock, cinders, and slag make a drive that's relatively inexpensive and impervious to freezing and thawing cycles. The major problem with a loose-fill drive is that repeated use and erosion

tend to deposit some of the fill on your lawn or flush it down the street's storm drainage system, forcing you to replenish the material every few years.

If your drive slopes steeply, loose fill simply can't stay put. Consider repaving with a hard-surface material such as concrete or asphalt. On fairly level terrain, retain the fill by installing curbing as shown below.

Before you begin, though, wait for a

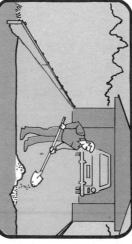

heavy rain and see what happens to the water. If it stands in puddles on the drive itself, you need to build up the low spots. To do this, spread out sand or a mixture of sand and crushed limestone, then add the loose-fill topping.

If water flows across the drive, taking loose fill with it, regrade the drive before adding the edging.

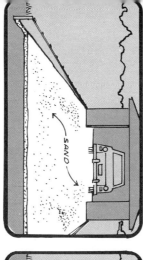

Add pressure-treated wood to both sides of the driveway, anchoring with stakes. Or set solid partition block.

Level any high spots and fill low ones. Surface should be as even as possible. Fill depressions with sand and loose fill.

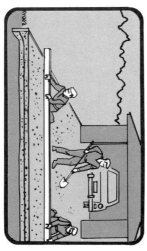

Have a truck dump fill in a series of piles along the length of your drive. Then spread out the fill with a shovel and rake.

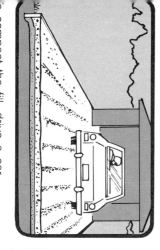

A sand base facilitates drainage. Use about 2 inches of sand for every 3 inches of fill. Level sand, then wet to compact.

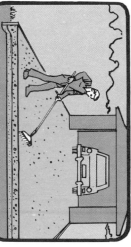

To compact the fill, drive a car back and forth across the surface. After several passes, add more fill to low spots.

Every spring and fall, rake the fill to level. Add more where necessary, and compact it with the wheels of your automobile.

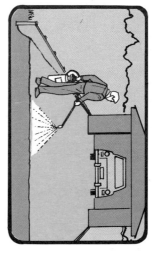

Level the fill with a 2x4, dragging its ends along curbing. Have one person shovel away excess fill in front of the 2x4.

Saturate the ground with weed killer to keep vegetation from peeking through the loose-fill material. Do this in the spring.

# LAYING NEW PAVING MATERIALS

Garden paving offers an excellent opportunity for you to learn about the basics of working with masonry. Unlike the bigger jobs of constructing a patio (see pages 158-166) or planning a drive (see page 199), you needn't move a lot of earth, prepare extensive footings and forms, or master any special techniques.

Certain projects go faster than others, of course. For a rustic pathway that rises and falls with the terrain, you need to excavate only a few inches, pour a loose-fill base of sand or gravel, then lay one or a combination of the materials shown below. On land that's high and drains reasonably well, you may not even need a base for the paving.

For the more formal look of an arrow-straight walk, you'll probably need a concrete base, but it needn't be more than 4 inches thick, and doesn't require reinforcement.

If you have a lot of paving to do, use materials that you can fabricate yourself or buy at home improvement centers. This way, you can do a few sections at a time, without a weekend-after-weekend work hangover.

If soil drains well, concrete walks can be as thin as 3 inches. Make forms from 1x4s and shape curves with 1/4-inch tempered hardboard. Broom-finish surface.

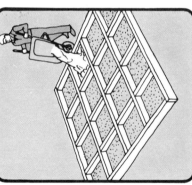

To cast your own stepping-stones, first build a form on a level spot. Then add a layer of sand and 2 inches of concrete. Screed the units with a 2x4.

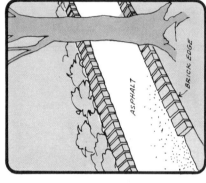

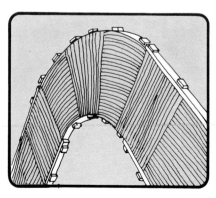

Brick—a paving classic—works well with formal or informal settings. Set paving bricks on sand as you would a patio (see page 159) or a mortar base (opposite).

Asphalt makes an economical paving material, but it needs a firm base of rock or tamped sand on which to lie. You can color asphalt with special paints.

Flagstones may be set on sand or in mortar. Use 2-inch minimum thickness over sand; 1/2 to 1 inch on concrete. Choose modular rectangles or irregular shapes.

Retain loose-fill materials with wood, brick, or block edging. Build forms as you would for a loose-fill drive (see page 195). Use various gravels for interest.

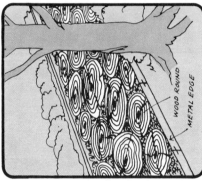

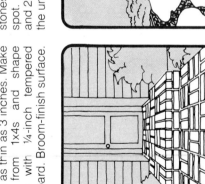

Wood blocks or rounds, made by slicing timbers or logs, give a rustic character to walks. Use redwood, cypress, cedar, or a rot-treated wood. Set in sand.

196

For a durable, dressy walk—to a front entry, for instance—consider veneering a concrete slab with flagstones, slate, or quarry tiles.

Flagstones—typically sandstone, limestone, or quartzite—are simply big flat rocks. They come in irregular shapes or precut squares and rectangles.

Because flagstones aren't uniformly thick, you must lay them on sand or in a 1-inch mortar bed, as shown below.

Slate tiles, sold in a variety of colors, are available in standardized thicknesses ranging from 1/4 to 1 inch. Choose either regular or irregular shapes. To trim slate, you'll need to rent a slate cutter. Set in a 1/2- to 3/4-inch mortar bed.

Quarry tiles are made in many different colors, and are 3/8 and 1/2 inch thick.

Choose square, hexagon, or curved shapes, and be sure to get a type meant for outdoor use. Trim and set as you would slate.

The drawings below illustrate the *dry-set* method of veneering with stones and tiles. First, bond paving units to the concrete, then grout the spaces in between.

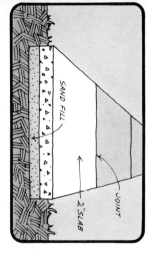

The concrete base—whether existing or new—should be at least 2 inches thick and poured over 1 to 2 inches of sand.

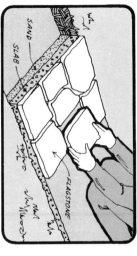

Dry-lay units to test pattern; allow 1/2-inch mortar joints. Adjust later if necessary. Align expansion joints with those in slab.

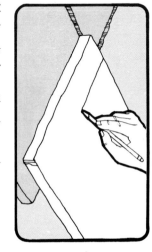

Mark units for cutting by overlaying adjacent stones, then tracing a line. For tile or slate, you'll need a special cutter.

To cut a flagstone, lay it on a solid surface and score along the line with a brick chisel. If necessary, score other side, too.

Slip a board underneath the stone along the scored line and gently tap with a sledge or hammer until the stone fractures.

Now remove several of the units. Wet the concrete well and trowel on a layer of 1:3 mortar mix or special dry-set mortar.

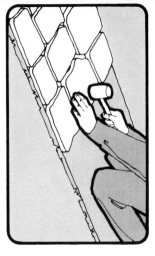

Embed the stones and tap them in place with a mallet. After laying several of them, check for level; units must be true.

Let mortar set 24 hours or more. Then pack joints with a soupy 1:3 mortar mix or premixed grout. Smooth the joints with trowel.

When the mortar is nearly dry, wipe off the excess with damp burlap. Cover with polyethylene and keep damp for a week.

**197**

# BUILDING STEPS

Well-constructed in-ground steps not only get you from one level to another, they also hold back erosion. Plan them as you would a retaining wall (see pages 181-183). Notch steps into slopes wherever possible; otherwise, they may begin to slide in a season or two.

Select materials to match or contrast with the pathways at either end. The drawings below show six popular options and there are dozens of other possibilities. Just be sure to firmly anchor whichever material you choose and provide adequate drainage. It's best to pitch treads slightly downhill or to one side so water will run off.

Once you have made a decision as to materials, you'll need to answer some questions. How many steps will you need to get from one level to another? How deep should you make each *tread* (the part you walk on)? How high should each vertical *riser* be?

Begin by measuring the vertical distance, *rise*, from the bottom to top level. To do this, first drive a tall stake at the bottom and stretch a line from the stake to the top. Level this line, then measure from the point where it joins the stake to the ground below. Double-check this measurement. If it's off even an inch or two, you could end up with unequally spaced risers—a sure way to cause people accidents.

Next, determine the approximate height you'd like the risers to be. This can vary from 3 to 9 inches. Low risers—usually with deep *treads*—provide a leisurely transition from one level to another; plan shallow treads and higher risers for service areas where you'll want to get from one level to another more rapidly.

Now, to determine the total *run*, measure the length of the line you've stretched from the stake to the top of the slope. By juggling this dimension and the height of the risers, you can compute both the number of steps you'll need and the distance each tread will measure from front to rear (more about this on page 170).

Make treads a minimum of 10 inches deep (12 to 15 inches is a more comfortable depth), but for a graceful, terraced effect, treads can be 3 feet deep or more.

Excavate carefully, using a spade to keep the cuts' sides straight. In calculating how deep to dig, be sure to include a couple of inches for a sand or gravel base—and don't forget to allow for the thickness of the treads in planning the height of each riser, especially at the top and bottom.

If you can't notch-in your steps, you'll have to build them up—a big job with most materials. If you choose masonry, be certain to pour footings first. Or construct a wood, open-riser staircase, as shown on page 170.

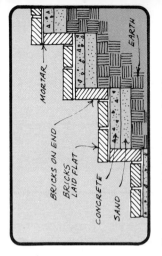

To construct brick steps, first lay down a bed of sand, set concrete slabs atop, then set the bricks in mortar, as shown.

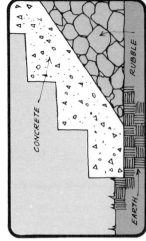

Cast concrete steps take lots of form-building and material. To save concrete, dump clean stones or bricks into form first.

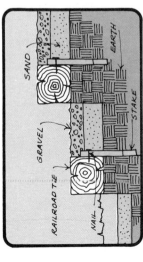

Solid concrete blocks offer a quick way to build steps. Sink them into a sand base. Be sure to pitch slightly for drainage.

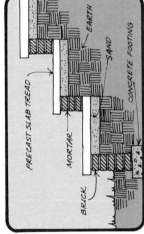

Precast slabs are usually heavy enough to hold themselves in position—but it's wise to put them on a firm base for stability.

Railroad ties make excellent risers. The treads shown here are gravel, but you could also use brick, block, or concrete.

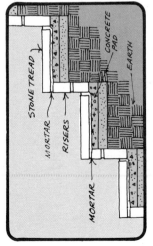

Flagstones rest on brick, wood, or broken stone risers. Set them on sand/concrete pads in mortar for the best stability.

# PLANNING A DRIVEWAY

Mainly because of the sheer magnitude of the project, most people don't ever attempt to pave a driveway themselves. And it's just as well. Although the planning and forming work isn't too difficult—providing you don't have lots of earth to move—the mixing, screeding, floating, and troweling is back-breaking. And besides that, few people have the time to devote to such a project.

But, if you decide you want to do the entire job yourself, be sure to order the concrete materials premixed.

The additional cost of having concrete delivered is small, especially when you consider the rental expenses you'd incur if you mixed the concrete yourself. The same is true for asphalt surfaces.

Where you can save dollars is in designing, laying out, and preparing the project for the professional.

If the ground on which you'll place the driveway is firm and has good drainage, don't disturb the soil. Rather, skim off all vegetation from the ground, set the forms, lay down a bed of sand, then pour the concrete.

If the earth is not solid, you'll have to add a base for the concrete—from 4 to 6 inches thick. For details on how thick yours needs to be (soil conditions and code restrictions vary from one place to another), check with a concrete supplier in your area.

Driveways vary in width from 10 to 14 feet, or about 3 feet wider than your car for a single garage or carport. Make the measurement 16 to 24 feet wide for two cars or a two-car garage.

If heavy trucks will frequent the driveway, make the surface material 6 to 8 inches thick. If only pickup-type trucks and cars will use the driveway, 4 inches will suffice.

To ensure that you have proper drainage, you should slope the driveway away from the garage, carport, or house. Figure on approximately 1/4 inch per running foot for the slope.

Use 2x4 or 2x6 lumber for the forms. Or, depending on availability, you may be able to rent metal forms for less than you'd pay for the lumber. The forms are held by stakes on the outside of the forming members. Use 2x2 stakes, pointed at the ends. Sledge-hammer them into the ground, and space from 24 to 30 inches apart. Drive the tops of the stakes below the top edges of the forms. This is a must: the concrete can't be leveled conveniently if the tops of the stakes are in the way. See pages 161, 164, and 165.

You may need a layer of plastic film for a moisture barrier and reinforcing rods or mesh for strength. Ask your materials dealer about this, since conditions vary with locality.

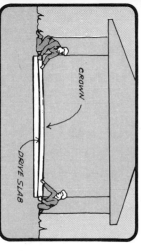

CROWN / DRIVE SLAB

Where drive intersects street, plan on having a 3- to 5-foot-radius curve. Other curves and turns in the drive need wider radii.

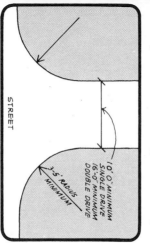

STREET / 10'0" MINIMUM SINGLE DRIVE 16'0" MINIMUM DOUBLE DRIVE / 3-5' RADIUS MINIMUM

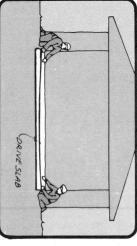

DRIVE SLAB

For a turnaround, plan an 18-foot radius and at least a 10-foot width. Make turnaround wider if it will serve as parking.

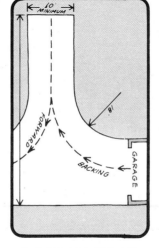

10 MINIMUM / 8' / FORWARD / BACKING / GARAGE

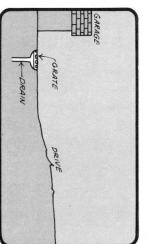

DRIVE SLAB

If the slope won't be severe, give the driveway a crown center so water will roll off to both sides of the drive.

For fairly long drives, or drives with severe slopes, plan a gutter center that will carry runoff water down the drive into street.

If garage is below street level, give the drive a gutter center and include a large drain directly in front of the garage door.

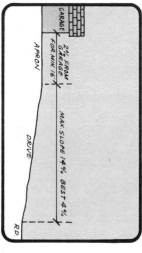

GARAGE / APRON / DRIVE / 2% FROM GARAGE FOR MIN 16' / MAX SLOPE 14% BEST 4% / RD

Maximum grade should not exceed 1¾ inches per foot. If more severe, cars will bottom out on humps or drag at street level.

GARAGE / GRATE / DRAIN / DRIVE

# GARAGES

A garage can be one of the best utilized and most serviceable areas of your home. Yet all too often—and usually out of laziness—people relegate the area to junk storage, leaving just enough space to squeeze in a car. Worse yet, they sometimes vacate the garage altogether and park outside.

If your garage isn't giving the service you expect of it, now's the time to correct the situation. Usually, simply adjusting a

garage door, repairing an automatic door operator remote control, or making any number of other minor repairs or improvements will put your garage back on the active list. This chapter shows you how to do these things, and more. There's even a section on building your own garage or carport.

As you can see from the anatomy sketches below, garage doors aren't overly complex. Most of them, whether

the *swing-up* or the *roll-up* type, utilize a *track* to facilitate opening and closing. A *cable and pulley system* usually does the actual lifting, with help from some type of *spring system*, which supplies the needed tension. The doors mount to the door jambs with *mounting brackets*, or ride in *tracks* that mount to the jambs.

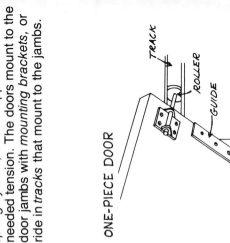

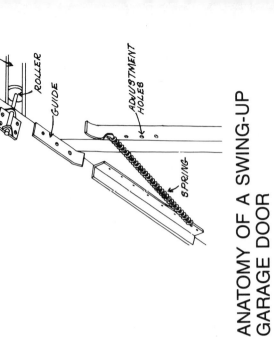

ONE-PIECE DOOR

## ANATOMY OF A SWING-UP GARAGE DOOR

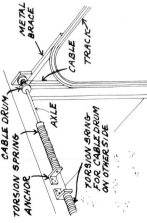

LIFTING MECHANISMS

## ANATOMY OF A ROLL-UP GARAGE DOOR

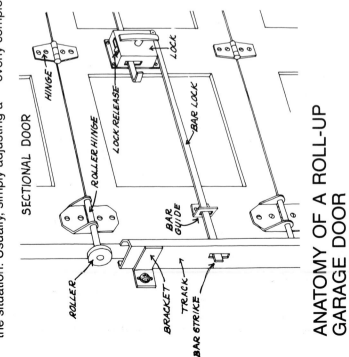

SECTIONAL DOOR

# SOLVING GARAGE PROBLEMS

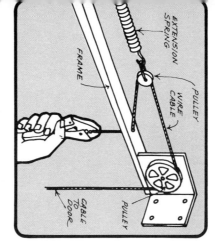

## TROUBLESHOOTING GARAGE DOORS

Unlike an electrical or plumbing problem, which may take a professional to diagnose, garage door maladies are not difficult to locate. If, for example, the door opens or closes too easily, look to the spring system. Or if the door sticks, check out the tracks or the door trim.

Below you'll learn about several common garage door problems that, when discovered, are easy to remedy.

Why do garage doors malfunction? Though not the sole culprit, moisture plays a large part. It warps doors, rusts hardware, and causes framing members

to rot away. So while you're looking for problems, check to make sure that water isn't being allowed to build up around or drip onto the door. If it is, make the needed repairs at once.

With swing-up garage doors, sagging is the biggest problem. The reason: the lifting mechanisms usually aren't adequate to support this weight. If this is the problem, replace—don't repair—the mechanisms. The new ones should be extra-heavy-duty, and positioned so the screws will be driven into new, solid wood.

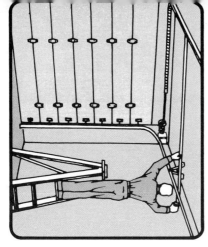

Too much cable slack can cause pulley-type doors to malfunction. Tighten the cable, but don't stretch the spring when you do.

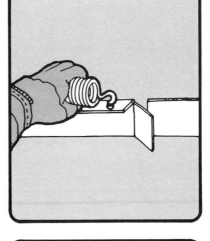

Tighten the springs on doors with tension springs: hook them into the next adjustment hole in the door framing or track support.

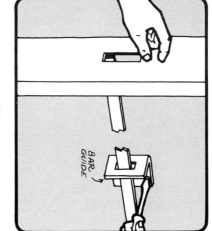

Bar locks won't lock if the assembly is out of alignment. Adjust either the lockset or the bar guide, and keep both lubricated.

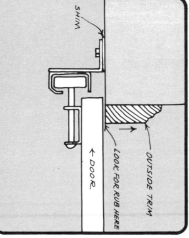

If the door rubs against the opening trim molding, either move the molding back, or adjust or shim out the track brackets.

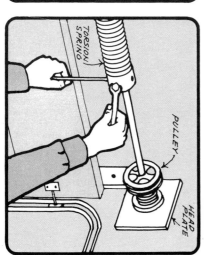

Though it's possible to adjust torsion spring-type doors yourself, don't do it. Rather, call in a trained serviceman.

The door's tracks must be parallel or the door will bind. Measure between them in several places, and make adjustments as needed.

**201**

# MAINTAINING GARAGE DOORS

As long as they continue to operate, garage doors don't get a second thought around most homes. That's unfortunate because this lack of attention almost always results in a back-wrenching episode at some time or other when the door won't open or close. (To learn about troubleshooting garage doors, see page 201.)

Keeping your door hardware clean and lubricated will prevent most problems. See the sketches below for the techniques involved.

Another thing to keep an eye out for is failing paint, or rust on a metal door—a sign that moisture is beginning to take its toll on the door. Blackish marks near the base of a wood door signal rot. Tend to

these danger signs as soon as possible to keep trouble to a minimum.

If your door is wood, remove the peeling or flaking paint down to the bare wood. Then spot-prime the area and give it two coats of exterior paint. If the door is metal, remove the rust or corrosion to the bare metal, prime the spots with metal primer, and apply two finish coats. You may have to repaint the entire door—wood or metal—so the new paint patches don't show.

Also replace any damaged hardware such as hinges, locksets, and tracks. These non-functioning parts can put additional strain on other components and result in future damage.

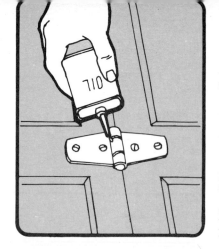

Lightly oil hinge pins, too. If the pins are rusty, remove them if possible, and clean the metal with steel wool or fine sandpaper.

Keep door edges, panels, and bottoms sealed with paint. Also repair any damaged concrete at the base of the door.

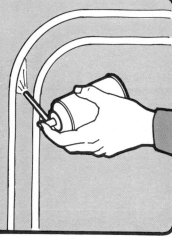

Relubricate the clean tracks with graphite or light machine oil. Distribute the lubricant by opening and closing the door.

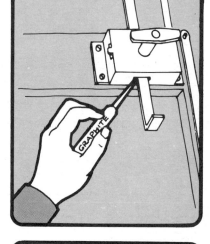

Use graphite, not oil or grease, for locksets. Puff the powder into the mechanism, as illustrated, and into the key channel.

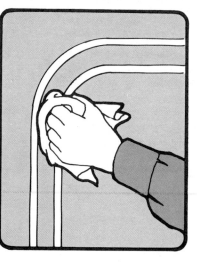

Clean grease and oil buildup from the door tracks. Lots of grease, combined with dirt, can cause the door to bind and jump.

Lubricate roller wheels and make sure they are in alignment with the track. You usually can adjust the metal wheel supports.

202

Unless they're attached to a house, garages generally aren't treated to the same energy-conserving building techniques afforded houses. Even attached garages leak a surprising amount of air, which comes in mostly through and around garage doors. You can tighten up your garage, though. Just implement the remedies shown here.

If your garage also doubles as your workshop or a crafts or play area, you'll probably want to insulate the sidewalls and rafters or ceiling. For more about insulating, see page 366.

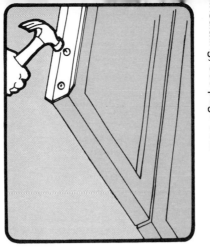

Seal the bottom of the door with garage door weather stripping. It compensates for unevenness in the threshold.

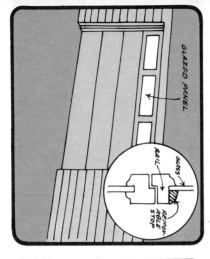

Replace broken windows in garage doors as you would any window (see page 144). The glazing, however, is a tack-on molding.

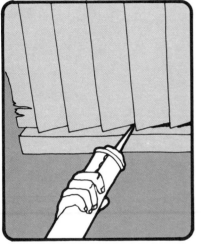

Seal the joints between window and door casings (trim) and the siding with a caulk formulated for exterior use (see page 131).

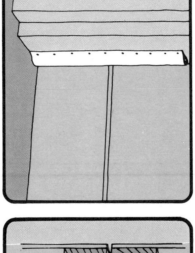

Outside, apply weather stripping to the top and side jambs to seal these areas when the door is in its closed position.

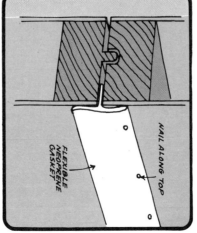

For panel joints, you can buy a neoprene gasket to seal out air and water. This weather stripping comes in several colors.

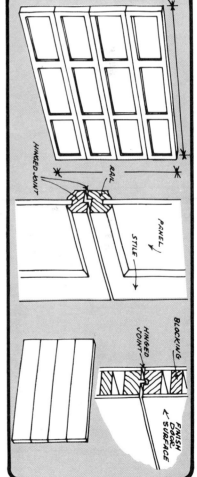

Sectional raised-panel doors leak air where they are hinged. Keep the hinges tight, and the joints free of dirt and paint gobs.

Flush-panel doors have the same problems as raised-panel doors. For tight joints, adjust tracks, rollers, and all the hinges.

# TROUBLESHOOTING ELECTRIC GARAGE DOORS

Occasionally, electric garage door operators go bad. But only occasionally. So before you start sleuthing for a problem in the unit itself, make sure that it's not the garage door itself that's at fault.

But even before that, make sure the operating unit is receiving electric power. You can check the power source by plugging a lamp or electric power tool into the receptacle used for the opener.

If all is well here, pull the emergency release cord or chain (see the anatomy drawing on opposite page). If you still can't move the door up or down, check to see if there are obstructions in the door tracks, or if something is caught on or in the chain or screw drive. Also check to see if the door has been damaged in any way—from an accidental hit by a car bumper, for example.

When you're satisfied that none of the above conditions exists, follow these procedures: let the motor of the opener cool for about 10 minutes; it may be overloaded. Then try to open the door with the auxiliary pushbutton control. If this doesn't work, the control could be defective.

If the opener works when you push this control but not when you use the transmitter, the batteries in the transmitter may be dead.

If the door opens for no reason, a neighbor's transmitter may be operating on the same frequency code as yours. If it's possible with your unit, try changing the code.

If the door opens, then stops partway open, the trouble may be in the travel adjustment. A door that starts down but stops before it's completely closed also requires adjustment.

And finally, if the transmitter activates the drive unit but the door doesn't move, chances are the drive belt needs tightening.

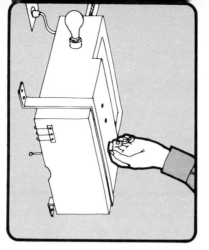

If the door reverses on its way up or down, or won't reverse when obstructed, adjust the safety sensitivity control.

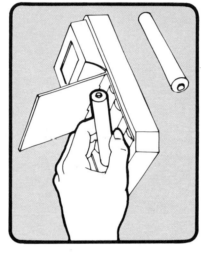

If the door won't open or close, the problem may be weak or dead batteries in the transmitter. It's smart to replace them annually.

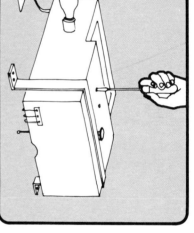

If the door doesn't open or close all the way, adjust the height adjustment screws. On some units, they're inside the housing.

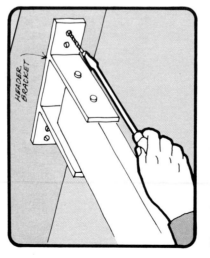

Through use, the header or door bracket can work loose and cause binding. Correct alignment and secure with long screws.

If the drive unit moves but won't raise the door, tighten the belt that connects the pulley to the motor. Don't overtighten, though.

# MAKING GARAGE IMPROVEMENTS

## CHOOSING AND BUYING GARAGE DOOR OPERATORS

An automatic garage door opener is one of those I-really-don't-need-one-of-those products that people thoroughly appreciate once they begin using it. And unlike many so-called convenience products, automatic door openers really do make sense in terms of effort saved—not to mention the added security they offer.

The safety and convenience features are intertwined. Once the door is down, the opener locks it automatically, and the only ways the door can be opened are with the transmitter, the auxiliary pushbutton control, or the manual emergency release cord inside the garage. A light, timed to shut off a minute or so after the door touches down, allows you time to exit the garage safely at night.

Most all automatic openers have safety devices that either stop the door or immediately reverse it in case it meets an obstruction while moving. Assuming the unit has been adjusted properly, the slightest resistance to the moving door will stop it from traveling any farther.

If the pushbutton transmitter malfunctions, you can pull an emergency release cord to disengage the unit from the door so you can operate the door manually. And, most operators feature motor-overload devices that automatically deactivate the motor if it overheats.

The anatomy sketch below reveals the relatively simple makeup of garage door openers. The drive unit, the heart of the opener, houses the motor, control terminals, a belt and pulley system, and a series of relay switches and gears or sprockets—all of which combine to make the unit function.

A trolley, attached to an opener arm, which in turn is connected to a door bracket, rides along a track to raise or lower the door upon receiving instructions from a remote control. The way in which the trolley rides along the track depends on whether your opener has chain drive or screw drive (see the sketch at right). With chain-drive units, the chain, activated by the motor/belt/pulley, moves back and forth around

a series of sprockets, taking the trolley with it. On screw-drive units, the trolley moves via a threaded rod that rotates in one direction to open the door, the other to close it.

The controls consist of a transmitter and receiver. The portable transmitter sends out a short coded signal to the receiver, which is mounted either within the drive unit or on the ceiling or nearby wall in the garage. The signal activates a relay switch, and the switch releases a low-voltage impulse, which activates the motor drive.

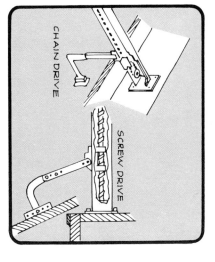

CHAIN DRIVE

SCREW DRIVE

## ANATOMY OF A GARAGE DOOR OPENER

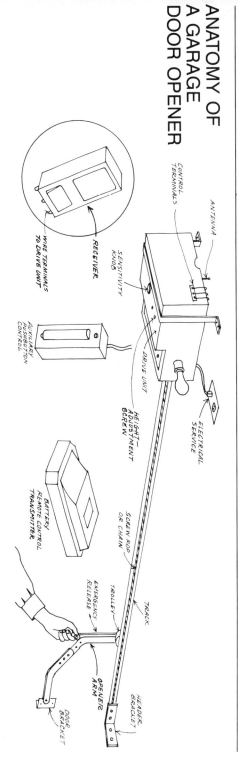

CONTROL TERMINALS

WIRE TERMINALS TO DRIVE UNIT

RECEIVER

SENSITIVITY KNOB

ANTENNA

AUXILIARY PUSHBUTTON CONTROL

DRIVE UNIT

HEIGHT-ADJUSTMENT SCREW

ELECTRICAL SERVICE

SCREW ROD OR CHAIN

BATTERY REMOTE CONTROL TRANSMITTER

EMERGENCY RELEASE

TROLLEY

TRACK

OPENER ARM

HEADER BRACKET

DOOR BRACKET

205

# INSTALLING A GARAGE
# DOOR OPENER

When you get home with your opener, sit down and study the assembly and installation instruction booklet first thing. This usually-thorough set of instructions will familiarize you with the unit and its parts, and lead you step-by-step through all the procedures necessary to install the unit correctly. The sketches below depict some of the steps involved in a typical installation.

After you've done this, give the garage door the once-over to make sure it's operating smoothly. (Balky doors put a severe strain on the small motors that power openers.) Make sure especially that the tracks are parallel to each other and that the rollers roll freely (see pages 201 and 202).

Then disengage any door-locking devices so they can't be used. The opener has a built-in lock that secures the garage adequately. Besides, additional locks can damage the opener.

You probably have most of the tools you'll need to complete the installation—stepladder, screwdriver, adjustable-end wrench, pliers, electric drill, wire cutters, hammer, and hacksaw.

Most likely, after installing the unit, you will need to make minor adjustments to ensure that the door opens and closes completely and that it will stop or reverse itself if obstructed on its downward path. Again, refer to the installation instructions (also see page 204).

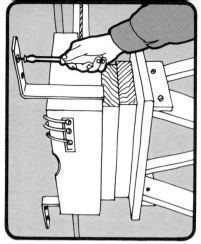

Fasten the drive unit to the garage ceiling or to the rafters or collar beams. The track must be perpendicular to the door.

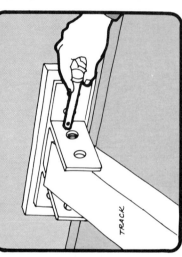

Slip the track into the bracket and secure it in position. You'll have to support the other end of the track during assembly.

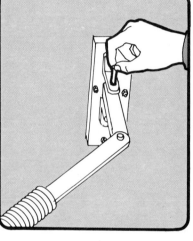

Close the door, then mount the opener arm parts to the track trolley and to the door bracket. Make electrical connections last.

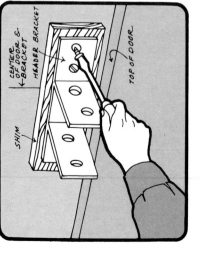

Locate the vertical center of the door, then fasten the header bracket about 2 inches above the high-arc point of the door.

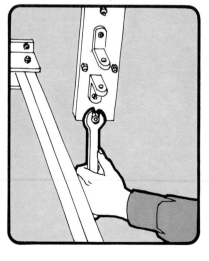

Mount the door bracket as shown, making sure the opener arm will pull straight up when connected to it. Otherwise, it may bind.

206

MAKING GARAGE IMPROVEMENTS

# CREATING
# STORAGE SPACE

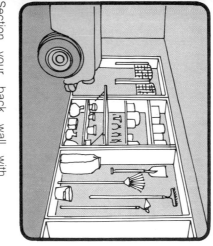

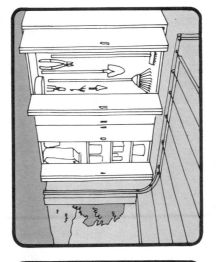

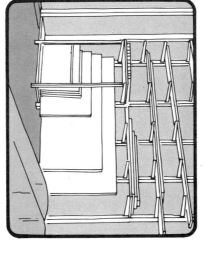

This page is dedicated to those people who, once or twice a year, decide it's high time they clean up that garage "once and for all."

Most garages have far more storage potential than we give them credit for. Here, the name of the game is to get everything up off the floor, making way for the more important things such as the family car(s). Obviously, you can't hang your lawnmower or motorcycle up on the wall, but you can lift most everything else out of the way.

The sidewalls of your garage are a natural for storing a multitude of items. So is the back wall. Hang garden tools and other smaller items from nails fastened to the studs or top plate. Or

devise a series of twixt-stud or surface-mounted shelves. See page 86 for a look at your shelf hardware options.

For larger items, consider making or buying cabinets, which can be as simple as a plywood box with a door on the front or as fancy as used kitchen cabinets. And don't forget overhead storage, either. Often, simply adding more crossties and nailing up plywood opens an entire level of new space. This area works well for seasonal gear.

Study the storage ideas below, do a little designing on your own, and maybe this time you *will* get your garage shipshape *once and for all.*

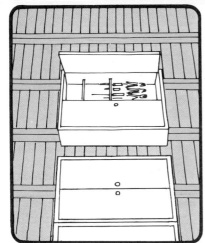

Section your back wall with plywood boxes fastened to the wall with metal angles. Fit shelves between the uprights.

Cabinets that lock are best for storing expensive tools, chemicals, paint, and other items that are attractive to children.

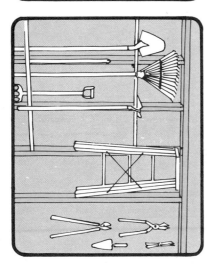

Build customized cabinets from plywood to utilize the space from the floor to the ceiling line. You can buy similar metal cabinets.

Inexpensive storage is easy to create with nails and scrap lumber. Just figure your needs, then divide up the space.

A storage setup like this keeps scrap lumber and sheet goods handy without taking up much space or looking cluttered.

**207**

MAKING GARAGE IMPROVEMENTS

# BUILDING A GARAGE

The next seven pages take you step by step through the construction of a typical garage—from the first rough sketches to the moment you pull the car inside and close the door.

Even if—like most of us—you never intend to take on a project of this magnitude, the drawings still deserve scrutiny. Why? Because the techniques they illustrate are part of a construction method known as *stud framing*, one of the two systems commonly used in all home structures...from a simple tool shed to your house itself.

Walls framed with studs distribute part of the roof's weight to each vertical member. Contrast this with the *post-and-beam* construction, which is shown and explained on page 215.

As with any structure, a garage has to begin with a careful site plan. Where, exactly, do you want your new garage and how big should it be? Let the drawing at right guide you in preparing a sketch,

then drive some stakes and stretch string between them for a life-size look at what you have in mind. At this point, pay special attention to the driveway basics illustrated on page 199.

Once you've formalized your design and made a to-scale drawing, you're ready to apply for a building permit. Officials will let you know if your plan violates any lot-line or other restrictions. The plan also will come in handy when you put together a building materials list. With it, you—or your suppliers—can accurately figure out the amounts of concrete, lumber, and other items you'll need.

Before you can get a garage off the ground, you need a slab and footings to set it on. If you decide to pour these yourself, too, reac pages 160–165 for information about working with concrete. The drawings below give some additional pointers. And building codes probably will dictate the required depth for footings.

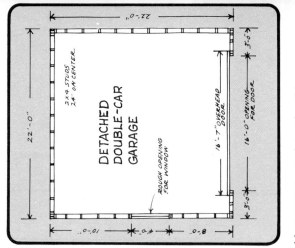

Most garages are based on this or a similar standard plan. Alter the dimensions to suit your individual needs.

## PLACING THE SLAB

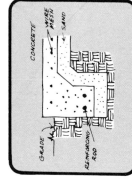

Install a floor drain before any concrete is placed. Stuff a rag into the intake so concrete and debris don't clog the pipe.

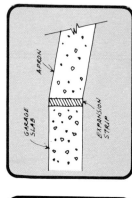

You might want to lay electrical conduit under the slab, too. Locate it in a corner. See pages 248-251 for outdoor wiring.

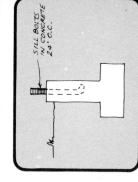

An integral slab and footing doesn't require extensive forming. Use reinforcing rod for the footings, and mesh for the slab.

A T-footing and slab needs forms. Footings must be below the frost line. Lay a polyethylene moisture barrier under the slab.

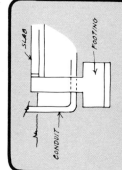

Expansion strips go between the garage slab and the driveway's apron, as well as between T-footings and the slab.

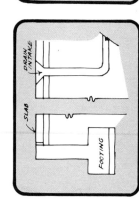

If you're using sill bolts, place them while the concrete is wet. Make sure they will accommodate the plate, a washer, and nut.

**208**

Framing the walls of your garage differs little from building a partition wall (see pages 48 and 49)—there's just more of them. Since you've got a ready-made flat surface in your concrete slab, preassemble the sections, then enlist a helper or two to help you set them up, as shown on page 210. Prefabricating spares you a lot of toenailing and ladder work.

Start by marking the location of each stud on the sill and top plates (usually 24 inches on center, though local codes may specify 16-inch centers). Then mark the sill-bolt locations on the sills by positioning the sills over the bolts and tapping the sills with a hammer to leave marks for drilling guides.

Drill the holes in the sill plate, then lay the top and sill plates on edge the appropriate distance apart and fill in between with studs. Create any window and door openings as you come to them. Secure the studs to the plates with two nails each at top and bottom.

For additional strength, double the headers and jamb studs at all windows and doors. For the garage door, figure on double or triple jamb studs and double headers—usually 2x6s or 2x8s or larger. Don't install windows or doors until the framing is complete.

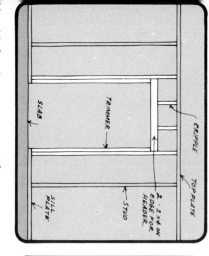

Drive nails flush with the faces of the top and sill plates; you needn't countersink them. Use two nails per stud at each joint.

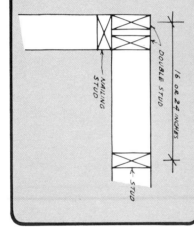

Make rough openings the size specified for the size window or door you've purchased. This information comes with the window.

This positioning of studs around the window opening provides maximum strength. Be sure sills and headers are level.

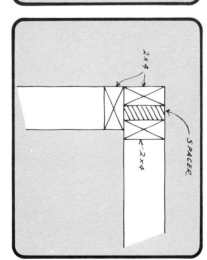

Use this framing arrangement for door openings. For side doors, use 2x4 headers; garage doors need 2x6s, 2x8s, or larger.

At corners, you have a couple of options. If you're not going to drywall the garage, just double the studs.

If you do plan to finish the walls, use the configuration shown here. It provides a surface for nailing on the drywall.

# ERECTING THE WALL SECTIONS

Raising the garage wall sections requires more care than skill. The reason: although the wall is tightly fastened together, its length will tend to produce a "twist" as you lift it. So have your helpers raise the wall at the same time, at the same speed, and from the same direction.

When the wall is up and on the sill bolts, fasten the sill plate to the sill bolts with wide, flat washers and nuts. Don't fully tighten them; just snug the nuts against the washers.

To adjust for level, force shims where needed under the sill plate. If the section isn't plumb, nudge it one way or the other. When the section is true, brace it at each end and in the center with 2x4

outrigger stakes tacked to one of the studs (see the illustration below) and tighten the nuts. Use the same procedures for remaining walls.

After positioning adjacent walls, join them by driving a series of 16-penny common nails.

With all of the wall sections in place, it's time to install the garage door header. Nail support studs at either side of the opening, then lift the header into position. Toenail it in place. Once the header is secured, add a second top plate to the walls. Make sure that all joints overlap. Also nail crossties to the top plates. Lend more support by nailing a 1x4 brace diagonally from the top plate to the sill plate as shown below.

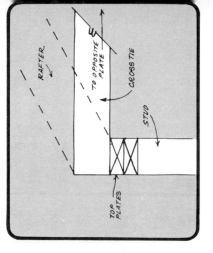

Cut trimmer studs to the appropriate length, then nail them to either side of the door opening. Secure them well.

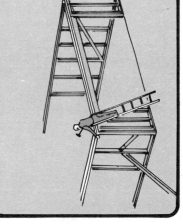

When the wall is level, tighten the sill bolts. Apply as much pressure as you can to prevent the plate from shifting later.

Level the wall with cedar shims positioned as needed. Then nudge the wall into plumb and nail outrigger stakes for support.

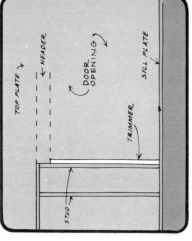

To further strengthen the structure, nail crossties to the top plates. One every 24 inches is ideal, but you can use fewer.

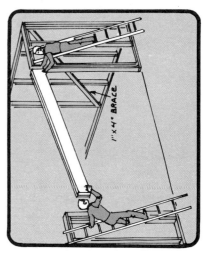

With the header in position, nail a second top plate all around the garage. Be sure to stagger the joints.

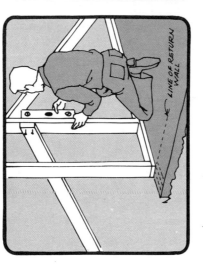

Set the garage door header on the trimmer studs. Check the header for evel, then toenail it to the studs and trimmers.

Cutting rafters accurately is a skill that takes even professional carpenters years to master. So if your budget will stand it, buy prefabricated trusses for the roof framing. Not only will they save you hours of measuring, marking, and cutting, but they're stronger than ordinary framing.

To buy roof trusses, you need only furnish the dealer with the measurement of the garage or structure—width and length. The two of you can then determine the design and roof pitch from these two measurements. The trusses will be delivered to the job site.

If you're a fairly accomplished carpenter and want to build your own roof framing, here's how to do it.

First decide on the roof pitch you want. A standard pitch is 4:12—4 feet of rise in 12 feet of run (see below). Codes may be restrictive as to the pitch, so check with the building officials in your community to make sure you don't violate any rules.

Then find the center of the width of the garage and mark this point. Triple-check the measurements. Next cut a length of 2x6 that spans the distance from the top of the top plate to where the bottom of the ridge board will be.

Nail the 2x6 to the front wall's top plate, plumbing the 2x6 as you fasten it. Do the same with another length of 2x6 at the back of the garage. Then, with a helper, position the ridge board atop the two 2x6s, level, and temporarily nail it.

With another 2x6, span the distance from the ridge board to the sidewall top plate. Include the roof overhang in this length. Mark the angle of the 2x6 where it joins the ridge board and where it meets the sidewall top plates. You now have established the pitch of the roof.

Cut all of the rafters, using the first as a pattern, then nail them to the ridge board. Work from the ends to the center.

When all of the rafters have been nailed to the ridge board and the top plates, and the gable ends have been filled in, remove the vertical members.

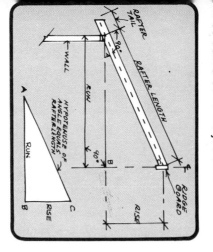

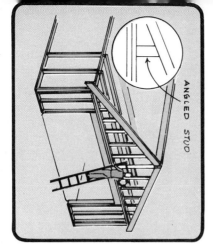

Cut gable studs at an angle and nail them flat to the rafters and top plates. Space them 16 inches on center.

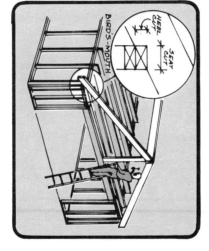

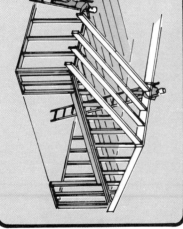

To figure the rafter length, square the rise and run in feet, then find the square root of the sum of these two figures.

Notch the rafters so they'll rest squarely on the top plates. For accuracy, use a framing square to mark the cuts.

Secure the rafters to the ridge board and the top plates with 16-penny common nails. Drive several at each joint.

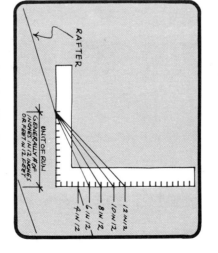

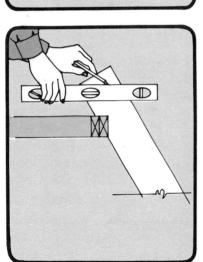

To check roof pitch with a framing square, lay it against the rafter as shown. Read the vertical scale for the exact pitch.

Cut the rafter tails after all of the rafters are in position. Use a level to plumb a cutoff line. Nail fascia to rafter ends.

## APPLYING THE SKIN

Closing in the garage won't cause you nearly as much grief as framing it. And chances are, you'll make faster progress because you'll probably use sheet material.

First, sheath the walls with board sheathing, plywood, or insulation board sheathing, which as the name implies, helps moderate the climate inside the garage. (Note: Because sheathing gives extra strength to the structure, you should especially use it if you'll be applying lap siding. With panel siding, the strength factor isn't as important. Some codes require sheathing, no matter what siding you use.)

Then, nail on the roof sheathing. Here, plywood works best because it covers a

lot of area fast. Be sure to buy sheets designed for exterior use, and specify that you want C/D grade.

After doing this, install the windows and doors—but not the garage door. Providing your rough openings are the right size, these should slip in easily. Nail through the outside trim into the jamb studs as shown below. (More about installing windows on pages 149-151.)

If you're applying wood panel siding, do it first, then install the doors and windows. Apply lap siding after the windows and doors have been installed.

Stagger the roof sheathing across the rafters, working from the bottom up to the ridge board. Be safe: wear rubber-soled shoes.

Wall sheathing may be applied horizontally or vertically. If you're dealing with board sheathing, apply it diagonally on the studs.

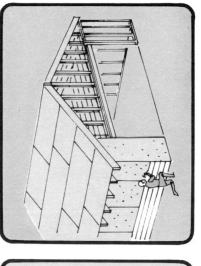

For lap siding, install sheet sheathing vertically. This gives you a stronger sidewall unit. Work from one corner to the other.

Nail lap siding to the sheathing and studs from the bottom up. Stagger the joints and work from openings outward.

After leveling them, nail windows and doors to the top and side jambs from the outside. No other nailing is required.

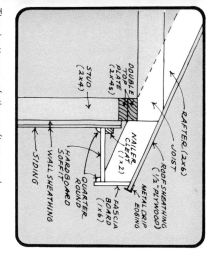

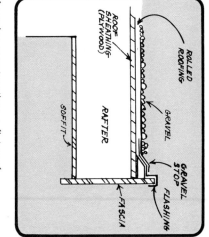

# FINISHING THE SHELL

Once all of the sheathing, windows, side doors, and siding are in place, your next task is to finish off the rafter tails. This is necessary in order to give your garage a finished look.

If you decide on open soffits, simply nail a fascia board to the plumbed rafter ends. Boxed soffits will take longer to build, but they yield a more finished look. For pitched roofs, boxing involves attaching soffit material (usually plywood or hardboard) to the underside of the rafters and to a cleat nailed to the siding, then facing the rafter tails with a fascia board. See the first two close-up

sketches below for specific details showing both pitched and flat roofs.

Now it's time to start shingling the roof. Pages 124 and 125 will tell you exactly what's involved in this operation. Allow several days for applying shingles, and try to get as much work done as possible during the cooler morning hours. Hot afternoons are no time to be working up on a roof. Not only are the temperatures insufferable, but you also risk loosening the shingles as you walk on them. The same goes for really cold weather, when shingles become brittle.

Caulking comes next. Be sure to seal all openings around windows, doors, and wherever gaps exist between materials. See pages 131 and 132 for information

about how to choose the right caulk and how to apply it correctly.

After this is done, give your garage a couple of coats of paint or stain. Exterior painting is covered in detail on pages 510-521, so read all of the information presented there before you begin applying the paint to the garage.

Actually, gutters and downspouts can be installed before or after painting. Prefinished components, of course, go up after you finish painting or staining. For more about gutter and downspout installation, turn to page 123.

---

The bottoms of the rafters and nailer cleats are level with each other. Trim the soffit with each board and quarter round.

If you're constructing a flat roof, just nail the fascia and soffit boards directly to the rafters as shown.

Shingle up from the eave to the ridge after laying down strips of asphalt-saturated building felt. Finish with ridge shingles.

---

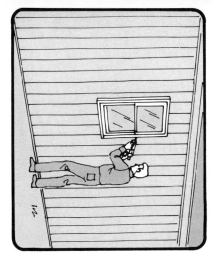

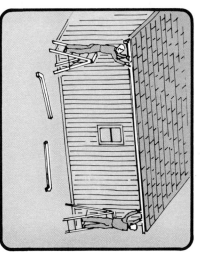

Caulking around all openings seals out the weather and protects raw edges of materials from troublesome moisture.

Apply a couple coats of paint or stain to all exterior surfaces. This coating beautifies as well as protects the materials.

Installing gutters and downspouts keeps water where it belongs—away from your garage's walls and footings.

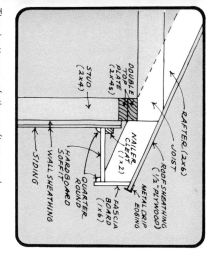

213

# INSTALLING THE DOOR

The cost of having a garage door professionally installed is fairly reasonable, yet you still can save quite a few dollars by doing it yourself. And since most garage doors are sold with complete assembly instructions, very little can go wrong. Note: Don't attempt to install a door that has a torsion-spring system, as adjusting the springs can be hazardous. Rather, stay with a tension-spring-and-pulley unit.

Before installing the door itself, first install any crossties or collar beams necessary to support the tracks (if your door requires them) or an automatic garage door opener.

The only trick to installing an overhead door is the proper installation of the tracks. If not perfectly parallel to each other, they'll cause the door to bind. To make sure that they're in alignment, measure the distance between them at several points and adjust as necessary.

Using lag screws, attach the tracks to the door jamb studs and to the collar beams or crossties. Usually, the tracks hang from a bracket that attaches to either of the above, or to the ceiling joists if your garage ceiling is finished off. Once you're satisfied with the position of the tracks, install the door, following the directions specified by the manufacturer.

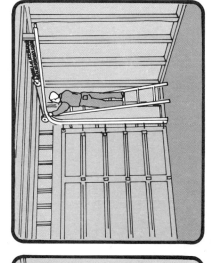

Attach the overhead track to the crossties. Then install the spring and pulley assemblies as directed in the instructions.

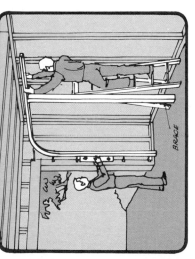

Plumb the tracks with a level. Also measure the distance between tracks at several points to keep them parallel.

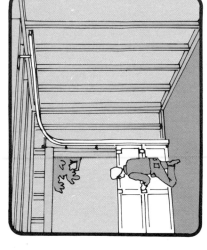

Slots in the brackets allow for adjusting the track. Do this after the entire door unit is assembled and in place.

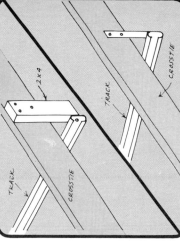

Measure the width of the opening, then make a mark to indicate the center of the door. Use this in locating the track hardware.

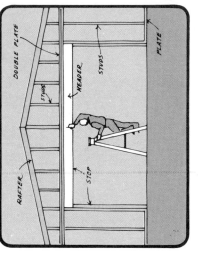

Assemble sectional doors one panel at a time in the tracks. Snug up the hardware, check for fit, then tighten it.

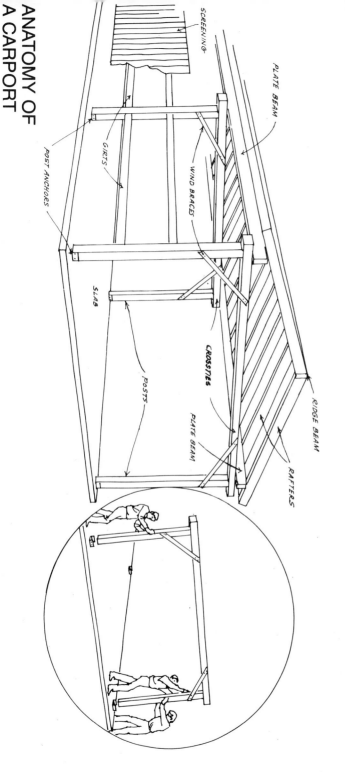

## ANATOMY OF A CARPORT

SCREENING
PLATE BEAM
GIRTS
WIND BRACES
POST ANCHORS
SLAB
CROSSTIES
POSTS
PLATE BEAM
RAFTERS
RIDGE BEAM

Though carports seemingly amount to little more than open-air garages, they're constructed in an entirely different way. Instead of framing out dozens of 2x4 studs and tying them all together with sheathing, as shown on the preceding pages, you erect just a few heftier posts and beams, then fill in the open spaces as you wish.

Post-and-beam construction—one of the earliest building techniques—still makes sense for any number of outdoor structures. Though the heavy timbers you'll need cost more than ordinary 2x4s, you'll probably save on materials in the long run—and you'll certainly get the framework up a lot faster.

What's more, whether you're planning a carport, deck, playhouse—or even a contemporary open-plan home—posts and beams offer design flexibility you just can't get with stud framing.

To familiarize yourself with the main elements of post-and-beam construction, consult the carport anatomy below. Like a garage, this one starts with a slab, to which *post anchors* have been attached. The *posts*—normally 4x4s or 4x6s—are tied together with *crossties* running the carport's width, and *plate beams* along its length. The beams can be four-inch material, or they can be assembled by nailing together two thicknesses of two-inch lumber.

Up top, you could build a roof like the one shown on page 211, add the *ridge beam* shown here, cantilever out from the ends or sides, or create almost any other profile your mind can envision.

The same goes down below. Here, *girts* serve as nothing more than nailers to which you can attach lightweight wood, plywood, or even fiber glass *screening.* Omitting the girts makes the structure only marginally weaker.

That's because the critical stresses in this type of construction happen where the posts join the beams. Here you might choose to use *wind braces* such as those illustrated below, or any of several different metal devices designed especially for the purpose.

Building with posts and beams calls for only simple carpentry, but careful engineering. As with any construction, you have to get everything plumb, level, and square. Instead of using nails, though, you usually secure all major joints with lag screws or bolts.

Post-and-beam work lends itself even more readily to prefabrication than stud framing does. On the ground, you lay out and assemble a series of *bents*, then lift them into position (see detail) and tie it all together with the plate beams. Build the bents and precut the beams ahead of time, invite some friends for a carport-raising, and you could get one like this under-roof in a single day.

## CHOOSING A CARPORT DESIGN

For a carport to be visually successful, it must complement the architecture of your home. You've probably seen carports that look tacked on—evidence that their owners neglected this very basic principle.

One of the best ways to select a design that will work is to drive around town looking for carports next to houses similar to yours. If you locate one you like, stop and chat with the owners.

Look, too, through current home service magazines, and visit home center planning stores. You may be able to adapt a design you find there, or one of those shown below.

If you simply can't find a design that appeals to you, consider retaining the services of a local residential architect. His fee for producing a design shouldn't be prohibitive.

In basic carport planning, keep the roo[f] line simple. It should match the roof of your home—or at least complement it in terms of its pitch and covering material. The same applies to the siding material. It should blend with the siding on your home—or complement it.

Chances are, you'll have to submit a rough drawing to building officials in you[r] community before they'll issue you a permit to erect a carport. Before you go t[o] obtain the permit, call to ask what you'll need to bring with you.

# SIZING POSTS AND BEAMS

Single-bay carports typically measure 11 feet wide and 21 feet deep; two-car versions run 18 to 20 feet wide; for each additional bay, add another eight or nine feet. These dimensions don't, of course, account for any storage units you might want to include.

To get an idea of how big posts and beams must be for a particular design, plot out all components, then check the chart at right. It's based on a roof load of 50 pounds per square foot—a typical code requirement—and a height of 10 feet or less.

Note, too, that lumber varies in strength according to its species. The chart presupposes that you'll be using "group 1" softwoods. For other groups, or for steel posts, consult your supplier before placing an order.

| If the Crosstie Span Is: | The Spacing Between Posts Is: | You'll Need Plate Beams That Are: | Posts and Crossties That Are: |
|---|---|---|---|
| 8 feet | 7 feet<br>11 feet | 4x8<br>4x10 | 4x4<br>4x4 |
| 9 feet | 6 feet<br>9 feet<br>10 feet | 4x8<br>4x10<br>4x12 | 4x4<br>4x4<br>4x4 |
| 10 feet | 8 feet<br>10 feet<br>13 feet | 4x10<br>4x12<br>6x10 | 4x4<br>4x4<br>4x6 |
| 11 feet | 6 feet<br>9 feet<br>10 feet<br>13 feet | 4x10<br>4x12<br>6x10<br>6x12 | 4x4<br>4x4<br>4x6<br>4x6 |
| 12 feet | 5 feet<br>8 feet<br>9 feet<br>12 feet | 4x10<br>4x12<br>6x10<br>6x12 | 4x4<br>4x4<br>4x6<br>4x6 |

# MAKING YOUR GARAGE A SAFE, SECURE PLACE

Potentially, a garage is a dangerous place. If this has never occurred to you before, just journey out into yours and take a quick look around. You'll probably find at least a few stray garden tools thrown in a corner; garden chemicals, paint, and gasoline within the reach of little hands; and a host of other hazardous items situated about. If you find that your garage fits this description, you'd best take some immediate action.

It's especially important that you gather up all toxic items and get them up off the floor—preferably into a locked storage cabinet. By doing this, you can rest easier knowing that children and pets won't accidentally sample any of the contents and become ill. For more about creating storage space in your garage, see page 207.

After putting things in their place, clean up any oil or grease spills on the floor. Both are real mishap makers, so get them up right away. See page 154 for remedies for these stains.

But getting organized and "spotless" is only half the battle. You should also prepare yourself for any emergencies that may arise. One of your best defensive weapons is a fire extinguisher, preferably one that will put out all three types of fires—combustible solids, flammable liquids, and electrical fires. Also have handy access to a first-aid kit, and make sure all family members know where both of these items are.

Personal and family protection against fire and accidents is one thing; protection from intruders is quite another. Your garage houses many items of value—and professional and amateur thieves alike know that. So it's up to you to dissuade them from coming around, and foil their attempts if they do. The security chapter of this book, which begins on page 382, discusses some of the measures you can take to protect yourself and your family.

If your garage doubles as the home workshop, be especially security conscious. Burglars delight in hitting workshops because tools sell like hotcakes "on the street." Keep under lock and key all portable power equipment and as many of your hand tools as possible. Your only defense for stationary power equipment is to keep the garage locked.

# YOUR HOME'S SYSTEMS

Energy! You can't really see it, but energy courses through your home in a variety of ways. It pushes electrons along wires, pumps water through pipes, adds heat in the winter, and subtracts it in the summer. Unbridled energy—such as fire and human violence—poses an awesome threat to life as well as property.

With energy so much on everyones' minds these days, we've devoted this entire section to the household systems designed to carry (and in some cases to retard) its flow. Even if you don't know an amp from a BTU, or a rim lock from a dead bolt, the chapters in "Your Home's Systems" will aid in your understanding of basic principles, guide you through the upkeep and fix-it jobs you can safely do yourself, and help you reduce your home's energy needs.

# ELECTRICITY

To most people, a household electrical system seems mysterious and even dangerous. Actually, its principles rest on elementary logic. Master them, observe a few precautions that will soon become second nature, and you can safely pull off a wide variety of electrical repair and improvement jobs.

## GETTING TO KNOW YOUR SYSTEM

Let's take a quick look at the overall system that keeps you comfortably supplied with electricity. Power from the utility comes in through a *service entrance*—either in overhead or underground wires—to a *meter* that keeps track of your household's consumption. Then the power continues

on to a *service panel* that breaks it down into a series of *circuits*. These circuits deliver current throughout the house. *Fuses* or *circuit breakers* at the service panel control individual circuits and protect against fire, which could develop if a circuit draws more current than it's designed to handle.

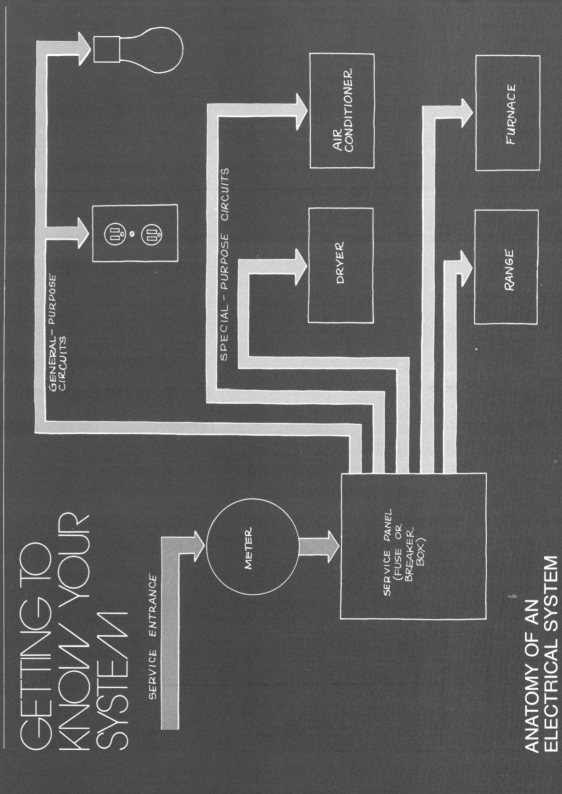

GENERAL-PURPOSE CIRCUITS

SPECIAL-PURPOSE CIRCUITS

AIR CONDITIONER

FURNACE

DRYER

RANGE

SERVICE PANEL (FUSE OR BREAKER BOX)

METER

SERVICE ENTRANCE

ANATOMY OF AN ELECTRICAL SYSTEM

## UNDERSTANDING ELECTRICAL TERMINOLOGY

Electrical *current* flows—under *pressure*—through the wiring in your house. That flow would come to an absolute halt if you were to disconnect every single appliance, light, and other device you have. But as soon as you start up one "customer," the flow in that particular circuit begins.

The amount of current (measured in *amps*) going through a wire at a given time is based on the number of electrons passing a certain point each second. The *pressure* that forces these electrons

along their route is known as *voltage* (measured in *volts*).

If you were to increase the voltage, you would not accelerate the flow of current; the electrons travel at a constant speed—the speed of light. But you would increase the *power* in your lines; that power is measured in *watts* and is the product you get when you multiply amps times volts. Your utility bills, incidentally, are based on the number of watts—in thousands—you consume each hour. The common term is *kilowatt-hour.*

When current flows to a plug outlet, for example, the electrons travel inside what's called a *hot wire*, which is black (or, in rare cases, a white wire with black paint or tape to indicate that it's

functioning as a hot wire). After current has flowed through a light or appliance, the electrons seek a direct route to *ground* (see page 225) and travel in white *neutral* wires to get there. These neutrals, also known as *system grounds*, complete every circuit in the system by returning its current to the ground.

Modern circuits have three wires, the third being a bare or green one that serves as an *equipment ground*. Its role is to ground all metal parts throughout your installation, such as conduit, armored cable, motors, and major appliances. This grounding wire protects against the danger of short circuits.

## COMPLYING WITH CODES AND INSPECTIONS

The National Electrical Code, published every three years by the National Fire Protection Association, is the most complete, detailed set of guidelines you're apt to find anywhere. So, if you're planning any major wiring job, get hold of a copy; the book is full of helpful tips. But despite the Code's strong influence nationally, the last word on what you can and can't do electrically comes from your local building code. Its provisions are

law and take precedence over anything you'll see in the national code.

A few localities won't even allow do-it-yourselfers to work on their own wiring; others make you get a temporary permit first. Some areas permit homeowners to undertake all but the final connection at the service entrance panel, so be sure to check with the building department in your community to find out what's in store for you. And, of course, expect to arrange to have your work inspected at the end of the project.

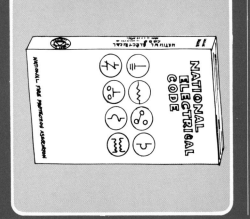

## HOW TO READ YOUR METER

Though you'll occasionally see a meter that looks like a car odometer, most types have a series of four or five dials. The leftmost dial indicates tens of thousands of kilowatt-hours; the next one to the right, thousands; and so on.

Read the leftmost dial first, then proceed to the right. When a pointer is between two digits, always read the lower number. If the pointer is right on a number, read the next lower number only if the dial to the right has not yet passed the zero mark.

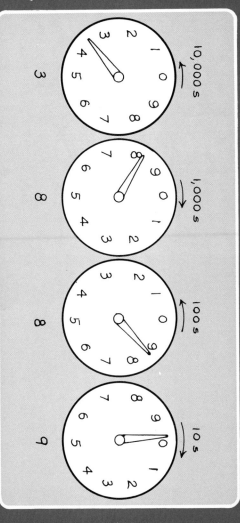

# CHECKING OUT YOUR SERVICE PANEL

## Circuit Breaker Panels

Most electrical projects begin at the service panel—also called a *breaker box* or *fuse box*. It's the heart of your system and home base for protective devices that automatically disconnect power to the entire house or to individual branch circuits in case of overloads or shorts. The panel also is the place you go to shut off the current manually when you want to work or a circuit or two.

In most newer installations, the safety devices protecting you are called *circuit breakers*. The typical service box (at right) will have one main cutoff breaker and several smaller breakers, each controlling its own branch circuit. After you find and correct the problem, reset the breaker by flipping the toggle switch to its *on* position.

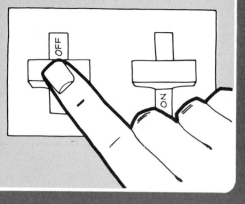

Unlike the switch-type breakers, this style has a button that you push in to turn off power, push in again to restore it.

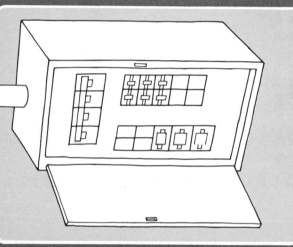

## Fuse Boxes

If you have an older home in which the original wiring is intact, chances are your service panel contains fuses rather than breakers. And instead of "tripping," which is what breakers do when problems occur, fuses "blow." Whenever the current builds up beyond the level intended for a particular circuit and its fuse, the thin strip of metal that carries the current through the fuse simply melts in a flash. As soon as this happens, the circuit is open, and current flow comes to a screeching halt.

Usually, you'll find a main pullout block with two cartridge-type fuses (see next page) mounted on its backside. Just grab the handle, pull out the block, and you'll shut off the entire house. (Some older boxes have a shutoff lever.) Most smaller branch circuits are protected by another kind of fuse—usually a screw-in plug fuse rated at 15 or 20 amps.

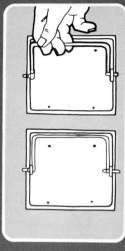

A plug fuse, threaded like a light bulb, screws into the fuse box. Handle only the rim when replacing this type of fuse.

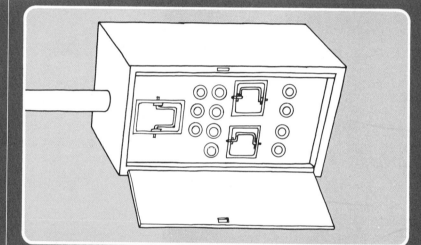

Larger 240-volt circuits for water heaters and the like generally are protected by small pullout blocks with cartridge fuses.

With the most common variety, the *plug fuse*, a metal strip melts and breaks the circuit in case of shorts or overloads.

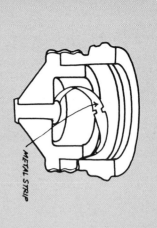

METAL STRIP

Use *time-delay* fuses for circuits that overload for just a few seconds. The *fuse* blows only for shorts or continuous overloads.

RELAY WIRE

The bases of *Type-S* fuses are sized by amp rating. Adapters installed permanently in the box accept only matching fuse bases.

HALF STAYS IN BOX

FUSE BASE

ADAPTER

For circuits larger than 30 amps, use one of two types of cartridge fuses. The *ferrule-contact* style comes in sizes through 60 amps.

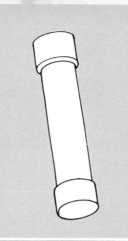

*Knife-blade-contact* fuses are rated higher than 60 amps. Both types of cartridge fuses can have time-delay features.

Use a plastic *fuse puller* to remove a cartridge fuse from an auxiliary fuse box or from the back of a pullout block.

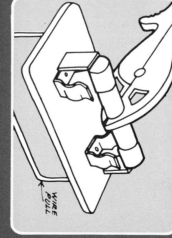

WIRE PULL

## HOW TO "READ" A BLOWN FUSE

Diagnosing the cause of a blown fuse is easy, mainly because the culprit usually leaves a telltale sign behind. An ordinary plug fuse will have a blackened window if a short has occurred. And in case of an overload, the metal strip will separate (see drawings at right). Time-delay fuses react the same way to shorts as do plug fuses. But if an overload hits a time-delay model, solder in the bottom of the fuse loosens and releases a metal strip that is pulled upward by a coiled wire.

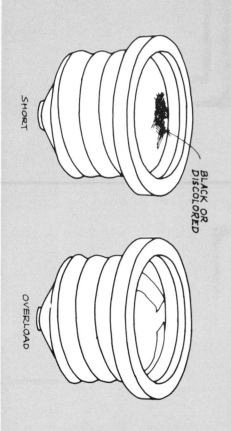

SHORT

BLACK OR DISCOLORED

OVERLOAD

# SOLVING ELECTRICAL PROBLEMS

## HOW'S YOUR HOUSE POWER?

Has your electrical system kept up with the demands placed on it by all the new work-savers you've accumulated recently? Chances are, it hasn't. A 100-amp service used to be more than enough for most homes. But today, you're likely to need 150 or 200 amps.

If a constant harassment of overloads keeps you busy changing fuses (or resetting breakers) and juggling appliances from one plug outlet to another, you already know you have a problem. Here's a scientific way to track it down.

Because circuits are rated at the service panel in terms of amps, you'll have to do some elementary arithmetic to get an amp rating for every electrical "customer" in your house. But before you start calculating, you'll need to take a

complete survey of your house, listing every electrical appliance and device *by circuit*. (When you're through, post a duplicate of that rundown next to—or inside the door of—your service panel. It can tell you at a glance which fuse to pull or breaker to flip when you want to work on a specific outlet or switch.)

Now, using the formula amps = watts ÷ volts, you can figure the amperage requirements of each electrical device on each circuit. Most of your circuits are 120 volts, and you should be able to find either a wattage figure or amperage figure for every bulb, appliance, and other electrical item you have. If you're lucky enough to find an amp figure, you're already there. And if you come up with a wattage figure, just divide it by 120 to determine the amperage.

The last step, of course, is to add up all of the amperage figures for each circuit and compare that total with the amperage capacity appearing on the

appropriate breaker or fuse. Now you'll know for sure if that circuit would face an overload if *every* customer tied into it called for current at the same time.

If your survey turns up some nerve-jangling match-ups, you should add circuits, shuffle outlets from one circuit to another, or do a little of both.

As you can see from the sketch below, so-called general-purpose circuits need 15-amp breakers or fuses, whereas the special-purpose circuits serving large appliances require greater capacities. In addition to the circuits depicted below, you should have at least two 20-amp small-appliance circuits in the kitchen. Also supply your workshop with its own—or a lightly used—20-amp circuit.

Individual 240-volt circuits are in order for central air conditioners, electric ranges, electric dryers, electric water heaters, electric furnaces, and heat pumps.

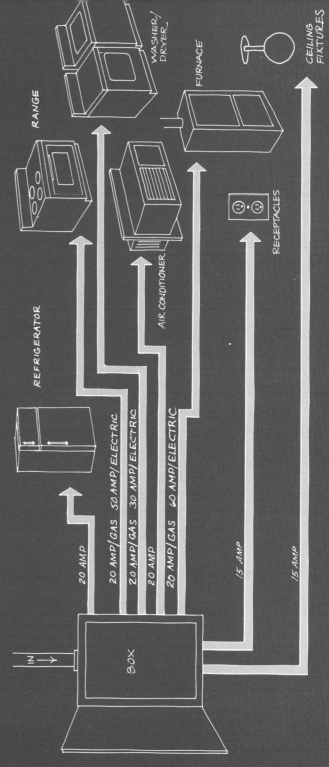

RANGE

WASHER/DRYER

FURNACE

CEILING FIXTURES

REFRIGERATOR

AIR CONDITIONER

RECEPTACLES

20 AMP

20 AMP/GAS 50 AMP/ELECTRIC

20 AMP/GAS 30 AMP/ELECTRIC

20 AMP

20 AMP/GAS 60 AMP/ELECTRIC

15 AMP

15 AMP

IN →

BOX

# IS YOUR ENTIRE INSTALLATION GROUNDED?

If you've ever stood on a wet basement floor and been jolted with a good, strong electrical shock, you've participated in a live demonstration of how electrical current seeks the shortest route to the ground. That time, it used you as its conductor; wire is a much more comfortable vehicle. When a short crops up in your wiring or in a device connected to it, your best protection is a properly grounded circuit.

There are several bits of background information you should know in order to minimize the chance of shock and electrical fire, and even damage from lightning. First, let's distinguish between two different kinds of grounding. *System grounding* is the grounding of current-carrying wires. *Equipment grounding* is the grounding of non-current-carrying portions of your wiring installation, such as the frames of motors and appliances,

as well as smaller metal items such as conduit, armored (BX) cable, and boxes for fixtures, switches, and receptacles.

Proper grounding starts in the service panel at the *grounding bus bar*, which is connected—literally—to earth by a cable (known as the *ground wire*). This is fastened either to a metal rod driven into the earth outside your house or to your incoming water-supply pipe. The bus bar, in turn, has solderless connectors or screw terminals to which two other types of wires are connected—*grounded wires* and *grounding wires*.

*Grounded* wires are the white neutral wires that complete each of your circuits by returning current to its source, and in so doing, ground the system. (Also connected to the bus bar is the incoming neutral wire from the utility company.) *Grounding* wires—usually bare, green, or green with yellow stripes—are the ones that ground the *equipment*.

One example will explain why it's so important to have an equipment ground. If a short circuit should crop up inside a

motor, there's a chance the motor would still run and that the fuse or breaker wouldn't react. The frame of the motor could then become "live," and anyone touching the live frame could complete the circuit through his or her body into the ground. A properly installed grounding wire would have routed that errant current safely back through the bus bar and into the ground.

There are two basic ways to obtain a good equipment ground, depending on the type of wiring you have. For circuits with individual wires strung inside metal conduit or armored (BX) cable, the conduit or cable must be mechanically connected to each box and to the service panel. A tight connection ensures proper grounding. Where nonmetallic-sheathed cable is used, the cable must contain three wires—a hot, a neutral, and a bare grounding wire. The grounding wire must extend from the metal switch or outlet box to the bus bar. In many older homes, neither of these situations exists.

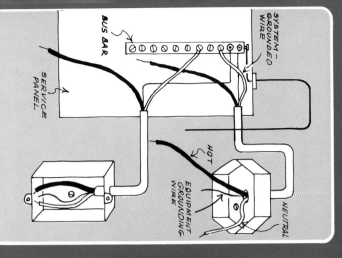

The bare equipment-grounding wires and the white system-grounding neutrals connect to terminals on the bus bar.

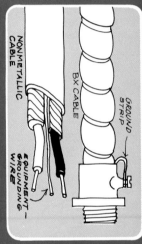

Shown here are two equipment grounds. The BX cable makes metal-to-metal contact; its ground strip adds extra insurance.

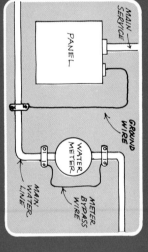

When using the water-supply pipe for a ground, add a bypass to keep the grounding complete in case the meter is removed.

A two-prong adapter is grounded only if the screw that holds the pigtail is in contact with a properly grounded outlet box.

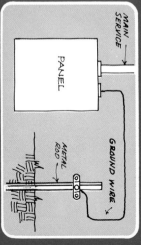

The alternative to using a water pipe as a ground is to attach the ground wire to a metal rod that's been driven into the earth.

## TOOLS FOR ELECTRICAL REPAIRS

You probably already have on hand a good number of the tools you'll need for electrical work—old standbys such as a hammer, drill, keyhole saw, chisel, screwdrivers, hacksaw, measuring tape, and the like. But there are a few special-purpose tools you'll want to buy, rent, or borrow before you take on an electrical project of any size. And if you decide to buy them, choose only quality tools. They'll work better and last much longer than their bargain-basket look-alikes.

The examples below represent the bulk of the tools you'll need to solve the electrical problems treated on the next four pages. To learn about a few more items necessary for bigger jobs, see page 236.

The *fish tape* can be bought with or without a reel. The two *testers* are musts and are described on the next page. Some electricians like to use the *combination tool* because it can both cut and strip wire and crimp special fasteners, whereas others prefer to stick

with the simpler *wire stripper.* You'll use the *side-cutting pliers* to snip wires in tough-to-reach places, and *lineman's pliers* have heavy square jaws that are ideal for twisting wires together. *Long-nose pliers* make quick work of curling loops on the ends of wires.

Also round up a sharp straight-bladed pocketknife or a *utility knife* to slit the sheathing lengthwise on nonmetallic cable. Use a *nut driver* to reach into places wrenches can't touch. And collect a good assortment of *wire nuts* in various sizes to help you make quick wire-to-wire connections.

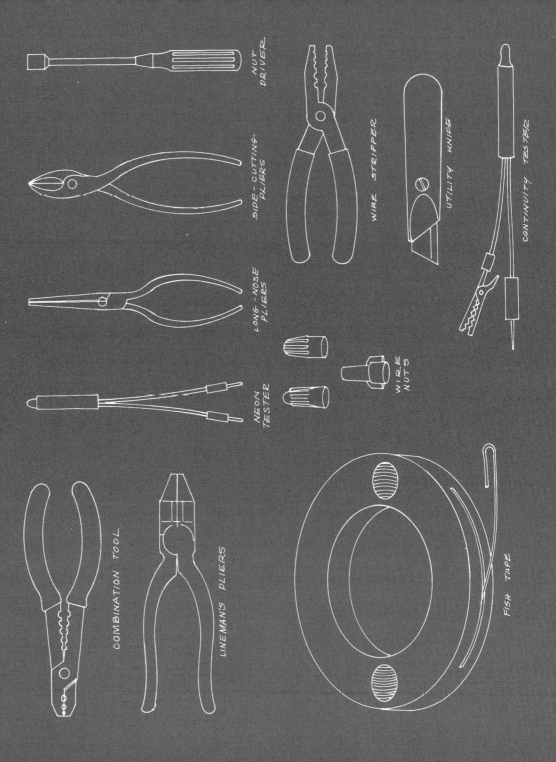

NUT DRIVER

SIDE-CUTTING PLIERS

LONG-NOSE PLIERS

NEON TESTER

COMBINATION TOOL

LINEMAN'S PLIERS

WIRE STRIPPER

UTILITY KNIFE

CONTINUITY TESTER

WIRE NUTS

FISH TAPE

There's a certain amount of detective work to be done when making electrical repairs (or improvements). That sleuthing is made much easier by the two testers shown here. You'll use the neon type mainly when the current is on, usually to find out if power is present at switches, lights, and receptacles.

Continuity testers, on the other hand, are used only with the power turned off. They have their own power source and are just the thing to test a switch, socket, cartridge fuse, etc.

If the neon tester lights up when touched to a receptacle box as shown, the plate screw is properly grounded.

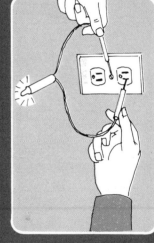

A lamp socket checks out OK if the continuity tester lights up when the alligator clip and probe are placed as shown.

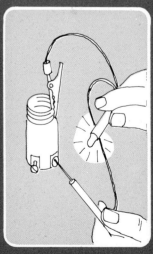

## MAKING CONNECTIONS

Whether you're joining wires to switches, receptacles, or in mid-circuit, for safety's sake make all connections inside a box. At switches and receptacles, you'll run into one of two types of terminals—screws and grip holes. The screw type is self-explanatory; you simply loosen the screw, strip and curl the end of the wire, and place the loop around the screw—clockwise. Then securely tighten the screw.

The devices that come with grip holes can be wired in a jiffy. After you've stripped the wire, just shove it into the appropriate slot where a locking piece will grab the wire tightly. If you ever want to remove the wire for any reason, press a small screwdriver against a release slot marked on the device, and the wire will slip out.

Solderless connectors (wire nuts) make a simple job of joining wires. See details below.

Remove the insulation—usually about ¾ inch—from each wire with a stripper. Wire size is indicated alongside each hole.

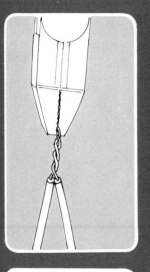

Use long-nose pliers to bend the end of the wire into a loop to curl around the shank of the terminal screw.

Be sure the screws are tight—but not too tight. An overzealous twist of the screwdriver can crack the plastic body.

Devices with grip holes have a strip gauge marked on them to show you exactly how much insulation to remove.

To ensure a solid connection when you use wire nuts, first strip the wires and twist them together with a lineman's pliers.

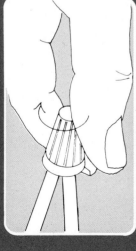

Shove the wire nut tightly against the wires as you turn it clockwise as far as it will go. Be sure no bare wire is exposed.

## TROUBLESHOOTING LAMPS

A table lamp is one of the simplest examples of electricity at work . . . and one of the easiest projects to troubleshoot. Whenever the bulb in one of your lamps won't light, the first thing to check is the bulb. If a new one won't work, the next place to look is the receptacle. The easiest way to find out if it's hot is to plug in another lamp. If it works, you've narrowed down the problem to one of three remaining areas—the plug, the cord, or the socket. Then check the table at right.

| Symptom | Cause | Cure |
|---|---|---|
| Won't light | Loose connection | Tighten connection |
|  | Broken wire | Replace cord |
| Blows fuse | Frayed cord | Tape or replace cord |
|  | Defective plug | Replace plug |
|  | Defective socket | Replace socket |
| Light flickers | Loose connection | Tighten connection |
|  | Defective switch | Replace switch |

## REPLACING A LAMP CORD

Cracked or worn lamp cords not only can cause a serious shock, they're also fire hazards. So why take a chance! Make the repair as soon as you spot trouble. And while you're at it, replace the old socket as well.

The easiest way to install the new cord is to tie a string between it and the old one so that new can follow old up through the lamp's base.

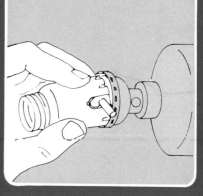

To expose the socket, push hard on the outer shell where it says "PRESS" and pull off the shell and insulating jacket.

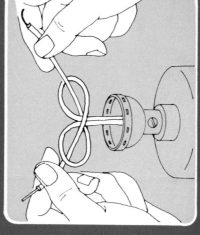

Loosen the terminal screws, remove the old cord (install the new one simultaneously), and tie an Underwriter's knot as shown.

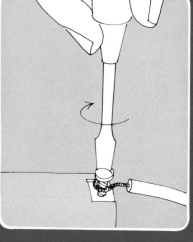

Twist the braided strands tightly, curl them as shown, and screw one wire to each terminal in a clockwise direction.

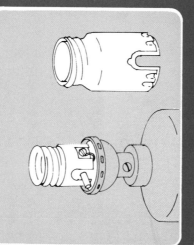

Gently pull the wire from below to draw the socket against its base, then replace the insulating and outer shells.

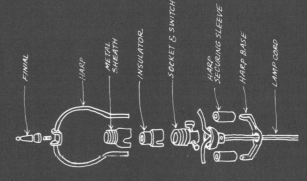

FINIAL
HARP
METAL SHEATH
INSULATOR
SOCKET & SWITCH
HARP SECURING SLEEVE
HARP BASE
LAMP CORD

228

# REPLACING PLUGS

If you find a plug with loose prongs, a cracked body, or a blackened spot (evidence of a short), replace it pronto—the expense is minimal, and the work is a breeze. Even if you don't see any obvious signs of problems, you might as well change the plug if you're replacing a worn cord—they're most likely of the same vintage.

You'll normally run into two types of plugs—some for round cords and others for flat cords. Vacuum cleaners, irons, and the like usually have a round-cord plug; flat-cord plugs come with lower-amperage appliances such as radios, clocks, and lamps. Be sure your replacement plug is the same basic type as the original.

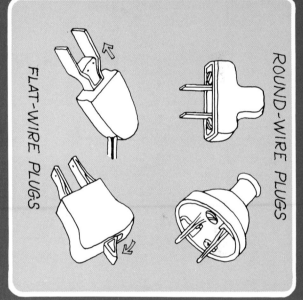

### ROUND-WIRE PLUGS

### FLAT-WIRE PLUGS

The two top plugs, designed for round wires, are hooked up as shown below. The other two accommodate a flat wire known as zip cord, the type widely used for lamp repairs. It consists of two conductors connected by a thin membrane that you can tear easily when you want to separate the wires.

To wire these plugs, insert the squared-off end of the zip cord into a slot and depress a lever (or push two parts together). Internal prongs penetrate the insulation and complete the circuit.

Remove the outer sheath, insert the cord, and tie the Underwriter's knot (see opposite). Then strip insulation from both wires.

Tightly twist the strands of each wire, loop each clockwise around a screw, then carefully tighten the screws. Tuck in stray strands.

With grounded plugs, insert the cord and tie together all three wires. Then pull the knot down snugly into the plug.

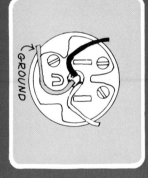

Strip insulation, twist strands to firm up wire, then loop and fasten under screws. Replace the protective insulating cover.

# CHOOSING EXTENSION CORDS

You can usually get by with a few 10-amp two-wire extension cords. But it's better to have at least one larger capacity cord—say, a 20-amp size—for hooking up appliances that draw more current than a radio or vacuum cleaner. For your workshop, you'll want a large-capacity three-wire cord—usually with No. 14 wire—to handle your power tools.

The longer the cord, the greater the chance of a current drop, so use the shortest cord possible. Check the table at right for buying guidelines.

| Use | Length | Size |
|-----|--------|------|
| Lamps, clocks, etc. to 7 amps | To 25 ft. | No. 18 |
| | To 50 ft. | No. 16 |
| | To 100 ft. | No. 14 |
| Small appliances, etc. to 10 amps | To 25 ft. | No. 16 |
| | To 50 ft. | No. 14 |
| | To 100 ft. | No. 12 |
| Large appliances, power tools | To 25 ft. | No. 14 |
| | To 50 ft. | No. 12 |
| | To 100 ft. | No. 10 |

Note: The larger the wire number, the smaller the wire's size.

229

## REPLACING RECEPTACLES

If a receptacle goes bad and you're elected to replace it, you won't need a cram course in wiring theory. The job's already done for you. All you need to do is wire the new outlet exactly as the old one was done. Note: in newer homes and

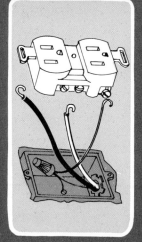

some older ones, there's often a (third) ground wire, which connects to the receptacle. This is an equipment ground wire. See page 225 for more information on grounding.

Before you start, remember to turn off the power at the main disconnect or circuit breaker. Then remove the faceplate.

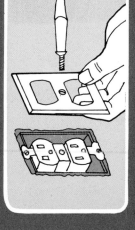

Before you disconnect anything, make a quick sketch to help you remember where each wire goes. Then remove the wires.

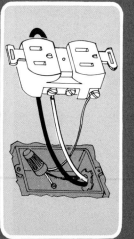

Remove the screws fastening the receptacle to the box at top and bottom, and pull the receptacle from the box.

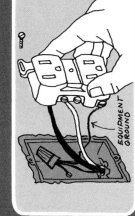

Hook up the new receptacle, using your sketch if needed. Test your handiwork by restoring power to the receptacle.

Working on a side-by-side installation is just as easy as a single receptacle. Just remember to sketch the wiring layout.

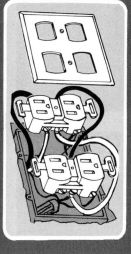

If you have small children, consider using child-proof safety receptacles. You have to twist a cover to expose the slots.

## REPLACING SWITCHES

Whether you're replacing a switch because it's bad or just because you want a different style, the job shouldn't

take longer than 15 minutes. And that includes a couple minutes to go to the service panel and cut the power to the circuit you're working on.

The common household switch is a *single-pole* variety that has two

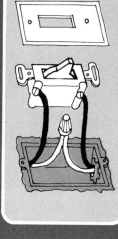

brass-colored terminals and—in some cases—a grounding terminal. (Some brands come with grip holes instead of screws.) A switch is wired only into the hot line, with the *source feed* usually connected to the top terminal.

In this exception to the color rules, the white wire in the cable is painted black to indicate that it's serving as a hot wire.

You won't always find the terminals on your new switch positioned the same as on the old one. Here they face the side.

The neutral wires in this circuit are independent of the switch and continue all the way back to the service panel.

**230**

## WIRE SIZES

Extending an existing circuit or adding a new one calls for more for careful thinking than for actual skill or hard work. Most components fasten together surprisingly easily, so your hardest task will be to become familiar with the vast array of electrical materials on the market. A good way to start is to visit a well-stocked electrical supply house and take a long, detailed look at the products on display. Try to figure out for yourself how one

component ties into another. If you're stumped, ask someone for help.

Then tour a home under construction that's still at the wiring stage. There—all exposed for you—is the whole story, from panel to light switch and all points in between. Take notes, make diagrams, pay attention to details, and digest what you see.

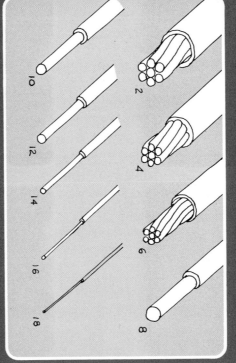

## WIRE COVERINGS

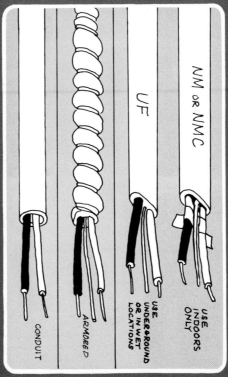

NM OR NMC

UF · USE UNDERGROUND OR IN WET LOCATIONS

USE INDOORS ONLY

CONDUIT

ARMORED

Though all of the wires above (about actual size) are used in homes, you're most likely to work with No. 14 and No. 12.

The smaller sizes (Nos. 16 and 18) are used mainly for doorbells and other installations involving small currents.

Nonmetallic sheathed cable is inexpensive and easy to work with. Use Type NM in dry places. NMC in wet areas. UF underground.

Steel armored cable is flexible and protects wiring from damage. Conduit, though rigid, can be bent with a special tool.

## RUNNING NEW WIRING

## HOW TO "READ" A CABLE

Codes specify the type and sizes of cable you may install. For indoor use, most permit Type NM, shown at right. Its outer sheath is usually a moisture-resistant, flame-retardant plastic that's soft and easy to strip away to get to the wires. You'll find two or three insulated conductors (wires) inside. If two, one will be black, the other white; if three, you'll see a red one in there, too. In addition to the insulated wires, you may find a bare one—the equipment ground.

The markings at right tell you that the cable contains two No. 14 insulated conductors and a grounding wire.

WIREMAKER TYPE NM 14/2 WITH GROUND 600 VOLTS (UL)

## WORKING WITH WIRE

Both nonmetallic sheathed cable and armored cable come with the wires already inside. And though the sheathed type is easier to work with, you may be required by local codes to use the armored variety.

Most often, either of these is concealed within walls where it runs little risk of being damaged. Run it vertically between the studs or horizontally through holes drilled in the studs. (Be sure the holes are at least 1½ inches from the front of the stud.)

When you buy armored cable, stock up on anti-short bushings; these prevent the cable's sharp edges from damaging the wires' insulation.

### Sheathed Cable

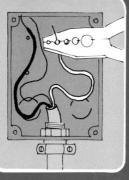

To tie sheathed cable into a box, first slip a box connector about seven inches onto the cable and tighten the screws.

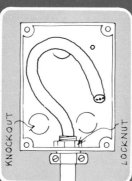

Remove a knockout from the side of the box and insert the threaded end of the connector. Then screw on the locknut.

After the cable is anchored to the box, slit and remove the outer sheath and cut away the spiraled layer of kraft paper.

Now use a wire stripper (match hole size to wire gauge) to remove about ¾ inch of insulation from both conductors.

### Armored (BX) Cable

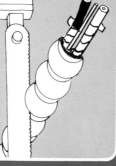

Partially cut armored cable—at an angle—with a hacksaw. Be careful not to nick the insulation on the wires.

Twist the cut end and pull it off. Unwind the kraft paper as far as you can, then give it a quick, hard jerk to tear it free.

Next, strip both wires back about ¾ inch. You'll find a wire stripper the best tool for this, but you also can use a knife.

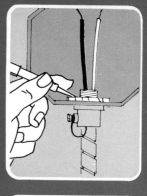

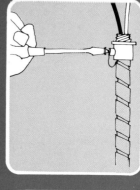

Remove a knockout, insert the connector, and screw on the locknut. Then pound a nail set against the lugs to tighten the nut.

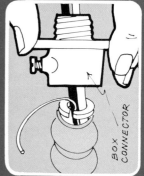

Wrap the ground strip around the screw on top of the connector and tighten the screw firmly with a screwdriver.

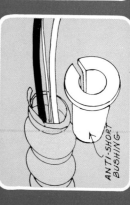

Fold back the ground strip, then shove a special box connector firmly onto the cable as far as it will go. Check for sharp edges.

Because the cut edges of the steel armor are rough, you're required to insert an anti-short bushing to protect the wires.

As mentioned earlier, unprotected electrical cable—unless it's tucked safely inside a wall, floor, or ceiling—is susceptible to damage. So whenever you're running wiring in an unfinished basement or garage, or for any special situation, protect yourself and your wiring with metal conduit.

Though there are four types of conduit available, you'll probably encounter only the *thin-wall* type (formerly called *electrical metallic tubing* in the Code). It's sold in 10-foot lengths that you can join end to end with fittings called

*couplings* and to boxes with *connectors*. Various types of these are shown below.

The trickiest part of working with conduit comes when you must bend it to get around corners or make the small offsets necessary at each box. To do this, you slip the conduit into a bender, as illustrated, then gently lever the bender toward you. Make a bend gradually, with a series of tugs along its radius. Pull too sharply at any one point and you'll crimp the tubing.

The importance of making smooth bends (and a minimum of them) becomes clear after you've installed a run of conduit and fitted boxes at either end. Now it's time to pull wires through the installation. Too many bends—and

any crimps at all—will hang up the wires, and you risk damaging their insulation when you pull.

Limit bends in any run between boxes to a total of 360 degrees. If an installation will traverse more than the equivalent of four quarter-bends, install an additional box.

Most codes specify that you use Type TW wires within conduit. Since each of these conductors is separately insulated, you'll need at least two (one black, one white) for each run. To pull the wires, first thread a fish tape through the tubing and attach the wires to it as shown below and on page 238. Never splice wires within conduit—a poorly made connection here could make the entire run "live."

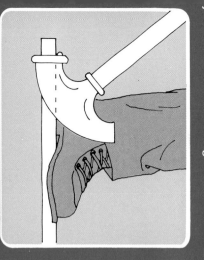

Bend conduit first, then cut it to length. You'll probably need to make a few practice bends before you master this knack.

Use a vise to hold the conduit while you cut it to size with a hacksaw. File off the burrs to prevent damaging the wiring.

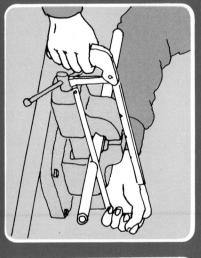

Shown are the three types of commonly used conduit couplings. The *indenter* version requires a special crimping tool.

Three main varieties of box connectors, which match the three couplings described above, secure the conduit safely in place.

Anchor ½-inch thin-wall conduit to the wall or ceiling with one- or two-hole clamps near boxes and at least every ten feet.

In short runs, you usually can push wires through conduit. On longer runs, pull the wires with a spring-steel fish tape.

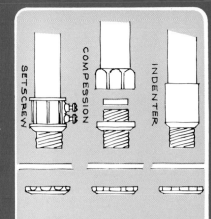

SET SCREW

COMPRESSION

INDENTER

CONDUIT

FISH TAPE

# USING SURFACE WIRING

## Metal Raceway

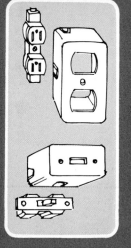

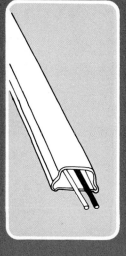

Surface metal raceways allow you an alternate method of adding circuits to your electrical system. Instead of tearing into walls and working in tight places, you install this product out in the open, usually along or near the baseboard.

Both commonly available types of raceway, the one-piece and the two-piece, install easily. The one-piece, which is simply a channel, attaches to the wall with couplings, clips, and straps. After you've mounted the hardware, you pull the wiring through the channels and make your connections. A host of fittings is available to help you build a raceway network suited to your particular needs. In a two-piece system, you mount the back to the wall, lay your wiring inside the cover, then snap the cover onto the back.

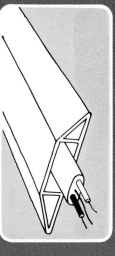

All types of elbows, T-connectors, reducing connectors—even receptacles and switches—tie into modular raceway systems.

For safety reasons, one-piece raceway must be exposed, except when it runs through a wall to continue into the next room.

There's even a one-piece "pancake" channel available for installations that require running wiring on top of the floor.

For two-piece raceway, you don't need a wall box. Power enters via cable connected to the wall-mounted backing plate.

# WHAT'S AVAILABLE IN BOXES AND ACCESSORIES

## For Exposed Walls

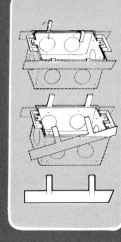

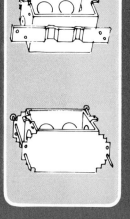

Because all switches, receptacles, fixtures (except fluorescents), and junctions must be protected by a box, you can appreciate why there are hundreds of different boxes on the market.

These boxes nail to the front of a stud. The brackets are recessed to allow for the thickness of the wall surface being applied.

You can nail either of these boxes to the side of a stud. The one at left has its own 16d nails; a bracket is attached to the other.

## For Finished Walls

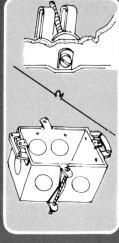

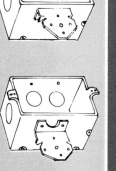

If you're faced with installing a box in a wall that's already finished off, the job's a little more complicated. But the toughest part of it is cutting the hole and fishing the wires—not mounting the box.

Fortunately, the products at right make the box-installation step a fairly simple process—even for beginners. Before you begin, refer to pages 30-37, 52, and 239 for information about cutting different wall materials.

With this type, you slip flat metal box supports alongside the box, then fold the tabs into the box to snug it against the wall.

Shove this box into the opening till the ears stop it. Then turn the two clamp screws to tighten the box against the wall.

234

## The Basic Box

You'll get a lot of mileage out of this box, especially if you use the style that comes with internal clamps. (That way, you won't have to fuss with special connector fittings.) The two-hole ears at top and bottom are adjustable and removable to suit differing wall thicknesses. This means you can join two boxes together by removing a side plate from each.

Internal clamps make for speedy hookups. The top one accommodates armored cable, the other two, nonmetallic sheathed cable.

To "gang" boxes, remove one side from each and join the boxes with the screws that formerly held the sides in place.

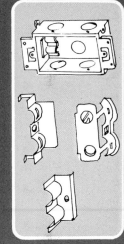

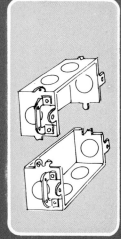

## Utility and Junction Boxes

All boxes must be made at least 1½ inches deep to comply with specifications in the Code. Most junction boxes—the ones in which you join wiring runs—are octagonal or square and are available only in the four-inch size. If you must mount a box on the surface of a wall, use the round-cornered variety called a utility or handy box.

Surface-mounted utility boxes come in 2- and 4-inch-wide sizes for one or two devices. Also use the square ones for junctions.

If the box won't be exposed, use one of these sharp-cornered types—for armored cable (left) or sheathed cable (right).

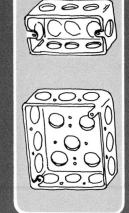

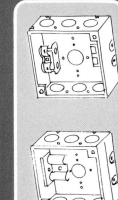

## Ceiling Boxes

Ceiling boxes, used most often to hold fixtures, are usually round, octagonal, or square. (For junction work, use the roomier square ones.) Because of the weight of most fixtures, you'll have to anchor the box very solidly. So if you can't gain access to the ceiling joists, you'll have to mount the box in the plaster or drywall span between joists. (More about this on page 240.)

Ceiling boxes come with internal clamps and/or knockouts for separate connectors. Boxes nail to or are suspended between joists.

The straps on the bar hanger at top are recessed into the plaster and nailed to joist bottoms. Install the other from above.

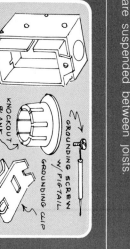

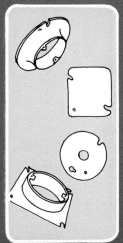

## Accessories

In addition to box connectors, many other accessories are available to solve about any wiring problem. For example, if you've installed thick planking over your old walls, your existing switch boxes are recessed too deeply to be safe. But a gadget called a *depth ring* can extend the box flush with the new surface. Check the sketches at right and electrical suppliers for more examples.

Accessories include a depth ring, grounding screw with pigtail, grounding clip, and a snap-in blank used to seal a knockout.

Every box must be covered in some way. Covers come in all sizes and shapes, ranging from metal disks to complex designs.

## WHAT SIZE BOX SHOULD YOU USE?

Our concern here is simple: an overcrowded box increases the chances of short circuits.

The chart below shows the sizes and number of wires that you can safely fit inside boxes of various sizes. As you work with the numbers, keep these exceptions in mind: (1) Wires from a fixture on the box to wires in the box aren't counted. (2) A wire that enters and leaves the box without a splice counts as just one wire. (3) If the box contains a cable clamp, hickey, or fixture stud, reduce the number of permitted wires by one. (The reduction is only one, no matter how many items are in the box.) (4) Attached connectors aren't considered as devices in the box; count only those that are integral with the box. (5) Reduce one wire for each receptacle, switch, or other device in the box. (6) If a wire starts and ends in a box—such as a ground wire from the green terminal to the box—don't count it. (7) And when one or more bare grounding wires from nonmetallic sheathed cable run into a box, reduce by one the number of wires allowed.

| Box Type | Size in Inches | Maximum Number of Wires | | | |
|---|---|---|---|---|---|
| | | No. 14 | No. 12 | No. 10 | No. 8 |
| Basic boxes (for switches and receptacles) | 3x2x1 1/2 | 3 | 3 | 3 | 2 |
| | 3x2x2 | 5 | 4 | 4 | 3 |
| | 3x2x2 1/4 | 5 | 4 | 4 | 3 |
| | 3x2x2 1/2 | 6 | 5 | 5 | 4 |
| | 3x2x2 3/4 | 7 | 6 | 5 | 4 |
| | 3x2x3 1/2 | 9 | 8 | 7 | 6 |
| Utility boxes | 4x2 1/8x1 1/2 | 5 | 4 | 4 | 3 |
| | 4x2 1/8x1 7/8 | 6 | 5 | 5 | 4 |
| | 4x2 1/8x2 1/8 | 7 | 6 | 6 | 5 |

| Box Type | Size in Inches | Maximum Number of Wires | | | |
|---|---|---|---|---|---|
| | | No. 14 | No. 12 | No. 10 | No. 8 |
| Ceiling and junction boxes | 4x1 1/2 round or octagonal | 7 | 6 | 6 | 5 |
| | 4x2 1/8 octagonal | 10 | 9 | 8 | 7 |
| | 4x1 1/2 square | 10 | 9 | 8 | 7 |
| | 4x2 1/2 square | 15 | 13 | 12 | 10 |
| | 4 11/16x1 1/2 square | 14 | 13 | 11 | 9 |
| | 4 11/16x2 1/8 square | 21 | 18 | 16 | 14 |

## TOOLS YOU'LL NEED FOR WIRING JOBS

On page 226, we talked about the tools you'll use to make general repairs. Now let's add a few more so you can work on those long runs between basement and attic.

Start out with a powerful *electric drill,* preferably one with a half-inch chuck. Arm yourself, too, with a good, sharp *spade bit* that can eat its way through 2x4s and their inevitable knots. Also buy an *extension bit* so you can make those deep cuts through double floor plates. And you'll need a carbide-tipped *masonry bit* to drill into masonry walls.

Round out your arsenal with a *conduit bender,* a *pipe cutter* (some pros still prefer a hacksaw), and the *fish tape* you bought for general repairs.

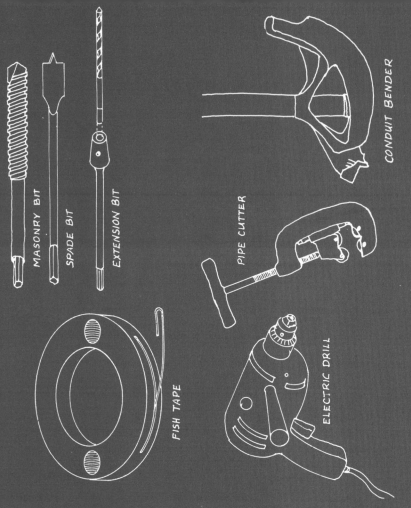

MASONRY BIT

SPADE BIT

EXTENSION BIT

CONDUIT BENDER

PIPE CUTTER

FISH TAPE

ELECTRIC DRILL

236

# EXTENDING EXISTING CIRCUITS

If you want to add just a couple of outlets or a new light fixture, you shouldn't have to go all the way to the service panel for your electricity. The two best places to borrow a little extra power are junction boxes and duplex receptacles.

If you have an unfinished basement, look there first. You should be able to find a junction box located as shown in the sketch below. If the circuit has excess capacity (see page 224) and your needs won't tax it, start your new line here. Or take your search to the attic, where you might find a box or two.

In the house proper, your best bet is a duplex receptacle like the one at right. Tie into one that has two unused terminals, providing the circuit has the power to spare.

Note the four terminals on this duplex receptacle—two hot and two neutral. Extend the circuit by tying into the two unused ones.

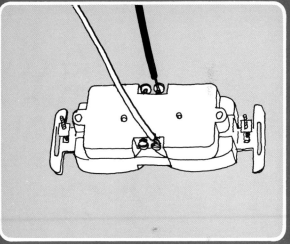

Extending a circuit from a junction box in the attic isn't difficult. Remove one of the knockouts and attach the cable.

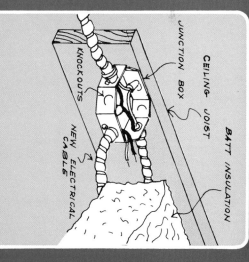

CEILING JOIST

BATT INSULATION

JUNCTION BOX

KNOCKOUTS

NEW ELECTRICAL CABLE

## Where Can You Tap In?

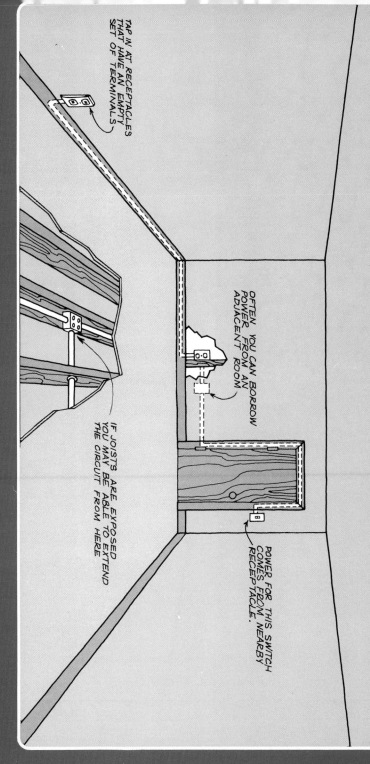

TAP IN AT RECEPTACLES THAT HAVE AN EMPTY SET OF TERMINALS

OFTEN YOU CAN BORROW POWER FROM AN ADJACENT ROOM

IF JOISTS ARE EXPOSED YOU MAY BE ABLE TO EXTEND THE CIRCUIT FROM HERE

POWER FOR THIS SWITCH COMES FROM RECEPTACLE NEARBY

237

# FISHING WIRES

Figuring out how to get your wiring from one spot to another—and then doing it—can be the biggest challenge of your electrical project. It takes time, patience, and a basic knowledge of construction techniques. But it also can be the most rewarding part of the job because once you've succeeded in pulling wires through an "impossible" maze of walls, ceilings, and floors, you know you've really accomplished something.

Expect to find a 2x4 plate in the bottom of each wall, double plates at the top, and possibly—heaven forbid—2x4 fire blocking crosswise between studs, halfway up the walls. If you have a chimney on an interior wall, try dangling a chain down alongside it; you may have found the best spot to run wire from the basement to the attic.

You'll have some patching jobs facing you when the wiring is completed, too. For a quick refresher course, check pages 34 and 36.

## From Unfinished Spaces

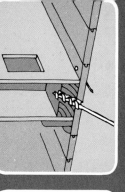
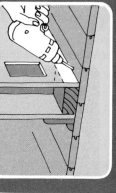
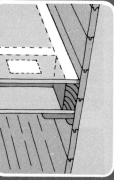

First, determine where you want the outlet, then check to make sure you're not cutting into a stud (see page 31).

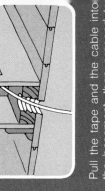

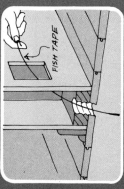

Cut the opening in the wall, then carefully remove the baseboard and drill an angled locator hole in the floor.

Thread fish tape up from below and have someone help guide the tip of it through the outlet hole and into the room.

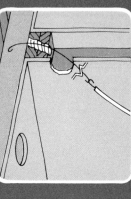

Slip a 16d nail into the hole to mark the spot, then angle up through the plate from below with a brace and long bit.

Hook the end of the sheathed cable to the tape and wrap the junction with electrician's tape to ensure a smooth pull.

Pull the tape and the cable into the basement, then proceed to wire the outlet and mount it in the wall hole.

## Through Finished Walls

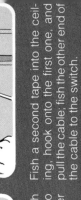

To get cable from a switch to a new ceiling fixture—without access from above—cut a hole in the wall near the ceiling.

Auger an angled hole up through the top plates, fasten the tape to the cable, then shove the other end of the tape into the cavity.

Fish a second tape into the ceiling, hook onto the first one, and pull the cable; fish the other end of the cable to the switch.

# MOUNTING WALL BOXES

When you have access to exposed studs, you literally can mount a box a minute. But if you have to hunt for the studs (see page 31), cut openings, and use special installation methods, plan on spending at least a half-hour per box—and sometimes a lot longer if you run into complications such as a framing member you hadn't expected to encounter.

When placing the boxes, remember that switches usually go 48 to 50 inches above the floor; receptacles, 12 to 16 inches above the floor. Also keep in mind that the Code requires that receptacles be placed so that no point along any wall is more than six feet from an outlet. Note:

always mount boxes so they'll be flush with the finished wall surface.

In finished spaces, your order of attack should be to locate and cut your openings, dry-fit the boxes, fish the cable, attach it to the box, then install the box permanently, as shown below. From that point on, it's a matter of patching the walls, if necessary, and hooking up your new switches, receptacles, and fixtures.

## In Unfinished Space

To mount a box away from a stud, just nail a 2x4 crosspiece between two studs and screw the box to the crosspiece.

This box comes with two 16d nails. Simply hold it where you want it and whack the nails into the side of the stud.

Place this box in the desired position on the wall. Then nail through the bracket and into the stud, as illustrated.

## In Paneling and Drywall

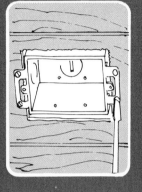

If the paneling is sturdy enough, just cut a hole, insert the box, and screw through the two ears into the paneling.

Shove this box into the drywall hole, then tighten the screws (these draw up holding clamps on each side of the box).

For a box without holding clamps, position box supports on each side of it (behind the drywall), and bend the flaps to anchor it.

## In Lath and Plaster

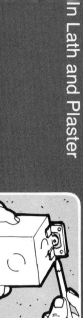

Cut a small peek hole so you can center the box on a lath. Then draw around the box or use a template to mark the cut.

Cut away the plaster with a chisel, drill starter holes, then carefully cut the lath with a sharp keyhole or compass saw.

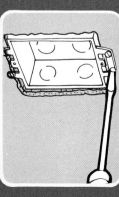

Enough lath should remain at top and bottom so you can screw the box directly to the lath strips through the ears.

## MOUNTING CEILING BOXES FROM ABOVE

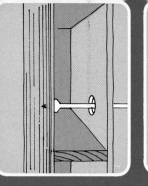

Drill a ¼-inch hole, slip an L-shaped piece of wire into it, and spin the wire to confirm an obstacle-free space above.

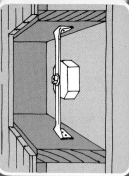

Widen the hole to an inch. Chuck a long extension and bit into your drill and bore a locator hole in the attic floor above.

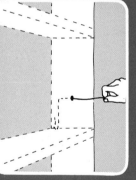

Cut out and save the flooring, draw an outline of the box, and drill starter holes all around the perimeter of the cutline.

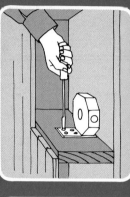

Cut the box opening with a keyhole saw. If you're working with plaster, deeply score it from below with a utility knife.

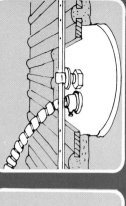

Otherwise, you'll need a box with its own adjustable bar hanger. Screw the ends of the hanger to neighboring joists.

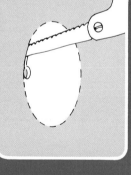

If you've spaced the hole the right distance from a joist, mount a box equipped with a bracket, as shown.

## MOUNTING CEILING BOXES FROM BELOW

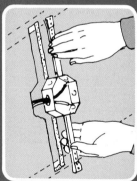

Remove the center knockout in a round ceiling box, slip the box onto the hanger stud, and screw on the anchoring nut.

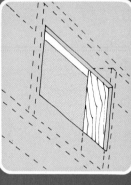

Insert a bar hanger and rest it on the ceiling. (Don't use this method to support anything heavier than a porcelain fixture.)

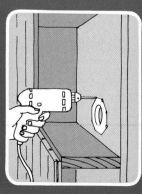

To mount a box where there's finished space above, mark the location of the box hole and cut it out with a keyhole saw.

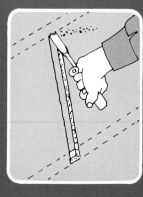

Cut a box hole in the center, and screw an offset bracket-and-box combination to the bottom of the joists; patch the grooves.

Here's a typical full-access installation for a recessed fixture (see page 61). Note the use of headers to provide support.

To handle heavier fixtures, first cut a groove in the ceiling, extending it to the joist on either side of the intended position.

# WIRING RECEPTACLES AND SWITCHES

Compared to the hassles often involved in getting wires to a new receptacle or switch box, installing the devices themselves is a breeze. And after you've completed this final "finishing" phase comes the moment of truth when you restore power and find out if everything really works.

Learning how to hook up receptacles won't take long. You simply connect a black, hot wire to one of the brass terminals on each device, and a white, neutral to one of its silver-colored terminals. If the circuit will continue on from there, you then connect a second set of hot and neutral wires to the second set of terminals.

Switches, on the other hand, require a bit more thinking. First, you have to figure out where the switch is located relative to the source and the fixture it will control. Will power flow through the switch to the fixture, or vice versa?

Second, remember that a switch interrupts only the hot leg of the circuit. This means that if current will come to the fixture first, you must make a "switch loop" by connecting the white wire to the power source and switch, and the black wire serves as a hot lead, it should be marked with black tape at each end.

If, however, current will come to the switch first and then to the fixture, you don't need to connect the neutral wires to the switch at all. You simply attach the black wires to each of the switch's terminals and "jump" the neutrals, as shown in the next-to-last drawing.

Note that in all the illustrations, we've left out grounding wires so the others will be easier to trace. To learn more about wiring switches and receptacles, see page 230; turn to page 255 for more about fixtures.

## Receptacles

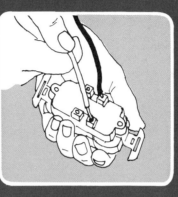

In slot-type (sometimes called back-wired) receptacles, you just shove the hot wire into one slot, the neutral wire into the other.

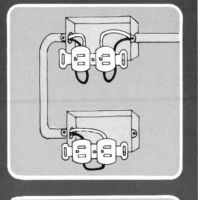

To tie a second receptacle into the line, run wires from the empty set of terminals on the existing receptacle to the new one.

Fold the wires carefully into the box, then screw the receptacle to the box; align the plate before tightening the screws.

## Two-Way Switches

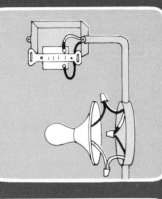

When you want the switch beyond a fixture (power comes from right), wire it like this. The white switch wire must be coded black.

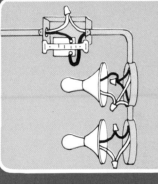

When the switch is in the middle of the run, wire it this way to control two fixtures; power comes from the bottom.

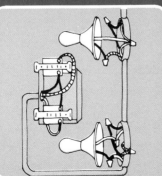

When two switches in the same box control separate fixtures, use a three-wire cable, as shown. Power comes from the left.

## Three- and Four-Way Switches

Three-way switches aren't what their name implies. They control lights from two locations, not three. Typically, you'll install one at the top of stairs, another at the bottom; both will operate the fixture lighting your stairway. But don't limit them to just this one use. Three-ways also are adaptable to many other lighting situations.

Though these switches are different from their simpler two-way cousins,

they're actually easy to understand if you learn these three bits of information: (1) A three-way switch has three terminals—a dark-colored one for the "common" wire, and two lighter-colored ones for the "traveler" wires. (2) Always attach the incoming hot wire (black) to the common terminal of one switch and always run a hot wire (black or a white wire marked black) from the common terminal of the second switch directly to the black wire on the fixture. (3) Always connect the two traveler terminals of one switch to the two traveler terminals on the other switch.

You'll need to get four-way switches into the act whenever you want to control a light from more than two locations. Just remember to install a three-way switch nearest the power source, another nearest the light, and the four-way switches in between.

The wiring diagrams below will show you how to handle the most common installations. (We've left out the grounding wires to make the sketches easier to follow.)

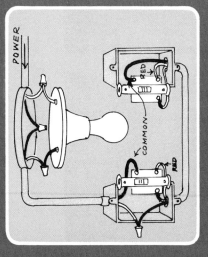

Here, the hot wire from the source passes through the fixture box and connects to the common terminal of the switch at left.

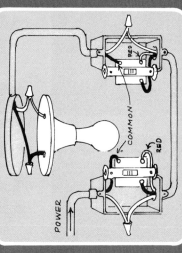

This is one of the fairly rare three-way installations in which the white neutral isn't pressed into service as a hot wire.

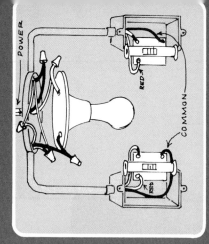

In this situation, the white wire serves as a traveler between switches. Indicate that it's "hot" with black tape or paint.

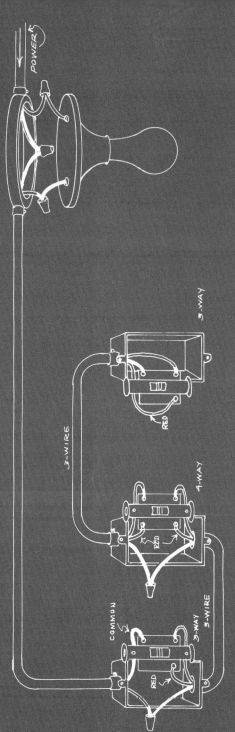

A four-way switch is wired between two three-way switches in this circuit so the light can be controlled from three locations. Note that two-wire cable (plus grounding wire) is all that's needed between the fixture and the first switch, but three-wire cable is re-

quired between switches. The neutrals take on added roles as travelers going from one switch to the next, and as the hot wire re-

turning from the switches to the fixture. You can easily pick out the four-way switch; it has an extra terminal.

Whenever you add on a room or take over unfinished space, you'll want to plan how you're going to run electricity to the new area. Chances are, you'll be doing two types of wiring jobs—burrowing behind and around finished surfaces, and breezing through the new construction.

The first step is necessary to get you from the service panel to the new space. From then on, you should be performing your craft after the rough framing is in, but before any finishing is done. (In a few rare cases, you won't have to go all the way to the service panel to start your circuits. Generally, though, an entire room will require more current than any

## Connecting to the Service Panel

This is the part of the job you may or may not want to do yourself. Some experts recommend hiring a licensed electrician to do all work inside the service panel (or box) itself; others say that if you take precautions and pay attention to what you're doing, you shouldn't have any trouble.

If you choose to make your own connections at the panel, the first thing you want to do is to remove or open the front cover and flip off the main breaker

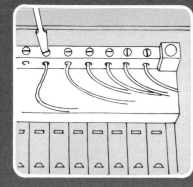

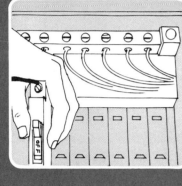

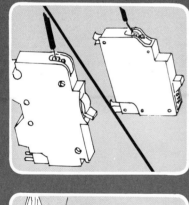

On many bus bars, you slip the end of the wire into a slot, then drive a screw tightly against the wire. Tug to be sure it's secure.

Installing this type of breaker is a one-handed job; simply push the breaker contacts into the appropriate slots.

The breaker shown at left is held in position by its friction ears; the style at right snaps in place after you've connected a hot wire to it.

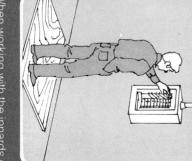

When working with the innards of a service panel, you're safest if you stand on a board and keep one hand in your pocket.

---

nearby circuit can supply via the tapping or splitting off the new circuits from the sub-panel.

Start at the service panel—but don't connect the wires to the box's terminals. Instead, fish all of your wiring (see page 238) through the walls, floors, and/or ceilings, as necessary. You'll probably be working with nonmetallic sheathed cable because you can't use rigid conduit without tearing out a lot of framing and finish materials. (Some local codes require the use of armored cable, so be sure to find out what's acceptable in your area.)

If your new room will require only a couple of circuits, you'll need to run only a single three-conductor cable from the panel; for a bigger multi-circuit add-on, consider running heavier cable from the main service panel to a new sub-panel

or pull the main fuses. (Caution: this shuts off all the branch circuits in your home, but those big wires coming into the box up top will still be live. Stay away from them!) Strip the wires you'll be bringing into the box, making sure they're long enough to curl around inside the box and reach the proper terminals. Then remove a knockout from the side of the box and anchor the cable or conduit to the box with a cable clamp or conduit connector.

For a fuse box, connect the black wire to the terminal screw on the fuse holder, and screw the white wire to the bus bar to which all of the other white wires are

connected. Attach the ground wire to the ground strip, which in some cases may be the same terminal used for the white wires. Screw in a fuse of the amperage you need, replace the inner cover of the box, and re-install the main fuses to test the circuit.

For a circuit-breaker box, attach the white neutral wire and bare grounding wire to the neutral bar. Fasten the black wire to a new circuit breaker, and install it. Flip the main breaker on and test the circuit. (Before you put the panel cover on again you'll need to remove the proper knockout(s) to accommodate the new breaker(s).)

in the new space, then splitting off the new circuits from the sub-panel.

When you get to the area of new construction, use a spade bit to drill wiring holes through the centers of the studs and joists. This minimizes the chances of a nail being driven into the wire later. If you're forced to drill a hole closer than 1½ inches from the front of the wood, cover the spot with a piece of metal plate at least 1/16 inch thick.

After the wiring is in, mount the boxes where needed (see pages 239 and 240). This stage of the project also will take place in the new area and should go quickly because you simply nail the boxes to the sides of the exposed framing. Then install the switches, receptacles, and fixtures (see pages 241, 242, and 252-258).

# HEAVY-DUTY CIRCUITS

Appliances that need heavy-duty circuits (120/240 volts or 240 volts only) must be wired according to strict guidelines, so find out what's required in your locality. You'll usually be working with special heavy-duty receptacles and plugs—even for built-in appliances that you'd normally expect to wire directly to a junction box. That's because the Code requires that you be able to disconnect a built-in unit in case of electrical emergencies. In some situations, this means a separate switch wired from the service panel, but usually the disconnect device is simply a heavy-duty receptacle into which a matching cord-connected plug is inserted.

Receptacles and plugs are commonly identified as 2-pole 2-wire, 2-pole 3-wire, 3-pole 3-wire, 3-pole 4-wire, and so forth. The number of poles indicates the number of wires that normally carry current. If there is one more wire than poles, this means the receptacle or plug has an extra connection for a separate grounding wire. Never connect a current-carrying wire to this terminal.

## 240-Volt Plugs and Receptacles

Hook together two 120-volt circuits and you have a 240-volt circuit. These consist of just two hot wires (plus an equipment ground); you don't need a neutral. This means that if you use ordinary two-wire cable (it will have a black and a white wire), you should mark the ends of the white wire with black paint or tape to indicate that the white wire also is hot.

Manufacturers of receptacles and plugs design their products so a plug of a certain voltage and wiring scheme generally will fit only a receptacle with identical characteristics, and will not mesh with a receptacle carrying a lower or higher amperage/voltage rating.

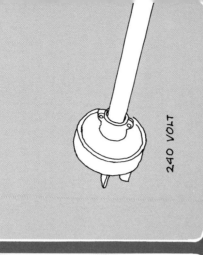

240 VOLT

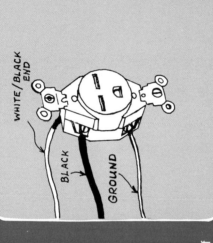

BLACK

WHITE/BLACK END

GROUND

In this 240-volt, two-wire-plus-ground receptacle, the top two terminals are for the current-carrying wires.

## 120/240-Volt Plugs and Receptacles

Sometimes, an appliance such as a range must be fed with a 120/240-volt supply. That's because the burners may need 240 volts at the higher settings but only 120 for lower heats. (The timers, lights, and so forth also run off 120.) So a special three- or four-prong plug and receptacle is made for this installation. (Three wires carry current; the fourth is for grounding.)

Heavy-duty components come in dozens of configurations—each for specific voltage and amperage requirements. (The chart opposite illustrates a few of the types.) Some plugs are designed so they can't be inserted or removed without twisting.

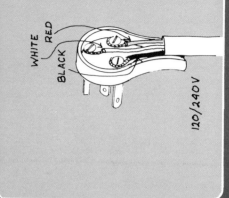

WHITE

RED

BLACK

120/240V

This 240-volt plug is a mate for the receptacle at left, and is wired identically. A protective sleeve covers the wiring.

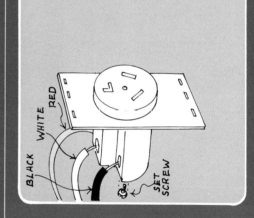

BLACK

WHITE

RED

SET SCREW

This 120/240-volt receptacle has three current-carrying wires—a white neutral (for the 120-volt portion) and a red and black.

When you get to the plug, simply match up its terminals with the receptacle terminals, then wire by color accordingly.

244

# INSTALLING MAJOR APPLIANCES

If you're running wiring for a new appliance, carefully read the articles of the Code pertaining to appliance circuits. Several decisions face you, the main ones being which size of wire and circuit breaker (or fuse) to use, and what types of plugs and receptacles are right for the job.

The chart below summarizes what your research will probably reveal—but be sure to check any appliance's rating before you size the circuit. (If it's given in watts, remember that you can simply divide by the voltage to get an amperage figure.)

Note, too, that 240-volt plugs and receptacles aren't as standardized as 120-volt devices. Not only do their configurations vary according to the amperages they're designed to handle, but sometimes even a receptacle and plug rated at the same amperage won't mate. The chart shows only some of the dozens of possibilities.

Will you need a special heavy-duty plug and receptacle at all? Again, the answer depends on what the Code says about the appliance in question. It talks about three types of appliances—portable, stationary, and fixed—and spells out different rules for each. A portable appliance, such as a microwave oven, is one that's quite mobile. The stationary variety (a slide-in range, dryer, etc.) can be moved fairly readily but is rarely shifted from its original point of installation. Fixed appliances (water heaters, cooktops, wall ovens, etc.) are permanently installed.

## SIZING HEAVY-DUTY CIRCUITS

| Appliance | Electrical Requirements | Wire Size | Plug/Receptacle |
|---|---|---|---|
| Electric dryer | 120/240 volts, up to 30 amps | #10 | 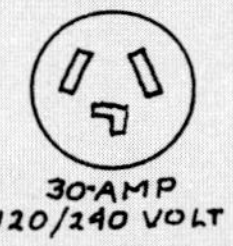 30-AMP 120/240 VOLT |
| Electric water heater | 240 volts, 20 to 30 amps | #12 for 20 amps or less #10 for 30 amps or less | 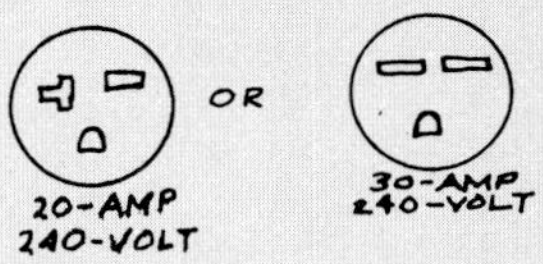 20-AMP 240-VOLT OR 30-AMP 240-VOLT |
| Range | Combination oven/cooktop units typically draw up to 50 amps at 120/240 volts. Check local code to determine if you need a plug and receptacle, or should wire directly to a junction box. | Most require two #6 hot wires and a #8 neutral; for small units, you may be able to use two #8 hot wires and a #10 neutral. | 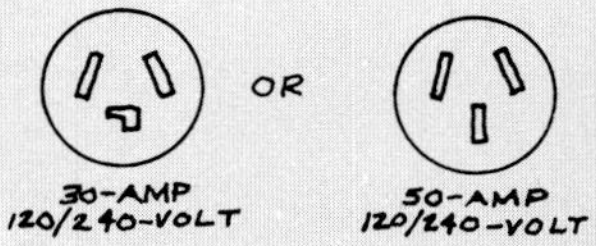 30-AMP 120/240-VOLT OR 50-AMP 120/240-VOLT |
| Separate oven and cooktop | Connect both to a single, 50-amp, 120/240-volt circuit, or provide separate 30-amp circuits for each. | For a single-circuit installation, see Range above; 30-amp circuits require #10 wire. | 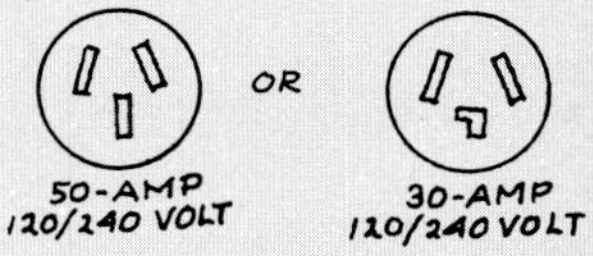 50-AMP 120/240 VOLT OR 30-AMP 120/240-VOLT |
| Microwave oven, refrigerator, dishwasher, clothes washer, gas dryer | These units typically draw less than 15 or 20 amps and require only a 120-volt circuit. Each should have a separate circuit, though. | #12 |  15-AMP 120-VOLT |
| Air conditioner | Window units vary according to their BTU capacity—from less than 15 amps at 120 volts up to 30 amps to 240 volts. More about air conditioners on page 358. | #12 for 20 amps or less #10 for 30 amps or less | 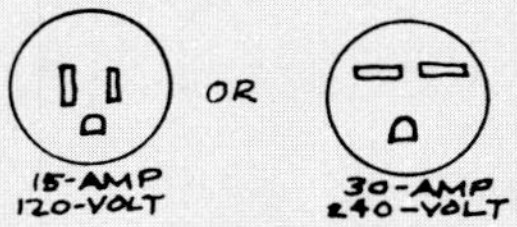 15-AMP 120-VOLT OR 30-AMP 240-VOLT |

## GROUNDING APPLIANCES

Big electricity-users should be grounded to provide added insurance against injury from shock if a circuit's fuse or breaker should fail to react when needed. If your home's receptacles are properly grounded (see page 225), the third wire of the appliance's power cord will ground the unit. Otherwise, or if local codes require it, you should ground your appliances as shown here.

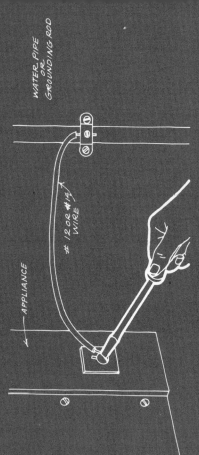

WATER PIPE OR GROUNDING ROD

# 12 OR #14 WIRE

APPLIANCE

## TROUBLESHOOTING APPLIANCES

When an appliance or power tool conks out—or begins to malfunction—you may need professional help to get it running smoothly again. But before you call for service, see if you can systematically isolate what's wrong using this process of elimination.

Start with the most obvious possibilities. Is the machine plugged in? Are its controls properly set? Next, go to the service panel and look for a tripped breaker or blown fuse. If you find one, reset the breaker (or replace the fuse).

If the circuit goes off again, you can be fairly sure that either there's a short within the unit or its cord, or that the entire circuit is overloaded. Sometimes, just unplugging an appliance and

peering into its innards will reveal a bare wire that has grounded out.

If, on the other hand, you don't find a breaker or fuse out, you know that the circuit is live. Double-check this by testing the unit's receptacle.

The drawings below illustrate where to look for problems. To learn about troubleshooting heating and cooling equipment, see pages 318-337.

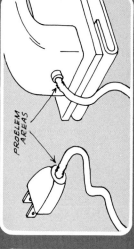

PROBLEM AREAS

Sometimes wiggling a switch gets results. If so, the switch should be replaced—a job you may not be able to do yourself.

When a cord goes bad, it usually happens at one end or the other. See pages 228 and 229 for how to replace cords and plugs.

With larger appliances, you may be able to track down the source of a malfunction with some careful listening.

If jiggling the plug gets an appliance going again, either the plug or—more rarely—the receptacle is faulty.

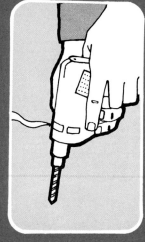

Motors that spark, smoke, or smell usually need new brushes. Don't use the device until it's been repaired.

Doorbells, chimes, intercoms, thermostats, and even some lighting systems run on low voltages that are "stepped down" by a special transformer from 120-volt household current to levels ranging between six and 30 volts. These electrical subsystems can be installed without boxes, circuit breakers, fuses, or special grounding procedures. Working with low-voltage circuits is ideal work for do-it-yourselfers, not only because the current is so limited that you can't cause fires, but also because the voltage is low enough that any shocks you get are at most a tickle.

If you're replacing old wiring, you'll probably be installing what's often called bell wire—a No. 18 gauge wire with a thin coating of plastic insulation. You splice it simply by twisting together two ends and covering them with tape. Be sure to buy different colors of wire so you'll know at a glance which is which when you're ready to make the final connections. And before you buy wire, find out whether you're working on a two-wire or three-wire system.

Of course, if you're installing a low-voltage device in a home where none exists, your first step will be to run a circuit from the service panel to a conveniently located junction box. Then add a transformer and go from there.

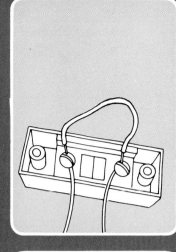

To check out a doorbell button, use a jumper wire, or a screwdriver as discussed in the copy below. If bell rings, button is shot.

## Doorbells and Chimes

The most popular use for low-voltage wiring is the common doorbell—or, in some installations, chimes. The low-voltage part of the system starts at the transformer, which is usually in the 6- to 8-volt range for doorbells, or 15 to 20 volts for chimes. A few models are even multi-voltaged, giving you the option of choosing the terminal—and voltage—you need. Transformers vary, so if you're replacing a bad one, be sure to get a unit that will be compatible with your existing system.

In old installations, you may find the transformer mounted near the junction box or even on the box cover. But in newer homes, it's usually fastened to the side of the service panel.

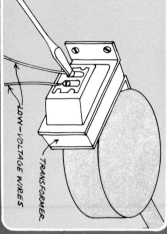

A threaded fitting on this transformer extends through a knock-out in the junction box and is held by a retaining nut.

LOW-VOLTAGE WIRES

TRANSFORMER

## Troubleshooting Procedures

Running down a problem in your doorbell (or chime) system is mainly a process of elimination. If the bell works sporadically, check out the button first. Unscrew it from the wall and hold a screwdriver across the two contact points. If the bell doesn't ring, clean the contact points with emery cloth and make sure the contacts touch when the button is pushed.

Assuming the button works, check the bell and transformer for loose connections. If they're tight, hold a screwdriver across the transformer's bell-wire connections. If you don't get a weak spark, replace the transformer. If you do see even the faintest spark, the transformer is fine, and your search narrows down to the bell itself or to the wiring. The easiest way to check the bell is to disconnect it, clean it thoroughly, rub the contacts with emery cloth, then hook it up directly to the bell-wire connections at the transformer. If you don't get a ring, the bell is shot; if you do, you'd better start replacing the wire—a tedious, last-resort measure.

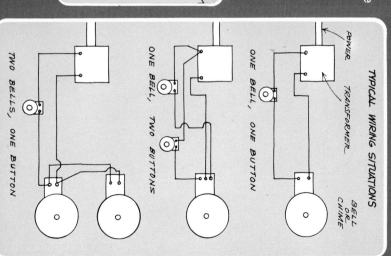

TYPICAL WIRING SITUATIONS

POWER

TRANSFORMER

BELL OR CHIME

ONE BELL, ONE BUTTON

ONE BELL, TWO BUTTONS

TWO BELLS, ONE BUTTON

# OUTDOOR WIRING

Whether it's an outdoor receptacle installation you've been considering, or a more extensive project such as running a branch circuit to a new shed or backyard light, the principles you learned for your interior work still apply outdoors. Only the equipment changes —and that only slightly.

Outdoor wiring does involve a few added precautions, though. For example, whenever undertaking any outdoor wiring project, use either metal conduit with Type-TW wires pulled through it, or UF cable, a tough, highly moisture-resistant sheathed cable. Some local codes specify one in particular, so check with code authorities on this. While you're there, also ask if there are any local restrictions concerning who does the work and how it's to be done.

If you use cable, you're still required to protect it with conduit whenever above ground. Keep in mind, too, that cable should be buried at least 12 inches below the surface. Rigid conduit need go only six inches underground; thinner conduit needs 12 inches of earth protection.

To guard against serious shock, always protect all outside circuits containing receptacles with a ground-fault circuit interrupter—GFCI—(see page 251).

The outdoor components shown below, though they look similar to the ones used inside, have watertight features such as gasket seals, spring-loaded covers, and rubber-sealed connections.

## WEATHERPROOF COMPONENTS

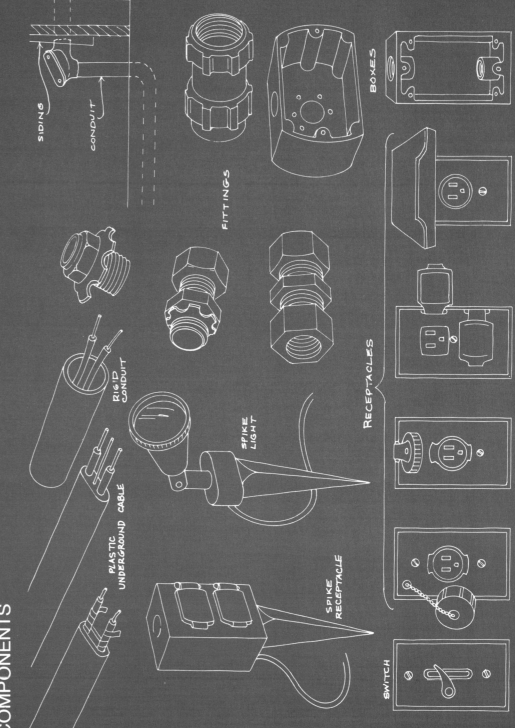

SIDING

CONDUIT

FITTINGS

BOXES

PLASTIC UNDERGROUND CABLE

RIGID CONDUIT

SPIKE LIGHT

SPIKE RECEPTACLE

RECEPTACLES

SWITCH

# GETTING WIRES THROUGH A WALL

Cutting a hole in an exterior wall isn't something you'll want to do without some planning. Where you make the incision should depend on your success in finding a circuit that's underused, as well as how far you have to go to tie into

a feeder line. Also see page 128 for a look at what you might encounter inside an exterior wall.

In some locations, you can run sheathed cable through the wall to the exterior box; in other places, you're required to use conduit or armored cable. Find out what codes permit.

In most cases, it's best to install a junction box back-to-back with the new

## INSTALLING AN EXTERIOR RECEPTACLE

The easiest outdoor electrical job of all is installing a receptacle. This amounts to little more than locating and cutting the hole, then mounting a weatherproof box on the surface or recessing it into the wall (this is the best way to go,

exterior box, then connect the two with conduit or armored cable.

Another way to get power for an outdoor add-on is to tap off of an existing exterior fixture. Special fittings and adapters make it easy for you to tie into the old fixture box. But before deciding on this approach, make sure that the present circuit has the extra capacity you need (see page 224).

even though it requires more work.) Remember that a ground-fault interrupter must be installed in any outdoor circuit to guard against a potentially dangerous shock if anything should go wrong.

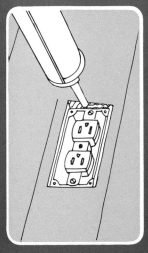

Install the receptacle (see page 251 for a ground-fault-protected type), and caulk as shown before screwing on the faceplate.

Carefully size the opening so the special waterproof box will fit snugly and minimize heat-robbing gaps.

## INSTALLING AN EXTERIOR LIGHT

One of the most overlooked—but obvious—locations for an exterior receptacle is the wall facing a deck or patio.

These days, security isn't far from anyone's mind. That's why it's comforting to know that a flick of a switch can turn a dark, shadowy backyard into one flooded with light. If you can't perform this kind of magic,

you'd be smart to install a security light or two. (See pages 250, 259, 383, and 390 for tips on where to put them to give you the most safety and security.) One of the easiest locations to work with is under an overhang.

Make an opening for a switch box in the room below, then fish a sheathed or armored cable to it through a hole in the soffit.

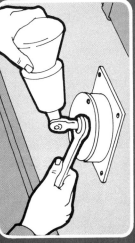

Fasten the cable to an outdoor fixture box with the appropriate box connector, screw the box to the soffit, and wire the fixture.

After connecting the cable wires to the fixture wires with wire nuts, mount the special outdoor fixture to the box.

## RUNNING WIRES UNDERGROUND

You'll quite literally "dig" running underground wiring, so plan on spending some time in the trenches. If you're planning a lengthy run, consider renting a trencher for a few hours. Though expensive, this tool makes quick work of this otherwise laborious task.

(See page 248 for depth requirements for cable and conduit.)

Start your project by planning your routes, including where you want to go through the wall. Then run power to a new junction box nearby, and drill through the wall. It's best to use a short piece of rigid conduit to make the through-the-wall connection between the box and an exterior connector called an LB fitting. This fitting enables you to

make the sharp 90-degree turn downward and also has a removable plate that takes the strain out of pulling wires.

Remember that you have to run conduit from the fitting to the bottom of your trench—and at the other end between the trench and the receptacle or lamppost. For tips on how to set posts, see pages 176 and 178.

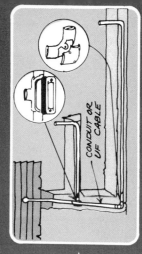

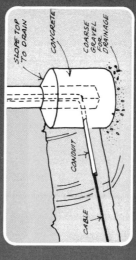
CONDUIT OR UF CABLE

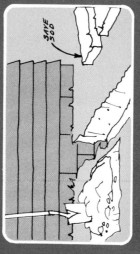
SAVE SOD

Carefully remove and save the sod before you dig the trench; pile the loose dirt on a tarp or piece of plastic sheeting.

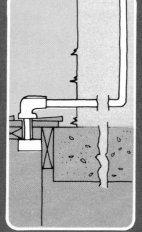

Though the LB fitting at the wall opening has a removable plate, there's not enough room inside to make connections.

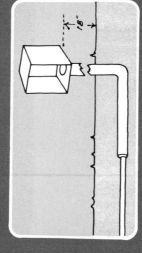

A receptacle should be at least 18 inches from the ground, and its wiring must be protected above grade by conduit.

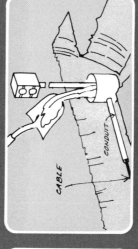
CABLE  CONDUIT

Stabilize all receptacles below ground with concrete; use either a big coffee can or a concrete block as your form.

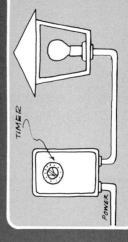
SLOPE TOP TO DRAIN  CONCRETE  COARSE GRAVEL FOR DRAINAGE  CONDUIT  CABLE

If you use rigid conduit throughout, you can buy special fittings called *bodies* to make the T-junctions and turns you need.

For lamps, run the conduit or cable up the center of the post, then set the post in a concrete pier with a sloped top.

## INSTALLING AUTOMATIC LIGHTING CONTROLS

One way to be sure your security light is on every night is to wire it directly to an automatic control. You'll find two types available—photocells and timers. Both usually come with easy-to-follow installation instructions. Photocells, of course, need to be outdoors, but timers should be installed inside.

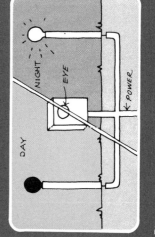
TIMER  POWER

Timers let you choose when the lights should go on and off. One model can take the place of a standard light switch.

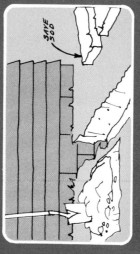

Photocells turn lights on at dusk, off at dawn. Include a switch as well, so you can manually override the photocell.

# INSTALLING GROUND-FAULT INTERRUPTERS

If one of your electrical tools or appliances goes haywire and starts leaking current, the grounding wire will carry off most of the errant electricity. But the key word here is *most*, because there may be enough other current zapping around to make you an instant conductor anyway. As little as 200 milliamperes—about enough to light a 25-watt bulb—can kill you if you happen to be touching plumbing components or standing on wet earth. That's why the Code requires that all new 15- and 20-amp outdoor receptacles and all new bathroom circuits be protected by a ground-fault circuit interrupter.

A GFCI is an amazing device in that it trips the circuit whenever even a tiny leakage occurs. And the shutoff action is so fast, there's not enough time for you to be injured. Shown at right are three commonly available types of GFCIs.

Install the GFCI at left in your service panel. Plug the other model into a receptacle, then plug an appliance or tool into it.

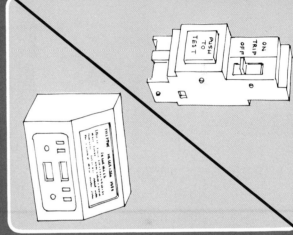

This GFCI replaces a standard receptacle and is a natural for outdoor use—mounted on a wall or on conduit in your yard.

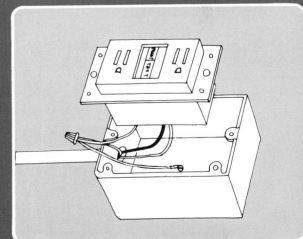

---

# USING ELECTRICITY WISELY

Ever wondered exactly how much it costs to burn a light or run an appliance? To find out, all you need to do is multiply the wattage the device consumes by the numbers (or fractions) of hours you use it. Divide this result by 1,000 and multiply it by the price you pay per kilowatt hour for electricity.

If you can't find a wattage figure on an appliance's rating plate, simply multiply its amperage by its voltage.

The table at right compares operating costs for major appliances and tells how you can reduce the amounts of energy they use. To learn about the even greater savings possible with heating, cooling, and water heating equipment, see page 359. For more about lighting, turn to the following chapter.

## HOW THRIFTY ARE YOUR APPLIANCE HABITS?

| Appliance | Relative Operating Cost | How You Can Save |
|---|---|---|
| Refrigerator, Freezer | The biggest energy eaters in any kitchen. Auto-defrost models use as much as 50 percent more than manual-defrost types. | If you can do without the convenience, buy a manual-defrost; if not, energy-saving automatic types are worth the extra money you'll have to pay for them. |
| Range | Usually the number-two consumer, depending on your family's cooking and baking needs. Self- and continuous-cleaning ovens are more costly. | Cook small meals in pressure cookers or other small appliances. A meat thermometer minimizes wasteful oven-peeking. |
| Dishwasher | Third or fourth. Most of the energy goes for heating water, so run only full loads and select short cycles. | Eliminating the drying cycle can cut operating costs by at least one-third. |
| Washer, Dryer | Third or fourth. Again, the less water a machine uses, the less it costs to operate. On dryers, auto-dry settings can save electricity, but actually not too much. | Run cold-water loads whenever possible and use the lowest water level necessary. Longer spin periods cut down drying times. |

251

# LIGHTING

Specialists in vision maintain that almost 90 percent of what we know and feel comes to us via our eyes—making lighting the most informative of your home's systems. In too many households, though, it's also one of the most neglected.

Few of us live totally in the dark, of course. But because our eyes tend to compensate for light levels that are a bit too dim or too bright, it's easy to ignore a lighting problem that causes eyestrain, fatigue, or even accidents.

Inefficient lighting wastes energy, too. Without enough illumination in a particular area, you may be turning on every lamp or fixture in the general vicinity—or overcompensating with high-wattage bulbs.

How much lighting is enough? And what can you do to achieve the proper level? This chapter begins by answering the first question, then goes on to explain the many different ways you can approach the second.

Good lighting starts with the right bulb. For most of the lamps and fixtures in your home, you probably prefer the warm color quality and high adaptability of *incandescent* bulbs. In these, electricity charges a metal filament, causing it to glow as white heat. The higher the filament's electrical resistance, the more watts it consumes and the more light it gives.

Note, though, that wattage figures don't truly denote the amount of light a bulb puts out. This is expressed in *lumens*, and not all bulbs are equally efficient on a lumens-per-watt basis. If you're interested in comparing bulbs in this way, you'll find a lumen output rating on the bulb's paper sleeve, though not on the bulb itself.

As a class, incandescent bulbs are the least efficient—much of the energy they use is wasted producing heat, which eventually burns up the filament. Long-life bulbs give off less heat—and correspondingly less light—for the same amount of electricity.

Fluorescent and high intensity discharge (HID) lighting, though each has its own drawbacks, use far less electricity per lumen output than incandescent bulbs, and can last 10 to 30 times longer. More about these money- and energy-savers on pages 257-259.

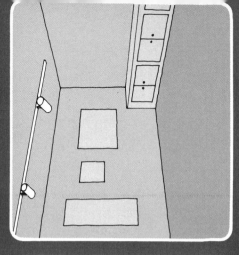

**General lighting** visually expands a room's size and provides basic brightness. It usually consists of a ceiling or wall fixture, supplemented with convenient portable lighting.

For living and sleeping areas, lighting experts recommend that you allow one watt per square foot with flush or pendant fixtures (see the opposite page), and 1.5 watts per square foot for recessed lights.

Kitchens, baths, and laundries need more illumination—as much as four watts per square foot for incandescent bulbs, and 1.5 watts for fluorescent tubes.

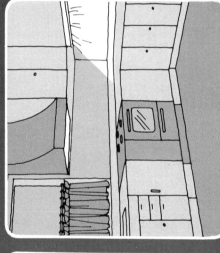

**Task lighting** lets you get a good look at what you're doing by focusing on countertops, sinks, workbenches, and your favorite reading spots.

Most tasks require 150 watts of incandescent or 40 watts of fluorescent lighting. For prolonged reading, though, you need 200 to 300 watts of incandescent, 60 to 80 fluorescent.

For countertops and workbenches, provide 120 watts of incandescent or 20 watts of fluorescent lighting for each three running feet of work surface. Fixtures should be mounted 14 to 22 inches above the surface.

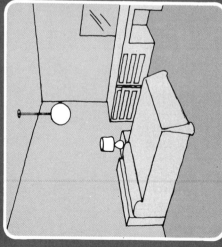

**Accent lighting** provides architectural flavor, and sometimes does the job of general lighting as well. Use it to wash a wall, play up interesting textures, spotlight a fireplace, or dramatize a dining table.

With accent lighting, let your imagination be your guide as to how much is enough. Do try, though, to give rooms a variety of different accent lights, separately switched, so you can vary moods and suit different requirements. A wide spectrum of bulbs—incandescent, fluorescent, and HID—adds even more possibilities.

# SELECTING FIXTURES

The most difficult thing about selecting light fixtures today is narrowing down the types of fixtures and some of their many uses. If after digesting this information, you're still not quite sure which type of fixture is right for you, go to a lighting store and talk with personnel there about your requirements. They should be able to guide you toward the most appropriate products.

The chart below discusses the various light fixtures available. There's a huge selection available. There's a fixture for every need, and for every budget. In fact, the possibilities are almost limitless once you realize that many lamp shops and hardware stores stock lamp components you can put together yourself.

## YOUR LIGHTING FIXTURE OPTIONS

| Type | Use |
|------|-----|
| Surface | This old standby mounts directly on the ceiling's surface, distributing very even, shadowless general lighting. These must be shielded with translucent material to minimize glare, and should have sockets for several smaller bulbs rather than one or two big ones. A variation, the surface-mounted downlight, looks like a can or cylinder and provides task or accent lighting. |
| Dropped (suspended) | Pendants, chandeliers, and other dropped styles have many of the same characteristics as flush-mounted fixtures, and you can easily substitute one for the other. Because these are closer to eye level, glare can be a problem. Try using low-wattage bulbs or dimmer switches (see page 255). Hang fixtures 12 to 20 inches below an 8-foot ceiling or 30 to 36 inches above table height. |
| Recessed | Recessed fixtures include fixed and aimable downlights, incandescent or fluorescent bulbs shielded by plastic diffusers, and even totally luminous ceilings. You can get a wide range of high-lights and shadows with recessed lighting, but it requires more wattage—up to twice as much. To learn about installing these, see pages 61-63. |
| Wall bracket | Wall-mounted fixtures conserve space in tight quarters, serving as either task or accent lighting. For reading, mount them 15 to 20 inches to the left or right of the page, and 48 inches above the floor. |
| Track | Track lighting offers great versatility. You can add, subtract, or rearrange fixtures at will, aiming them in any direction you please. You get a very broad choice of modular fixtures, too—ranging from simple spot and floodlight bulb holders to framing projectors with special shutters to exactly control the spread of light. To learn about installing track lights, see page 256. |
| Cornice | Cornices mount at the intersection of a wall and ceiling, bathing the wall with soft, downward light. To dramatize draperies or other wall treatments. You can build a cornice treatment with 1x2 and 1x6 lumber. Mount the tube so its center is 6 inches from the wall. |
| Valance | Valances resemble cornices, but they're installed lower on the wall often over draperies, providing both up- and downlight. To build one, you'll need 1x2- and 1x6-inch material and angle brackets, as shown at right. Top off the unit with a strip of plastic and you can also use it as a display shelf. |
| Cove | Cove lighting dramatizes a ceiling. You can buy commercial metal or plastic fixtures, or make your own with wood and angle brackets, as illustrated. Mount the light about a foot below ceiling level, and paint the inside white to maximize reflection. |
| Under-cabinet | The simplest way to shed light on countertops is to attach fluorescent tubes to the undersides of cabinets, as shown. Shield them with skirting. Use the longest tubes that will fit, and fill at least two-thirds of the counter's total length. |

# INCAN-DESCENT LIGHTING

Incandescent fixtures operate much like the ordinary table lamp shown on page 228. A pair of *leads* serves as the cord, connecting the fixture's socket or *bulb holder* to house wiring. (For safety, these connections must always be made in a ceiling or wall box.)

But because fixtures don't permit as much air circulation, they get much hotter than table lamps. That's why bulb holders are usually made of non-melting material, such as porcelain, and wired with high-temperature conductors.

It's also why you should never exceed the wattages specified on the unit's *canopy plate*—heat could melt the wires' insulation, causing a short circuit, a fire, or both.

Support systems vary (see below), but all of them secure the fixture to its electrical box—usually a four-inch octagon—and in some cases to the ceiling as well. Never support a fixture only with its leads.

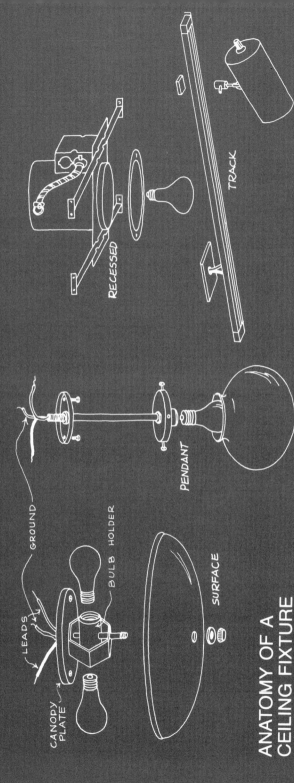

LEADS

GROUND

CANOPY PLATE

BULB HOLDER

SURFACE

RECESSED

PENDANT

TRACK

## ANATOMY OF A CEILING FIXTURE

## TROUBLESHOOTING FIXTURES

With a roll of electrical tape, a screwdriver, a pair of pliers, and a neon test light, you can track and solve most fixture problems. To eliminate any possibility of electrical shock, shut off power to the light, then double-check with your tester before touching the fixture. You may have to turn on the power later to make some of the tests called for below.

### THINGS TO CHECK

| Symptom | Causes | Cures |
|---|---|---|
| No light | A burned-out light bulb. A broken or loose wire in the ceiling box. Switches occasionally go bad, too. | Replace bulb. Drop the fixture as shown on the opposite page, then check and tighten all connections. Check out the switch with a neon tester (see page 227); to learn about replacing switches, see page 230. |
| Fixture blows fuses | Frayed wires in the ceiling box may be shorting out, or a bulb socket may be defective. | Drop the fixture and examine the wires carefully; tape any bad spots. Test the socket (see page 227). Some sockets can be easily re-placed; with others, you'll have to get a new fixture. |
| Light flickers | Suspect melted insulation or a failing socket. A dimmer may be going bad. | Tape or replace any wires that look dubious. Next, test the socket. If you still have a problem, you may have to replace the dimmer. |

254

# REPLACING A FIXTURE

Substituting a new fixture for an old one usually takes only a few minutes, if you have the right hardware. First shut off power at the service panel. Wall switches interrupt only the fixture's "hot" wire, so

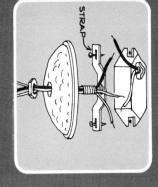

you still could get a shock through the neutral if the circuit is live.

Next, examine how the old fixture is attached. Some secure with bolts to a *strap*, as shown in the first drawing below; others mount with a *hickey* to a *stud* in the center of the box (third drawing); still others use a combination of these systems.

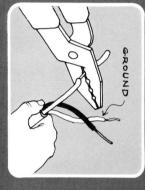

After that, just follow the sequence illustrated. Take care not to undo any other connections you may find in the box, and handle fixtures gently—most are made of lightweight metal that can be bent easily.

To learn about getting power to a location that had none before, see pages 231-243.

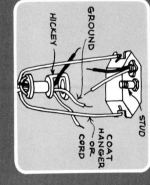

Temporarily support a heavier fixture with a coat hanger or strong cord, as shown. Preassemble everything first.

Make sure all of the wires exit via the hickey's side, screw a nipple into it, then thread the hickey onto the stud.

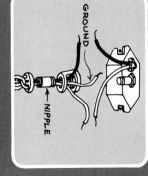

As you dismantle the old fixture, note how everything fits together. Strap mounting works best with lighter units.

Now strip about 3/4 inch from the new fixture's leads. If the wires are stranded, twist their bare ends slightly.

After the fixture is mechanically secure, make the electrical connections, then carefully coil up wires within the box.

Check your installation by turning on the power. If the fixture lights, shut off power again, and raise and secure the canopy.

# INSTALLING A DIMMER SWITCH

Dimmers let you select lighting levels according to your needs and moods. And by reducing a bulb's wattage, they conserve some electrical energy and greatly prolong the bulb's life.

Install one as you would any switch (see page 230); don't overload the dimmer beyond the wattage limits specified on its housing. In three-way installations, make sure to use a dimmer designed for this use. Otherwise, you could burn out the unit.

And note that incandescent dimmers should be used only in incandescent lighting circuits, not to control motors or fluorescents.

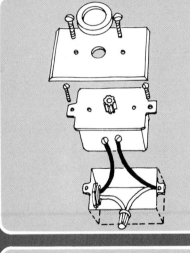

Hook up a rotary-type dimmer as shown. Tuck the switch, wires, and connectors back in carefully—space can be tight.

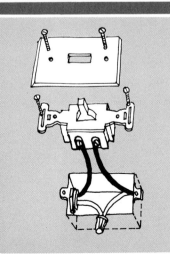

High-low dimmers are a bit larger than an ordinary switch. These give just two settings, but cost less than rotary dimmers.

# INSTALLING TRACK LIGHTING

Track lights might be called "unfixed fixtures." Instead of a single light source glaring mercilessly overhead, a track system lets you ring a room with soft, balanced illumination, play up a ceiling, spotlight architectural details . . . and change it all around whenever you feel like it.

Lightweight and modular, track light components assemble fairly easily. However, even a relatively modest layout may require a dozen or more different pieces. Plan carefully to know exactly how many of each you need.

The tracks themselves come in two-, four- and eight-foot sections that can be plugged end-to-end to any length you like. T, X, and L couplings let you change directions, too. And with two- or three-circuit components, you can wire in separate switches to control different lights at any point along the track runs.

In plotting out an installation, you first must provide a power source. Most tracks can be fed from one end, at a coupling, or—in some cases—at any point in between. If the room already has a switch-controlled fixture, you can probably tap into its box—though that may involve fishing cable and installing a new box at the right spot, as shown on pages 237-240.

If you don't already have power up there, check with an electrician for the cost of installing a new ceiling box and wall switch. Or consider just running a switch-controlled power cord from a receptacle to the ceiling. A special adapter lets you hook in at one end of the tracks.

You also have to decide how you're going to attach the tracks to your ceiling. The drawings below show two ways to go. You also can buy special kits for attaching the track to the T-bars of a suspended ceiling or for dropping it a foot or so below a conventional ceiling.

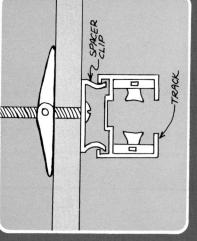

Spacer clips drop the tracks a bit so they can ride out uneven surfaces. Mount the clips first, then snap the tracks into them.

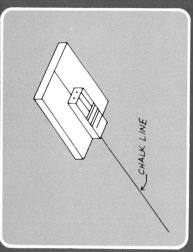

Next, snap chalk lines from the connector's center along the route you want the tracks to follow. Measure carefully.

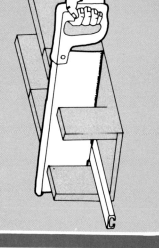

If, at the end of a run, you must cut a track, use a hacksaw and miter box. Once a unit has been cut, you can't add to it.

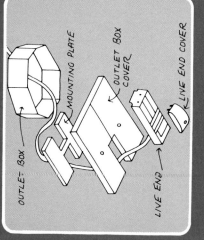

Shut off the power first, then mount a connector—either the live-end type shown here or a center feed—to the ceiling box.

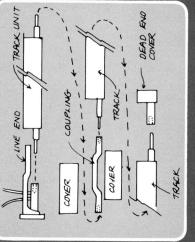

Push the couplings and tracks together as you go. Special snap-on covers give the installation a finished appearance.

# FLUORESCENT LIGHTING

Switching on the power to a modern-day rapid-start fluorescent light kicks off the chain reaction illustrated here. First, a *ballast* sends current to *cathodes* at either end of the tube. These excite a gas, creating barely visible *ultraviolet* rays. The rays then strike a *phosphorous coating* on the tube's inner surface, causing it to glow.

Because fluorescents don't "burn" the way incandescents do, they operate much more efficiently. A 40-watt incandescent bulb, for instance, typically produces 450 lumens—compared to over 2,000 from a 40-watt fluorescent tube.

Cooler operating temperatures help fluorescents last much longer, too. In fact, the number of times you start one—not the length of time it runs—determines the tube's life-span.

Thrifty as it is, though, fluorescent lighting has a few drawbacks. It's much less flexible than incandescent lighting because you can't interchange tubes of different wattages in the same fixture. And its illumination has a diffuse, flat quality that's ideal for task lighting, but monotonous in other situations.

You needn't, however, settle for the bluish cast that emanates from "cool white" tubes. "Warm white" and "warm white deluxe" versions more closely resemble incandescent light.

## ANATOMY OF A RAPID-START FLUORESCENT LIGHT

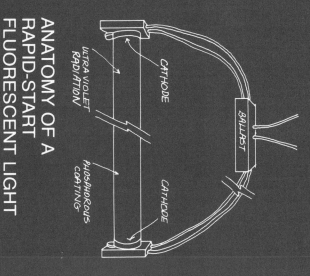

Labels: ULTRA VIOLET RADIATION, CATHODE, CATHODE, BALLAST, PHOSPHOROUS COATING

## REPLACING A STARTER

A fluorescent fixture that flickers for a few moments before lighting up probably has one additional component not shown on the anatomy above. Delayed-start fixtures preheat the cathodes with the glow from a *starter*.

When one of these goes bad (see the chart below), remove the tube, twist out the old starter, and twist in the new one (see illustration at right). Delayed-start fixtures use less electricity than rapid-start types.

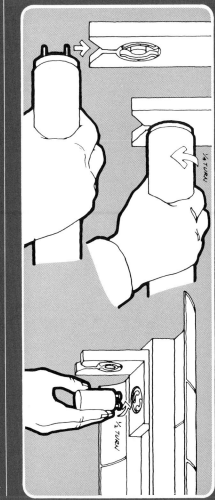

¼ TURN

½ TURN

## TROUBLESHOOTING FLUORESCENT LIGHTS

| Problem | Causes/Solutions |
|---|---|
| No light | It's rare for a fluorescent tube to abruptly burn out the way an incandescent bulb does, so check electrical connections first (see page 258); replace the starter, tube, and ballast—in that order. |
| Partial light | If the ends light up but the center doesn't, suspect the starter. If the ends are blackening, the tube is beginning to fail. Uniform dimming may mean that the tubes are failing or dirty. |
| Flickering light | Tubes often blink when they're brand new, at temperatures below 50 degrees F., and just before they go out. If a tube blinks, it or the starter may not be properly seated. |
| Humming; acrid smell | These almost always indicate a ballast problem. Tighten all ballast connections, and replace if necessary. |

## INSTALLING FLUORESCENT LIGHTING

To put up a fluorescent fixture, you follow essentially the same procedure shown on page 255, securing the unit to a ceiling or wall box with either a hickey or strap. You may, however, need to provide additional support, depending on the fixture's length and whether its electrical feed will be at one end or in the center. For more about this, check the drawings below.

Making the electrical connections is equally simple—you just hook the fixture's black wire to the black house wire, and the white to white.

Note, though, that most fluorescents also have a third green grounding wire. If the ceiling box has a separate ground wire, connect to this; if not, attach the ground to the box itself with a screw or special grounding clip.

If you're installing a series of fluorescent fixtures, such as you would for the luminous ceiling system shown on page 63, plan to provide intensity

controls so you can vary lighting levels to suit your needs.

The best way to do this is to connect some fixtures to one switch, others to another. Or hook them all to a single, *fluorescent-only* dimming control (ordinary dimmers just don't work with fluorescent lighting). The trouble with these, though, is that you must install a special ballast in each fixture—a costly and time-consuming proposition.

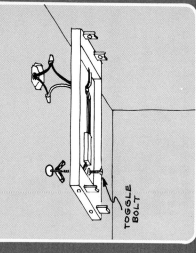

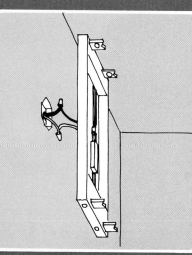

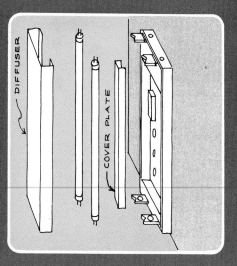

Begin by removing the diffuser, tube, and cover plate. A series of knockouts lets you bring in power from almost any direction.

To drop a fixture closer to a work surface, suspend it with light-weight chains. Thread its wires through the links.

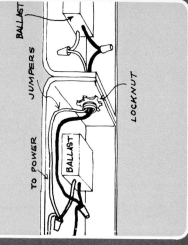

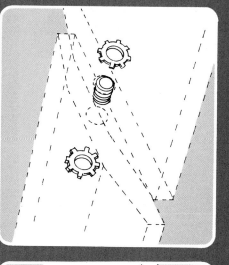

If you'll be feeding the power from one end, support the other with a screw into a joist, or a toggle bolt into the ceiling.

For a center-feed installation, re-move the center knockout and mount the unit as you would an incandescent fixture.

With multiple installations, you can make electrical connections within the fixtures themselves, as shown here.

Additional knockouts and some threaded nipple couplings let you tie two or more fixtures together end-to-end or side-to-side.

258

# H.I.D. LIGHTING

Mercury, metal halide, and sodium-vapor lights—known collectively as high intensity discharge (HID) types—combine elements of both fluorescent and incandescent lighting.

These efficient lamps use a ballast to energize the same chain of events that takes place inside a fluorescent tube (see page 257). Instead of tubes, though, HID lights feature bulbs that can be aimed almost as effectively as incandescent lights. The result: brilliant, economical illumination that can floodlight your yard, drive, or entry walk just as effectively as it does public roadways and parking lots. HID lights vary in efficiency (see the chart below), but all put out far more light than incandescent bulbs of the same wattage—and last up to 30 times longer as well.

HID lights take three to 15 minutes to warm up, though, so don't plan to use them in frequent on/off situations. And select wattages carefully—you can't change to a bigger or smaller bulb unless you change ballasts, too.

## COMPARING H.I.D. LIGHTS

| Type | Properties | Uses |
|---|---|---|
| Mercury | Available in 50- to 1,500-watt sizes, these produce about twice as much light as an incandescent bulb of the same size. Some mercury lamps come close to matching incandescent's color quality, too. | Fixtures range from homey-looking post lanterns to no-nonsense industrial styles. Select a 50- or 75-watt lamp to illuminate a yard or driveway, and 175-watt eave lights for security. |
| Metal halide | Wattages range from 175 to 1,000 and are about four times as efficient as incandescent lights. Metal halide lamps cast a strong, green/white light. | These work best for floodlighting a yard or house. As with any HID type, you can control them with either a switch or an automatic light-sensitive control. |
| Sodium-vapor | Usually available in 250-, 400-, and 1,000-watt sizes, they're six times as efficient as incandescents, and emit the same yellow hue cast by street lights. | Where you really need a lot of light, sodium-vapor can do the job most economically. Combining these with metal halide lamps helps cool the color. |

# LOW-VOLTAGE LIGHTING

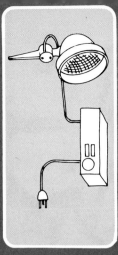

Low-voltage systems step down house current to a six- or 12-volt trickle, which means you can safely string together a series of fixtures like so many Christmas tree lights.

Indoors, low-voltage lets you add new fixtures almost anywhere, hooking them up with surface wiring that resembles ordinary telephone cable. You can run it easily along baseboards, window casings, and other trim.

Outdoors, low-voltage lighting is even more versatile. You simply plug a transformer into a standard 120-volt receptacle and run lightweight cable to spiked fixtures such as the one shown here. Because there's little shock hazard, you can bury the cable a few inches below ground or lay it right on the surface. Contrast this with the far more arduous job of installing underground

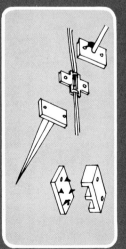

120-volt wiring shown on pages 248-251.

Best of all, you can alter a low-voltage layout any time you wish—moving lights around as flowers come into bloom, for instance, or setting the stage for a patio party.

Don't, however, count on low-voltage equipment for all your outdoor lighting needs. Bulb sizes are a modest 25 and 50 watts, and don't give as much light as comparable 120-volt bulbs. For more about working with low-voltage wiring, see page 247.

Transformers typically provide enough power to supply about 300 watts of lighting, to distances of 100 feet.

Special connectors let you snap wires to the fixtures or to each other without splicing or installing junction boxes.

# PLUMBING

The oldest and simplest of a home's systems, plumbing seems mysterious only until you realize it relies on just two physical principles—pressure and gravity. Turn on a faucet full-blast and you can feel the pressure that pushes water through pipes to your fixtures; pull a drain plug and gravity carries it away.

Because of this simplicity, the hidden parts of your plumbing system—its pipes and the fittings that tie them together—rarely give trouble. When something does go wrong, it usually happens at a fixture or in a drainpipe, either of which you can easily service yourself.

This chapter begins by introducing you to your system's inner workings, tells how to cope with plumbing emergencies and repairs, then goes on to illustrate what you need to know about upgrading your home's waterways.

## GETTING TO KNOW YOUR SYSTEM

Your home's water supply, which comes either from the city or a well, enters via a sizable pipe. If you're on city water, this pipe connects to a *meter* that reads the amount of water entering. Next to the meter is a *shutoff valve* that lets you stop all flow of water, if necessary. The supply pipe then travels to a *water heater*, or in the case of private systems, to a *pressure tank* and then to a water heater.

From the heater emanates a *hot water supply line*. This line and a *cold water supply* run parallel throughout your home to serve the various *fixtures* (water faucets, lavatories, bathtubs, toilets, etc.) and *appliances*, such as clothes- and dishwashers. The supply lines are under constant pressure—usually 50 to 60 pounds per square inch.

Another system of pipes, the *drain-waste-vent pipes* (DWV), carries away water and waste to a *city sewer* or a *septic system*, and vents potentially harmful gases to the outside. Not under pressure, these pipes depend on gravity to perform their function.

## ANATOMY OF A PLUMBING SYSTEM

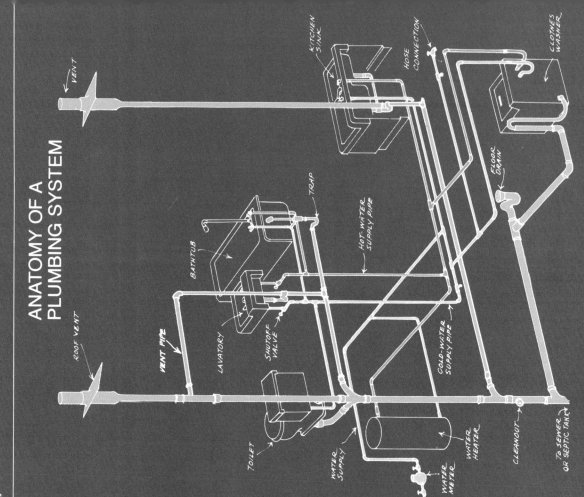

VENT

ROOF VENT

VENT PIPE

BATHTUB

TRAP

KITCHEN SINK

HOSE CONNECTION

CLOTHES WASHER

LAVATORY

SHUTOFF VALVE

HOT-WATER SUPPLY PIPE

COLD-WATER SUPPLY PIPE

FLOOR DRAIN

TOILET

WATER SUPPLY

WATER METER

WATER HEATER

CLEANOUT

TO SEWER OR SEPTIC TANK

# SHUTOFF VALVES

The cold and hot water supply system in your home features a series of *shutoff* valves—sometimes called *stops*. Think

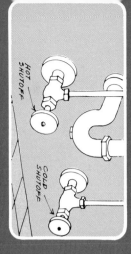

Water supply lines at sinks, lavatories, and flush tanks also may be equipped with shutoff valves. Water heaters have one, too.

of them as on/off switches that provide you with an easy-to-find, quick-to-close turnoff network in the event the piping system springs a leak or if you want to make repairs or replace any of the system's components.

Look for stops near the point where supply lines enter a fixture or an appliance. If you don't find any there, use the main shutoff on the meter's street side. Closing this valve turns off your entire water system.

With some fixtures, such as tubs, the shutoff may be beneath the floor, as shown, or hidden behind an access panel.

If your home has a meter, you'll find two main shutoffs. Use the one on the supply side so pressure doesn't damage the meter.

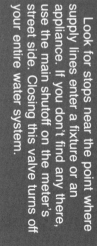

# TRAPS

Traps perform the useful function of preventing dangerous gases generated in the drain-waste lines from backing up and infiltrating your home. These simple, yet effective devices do this by creating an automatic water seal (see sketches at right), which forces the gases to rise up the soil stack. Running water flushes the trap, but gravity ensures that some will always remain.

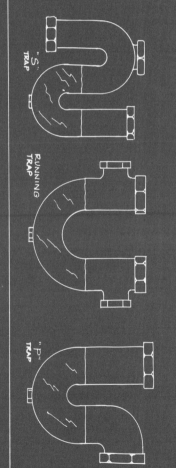

"S" TRAP

RUNNING TRAP

"P" TRAP

# PLUMBING CODES

For everyone's protection, a national plumbing code spells out specific guidelines for all plumbing operations.

Most cities, towns, and communities have adopted this code and amended it to fulfill local requirements and conditions.

Before you install new plumbing, read or ask about the plumbing codes in

your area to make sure your intended project conforms with the code. A permit may be required for new plumbing work. You'll probably also have to have a plumbing inspector check your installation.

# READING A METER

Whether your meter is a direct-reading type like the one shown at near right, or has a series of dials like the one at far right, determining consumption is an exercise in subtraction.

With dial types, note the position of each pointer, wait a few days, then note their positions again. Subtract the first reading from the second for the number of gallons of water used.

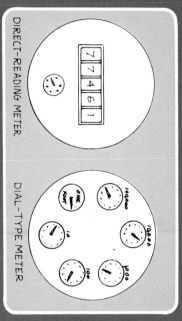

DIRECT-READING METER

DIAL-TYPE METER

If you suspect a water leak but can't locate it, give your water meter a leak test. First, turn off all the faucets and water-using appliances in your home. Then take a look at the scales on your water meter (see sketch at left). Watch the one-cubic-foot scale for 20 minutes or so. If the dial moves at all during this time, the water supply system is leaking, probably behind a wall or underground.

# SOLVING PLUMBING PROBLEMS

When confronted with a plumbing problem—even one of those "nuisance" repairs such as fixing a dripping faucet or unclogging a drain—too many people simply throw up their hands and call a plumber. Then, often as not, they wait hours or even days for a repair that takes only a few minutes, but costs a lot of money.

If that's happened at your house, the next 20 pages are for you. They delve into just about any difficulty you're likely to encounter, explain the relatively simple components you'll be dealing

with, and present the know-how you'll need to handle a situation confidently and effectively.

After you've mastered these repair basics, you may then want to go on an try out some of the improvements covered later.

Note that one aspect of home plumbing is *not* covered here—the sub system of pipes, valves, and appliance that use natural or LP gas. To learn about this one, see pages 308-315.

## BASIC TOOLS

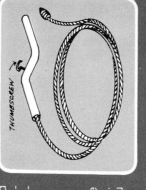

A "plumber's helper"—also called a *plunger* or *force cup*—dislodges debris from drains by creating suction.

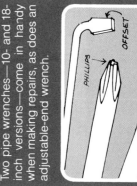

A flexible *plumber's snake* can be threaded through drain pipes. Locking the thumbscrew lets you crank to break up debris.

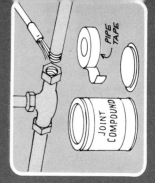

Plastic electrician's tape will tem porarily stop a pinhole leak in a water supply pipe. The bad pipe must be replaced, however.

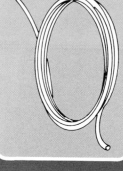

Chemical drain cleaners, used periodically, keep drains open and functioning perfectly. They're tops for preventive maintenance.

Use joint compound (pipe dope) or pipe tape to seal threads when you reassemble an old connection or assemble new piping.

Two pipe wrenches—10- and 18-inch versions—come in handy when making repairs, as does an adjustable-end wrench.

Packing for faucet nuts looks like heavy twine that's been coated with black or brown caulk. Keep the packing sealed.

To clean corroded valve seats in faucets, you'll need a valve-seating tool. The cutting end fits into the faucet.

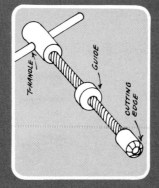

For faucets, buy a bag of assorted washers, which usually includes needed screws and O-rings in a variety of sizes.

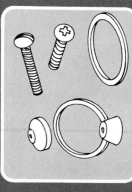

For plumbing fixtures, you'll need screwdrivers with standard, Phillips, and *offset*-type blades. *Allen* wrenches are also handy.

262

The patch can be any material that will stop the flow of water: a piece of rubber and a C-clamp, several layers of plastic tape, even a length of garden hose split and tied around the pipe. Far better, though, is an emergency patch kit. Several inexpensive solutions are shown below.

When you notice a leak, turn off the water at the main supply valve or a shutoff valve (see page 261) first thing. This takes pressure off the line. After

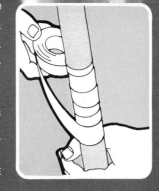

this, diagnose the exact damage and administer the appropriate repair.

If the leak is behind a wall, in a ceiling, or under a floor where you can't get at the pipe, shutting it off is about all you can do. If, however, the leak is visible and patchable, just apply the patch as described below.

If the leak is more of a drip than a squirt, it may be water condensation, not a break in the pipe, joint, or fitting. If this is the problem, see page 372.

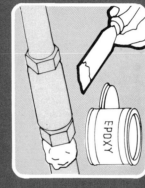

EPOXY

This special metal clamp has a rubberlike inner lining insert. You can tighten the clamp with a screwdriver.

An auto hose clamp and a piece of rubber make an excellent emergency leak stopper until you can replace the leaky pipe.

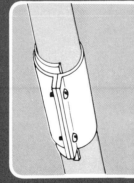

For tiny leaks, wrap the pipe with several layers of plastic electrician's tape. Wind the tape 6 inches each way from the hole.

Epoxy putty works well for leaks at connections. Spread it around the leak with a putty knife; it dries quickly.

Sometimes it almost seems as if pipes schedule leaks to correspond with the closing hours of hardware stores and plumbing outlets just to confound you. If you find yourself in this untimely predicament (and you will sometime or other), and if the flow isn't of gusher magnitude, you can get by temporarily by making an emergency patch.

## THAWING FROZEN PIPES

Having water pipes that freeze during the winter not only is frustrating, it's downright dangerous. If you don't thaw them soon after they freeze, you're asking for burst water lines, and sooner or later your request will be granted.

Before attempting any of the thawing techniques shown here, be sure to open the faucet the frozen pipe supplies. The steam created by the heat you'll apply must be able to escape. Otherwise, your pipe will burst.

If the frozen pipe is behind a wall or in a ceiling or floor, you're best off placing a heat lamp as near the faucet as possible.

If you use a propane torch to thaw a frozen pipe, be extremely careful of fire. Don't use open flame to thaw frozen pipes behind walls, ceilings, or floors, or near gas lines.

If freezing pipes are a constant threat in your area, wrap the pipes with insulation made in narrow widths especially for pipes, or buy wool felt, plastic foam, air-cell asbestos, or pipe jackets to minimize freezing.

Sometimes other tactics work, too. If pipes under a kitchen sink that's on an outside wall are a problem, try putting a small lamp down there—or just open the cabinet doors and let room heat warm the pipes.

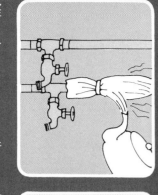

TIN OR HEAVY FOIL

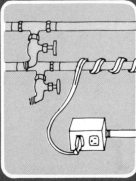

PROTECTIVE MATERIAL SUX DRYWALL OR WOOD

Although messy, you can thaw a pipe by wrapping it with layers of cloth, tying the cloth to the pipe, and pouring hot water on it.

A heat lamp is excellent for exposed or concealed pipes. But protect other materials around the pipe—heat lamps can scorch.

For exposed pipes, use a propane torch, but watch out for fire. Work from the faucet toward the frozen area. Open the faucet.

Electric heat tape runs on house current. Wrap it around the pipe and plug it into an outlet. A thermostat controls the heat.

# OPENING CLOGGED DRAINS

Impossibly stopped-up drains call for a professional with the electric equipment only pros can afford. But fortunately, most drain problems don't fall into this category, and often you can handle them yourself.

First realize that your home has three types of drains: fixture drains such as those at sinks and toilets; main drains, which lead from the fixture drains to the main pipe that carries waste from your home; and sewer drains, which run underground to the community sewer or septic tank.

Your problem can originate in any of the three, so your most immediate chore is to locate the blockage. Almost always it will be in or next to a pipe connection that makes a turn, or in a trap.

To pinpoint the difficulty, open a faucet at each sink, tub, or other fixture—but don't flush a toilet; it could overflow. If only one fixture is stopped up, the problem is right there or nearby. If two or more fixtures won't clear, something has lodged itself in a main drain. And if no

drains work, the blockage is farther down the line—either near the point where the main drain or drains connect to the sewer drain, or in the sewer drain itself.

Bearing in mind that waste water always flows downward through pipes of increasingly larger diameter lets you logically ferret out an obstruction you'll almost certainly never see. The drawings here and on the opposite page show what to do once you've found it.

## Sinks

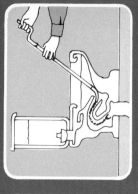

Hair, bits of soap, and other debris can gum up a lavatory stopper. To remove some types just turn and lift.

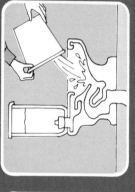

A plunger with a molded suction cup is ideal for toilets or rounded lavatory bowls. Flat plungers work best on flat surfaces.

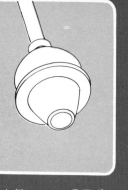

If a sink has an overflow outlet, plug it with a cloth and make sure the plunger seals tightly over the drain outlet.

If a plunger won't work, try an auger snake. Thread it down and through the trap, or open the cleanout and work from there.

If augering doesn't do the job, remove the trap (see page 273) and flush it. This also lets you get a snake into the main drain.

## Toilets

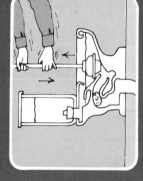

Use a plumber's friend over the hole in the bottom. Work the plunger hard and vigorously, and don't give up too soon.

If the toilet doesn't have water in the bowl, fill it to the rim. Spread petroleum jelly on the plunger's rim; this aids suction.

If a plunger doesn't work, use a special snake called a closet auger. As you crank, it wends its way through passages.

## Main Drains

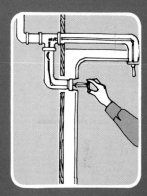

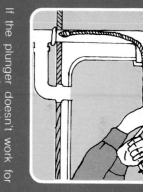

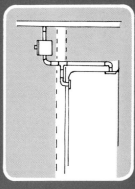

Remove and clean the stopper/strainer. Try the plunger treatment, blocking the overflow drain with a wet piece of cloth.

If the plunger doesn't work for you, remove the tub's pop-up or trip-lever assembly and run a snake through the overflow tube.

Some tubs have a drum-type plug, accessible by removing a plug that is in or under the floor beside the tub.

There may be more than one cleanout in your home's drain system. If so, find the cleanout plug nearest the sewer line. Clean out this pipe first, then check to see if the stoppage has been removed. If not, move down the line of plugs from the sewer line back.

Sometimes you can save yourself some muscle simply by loosening the cleanout plug. If water drips or forms around the threads of the plug when you loosen it, the trouble is between this plug and the sewer.

With a pipe wrench or adjustable-end wrench, unscrew the clean-out plug. Have a large bucket handy to catch any residue.

Thread an auger or snake into the cleanout opening and toward the sewer line. Once you break through, flush with a garden hose.

On a U-trap, work from the clean-out plug nearest the sewer line. If the obstruction isn't in the trap, continue up the main drain.

## Sewer Drains

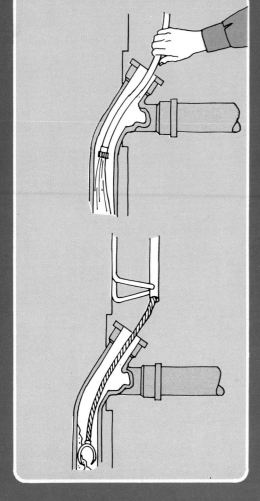

The sewer drain, the largest of your home's drains, rarely gets clogged. If it does, though, first remove the cleanout plug. Then thread a garden hose into the line and turn on the water full-blast. Push the hose through the blockage, letting the water pressure clear away the debris. Or insert an auger-type snake into the pipe and twist it through the blockage. If your problem persists, rent an electric auger with flexible blades that snip away the debris, or call in a pro.

## MAKING FAUCET REPAIRS

Unless your ears have long since tuned out such noises, it probably hasn't been too long ago that you heard the plop-plop-plop of a leaky faucet. And you can bet you'll hear it again. No matter how hard you try, wishing away leaky faucets doesn't work. So you might as well learn how to stop that drip.

Though faucets vary considerably in style, all fall into one of two broad categories—*compression* and *non-compression* faucets. Chances are, you've got some of each in your home. Compression types, also known as *stem* faucets, always have separate hot and cold controls. Turning a handle to its *off* position rotates a threaded stem. A *washer* at the bottom of the stem then compresses into a *seat* to block the flow of water, as shown in the first anatomy drawing below. To learn about repairing stem faucets, see the opposite page.

Most non-compression faucets have a single lever that controls the flow of both hot and cold water. Inside, a single-lever non-compression faucet may have any of four different operating mechanisms, also illustrated here.

Moving the lever on a *tipping-valve* faucet activates a *rocker cam*, which in turn opens spring-loaded valves in the hot and cold water lines. Temperature-blended water then flows through the spout. More about these on page 268.

A *disk faucet* mixes water inside a *cartridge.* At the bottom of the *mixing chamber*, a pair of disks raises and lowers to regulate the volume of water, and rotates to control its temperature. For repair information, see page 268.

A *rotating-ball* faucet consists of a ball with openings that line up with the hot and cold inlets and with the spout. Rocking its lever adjusts both the temperature and the flow. Repairs are explained on page 269.

A *sleeve-cartridge* faucet operates something like a disk type—lifting the handle controls the flow, moving it from side to side regulates the temperature. Inside, though, the workings include a cartridge and sleeve arrangement instead of disks. For repair procedures, see page 269.

Any of these five types of faucets may have aerators, divertors, and strainers that can clog and choke the flow of water. If you have a problem with any of these items, turn to page 271. Note, too, that tipping-valve faucets sometimes have another set of strainers inside their housings, as explained on page 268.

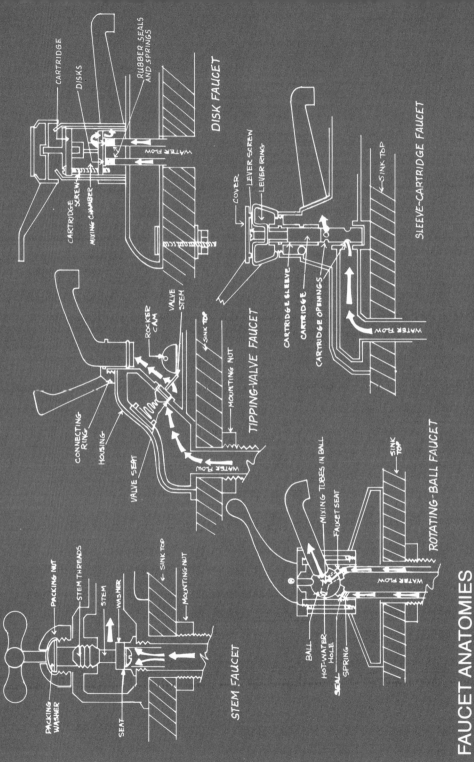

## FAUCET ANATOMIES

**STEM FAUCET**

**TIPPING-VALVE FAUCET**

**ROTATING-BALL FAUCET**

**DISK FAUCET**

**SLEEVE-CARTRIDGE FAUCET**

266

# Repairing a Stem Faucet

Stem faucets—the most leak-prone of all types—develop the sniffles for one or more of the following reasons: a worn washer, a pitted or corroded valve seat, or deteriorated packing.

Examine the anatomy drawing on the opposite page and you'll see that the washer must withstand the pressure of repeated openings and closings. As the washer wears, you have to apply more and more muscle to turn off the water—until finally, no amount of turning can stop the flow.

Fortunately, replacing a washer is a simple procedure, as illustrated below.

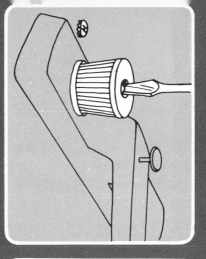

You'll need only an adjustable wrench, a screwdriver, and a faucet repair kit that includes an assortment of washers to fit most stems. The package generally also includes O-rings and new screws for attaching the washers to the stems.

If you have to replace faucet washers often—every month or two—you're probably dealing with a pitted or corroded valve seat. Abrasion here wears out washers rapidly. Again, the solution is simple, though you'll need one specialized tool—the seat grinder shown below and on page 262.

Washer and seat problems cause drips. If, on the other hand, a faucet is leaking around the handle, its packing has worn out. With newer faucets, which

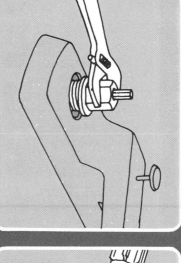

don't use packing, the problem may be a faulty O-ring.

While you have a faucet apart, note whether the threads around its stem show signs of heavy wear. If so, you'll be money ahead to replace the entire unit, preferably with a washerless noncompression type. Installation is fairly easy; see pages 298 and 299.

And whenever you work on a faucet, be sure first to turn off the water at the main entry or at the shutoffs below the sink or lavatory, as shown on page 261. Forget this step and you'll have a real mess on your hands.

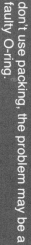

---

Pry out the decorative escutcheon on the faucet handle. Back out the screw and remove the handle. Lift it straight up.

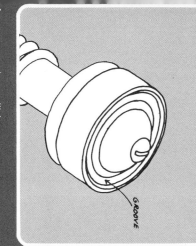

Remove the packing nut. Use an adjustable wrench or a pair of slip-joint pliers for this. Then simply turn out the stem.

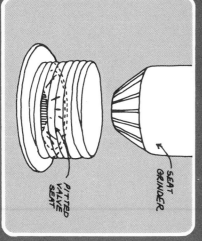

The seat washer, held in place by a screw, is at the bottom of the stem. You may have to replace the stem's O-rings as well.

---

A worn washer will be grooved, pitted, and/or frayed. When you replace it, clean the entire valve stem with fine steel wool.

To smooth a worn seat, insert a grinder, apply light pressure, and turn clockwise several revolutions. Blow out chips.

Before you reassemble an older faucet, be sure to wind packing around the stem, then install the packing nut.

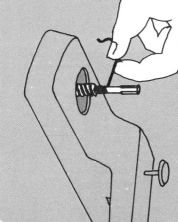

267

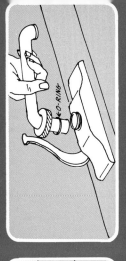

## Repairing a Tipping-Valve Faucet

Unlike compression faucets, tipping-valve units have no washers—but worn valve-seat assemblies can cause them to drip anyway. To get at these, you remove the spout and housing, as shown. Then replace the assemblies—valves, seats, seals, and all—with parts sold in kit form. With some, you may need a seat wrench to get the seat out.

Sometimes sediment can gum up strainers in the valve assemblies, making it seem as if there's something lacking in your water pressure. Rinse out the strainers and water will flow again.

When water oozes up from the spout's base, the O-ring has probably gone bad. Take care in removing it that you don't scar the metal underneath. Lubricating with petroleum jelly helps you slip on a new O-ring and makes a better seal.

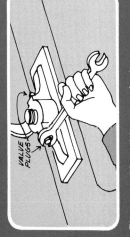

First turn off the water supply, then pad the jaws of a wrench with tape and loosen the nut at the spout's base.

Now lift the spout straight up and out, taking care not to damage the O-ring. Lift or pry off the housing, too.

Plugs on either side—one for hot, one for cold—secure the valve-strainer assemblies. Remove these and pull out the parts.

Each assembly consists of a gasket, strainer, spring, stem, and seat. Take these along when you shop for replacements.

## Repairing a Disk Faucet

The disks in most disk faucets are made of ceramic material and won't wear out. But their inlet holes (see below) can become constricted by lime deposits in the water. When this happens, you have to dismantle the faucet and clean out the debris. If the faucet leaks at its base, you must replace the inlet seals in the cartridge's underside.

Another type of disk faucet (not shown) resembles the compression versions shown on pages 266 and 267 in that it has separate hot and cold controls. Take one apart, though, and you'll find a cone-shaped rubber diaphragm at the end of the stem where you'd expect to see a washer. If this is worn, pry it out and replace it. These are sometimes called "washerless" faucets.

You can buy repair kits for both ceramic and diaphragm-disk faucets, but take along the old assembly when you shop; sizes vary. As with any faucet repair, shut off the water and drain the tap before you begin.

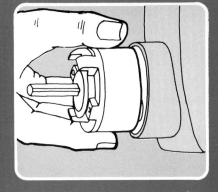

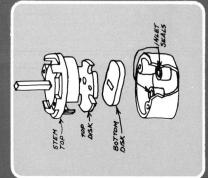

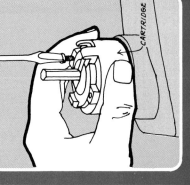

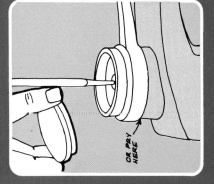

Pry off the decorative cap, then remove the screw and handle. With some, you pry as indicated to get at the handle screw.

Now remove the two screws that hold the cartridge in place and lift it out. This entire unit can be replaced if necessary.

Insert the new or repaired assembly back in place, carefully aligning it so the screws mesh with holes below.

But first check to be sure that dirt hasn't lodged between the disks and that the inlet seals are in good condition.

# Repairing a Rotating-Ball Faucet

Ball faucets serve for years without trouble. When one begins to drip, you can be almost certain its springs and seats need replacing. Leaking around the handle, on the other hand, means it needs new O-rings. Neither of these repairs is a difficult job.

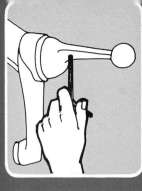

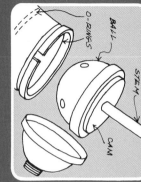

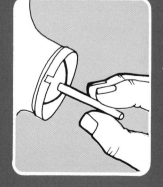

The procedure for getting at faucet parts varies somewhat, depending mainly on whether the unit has a fixed or a swiveling spout. With fixed-spout models, you simply remove the handle and a cap underneath, as shown here; with swivel-spout types, you have to lift off the spout as well.

While you have the unit apart, check the ball itself for wear or corrosion and replace it, too, if necessary. Repair kits include springs, seats, O-rings, and other seals—but you'll need the make and model number or the old parts to get the right components.

Reassemble the parts in order and replace them in the housing. With a swivel-spout model, push the spout straight down until you hear it click against a slip ring at the base of the housing. Since the O-rings create lots of tension, you'll have to push hard.

When you replace the ball, be sure to align a slot in its side with a pin inside the housing. The cam has a lug key, too.

After turning off the water, loosen but don't remove) the handle's setscrew with an allen wrench, then remove the handle.

The cap comes off next, then pull out the cam, ball, and stem assembly. Remove the O-rings if they're worn or cracked.

Pull out the seats and springs with long-nose pliers. Replace these according to directions that come with the repair kit.

# Replacing a Sleeve Cartridge

When a sleeve-cartridge faucet goes bad, you'll have to replace either its O-rings (if there are any), or the entire cartridge. These assemblies don't lend themselves to repairs—but they're not prohibitively expensive.

The key to dismantling one lies with a small "keeper" or retainer clip at the base of the handle assembly. With some faucets, you can see this clip at the point where the handle meets the base. With others, you must first remove the handle and—in the case of a swivel-spout faucet—the spout.

Under the handle, you'll probably find a ring or tube that simply slides off to expose the keeper. Pry out the clip with a screwdriver or long-nose pliers and the cartridge will pull out with little difficulty.

When you assemble the faucet, look for a flat spot, arrow, or other mark on the cartridge stem. Usually this must be pointing up for the faucet to work properly.

A typical cartridge faucet looks like this. A keeper ring must be pulled back to expose the keeper clip for removal.

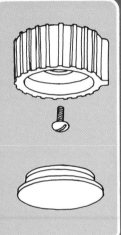

With a screwdriver, carefully pry off any decorative cap, and back out the screw in the handle. Then withdraw the cartridge.

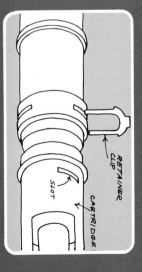

The clip may not be hidden at all. Some faucets also have a second retainer clip located near the handle.

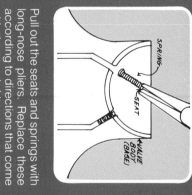

## REPAIRING TUB/SHOWER FAUCETS

Like sink and lavatory faucets, wall-mounted faucets also fall into two categories: compression and non-compression types. The non-compression version usually has a single handle pull-on, push-off configuraton, with a cartridge assembly beneath. When it leaks, this assembly usually requires replacement. Compression faucets, the two-handled types, feature O-rings and washers, which you can replace. An example of each type is shown here.

Problems with shower heads usually stem from lime deposits and/or corrosion. Often, you can disassemble the head and clean its screens and strainers. If you can't take your unit apart, replace it with a new one.

To repair compression faucets, pry out the handle insert and remove the knob. Under this you'll find a packing nut. Loosen this nut and replace the handle on the stem. Then, turn the handle to remove the stem.

If the stem has worn O-rings or a worn seat washer, which you'll find at the bottom of the stem, replace them. Thinly coat the O-rings with a heat-resistant lubricant jelly. Replace worn packing, too, if your stems have it.

PACKING NUT

PACKING

STEM WASHER

STEM

HANDLE

ESCUTCHEON

SEAT WASHER

STEM SLEEVE

TO SHOWER HEAD

COMPRESSION-TYPE FAUCET

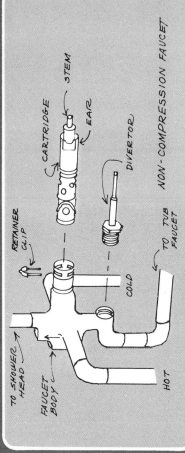

RETAINER CLIP

CARTRIDGE

STEM

EAR

DIVERTOR

COLD

TO TUB FAUCET

TO SHOWER HEAD

FAUCET BODY

HOT

NON-COMPRESSION FAUCET

To repair leaky single-handle faucets, you need to replace the cartridge. Remove the handle and retainer clip, then the cartridge.

To insert the new cartridge, push it into the housing until the ears are flush with the housing. Align parts, then insert clip.

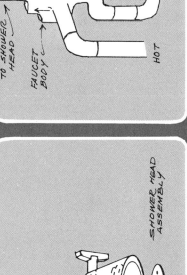

SHOWER HEAD ASSEMBLY

Unscrew shower heads as shown in this sketch. This will expose the screens and strainers for cleaning or replacement.

270

Whenever divertors, sprays, or aerators act up, you'll usually find the culprit to be a worn washer or a clogged strainer.

*Divertors* channel water from a faucet to a shower head or spray attachment. You can make minor repairs such as replacing worn O-rings, packing, or washers by backing out the divertor assembly. However, if the divertor assembly is leaking, you'll have to replace it. Take the old unit to a plumbing shop so you can match it with a new one.

*Sprays* have a hose and nozzle head. Troubles can develop in the connections,

washers, or the nozzle. But before you rip into the assembly, try tightening connecting nuts to stop leaks, and make sure the hose is not kinked.

*Aerators,* those tiny spray devices connected to the spouts of faucets in sinks and lavatories, have threads that let you screw them to the spout. Corrosion in the form of rust or lime deposits blocking the screen or strainers causes most all the problems you'll encounter with these devices. If a malfunctioning aerator is an old one, replace it with a new assembly.

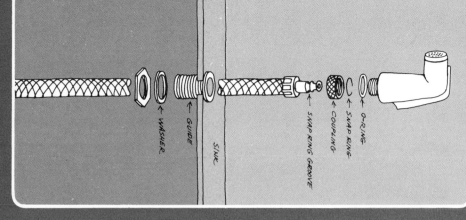

← WASHER
← GUIDE
← O-RING
← COUPLING
← SNAP RING
SNAP RING GROOVE
SINK

A spray attachment has washers and couplings that can leak. You can stop most leaks by tightening these.

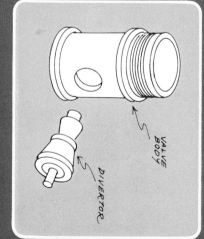

HOT-WATER SUPPLY
SPRAY HOSE
DIVERTOR ASSEMBLY
O-RING
SWIVEL SPOUT

The divertor on sink faucets is positioned on top of the faucet housing. The spray hose connection is under it.

Remove the faucet handle and unscrew the stem nut to release the innards of a shower divertor assembly.

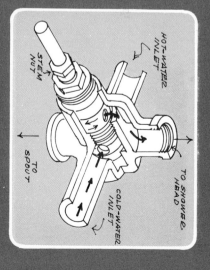

HOT-WATER INLET
STEM NUT
TO SPOUT
TO SHOWER HEAD
COLD-WATER INLET

Lime deposits can clog a faucet's divertor. With the type shown, remove and replace the assembly. You can clean some kinds.

VALVE BODY
DIVERTOR

Assemble aerators in this order. You can clean the basket and screen by flushing them with water or brushing the mesh.

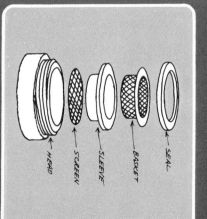

← HEAD
← SCREEN
← SLEEVE
← BASKET
← SEAL

## REPAIRING DRAINS AND TRAPS

Compared to faucets, the components that carry water away from a fixture are relatively simple. Since gravity does most of the work, drainage systems need to handle only moderate pressures. And except for the rudimentary linkages that operate pop-up and trip-lever assembles (see below), you'll find no moving parts underneath a lavatory, sink, or tub.

When trouble does occur, it almost always falls into one of two categories—a clog or a leak. If the flow seems just a little slower than it should be, try running hot water down the drain for about 10 minutes; often this will be enough to dissolve any accumulated grease or soap.

If hot water doesn't do the job, try a commercial drain cleaner. Follow the manufacturer's instructions to the letter, though. And don't use drain cleaner in a completely stopped-up fixture—if it doesn't work and you have to dismantle the trap, as shown opposite, you'll be working with dangerously caustic water. For more about clearing clogged drains, see pages 264 and 265.

Leaks call for some sleuthing to pinpoint exactly where the water is coming from. First set up a strong light under the fixture and wipe all drainage components dry. Now run tepid water (cold water can cause misleading condensation) and methodically check each connection, starting up top where the drain exits the fixture. Don't rely on your eyes alone. Instead, wipe each fitting with your fingertips, then look for moisture on them.

If you find a leak at a connection, often simply tightening its slip nut will solve the problem. Take care not to apply too much pressure, though; because they're made of soft, lightweight materials, drain fittings can be easily cracked or crushed.

If tightening doesn't do the job, prepare to dismantle the assembly, as shown opposite.

## Adjusting Pop-Ups and Trip-Levers

Have you ever filled a lavatory or tub, stepped away for a few minutes, and returned to discover that the water level had dropped? If so, the fixture's pop-up or trip-lever mechanism is letting you down.

Start by lifting or turning out the *stopper* and flushing away any hair, soap, or other debris that might be preventing it from seating properly. Wipe off the *flange*, too, and inspect it for any signs of wear or damage.

After you replace the stopper, check to see if the lifting assembly pulls it down snug. If not—and you're dealing with a lavatory pop-up—get under the basin and take a look at the *pivot rod*. It should slope slightly upward from the *pivot* to the *clevis*.

To adjust this, loosen the clevis's set-screw, push the stopper down hard, and retighten the setscrew. Now the lavatory will probably hold water, but its *lift rod* may not operate as easily as before. If this is the case, adjust the linkage between the pivot and clevis so they meet at nearly a right angle.

Occasionally a sink pop-up will leak at its pivot. Sometimes tightening the retaining nut here will stop the drip. If not, remove the nut and replace any washer or gasket you find underneath.

Tub pop-ups—and a variation called a trip-lever—work in much the same way, except that they are housed within the overflow tube. To adjust them, you remove the stopper, unscrew the overflow plate, and pull out the entire assembly.

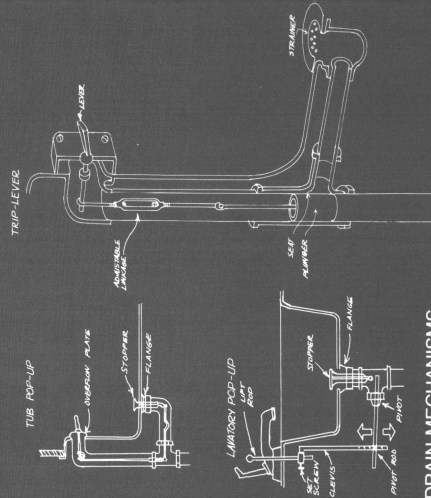

TRIP-LEVER

LEVER

STRAINER

ADJUSTABLE LINKAGE

SEAT

PLUNGER

TUB POP-UP

OVERFLOW PLATE

STOPPER

FLANGE

LAVATORY POP-UP

LIFT ROD

STOPPER

FLANGE

SET SCREW

CLEVIS

PIVOT ROD

PIVOT

DRAIN MECHANISMS

# Dismantling a Trap

Clogged drains, missing rings, and the ravages of time make it almost inevitable that you'll have to take apart a trap at some time or other. Master the steps depicted here, though, and you'll be out from under the problem in just a few minutes, and with a minimum of aggravation.

The secret to the way trap components fit together lies with the special slip-joint connections depicted below. Only the trap itself is threaded, not the tailpiece or drainpipe that slips into either end. This arrangement lets you twist everything around to align the assembly. Then you tighten slip nuts to secure it.

Although most slip fittings utilize rubber washers, some older slip fittings

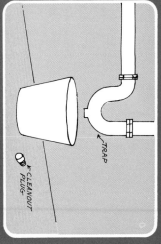

may be packed with lamp wick, which looks like ordinary cotton string, but makes a more watertight seal.

Whenever you have a trap apart, inspect it carefully for signs of corrosion. These usually show up first at the bend along the sides and bottom. Before going shopping for a new trap, measure the diameter of the tailpiece. This is usually 1¼ inches.

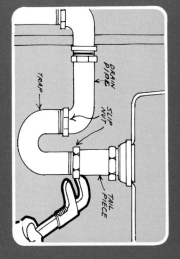

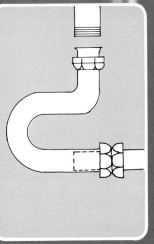

First shut off water at the fixture stops or take knobs off the faucets. Don't chance inadvertently turning them on.

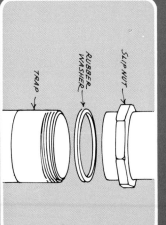

Next, slip a bucket or tray underneath to catch water in the trap. Open the cleanout if the trap you're working has one.

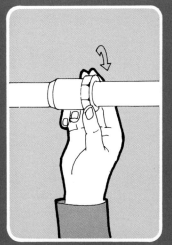

When you reassemble drain fittings, be careful not to overtighten them. Start by turning the slip nuts hand-tight.

Leaks often result from worn-out washers rather than from the trap itself. Tighten the slip nut or replace the washer.

Then go another quarter-turn with a wrench. Select one with smooth jaws—or pad serrated jaws so they don't mar the plating.

When you loosen slip nuts at the tailpiece and drainpipe, this type of trap will simply drop loose or come off with a tug.

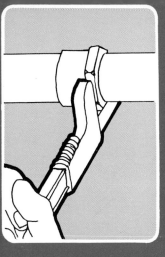

With a fixed trap, such as this one, you slide down the tailpiece, then turn the trap loose from the drainpipe.

To test a trap for leaks, completely fill the basin, then open the drain and check all connections closely for signs of moisture.

**273**

# REPAIRING TOILETS

Repairing a problem toilet isn't anyone's idea of a good time, but you'll have to do it every so often nonetheless. Most toilet maladies happen inside the tank where all the mechanical parts are located. Only rarely will other problems develop.

Lift the top off a home toilet tank and you'll find—mostly submerged in water—an assortment of balls, tubes, and levers similar to those illustrated at right. To understand what they do, first realize that flipping the handle sets in motion a chain of events that releases water to the bowl, then automatically refills both the tank and the bowl.

In the flushing cycle, moving the *handle* activates a *trip lever* that lifts a *flush ball* at the bottom of the tank. Water then rushes through a *seat* into the toilet bowl. After the tank empties, the flush ball drops back into its seat.

Flushing also triggers the refill cycle, thanks to a *float ball* that goes down along with the water level and opens an *inlet valve.* This brings fresh water into the tank via a refill tube; it also sends water to the bowl through a second refill tube that empties into an *overflow tube.*

As the water rises, so does the float ball. When it reaches a point ¾ inch or so below the top of the overflow, the float shuts off the inlet valve.

The following pages take you step by step through just about everything that can possibly go wrong inside a toilet tank, and tell what to do about each situation. To learn about toilet bowls and how to install a new unit, see pages 300 and 301.

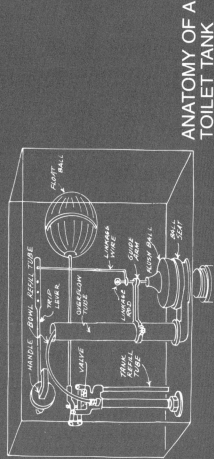

## ANATOMY OF A TOILET TANK

# TROUBLESHOOTING TOILETS

| PROBLEM | SOLUTION |
|---|---|
| Toilet won't flush | Check the handle, trip lever, guide arm, flush ball, and the connections between each one of the parts to make sure all are functioning. The handle may be too loose or tight; the trip lever or guide arm may be bent or broken; the connection between the trip lever and guide arm may be broken or out of adjustment so it doesn't raise the flush ball far enough. |
| Water runs, but tank won't fill properly | The handle and trip assembly may be malfunctioning. See above. Check the flush ball for proper seating; check the seat for corrosion; and check the float ball for water inside. |
| Water runs constantly after the tank is filled | You may have to adjust the float ball downward. Check the float ball to make sure it's not damaged. It could be full of water, causing it to float improperly. The inlet valve washers may be leaking and need replacement. Check to see that the flush ball is seating properly. Check the ball seat for corrosion. |
| The water level is set too high or too low | Gently bend the flush tank float downward to lower the water level. Bend it upward to raise the water level. Or, use the adjustment screw on top of the inlet valve to set the float arm. The water should be ¾ inch below the top of the overflow tube. |
| Toilet won't flush properly | Water may be too low in the tank. If so, bend the float ball up to permit sufficient water to flow into the toilet bowl. |
| Water splashes in the tank while it refills | Adjust the refill tube that runs into the overflow tube. You may need to replace the washers in the inlet valve. |
| Tank leaks at the bottom | Tighten all the nuts at the bottom of the tank. If this doesn't work, replace the washers. |

# Repairing Flush Mechanisms

An occasional gurgle, a constant flow of water—both are sure signs that your toilet's got troubles. But don't panic! Almost 100 percent of the time, you can trace the problem to the flushing mechanism, which controls the water in the flush tank. And, usually, correcting the problem involves only a very simple adjustment, or, in some cases, a few new parts.

If the working parts are metal (usually brass) and aren't too old, you're best off replacing the individual malfunctioning parts. But if the parts are plastic or have been in service for several years, replace the entire assembly. These come in kit form with easy-to-follow installation instructions.

Not covered here are trip arms and linkage wires. These parts often corrode and break before the inlet valves, refill tube, and flush-ball seat go on the fritz. To learn about trip arms and linkages, see page 277.

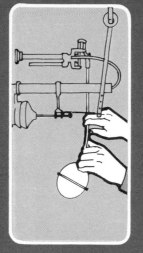

To adjust the position, carefully bend the float rod so the float ball is about ½ inch lower. Flush the tank to check the float.

A collar you can buy allows more accuracy when adjusting float position. Also look for an adjustment screw on the inlet valve.

Only half of the float ball should be submerged. If it sinks lower, check it for leaks. Replace the float, if necessary.

Lift the float rod gently. If the water shuts off, the float ball position has to be changed slightly to close the valve.

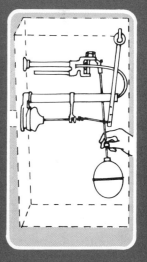

To adjust the position, carefully bend the float rod so the float ball is about ½ inch lower. Flush the tank to check the float.

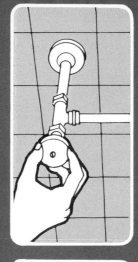

Before making valve-assembly repairs, turn off the water at the shutoff valve below the tank (or at the water meter).

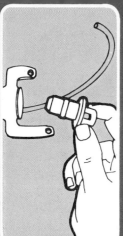

If the water doesn't shut off when you lift the float, the washers may be worn. To open the valve, remove two pivot screws.

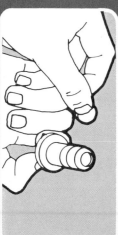

Slide the float, rod, and linkage out of the valve. On some assemblies, you remove a cap that covers the inlet valve.

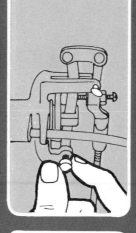

To remove the plunger from the valve, pull upward. If it's stuck, use a screwdriver to gently pry it out. Don't damage the metal.

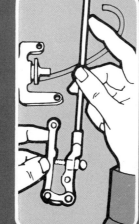

A washer at the base of the plunger shuts off the flow of water. In most cases, you simply push the new washer in position.

Some plungers have two washers. The second washer fits into a groove in the valve. Remove any corrosion from the plunger.

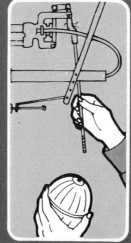

275

## Repairing a Leaky Flush Ball

Generally, you'll find one or more of the following conditions responsible for water leaking via the flush ball from the tank into the bowl: a misaligned guide arm and wire, a bent linkage wire, a worn flush ball, or a pitted or corroded flush-ball seat.

You generally can pinpoint the problem by flushing the toilet and watching these parts operate. (See page 274 for a sketch that identifies them.)

To check the ball seat, lift the ball with the flush handle and run your fingers over the seat. If it feels rough, chances are good that it's corroded or pitted—a job for an abrasive or steel wool.

If your problem is a worn flush ball, buy a replacement. Just unscrew the old

ball and screw on the new one. You might want to upgrade the assembly at this time with a new flapper-type ball unit or a "water saver" valve-and-ball device. Both are easy-to-install replacements you'll find at most home center stores. More about these at the bottom of the page.

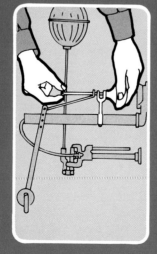

Raise the linkage rod and test the flush ball for wear. To replace the ball, unscrew the linkage rod by hand or with pliers.

With the flush ball removed, clean the ball seat. Use fine steel wool for this, and buff the metal seat until it's shiny.

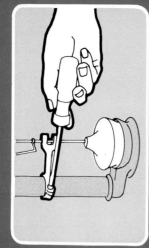

Adjust the linkage rod so it allows the ball to seat. To adjust the guide arm, loosen the setscrew as shown.

Align a flapper-type ball unit over the ball seat by twisting it on the overflow tube. A chain serves as the linkage wire.

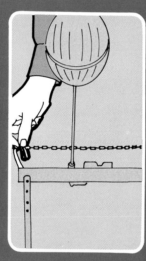

Adjust the lift chain to the proper length and fasten it to the trip arm. If the lift chain is broken or badly corroded, replace it.

## Upgrading a Flushing Mechanism

Like anything mechanical, a flush-tank assembly eventually wears out. Its life-span depends on how often it's used and the hardness of the water in your area. Some water can quickly corrode parts, and lime deposits can quickly clog them up.

Almost all flush-tank mechanisms are replaceable by the piece, so you don't

have to buy the entire unit. Flush balls, floats, lifts, and guides are "standard," so they usually fit any flush-tank make or model. However, if you're having trouble with the assembly, it might be smarter to replace the entire unit, a not-too-difficult project.

Several new flush-tank mechanisms depart from the traditional designs. One, a flapper-ball unit, features quietness of flush and an extremely long life-span. Another type—called a water-saver—doesn't use a float-ball component.

Instead, water pressure regulates the water-inlet valve. This, in turn, meters out the exact amount of water needed in the tank for a full flush. This feature, in time, can save a considerable amount of water, and can eliminate the need to adjust a float arm and float ball.

If you choose to stick with a standard assembly, invest in a quality product. The cost may be a bit more at the outset, but your troubles with the unit should be minimal.

276

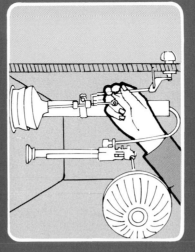

## Adjusting Tank Linkage

No toilet flushing action can take place until you flip the handle on the tank. This mechanism is the key to the assembly, and it's also the most prone to malfunction. The tank linkage is made up of a handle, trip lever, linkage wire or chain, and connecting devices. If any one of them gives out, it affects the entire assembly.

Corrosion, the assembly's biggest enemy, usually occurs around the handle where it goes through the tank and connects to the trip lever. If you spot trouble here, remove the handle (a nut holds it tight) and clean the parts

with fine steel wool. Then lightly coat the parts with a waterproof lubricant and reassemble them.

Be extremely careful when you remove the handle (use a wrench). Too much pressure can crack the flush tank. If this happens, you'll have to buy a whole new tank. If you can't remove the nut, you'll have to cut through the bolt with a hacksaw. Again, take care that you don't crack or chip the tank.

Trip-lever troubles start when the lever becomes bent or misaligned with the lift chain or linkage wire. The lever is set at a slight angle to the handle so it may operate freely without rubbing against the side of the tank, the inlet valve, or the overflow tube.

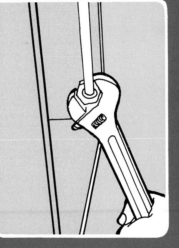

Flip the handle several times to make sure the trip lever is operating freely; if it isn't, try gently bending the arm toward the center of the tank for necessary clearance. As you bend the arm, hold it with one hand near the flushing handle.

The fastener or chain between the end of the trip lever and the linkage wire or chain often presents a problem. The water corrodes this part, and it actually rots away. Fortunately, replacing this connector is extremely simple. If the new part is made of brass, it will survive longer in the water.

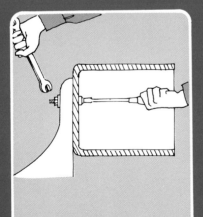

## Stopping Tank and Bowl Leaks

Occasionally a toilet will develop an external leak at one of three points—around the water-supply pipe, where the tank joins the bowl, or around the base of the bowl.

To solve a water-supply-pipe problem, first tighten the nut that holds the fitting to the tank. If that doesn't work, shut off the water supply, remove the fittings, and install new washers, or a new pipe if necessary.

A leak where the tank joins the bowl may simply mean the tank's hold-down bolts have loosened. Drain the tank and try tightening the bolts as shown at right.

If that doesn't stop the leak, you'll have to remove the bolts and install new washers.

With some older-model toilets, the tank is attached to the wall and connected to the bowl via an elbow fitting. If you spot leaks here, try tightening the elbow's slip nuts; if that doesn't work, repack them.

When a leak appears on the floor at the bowl's base, check the bowl's hold-down bolts. Chances are, they've loosened and allowed the bowl to rock on the seal underneath. Tightening the bolts might solve the problem; if not, you'll have to remove the entire toilet and install a new seal, as explained on page 301.

Straighten the linkage wire connected to the trip lever. Lift the flush ball off the seat to prevent suction.

Take care when tightening or loosening the handle nut. Clean and coat the parts with water-proof lube.

Apply penetrating oil to the tank bolts, loosen, then carefully re-tighten them. Too much pressure will crack the tank.

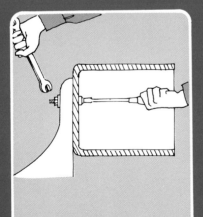

277

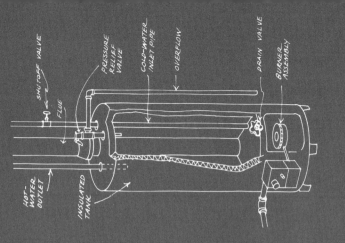

SHUTOFF VALVE
PRESSURE RELIEF VALVE
COLD-WATER INLET PIPE
OVERFLOW
FLUE
DRAIN VALVE
BURNER ASSEMBLY
HOT-WATER OUTLET
INSULATED TANK

## MAINTAINING A WATER HEATER

Today's water heaters generally provide years of trouble-free service, with or without maintenance. But just a little effort on your part can extend your water heater's life and cut down on its energy consumption.

Some manufacturers recommend that new gas or electric units be drained every two months for the first year they're in operation, then every six months after that. Doing this rids them of sediment, which builds up over time, impeding efficiency and providing you with less hot water at any given time.

To drain a water heater, first shut off the water supply by turning the shutoff valve at the top of the heater or at the meter. Next, place a bucket under the tank's drain valve, or fasten a garden hose to the valve and run the hose to a floor drain.

Now open the drain valve and let off water until it runs clear; then close the drain valve and open the supply valve.

You should also periodically check the heater's *pressure-relief valve* to be sure it's capable of letting off steam if pressure builds up in the tank. Just lift this valve's handle; if it's functioning properly, hot water will be released through the overflow.

If yours is a gas-fired heater, like the one shown here, inspect the flue assembly every six months or so. The draft divertor should be aligned with the flue, and the asbestos tape that seals joints between flue sections should be intact. (More about this essential safety check on page 322.)

The ports of a gas burner may have to be cleaned every two years or so—as explained in the chart below. And if you're plagued with a pilot light that just won't stay lit, see pages 309 and 310, and page 323.

## TROUBLESHOOTING WATER HEATERS

| Problem | Solution |
| --- | --- |
| Water won't heat (electric) | Check the fuse box or circuit breaker for a blown fuse or a tripped switch; reactivate. If the heater continues to blow fuses or circuits often, call in a pro. |
| Water won't heat (gas) | Pilot light isn't burning; relight it (see page 309). Unclog burner ports as explained below. Make sure the gas connection shutoff valve is fully open. Check temperature control knob for proper setting. |
| Water too hot | Check the thermostat setting; turn back setting, if necessary. The thermostat may be malfunctioning or not functioning. If you suspect this, call in a professional. |
| Water tank is leaking | Turn off the heater's water and gas or electrical supplies and drain the tank. It'll probably have to be replaced. To learn about installing a new unit yourself, see pages 302 and 303. |
| Water supply pipes leak | Tighten the pipe fittings. If this doesn't work, turn off the water and replace fittings. If water is condensing on the cold water supply pipe, wrap the pipe with standard pipe insulation (see page 372). |
| Clogged gas burner ports | Remove the debris with a needle or the end of a paper clip. Do not use a wooden toothpick or peg; either can break off in the portholes. |
| Gas flame burns yellow | The burner may not be getting enough primary air. Also check the pilot light (see page 310); the flame should be about ½ inch long. Call in a pro for any necessary adjustments. The burner of a gas water heater should be serviced professionally every 24 months or so. |
| Heater smells of gas | Immediately turn off the gas at the main supply valve. Open the windows and let the gas out. Turn on the gas at the main valve and coat the pipe connections with soapy water. If bubbles appear, the connection is leaking. Do not relight until the gas leak has been repaired. |

# WINTERIZING PLUMBING

Winter cold can wreak havoc with a plumbing system—and today most homes are plumbed with this in mind. Still, many homeowners have found out the hard way what happens to pipes in vacant houses with little or no heat.

Completely shutting down a plumbing system is neither difficult nor costly. Follow the procedures outlined here and in the drawing below.

On the day of the shutdown, turn off water at the meter or—better yet—schedule with the city water department to turn off service at the valve outside your home. (This is usually located in the front or backyard, and requires a special key or wrench to operate.) Then, starting at the top of the water supply system, open every faucet—bathtub, shower, lavatories, and so on. Be sure you don't miss any you don't normally use, such as an outside sill

cock or underground sprinkler system. (These should be drained every fall anyway, whether your home will be heated or not.)

Turn off power to the water heater and drain it, too. By the time you reach your system's lowest point, its supply pipes should be completely empty. Make sure, though, that there's an outlet at the lowest point. This might be the water heater, a basement laundry tub or washing machine, or a valve installed specifically for draining the system.

Now you have to go through the entire house a second time to freeze-proof its drainage system. Start by removing the cleanout plugs on all sink and lavatory traps (see page 261) or, if a trap doesn't have a cleanout plug, dismantle and empty the trap itself, as shown on page 273. After you've emptied each trap, replace it or its cleanout plug, then pour in automotive antifreeze mixed with water in the proportions specified for cars in your climate.

You won't be able to drain some traps, such as the ones in toilets and perhaps those under tubs as well. With toilets, first flush them, pour a gallon of the antifreeze solution into each tank, then flush again. With bathtubs and other traps you can't get at, use the antifreeze full strength—at least a quart.

Water collects in dish- and clothes-washers, too. This you'll have to completely siphon out—but don't pour antifreeze into these appliances or any fresh-water pipes. Finally, fill your home's main trap with antifreeze.

To refill a system that's been drained, you simply turn off all faucets, then open the water supply valve. Expect some sputtering at first as the water pushes air out of the lines. Don't worry about the traps; antifreeze in them will clear away automatically.

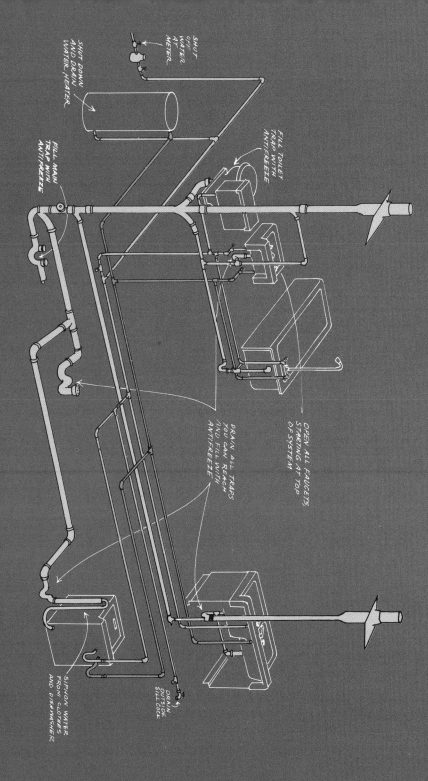

SHUT OFF WATER AT METER.

SHUT DOWN AND DRAIN WATER HEATER.

FILL MAIN TRAP WITH ANTI-FREEZE

FILL TOILET TRAP WITH ANTI-FREEZE

OPEN ALL FAUCETS, STARTING AT TOP OF SYSTEM

DRAIN ALL TRAPS YOU CAN REACH AND FILL WITH ANTI-FREEZE

DRAIN OUTSIDE SILL COCK.

SIPHON WATER FROM CLOTHES AND DISHWASHER.

# QUIETING NOISY PIPES

Pressure can get to any of us from time to time, and believe it or not, the same thing is true of your water system. Most generally under the considerable load of 60 pounds of pressure per square inch (psi), your home's pipes can make a nerve-racking array of noises. But don't assume that you can't do anything to silence them—because you can. Discussed below are the more common maladies and how to cure them.

*Water hammer*, the loud bang you hear when you open a faucet, run the water, and quickly close the faucet, is

terribly common. Automatic washing machines also produce this sound when a solenoid valve snaps shut. Most house fixtures have an air chamber, which eventually fills with water and causes "hammer." To fix, first drain the system. Then refill the pipes (the air chamber will fill with air again and shouldn't act up for several years).

If your system isn't outfitted with chambers, install one at the faucet fixture. This chamber provides a "cushion" of air on which the bang can bounce (see below).

*Machine-gun rattle* signals a faucet problem. Try replacing the washer.

A *whistle* indicates that a water valve somewhere in the system is partly

closed. The water, under pressure, narrows at the valve and causes the whistle. Simply open the valve as far as you can. If a toilet whistles, adjust the inlet valve (see page 275).

If you hear *running water*, check for leaks at toilets, sill cocks, your furnace humidifier, and your water softener.

Generally, you can trace *soft ticking or cracking* to a hot water pipe that was cool, then suddenly was reheated with water. Muffle with insulation.

*Bangs* may result from water pressure in the pipes that causes them to bang against their metal hangers. Have someone quickly open then close the faucet to cause a bang; often you can see the pipes move.

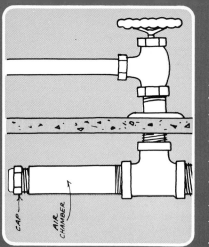

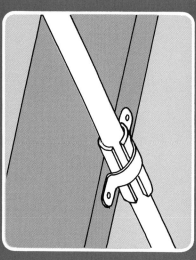

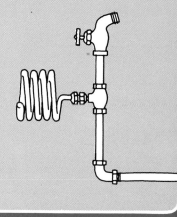

An air chamber is a length of pipe rising above the supply pipe, usually located near a faucet or fixture shutoff.

"Soundproof" pipes that touch hangers with short lengths of rubber hose. Split the hose lengthwise and slip it around the pipes.

Copper-coil air chambers are available at plumbing stores. To install them, break the supply line and add a tee fitting.

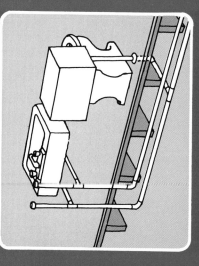

To stop bangs and squeaks, nail pipe hange's as shown. Be sure not to use galvanized hangers on copper.

If you're extensively remodeling or building a new house, here's an air-chamber hookup diagram for a lavatory and toilet.

Water pressure is one of those things you can have too much or too little of. Too little pressure results in trickles rather than streams of water, the results of which are obvious. Too much pressure, although a much rarer problem, can wreck faucets and weaken connections in your system.

If you have too much pressure in your lines, you need a pressure reducer, a device you can easily install.

If you're suffering from too little pressure, your immediate task is to locate the source of the problem. Start

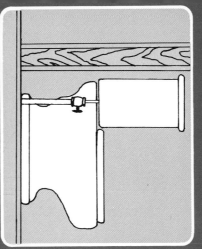

by removing aerators and shower heads from fixtures. If the strainers in these units are blocked with sediment and lime deposits, clean the strainers.

Next, make sure all shutoff valves are fully opened; partly closed valves slow water flow considerably.

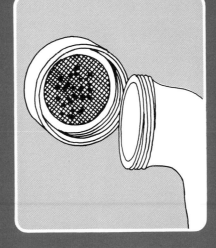

If your water source is a well and you have an automatic pump, the pressure regulator at the pump may be set too low. Also check for a loose pump belt. In the winter months, low pressure can be caused by a frozen pipe or pressure switch.

If none of the obvious checks produce any results, break a connection in the water system. If you find lime deposits inside the pipe, you may have to finance

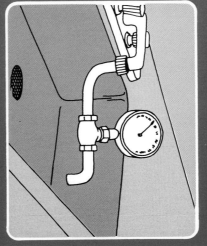

a new plumbing job. Under no circumstances should you try to flush a limed system with chemicals. You can, however, have sediment flushed from the pipes, which may restore much of the pressure. This is a job for a professional plumber; don't attempt to do it yourself.

If liming is a problem in your area, the cheapest and easiest way to correct it is to install a water softener on cold as well as hot lines. (See page 306.)

But before calling in a plumber, call the water department and ask them to check the water main leading into your home. It could be faulty.

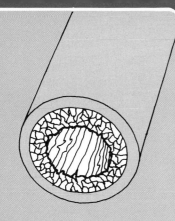

Make sure all supply valves are open. Also turn off water at the main, and check valve parts for damage, corrosion, or liming.

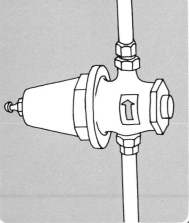

Unscrew aerators on faucet spouts to clean out any debris. If the wire strainer is badly corroded, replace it.

To decrease pressure, buy a pressure-reducing valve. The further you open the valve, the less pressure you should have.

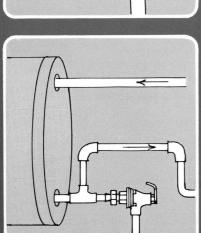

Limed pipes slow water to a trickle. If flushing the system doesn't help, you'll have to have your house re-plumbed.

An inexpensive pressure gauge is a fast, easy way to check the water pressure. It should register 50 to 60 pounds per square inch.

If your water heater doesn't have a relief valve, install one this way. Without one, hot water pressure could reach dangerous levels.

# MAKING PLUMBING IMPROVEMENTS

Like carpenters, plumbers divide their work into two general categories—*roughing-in* and *finishing*. In the roughing-in stage, you cut sections of pipe to length and piece them together with a variety of standardized *fittings*. Then you finish off the job by hooking a *fixture* to the new lines.

The balance of this chapter takes you step by step through both phases of a plumbing project—from those critical first measurements to the moment you turn on the water and check your work for leaks.

The key to visualizing the way any plumbing run will go together lies with the fittings illustrated on the opposite page. Plumbing components are made from a wide variety of materials (see page 284), but all join with similar elbows, couplings, tees, and other connecting devices.

Note, though, that we've divided the chart into different sections for supply and DWV piping. These fittings are not interchangeable, even when they're made of the same materials. That's because drainage fittings have smooth insides. Since supply fittings are under pressure, their slight restrictions don't critically impede the flow.

## MEASURING PIPES AND FITTINGS

Before you can buy the parts for any pipe-fitting project, you first have to know the diameters you'll be dealing with, and sometimes—especially if you're purchasing pre-threaded stock—the exact lengths as well. Computing both can be tricky until you get the hang of it.

Start by realizing that pipes are always sized according to their *inside* diameters. This means that the best way

to get an accurate fix on what you need is to break open the run you'll be tying into and measure the pipe—not its fittings—as illustrated below.

Secondly, don't be surprised to discover that the inside diameter turns out to be slightly larger or smaller than a standard pipe size. So-called "one-inch" steel pipe, for instance, may be slightly greater or slightly less than an inch inside, depending on the thickness of its walls. Rounding off your measurement to the nearest ⅛ inch gives the *nominal dimension* you'll need.

The thing to keep in mind when you're figuring lengths is that you have to account for the distance each pipe engages in its fittings, as well as the distance between fittings. To do this, first measure from *face to face*, then add on the *socket depths*, as shown here. Socket depths vary somewhat from one pipe material to another, but remain the same for all fittings of a given material.

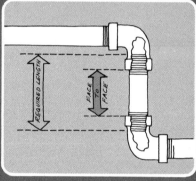

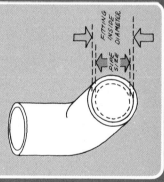

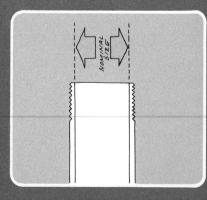

Always measure inside—not outside—pipe diameters. Actual and nominal dimensions can vary by ¹⁄₁₆ inch or so.

Fittings are also sized according to the pipe's inside dimensions, so measuring a fitting doesn't tell you much.

A pipe that's a little too short may leak at one or both ends. For accuracy, compute the length from face to face.

Now check the socket's depth. Since pipes have fittings on both ends, multiply by two, then add the face-to-face length.

## KNOWING PLUMBING FITTINGS

| Water Supply Fittings | | Uses |
|---|---|---|
| Elbow |   | You'll need an elbow anywhere a plumbing run changes direction. Most make 90- or 45-degree turns. *Reducing elbows* (not shown) connect pipes of different diameters. *Street ells* have female connections on one end, male on the other. These let you couple one with another fitting. |
| Tee |   | Use this one wherever two pipes intersect. *Reducing tees* let you connect pipes of different diameters, as you might in taking a ½-inch branch off a ¾-inch main supply line, for example. To order, give the dimension of the main line first, then the branch line—¾x½ in the case cited here. |
| Coupling |   | This fitting connects lengths of pipe in a straight run. Once you've assembled pipe with couplings, you can't break into it without cutting at some point. *Reducers* let you step down from one pipe diameter to a smaller one. *Slip couplings* (see page 293) let you connect to an existing copper or plastic line. |
| Union | 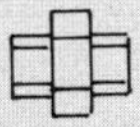 | Used mainly with threaded stock, a union compensates for the fact that all pipes have right-hand threads. You'll need at least one in any run of threaded pipe, and might want to add others so you can easily dismantle sections at a future time. More about this important fitting on page 293. |
| Cap, Plug, Bushing |  | To close off the end of a pipe, install a *cap;* these are available for both threaded and non-threaded pipe. To seal an opening in a threaded fitting, screw in a *plug*. Need to insert a pipe into a larger-diameter fitting? If so, a *bushing* is the answer. It's threaded both inside and out. |
| Nipple |  | Actually just lengths of threaded pipe that are less than 12 inches long, nipples are sold in standard sizes because short pieces are difficult to cut and thread. Get an assortment of these to join fittings that will be close together. A *close nipple* has threads from one end to the other for really tight situations. |
| Valve | 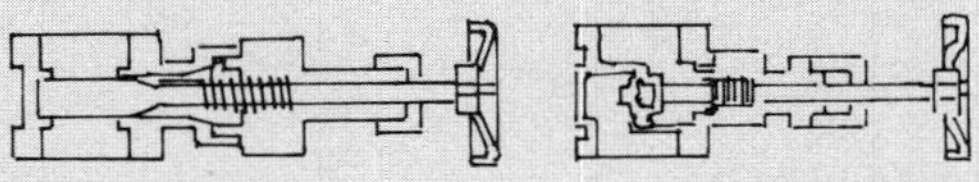  | *Gate valves* slide a gate-like disk that completely opens or closes the flow; these must be turned fully on or fully off. *Globe valves* operate like a compression-type faucet (see page 266); with these, you can regulate the flow as well as stop it. Even when wide open, globe valves constrict the flow somewhat. |
| **DWV Fittings** | | **Uses** |
| Bend | 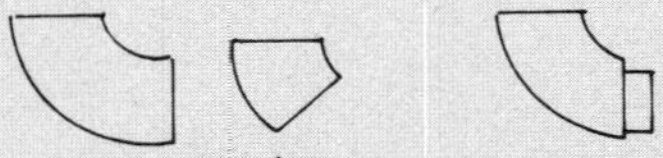  | Use these to change direction when running DWV pipe. Note that they have a gentle curve, rather than an abrupt angle where waste might lodge. Select ¼ bends for 90-degree turns, $^1/_5$ for 72-degree angles, $^1/_6$ for 60 degrees, ⅛ for 45, and $^1/_{16}$ for 22.5. A *closet bend* connects a toilet to a main drain. |
| Tee, Wye, Cross |  | Available in a wide variety of shapes for different situations, these *sanitary branches* serve as the intersection where two or three drains converge. For vent piping, you can simply invert the same fittings. Like bends, these are shaped for a smooth downward flow of liquids and waste. |

# SELECTING PIPES AND FITTINGS

If you've been under the impression that pipe is pipe, prepare for a surprise before you check out the table below. It compares no fewer than a dozen different materials.

Which you'll want to purchase for a particular project depends first of all upon the plumbing code in your area. Begin by learning which materials are allowed and which ones aren't.

Next, consider what function the pipe and fittings must serve. Some can be used only in drain-waste-vent systems;

others can't carry hot or drinking water. A few work for almost anything.

Finally, determine what the existing pipes in your home are made of. You needn't stick with the same thing—but you'll have to order special fittings to join dissimilar materials.

To help clarify matters, we've divided the dozen possibilities into four broad categories—copper, threaded, plastic, and cast iron.

Of the four, copper easily wins out as the most widely used, and virtually all codes permit it. Though somewhat more expensive than other types, it's lightweight, extremely versatile, and highly resistant to corrosion.

Threaded pipe—especially galvanized steel—has all but seen its day. Lifting, cutting, threading, and turning threaded pipe calls for lots of muscle work. What's more, steel limes up badly and can rust out in a decade or two. If yours is an older home, chances are it was originally plumbed with galvanized steel.

If codes permit you to use plastic pipe, count yourself fortunate. This one is the easiest of all for amateurs to work with.

You can't use it in every situation, though. Cast iron pipe does only drain-waste-vent duty. It's far and away the heaviest and most difficult to work with, though no-hub clamps (where allowed) make smaller jobs feasible for do-it-yourselfers.

## COMPARING PIPE MATERIALS

| Material | | Uses | Joining Techniques/Features |
|---|---|---|---|
| **Copper** | Rigid | Hot and cold water lines; DWV | Usually sweat-soldered together, as illustrated on the opposite page. Light weight makes copper easy to handle. |
| | Flexible | Hot and cold water lines | Sweat-solder, flare, or use compression fittings (see page 286). Comes in long coils that can be easily bent. Too soft for exposed locations; fittings are relatively expensive. |
| **Threaded** | Galvanized steel | Hot and cold water lines; DWV. *Don't use as a gas line.* | Comes in standard 21-foot lengths that you cut, thread, and join with standard fittings. Cumbersome and time-consuming. |
| | Black steel | Gas and steam or hot water heating lines | Same joining techniques and features as galvanized, but as black pipe rusts readily, it's not used for household water. |
| | Brass and bronze | Hot and cold water lines | Again, you cut and thread. Because these are costly, they're rarely used in homes. Very high resistance to corrosion. |
| **Plastic** | Rigid ABS | DWV only | Cut with an ordinary saw, then solvent-weld sections together as shown on page 288. Lightweight and very easy to work with, but not all plumbing codes permit it. |
| | Rigid PVC | Cold water and DWV only | Same as ABS |
| | Rigid CPVC | Hot and cold water lines | Same as ABS |
| | Flexible polybutylene | Hot and cold water lines | Goes together with special fittings like the ones shown on page 289. Costly and not widely used in home plumbing systems. |
| | Flexible polyethylene | Cold water lines only. Used mainly for sprinkler systems. | Same as polybutylene |
| **Cast Iron** | Bell and spigot | DWV only | Joints are packed with oakum, then sealed with molten lead—a job for a professional plumber. More about this one on page 290. |
| | No-hub | DWV only | You join sections with gaskets and clamps, as shown on page 291. Not overly difficult for an amateur to work with. |

Arm yourself with a tubing cutter and a propane torch, master the knack of sweating joints illustrated below, and soon you'll be "running copper" like a professional plumber.

Rigid copper pipe comes in 10- and 20-foot lengths, in one of three wall thicknesses. The thinnest of these, Type M, is approved for interior use by most local codes, though a few of them call for medium-wall Type L. Type K has a thick wall and is required for applications that run underground. Fittings include almost all of those that are shown on page 283.

Most pros preassemble runs of copper pipe, fluxing and dry-fitting each joint, but not soldering yet. Then when they're satisfied that everything fits properly, they go back and torch it all together.

After you sweat each joint, carefully look for any gaps around its perimeter. Leaks that don't show up until after you turn on the water mean you have to completely drain and dry out the joint before you can re-sweat it.

When you're using the torch, protect flammable surfaces with sheet metal, asbestos board, or wet rags.

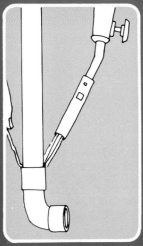

A tubing cutter does a fast, neat job of cutting pipe to length. If you use a hacksaw, take care to keep the cut square.

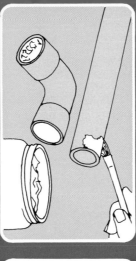

Remove all metal burrs from the cut with a file. Don't nick the metal; it could cause the connection to leak.

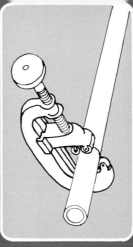

Shine the ends of the pipe to be connected with a fine-grit abrasive or steel wool. This will remove grease and dirt.

Apply rosin- (not acid-) flux soldering paste to the outside of the pipe and to the inside of the pipe fitting.

Slip the fitting onto the pipe. If the fitting has a hub or shoulder, make sure the pipe is seated against it.

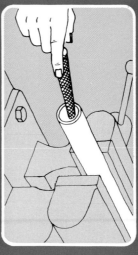

PROPANE TORCH

Heat the pipe and fitting where both components join. The tip of the inner flame produces the most heat. Don't overheat.

Test the pipe for temperature. If the solder melts, the temperature is right. The solder will flow into the connection.

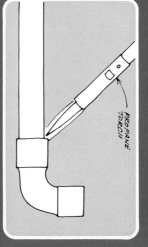

BEAD

The solder will form a solid bead around the connection. When the bead is complete, remove the solder and heat from the pipe.

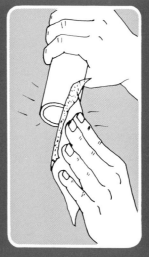

To give the joint a professional appearance, wipe it with a cloth as shown. Be careful not to get burned, though.

# WORKING WITH FLEXIBLE COPPER TUBING

As its name implies, flexible copper tubing distinguishes itself by being exceptionally workable. It goes places that rigid copper pipe just can't, and so is ideal for many close-quarters situations. Do use care when bending it, though. Flexible copper tubing kinks easily, and once kinked it's practically impossible to bend back into its original round shape. Don't use kinked tubing—it impedes water flow.

There are two weights of flexible copper tubing: Type K, generally used for underground installations, and Type L, the interior product. Both generally come in 15-, 30-, and 60-foot rolls at plumbing and home center stores.

You can assemble runs with solder and standard connections (as shown on page 285), with flare fittings, or with compression fittings. Flare and compression fittings cost more than solder fittings, but they do assemble more easily and don't require heat, a big advantage when working in close quarters between wall studs and floor joists.

Consider soldering connections you'll never need to break; save the more costly fittings for hooking up fixtures that might need to be removed someday.

To form flare fittings, you'll need a flaring tool, a fairly inexpensive item (see below). Once you've flared the tubing ends, you just screw special fittings together. Be sure to put flare nuts on the tubing before flaring the ends, though.

With compression fittings, the pipe doesn't have to be flared. You simply slip a compression ring over the tubing. The ring compresses (and seals) when the fittings are screwed together. The drawings below show how to join flexible tubing with either flare or compression fittings.

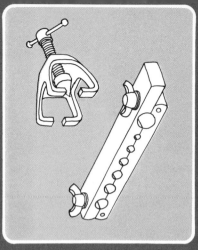

A flaring tool is a two-piece unit. Different-sized, beveled holes in the block accommodate several different sizes of tubing.

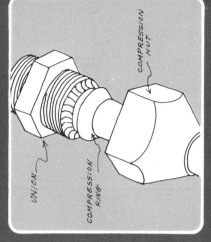

A compression joint has a ring that compresses under pressure of the fitting, producing a leak-free joint.

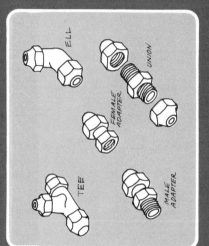

Fittings include tees, ells, unions, and a variety of copper, steel, and plastic adapters for hooking to other types of pipe.

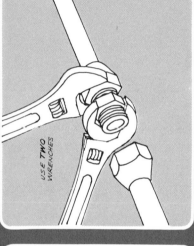

After the flares are made, use two wrenches to connect the joint. If the joint leaks under water pressure, re-flare the joint.

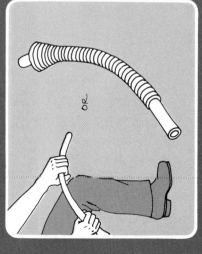

Bend flexible copper tubing over your knee, or use a spring tube bender. Work with gentle bends, not acute angles.

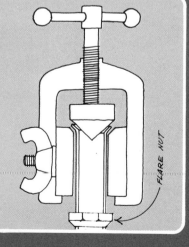

Clamp the tubing in the block. Attach and center the flaring part of the tool over the tubing. Then tighten, turning clockwise.

286

# WORKING WITH THREADED PIPE

Though copper and plastic now offer better ways to go, plumbers have been threading together steel, iron, brass, and bronze pipes for a century or so—and unless yours is a fairly new home, at least some of its plumbing probably uses this old-fashioned system.

Need only a few sections of threaded pipe? Measure carefully, then order them precut and threaded. For bigger jobs, it may pay to thread your own.

Threading tools (these are best rented) include a vise, pipe cutter (you also can use a hacksaw), a threading die, die

stock, reamer, and two 10-inch pipe wrenches.

The key to threading pipe is to start the die squarely on the pipe. You must get it right the first time or the threads won't thread, so take your time until you get the hang of it.

The size of the pipe you're using determines how far it must be turned into the fittings. For ⅛-inch pipe, the distance is ¼ inch. For ¼-inch pipe, it's ⅜ inch. One half- and ⅜-inch pipes need ½ inch of threads; and ¾- and 1-inch pipe requires a ⁹⁄₁₆-inch distance.

To measure the length of pipe needed, figure the distance between the face of each fitting, plus the distance into the fittings. For example, if you're working with

¾-inch pipe and the distance between the face of each fitting is 4 feet, you'll need a piece of pipe 4 feet, 1 inch long.

If you're replacing a piece of pipe and threading the pipe yourself, remember to include a union fitting in the measurement. The same threading distance applies to unions as for the other fittings.

When threading brass pipe, you must be extra careful not to scratch or mar the finish as you thread it. And when cutting and threading galvanized or black pipe, be sure to wear gloves to protect your hands against sharp metal slivers and shavings.

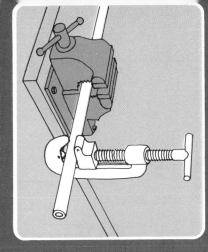

To cut pipe, first clamp it tightly in a vise. Then make the cut with a pipe cutter. The sharp metal wheel does the cutting.

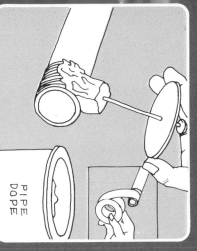

Apply pipe dope or pipe tape to the pipe threads (but not to the fitting threads) before twisting on the fitting.

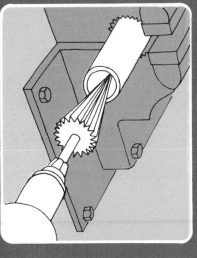

Remove burrs from the inside of the pipe with a reamer powered by a brace or drill. Remove just the burrs, not the metal.

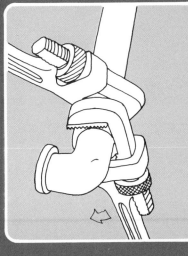

To use pipe wrenches as shown below, turn the fitting onto the pipe. To avoid leaks, tighten down as far as you can.

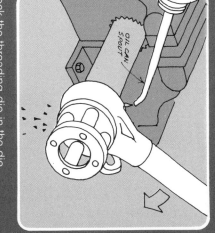

Lock the threading die in the die stock. Place the die squarely on the pipe and begin turning it. Apply oil as you cut the threads.

287

## WORKING WITH RIGID PLASTIC PIPE

Rigid plastic pipe, though only a recent introduction to the plumbing industry, offers great promise for pros and do-it-yourselfers alike. It's the lightest of all pipe materials, cuts with an ordinary saw, and glues together with fittings and a special solvent cement.

Be warned, though, that since plastic pipe hasn't yet been subjected to the test of time, many localities still prohibit or restrict its use—so before you spend a dime on plastic pipe or fittings, check the codes in your area to find out if they're allowed and in which situations.

And note that of the three types available—CPVC (Chlorinated Polyvinyl Chloride), PVC (Polyvinyl Chloride), and ABS (Acrylonitrile Butadiene Styrene)—only CPVC can be used for hot water supply lines. Don't mix these materials; they require different cements and expand at different rates.

Keep expansion in mind, too, when you're assembling runs of plastic pipe, especially CPVC. Provide plenty of clearance between fittings and framing, and bore oversize holes everywhere the pipes pass through wood. Otherwise, the system will creak, squeak, groan, and maybe even leak every time you turn on a water tap or run hot water into a drain line.

Check the drawings below and you'll see that solvent-welding plastic fittings calls for no special tools or skills. Alignment is critical, though, because once you've made a connection, the joint is permanent. Make a mistake and you have no choice but to cut out the fitting, throw it away, and install a brand-new one.

Realize, too, that solvent-welded joints don't reach working strength for periods of anywhere from 16 to 48 hours. This means your family may have to do without running water for a full day or even two after you've completed an installation.

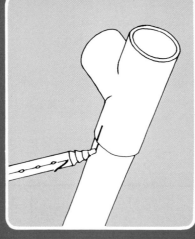

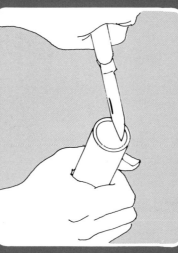

Very carefully remove the burrs made by the hacksaw with a sharp knife. Keep the pipe tipped downward so debris will fall out.

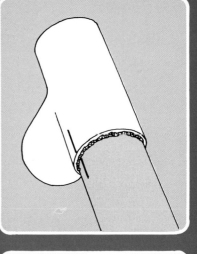

To ensure proper alignment of the pipe and fitting, dry-assemble them before applying the solvent. Mark the alignment as shown.

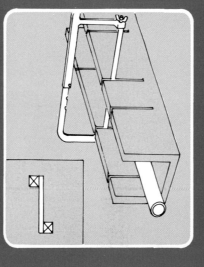

Using a bench jig or miter box, cut rigid plastic pipe with a hacksaw. Be sure the cut is absolutely square.

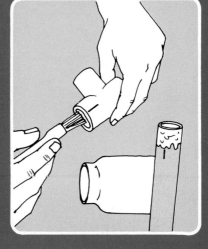

Very lightly sand the outside tip of the pipe. Then wipe it with a clean cloth and apply cement to both the pipe and connection.

As you assemble the connection, give it a quarter turn to distribute the cement. A small bead should form around the fitting.

288

Of all the types of pipe available today, flexible plastic has seen less duty than any other. In fact, most people have never even heard of it. That's due to two factors. First, it's costly, and second, there are some limitations as to where it can be used. For example, only the pipe made from polybutylene can stand up to the heat generated by a hot water line. The polyethylene type won't. If you do decide to use flexible plastic pipe, you'll find that it's available in three different water-pressure ratings: 125 psi; 100 psi; and a low-pressure product, which is so specified.

Unlike its rigid cousin, flexible plastic pipe goes together with clamps instead of cement. You can buy a potpourri of fittings—tees, ells, and straight connections—in a variety of diameters to fit various pipe sizes. You also can buy conversion fittings that let you join the pipe to copper and galvanized plumbing.

Although flexible plastic pipe is "flexible," don't overdo it; it can kink. Rather, bend it into gentle curves. The product is rigid enough to support itself on fairly long runs, although it's usually smart to use hangers for support.

There are no special tricks or stunts involved in working with flexible plastic pipe (see the basic techniques below). You should, however, keep in mind that the polyethylene pipe "softens" somewhat when it becomes warm. Connections on above-ground installations can expand in the hot summer months, causing leaks. Check these connections from time to time and tighten the holding clamps if needed.

Flexible plastic pipe that's exposed to the elements should be drained during cold weather to prevent frozen water from cracking and breaking it. But since the plastic is weather-resistant, you needn't disconnect the system and store it during cold weather.

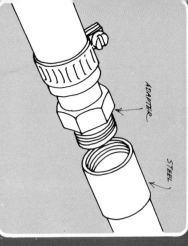

A hacksaw is the best tool for cutting flexible plastic pipe. Make the cut square, and remove saw burrs with a sharp knife.

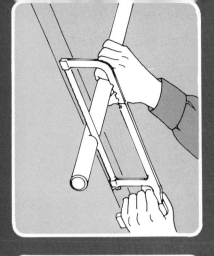

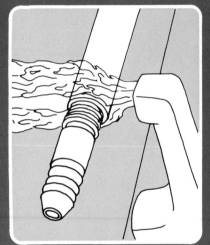

Always use an adapter when joining plastic to other materials. You'll need both pipe and adjustable wrenches for this job.

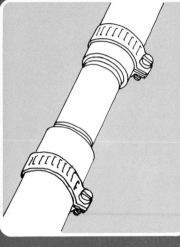

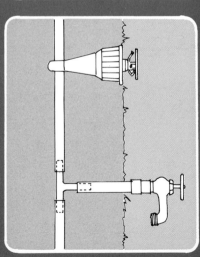

If you want to break a clamped connection, soak the connection in hot water to loosen it. Do not use a propane torch for this.

Use stainless steel worm-type clamps to fasten fittings to the pipe. Slip the clamp over the pipe before you add the fitting.

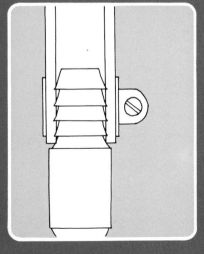

Position the clamp on the pipe so the clamp tightens against the entire shoulder of the fitting. This keeps the pressure even.

A hookup for an underground sprinkler utilizes tees and ells to turn corners. Tight bends will kink the pipe.

# WORKING WITH CAST IRON PIPE

Until recently, installing cast iron DWV systems was all but out of the question for amateur plumbers. Traditional "hub-and-spigot" joints—a lipped *spigot* on one section slips into a bell-shaped *hub* on the other—had to be packed with oakum, then caulked with molten lead.

With one newer system, joints are sealed by inserting a neoprene gasket into the hub end of a pipe then forcing the bald (straight) end of the next pipe into it.

By far the easiest system, though, employs *no-hub* cast iron pipes.

With these, you simply couple sections with a special neoprene gasket and an automotive-type clamp, as shown on the opposite page. You need no special tools, and if a fitting comes out a little cockeyed, it takes only a minute to loosen the clamp, twist everything the way you want it, and retighten it.

Best of all, no-hub components are compatible with hub-and-spigot piping, so if you ever have to cut into an existing cast iron soil pipe, you can simply cut away a section and slip in a no-hub tee (see the opposite page).

No-hub joints eliminate most, but not all of the hassles involved in working with cast iron. Wrestling 5- and 10-foot lengths of this heavy material into place is heavy

work. And cutting can be a problem, too unless you rent specialized equipment, or measure and buy precut lengths.

That's why, faced with a sizable DWV installation that calls for a new soil stack you might be wise to have a pro install the stack. Then you can run lateral drain and vent lines from fixtures to the stack.

Plan these runs so they'll require a minimum of bends, and be sure to pitch drain lines back to the stack. (For more about laying out a DWV system, see pages 292-294.)

Be sure, too, that you properly brace the pipes with supports at each fitting and every four feet on straight runs. Drawings on the opposite page show commonly available hangers.

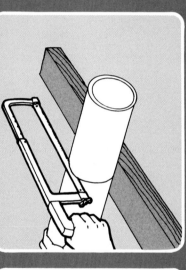

To cut cast iron, measure the length you need. Then scribe the cutoff line on the pipe with a wax-type pencil

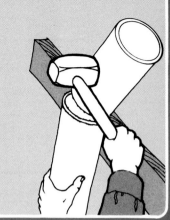

Elevate the pipe by placing it on a piece of 2x4 or 2x6. Make a 1/16-inch cut around the pipe's circumference.

Along the hacksaw kerf, rap the pipe with a baby sledge. Tap the pipe smartly; it should fracture cleanly at the cut.

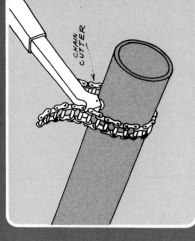

A chain-type cutter handles larger diameters. The chain secures the pipe while the cutting wheel scores the surface.

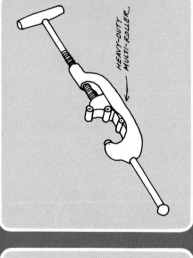

For small-diameter cast iron pipe, you can rent a roller-type cutter like this one. It will save you a lot of effort.

A jagged break can be evened up by tapping with a cold chisel. You don't have to get the edges glassy smooth.

290

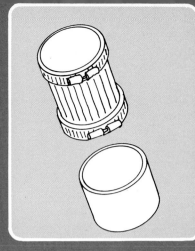

A no-hub connector consists of a neoprene sleeve and a metal clamp that tightens with two worm-drive screws.

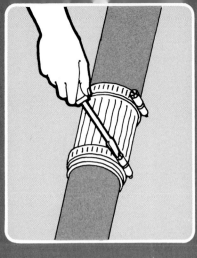

To assemble joints, remove any burrs from the pipes' cut ends, then slip the clamp and sleeve onto the pipes as shown.

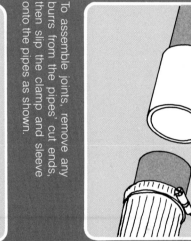

Be sure when you shove the pipes together that their cut ends butt together, separated only by the sleeve's inner ridge.

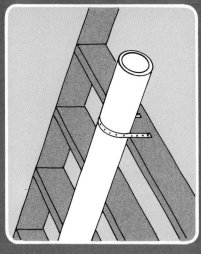

Now center the clamp and tighten it securely with a screwdriver or special T-wrench. Be careful not to overtighten, though.

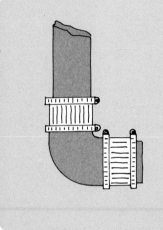

Bends and all other no-hub fittings go together the same way. You'll need a sleeve and clamp for each end of the fitting.

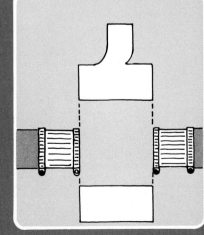

Here's how to fit a no-hub tee into an existing pipe run. Slip clamps over the cut ends, then position the fitting.

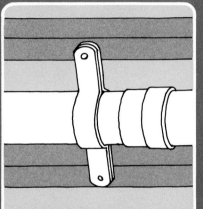

Support horizontal runs with pipe straps or hangers. This type attaches to the faces of floor joists.

Two-piece hangers serve as a clamp to hold vertical runs. Install one below each joint and at floor level.

## CONNECTING TO DWV LINES

Thinking about adding a new fixture at your house? If so, you've probably already wondered where the water's going to come from—and where it's going to go.

Of the two parts to this problem, the first is relatively easy to solve. Small-diameter supply lines can zigzag easily through tight spots—and because they're ur der pressure, you can extend them almost any distance.

Drain-waste-vent lines are another matter. First, they're much larger and more difficult to conceal. Second—and even more critical—you have to ensure that any new fixture is properly vented. Otherwise, vacuum in the drainage system could suck water from the fixture's trap and let sewer gas back up into the house.

Does this mean you have to install a vent, as well as a drain, for each and every fixture? Fortunately, most plumbing codes let you dispense with individual venting under certain circumstances (see below).

Note that the most common of these exceptions—*wet venting*—requires locating the fixture within a specified distance from your home's soil stack—and the fixture must drain only liquid wastes. This means you can wet-vent a lavatory, tub, or shower, but not a toilet or kitchen sink. Get advice from a pro before you plan DWV hookups for these solid-waste carriers.

Clearly, it makes sense to situate a new fixture as close as possible to existing lines. Your alternative is to opt for an entirely new stack—one you might consider if you're contemplating a major installation such as a new bath.

When you're measuring out distances, don't neglect to allow for a slope of ¼ inch per foot (or whatever local code calls for) from the fixture to the main drain. You may end up having to elevate a tub or shower to provide proper drainage.

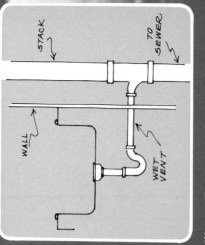

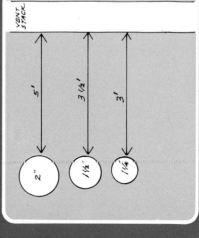

Wet venting lets a portion of the drain line serve also as a vent. Not all fixtures can be wet-vented (see above).

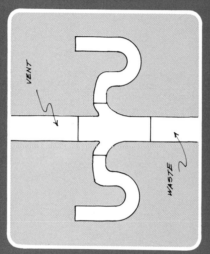

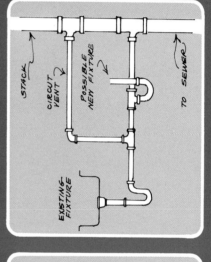

Unit venting lets you locate fixtures back to back, discharging into the same vent-waste line. Each has its own trap.

Existing fixtures may tie in via a *circuit vent*. If so, you can install a new fixture between the main and the circuit.

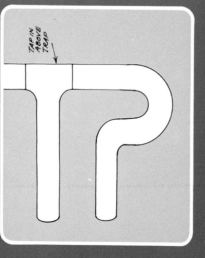

Often you can drain two lavatories or sinks into the same trap—provided their drain outlets are no more than 30 inches apart.

Maximum wet vent distances depend on the size of the fixture's drain. These are typical, but check your code.

## Saddle Tees

Looking for a way to run a new pipe off of an existing one without breaking a connection in the old run? Simply clamp on one of the saddle fittings shown at right, drill a hole, and hook up your new run.

Turn off the water first, of course, and open a faucet to drain the pipe. Next, strap on the saddle. Some come with drill guides so you can bore the hole without removing the fitting; with others, you mark the hole with a center punch, remove the saddle, and drill. File away any rough edges.

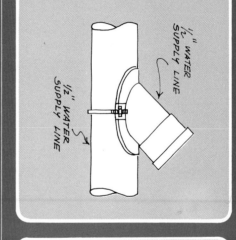

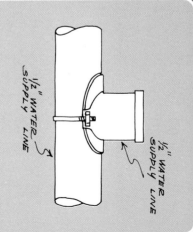

## Slip Rings

Try to insert an ordinary rigid copper or plastic tee into an existing run and you may discover the line doesn't have enough flex to pop into the tee's socket. This means you'll either have to install a union, as explained below, or a slip ring, like the one shown here.

When you cut the line, remove a section big enough to accommodate the tee and a spacer that will help tie the tee into the existing line (see sketches at right). Fit the tee, spacer, and slip ring into the run, slide the ring into position, and solder or solvent-weld.

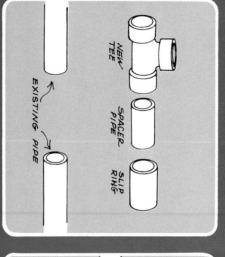

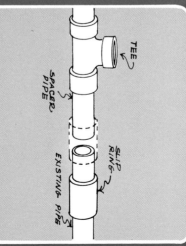

## Unions

Unions are the keystones in threaded-pipe systems. These three-part devices compensate for the fact that all pipe threads in and out in the same direction.

If there's a union in the existing run, loosen its union *nut*, pull apart the fitting, and remove pipe on one side or the other. Now install a new tee and nipples, then reassemble as illustrated.

If there's no union in the existing run, simply cut in wherever you wish and add one. You may also need a second union at some point in the new run.

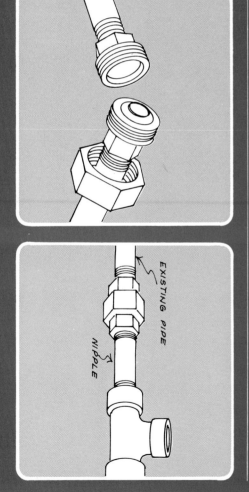

# ROUGHING-IN

## Plotting Dimensions

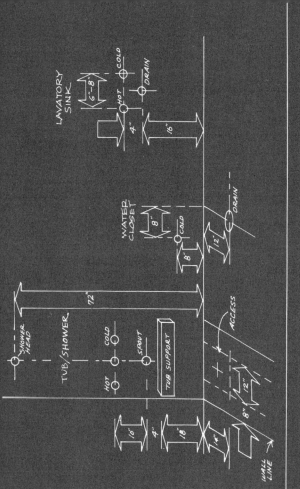

Once you know where and how you're going to tie into your home's existing plumbing system, it's time to pinpoint exactly where new lines will go. The best way to do this is to purchase your new fixture or fixtures then mark the "rough" dimensions on the floor and wall, as shown at right.

Don't let the word *rough* mislead you. Accuracy is essential—miss by an inch or so and you'll have to do a lot of work over again. These measurements are typical, but check your fixtures (or cut-outs that come with them) for specifics.

## Supporting Exposed Pipes

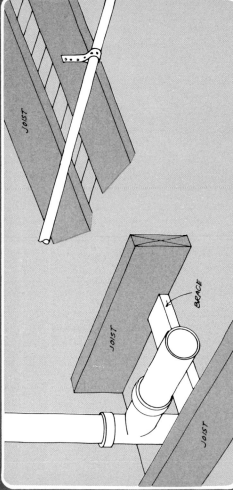

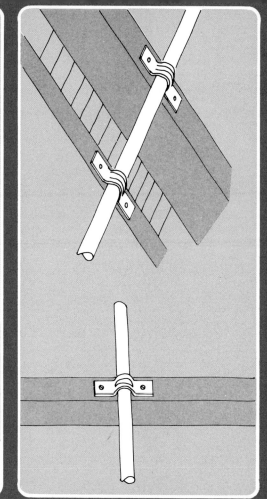

Iron, steel, copper, and plastic pipes are tough customers, yet all of them must be supported to take the weight off threaded, soldered, or cemented connections. You can do this with any one of several types of pipe hangers, or with wood scraps or wire. Installation techniques are shown at right. Caution: If using metal pipe, make sure to use only hangers made of the same metal.

Unless otherwise specified by codes, space hangers every three feet. At points where pipes (especially cast-iron pipes) make 90-degree turns, support the pipe with a piece of wood or use a strap hanger to support it.

Plastic and copper pipe need support more often than galvanized steel pipe. Although plastic and copper won't kink, they tend to belly-down when filled with water. This weight can quickly break connections and cause a serious leak. Note, too, that plastic needs more room for expansion and contraction, as explained on page 288.

If the pipe snakes along a masonry wall, the hangers sometimes can be installed with concrete nails. Drive the nails flush with the hangers, then stop hammering—extra "finishing" taps will loosen the nails. If concrete nails won't work, you'll have to use fiber plugs or lead anchors (see page 32).

**294**

# Notching Studs and Joists

Supporting pipes that pass through walls, under floors, or over ceilings is easy—you just cut notches in the framing members, or bore holes through them. Some plumbers prefer to notch; others bore. Generally, boring weakens a member less, but may create problems in assembling long runs.

Whichever method you choose, take care that you don't critically undermine a stud's or joist's load-bearing strength. Exactly how much you can safely cut away depends on where the notch or hole will be located.

If a notch will be in the upper half of a stud—usually four feet or more above the floor—you can safely cut away up to two-thirds of the stud's depth. In the lower half of a stud, though, don't notch

more than one-third of its depth, unless you reinforce it as shown below. You can bore anywhere along a stud's length, provided you leave the clearance indicated.

With joists, never notch more than one-fourth of its depth—and keep the notch toward the ends, never near the center. Always reinforce joists, too.

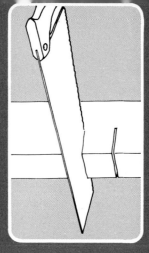

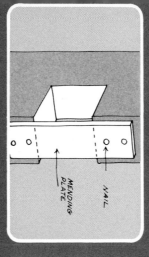

Make the cuts for notches with a handsaw or backsaw. Measure and lay out the cuts; don't guess at their width and depth.

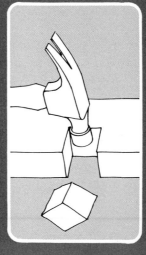

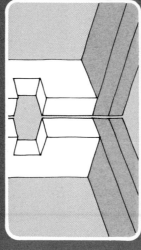

With a chisel, score a line on the framing member that connects the saw cuts, then knock out the notches with a hammer.

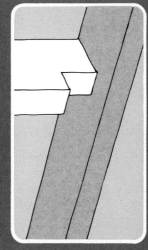

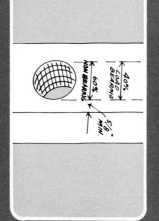

If the notch will be made next to a header or sill, use a hacksaw to make the cut. If you cut through a nail, renail the member.

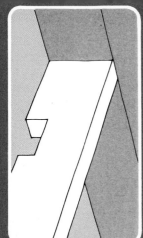

MENDING PLATE

NAIL

Reinforce deeply notched studs with a metal mending plate. You'll have to mortise it if the studs will be covered.

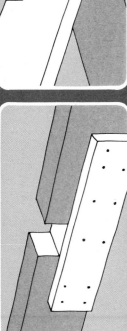

Notch a corner this way, taking half the notch from each framing member. A 90-degree pipe ell will fit snugly in the notch.

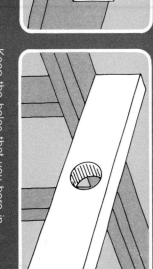

40% LOAD BEARING  
60% NON BEARING  
5/8" MIN.

Leave at least 5/8 inch of wood around holes bored for pipes. The pipe should fit fairly snugly in the hole. Don't go oversize.

Notch joists near the ends, never near the center. Always cut the notch to fit the pipe. Big, sloppy cuts weaken the framing.

Reinforce joists with short lengths of wood nailed to both sides of the framing member. You can notch the patch, too.

Keep the holes that you bore in joists near another support member to avoid undue stress on the joist.

# INSTALLING SINKS AND LAVATORIES

Once you've roughed in new hot, cold, and drain lines for a new sink, about 75 percent or more of your work is completed. All that remains is to fasten a faucet assembly to the fixture (see page 298), mount the fixture itself, and fit it with a trap (see page 273).

Sinks and lavatories are generally made of steel (either enameled or stainless) porcelainized cast iron, plastic, or vitreous china. Deck-mounted types fit into a countertop or cabinet; wall-hung versions rest on brackets, and also may be supported by a pair of legs.

To install a deck-mounted sink, you first need to make a cutout for it. Most come with a pattern or basic dimensions you can use to make a template. Take care in laying out the cut, paying special attention to how the drain and supply lines will tie into the fixture.

Now cut the opening with a saber or keyhole saw; in a butcher-block counter, you may need to make pocket cuts with a circular saw, as illustrated on page 410, then finish up with a saw capable of making curved cuts.

Deck-mounted units may be either rim type or self-rimming, as shown below. With some models, you need to cut a recess around the opening. The manufacturer usually supplies full installation instructions. Follow these carefully to avoid difficulties.

Try to mount the faucet assembly before you set a sink or lavatory into place; with the bowl upside-down you'll find it much easier to get at the faucet's locking nuts underneath.

Wall-mounting systems vary, but with most of them you fasten a bracket to the wall with toggle bolts, or first mortise in a hanging strip (see below). Make sure the brackets are absolutely level, then align slots or lugs in the lavatory's back and lower it into place.

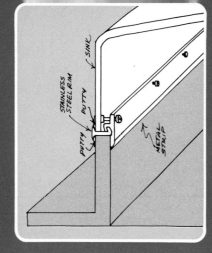

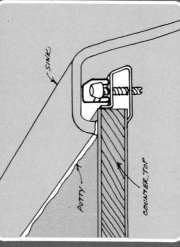

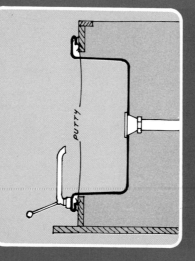

A self-rimming fixture has this profile. The counter or cabinet top may need to be recessed to accept the rim.

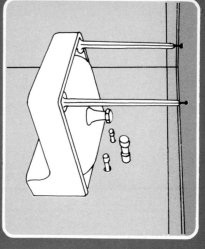

A rimmed fixture usually has a preformed metal strip in which the edge of the fixture is sandwiched. Secure with clips or screws.

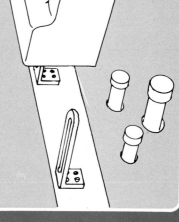

On lighter weight self-rimming sinks, screw-down clips similar to the one shown hold the sink tight against the countertop.

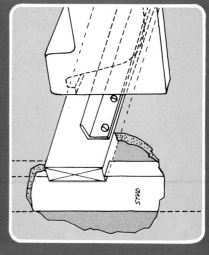

Recess a 1x8 into two wall studs for wall-mounting brackets. Position the face of the 1x8 flush with the finished wall.

Brackets are screwed to the 1x8 mounting piece. The style of the brackets depends on the fixture design. Brackets must be level.

Attach the legs under the fixture apron. Unscrew them until they fully support the weight of the fixture.

296

Of all plumbing fixtures, bathtubs and showers are the most "fixed." If you're constructing an all-new bath—or you're constructing an all-new bath—or adding a basement shower—plan your framing around the installation and you can set in these bulky items without too much difficulty.

Start by selecting the unit you prefer. Standard tubs measure 4½, 5, and 5½ feet long—and you'll find lots of non-standard sizes, styles, and shapes to choose from.

You get a choice of materials, too. Baked-enamel steel tubs are relatively lightweight and inexpensive. They're prone to chipping, though, and can be noisy unless you insulate under and around the unit.

Cast-iron tubs are far more durable, somewhat more costly, and quite heavy. Plan to beef up floor joists under these. Though more expensive than either steel or cast-iron versions, fiber glass tubs usually include molded wall panels so you needn't worry about tiling or otherwise waterproofing around them.

For a shower, you can buy a standard receptor base and build your own enclosure, or purchase the entire unit base, walls, and a sliding or folding door—in knock-down kit form. The drawings below illustrate how each of these fixtures fits into new framing.

Thinking of replacing a deteriorated old tub with a new built-in? If so, prepare for a much bigger project. First comes the problem of getting the old tub out of a space that was probably built around it—major surgery that usually involves chopping into tile work and may entail removing a wall as well. Next you have to wrestle the new unit in, then adapt framing and plumbing to suit its dimensions.

## Tying Into Framing and Plumbing

Check the anatomy drawing at right for the basics of a typical tub/shower installation. Drain connections call for dropping a trap below floor level—in space between joists or within a plumbing wall. If this isn't feasible, you'll have to elevate the tub a step or two. Position the faucets, spout, and shower head as indicated.

This tub, an enameled-steel type, has a flange around its edges that rests on 1x4 cleats and also is nailed to the studs. Recess another 1x4 into the studs to support the shower pipe.

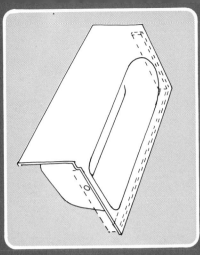

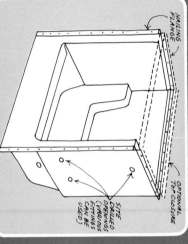

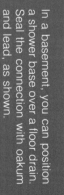

A cast-iron tub simply rests on 1x4 cleats. Its heavy weight keeps it stable, so you needn't nail it in place.

Molded fiber glass tub/shower units also have flanges for nailing to studs. Some dismantle to get into existing space.

In a basement, you can position a shower base over a floor drain. Seal the connection with oakum and lead, as shown.

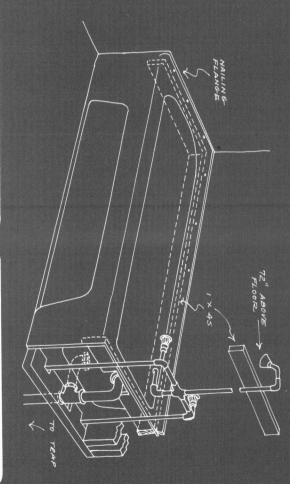

NAILING FLANGE

72" ABOVE FLOOR

1 X 4S

TO TRAP

TERAZZO, TILE OR FIBER GLASS RECEPTOR

OAKUM

LEAD

TO TRAP

STRAINER

FLOOR DRAIN

## INSTALLING NEW FAUCETS

Selecting a new faucet is about like choosing a pair of shoes—first you pick out the style you like, then you make sure it fits properly.

If you're simply replacing an existing faucet, measure the distance between its pipe connections, as shown below. Or, better yet, disconnect the old unit and take it along to the store. The new faucet must fit the holes in your fixture exactly.

If, on the other hand, you'll be installing an entirely new fixture, choose the fixture first, then buy a faucet that's compatible. Don't worry about supply connections; flexible tubing connectors—often sold in kit form with shutoff valves—let you compensate for any differences here.

Disconnecting an old faucet can be tricky if the old connections are corroded or tough to get at. First, shut off the water and slip a bucket underneath to catch any water that may remain in the pipes. Now carefully fit a wrench to the connector nuts (you may need a basin wrench like the one shown below) and make sure the wrench has a good grip before you apply pressure—a slip could crack or dent the fixture.

If the connections won't budge, apply penetrating oil, wait for 20 minutes or so, and try again. As a last resort, heat the nuts with the flame from a propane torch, then turn them loose.

Faucets typically connect via a compression fitting that threads onto their inlets and is either threaded or soldered to the supply lines. If you have to solder, dismantle the faucet's working parts first (see pages 266-270) so they won't be damaged by the heat.

## Deck-Mounted Units

Some copper tube connections have flared or compression fittings with nut connections. Take care not to bend the tubing.

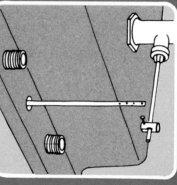

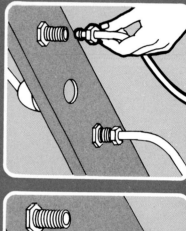

If using copper tubing, bend it to fit the connections, but don't kink it. Then tighten the connections with a wrench.

Turn on the supply valves and test the pipes and faucet for any leaks. If you spot any, try tightening the connections.

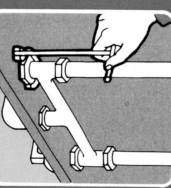

A sink pop-up may be connected to the faucet. If so, remove the connection on the slide rod below the faucet unit.

To connect or disconnect pipes in tight quarters, you may need to use a basin wrench. It can adjust to several positions.

Tighten the locking nuts below the deck, then make the water supply connections. Use pipe dope or tape on threads.

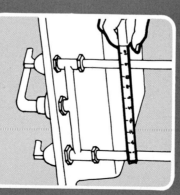

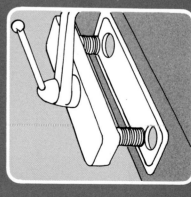

To find the distance between the centers of pipes (or any rounds), measure from the outside edge of one to the other's inside edge.

Insert the new faucet connections in the holes in the deck. Refer to the installation instructions for particulars.

298

## Wall-Mounted Faucets

Though you gain access to wall-mounted faucets differently than deck-mounted faucets, the same installation techniques apply. Carefully measure the distance between the water supply lines, or take the old faucet to the store to match the fittings on a new faucet.

Since the fittings of wall-mounted faucets usually are plated with chrome or another finish, be careful when you turn them. A wrench or slip-joint pliers can leave marks. To prevent this, pad the jaws of tools with adhesive bandages.

## Tub/Shower Faucets

To replace or add faucets to shower and tub assemblies, you'll have to get in back of the finished wall to reach the connections. And unless the builder/plumber left an access panel for this purpose, getting there may mean poking a hole in the wall. Regardless of whether you cut into the wall from the front or the back, make sure the panel you cut allows you plenty of working room.

Once you gain access, close the shutoff valves controlling the water supply to the tub and disconnect the faucet. If you'll be removing soldered connections, protect the wall surfaces from heat and possible damage with a sheet of asbestos board.

Start by removing the faucet handles, escutcheons, and spout as shown. Don't mar plated parts.

Cut an access panel in the wall with a keyhole saw. See pages 34 and 36 for repair techniques.

## Installing a Hand Shower

As you can see at right, hand showers can mount at either the shower head or the spout. Combination hand and stationary showers, though, connect to the shower pipe. These units have a bracket that holds a hand shower.

An existing shower head usually is connected to the water supply pipe with a threaded fitting. Simply loosen the fitting to remove the shower head. If you don't have the water supply pipe for a shower, you can replace your existing spout with a divertor type that has a connection for a hand shower.

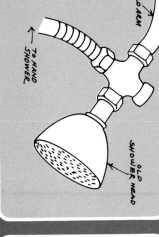

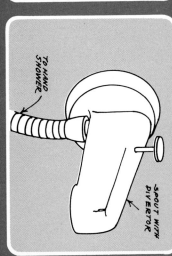

A standard or cross-tee fitting may be used for the addition of a hand shower. Make sure the tee fits all three connections.

Divertor spouts also channel water to the hand shower. Make absolutely sure the new spout's threads match those of the pipe.

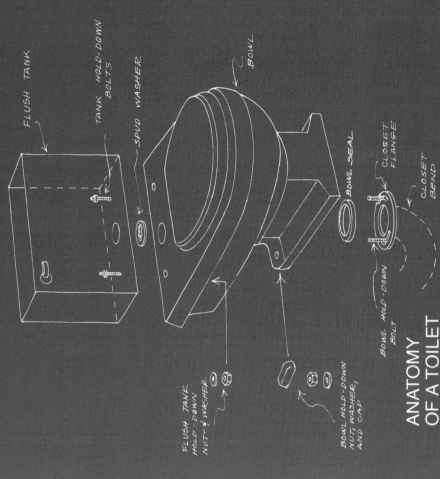

*FLUSH TANK*

*TANK HOLD-DOWN BOLTS*

*SPUD WASHER*

*BOWL*

*BOWL*

*BOWL SEAL*

*CLOSET FLANGE*

*CLOSET BEND*

*FLUSH TANK HOLD-DOWN NUT-&-WASHER*

*BOWL HOLD-DOWN BOLT*

*BOWL HOLD-DOWN NUT, WASHER, AND CAP*

## ANATOMY OF A TOILET

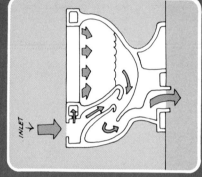

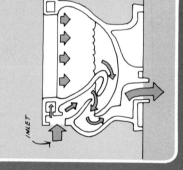

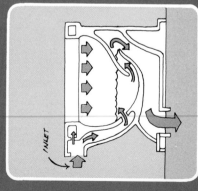

## CHOOSING AND BUYING A TOILET

All of a toilet's mechanical action takes place in its *flush tank*. Since most of what can go wrong happens there, we show its components in an anatomy drawing on page 274, and devote the three pages that follow it to explaining how to make repairs.

When you're shopping for a new toilet, though, it also helps to know about the elements illustrated at right. Both the *tank* and *bowl* are molded of vitreous china, then fired in a high-temperature kiln. This produces a glaze that's impervious to just about anything but chipping, scratches, and cracks. Top-of-the-line versions combine the tank and bowl into a single piece, eliminating the *spud washer* and quieting the flushing action.

Flushing actions differ, too. All depend on water pressure to create a siphoning action—but some do this more efficiently and quietly than others. The drawings below compare the three basic types.

Regardless of design, all floor-standing toilets mount in the same way. A *closet flange* atop a *closet bend* accommodates *hold-down bolts*. These, plus the unit's considerable weight, maintain pressure on a wax or rubber *bowl seal* that prevents leaks. More about these on the opposite page.

*Washdown* toilets flush through an opening at the bowl's front. They're inexpensive, inefficient, and prohibited by some codes.

*INLET*

Better, *reverse-trap* toilets flush through the rear for a quieter and much more efficient siphoning sort of action.

*INLET*

*Siphon-jet* types improve on the reverse-trap design with more water surface and bigger passages to reduce clogging.

*INLET*

Before you buy a toilet, check this measurement. Most have a 12-inch "rough." A ten-inch version fits tight situations.

*WALL*

*USUALLY 12"*

*CENTER OF FLOOR FLANGE*

Whether you're replacing an existing fixture or mounting a new unit on a closet bend that's already in place, setting and hooking up a toilet is a surprisingly simple operation.

Besides the toilet itself and a few ordinary plumbing tools, you'll need some plumber's putty, a bowl seal, and—for a new installation—a closet flange.

With an existing fixture, first shut off and disconnect the water supply, flush the tank, then swab out water that remains in the tank and bowl with an old towel or sponge.

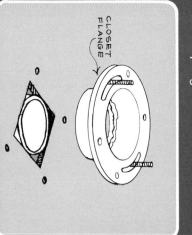

CLOSET FLANGE

Apply cement to both the closet bend and the flange as shown. Press the flange into place, and screw it to the floor.

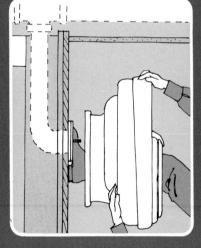

Set the bowl in place with a slight twisting motion, but don't rock or lift it again—you could break the seal.

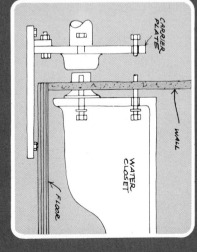

Wall-mounted toilets attach to a carrier plate behind the wall. These have a similar flange-and-gasket arrangement.

CARRIER PLATE
WALL
WATER CLOSET
FLOOR

Next, check to determine if the tank is connected to the wall. Some older units attach via screws through the rear and have an elbow connection to the bowl. If that's the case with yours, disconnect these and remove the tank. If the tank sits atop the bowl, the toilet can be removed in one piece, though you may need help to lift it.

Now pry off the caps that cover the bowl's hold-down bolts. Remove the nuts—or cut the bolts with a hacksaw—and just lift the bowl off the flange. Get it out of the way so you'll have room to maneuver the new unit.

Before you install the new bowl, temporarily set it on the flange and check for level—front to back as well as side to side. Shim, if necessary, with rustproof metal washers.

Now lift the bowl off again, turn it upside-down (on padding to protect the rim), and fit the seal around the bowl's outlet. Run a bead of putty around the outer rim of the bowl's base, too, so dirt and water won't get underneath.

Set the bowl in place as illustrated below, check for level once more, and install nuts on the hold-down bolts.

Finally, fit a spud washer and the tank over the bowl's inlet opening, secure with bolts, and hook up the water supply. If you don't have one, now's the time to install a shutoff, too, as shown at the bottom of the page.

Tired of turning off your entire water system every time you need to replace a faucet washer or work on a flushing mechanism? Fixture shutoffs—often sold in easy-to-hook-up kit form—spare hassles and trips to the basement.

Before you set out to buy the parts, measure the supply pipe or pipes you'll be attaching to and note whether they're threaded steel, copper, or plastic. Each requires different fittings or adaptors. For installation, refer to the appropriate pipe-fitting techniques on pages 282-289.

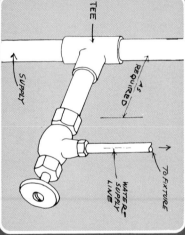

TEE
SUPPLY
AS REQUIRED
WATER SUPPLY LINE
TO FIXTURE

Angle stops suit cases where pipes come out of the wall. Flexible tubing connects with compression fittings to the fixture.

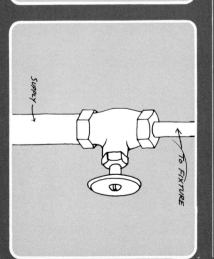

SUPPLY
TO FIXTURE

If pipes exit from the floor, choose an in-line stop. Stop outlets are usually smaller in diameter than house plumbing.

# INSTALLING A WATER HEATER

Most water heaters serve dutifully for many years, but sooner or later all succumb to rust and corrosion and need replacement. When you find yourself faced with this situation, consider whether or not you really need a pro to install a new one.

There's nothing especially difficult about hooking up a water heater. Even if you want to increase—or decrease—your water heating capacity, you can usually find a replacement with almost the same overall dimensions as the old equipment. This spares you the trouble of retailoring plumbing lines for the new unit.

Before you rush out to get a new heater, though, make sure it's really the tank that's leaking—not the overflow or a poor connection. (To learn about troubleshooting water heaters, see page 278.)

If you do need a new unit, arrange to have a helper on hand when it arrives. Traversing stairs with a tank that weighs 125 to 200 pounds can be tricky. In some cases, you might be better off to remove a basement window, set up a ramp with planks, then slide the new unit in and the old one out.

After you uncrate your purchase, set it up next to the old heater, study the installation instructions that come with it, and determine whether you need any new plumbing or flue fittings. Some economy-minded plumbers don't bother to install unions. If that's the case at your house, you'll have to cut the lines to remove the water heater. To save trouble in case anything goes wrong in the future, invest in a couple of unions—and a shutoff valve, too, if you don't already have one.

For information about saving water heating energy, see pages 251 and 359. And to learn about the principles of solar water heaters, turn to page 355.

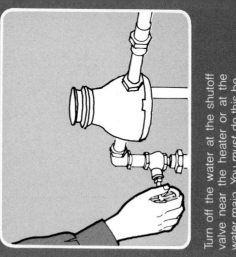

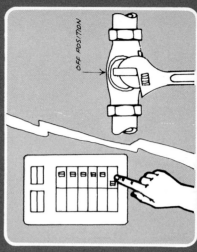

Turn off the water at the shutoff valve near the heater or at the water main. You *must* do this before starting any other work.

Shut off the power at the service panel, or halt the supply of gas by closing the shutoff valve leading to the water heater.

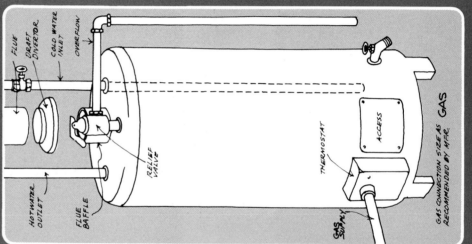

A gas water heater, in addition to hot and cold water hookups and a relief valve, also has a gas line and a flue stack.

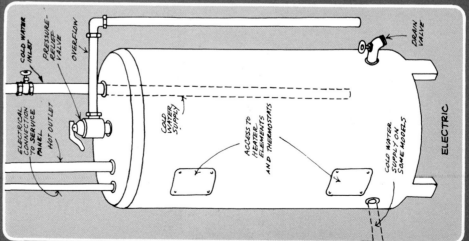

An electric water heater has four hookup points: hot and cold water supply lines, electric power, and a pressure-relief valve.

302

**After the water to the tank has been turned off, drain the tank. This can take several hours, so connect a hose to the drain valve.**

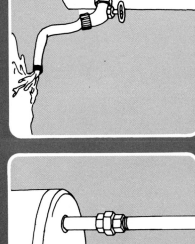

**Disconnect the water and gas lines. See pages 285 and 287 if you have to cut the pipes. Slide the old unit out of the way.**

**Don't make any connections until the new heater is level. You can level it with cedar-shingle shims or pieces of rot-resistant wood.**

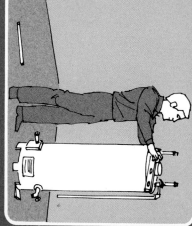

**Connect the pressure-relief valve and reconnect the power source to the heater. You may be able to use the old connection.**

*CONNECTION FOR OVERFLOW PIPE*

**Install the draft divertor and position it over the flue baffle. Then connect the flue pipe. The parts usually are in the new kit.**

**On new connections, check for gas leaks with a solution of soap and water. Use an old brush to swab the joint; look for bubbles.**

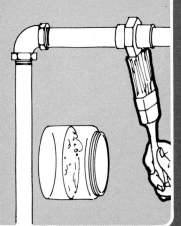

**Turn on the water and fill the tank. Then open a hot water faucet in the kitchen. When the water flows, fire the unit.**

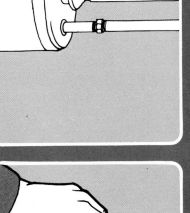
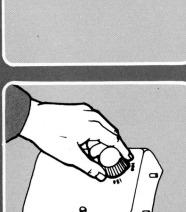

**Set the thermostat at about 140 degrees F. after the power is on. Lowering the setting a few degrees will save some energy.**

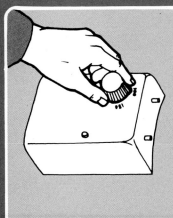

**Drain the new hot water heater every two months the first year; every six months afterward. Draw off about two gallons of water.**

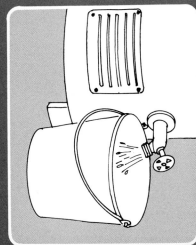

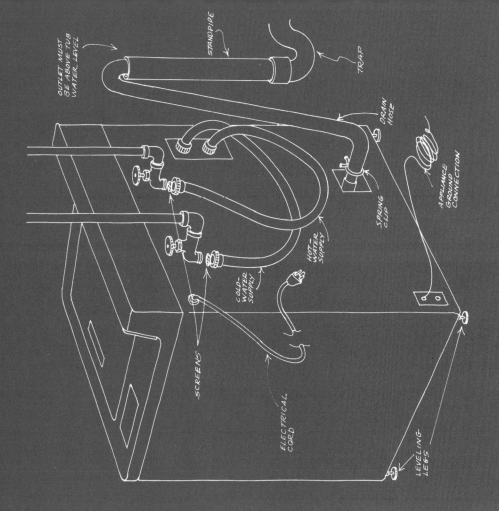

## CONNECTING AN AUTOMATIC WASHER

Washer hookups are only semi-permanent. You simply thread hoses to valves on hot and cold water supply lines, and insert the *drain hose* into either a *standpipe*, as shown at right, or a laundry tub.

First move the machine into position and level it by adjusting *leveling legs* at the corners. Make sure all four feet are in firm contact with the floor and that you firmly tighten their locknuts up against the bottom of the washer frame. An improperly leveled machine can "walk" during some cycles.

Now move the unit out again, if necessary, to get at the supply and drain connectors. Pull supply hoses clear from the cabinet and watch that they don't kink when you make these hookups. Be sure, too, to install *screens* in the hose fittings.

If yours is a standpipe installation, ward again*st* overflow by making sure the pipe stands higher than the machine's water level. Also note that the pipe must be larger than the hose. This provides an air gap so the machine can't back-siphon dirty water.

In some communities, you can simply plug a washing machine into a properly grounded electrical outlet; in others, you must wire a separate appliance ground (see page 246).

## ANATOMY OF A WASHER HOOKUP

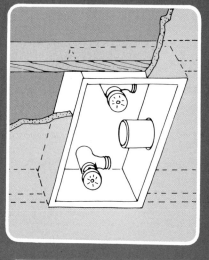

For a really tidy installation, recess the hose valves and standpipe between studs. Make sure the valves are easy to reach.

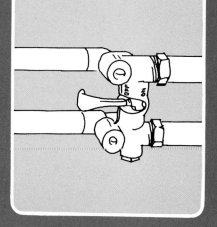

A lever valve lets you shut off both hot and cold water with a single throw. Always close valves when the unit's not in use.

# CONNECTING A DISHWASHER

Installing a built-in dishwasher calls for relatively simple hot-water, drain, and electrical connections—plus a few carpentry chores.

Begin by uncrating the machine and studying its installation instructions. Most units are designed to replace a 24-inch-wide base cabinet, so your first job will be to remove a cabinet or tailor a space to fit. (More about cabinets on pages 88 and 89.)

Next, figure out where you want to tie in the water and drain lines. If your new dishwasher will be located near the sink, that's the logical place to go—but you

can also choose to drop through the floor and connect to basement plumbing. Both of these alternatives are shown below.

For the supply line, use flexible copper tubing, sized according to the manufacturer's recommendations and code specifications. A saddle-tee (see page 293) lets you make short work of this connection. Just be sure to provide a shutoff. (For more about working with flexible copper pipe and shutoffs, refer to pages 286 and 301.)

Dishwashers drain through a hose that you can clamp to either a new tee under the sink, or—if you have a garbage disposer—to a fitting on the side of the disposer's housing. Some

codes, however, require that you also provide an air gap to ensure that the machine can't accidentally back-siphon water from your home's drainage system. The drawings below depict all three of your options here.

For electricity, you'll need a separate 15- or 20-amp branch circuit. Provide a junction box near the unit so you can easily disconnect it for repairs. And in some communities, you also must ground the machine's frame. (To learn about running new circuits and grounding appliances, see pages 231-243, and page 246.)

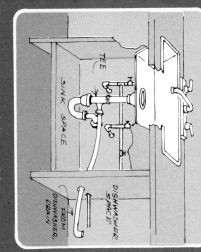

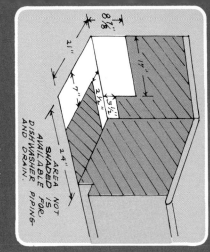

Before you run supply and drain lines, check specifications to see where they can and can't be located. These are typical.

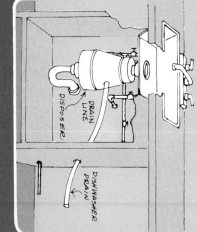

Usually the easiest way to bring hot water to a dishwasher is to tap a sink supply line. You make final connections at the front.

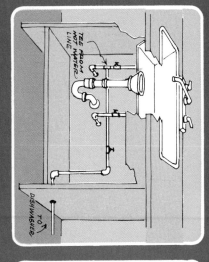

Before you can hook into a sink drain, you'll need to install a special tee fitting. More about drains on page 272.

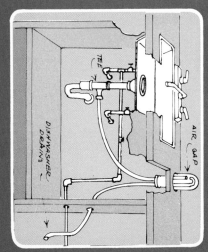

With a disposer, you remove a knockout or threaded plug, then connect the drain line. Dealers often have installation kits.

If there's an open ceiling under your kitchen, you might prefer to go that way for hot water. Locate the shutoff there, too.

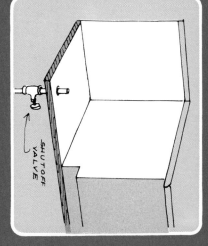

If your plumbing code calls for an air gap, you'll need this arrangement. It requires a hole in the sink or countertop.

305

## TREATING WATER

How's the water at your house? If it leaves rings around the tub, rust-stains fixtures, or smells or tastes bad, yours is among the estimated four out of five homes in the United States and Canada that need treatment of some kind.

Hardness—far and away the most common problem—comes from an excess of calcium and magnesium. These minerals combine with soaps and detergents to inhibit cleaning action. Heated hard water also builds up constricting scale inside pipes, faucets, water heaters, and appliances—impairing their efficiency and shortening their lives.

To find out if your home has a hard-water problem, draw off a pint of tap water into a bottle you can cap, add 10 drops of detergent, and shake well. If the solution foams readily, your water is relatively soft. If you get a curd-like film instead of foam, consider investing in a water softener.

(For more scientific information, call your water department and ask how much calcium carbonate is in your community's water supply. Water with less than one grain per gallon is considered soft; from 3.5 to 7.0 is hard; 7 and over is very hard.)

Water softeners remove calcium and magnesium via a process called *ion exchange*. Water passes through a bed of plastic resin beads that absorbs the minerals and replaces them with sodium, derived from common salt. Periodic backwashing removes the built-up calcium and magnesium and also replenishes the "salts."

Other minerals—iron and/or manganese, hydrogen sulfide, and sodium—also can taint water. Removing these calls for one or a combination of devices. An *oxidizing filter* removes excessive iron deposits. An automatic *chlorine feeder*, in tandem with an *activated carbon filter*, gets rid of manganese or hydrogen sulfide, and disinfects water from a contaminated or questionable source.

*Neutralizing filters* include a cellulose element that strains out sediment, silt, and cloudiness. For really bad water, consider a *reverse osmosis* filter. This one has a plastic membrane that catches dissolved salt, pesticides, detergents, and organic and even radioactive matter. More about all of these on the opposite page.

## Connecting a Water Softener

With water softeners, you have three options—buy one outright, rent a unit and maintain it yourself, or have the equipment installed on a service basis and let the company take care of the upkeep.

Buying or renting costs less in the long run, but owner-maintained water softeners require drain and electrical connections so you can periodically flush and recharge them. Service units don't; instead, the dealer simply brings a fresh tank and regenerates the old one at his plant. Both types of water softeners use the ion-exchange process described above.

Both types tie into a home's plumbing system as shown at right. Note that you really need to treat only water that's used for cleaning, laundering, dishwashing, and bathing. This means you might want to divert hard water to toilets and outside sillcocks with the tee arrangement illustrated.

From there, water flows through the softener, then on to cold-water faucets and the water heater. A *bypass valve* lets you or the dealer service the unit without totally shutting down your home's water supply.

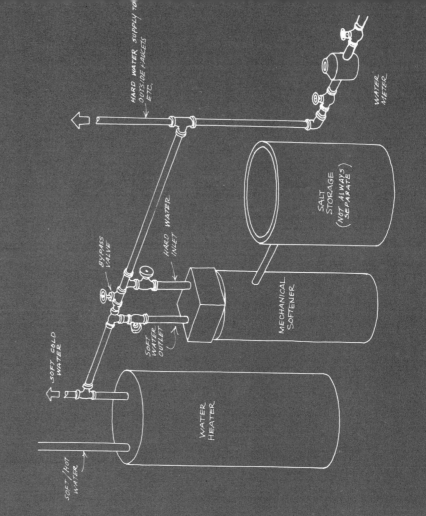

## ANATOMY OF A WATER SOFTENER HOOKUP

HARD WATER SUPPLY TO OUTSIDE FAUCETS, ETC.

WATER METER

BYPASS VALVE

HARD WATER INLET

SOFT COLD WATER

SOFT WATER OUTLET

SOFT HOT WATER

WATER HEATER

MECHANICAL SOFTENER

SALT STORAGE (NOT ALWAYS SEPARATE)

# Connecting a Water Purifier

Water softeners improve water's cleaning power; they don't clean the water itself. For this you need a purifier installed somewhere in your cold-water supply system.

Two-stage units combine neutralizing and carbon filters to provide crystal-clear, good-tasting water. Others also include a reverse-osmosis (RO) module that catches dissolved contaminants. A third type, the chlorine feeder system described on the opposite page, chemically treats all household water.

Feeder systems should be installed by a professional, but you can hook up the other two types yourself. They require no electrical connections and only minimal plumbing modifications.

For a two-stage purifier, you simply break into a supply line and hook in the unit, as shown at right. RO filters also need a drainage connection, which you can usually make with flexible ¼-inch tubing. Most come with installation instructions an amateur plumber can follow.

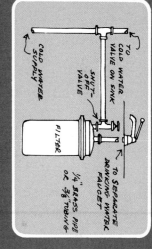

To cold water valve on sink

Shut-off valve

Cold water supply

To separate drinking water faucet

¼" brass pipe or ⅜" tubing

FILTER

An under-sink filter serves just one tap. This is a good location for models that include a reverse-osmosis module.

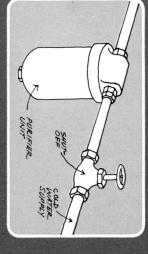

Purifier unit

Shut-off

Cold water supply

Two-stage purifiers fit into any cold water line. Be sure to include a shutoff so you can easily service the unit.

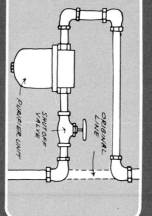

Purifier unit

Shutoff valve

Original line

Purifiers must be installed horizontally. In a vertical run, you'll need to use this plumbing arrangement for a unit to work properly.

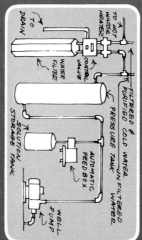

To hot water heater

Control valve

To drain

Water filter

Filtered & purified cold water

Pressure tank

Filtered & un-filtered cold water

Solution storage tank

Automatic feed box

Well pump

Feeder-filter systems include several bulky components and are much more complex. This one purifies well water.

## WATER TREATMENT PROBLEMS AND CURES

| Problem | Symptoms | Cures |
|---|---|---|
| High iron content | Stains on fixtures and the laundry; bad-tasting water; water will appear somewhat rusty after it stands for several minutes; rust dust on surfaces. | Install a water softener. If amounts of iron are excessive, use a special iron (oxidizing) filter in the water softener unit. |
| High manganese and iron content | Cloudy or hazy-looking tap water. It may leave blackish stains on fixtures or hard surfaces such as kitchen countertops or bathtubs. | A water softener with iron filters, plus a chlorine feeder, may solve the problem. The chlorine, after performing its function, is removed from the water by means of charcoal filters. |
| High corrosive hydrogen sulfide content | Rotten-egg odor to the water. | To rid your system of this problem, use a water softener with the chlorine treatment described for high-manganese problems. Also use a water purifier with an activated carbon filter and a water softener with a neutralizing element and a cellulose element. |
| High sodium content, pollution | Salty, black-colored water. | Install a reverse-osmosis and de-ionization unit, as explained above. |
| "Hard" water | No suds when detergent is added to water. | Install a water softener as shown on the opposite page. |

# GAS

Think of a gas system as a special, simplified sort of plumbing network. Like its water-carrying cousin, a gas system consists largely of pipes that thread their way under floors and through walls to supply fixtures or appliances. Unlike other plumbing, however, gas systems have no drainage lines—and, of course, their medium is a gas, not a liquid.

Most people are wary of gas—and with good reason. A leak can cause fire,
explosion, or suffocation. That's why most suppliers scent their product with odoriferous mercaptan so you can smell a heavy concentration of gas. If you do, first open doors and windows, then shut down the system as explained below. Don't attempt to make repairs yourself—call the gas utility or a professional plumber.

## GETTING TO KNOW YOUR SYSTEM

The anatomy drawing below illustrates the pathways gas follows through a home. Liquefied petroleum or natural gas, supplied privately or by a utility, enters via a *supply main*. If the gas is coming from a utility, a *meter* here keeps track of usage.

From the meter, gas then travels to the various units it serves through black steel pipes, sometimes known as *black pipe*.

*Shutoff valves* located at the meter and at each unit allow for shutting down the entire system or any component. Some shutoffs have handles that can be manually operated, as shown in the detail
at upper left; others (upper right and bottom) have a key that can be turned only with a wrench. Both types are open when their handles or keys are parallel with the pipe, off when they're perpendicular to it.

*Venting pipes* on gas furnaces and water heaters complete the system by carrying off the harmful carbon monoxide produced during combustion. On water heaters, a *draft diverter* prevents outside air in the vent stack from reversing itself and blowing out the pilot light.

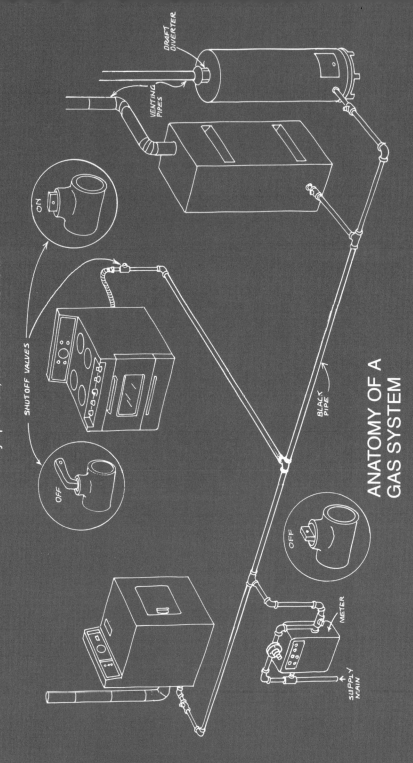

ANATOMY OF A GAS SYSTEM

DRAFT DIVERTER

VENTING PIPES

ON

OFF

SHUT OFF VALVES

OFF

METER

BLACK PIPE

SUPPLY MAIN

## TESTING FOR LEAKS

Any gas leak calls for immediate action. If you ever detect the unmistakable aroma of escaping gas, follow the steps explained on the opposite page.

If on the other hand, you merely *think* you smell gas, the first drawing at right shows how you can check out your suspicion without the expense and delay of a service call.

Vent pipes sometimes leak too—and they can easily go unnoticed because you won't smell anything. For these, see the second drawing and page 322.

Because they're so simple, gas systems rarely give trouble. When one does, you'll most likely find the cause at the *pilot light*—a small, continuous flame that ignites the main burners in all but the most recently manufactured gas appliances. (Some of these ignite electrically; see page 312.)

A few other problems sometimes crop up as well. Tiny leaks—usually at a

connection that's been jarred—pose an obvious safety hazard. A poorly adjusted pilot may be wasting energy. And most burners need an occasional tune-up.

This and the following two pages show how you can safely cope with these troubleshooting and repair jobs.

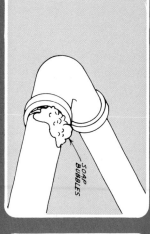

Brush a frothy solution of dish detergent and water onto any gas fitting you suspect is leaking. Bubbles indicate a leak.

Check vent systems with a match. If the flame is drawn to a joint, there's a leak. Don't ever use this method to check supply lines.

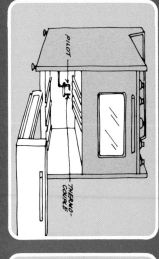

## LIGHTING PILOTS

Most of us are called on to light a pilot at some time or other . . . and the exercise can be a frustrating one if you don't follow the manufacturer's instructions to the letter.

Range burner pilots rarely pose a problem; you just touch a match to them, as shown below. But other

appliances—such as ovens, furnaces, and water heaters—require a slightly more complicated procedure, usually spelled out on a plate affixed to the unit.

The difficulty comes because their pilots include an important safety device called a *thermocouple*. A bulb-like sensor that's warmed by the pilot flame, the thermocouple tells the main burner control whether or not the pilot is burning. If it's not, the thermocouple cools and

shuts off gas to both the burners and pilot.

To relight the pilot, you need to either warm the thermocouple for a moment with a match (this works with most ovens), or you temporarily defeat it by holding down a reset button.

Procedures vary, so check out the instruction plate on the pilot assembly. If the plate is missing or illegible, see below and page 323.

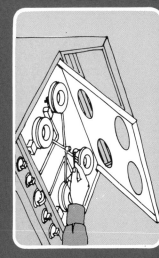

To light a range burner pilot, turn off the controls, then hold a match to the pilot. You may have to lift the top for access.

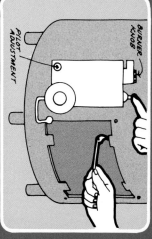

To get at an oven pilot, you may have to remove the broiler. Let the match warm the thermocouple and the pilot will light.

With other pilots, turn the burner knob to "pilot," strike a match, then hold down the reset or the knob itself for a minute.

## ADJUSTING PILOT LIGHTS

When was the last time you took a close look at the pilot flames on your gas appliances? Chances are you never have—and may be paying for more gas than you need to.

Natural gas pilot light flames should be blue with perhaps just a tinge of yellow at the tip. If yours is an LP system, you should see a blue-green inner flame, again with no more than a fleck of yellow at the tip.

Before you make any adjustments, be sure that the gas supply line is completely turned to its *open* position. A valve that's partially closed may be constricting the flow of fuel.

Also check to see that the unit is getting an adequate supply of the air it needs for combustion. Boxes and other paraphernalia stacked too close could be partially suffocating the flame.

Pilot light adjustments are usually made with a small screw that you turn in one direction or the other until the flame is just right. The job only takes a few minutes, but first you have to locate the right screw. Manufacturers often conceal these (so they won't be accidentally tampered with), and the hiding places vary from make to make.

If you have the unit's operating and maintenance guide, it will probably tell where to look. If not and the screw isn't out in the open—try removing control knobs, nameplates, or anything else that looks like it'll easily pry off. In some models, the adjusting screw is covered by a larger cap screw.

If all else fails, call in a pro and watch what he does. Then you can do the job yourself the next time. The drawings below illustrate the basics of getting an efficient flame.

(Note: with a furnace or water heater, turn the control knob to its *pilot* setting before you begin. This prevents the main burners from firing while you adjust the pilot flame.)

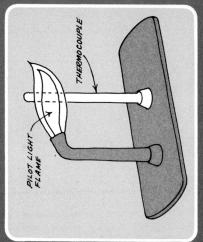

THERMOCOUPLE

PILOT LIGHT FLAME

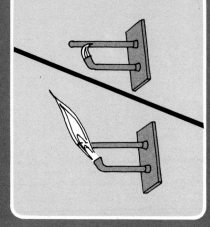

If the pilot has a thermocouple, adjust the flame so it touches the thermocouple about ½ inch from the end of the device.

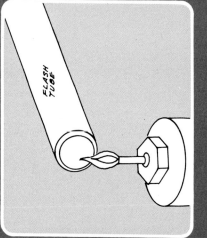

FLASH TUBE

For the proper pilot flame setting, turn the adjustment screw until the pilot flame's tip is centered in the flash tube.

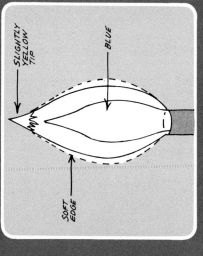

High gas pressure causes a lifting, flowing flame; low pressure, a small blue flame. With either, call your utility or supplier.

Dirt in a pilot will cause a flame like the one at left. A draft will cause the flame to flicker like the one at right.

Adjustment screws for this range are near the front of the gas valve body. Pulling off a control knob provides access to it.

SLIGHTLY YELLOW TIP

BLUE

SOFT EDGE

If the pilot flame appears mostly yellow, lack of air is the problem. Clean the tip of the pilot tube. The flame should look like this.

# ADJUSTING GAS BURNERS

Most burner troubles result from cooking grease and combustion by-product buildup. So always check out this potential troublemaker before making any adjustment on the flame controls.

The surface burners of a gas range should be adjusted so they produce an inner-cone flame about 1/2 inch high. To do this, slide the air shutter until you get a medium-sharp flame coming out of the burner orifices.

Some newer gas burners feature an automatic-control thermostat that's stimulated by heat reflected from pots or

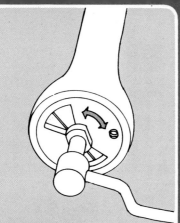

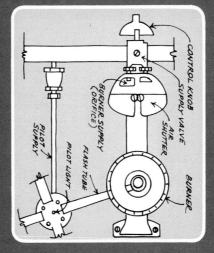

pans on the burner. When the reflected heat reaches a certain level, the thermostat "turns down" the gas supply.

To adjust controlled burners, first open the control knob completely and light the burner. Then unscrew the knob and remove the trim. To lower the flame, carefully turn the pilot/flame adjustment screw clockwise. To raise it, turn the screw counterclockwise. The sensing head should be adjusted so it's 3/16 inch below the surface of the utensil grate.

Several conditions can cause oven burner malfunctions—a control knob that's not adjusted properly, an improperly set thermostat, or a faulty thermocouple. If the pilot light is working properly and the burner ports aren't

clogged, call in a pro to make the necessary adjustments or repairs.

Burners in furnaces can become clogged with combustion debris or rust. And though you sometimes can clean the burners by gently brushing along the ports with a wire brush, you'll generally need to call in a service technician to solve this problem.

Have your furnace serviced before every other heating season. Be sure to get your call in early, though, to reserve a time. The money you spend for a checkup can save you plenty on extra fuel, and it lessens the likelihood of having to deal with a malfunctioning part on some cold, snowy night.

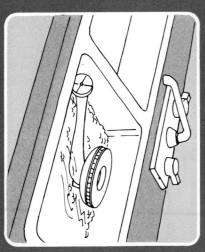

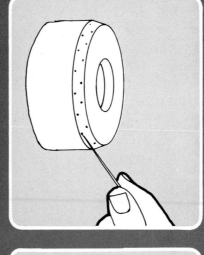

Typical burner assemblies have a gas control, a burner unit with a perforated ring, and a flash tube from the pilot to the burner.

If the burner flame is uneven, it may be due to one or more clogged ports in the burner ring. Clean these with a needle or pin.

You can lift out most burner units for cleaning. Wash them with warm water and detergent. Replace them when thoroughly dry.

If a burner won't light easily, suspect dirt in the orifices near the base of the burner. Clean these, too, with a needle or pin.

To adjust the burner flame, loosen the screw and turn or slide the shutter. When you get the right setting, tighten the screw.

# MAKING GAS IMPROVEMENTS

Though most people go ahead and pay to have new appliances hooked up by a professional, this isn't necessary in many situations. If you're replacing an old unit, for example, the work of running a gas pipe to the appliance was done long ago. All that's left for you to do is to make one simple hookup.

However, if you're changing the location of an appliance or dealing with an entirely new installation, hiring someone who knows the tricks of the trade is money well spent. Here, some fairly sophisticated hookups may be necessary. Also much too complicated for most do-it-yourselfers is any installation work for a gas furnace.

If you decide to run a gas line yourself, make sure that the pipes and connections you use for the hookup meet code requirements. Call the local gas utility and ask personnel there for this information; don't rely on an appliance dealer, as he or she may not know the very latest regulations.

## CHOOSING AND BUYING GAS APPLIANCES

Set out to purchase a new range, water heater, dryer, barbecue grill, or other gas-fired appliance and you'll find an astonishingly broad selection to choose from. Exactly which features you prefer depends, of course, on your needs and budget—but in general, you'll usually find the best values with models that are one or two notches below the top of the line.

Why? To keep prices competitive, manufacturers all too often cut quality corners with so-called "economy" models. Medium- to upper-level appliances, on the other hand, usually have the same basic machinery as the very best—but with fewer frills.

Another good reason for aiming high is that here's where you'll find energy-saving devices that can pay for themselves several times over during an appliance's lifetime. These include electric ignition systems instead of pilot lights, heat sensors that automatically turn down burners, and humidity sensors that shut off dryers when clothes are dry. These options make good sense, especially when you consider that something as seemingly insignificant as a pilot light can account for one-third to one-half of the total fuel needed to operate a particular appliance.

Some manufacturers now are labeling their gas and electric appliances with their approximate consumption of energy over normal lengths of time. This is similar to automobile manufacturers' disclosures of how much gasoline their cars burn per mile in city and highway driving.

Many gas appliances can be adapted to burn natural gas or LP gas. Conversion usually involves unscrewing and turning over a plug in the appliance's burner assembly. Check with the dealer to find out if this is possible with the unit you're considering.

When making your decision to buy, weigh the added convenience of each of these features against the amount of money it will cost. You may find that you can get along quite nicely without this or that.

Also take your family's size and life-style into consideration when determining your needs. If you're in the market for a water heater, for example, you need a unit large enough to supply you with all the hot water you need whenever you need it. An oversized heater, on the other hand, can waste a lot of energy warming water you don't need. Average families can get by with a 40-gallon water heater.

With water heaters, also take note of a unit's "recovery rate"—the amount of water that it can heat in a half- or full-hour period. If your family doesn't use a lot of hot water, this probably won't make much difference—but if demand is heavy during certain periods of the day, a medium-size, quick-recovery unit might use less gas overall than a larger, low-recovery model. Again, you won't be paying to heat water when you don't really need it. (To learn about installing a water heater, see pages 302 and 303.)

And before making any commitments, ask the dealer the following questions. The answers he gives will enable you to determine whether or not you're buying the best for the least.

● How long are parts warranted on the appliance? What is the replacement warranty, if any, on the entire unit?
● Is there a charge for delivering the appliance to your home?
● Is there a charge for connecting the appliance? Does this include parts?
● What is the delivery timetable?
● Will the dealer disconnect and haul away the appliance you're replacing? Is there any charge for this?
● Does the dealer have a service department, or must you call in another repair service if you have trouble?
● Does the dealer offer financing terms? If so, what are the terms?
● Will the dealer give you a trade-in allowance for your old appliance?

# INSTALLING A GAS RANGE

Provided you already have a gas line where you need it, hooking up a range calls for more homework than actual labor. Start with a careful reading of the installation instructions that came with the appliance.

If you don't have these, look for the unit's rating plate, usually affixed to the inside of its broiler or oven. Here you'll find the manufacturer's recommended clearances to combustible surfaces. Most modern-day ranges can be installed with zero clearance at the rear and to cabinets on either side—but must be

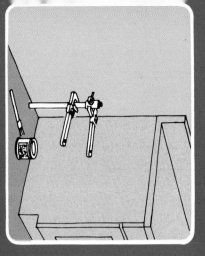

situated 12 inches or so from a corner. Next, check with your utility to learn if codes in your community permit the use of a flexible connector. If they do, buy one only slightly longer than you'll need, don't thread it through walls or cabinets, or position it any place it might be physically damaged. Note, too, that ammonia can cause these devices to deteriorate.

If "flexible" isn't allowed in your area, you'll have to make a rigid connection instead. Use black steel pipe, and see pages 282–284, 287, and 293 for how-to. Whichever type of connection you decide to use, it's wise to install a branch line shutoff as well.

Finally, what sort of electrical connection will your gas range need?

Slide-in types—such as the one shown here—can be simply plugged into a nearby receptacle. Most drop-in and countertop units, however, should be permanently connected to a wall box (see pages 235-237).

With these points settled, you're ready to shut off the gas and make the connections. Most ranges have enough clearance to slide into place without damaging fittings, but check this as you push the range into position. If anything gets broken, stop work at once and replace the damaged items with new ones.

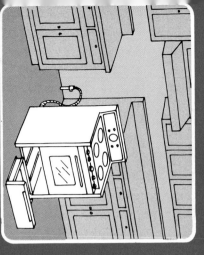

Now you're ready to slide in the range and connect it. With most models, you remove the broiler to get at connections.

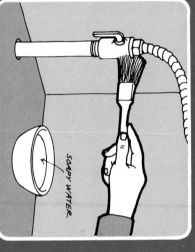

Coat the pipe's threads with a sealer, then install the shutoff. Use two wrenches so you can get a tight connection.

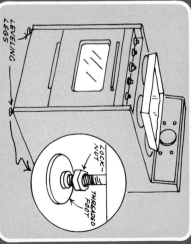

Turn on the gas, open the shutoff, then open a burner until you smell gas. Turn off the burner again and check for leaks (see page 309).

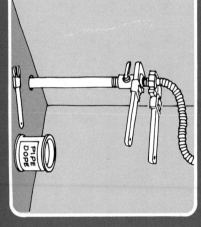

Apply more sealer and attach the flexible connector. Don't exert too much pressure or you'll crack the brass fittings.

SOAPY WATER

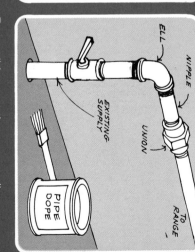

For a solid connection, use an ell, nipple, and union as shown here. You also may need a reducer at the range's gas inlet.

PIPE DOPE · ELL · NIPPLE · UNION · EXISTING SUPPLY · TO RANGE

Once the unit is positioned, level it by unscrewing its front legs. A pan of water is easier to read than a conventional level.

LOCK NUT · LEVELING LEGS · THREADED FOOT

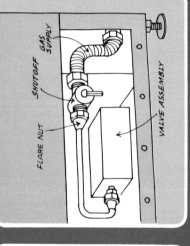

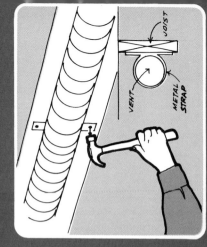

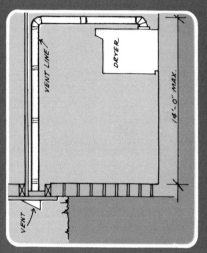

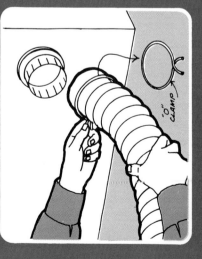

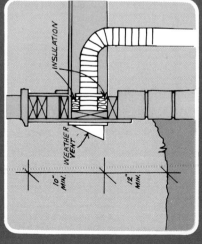

# INSTALLING A GAS DRYER

Not surprisingly, hooking up a gas dryer involves about the same amount of work as connecting a gas range. The only additional step involves venting the unit to the outside.

For the vent pipe, you have two options: rigid metal, which requires an elbow at every change in direction, and flexible vinyl, which doesn't. Which you choose depends largely on the path your vent will follow.

Longer runs, especially any that pass through interior walls, floors, or ceilings, call for rigid. Use flexible only for

out-in-the-open distances of 10 feet or less. Either flexible or rigid dryer vents should be no less than four inches in diameter.

In planning duct runs, try to keep them as short as possible—but don't exhaust into a chimney, under a floor, or into a crawl space. Lint could build up in these spaces and create a fire hazard. Don't put screws or a damper inside vent pipe, either. They catch and hold lint. Secure joints with duct tape instead.

You will need a hooded damper at the outside, though, to keep cold air from blowing back through the run. And add insulation around the pipe where it passes through an exterior wall or a space that's not heated. Cool pipes are

prone to condensation, which also collects lint.

To perform properly, a dryer must be installed dead level and located on a firm footing. If not, its spinning action can beat the machine to pieces in a short time. If your floor is at all shaky, beef it up with more bridging between the joists, as illustrated on page 11.

The drawings below illustrate only the steps in a dryer installation that differ from those you'd follow in hooking up a range, so check page 313 as well.

Both rigid and flexible ducting should be anchored with hangers every 6 feet. Stretch flexible slightly; don't let it coil up.

Make sure the unit is absolutely level and solid before loading it with clothes. Don't install a dryer on carpeting.

Flexible ducts are easiest to install. You can buy these in kit form, complete with clamp and an outside damper.

A rigid duct run with two elbows can go up to 14 feet. Deduct 4 feet from this maximum for each additional elbow.

If the dryer won't fire, purge air from the gas line by loosening the flare nut and opening the shutoff for a few seconds.

A vent should exit at least 12 inches above ground level, with a minimum of 10 inches to any window above it.

314

# INSTALLING A GAS GRILL

Tired of messing with charcoal briquettes, lighter fluid, smoke, ashes, and uneven cooking temperatures? A gas-fired grill takes all the bother out of outdoor cooking—without sacrificing any of its fun and flavor. You can even install one indoors, provided you top it off with a powered ventilating hood to draw off cooking odors (see page 381).

The key to the way a gas grill works lies with its permanent briquettes. Fired by natural or LP burners, these volcanic rocks catch meat juices, then smoke and flare up just as charcoal does. It's this action—not the smell of charcoal itself—that gives grilled food its unique taste.

Gas grills can be permanently mounted on a post or in a countertop, attached to a roll-around cart and plugged into your gas supply with a flexible, quick-connect hose, or supplied by an LP gas bottle that rides on the cart.

If you decide on a permanent mounting, you can make the hookup with small-diameter, flexible copper tubing, as shown below. First check with your gas supplier and ask how deep the line should be buried—and hire a pro to connect it to your house's system. (For more about working with copper tubing, see page 286).

Set the grill post in the ground with concrete, as you would a fence post (see page 178). If you plan to install the post on a concrete patio, you can either remove a small circle of concrete and dig a hole for the post, or use concrete expansion anchors and lag bolts to attach the post directly to the concrete. With brick, just remove a few bricks, dig a hole, and set the post.

If the grill will set on a wooden deck, bolt the post to the deck. Or, if the deck sits just off the ground, cut out a decking board and sink the post into the earth. Install headers where you cut into the deck.

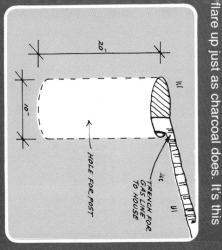

HOLE FOR POST

TRENCH FOR GAS LINE TO HOUSE

20"

10"

To set the grill post, dig a hole 10 inches in diameter and 20 inches deep. Run the trench for the pipe after you dig the hole.

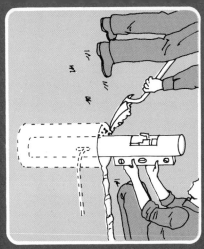

Set the grill post in the hole, then enlist someone to help keep it level while you shovel concrete around it.

Ever so gradually, bend the tubing at a 90-degree angle. Attempt the bend as shown, or if desired, use a spring bender.

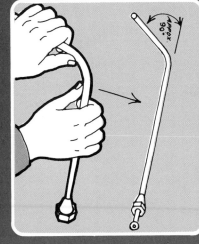

APPROX. 90°

Assemble the pressure regulator or manifold valve according to the manufacturer's instructions. Insert the tubing and connect it.

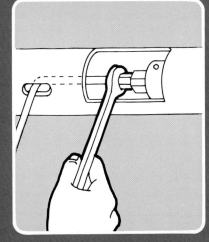

Connect the tubing to the gas supply line. Turn off the controls, turn on the gas, and test for leaks. Then assemble the unit.

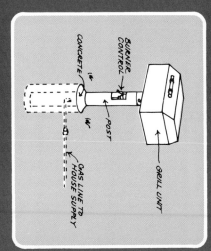

BURNER CONTROL

CONCRETE

POST

GRILL UNIT

GAS LINE TO HOUSE SUPPLY

**315**

MAKING GAS IMPROVEMENTS

# HEATING AND COOLING

How's the climate in your home right now? Whether you feel too hot, too cold, or just right depends largely on the temperature and humidity of the air around you. And it's your home's comfort system—whether it be an air, piped, or radiant one—that regulates the air's temperature by adding or removing heat; many also control the humidity level by adding or removing moisture.

The following pages tell how heating and cooling systems work, how you can maintain and improve their efficiency, what your choices are in new equipment, and—most importantly—what you can

do to slow the flow of energy dollars to your gas, oil, or electric company.

Begin by understanding that though heating and cooling components vary enormously, all take advantage of heat's inherent tendency to move from a warmer object or space to a cooler one. This means you can couple a *heat source* such as a burner, electric resistance element, or heat pump with a *heating plant*—usually a furnace or boiler—then send heated air, water, or steam via a *distribution network* to a home's various rooms. After the medium gives off its heat, it then recirculates

to the heating plant. A *control unit*, almost always a thermostat, maintains a preset temperature by switching the heating plant on and off.

Note that in a sense, this chapter presents *more* than you really need to know about heating and cooling. Since no one system would include all the components we show, you'll need to read selectively.

Yet in another way, the chapter tells *less* than the full story. Equally important is the way you conserve heating and cooling energy with insulation and ventilation—that chapter comes next.

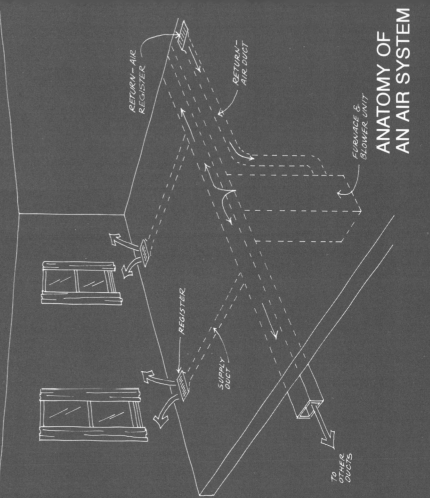

**ANATOMY OF
AN AIR SYSTEM**

## GETTING TO KNOW YOUR SYSTEM

"Ducted" systems use air as the heat distributing medium, circulating it from a *furnace* to *registers* in each room via a network of *ducts*. Modern-day versions have a *blower* that pushes treated air through *supply* ducts and pulls it back through *return* ducts.

If yours is an older home, it may have a less-efficient *gravity* system, which works the same way, but without the blower. Heated air rises from the furnace to the rooms, and cool air falls through the returns.

Blower-driven "forced-air" systems have one big advantage over the types illustrated or the opposite page—they can be easily adapted to centrally cool as well as heat your home (see pages 318-327, 335, and 336).

# ANATOMY OF A WATER OR STEAM SYSTEM

In a "piped" system, water or steam serves as the distribution medium. Here the heating plant, called a *boiler*, sends hot water or steam up *supply lines* to *radiation units* in each room. These transfer heat to the air, then direct cooler water back to the boiler via *return lines*.

Steam and hot-water systems have the same basic components, but differ somewhat in operation. Because steam always rises, it doesn't require the *circulator pump* shown here. Not all hot-water systems have pumps, either. "Gravity" types rely on water's tendency to expand when it's heated and contract when it cools. In "forced" or *hydronic* systems, the pump merely helps to move the water along.

If your home has hot-water or steam heat, turn to pages 328-333 for more detailed information.

# ANATOMY OF A RADIANT SYSTEM

Radiant heating directly warms the floor, ceiling, or baseboard units in a room, providing even and totally inconspicuous distribution. Some do the job with little more than electric cables, as shown at right; others circulate hot water through small-diameter tubing embedded in concrete.

Because they have no moving parts (and no heating plant), electrical radiant systems rarely give trouble. When they do, the problem usually happens at the breaker box (see pages 222 and 223) or because a cable has been damaged. If your home has this type of system, avoid boring or breaking into radiant surfaces. And don't confuse radiant heating with the electric-resistance furnace shown and discussed on page 321.

Not much can go wrong with a radiant water-distribution system, either. It depends, however, upon a boiler to supply the heat (see pages 332 and 333).

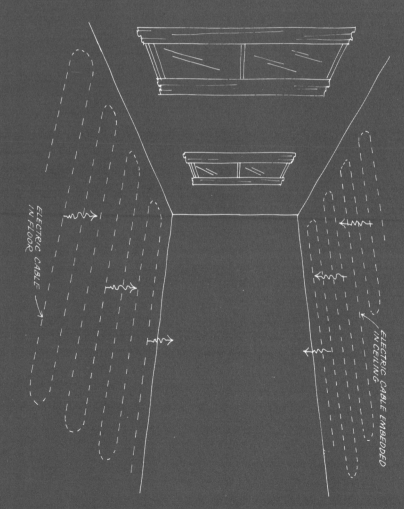

ELECTRIC CABLE IN FLOOR

ELECTRIC CABLE EMBEDDED IN CEILING

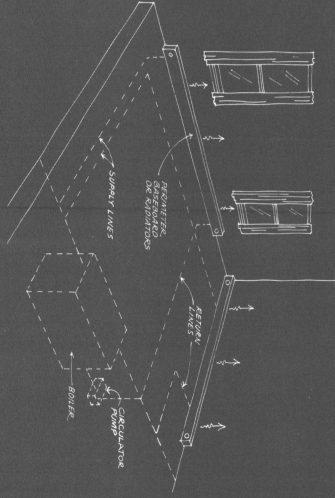

SUPPLY LINES

PERIMETER BASEBOARD OR RADIATORS

RETURN LINES

BOILER

CIRCULATOR PUMP

# MAINTAINING AND TROUBLESHOOTING AIR SYSTEMS

Consider that a forced-air heating/cooling system completely changes the air in your home as many as three times every hour, and you can see that it has a big job to do. Fortunately, most of its components are surprisingly easy to take care of—once you know what and where they are.

Begin by noting which registers supply treated air and which ones return it to the furnace. Most rooms have at least one

supply register; these usually include a movable damper that lets you modulate the air flow or shut it off entirely.

Return registers typically are larger and less numerous—many homes have only one per floor, located in a hallway or other central spot. Returns never have dampers, since shutting one off would partly suffocate the system.

While you're surveying your air registers, make sure none is blocked by

furniture, draperies, or carpeting. Supply registers must have unobstructed space above, and returns must be open to air currents from all directions.

Next, take a trip to the basement. If it has an exposed ceiling, you can easily trace the entire duct network. The drawing below shows how ducts connect to the furnace and what goes on in there.

## KEEPING AIR MOVING

Regardless of your furnace's shape or source of energy, it works like the one illustrated here. *Return air*, fed through a duct that's rectangular in cross-section, passes through an *air filter* into a compartment that houses the *blower*, essentially just a large, motor-driven fan. The blower then pushes air into a second compartment where it's warmed by a *heat source*. This might be a gas- or oil-fired *heat exchanger* (see pages 322 and 324), electrical *heating elements* (page 321), or a *heat pump* (page 326). If your home has central cooling, a *cooling coil*, situated in the supply duct above, extracts heat from the moving air. (More about this on pages 335 and 336.)

The heated or cooled air then moves into a *plenum* that feeds the various supply ducts. This may be a long, rectangular run like the one shown here —called an *extended plenum*—or it might look like a large, squarish box from which *perimeter ducts* radiate.

Note that air enters this particular furnace configuration at the bottom and exits at the top. Known as an *upflow* type, it's best suited to basement installations. For shapes that fit other locations, see page 353.

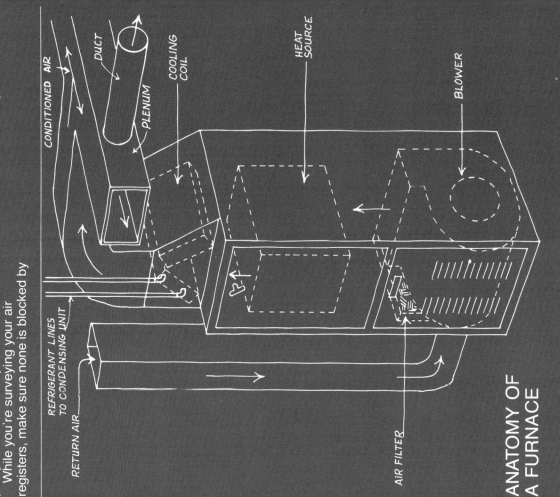

CONDITIONED AIR
DUCT
PLENUM
COOLING COIL
HEAT SOURCE
BLOWER
REFRIGERANT LINES TO CONDENSING UNIT
RETURN AIR
AIR FILTER

## ANATOMY OF A FURNACE

## Replacing Filters

One minor disadvantage of forced-air heating/cooling systems is that they tend to stir up dust and dirt. Situated upstream in the flow of air through a furnace, the filter serves as a net that catches many of these particles before they gum up the blower or heat source—or redeposit themselves on walls and baseboards around supply registers.

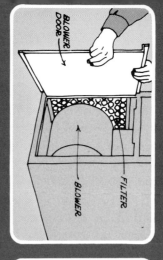

Neglect a filter and it can turn into a dam that throttles the air flow, makes the unit work harder, and wastes energy. A severely clogged filter can even cause a furnace to overheat, in which case a safety control—called a *limit switch* —will shut it down.

Check filters monthly during the heating and cooling seasons. Just pull out the old one, as shown below, and hold it up to a light; if you can see light through the filter, it's still usable.

Now just slide the filter out of its channel. Look for dirt on or around the blower, too. Vacuum the entire area if necessary.

Most disposable filters consist of oil-treated fiber glass in a cardboard frame. Be sure to install these so air strikes the oiled side first. Cleanable dry-foam filters can be vacuumed or washed.

Realize, too, that standard filters trap only larger airborne particles. To remove the fine dust and pollen that cause hay-fever sufferers so much grief, consider installing an electrostatic air cleaner, as shown on page 342.

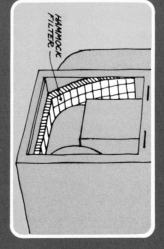

Some furnaces have a "hammock"-type filter that wraps around the base of the blower. They're also easy to replace.

---

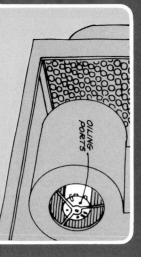

Most blower compartment doors lift or swing open easily. On counterflow models (see page 353) the door will be up top.

## Oiling and Adjusting Blowers

Make blower maintenance a part of your seasonal tune-up schedule—and check out the unit any time air seems to be moving faster or slower than usual.

Some blowers have direct-drive motors; others operate with an adjustable V-belt-and-pulley setup. You needn't

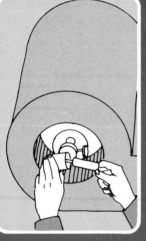

worry about adjusting the direct-drive type, but check the manufacturer's instructions about oiling; or look for lubrication ports, as shown below. If you find some, add a few drops of SAE-10 non-detergent oil at the beginning of each heating and cooling season.

Belt-drive blowers require just the right amount of belt tension (see below). Check the belt for fraying, cracks, and signs of wear, too—and consider

keeping a spare one on hand. An adjustable motor pulley lets you change the speed of a belt-drive model. You simply loosen a setscrew, then push the pulley's faces together to make it bigger (faster), or separate the faces to slow down the blower speed.

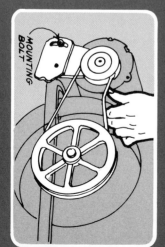

If a motor has oiling ports, they'll be located at each end of the shaft. Also check for lube points on the blower fan.

Blower fans usually have grease cups that you turn once annually. When they're empty, refill with bearing lubricant.

Adjust the belt so it's as loose as possible without slipping; it should depress about one inch. Keep mounting bolts tight.

## Balancing an Air System

If certain rooms in your home seem chronically too hot or cold, don't be too quick to blame the furnace. Instead, prepare yourself for a simple but time-consuming project called *balancing*.

To balance a heat-distribution system, you throttle down the air flow to a room that's usually too warm—a kitchen, for instance, or a family room with a southern exposure. Dammed-up air then gets a better chance to reach colder areas, typically those located farthest from the furnace.

Chances are, you've already tried a crude form of balancing by partially or totally closing registers in the hotter rooms. This cools them off, but it doesn't do much about redirecting the air. Instead, look for dampers in the ducts themselves. These usually are controlled by a handle or a locknut arrangement like the one shown below. You'll find one at the point where each duct takes off from the plenum.

(Note that not all duct systems have dampers. If this is the case at your house, consider installing them, as shown on page 339.)

Next, identify which ducts serve each room and label their dampers. If you have doubts, simply close them one at a time and determine which room isn't getting any air.

Now wait for a cool day, when the furnace will be running most of the time, and begin your balancing act. You'll need a handful of inexpensive thermometers, masking tape, and plenty of time. Most of that time will be spent waiting for temperatures in the rooms to catch up to the new damper settings.

If only one or two rooms have air-flow problems, you might be tempted to adjust only their dampers. This might work, but since balancing is a robbing-Peter-to-pay-Paul proposition, you'll get better results by tuning the entire system. Best of all, you may end up using a lower thermostat setting when everything's in harmony.

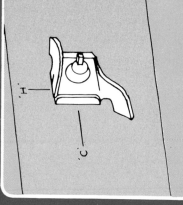

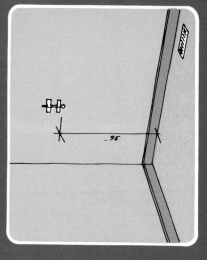

Now distribute the thermometers to various rooms. Tape them two to three feet from the floor, and not directly above registers.

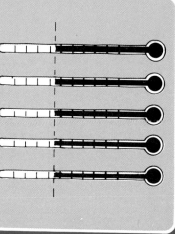

Synchronize a series of thermometers by laying them out together for 30 minutes or so and noting any discrepancies.

If you have central cooling, you may have to balance again in the summertime. Mark seasonal settings right on the duct.

Note any increase in air delivery to other rooms. Check temperatures again and make only very slight damper adjustments.

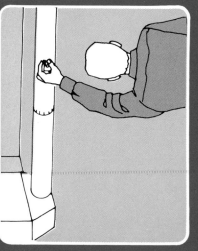

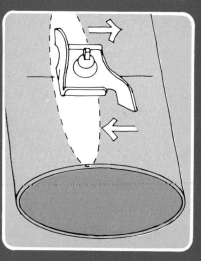

Begin by opening all registers and dampers. Loosen each damper's locknut and turn it to a position parallel with the duct.

After another 30 minutes, begin to partially damper rooms, beginning with the one where the thermostat is located.

# UNDERSTANDING AN ELECTRIC-RESISTANCE FURNACE

To envision how an electric-resistance furnace operates, think of a giant toaster with a fan blowing through it. Current flows into a series of *heat elements* —high-resistance electric wires or rods that glow like the much smaller elements in a toaster. As air pushed by the blower moves through these elements, it picks up warmth, then continues into the plenum and ducts to registers in each room.

Because there's no combustion in an electric furnace, it doesn't require the flue or heat exchanger gas and oil furnaces must have. And since there are no moving parts (other than the blower unit), maintenance is almost nil. Operating costs, however, usually run substantially higher.

Check the anatomy drawing at right to learn where you'll find the controls. An *air circulation switch* lets you run the blower continuously, if you wish. Underneath, accessible through a removable cover, a *fuse* or *breaker block* provides fuses or breakers for each of the heating elements. A *transformer* steps up amperage to the high levels needed for heating. And *relays* turn the elements on or off according to instructions from the thermostat.

The chart below lists the few things that can go wrong with an electric furnace and what you can do about them. Always shut off the furnace's main circuit breaker before removing the control or access panels. You'll find the breaker located next to the furnace or in your home's main service panel. (For more about breakers and fuses, see pages 222 and 223.) And finally, don't attempt to get at the heat elements at all—that's a job for a professional serviceman.

If your home has a heat pump (see pages 326 and 327), it may be backed up by resistance-type *duct heaters* like the one shown here. These mini-furnaces automatically pitch in when the temperature drops below what a heat pump can handle by itself.

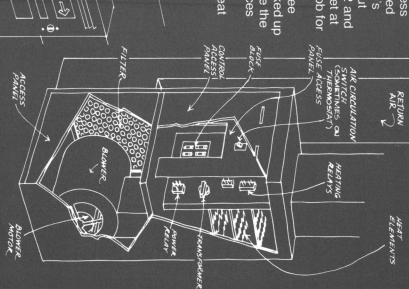

RESISTANCE COILS · DUCT · HEATER UNIT

RETURN AIR · AIR CIRCULATION SWITCH (SOMETIMES A THERMOSTAT) · FUSE ACCESS · CONTROL ACCESS PANEL · FUSE BLOCK · FUSE PANEL · HEATING RELAYS · HEAT ELEMENTS · ACCESS PANEL · FILTER · BLOWER · POWER RELAY · TRANSFORMER · BLOWER MOTOR

## What To Do Before Calling For Service

| Problem | Causes | Solutions |
|---|---|---|
| No heat | Furnace switch or main breaker is open; thermostat is set too low. | Check switch, fuse or breakers, and the thermostat. If the blower runs but there's no heat, check the fuse or breaker block. |
| Cycles on and off too often | A clogged filter or failing blower unit may be causing the unit to overheat. | Replace the filter, or oil and adjust the blower, as shown on page 319. |
| Not enough heat | Improper thermostat setting, a defective heating element, or a clogged filter or duct. | Check the thermostat first, then the fuse or breaker block. Replace the blown fuse (or flip on the breaker). If the fuse blows when you turn on the power, or if the breaker trips again, it's time to call in a serviceman. Replace the filter. |

321

MAINTAINING AIR SYSTEMS

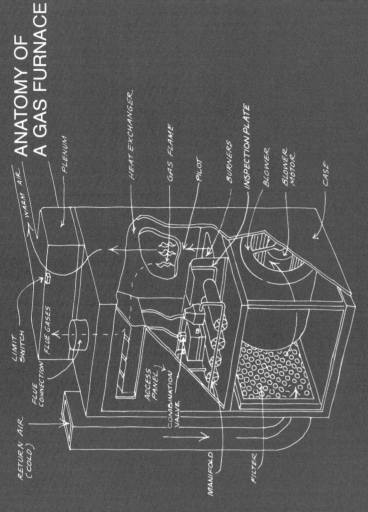

# ANATOMY OF A GAS FURNACE

Labels: WARM AIR, PLENUM, HEAT EXCHANGER, GAS FLAME, PILOT, BURNERS, INSPECTION PLATE, BLOWER, BLOWER MOTOR, CASE, RETURN AIR (COLD), FLUE CONNECTION, LIMIT SWITCH, FLUE GASES, ACCESS PANEL, COMBINATION VALVE, MANIFOLD, FILTER

## UNDERSTANDING A GAS FURNACE

The burners in a gas furnace differ little from the burners atop a gas range—they're just bigger and more numerous. Complexity enters in, though, when you consider the various controls needed to automatically turn the burners on and off and to provide a virtually foolproof safety system.

Examine the drawing at right and note that the burners themselves are housed behind an *inspection plate*, as is a series of sealed tubes called a *heat exchanger*. Another set of tubes, called *manifolds*, feeds the burners a mixture of gas and air, which is then ignited by the *pilot*. As the heat exchanger warms up, the blower pushes air through it and up to the plenum. Meanwhile, gases, primarily carbon monoxide, exit past the exchanger through the *flue* and up the chimney.

The safety devices include the pilot itself, which is connected to an assembly called a *combination valve*. If the pilot goes out and can't fire the burners, these units automatically shut off the gas. (More about pilots on the opposite page.)

A second safety control, the *limit switch*, is located in the plenum just above the heat exchanger. This turns off the gas if the plenum gets too hot; it also stops the blower when the temperature

drops to a certain level after the burners have shut down.

Beyond checking for flue leaks (see below), relighting the pilot, replacing filters, and servicing the blower (see page 319), there's very little you can or need do with a gas furnace.

Call a heating contractor for a routine tune-up every other fall, though. Rust and scale eventually clog some of the burner orifices, reducing their efficiency. Cleaning the burners isn't a big job, but you risk jarring the shutter settings on their manifolds—and adjusting these calls for an expert's eye to get the flames right. For more about gas appliances, see pages 308-315.

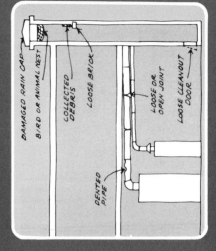

Labels: DAMAGED RAIN CAP, BIRD OR ANIMAL NEST, COLLECTED DEBRIS, LOOSE BRICK, LOOSE OR OPEN JOINT, DENTED PIPE, LOOSE CLEANOUT DOOR

Any of these points could leak carbon monoxide. If you suspect any flue pipe, shut down the furnace and replace the pipe.

Hold a candle to the opening in the top access panel while the furnace is running. If there's a leak, it will blow out the flame.

## Checking Out the Chimney and Flue

Very rarely does a gas furnace catch fire or blow up. But flues can develop leaks, releasing carbon monoxide—a colorless, odorless, and highly lethal by-product of combustion—into your home's air. And various things can clog a chimney.

These dangers warrant an annual check when you start up for the heating season. Inspect all of the points illustrated at far right, paying special attention to the pipe between the furnace flue and the chimney. For more about chimneys and flues, see pages 94 and 95, 118, and 314.

322

# Lighting a Pilot

Some newer gas furnaces ignite with an electrical spark system similar to the one used on oil burners (see page 324). Most, however, depend on a gas pilot light for firing—and when the furnace fails to operate, it's usually because the pilot has gone out or needs adjusting.

Procedures for relighting a pilot differ somewhat, so follow the steps listed on the instruction plate attached to the furnace or pilot assembly. With most, you'll find a *gas cock* with three settings—*off, pilot,* and *on.*

You turn the cock to "off," wait a few minutes for any residual gas to clear, then switch to the "pilot" setting. Now hold a match to the pilot, depress a *reset button,* and hold it down for the amount of time specified on the instruction plate.

If the pilot stays lit, turn the cock to "on" and the burners will fire. If the pilot goes out again after you release the reset, repeat the entire procedure, holding the reset down a little longer.

If you can't get the pilot lighted after two or three tries, call your utility company or a serviceman. The failure most likely indicates a problem with the *thermocouple,* a sensing device that keeps the main valve to the burners open. When the pilot goes out or the thermocouple malfunctions, it signals the main gas valve to close.

A weak or wavering pilot flame can also cause a thermocouple to shut everything down. The flame should be blue, with the tip barely flecked by yellow, and it should hit the sensing tube about 1/2 inch from the end.

If the flame doesn't fit this description, first make sure it isn't being buffeted by a draft. Next, try cleaning out the pilot opening with a toothpick or wood matchstick.

If that doesn't do the job, you'll need to adjust the pilot flame, as explained on page 310.

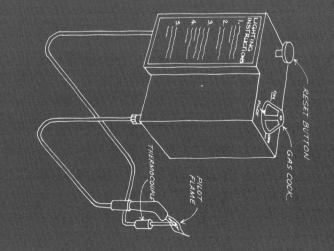

RESET BUTTON

GAS COCK

LIGHTING INSTRUCTIONS
1.
2.
3.
4.
5.

ON
PILOT

THERMOCOUPLE

PILOT FLAME

# What To Do Before Calling For Service

| Problem | Causes | Solutions |
|---|---|---|
| No heat | Thermostat set too low; furnace switch, fuse, or circuit breaker open; gas shut off at the furnace or meter; pilot out. | Check the thermostat, switch, and fuse or breaker; to learn about opening and closing gas valves, see page 308; relight the pilot. |
| Cycles on and off too often | Usually the result of a clogged filter, or a blower problem. | Replace filter; oil and adjust blower (see page 319). |
| Not enough heat | Again, a clogged filter; or the burners may need cleaning. | Replace filter; have burners cleaned by a serviceman. |
| Blower runs continuously | Fan switch is set for continuous circulation, or limit control is out of adjustment. | Reset fan switch on front of furnace or thermostat, or adjust limit control (see page 343). |
| Furnace squeals or rumbles | A squealing sound means the blower belt is slipping or its bearings need lubrication. Rumbling when the burners are off means the pilot needs adjusting; a rumbling sound when burners are on means the burners need cleaning. | Oil the blower and adjust its belt (see page 319); adjust the pilot (see page 310); have serviceman clean the burners. |
| Ducts vibrate | Vibration, or a whooshing sound, indicates that the blower is running too fast. | Adjust blower motor pulley (see page 319). |

323

## UNDERSTANDING AN OIL FURNACE

Compared to gas and electric furnaces, an oil-fired forced-air heating plant has quite a few more components. It starts out with the same filter-and-blower unit common to the other types. This pulls in return air and forces it through a *heat exchanger*, just as in a gas furnace.

But the heat producer in an oil furnace—its *burner*—includes a second motor/blower setup. This one supercharges oil with air, ignites the mixture with an electric spark, then blasts a torch-like flame into a fireproof compartment just below the heat exchanger.

To learn about the burner's major parts, examine the detail in the anatomy drawing below. The *combustion air blower* pulls in air through an adjustable *shutter*, mixes it with oil in an *air tube*, sets it afire with a pair of electrodes, then forces it through a *nozzle* into the *combustion chamber*. An *ignition transformer* steps up voltage to the electrodes. In some models, a *primary safety control* keeps an electric eye on the flame; if it fails to ignite, the safety shuts down the burner. Other types do the same job with a heat sensor in the flue pipe.

The combustion air blower's motor also drives an *oil pump*. This pulls oil through lines from the tank. An automotive-type *filter* strains any sediment from the fuel.

Despite their complexities, modern-day oil burners provide surefire heat. They do, however, require a regular —usually monthly—maintenance program and an annual tune-up. Neglecting these greatly undercuts the burner's efficiency, adds to your oil bills, and could lead to costly repairs.

Maintenance procedures vary, so check the manufacturer's literature for specifics. Here are the jobs that generally need doing.

• Clean or change the oil filter at least once a year. Some types have a replaceable cartridge; other, basket-types should be washed out in kerosene. With either, make sure to install a new gasket when you reassemble.

• Clean the pump strainer annually, if your unit has one. Again, soak it in kerosene and replace the gasket.

• Clean the fan blades monthly. Dust here greatly impedes the burner's efficiency. Do this with a long-handled brush.

• Lubricate the burner motor every month or two, unless it's permanently lubricated. Most require only a few drops of light, non-detergent oil. Look for instructions on the housing.

• Check all flue connections annually, as explained on page 322.

• Call for a tune-up every fall at the start of the heating season. Insist that the serviceman take instrument readings for combustion efficiency, smoke density, and draft. He also should check out the firing system, clean the ignition electrodes, and clean or replace the nozzle.

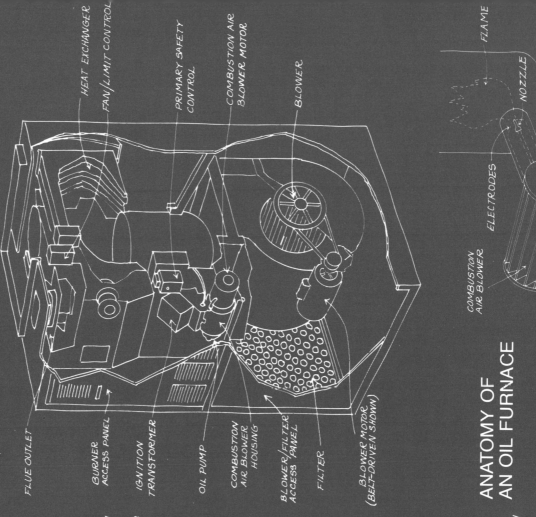

HEAT EXCHANGER

FAN/LIMIT CONTROL

PRIMARY SAFETY CONTROL

COMBUSTION AIR BLOWER MOTOR

BLOWER

FLUE OUTLET

BURNER ACCESS PANEL

IGNITION TRANSFORMER

OIL PUMP

COMBUSTION AIR BLOWER HOUSING

BLOWER/FILTER ACCESS PANEL

FILTER

BLOWER MOTOR (BELT-DRIVEN SHOWN)

## ANATOMY OF AN OIL FURNACE

FLAME

NOZZLE

COMBUSTION AIR TUBE CHAMBER

BLOWER MOTOR

COMBUSTION AIR BLOWER

ELECTRODES

SHUTTER

# Checking Safety Controls

Every oil burner includes a safety device that monitors its operation and turns off the unit if something goes wrong. Often, though, the reason for a shutdown lies with the safety itself. Here's how to troubleshoot the two different types.

With either type, reset the safety and try again, as shown below. If the burner

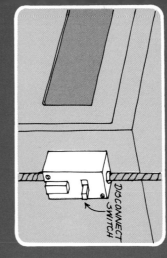

DISCONNECT SWITCH

kicks off again, shut off all power. (The burner motor and ignition may be protected by separate fuses or breakers.)

If your burner has an *electric-eye primary safety*, look for an access cover that lets you get at its photocell. Wipe this with a clean rag or tissue to remove any soot, reassemble, turn on the burner, and see if it fires.

The second type of safety—called a *stack switch*—mounts on the flue.

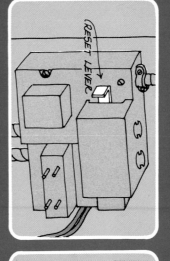

(RESET LEVER)

If the primary safety or stack switch is locked out, wait five minutes, then press the reset lever or button.

Remove the screw that holds the unit to the stack, carefully slide it out, and wipe off the sensor rod.

Don't continue trying to restart a balky burner. Unburned oil could accumulate in the combustion chamber and "flash back" if you get ignition. If the furnace won't fire after two or three attempts, call for service.

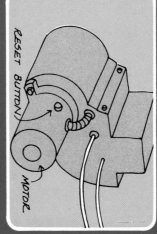

RESET BUTTON

MOTOR

Combustion air blower motors are also usually protected by an overload device. Restart one by pressing the red reset button.

## What To Do Before Calling For Service

You'll probably find one burner-disconnect switch on the side of the furnace and perhaps another outside the furnace room.

| Problem | Causes | Solutions |
|---|---|---|
| Burner doesn't run | Thermostat setting may be too low; the main switch, a circuit breaker, or fuse may be open; the motor may have overheated. | Set the thermostat five degrees higher than usual; check switches, breakers, and fuses; oil the motor and press its reset. |
| Burner runs but won't fire | This usually means that oil or spark isn't getting to the unit, or that the safeties are sooty. | Check to be sure oil valves are open and that there's oil in the tank—dip a rod into it, don't trust the gauge; clean safeties. |
| Burner cycles on and off too often | Clogged blower filter or other blower problems; improperly set limit control. | Check filter and blower (see page 319); check limit control (see page 343). |
| Burner smokes or squeals | Combustion air blower motor needs oiling. | Shut the unit off immediately, let it cool, and fill the oil cups. Check them again after the motor has run for an hour or so. |
| Chimney smokes | A cold flue may cause this when the burner first fires, but if smoking persists, it's a sure sign of incomplete combustion, which means the unit is wasting fuel. | Call for service and request the instrument tests listed on the opposite page. Don't attempt to adjust a burner yourself. |

# UNDERSTANDING A HEAT PUMP

Of all modern-day heat producers, a heat pump is one of the most difficult to comprehend. Begin by thinking of it as a reversible air conditioner. Like an air conditioner, it can lower indoor temperatures by removing heat from the air and dispelling it outside—but it's also capable of extracting heat from relatively cool outside air and pumping it indoors. (Surprisingly, even at 0 degrees F., air still has more than 80 percent of the heat available at 100 degrees.)

To do its job, a heat-pump—like all refrigeration devices—takes advantage of a liquid's tendency to absorb heat as it turns into a gas. Compressing the gas intensifies the level of heat, which is then either circulated through the house or dissipated outdoors (see the diagrams at right).

Study the anatomy of a split heat pump system (shown in the heating mode) and note that it has two sections. In the *outdoor unit*, a *fan* moves air through a coil, which absorbs heat.

A compressor then superheats the vapor and sends it through refrigerant lines to a second coil in the furnace. Here a blower unit pushes return air through the coil, warming the air and forcing it into the plenum and ducts beyond.

Meanwhile, refrigerant travels back to the outdoor unit to begin another full cycle through the pump.

The process reverses itself in the cooling mode by means of a *reversing valve*. This device automatically switches from one mode to another. It must be automatic because at certain temperatures—usually right around freezing—heat pumps tend to ice up. When this begins to happen, a sensor activates the reversing valve and the unit defrosts itself.

Some heat pumps include all components in a single outdoor cabinet, as shown at right. Here, the compressor, fan, both coils, reversing valve, and blower unit fit into one low-slung package. Only the system's main supply and return ducts penetrate exterior walls; there's no separate furnace.

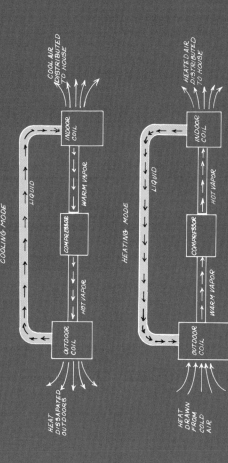

COOLING MODE

COOLER AIR DISTRIBUTED TO HOUSE

INDOOR COIL

LIQUID

WARM VAPOR

COMPRESSOR

HOT VAPOR

OUTDOOR COIL

HEAT DISSIPATED OUTDOORS

HEATING MODE

HEATED AIR DISTRIBUTED TO HOUSE

INDOOR COIL

LIQUID

HOT VAPOR

COMPRESSOR

WARM VAPOR

OUTDOOR COIL

HEAT DRAWN FROM COLD AIR

## ANATOMY OF A SPLIT-SYSTEM HEAT PUMP

AIR SUPPLY

COIL

FURNACE

BLOWER

LIQUID

VAPOR

REVERSING VALVE

OUTDOOR UNIT

COIL

FAN

COMPRESSOR

## ANATOMY OF A SINGLE-UNIT SYSTEM

SUPPLY

RETURN

OPTIONAL HEATING ELEMENT

BLOWER

REVERSING VALVE

ACCUMULATOR

COMPRESSOR

COIL

FAN

COIL

# Operating a Heat Pump

Heat pumps work most efficiently at temperatures down to about 15 degrees F. Below that, most systems require supplementary backup heating, usually electric-resistance elements installed in the furnace, ducts, or—in the case of a single-package unit—the pump cabinet itself. These units also take over for the pump while it's defrosting.

When a heat pump's defrost cycle runs continuously—or not at all—the backup system automatically takes over, a problem you might not be aware of until your next electric bill arrives. That's why it pays to familiarize yourself with what happens during a normal defrost cycle.

You'll probably notice that when the temperature hovers around freezing, frost will periodically form on the outdoor coil. When this occurs, the reversing valve should activate a five- to 10-minute cooling cycle to melt the ice. You may hear a gurgling sound as the valve operates, or see steam rising from the outdoor unit.

A heavy accumulation of ice on the outdoor coil means the unit isn't defrosting; no ice, or defrost cycles that last longer than 15 minutes, indicate that the pump is stuck in its cooling mode.

For either condition, first check the outdoor coil. You may find that leaves, snow, or other matter is cutting off the flow of air through the coil; clear the obstruction and the system should return to normal operation within an hour or so. If it doesn't and the coil remains coated with ice, the reversing switch may be stuck. You can try freeing it by switching the thermostat to the cooling mode. If the ice remains after an hour, flip the system selector switch to the "emergency heat" setting and call a heating contractor immediately for service.

The chart below identifies the most common heat pump maladies and what to do about them. Note that if all power has been off for more than an hour at temperatures lower than 50 degrees F, either because of a power outage or because a circuit breaker has tripped—you should not attempt to restart the pump for at least six hours after power has been restored. This gives a heating element in the compressor's crankcase time to warm up the lubricant and prevent valve damage.

Instead, turn the system selector switch to "emergency heat," wait six hours, then return to the normal heat setting; turning the system switch to "off" doesn't shut off the heater.

## What To Do Before Calling For Service

| Problem | Causes | Solutions |
|---|---|---|
| Pump does not run | Power isn't getting to the unit, or the thermostat isn't demanding heat. | First check the thermostat setting, then go to the electrical disconnect switch and fuses or breakers; most pumps also have a "reset" switch in the outdoor unit's cabinet. IMPORTANT: See above before restoring power. |
| Pump short-cycles | This may result from an obstruction blocking the outdoor coil, a malfunctioning blower unit, or a clogged filter. | Clear the outdoor coil (see above); check the filter and blower unit (see page 319). |
| Long or frequent defrost cycles | Defrosting that lasts longer than 15 minutes or that occurs more than twice an hour could mean the outdoor coil is blocked. | See above for symptoms and what to do. |
| Uneven heating | Heat pump systems deliver a stronger and cooler flow of air than you may be used to. Also, indoor temperatures may drop 2 to 3 degrees at or below the system's balance point—where backup heating kicks in; this is normal. | You can minimize air flow discomfort by carefully balancing the system (see page 320); to offset the balance-point differential, you may have to raise the thermostat setting in colder weather. |

# MAINTAINING AND TROUBLESHOOTING PIPED SYSTEMS

The difference between hot water and steam might seem merely one of degrees, but that's not always the case. In many hot-water systems, the water reaches a temperature of 240 degrees F., far above the 212 needed for steam.

What actually distinguishes the two is that water systems are sealed, with only

carefully controlled amounts of air in the radiation units, piping, and boiler; steam systems, on the other hand, must "breathe."

This explains why you can usually hear steam coming up, often to the accompaniment of banging pipes and hissing radiators. The steam has to push

air ahead of it up the "risers" and out vents on each radiator.

Conversely, hot water has little air to impede its progress, and circulates smoothly through the system, generally with nothing more than a few muffled thumps to let you know it's operating.

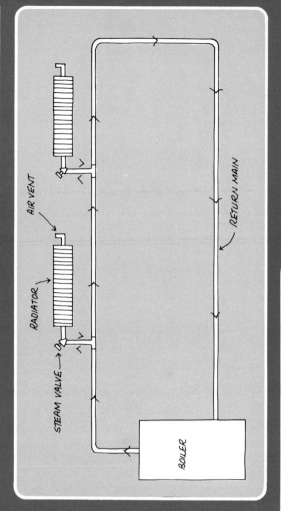

## KEEPING STEAM OR WATER MOVING

Steam systems usually—though not always—employ what's called a "one-pipe" distribution network like the one shown at right. A single line serves as both supply and return for each radiation unit.

Steam from the boiler rises via a *supply main* to the radiators, gives off its heat, and condenses to water. Then, because water is heavier than steam, the condensate drops back down the same pipe to a *return main*. This feeds the boiler with water to be boiled for the next steam cycle.

A few steam systems—and almost all hot-water systems—use the "two-pipe" arrangement illustrated at left. Here water or steam flows through radiation units, exiting via separate pipes to the return main.

Note the *expansion tank*, a feature of all hot-water systems. Partially filled with air, it serves as a cushion that prevents the heated water from turning into steam. Instead, the water increases in pressure, helping it circulate more readily.

In yet a third variation, called the "series loop" (not shown), steam or water flows from one radiation unit to the next; there are no mains. Turning off one radiator stops the flow of steam or water and shuts them all off.

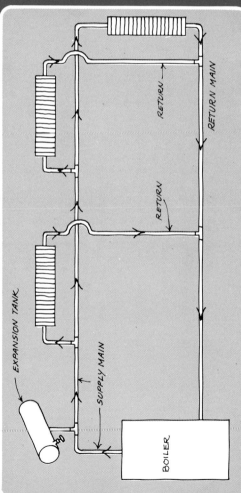

# Maintaining Radiation Units

Steam and hot-water radiation units—whether they're old-fashioned radiators or the more up-to-date convectors and baseboards shown on pages 344 and 345—amount to little more than pipes specially shaped to dissipate heat. Maintenance consists of making sure that water or steam can flow through. When a unit isn't heating up, first check its air vent. Liquids and gases can't get into a pipe that's full of air. Hot-water radiators—especially the one located farthest from the boiler—may need to be bled every fall, as shown below. Steam radiators bleed themselves with each heating cycle—provided their vents are working.

Realize, too, that like all plumbing components, radiation units depend on pitch for drainage. If one doesn't slope slightly toward its return outlet (or the inlet, in a one-pipe system), entrapped water will keep it from heating up.

What can you do about a radiation unit that's *too hot*? If yours is a hot-water system, you might get some relief by adjusting its inlet valve.

Better yet, try balancing the entire system, as you would with forced air (see page 320). With some piping, "flow" valves near the mains serve the same function as duct dampers. If your system doesn't have these, just methodically tune each inlet valve. When you get the balance you want, remove their handles so the settings can't be tampered with.

Steam radiators are difficult to regulate. Their inlets consist of on-off "gate" valves (see page 283); turning these to an in-between position not only won't modulate the heat, it will cause the unit to bang.

Instead, check with plumbing and heating suppliers to see if you can locate an adjustable air vent. By decreasing the size of the vent's aperture, you can slow down the rate at which steam enters the radiator.

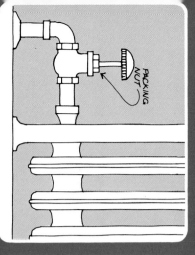

If an inlet valve leaks, first try tightening its packing nut; if that doesn't work, repack it as shown on page 267.

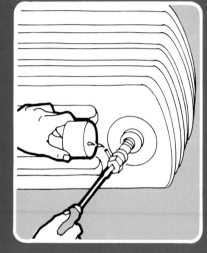

Bleed a hot-water radiator by opening its vent with a screwdriver or special key. When water squirts out, close it again.

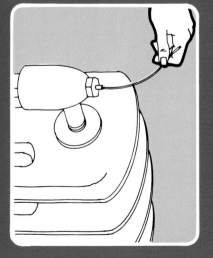

If a steam radiator won't heat, clean out the orifice of its air vent with a fine wire. You may have to replace the vent.

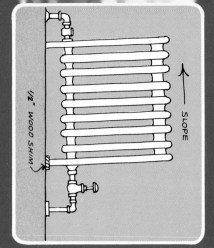

If a radiator warms only slightly but evenly, water may be trapped inside. Check to be sure it's pitched as shown.

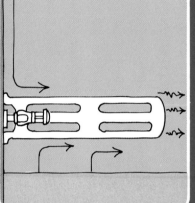

Any radiation unit depends on air circulating freely through it. Don't obstruct this with draperies, furniture, or solid enclosures.

To add humidity to a too-dry room, place a large, shallow pan of water atop a radiator. Some enclosures include pans.

## UNDERSTANDING A STEAM BOILER

In principle, a steam boiler works like a giant tea kettle. A gas or oil burner or electric-resistance elements heat water to the boiling point, sending steam to radiators throughout the house.

Actually, however, modern-day boilers are considerably more complex. First of all, the water doesn't simply lie inside a big kettle that would take hours to heat up; instead, it circulates around the heat source through a series of tubes or passages.

Second, boilers require several controls to automatically monitor and regulate their operation. These include a *pressure gauge and regulator* that shuts down the heat source when steam reaches a certain preset level; a *pressure relief valve* that releases steam if the regulator fails; and a *low-water cutoff* that shuts down the system if the boiler's water level gets dangerously low.

Some boilers also have an *automatic feed,* usually combined with the low-water cutoff, that supplies fresh "makeup" water when it's needed; with others, you have to manually open and close an ordinary valve.

Preventive maintenance calls for checking these controls monthly and occasionally flushing rust from the boiler's passageways. Both of these routines are illustrated in the drawings below.

To prolong your boiler's life and maximize its efficiency, schedule an annual professional checkup as well. Ideally, this should be done in the spring just before you shut down the heating system. Rust—a boiler's biggest enemy—thrives during periods when the unit is idle.

Also ask the serviceman about the feasibility of chemically treating your boiler's water. By their nature, steam systems include a lot of air, and it's aerated water that causes rust. Adding a special chemical can greatly reduce the oxygen content.

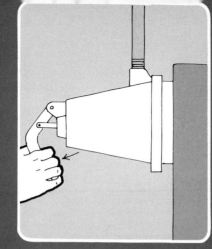

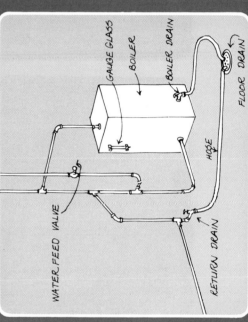

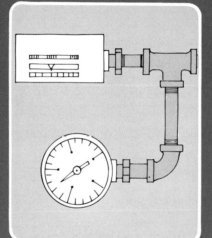

Periodically lift the lever on the relief valve to make sure that it's working properly. It should expel steam when the unit is running.

The pressure gauge should not exceed the level shown by the pointer beside it. If it does, shut down the boiler; call for service.

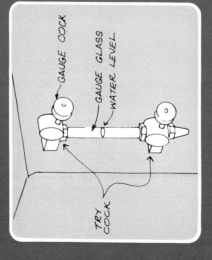

The gauge glass tells you how much water is in the boiler. To make sure the gauge is working, open the try cocks occasionally.

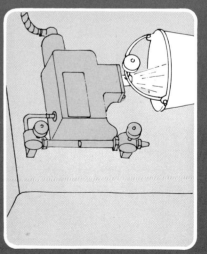

Open the blow-off valve on a low-water cutoff monthly to flush out any sediment. Do this until the water runs clear.

If the water in the gauge glass is rusty, and flushing the cutoff doesn't clear it, it's time you flushed the entire boiler. To do this, first shut off the power and auto feed, if you have one. Now attach hoses to the boiler and return drains, open them, and let the water run out.

Next, shut the drains, refill the boiler, and drain it again. You may need to repeat the process several times until water in the gauge is clear.

# TROUBLESHOOTING A STEAM BOILER

When a boiler goes cold, first check to be sure its main switch hasn't been inadvertently turned off, then look for a blown fuse or tripped circuit breaker. Also try upping the thermostat setting.

If the unit is getting power, next look at its gauge glass and determine if the boiler has enough water, as shown on the opposite page. When the water level drops below a certain point, the low-water cutoff activates a switch that turns off the burner or electric heating elements; otherwise, heat would soon "cook" the tank.

You can easily add water to a thirsty boiler—but first examine the return lines for any signs of leakage. Most steam systems gradually lose water through evaporation, but a big return leak can trip the low-water cutoff after just a couple of heating cycles. (Since supply lines carry only steam under relatively low pressure, they rarely develop leaks.)

If you have a leaking return, call a plumber, not a heating specialist. One of the emergency repair techniques shown on page 263 might let you run the system until help arrives.

When you do add water to a boiler, take care that you don't overfill it. Steam systems depend on an air space above the waterline—called a "chest"—where the steam builds up a head. Flooding the chest could cause water to back up the return lines or trip the relief valve—both messy situations.

If your boiler has an automatic water feeding device, you won't, of course, notice any problems with the water level; the auto feed will make up any shortage with each heating cycle. This means that a leak could go unnoticed for quite some time, and constantly introducing fresh, cold water to the system will add to fuel as well as water bills. This is why you should shut off the feed every so often—most have valves or bypass piping for that purpose—and keep an eye on the water level for a few days.

Also, don't neglect to flush the automatic feed at the intervals recommended by the manufacturer. A sticking feed could flood the boiler.

## What To Do Before Calling For Service

| Problem | Causes | Solutions |
|---|---|---|
| No heat | No power to the unit; no water; burner problems. | Check the thermostat, switches, and fuses or breakers; check the water level (see above). Boiler burners differ very little from those used on furnaces; to learn about them, see pages 322-325. |
| Poor heat | Rust and scale constrict the water passages that honeycomb a boiler, reducing efficiency and increasing fuel consumption; soot and corrosion from combustion also can build up on heating surfaces. | Flush the boiler, as shown on the opposite page; cleaning the heating surfaces is a job for a serviceman. |
| Chronically low water level | Leaking return lines or, more serious, a leak within the boiler itself. | For return-line leaks, see above; boiler leaks require major repairs, and may mean you'll have to buy a new unit. |
| Clouded gauge glass | This usually means the boiler needs flushing, but sometimes the glass itself also must be cleaned out. | Flush the boiler (see opposite page). To remove the glass, loosen the nuts above and below; lift the glass up, then pull it out; clean it with a brush. (To be sure a gauge is working open the try cocks—steam should come from the one on top, water from the one below. |
| Noisy pipes | Probably the result of water entrapped in return lines or in the return main. | With a level, check the pitch of all returns—they must slope back toward the boiler; if you find one has tilted the other way—usually because the house has settled—adjust the slant with new pipe hangers. |

# UNDERSTANDING A HOT-WATER BOILER

Hot-water and steam systems use the same boilers, fired by similar burners or electric heating elements, and both have pressure-relief valves designed to "blow" if pressure in the system gets too high. But hot-water heating plants are controlled by a different set of devices—and they have a few additional components that need tending from time to time.

The controls include a *combination gauge* that lets you keep an eye on both water temperature and water pressure, and tells you when the boiler needs water or is otherwise malfunctioning. With some systems, a *pressure-reducing valve* takes care of the water problem automatically. Both are shown below.

All hot-water systems also depend on an *expansion tank* that must be properly charged with air to prevent the water from boiling. With newer installations, you'll find this hung from the basement ceiling near the boiler, as in the drawing below, right. In older homes, it may be located in the attic.

Newer-type expansion tanks include a *purge valve* that simultaneously releases water and lets in air when it's opened. The older versions have only a gauge glass, like the one on a steam boiler (see page 330) to let you know how much water is inside. For more about expansion tanks and their ills, see the opposite page.

If yours is a forced-water (hydronic) system, look for one or more motor-driven pumps—called *circulators*—on return lines near the boiler. Some circulator motors are permanently

lubricated and need no maintenance. Others require a few drops of light, non-detergent oil every heating season. Note and heed the instruction plate attached to the motor; over-oiling can cause problems.

Systems with more than one circulator may or may not be zoned for independent temperature control of different areas within the house. Zoned systems have low-voltage, motor-driven *zone valves* on their supply lines. Each of these opens or closes according to orders from its own thermostat. These require no regular maintenance, but one does occasionally fail, as explained in the chart on the opposite page.

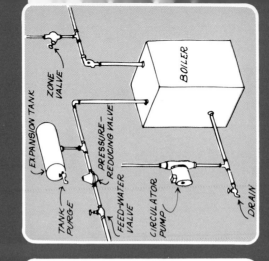

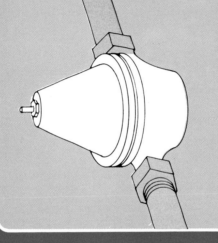

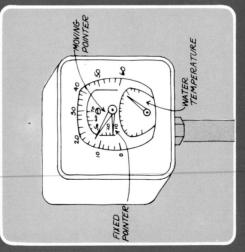

A combination gauge at the side or on top of a boiler has three indicators. The moving pointer tells the actual pressure; the fixed pointer registers the minimum pressure for which a system has been set. If the moving pointer drops below the fixed one, the system needs water.

The lower, temperature gauge indicates the water's temperature. The maximum temperature is also preset—by moving a pointer along the sliding scale of a separate device called an *aquastat* (not shown). Don't tamper with an aquastat setting.

If your system has a pressure-reducing valve like this one, it should automatically maintain the correct water pressure. To be sure it's doing its job, check the combination gauge every so often, as explained at left, and call for repairs if necessary.

If you don't have a pressure-reducing valve, you may have to manually feed the boiler monthly. Just open the feed water valve and close it again when pressure reaches 12 pounds. High water consumption means there's a leak somewhere in the supply or return piping or in the boiler itself.

Hot-water boilers rarely need to be flushed, but check yours every year or so by opening the drain and running off a bucketful of water. If it comes out rusty, shut off all power, then open the drain cock and the air vents on the system's highest radiation units (see page 329). If your boiler has a manual feed, open it, too.

When the water runs clear, close the drain and air vents, and wait until the pressure reaches 20 pounds. Now bleed each radiation unit. If pressure still exceeds 20 pounds, drain water off; if it falls below 12 pounds, add more.

# TROUBLESHOOTING A HOT-WATER BOILER

## What To Do Before Calling For Service

Despite their complexity, hot-water boilers give troublefree service for years on end—and when a problem does develop, it usually lies within the expansion tank or a circulator, not the boiler itself.

Water spurting from a pressure-relief valve (see page 330) means there's not enough air in the tank. Instead, the tank has filled with water, which expands as it heats up and trips the safety. You can double-check this by lightly touching the tank. Normally its bottom half will feel hotter than the top; if the top seems hot, too, the tank has filled with water and must be bled.

With most tanks, you simply let the system cool, attach a hose to the tank's purge valve, and run off two or three bucketsful of water. The valve lets in air at the same time. An older tank might have an ordinary valve rather than the purge type. With these, you first close a second valve in the line between the tank and boiler, then completely drain the tank.

After you've bled the tank, return all valves to their normal settings and start up the boiler again. Let it run an hour or so, then check the system's pressure, as indicated by the combination gauge. When a circulator fails, its motor may continue to run. That's because the motor and pump are connected by a special, spring-loaded coupling designed to break if the pump jams. Usually the broken coupling makes a loud clamor. Water trickling from a circulator means the pump seal has given out and must be replaced. Call a serviceman for either of these circulator repairs.

| Problem | Causes | Solutions |
| --- | --- | --- |
| No heat | No power to the boiler; low water level; burner problems. | Increase the thermostat setting; check all switches and fuses or circuit breakers; check the water level (see opposite page); trouble-shoot the burner's safety controls (see pages 322-325). |
| Poor heat | A sudden drop in heating efficiency usually means water problems—either the system has too much or too little; gradual deterioration results from rust or scale within the boiler's water passages or on the surface of its heat exchanger. | First check the combination gauge (see opposite page), then look for expansion-tank problems (see above). If the problem has come on slowly, try flushing the boiler (opposite page), then call a serviceman for a tune-up. |
| Leaks | Water may be coming from a circulator, the pressure relief valve, piping, or (more rarely) the boiler's tank. | Carefully investigate the water's source. Is it emanating from the pressure-relief valve, the underside of a circulator, or supply or return pipes? Bear in mind that water may travel quite a distance from a leak, but always in a downward direction. For leaking pipes, call a plumber, or shut down the system and repair them yourself, as shown on pages 263 and 282-291. |
| Only some radiators heat up | Suspect air entrapped in the units, especially if they're located far from the boiler; if an entire zone is cold, the problem lies with a zone valve or its circulator. | Bleed air from the cool units (see page 329); check the circulator (see above). If a zone valve is stuck, you'll feel heat in the pipe from the boiler to the valve but not beyond. Touch pipes gingerly. |
| Clanking pipes | With a sudden racket, you can be almost certain a circulator has gone bad; chronic banging noises may be the result of improperly pitched return lines. | Check the circulator; for banging, hold a level to all return lines, as explained on page 331. |

333

# TROUBLESHOOTING A THERMOSTAT

Pop the cover from a thermostat and you'll discover that your heating system's "brain" has remarkably few components. That's because it amounts to nothing more than a temperature-sensitive on/off switching device.

The sensing is done by a coil or strip of two metals that expand and contract at different rates. As room temperature drops below the setting you've selected, this *bimetal* coil or strip closes a set of electrical *contacts*, sending a low-voltage signal to a transformer that turns on the heating plant. When air warms above the thermostat setting, the bimetal opens the contacts again, shutting off the heat. (Switching to the cooling mode, of course, simply reverses these cycles.)

Thermostats are as reliable as any other switch. When a heating or cooling problem comes up, first make sure the temperature setting is at the right level—sometimes turning the dial up or down a few degrees will get things going again. Next, troubleshoot the system's other components, as shown on the preceding pages. If they're all in working order, shut off the main power switch, return to the thermostat, and try the procedures shown below. (For information about installing a new thermostat, see page 350.)

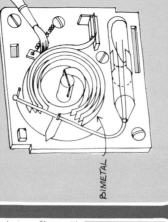

BIMETAL

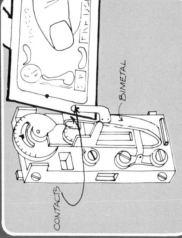

CONTACTS
BIMETAL

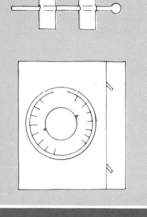

BIMETAL
MERCURY SWITCH

With newer thermostats, the contacts usually consist of a mercury switch sealed in a glass tube. These never need cleaning.

In older devices, exposed contacts may collect dirt. Clean by rubbing a new dollar bill between them. Don't use sandpaper.

Dust or lint on the bimetal will impair the efficiency of either type. Clean this with a small brush or with dry air.

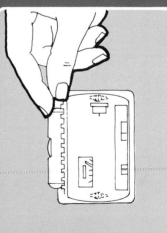

To check a thermostat's accuracy, tape a thermometer to the wall. If there's any discrepancy, a serviceman can re-calibrate the unit.

To operate properly, a thermostat must be level. To reposition, remove cover and adjust screws in the mounting plate.

# MAINTAINING AND TROUBLESHOOTING COOLING SYSTEMS

You've probably noticed that degree for degree, cooling consumes far more energy than heating. Why?

The answer lies in the nature of the cooling process. First, of course, the cooling unit must absorb heat from the air—a big task in itself. Secondly, it also has to reduce humidity to a more comfortable level. This it does by over-chilling the air, then pushing controlled amounts of warm, humid air through the cooling coil—causing moisture to form on the coil. This moisture is carried away through a condensate drain.

What's more, cool air weighs more than warm air, and unlike heat, it doesn't tend to rise of its own accord. The result: you first pay dearly to lower temperature and humidity in the air, then you need additional energy to move it around.

Any inefficiency in a room air conditioner or a central system just compounds the already heavy electrical load it needs; to minimize this energy draw, you must keep your home's cooling equipment in top operating order. The following pages show how.

Begin by familiarizing yourself with the principal components in any cooling system. These include a *condensing unit* where refrigerant is condensed into a liquid. You'll always find this one located outside, where it can release heat (and almost all of the system's noise) to the outdoor air.

The condensing unit then sends the now-cool refrigerant to an *evaporator coil* situated indoors. Here a *blower* moves air through the coil to cool and dehumidify it. If yours is a central system, its evaporator coil is located in the furnace plenum, as illustrated below.

Room units house all their parts in a single, two-compartment cabinet, such as the one shown on page 337. Heat pumps—essentially two-way air conditioners—have a few additional components. For more about these, turn to page 326.

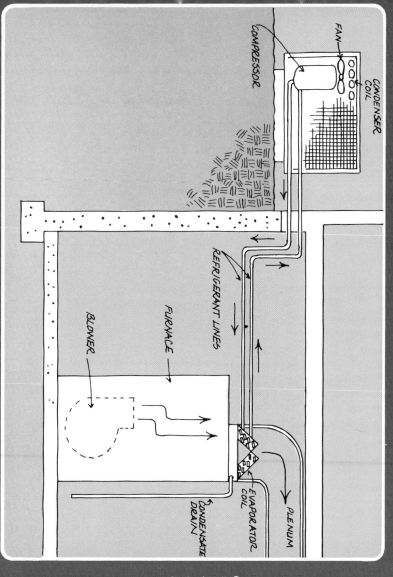

## ANATOMY OF A CENTRAL COOLING SYSTEM

To trace the circuits of heat and cold through a whole-house air conditioning system, study the drawing at left. Begin at the condensing unit outside.

Here a *compressor* and *condenser coil* "make cold" by pressurizing refrigerant gas, which loses heat as it turns into a liquid. The coil, a network of tubing and fins, dissipates the heat into outdoor air pulled through it by a *fan*.

Next, cool refrigerant flows through copper tubing to a second coil, the *evaporator*. In this one, the refrigerant absorbs heat from air pushed through it by the furnace *blower*.

Cool, dry air then moves into the *plenum*. Meanwhile, water condensed from the air leaves via a *condensate drain*, and the refrigerant, a hot gas once again, returns to the condensing unit for another cycle.

335

## MAINTAINING A CENTRAL AIR CONDITIONER

Factory-sealed components, charged with pressurized refrigerant, keep central cooling systems humming for years—and when something does go wrong, only a service contractor should attempt repairs.

Don't wait until a unit breaks down, though, before calling for service. Instead, schedule a tune-up for the start of every cooling season. Some of the refrigerant may have leaked out, for example—a condition that gradually diminishes your system's efficiency.

Also, keep a monthly eye on the points illustrated below, making sure air flows freely through the condenser and evaporator coils and your furnace's blower unit. Examine one of the coils and you'll see that it resembles an automobile's radiator—loops of tubing laced through a honeycomb of aluminum fins. Leaves, debris, even a heavy accumulation of household dust on these fins can choke off the air flow any cooling system depends on.

When you clean the fins, treat them gingerly; they bend easily, and sharp tools could puncture the relatively soft copper tubing.

Don't neglect your furnace's blower unit, either. Moving cool, heavy air strains belts and bearings. To learn about keeping blowers blowing, see pages 318 and 319.

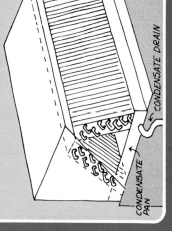

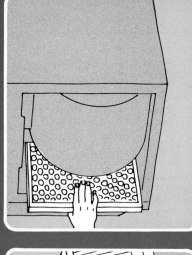

CONDENSATE DRAIN

CONDENSATE PAN

Keep the condensing unit clear for maximum air flow. Hose out leaves or other debris, and keep shrubbery pruned back.

During humid weather, check the condensate drain every so often to be sure that it's carrying off excess moisture.

A clogged furnace filter can shut down a unit. Change this two or three times per season, and never run a unit without a filter.

### What To Do Before Calling For Service

| Problem | Causes | Solutions |
| --- | --- | --- |
| System not running | Almost always the result of an incorrect thermostat setting or because power's not getting to the unit. | Check to be sure room temperature is above the thermostat setting; investigate circuit breakers and the main power switch. |
| System runs but doesn't cool | This may mean the unit needs refrigerant, or it could be caused by air flow problems. | First check for a clogged filter, and make sure the blower is functioning properly (see page 319). Next look for blockages at the condensing unit; refrigerant must be recharged by a repairman. |
| System cycles on and off too often | Again, you could have air flow problems—or the thermostat could be defective. | Check the condensing unit's air flow first, then the filter and blower; for more about thermostats, see page 334. |
| Uneven cooling | If some rooms are too cool and others too warm, the duct system needs balancing. | To learn about balancing an air system, see pages 320 and 339. Not quite enough cooling? The unit may be undersized. |

# MAINTAINING AND TROUBLESHOOTING A ROOM AIR CONDITIONER

window or through-the-wall cooling unit—as all the same components you'd find in a central system—but they're scaled down to fit into a two-section enclosure.

The enclosure's smaller inside cell includes a *blower, evaporator coil,* and *thermostat sensor* that reads the temperature of air coming into the evaporator coil. The thermostat itself is located behind the *control panel,* as are all other switches. A removable *front panel* covers everything over, and often holds the *filter* as well.

An *isolation panel,* usually made of sound-resistant material, separates the inside and outside compartments. This may or may not have a shutter that you can adjust from the control panel to bring in outside air.

Outside, the *fan* moves air through the *condenser coil,* where the refrigerant is liquefied and sent to the evaporator coil. A few older room units may require occasional oiling of blower bearings—accessible by sliding the chassis out of its enclosure. But most air conditioners are now permanently lubricated; routine upkeep consists of keeping their filters and coils clean, as shown below.

When a unit refuses to run, make sure its filter is clean and that the power cord is plugged in. Next, go to your home's

main service panel and look for a blown fuse or tripped circuit breaker. But don't restart an air conditioner within five minutes after it kicks off; let built-up heat dissipate first.

If the unit cycles too often or otherwise runs erratically, suspect thermostat problems. Often this means that the sensor has been knocked out of position. It should be near the coil, but not

touching it; adjust by carefully bending the wire.

If you hear a gurgling noise, or if water drips from the front panel, shut off the power and check with a level to make sure the cabinet's outer section slopes toward its condensate drain.

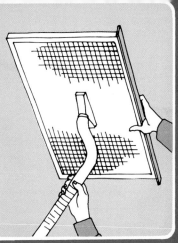

Some types of filters should be vacuumed, others washed or replaced. Clean or change the filter every two to three weeks.

Every month, check the condenser coil and intake vents for any obstructions. Hose out this part of the unit every spring.

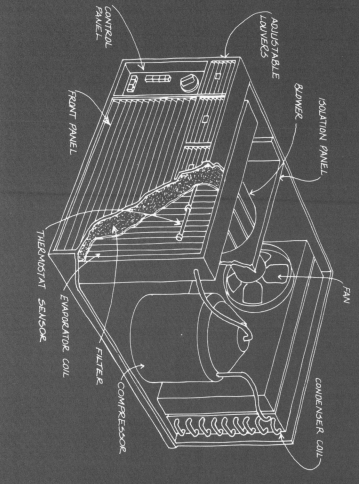

CONTROL PANEL

ADJUSTABLE LOUVERS

ISOLATION PANEL

BLOWER

FRONT PANEL

THERMOSTAT SENSOR

EVAPORATOR COIL

FILTER

COMPRESSOR

CONDENSER COIL

FAN

VENT

CONDENSATE DRAIN

Also check the condensate drain outlet. If it's plugged or the unit is not properly pitched, humidity can't run out.

# MAKING HEATING AND COOLING IMPROVEMENTS

If you've studied the heating and cooling basics on the preceding pages, you may have already realized an anatomical fact. Though the "heart" of your home's comfort system can be complex, its "arteries" and "veins" amount to little more than runs of ducts or pipes. And its thermostatic "brain" is really nothing but a temperature-activated on/off switch.

You'll want to leave heart surgery to a heating specialist, of course. But with only a few talents and tools, you can safely operate on your home's circulatory system, replace its brain with a more sophisticated one, and even implant another heart in the form of an auxiliary space heater. Following are a dozen examples.

## ADDING A WARM AIR OUTLET

You've got an "under-aired" room that's too cool in the winter and too hot in the summer. Or you've just finished off an unheated part of your house. How do you make them comfortable? If your heating/cooling system isn't already running continuously in very cold or warm weather, extending the plenum or tapping into it as shown below is the answer. (If, on the other hand, your system is already working at its capacity, consider solving the problem by installing one of the independent space heaters shown on pages 346-349.)

Before going to a sheet-metal supplier for materials, draw a rough sketch of what you're trying to do. Measure the length of the new run and also the diameter of the pipe that's used for existing runs.

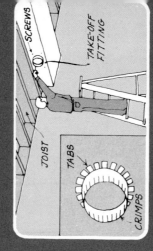

"Take-off" fittings come with flanges designed to be inserted into the plenum, then folded flat. Secure them with screws, too.

If you can't extend an existing duct run, you'll need to tap directly into the plenum. Cut an opening in its bottom or side.

Finally, fit an "elbow" to the boot and assemble the rest of the run. Secure each connection with screws and duct tape.

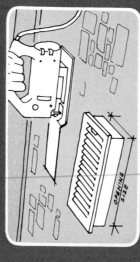

Try to locate your new register along an outside wall, keeping its supply run as straight and short as possible.

Most registers connect to their ducts with a "boot" fitting. Nail or screw it securely to the subflooring, as shown.

# ADDING AN IN-LINE DAMPER

Dampers—essentially doors located in supply ducts—offer a way to control the flow of heated or cooled air to your home's various rooms. With them, you can cut down the flow to a spot that's "over-aired" and redirect it to one that's not getting enough air.

The process, called "balancing," lets you equalize temperatures to make up for differences in exposures, the length of duct runs, heat-producing appliances, etc. To learn how to do a thorough balancing job, check out the information on page 320.

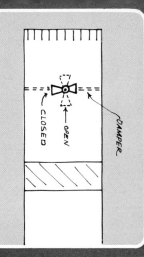

If your ducts don't already have dampers, installing them is simple. Just buy the right components and locate them in the right places.

Dampers for round ducts come preassembled in duct sections that simply fit into existing runs, as shown here. When buying them, specify the size of your present ducts—usually 5, 6, or 7 inches in diameter.

Rectangular ducts vary in size and cross-section, so you may need to have these made to order by a sheet-metal fabricator. He also can show you how to install them.

Where you locate dampers depends largely on whether your system has an "extended plenum" or "perimeter

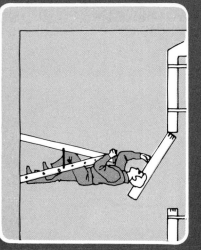

ducting." With an extended plenum, such as the one illustrated on page 318, install a damper in each branch just past the point where it exits the plenum. To get at these (sometimes you can't), you may have to work your hands and tools into cramped quarters.

Perimeter ducts fan out from a central, box-like plenum. Here again, install dampers slightly beyond the branches' exit collars.

Most duct runs dismantle more easily than you might think. You'll find them secured with just one or two screws at each joint. Unscrew either end of a section, and maybe the boot as well, and you can usually create enough play to wrestle the section loose.

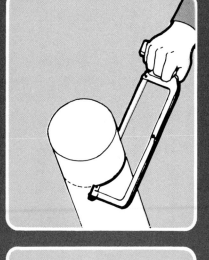

Gently pulling a section away from the furnace disengages its uncrimped end; once it's loose, slide the other end free.

Now cut a piece from the non-crimped end of the duct. The piece should be 4 inches shorter than the damper section.

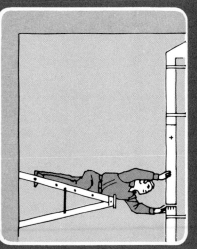

As with any duct run, slip the plain end over the previous section's crimped end. Secure with screws; wrap with duct tape.

Finally, reassemble the run and tape all joints. Note that the sections' crimped ends always point away from the furnace.

In its fully open position, the damper lever will be parallel to the duct; fully closed, it will be perpendicular.

## INSTALLING A HIGH-WALL RETURN

One small difficulty with using the same duct network for both heating and cooling is that warm and cool air behave differently.

For heating, it makes sense to locate both supply and return registers at or near floor level. Heated air rises from the supplies, while heavier cool air settles to the returns.

In its cooling mode, a furnace's blower pushes cooled air with enough force to boost it toward the ceiling. But unless warm air up there can get back to the cooling unit, the air in the room tends to stratify in layers—the warmest toward the ceiling, the coolest at the floor.

If this is happening at your house, you needn't rip open an entire wall to install a return register near the ceiling. Most interior walls—the best places for returns—have hollow cavities between their studs, and there's no reason why you can't let one of these serve as a return duct.

The drawings here show how you can tap into a wall cavity—and possibly utilize space between the floor joists as well. In planning the right spot, be sure to avoid any other heating or plumbing runs. (Don't worry about wiring, though; it won't impede air flow to any appreciable extent.)

Also, study the anatomy of an interior partition shown on page 30. Note that if your wall includes fire blocking, you'll need to make a third opening in the center to remove it. Typical floor construction is illustrated on page 10.

How you'll cut into your walls and patch them afterward will depend on whether they're surfaced with drywall, plaster, or paneling. More about these on pages 34-37.

Once you've installed a high-wall return, you'll notice a big improvement in the room's comfort level, and your cooling system will run more efficiently, too. You may need to rebalance the system, however (see page 320).

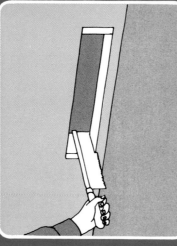

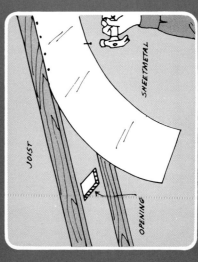

Now make another opening directly below at floor level. Saw out the sole plate, and cut a hole in the subflooring.

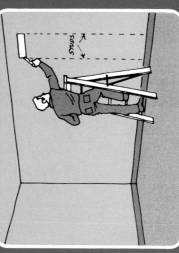

Locate studs (see page 31), then cut an opening to accommodate a return grille. It should be about 6 inches from the ceiling.

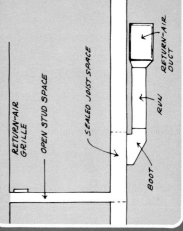

RETURN-AIR GRILLE
OPEN STUD SPACE
SEALED JOIST SPACE
RUN
BOOT
RETURN-AIR DUCT

Or, drop a boot below the joists for the run back to your home's main return. The joist cavity must be sealed.

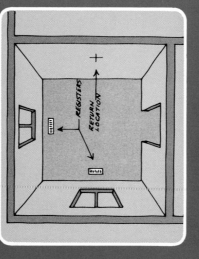

REGISTERS
RETURN LOCATION

So air can circulate entirely through the room, locate your new return on an interior wall opposite any supply registers.

JOIST
SHEETMETAL
OPENING

If joist cavities run in a convenient direction, let one double as a duct by enclosing it with sheet metal, as shown.

# ADDING A POWER HUMIDIFIER

Many forced-air heating systems don't just heat the air they move, they treat it as well. Specifically, they add moisture to make up for the dryness that comes with winter weather. (The colder air gets, the less humidity it can hold.)

If your furnace isn't equipped with a humidifier, or if it has only a passive, evaporative-plate humidifier (a small, drawer-like affair), your home's air isn't being treated effectively. You need something that can cope with the big volumes of arid air that pass through a heating system.

Power humidifiers can. Some motorized models spray a fine mist directly into the air stream; others rotate a porous water wheel through the heated air. Still others pull the air through a moist pad.

Better units are controlled by a *humidistat*—a moisture-sensing device similar to a thermostat. When the air's relative humidity reaches a preset point in the 30-to-50-percent range that most people find comfortable, the humidistat turns off the humidifier until the moisture level drops again. The unit also cycles on and off with the furnace blower.

Besides cutting a hole in a plenum or duct, installing a power humidifier involves hooking into a cold water line,

routing any overflow to a nearby drain, and making electrical connections to a 120-volt house current, the furnace's transformer, or both.

If your home has copper or plastic plumbing, you can easily tap into the existing water line with a "saddle-T," as shown on page 293. With steel pipes, use the conventional T-and-union arrangement explained on the same page. For help with the electrical work, see pages 231-237.

Most power humidifiers mount on the furnace plenum, as illustrated here. A few, however, attach to the main return, or to a bypass between the two. Consult the manufacturer's instructions before installing these.

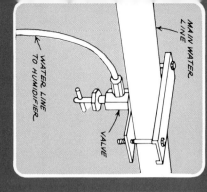

MAIN WATER LINE
WATER LINE TO HUMIDIFIER
VALVE

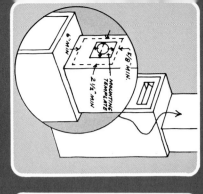

6" MIN.
5/8" MIN.
2 1/2" MIN.
MOUNTING TEMPLATE

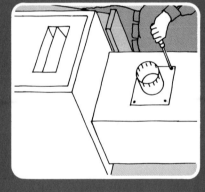

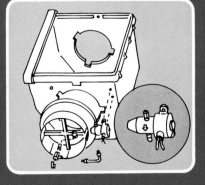

Most units come with a template you tape in place to locate the unit. Choose a spot you can easily get at for service.

Now cut an opening in the duct with a pair of aviation snips. You'll also have to drill holes for the mounting hardware.

Slip the mounting collar into place and secure it with sheet metal screws. Caulk its flange, too, for an airtight fit.

As you assemble the humidifier, make sure the arrow on its solenoid valve points in the same direction as the water flow.

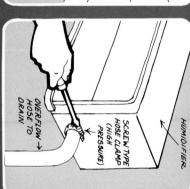

RETURN DUCT
RETURN-AIR FURNACE PLENUM
RETURN DUCT
WIRE TO HUMIDIFIER
HUMIDISTAT

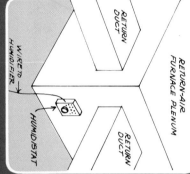

OVERFLOW HOSE TO DRAIN
SCREW TYPE HOSE CLAMP (HIGH PRESSURE)
HUMIDIFIER

When you connect the water line, install a shutoff valve so you can easily remove the unit if it ever needs servicing.

Position the humidistat on the main return duct. Check the manufacturer's instructions for wiring specifics.

For the overflow piping, you can use a length of flexible plastic or rubber tubing. Attach it to the humidifier with a hose clamp.

341

## CHOOSING AND BUYING AN ELECTRONIC AIR CLEANER

The mechanical filter on a furnace or air conditioner—really nothing more than a simple screen—does an excellent job of snaring relatively large bits of dust. But airborne pollen, smoke, bacteria, mold spores, and other microscopic particles pass right on through.

An electronic air cleaner, on the other hand, uses a magnetizing process called *ionization* to remove more than 90 percent of the pollutants in your home's air. It does this by giving the very tiny particles a strong positive charge, then attracting them to a series of negatively charged plates. The collected particles then cling to the plates until they're washed away.

Electronic air cleaners range from portable models no larger than a radio to whole-house units that turn a heating/cooling/humidifying system into true air *conditioning* (see below). All depend on a continuous flow of air through the unit, usually requiring three changes of air per hour for maximum efficiency. Maintenance consists of periodically washing the collecting plates; with some types, you must also replace a charcoal filter every three or four months.

Central air cleaners usually mount on the furnace's return side. Some models

also include a light that tells you when the collector needs cleaning, and a test button to let you know if the unit is working properly.

To install a furnace-mounted air cleaner, you need to tap into ductwork, make power connections, and sometimes—with wash-in-place models like the one shown below—provide a water line and a drain. Bigger, more complex systems should be sized and installed by a professional. Some others come in kit form, with instructions oriented to do-it-yourselfers.

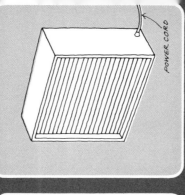

POWER CORD

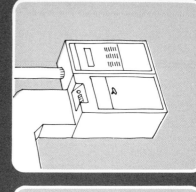

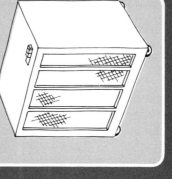

Console-style models roll on casters and work efficiently in spaces up to about 500 square feet. Most have two-speed fans.

For smaller heating/cooling systems with only one return register you can get a unit that doubles as a register grille.

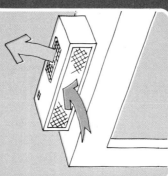

An electronic air cleaner's *pre-filter* catches big particles before the smaller ones are ionized and collected.

PRE-FILTER SCREEN

CLEAN AIR

COLLECTING SECTION

IONIZATION SECTION

DIRTY AIR

Tabletop cleaners adequately handle a room up to about 250 square feet in size. You can plug these in anywhere.

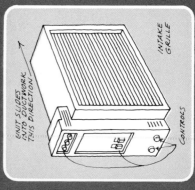

To clean most types, you simply slide out the collector plate and scrub or rinse it off in a laundry tub or a big tray.

You needn't manually clean the collectors of wash-in-place air cleaners. These large units install adjacent to the furnace.

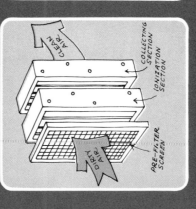

UNIT SLIDES INTO DUCTWORK THIS DIRECTION

INTAKE GRILLE

CONTROLS

Other models mount in the return duct, just ahead of the blower unit. These adapt well to different furnace layouts.

# SETTING A FURNACE FOR CONTINUOUS AIR CIRCULATION

Adjusting your blower for continuous air circulation guarantees an ever-moving supply of conditioned air in your home 24 hours a day. Your heating, cooling, and humidifying equipment won't be running all that time, of course; will still kick in and out as needed. But keeping the air in motion helps extract every bit of efficiency from these components.

With continuous circulation, you'll notice fewer temperature fluctuations and more even heating and cooling. If

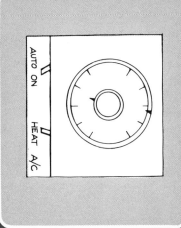

adjusting your blower for continuous air circulation guarantees an ever-moving motion draws off body heat and consequently tends to feel cooler than it actually is.

Note, too, that adjusting a system for continuous circulation may or may not reduce your home's total energy consumption. You may save on heating and cooling energy in certain instances, but what about the electrical cost of running the blower constantly. Whether or not this will exceed your fuel savings depends on what you're paying for the different forms of energy, how tightly your

your system has an electronic air cleaner, it will operate continuously, too.

Not everyone will find this option acceptable, though, especially on cold evenings between heating cycles. Air in

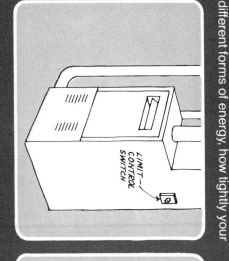

LIMIT CONTROL SWITCH

house is weather-stripped, and several other individual factors.

It takes only a few minutes to switch a blower from intermittent to continuous operation, so the best way to find out is to experiment for yourself. Give continuous air circulation a trial period, keep a careful tally of your energy bills, and ask family members if they feel comfortable with the blower on.

If you get complaints, try slowing down the blower as explained below. With direct-drive blowers, a serviceman may be able to make a simple electrical speed adjustment.

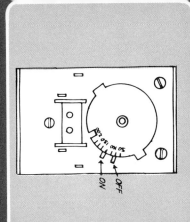

f your thermostat has a blower switch control, simply turn it to the "on" or "continuous" setting for constant air circulation.

If you don't have a switch on your thermostat, you'll have to adjust the fan's limit control, usually located as shown.

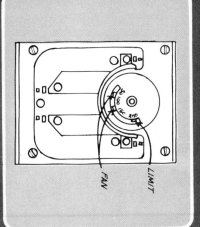

FAN
LIMIT

With this type control, move the fan levers to their lowest settings. Again, be careful not to move the limit control.

Remove the control's cover. If it looks like this, move the fan control to its lowest setting. Don't touch the limit setting.

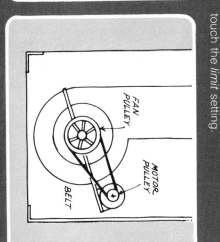

FAN PULLEY
MOTOR PULLEY
BELT

To slow air flow with a belt-driven blower, adjust the motor pulley or replace it with one smaller in diameter.

If it looks like this, move both levers to their lowest settings. To restore intermittent operation, reset the levers to 115° on, 90° off.

**343**

# CHOOSING AND BUYING RADIATION UNITS

*Radiator*—a hot surface's tendency to "throw" heat into the air around it—actually accounts for only part of the way a so-called "radiator" works. Hold your hands below and above one and you can feel cold air rushing in at the bottom and heated air rising from the top. This process, called *convection*, helps distribute the heat evenly.

That's why, whether you're shopping for a charming antique unit or a modern-day baseboard-style heater, the shape of what you select may be more important than its physical size. Longer, lower types don't put out any more heat than their upright counterparts, but they do spread it out over a broader area.

As for size, a large unit may or may not radiate more heat than a smaller one. Here the critical consideration is the area of heating surfaces exposed to air passing through as well as around the heater. You may not be able to see all of it, much less measure it, so manufacturers commonly specify the square inches of radiation a unit offers. With some help from your heating contractor, you can compute the number of square inches you'll need to warm a given area of your home.

Finally, in evaluating the potential performance of any radiation unit, you

must consider the metal it's made of. Cast iron gains and dissipates heat slowly, stretching the cooling-off period between heating cycles; units of steel, copper, aluminum, or combinations of these heat up rapidly, and cool just as quickly. This means that one fin-type convector in an otherwise iron system could result in a room that's alternately too hot and too cool.

The drawings below illustrate the various radiator/convector units you'll encounter. Note that baseboard types come in one- to eight-foot-long sections that can be joined end to end.

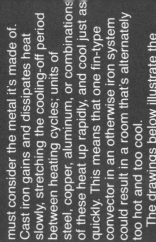

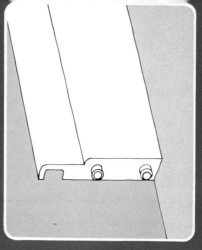

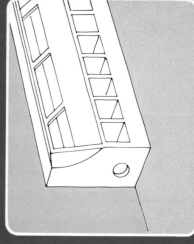

Lower-output *Type-R* units make sense for longer runs, which give off heat more evenly than shorter ones.

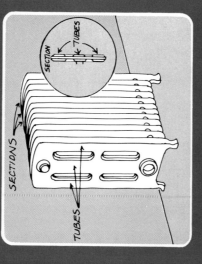

The size of a radiator depends on how many *tubes* as well as how many *sections* it has. To match the output, count both.

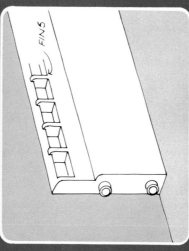

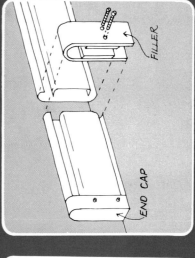

*Type-RC* cast-iron baseboards have fins inside and out to increase convection output. Use these for shorter runs.

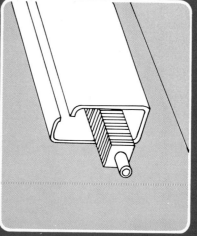

Electric baseboards warm mainly by radiation. Actually space heaters, each one can be controlled by its own thermostat.

You also can order dummy baseboard accessories to fill the spaces between convector units and hide piping.

*Fin-tube* units rely primarily on convection, and heat and cool rapidly. Use them only in hot-water—not steam—systems.

**344**

# INSTALLING NEW RADIATION UNITS

Thinking of replacing an unsightly old radiator with a sleek new baseboard system? If so, you have some fairly easy plumbing and carpentry chores—and one muscle job—ahead of you.

The heavy work comes first when you have to wrestle that ancient iron behemoth out the door. Don't try to pick up a radiator; even small ones are amazingly heavy. Instead, with a helper, topple the unit onto a rug and drag it.

Next, assess your existing plumbing layout. Ideally, baseboard units should run along outside walls and under

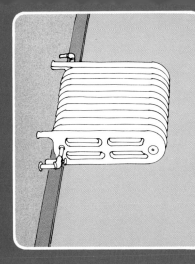

windows—regardless of where the old radiator may have been located. This means you might have to re-pipe supply and return lines to the right spots—a not-too-difficult chore if you're familiar with the plumbing basics covered on pages 282 through 295.

For heating work, you can use copper or threaded black steel pipe, in sizes specified by the manufacturer. Be sure, though, to install a special adapter wherever steel and copper meet to prevent electrolytic corrosion. And don't forget to provide unions at either end in case you ever need to disconnect the baseboard units.

Note, too, that you'll probably want to include a supply valve, and most

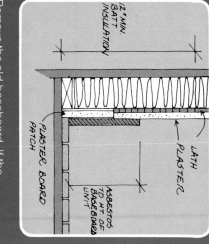

certainly an air vent at the return side. For a steam system, get a "gate" valve; for a hot-water system, a "globe" valve. In some situations, you may also need a valve at the return outlet.

Mounting procedures vary, so follow the manufacturer's instructions, bearing in mind that you must always provide enough pitch for condensate or cool water to drain to the return lines.

After you've finished installing your new baseboard heaters, fire up the boiler, wait an hour or so, then bleed air from the new run. To learn about this and other radiator basics, see page 329.

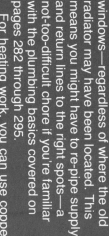

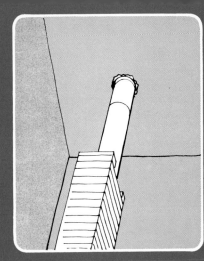

Count the number of tubes and sections in your old radiator. Knowing this, your dealer can compute what you'll need.

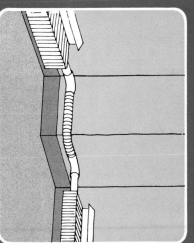

Remove the old baseboard. If the wall isn't insulated, open it up and stuff with batts, as shown. Then staple up heavy asbestos.

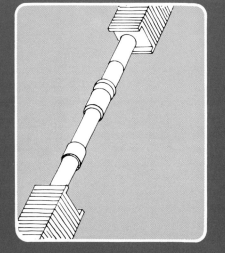

Flex couplings allow for thermal expansion with fin-tube convectors. You'll need a special wrench to join iron sections.

You can run heating pipes right through walls, but leave a ⅛-inch clearance to prevent creaking from expansion.

Flexible piping lets you clear obstructions in fin-tube installations. Cover the pipes with dummy panels.

# CHOOSING AND BUYING SPACE HEATERS

Most furnaces and boilers are bigger than they need to be, which means that in all but a few instances you can easily add a few more registers or radiation units, as shown on the preceding pages. If, however, you want to warm a sizable space—and especially if you need only part-time heat—an independent space heater might offer a better way to go.

In shopping for a self-contained heating unit, you'll find a multitude of models to choose from. (The drawings below illustrate the major possibilities, and there are dozens of variations.)

To narrow the field, first ask yourself exactly what job you want the heater to do. Will it be used only occasionally or briefly for backup or auxiliary heating? If so, an electric wall, ceiling, or baseboard unit might be the answer. These are inexpensive to buy, easy to install, and economical on floor space. Running one for extended periods could add a lot to your electric bill, though.

At the other end of the energy-cost scale is the old-fashioned stove. Advances in wood-burning know-how have turned it into a truly efficient modern heater. But unless you plan to cut your own wood, check on wood prices before you invest in wood-burning equipment—and realize that even the most efficient

units must be tended once or twice a day. Veterans of wood heat point out that cutting wood, stacking and carrying it into the house, and removing ashes can demand enormous expenditures of *human* energy.

What about fireplaces? We didn't include them in this lineup because, though a few do a good space-heating job, most don't—and many actually rob heated air from your home. For a complete discussion of fireplaces, see pages 92-99, and note especially the heat-efficient versions illustrated on page 96.

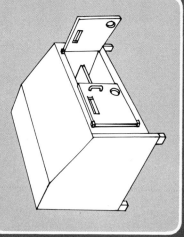

Airtight stoves use a variety of special drafting systems to extract maximum heat from each load of logs.

Electric-resistance heaters install almost anywhere and come in many different models. More about these on page 348.

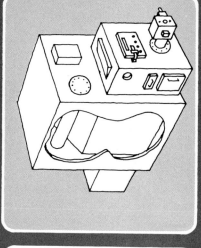

Multi-fuel furnaces burn wood, coal, gas, or oil, letting you maintain heat even when you're gone for long periods.

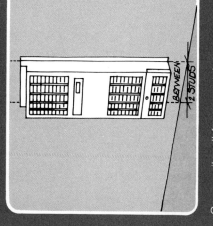

Gas or oil wall furnaces take up little space, but must be vented to the outside. They also need fuel and power hookups.

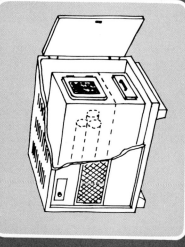

Highly efficient wood-burning heaters even have thermostatic controls. They can warm a small house. See page 349.

# INSTALLING A GAS WALL FURNACE

A wall furnace packs all the elements of a forced-air heating system—burner, heat exchanger, blower unit, filter, and supply and return registers—into a cabinet compact enough for mounting in or on an exterior wall.

With direct-venting models, a pair of metal pipes—one running inside the other—penetrates the wall. One pipe supplies fresh air for combustion; the other exhausts fumes. Direct venting means you don't need to run a chimney to the roof. And since the fire is fed with unheated outside air, rather than warm

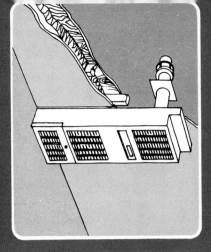

house air, the system conserves indoor heat.

Check community codes before buying a direct-vent furnace. Some restrict the type you can use or may require that units be professionally installed.

Except for running the gas line, however, there's nothing dangerous or tricky about tackling an installation yourself. You'll need to make a wall opening, of course. And if you choose a horizontal console model, you'll have to cut a stud and fit in a header. (Both of these tasks are explained on page 150.)

Try to position the furnace near the center of the wall, where doors, draperies, or furniture won't block its air flow. Outside, the vent should be at least

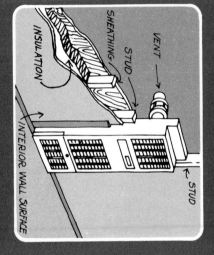

24 inches below eaves or any other overhead projection, and at least 12 inches above ground level.

When handling the unit, be careful not to crack the connections where the vent pipes attach to the furnace and where the door opens for access to the burner and pilot. Leaks here will blow out the pilot.

The drawings below show the typical procedure for installing an upright unit. To learn about gas hookups, see pages 308-315. You can probably tap electrical power from a nearby wall outlet or basement ceiling box, as shown on pages 227 and 231-239.

Now determine where the flue will go, drill a hole through the exterior wall, and enlarge the opening with a saber saw.

Many also can be recessed into the wall. To do this, locate studs and cut away the drywall or lath and plaster.

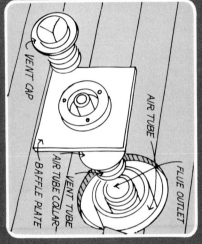

If your heater has an external thermostat, locate it as shown. Avoid hot and cold spots, corners, and alcoves.

Once the furnace is secured in its niche, assemble the vent as shown. Make all connections airtight, and caulk the baffle plate.

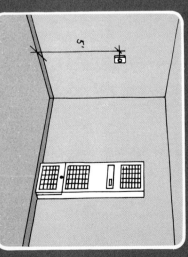

To minimize carpentry work, you can hang most units directly on the wall's inner surface with special mounting brackets.

Next, drill holes for gas and electrical supply lines. Note that these can come through either the wall or floor.

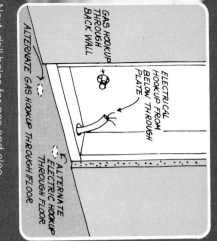

# INSTALLING AN ELECTRIC HEATER

Electric units put out quiet, almost instantaneous heat—just what you need to take the nip from chilly bathroom air, warm a basement shop, or boost the temperature in a chronically cool room. And since electric heaters needn't be vented, you can tuck one almost anywhere.

Although these heaters aren't cheap to operate, using one strategically could help cut the cost of running your central heating system. Consider, for instance, installing a baseboard unit in a room that's used only occasionally. You could

then shut off the room's registers or radiators and heat the space only when needed.

Electric heaters require lots of power. With smaller 500- to 1,000-watt models, you may be able to tap into a receptacle on a lightly used circuit, as shown here. If a unit draws more than 1,000 watts, though, it should have its own 20-amp circuit. And really high-output types require 240-volt current. Wiring either of these is a job for a professional electrician.

He might also be able to easily provide you with a remote switch next to a door or in some other convenient location. Special timer switches save energy by automatically shutting off a unit after it's

operated for a preset period (usually up to 30 minutes).

For safety, don't locate either the switch or the heater itself within reach of a bathtub or other wet place—and make sure its grille can't be penetrated by a child's fingers.

Most units come with installation instructions. The drawings below show how to recess a fan-powered model into a wall. Radiant baseboards should be backed with insulation and asbestos, as illustrated on page 345. Ceiling lamp-type heaters also may include an exhaust fan. For more about these, turn to pages 378-381.

Now's the time to bring in the electricity. You'll need to determine if your heater will require a special circuit.

Most wall heaters fit easily between studs. Locate the studs, then carefully cut an opening with a keyhole or saber saw.

If you've chosen an outside wall, you'll probably find insulation in the cavity. Cut it off above and below the opening.

Finally, slip the heater into its box and complete the electrical connections. Screws make the grille more tamper-resistant.

Most units come with mounting flanges for attaching to either plaster or drywall. Connect the electrical cable first.

# INSTALLING A WOOD-BURNING HEATER

Descended from yesteryear's pot-belly stoves and Franklin fireplaces, newer wood-burning heaters can keep a load of logs glowing for 12 hours or more. And they burn them so completely, you need to shut down only about once a week to clean out the ashes.

To maintain this long-burning fire, wood heaters carefully control the combustion process. Designs vary, but most feature airtight construction and an automatically regulated draft that gives the flames no more air than they really need. The result: wood-burning heaters draw very little air and lose a minimum of heat up the chimney.

You pay a price for this efficiency, though. Slow-burning fires tend to produce creosote, which can build up in a chimney and possibly ignite. Because of this, you'll need to follow some strict installation and maintenance procedures. You should use only a masonry chimney, or a metal chimney with a Class-A rating from Underwriters Laboratories. Follow the heater or chimney manufacturer's requirements to the letter, and check local building codes, too.

As you assemble a metal chimney, note that, unlike warm air ducts, flue sections fit together with their crimped ends toward the heater. This allows any condensation in the vent to flow back to the fire. For airtight assembly, seal each joint with furnace cement and secure it with three metal screws.

Break in a new wood heater with only small fires the first few times you kindle it; otherwise, heat could crack a casting. Proper maintenance is important, too. Remove ashes at recommended intervals to prevent warping and burnouts, and clean the flue annually (see page 118).

When wood-burning equipment smokes or won't draw properly, first make sure it's getting enough combustion air. If that's not the problem, your chimney might not be tall enough. More about these symptoms on pages 94 and 95.

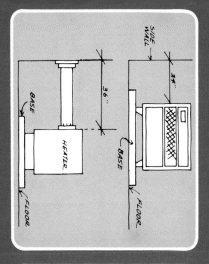

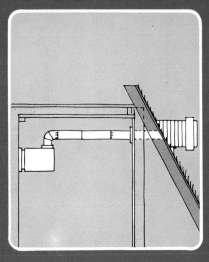

Check heater instructions for minimum distances to a combustible wall. Most also call for a masonry base.

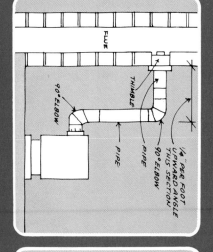

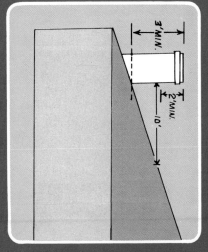

To connect to a masonry chimney, assemble the components as shown. Keep runs short and don't use more than two elbows.

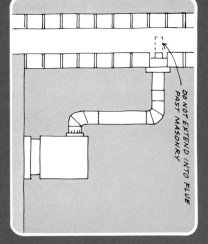

At the chimney, take care that the pipe doesn't extend into the flue. Make the connection at least 18 inches below the ceiling.

For safety, try to extend your chimney above the roof peak. If that would make it unwieldy, be sure to allow these clearances.

If you don't have a masonry flue, go up through the roof with a Class-A metal type. More about these on page 99.

**349**

## INSTALLING A TIMED THERMOSTAT

Programming your heating and cooling system to run at a more economical thermostat setting while you sleep or when no one's home can result in a sizable reduction in your energy bills. How much you'll save depends on a variety of factors, but generally speaking, the greater the spread in degrees between settings—called the *setback* —the more savings you'll realize.

Timed thermostats such as the one shown below include a 24-hour clock. With these, you select the times you'd like the setback period to begin and end, and then forget about it. Others are equipped with timers that you must manually start before going to bed or leaving the house. Still a third type uses a photocell to switch from one setting to another at dusk and dawn.

Regardless of the type that best suits your needs, select a model that's compatible with your furnace's control circuit. In most cases, furnace switches operate on 15- to 30-volt current, as do all timed thermostats. Don't try to connect one to a 120-volt system.

Any thermostat depends on good air circulation for proper operation. Locate yours about five feet above the floor and away from drafts, direct sunlight, and dead spots behind doors or in corners.

Also make sure there are no heating ducts, pipes, or flues in the mounting wall. Most times, your existing thermostat location already will satisfy these criteria.

Adjusting the setback may call for some experimentation. Begin by trying a setting 10 degrees lower or higher than your normal heating and cooling levels. If the house cools down or warms up too much, decrease the setback to eight degrees. You also will have to adjust the timings on the setback cycle to accommodate your schedule.

Note: if your home has a heat pump, consult your heating contractor before buying a timed thermostat. Using one of these devices with a heat pump may actually add to your utility bills.

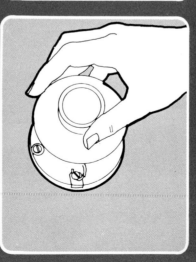

Shut down the furnace, remove the old thermostat from the wall, and disconnect its leads. Some units fit over existing thermostats.

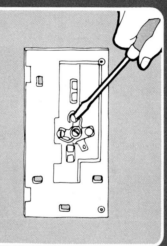

Pull wires through openings in the new unit's back plate and connect them to its terminals. These usually are color-coded.

Now carefully level the plate, install its mounting screws, and check the level again. You can still make minor adjustments.

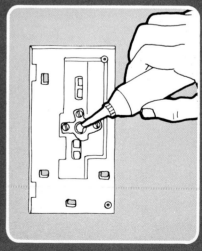

Push all excess wire back into the wall and caulk around it. Otherwise, drafts from the wall cavity could affect settings.

Next, fasten the thermostat to the plate. Double-check your installation, then turn on the system for a test run.

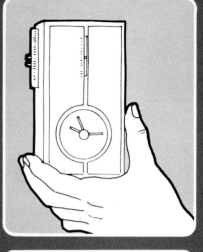

Do any fine-tuning recommended by the manufacturer before you snap on the cover plate. Wait a few days before adjusting further.

he worst possible time to select a new furnace or air conditioner is the day the old one breathes its last. Split-second decisions then can mean years of higher-than-necessary fuel bills if you make a poor choice of equipment—and with new developments in this fast-changing field, the choice can be confusing.

The remainder of this chapter takes you through the steps a good contractor should follow before he submits a written bid, and then tells you about some of the equipment he may recommend.

As you solicit bids for your new system, make sure that each one spells out exactly how much heating or cooling you're being asked to buy, as well as the ultimate price tag. The glossary below introduces you to the terms you're likely to encounter.

## Understanding Heating/Cooling Terminology

A *backup system* is a supplementary heating unit that kicks in when the main heat source—usually a heat pump or solar setup—can no longer handle the load by itself.

A *British thermal unit (BTU)* is the amount of heat needed to raise the temperature of one pound of water one degree Fahrenheit. Heating and cooling equipment is sized by the BTUs it can deliver in a single hour (*BTUh*).

*Collectors* capture heat in a solar installation.

The *coefficient of performance (COP)* is a ratio calculated by dividing the total capacity of a heating unit by its total energy output. This gives you a measure of its efficiency.

*Design temperature* is the temperature level that you want to maintain in your home.

The *energy-efficiency ratio (EER)* is a measure of efficiency derived by dividing the unit's cooling capacity by its energy input in watts.

*Heat gain* is the amount of heat coming into your home from sources other than its heating/cooling system. Most heat gains come from the sun, but lighting, appliances, and even body warmth also make contributions.

*Heat loss* is the amount of heat escaping from your home, usually to colder outside air. Like the capacities of heating and cooling equipment, heat gains and losses are expressed in BTUh.

*Payback* refers to the length of time before the energy savings from new equipment will equal your investment. To figure payback, divide your estimated annual savings into the purchase price.

*Tons* is another way of expressing the output from an air conditioner or heat pump. One ton equals 12,000 BTUs.

A *watt* is a measure of the work energy of electricity. Electrical inputs—and your electric bill—are measured in kilowatts per hour (*KWH*).

## Shopping for Energy

What exactly would be the relative costs of heating your home with oil, natural gas, LP gas, and electricity? You probably don't have all of these options, of course, but most of us can choose between electricity and at least one of the fossil fuels.

To find out which would be your most economical choice, you need to get the unit cost of each form of energy from your power, gas, or oil supplier, then do some math on a calculator.

Energy units differ. Utilities price electricity by the *kilowatt hour (KWH)*; natural gas comes in increments of 100 *cubic feet (CCF)*; and oil and LP gas are sold in *gallons*. Rating these units might seem like comparing apples and oranges until you realize that each unit yields a predictable number of BTUs. And it's BTUs—millions of them—that you need to heat your home.

Here are the BTU yields you can expect to get from each energy unit.

1 KWH electricity . . . . . . . . . .3,413 BTUs
1 CCF natural gas . . . . . . . . 100,000 BTUs
1 gallon #2 fuel oil . . . . . . . . 138,000 BTUs
1 gallon LP gas (propane) . .92,000 BTUs

To figure the cost of each BTU to be generated by your new heating plant, first divide the cost of each energy unit by its yield. Not all forms of heating are equally efficient, though, so you also have to factor in the coefficients of performance for the equipment you're thinking about buying. If you don't have these, divide the cost per BTU by .70 for natural gas, oil, and LP gas heating plants; by 1 for electric-resistance heating; and by 1.5 for a heat pump.

Finally, since a single BTU doesn't amount to much, multiply everything by one million. Your final computation should look like this: cost of the energy unit ÷ its yield in BTUs ÷ COP × 1 million = cost per million BTUs.

351

# SIZING UP YOUR HEATING NEEDS

Once upon a time, a heating contractor might take a quick walk around your home, guesstimate its size, then—to allow a wide margin for error—order a furnace or boiler with considerably more capacity than you'd ever need.

Such seat-of-the-pants engineering guarantees that you'll always be warm, but oversized heating equipment wastes energy and may create wide swings in comfort levels as well.

That's why knowledgeable contractors now arrive for estimates armed with forms to help calculate the exact amount of heat your house loses every hour—its *heat loss*. Next, they compute this loss as it relates to your geographic region, using one of the *design temperatures* indicated on the map below. The result, expressed in BTUs per hour, provides a guide for sizing the heating plant.

If, for example, your home has a heat loss of 93,000 BTUs per hour, you'll need a furnace or boiler with at least that much output, and maybe up to 100,000 BTUh (BTUs per hour).

If you're simply replacing a wornout furnace or boiler, you may be able to get by with matching the output of the old one. Make sure first, though, that it wasn't oversized to begin with. (Properly sized units run almost all the time in very cold weather; oversized ones seem to be loafing.) And consider whether new insulation, storm windows, or weather stripping might substantially reduce your home's heat losses.

## Calculating Heat Losses

Every part of a house loses some heat to the outdoors, but at different rates. To accurately asses your home's heating needs, a installer first computes the volume of air to be treated, then assigns heat transfer values to each exterior surface.

Arrows on the drawing at left illustrate the relative rates of loss for the roof, chimney, walls, windows, doors, and foundation. The longest vectors denote the biggest losers. For more about heat losses, see pages 72, 73, and 366-375.

## Selecting a Design Temperature

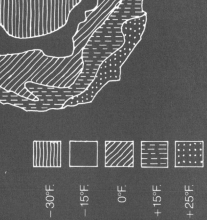

| | −30°F. |
|---|---|
| | −15°F. |
| | 0°F. |
| | +15°F. |
| | +25°F. |

Once a home's heat losses have been tabulated, the contractor then consults tables that tell the coldest normal outdoor temperatures in your geographic region. (See the map at right and note that these are not necessarily the coldest on record.)

Subtracting this *outside design temperature* from the *inside design temperature* you want to maintain provides the *design temperature difference*—and determines the load your new furnace will be expected to handle.

Once he's thoroughly calculated your home's heating needs (opposite page), a skilful contractor can go one step further. With the energy-yield data explained on page 351, plus temperature norms available from the U.S. Weather Service, he can come surprisingly close to estimating what you'd actually pay per year to operate a particular system.

Get this estimate in writing, if you can. It helps you predict the *payback period* for equipment that might be more costly to begin with, but more economical in the long run. If, for example, heating unit A is

priced $500 more than unit B but would save $100 a year in energy bills, its payback period would be five years.

Figuring payback periods calls for guesswork, of course. Not even experts can say exactly what will happen to relative energy costs in the years to come. And it's hard to make allowances for auxiliary equipment that adds to your comfort by cooling, humidifying, or cleaning the air as well as heating it. (To learn more about these amenities, see pages 341-343, 356, and 357.)

Imprecise as they may be, payback computations offer the best way to make sure you're getting your money's worth when you buy a new heating unit. Just be sure to investigate all the alternatives.

For instance, the drawings immediately below show ways you can install a forced-air furnace and its ductwork in a house that doesn't already have them. And at the bottom of the page, you'll find information about two devices that can improve the efficiency of a fossil-fuel furnace.

How long you must wait before a heating plant pays for its added cost becomes even more important when you delve into more sophisticated (and expensive) apparatus such as solar units and heat pumps. Paybacks for these can be lengthy. More about them on the following pages.

## Fitting in a Furnace

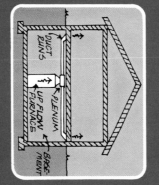

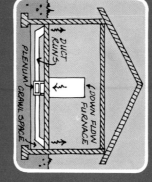

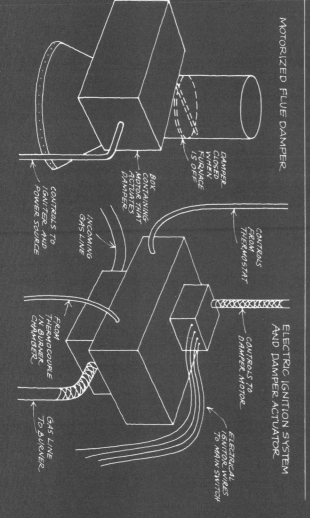

*Upflow* furnaces, the most common type, make sense for basement installations. Usually most ducts are down there, too.

If your house has a crawl space underneath, conceal a *downflow* furnace in a closet, then run ducts through the crawl space.

*Horizontal* furnaces can be installed in either a crawl space or an attic. Cool air enters one end; warm air exits the other.

## Energy-Saving Devices

At best, gas- and oil-fired furnaces lose about 20 percent of the heat they generate up the flue. On gas models, "standing pilots," which burn constantly, waste still more energy.

A *motorized flue damper*, like the one shown at near right, recovers the heat that would normally escape immediately after a unit has cycled off.

*Electric ignition systems* (far right) are usually coupled with the control that actuates a damper. When it's time for the furnace to fire, these open a valve and light a pilot. The pilot ignites the burners, then shuts down.

To learn about another energy-saving tactic—getting fresh air to your furnace—see page 376.

MOTORIZED FLUE DAMPER.

DAMPER CLOSED WHEN FURNACE IS OFF

BOX CONTAINING MOTOR THAT ACTUATES DAMPER.

CONTROLS TO IGNITER AND POWER SOURCE

INCOMING GAS LINE

CONTROLS FROM THERMOSTAT

CONTROLS TO DAMPER MOTOR

FROM THERMOCOUPLE IN BURNER CHAMBER.

ELECTRICAL IGNITOR WIRES TO MAIN SWITCH

GAS LINE TO BURNER.

ELECTRIC IGNITION SYSTEM AND DAMPER ACTUATOR.

# UNDERSTANDING SOLAR ENERGY

Probably the most promising energy "discovery" of the 1970s was that sunlight—an abundant, non-polluting, and best of all, free resource—could supply most of the heat a household needs. Is there a solar system in your home's future?

Chances are, you could team the sun with your existing water heater right now. Solar water heating has advanced well beyond backyard and laboratory prototypes. The anatomy drawing on the opposite page shows one version, available in component form from a major heating manufacturer.

Such a system could provide 40 to 90 percent of the hot water your family uses—but you'll want to carefully figure the payback period for solar water heating equipment before investing in it (see page 353). Solar gear can be quite difficult to install, though a few companies do offer components a fairly proficient amateur plumber could handle.

Solar whole-house heating also merits careful investigation—especially if you're building a new home. You'll need a site that gets lots of direct sunlight, of course, plus a southern exposure for the flat-plate collectors used in most present-day installations.

Realize, too, that solar components require lots of space. Besides room on the roof for a dozen or more sizable collectors, you have to find a place for a several-thousand-gallon storage tank (see the anatomy drawing below) or an even bigger rock pit.

And prepare yourself for a major initial investment. Solar systems can easily cost two to three times as much as conventional installations—in part because you also need a backup heat source that can take over during periods of prolonged cloudiness. This might be a standard gas, oil, or electric furnace, a series of radiant electric units, or a heat pump especially tailored for solar compatibility.

Your payback calculations will, of course, have to account for the energy costs of operating the backup system, as well as the "free" heat you'll be getting from the sun. If the payback period seems unacceptably long—or if you simply haven't the money to spend on a solar installation right now—try at least to plan a solar "capability" into your new home.

This means thoroughly insulating and weather-stripping to minimize heat losses (pages 360-375), siting so that windows take advantage of "passive" solar heat gains (see page 72), and opting for a forced-air system into which you can easily plug solar components.

## Anatomy of a Solar Heating System

To understand how a solar *collector* captures sunlight, think about what happens to the temperature inside a car parked in a sunny spot. It goes up because the car's windows trap far more heat than they radiate back to the cooler air outside.

A collector's glass surface does the same thing, only more efficiently. Then the heat it traps is absorbed by a *transfer fluid*—usually an antifreeze-water solution—that's circulated through black-coated tubing just beneath the glass. This warmed fluid carries heat to an *indoor coil* in your furnace, or to a huge insulated *storage tank* that the furnace coil can draw on when the sun isn't shining.

A *backup system*, such as the heat pump shown at right, cuts in only when the solar components can't handle the heating load. Then lukewarm fluid is diverted through the pump, which first boosts the fluid's temperature with heat extracted from the outside air and then routes it to the furnace coil. (More about heat pumps on pages 326, 327, and 356.)

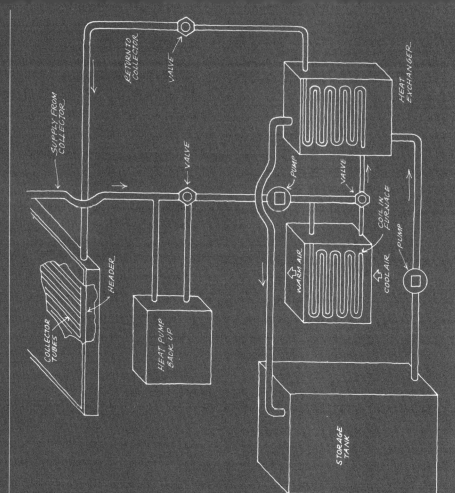

354

# How Much Heat Can the Sun Give?

The answer depends largely on where you live. Check the map at right to learn the average percentage of sunny daylight hours in your region.

This figure gives a rough idea of the *theoretical* savings solar energy could offer. (The actual savings will be determined by, among other things, the number of collectors you choose to invest in and their efficiency.)

If your area gets less sunshine than others, don't be discouraged. Because you've probably been buying larger quantities of conventional energy to begin with, your actual dollar savings could still be substantial.

## Heating Water With the Sun

Water heating typically accounts for about 20 percent of a family's energy load. Sunlight can greatly lighten that load, and even take it over entirely during certain periods of the year.

Depending on your hot water needs and the region in which you live, you'll need from one to five collectors like the one illustrated here. These send heat, via an antifreeze transfer fluid, to a storage tank installed next to your existing water heater.

Here fluid circulates through the tank's heavily insulated jacket, giving off heat to the water inside. A pump sends fluid back to the collector, continuing the cycle as long as the sun is providing heat.

Solar-heated water can sometimes reach temperatures of 200 degrees F. or more, so a tempering valve in the link between the storage tank and the water heater automatically adds cold water to maintain the temperature needed for household use.

If you're a moderately skillful amateur plumber and can make simple electrical connections, you might be able to install modular components such as these yourself. Manufacturers usually provide full instructions.

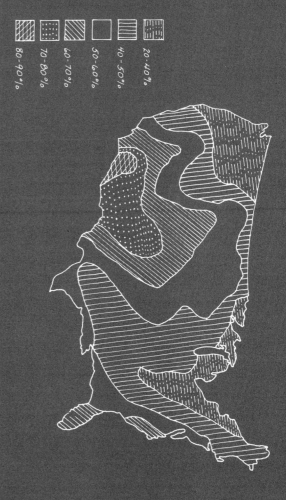

Legend:
- 20-40%
- 40-50%
- 50-60%
- 60-70%
- 70-80%
- 80-90%

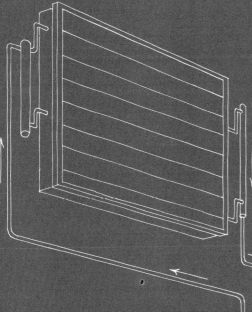

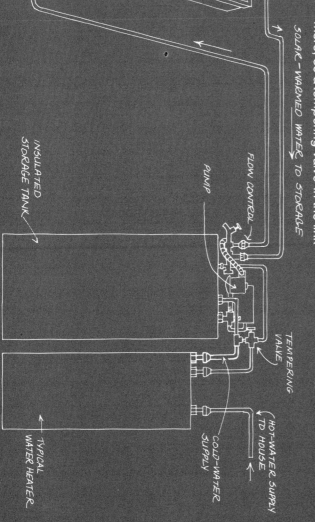

COLD FLUID TO COLLECTOR

ROOF-MOUNT COLLECTOR

SOLAR-WARMED WATER TO STORAGE

PUMP

FLOW CONTROL

INSULATED STORAGE TANK

TEMPERING VALVE

HOT-WATER SUPPLY TO HOUSE

COLD-WATER SUPPLY

TYPICAL WATER HEATER

## SELECTING REFRIGERATION EQUIPMENT

If the *energy efficiency ratio (EER)* expresses the relationship between a cooling unit's input in watts and its output in BTUs, and a watt yields only a predictable number of BTUs, how come EER ratings vary so widely? Closely analyze some, in fact, and you may conclude that certain models put out two or three times as much energy as they consume. Is this true?

Yes and no. Under certain conditions, a refrigeration unit can indeed deliver more than 100 percent of the energy it draws. But that's because it's using those watts to *move* heat, not to *produce* it. An air conditioner, remember, simply extracts heat from indoor air and moves it outside. Similarly, a heat pump squeezes heat from outside air and transfers it indoors.

What's more—unlike combustion- or electric resistance-type heat *producers* —a heat-mover's efficiency relates inversely to the difference between indoor and outdoor temperatures. As this increases, the EER drops.

The same goes for the *coefficient of performance* (COP) figures used to rate the heating efficiency of heat pumps. Air conditioner and heat pump manufacturers commonly give the top EER and COP ratings for their units; these are usually certified by the Air-Conditioning and Refrigeration Institute, as explained and illustrated below.

These ratings let you easily compare the relative efficiencies of different makes and models. The higher the COP or EER, the more heating or cooling per dollar you can expect.

However, EER and COP figures don't help much in predicting your actual operating costs. To do this, you—or your contractor—also need to know the capacity required for your home and climate, and the indoor temperature level you want to maintain. More about these on the opposite page.

Specifications for some newer heat pumps and air conditioners include two sets of EER and COP ratings, one for each of the speeds at which the equipment was designed to run. Two-speed units loaf along at a lower rpm during mild weather, then automatically shift into high gear for extreme outside temperatures. Since the lower speed draws only about half as much power as the higher one, you aren't paying for capacity you don't need.

You may find two-speed cooling units rated according to their *seasonal energy-efficiency ratio* (SEER)— basically the EER prorated over an average cooling season. Here again, the higher a model's SEER, the better.

## Labels To Look For

One or a combination of the symbols at right tells you that an air conditioner, heat pump, or humidifier has been certified by the Air-Conditioning and Refrigeration Institute—an industry organization that independently tests manufacturers' products and rates them according to the same standards.

ARI ratings ensure that you're getting the BTUh or humidification capacity you've been promised, and they sometimes certify that a unit meets certain noise standards, as well.

Note, though, that companies who don't participate in this voluntary program aren't necessarily overrating their units. With these, you can often depend on the manufacturer's reputation.

Humidification Level

Heat-Pump Capacity

Cooling Capacity

Sound Level

# SIZING UP YOUR COOLING NEEDS

air conditioners, like hats and shoes, must fit just right if you're to get the comfort you're paying for. As you might imagine, a grossly undersized unit just can't keep up on those really hot days. But oversized units can be even worse. These cool in short, energy-wasting bursts, then shut down for lengthy intervals. Meanwhile, the humidity level climbs and the air begins to feel clammy. A properly conditioned air, remember, is drier as well as cooler.

Ideally, any cooling unit—whether it's a room or central type—should have a capacity just large enough to cope with prolonged hot spells. At those times, you can expect it to run almost constantly, controlling humidity as well as temperature.

This means that the unit's output, in BTUh, must roughly equal the sum total of your home's or room's heat gains. If you're shopping for a central system, get bids from several installers and let them compute the gains as explained below. For a room unit, you can do the figuring yourself without too much trouble (see page 358).

In comparing capacities, you'll find that some manufacturers size their equip-ment's output in tons rather than BTUs. To convert tons to BTUs, just multiply the tonnage by 12,000.

Chances are, you won't be able to get an exact BTU-for-BTU match between a model's capacity and your home's heat gains. Generally, it's safer to go to the next *smaller* size. With a slightly underpowered unit, indoor temperatures might rise somewhat on really hot days, but continuous dehumidification will maintain a tolerable level of comfort.

## Calculating Heat Gains

When a cooling contractor prepares a bid, expect him to fill out a lengthy work sheet—similar to the one used for computing heat losses (see page 352), but even more detailed.

Besides assigning BTUh gains to the exterior factors shown at right, he'll also need to know about any hot or cold spots inside, how many appliances you have, and even how many people are in the family. For more about heat gains, see pages 72 and 73, and 366-375.

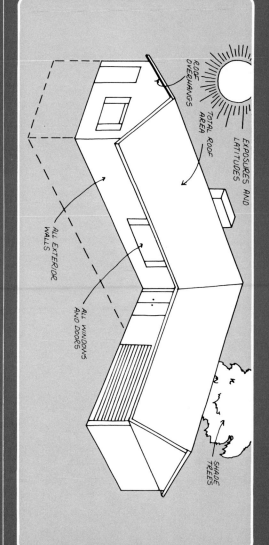

ROOF OVERHANGS

TOTAL ROOF AREA

EXPOSURES AND LATITUDES

ALL EXTERIOR WALLS

ALL WINDOWS AND DOORS

SHADE TREES

## CHOOSING AND BUYING CENTRAL AIR CONDITIONING

Once he has a fix on your home's heat gains, an installer will check your furnace's blower and ductwork to determine if they can handle heavier, cooled air. You may need a new blower, a bigger plenum, or new branch ducts. While he's looking at the plenum, ask him if it can be easily modified to accept an electronic air cleaner, a power humidifier, or both. Even if you can't afford these items now, allowing for them can save on installation charges later. (More about humidifiers and air cleaners on pages 341 and 342.)

You also may want to consider a zoned system that gives you separate control over two or more sections of your house. With it, you could save energy by keeping daytime temperatures higher in empty bedrooms.

Two-speed condensing units offer another way to minimize operating costs, in effect tailoring a system's capacity to its needs at the moment. Lights on the thermostat let you know whether one of these is running at high or low speed, giving you a chance to raise the temperature setting and reduce demand when you choose.

And if your area has natural-gas service, you also can consider a gas-powered system. It will cost more than an electric air conditioner to install, but you may recover the difference—and more—through lower operating costs, less maintenance, and longer life. This, of course, depends on your energy costs.

Finally, don't be surprised to find a wide range of prices for equipment with similar BTU capacities. Quality differences account for most of this variance: some components are designed to last five years, others ten.

## CHOOSING AND BUYING A ROOM AIR CONDITIONER

BTU for BTU, a central cooling system offers greater efficiency at lower operating cost than a series of room air conditioners adding up to the same capacity. Settle for less cooling, though, and you might come out dollars ahead with the room units.

Your initial investment will be much lower, of course, especially if your home doesn't have forced-air heating. And if you get in the habit of turning units off or to a higher temperature setting when you're not using the spaces they cool, you can hold down operating costs, too.

Before you begin shopping for a room air conditioner, consider what you want it to do and where you'll be mounting it. A location opposite a doorway, for instance, may let you cool several rooms with the same unit, though you may need to set up a fan or two to help air circulate.

Most room units are designed to fit into a double-hung window. If your windows are a different style, you may need to modify one, or shop for a narrow-chassis air conditioner sized for casement windows.

Better yet, consider a through-the-wall installation. You'd have to do some carpentry work first, of course, but wall-mounted units don't obstruct views and run more quietly. (To learn about making openings in exterior walls, see page 150.)

Next, calculate how much capacity you need, as explained below, then try to find an air conditioner with a BTUh rating within 10 percent of that figure.

As you shop, compare features and EERs carefully. As with all cooling equipment, the higher the EER, the less electricity a unit will draw. High-efficiency models often feature more sophisticated controls, too—such as built-in timers an[d] switches that let you choose whether or not the fan will run when the compresso[r] is off.

Most room air conditioners come with complete installation instructions, and you can expect to do a typical, window-mount job in a couple of hours. You'll need help, though, when it comes time to set the heavy, awkwardly balanced chassis in place.

Finally, check for air leaks around the housing or sashes, and seal any gaps with spongy air-conditioner gasket or weather stripping (see pages 361-363). you'll be leaving the unit in place year-round, you might want to custom-fi[t] a storm window around it and replace th[e] side panels supplied by the manufactur[er] with material that has a higher R-value.

| Cooling Area | Capacity |
| --- | --- |
| 265 sq. ft. | 6,000 BTUh |
| 300-350 sq. ft. | 7,500 BTUh |
| 350-450 sq. ft. | 9,000 BTUh |
| 450-520 sq. ft. | 10,000 BTUh |
| 520-600 sq. ft. | 11,000 BTUh |
| 600-750 sq. ft. | 12,500 BTUh |
| 750-900 sq. ft. | 15,000 BTUh |
| 900-1,050 sq. ft. | 16,500 BTUh |
| 1,050-1,250 sq. ft. | 19,000 BTUh |
| 1,250-1,600 sq. ft. | 23,000 BTUh |

### Calculating Room Cooling Needs

Most retail outlets size room units according to the number of "rooms" you want to cool—figuring 6,000 BTUh for the first room, then adding 3,500 to 5,000 for each additional space.

How big is a typical room, though? And how do you account for factors such as exposure, insulation, the number of windows and doors, heat gains from appliances, and the number of people who will use the space?

If you want to make a truly thorough computation, ask an air conditioning contractor for a standardized *cooling-load estimate form*, along with the BTU factors he normally uses.

Otherwise, use the chart at right as a guide, going to the next larger size for hot spots and spaces with ceilings over eight feet high.

### Getting Power to a Unit

If yours is a smaller 120-volt model, you can probably just plug it into an existing lightly loaded circuit. Make sure, though, that the connection is properly grounded (see page 225). And see that the circuit has a time-delay fuse or ordinary circuit breaker that can ride out momentary power surges without blowing.

Larger 120-volt air conditioners and all 240-volt models need circuits of their own. If, incidentally, you have a choice between 120- and 240-volt units with similar capacities, select the 240-volt equipment, especially if you'll have to run a new circuit anyway. Higher-voltage air conditioners use somewhat less electricity.

Plug and receptacle patterns for 240-volt appliances vary according to the amperages they're meant to carry. The drawings at right show the ones you'll most likely encounter. Don't exchange an existing receptacle for another unless you're sure the circuit can handle the new load.

To learn about adding new circuits and installing major appliances, see pages 244-246.

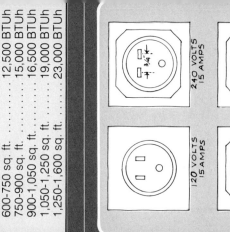
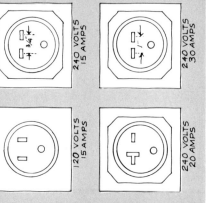

120 VOLTS 15 AMPS  
240 VOLTS 15 AMPS  
240 VOLTS 20 AMPS  
240 VOLTS 30 AMPS

# CONSERVING ENERGY

Energy conservation starts with efficient equipment that's also conscientiously maintained. In the following chapter, "Weather Stripping, Insulation, and Ventilation," we tell you how you can minimize the work they have to do.

But in the end, the way you operate your home's climate system is as vital to its economy as your driving habits are to your car's fuel consumption. Rushing to the thermostat every time you feel a bit too hot or too cold wastes energy just as surely as keeping a lead foot on the accelerator.

The chart below explains how you can control your heating and cooling components with the same light, steady touch you use—or should use—behind the wheel. For other energy-saving tactics, see pages 72, 73 and 251.

## HOW THRIFTY ARE YOUR HEATING/COOLING HABITS?

| Component | Tactic | How you save |
|---|---|---|
| **HEATING** | | |
| Thermostat | Set back 8 to 10 degrees at night. (To learn about installing clock devices that do this automatically, see page 350.) And when you're away from home for more than a day or two, drop the home's setting to 55 degrees. | Figures depend on the climate and your home's insulation, but savings of 8 to 15 percent are not unusual. |
| Fireplace | Don't expect fires in an ordinary fireplace to help much in reducing your heating bill. Some, in fact, draw off more heated air (for combustion) than they add. What's more, an ill-fitting damper—and most are—leaks heat even when it's closed. Consider sealing off a fireplace with a glass fire screen. More about fireplaces on pages 92-99. | A tightly sealed glass screen will definitely cut your heating bills. Close it before retiring and the fire will burn itself out. |
| Ventilation | Leaving a range hood or bath-room fan running can exhaust all the heated air in your home in just an hour or so. Consider controlling bath units with timers so they can't run indefinitely; use range hoods sparingly in cold weather. More about fans on pages 378-381. | Indiscriminate use of fans could be *adding* to your heating costs. |
| Water heater | If you never run out of hot water, try lowering the heater's setting 5 or 10 degrees—but not below 120° F. Water tanks are already fairly well insulated, but more insulation, which you can buy in kit form, might make sense if your unit is located in an unheated space. More about water heaters on pages 302 and 303. | Exact amounts depend on where you live. Lowering the setting saves more with electric units than with gas. |
| **COOLING** | | |
| Thermostat (central cooling) | Cooling uses enormous amounts of electricity, and the cooler you like it, the more—proportionately—you'll pay. Keep the setting no lower than 78 degrees, and on really hot days, try turning it up. Regardless of the temperature outside, you'll feel comfortable if indoor levels are 15 degrees lower. Don't juggle settings a lot, though; you could blow a fuse. | One study found that *dropping* from 78 to 77 degrees cost about 8 percent more; to 72 degrees as much as 60 percent more. |
| Room units | Since most temperature controls aren't graduated in degrees, set up a thermometer to determine which setting will maintain a 78-degree room temperature, then mark it for future reference. | Same as for central units. |
| Appliances | Operate heat-producing washers, dryers, dishwashers, etc. at night or in early-morning hours so heat and humidity don't add to the peak cooling load. | Expect some energy savings and more comfort, too. |
| Ventilation | An attic fan, coupled with proper attic insulation, can make a big difference in your home's cooling load (see page 379). If you don't have power ventilators to dispel excess humidity in your kitchen or bath, consider adding them, as shown on page 381. | An attic or whole-house fan uses only about 1/10 the energy consumed by a central air conditioner. |

# WEATHER STRIPPING, INSULATION, AND VENTILATION

The preceding chapter acquaints you with heating and cooling equipment, the biggest energy users in most homes. Here you meet their silent partners—the weather stripping, insulation, and ventilation systems that help you make the most of that precious energy.

These elements work to control the heat your home loses in the winter and gains in the summer. Weather stripping seals outside walls, keeping outside air out, and inside air in. Insulation retards heat transfer through solid surfaces. And ventilation exhausts excess heat, as well as stale air and humidity.

Chances are, your home could stand some upgrading on all of these counts

(see the drawing below for points you should check). But why not start with your weather stripping; it's the easiest and least expensive component to deal with. You need a tight seal at all doors, windows, and anything else you can open. Note, too, that caulk, a form of weather stripping, fills gaps between immovable elements where air could penetrate. For caulking basics, see pages 131 and 132. And window putty (also called glazing compound) seals the joints between glass and wood. More about this on pages 144 and 145.

Once your home is snugly weather-stripped, you can begin to assess the effectiveness of its insulation.

Since heat rises, you need the most material up top, either under your attic floor or between the roof's rafters. Next come exterior walls. And if your home sits atop a crawl space or unheated basement, you should have insulation down there, too—around ducts and pipes, as well as under the floor or around the space's perimeter.

After you've tightened up your home's weather stripping and insulation, take a fresh look at its ventilation. Roof, soffit, and gable vents let an attic breathe (also see page 119); fans do the same for other areas of the house.

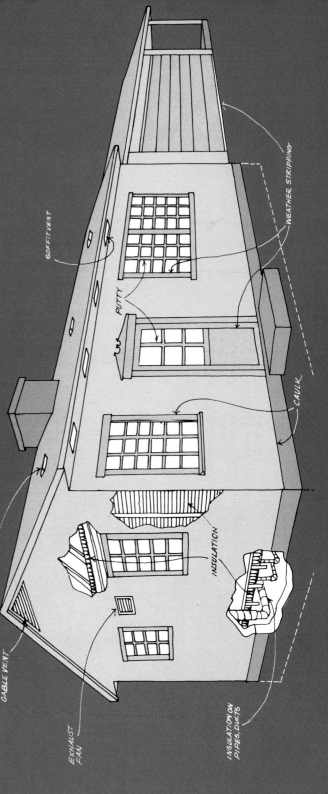

SOFFIT VENT

WEATHER STRIPPING

PUTTY

CAULK

ROOF VENT

GABLE VENT

EXHAUST FAN

INSULATION

INSULATION ON PIPES, DUCTS

# ADDING/UPGRADING YOUR HOME'S WEATHER STRIPPING

Usually you can feel the kind of heat leak caused by inadequate weather stripping. Wait for a cool day and systematically pass your hand around the perimeter of a door, window, or any openable part of your home. Feel a breeze? If so, you've located one air gap that needs to be sealed.

Continue searching and you may find others, too. Note, though, that some other types of heat loss, such as radiation through single-pane windows, seem to produce a draft, but actually don't. If you have doubts about which type of problem you're dealing with, tape polyethylene over the entire opening. If the plastic moves, you need weather stripping here as well.

## CHOOSING AND BUYING WEATHER STRIPPING

As you make the "hand-y" survey for air leaks outlined above, bring along a tape measure and write down the dimensions of any door or window that needs weather stripping. If you feel a leak along just one jamb, you might be able to get by with adding or replacing material only at that edge—but take a close look at the others just to be sure.

Now total up your measurements, add about 10 percent for waste, and make mental notes of how each window and door fits into its frame. You need to pay attention to this because weather stripping—whether it's made of metal, vinyl, felt, rubber, or a combination of these—depends on a tight squeeze-fit to seal out drafts. Some materials work only with swinging doors or sashes; others fit sliders as well.

The chart below briefs you on the products you're likely to encounter. To learn what each looks like and how to install it, see the drawings on the following pages.

## Comparing Weather-Stripping Materials

| Material | Installation | Relative Cost | Durability |
| --- | --- | --- | --- |
| Spring metal | Fairly easy. Cut it with snips, then tack it in place. Makes an invisible installation. | Moderate | Excellent |
| Rolled vinyl and felt | Also fairly easy to install. Cut with scissors or snips, then tack in place. These are visible when installed. | Moderate | Good |
| Self-adhesive foam | Very easy. Snip it with scissors, peel off the backing, and press it in place. | Inexpensive | Only fair; friction can pull it loose. |
| Interlocking metal strips | Several different configurations, all fairly difficult to install because you must align them exactly. These work only on doors and casement windows. | Expensive | Excellent, but some exposed types are subject to damage. |
| Door shoes, sweeps, and thresholds | Some mount on the bottom of the door; others replace an existing threshold. Installation can be tricky for some types, but relatively easy for others. | Moderate to expensive | Fair to excellent |

## WEATHER-STRIPPING WINDOWS

Tightly zipping up a window against air infiltration calls for only a few tools and no special skills—but the job could take a while, depending on the number of sashes you have to seal. Try to plan your work for moderately cool weather; though you'll have to open each window to get at its edges, you'll also want to feel for any air leaks that might remain.

And before you begin, inspect each window carefully to make sure weather stripping is all it needs. Outside, first look for loose or missing chunks of glazing compound, which holds the panes in place. (See page 144.)

Next, check for dried-out caulk around the window's outer frame. (For remedies for this and other caulk-related problems, see pages 131 and 132.) Complete your exterior inspection by examining the sill. Weather-stripping along the window's bottom edge can compensate for some deterioration or warping here, but badly rotted sills and bottom rails let in moisture as well as air. (For help with replacing a sill, see page 146.)

Inside, test latches to be sure they pull their sashes snug. Also, put each window in smooth operating order (see pages 64-69), or consider caulking it tightly shut.

In a big, drafty house, you may have to break down a thorough repair/weather-stripping project into phases, perhaps working on one exposure at a time. You'll begin to realize energy savings almost right away, though.

## Installing Spring Metal

Though not quite as easy to work with as some other weather strippings, bronze, aluminum, or stainless steel spring metal makes the best seal for most types of windows. Designed to fit inside window channels or frames, its out-of-harm's-way location helps it survive years of openings and closings, and makes the strips all but invisible.

This material comes in kit form—with enough strips and nails to treat a typical window—or you can buy it by the running foot in coil form. Get the type with pre-drilled holes.

The drawings below show how to fit spring metal around double-hung and casement sashes, but you can easily adapt these techniques to suit other types, too. Just be sure the metal compresses when the window shuts.

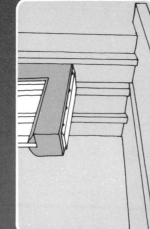

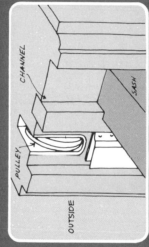

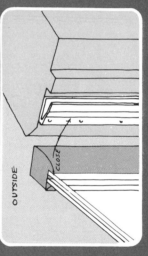

Align strips carefully and nail in place. After each strip is attached, pry the leaf up gently to get the best possible seal.

For double-hung windows, fit the strips in the lower half of the inner channel, the upper half of the outer one. Don't cover pulleys.

Fasten a strip to the bottom of the inner window's lower rail. Do the same to the top rail of the window's upper sash.

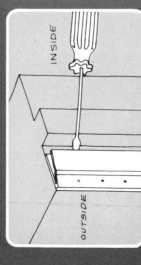

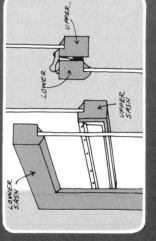

Where the sashes meet, nail a strip to the bottom rail of the upper sash. You may need to flatten the strip to make it fit.

On casement windows, tack strips to the frame as shown. Be sure to install them spring-side-in so sashes will open freely.

Rolled vinyl, felt, and other "gasket" weather strippings attach to the window frame or the sash, making a flap that compresses to seal air leaks. You'll find a wide variety of materials and styles to select from, including versions attached

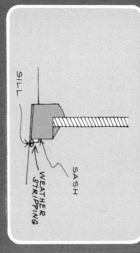

Attach gasket weather stripping so its edge will compress when the window is latched. A bulbous edge does this best.

to rigid or flexible metal strips, as well as the soft goods shown here.

Choose carefully. Though all are easy to install, some—such as felt—must be mounted on the inside of windows and can be an eyesore. Felt also deteriorates fairly rapidly.

Besides being less conspicuous, outside installations also provide a tighter seal against air infiltration. Note, though,

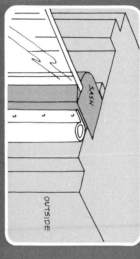

For the sides of double-hung windows, attach strips to the sashes as shown. Make sure the window still operates smoothly.

that you may need to do some ladder work. Avoid leaning way out of an upper-story window to drive those last few nails.

Stretch the gasket material slightly as you attach it, making sure that there are no gaps at corners.

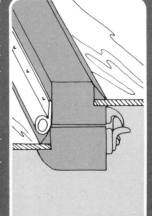

Seal the joint between sashes by tacking a strip to the bottom of the upper sash. It should completely cover the gap.

---

## Installing Foam Strips

Chances are, you've already discovered that self-adhesive foam tape can't resist friction very well—and that even when you can keep it stuck, it doesn't last long.

Still, there are compression-only situations where foam will work well for you. When foam flattens out, it's time to replace it, though.

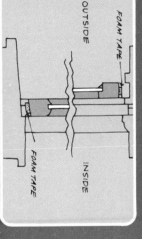

With double-hung windows, use foam only on the top and bottom rails. These strips can take compression but not friction.

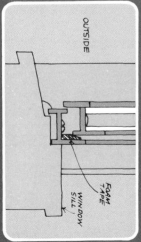

On metal casement or awning windows, install foam tape on the frame. Apply it to all four sides of each opening.

To seal at top and bottom, attach a strip to the outside of the upper sash's top rail and the lower sash's bottom rail.

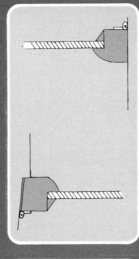

On awning or casement windows, attach strips to the sash or the casing, whichever location provides a tighter squeeze.

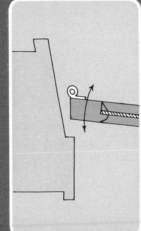

363

## WEATHER-STRIPPING DOORS

A poorly weather-stripped exterior door can leak up to twice as much air as a window in the same condition. Couple this with the fact that most doors also are used far more often than windows, and you can see why their seals merit a careful looking-at every so often.

First, check for crimped, flattened, or missing weather stripping at the top and sides. You might be able to adjust spring metal—the most commonly used door material—by prying lightly, as shown on page 362. Other types probably will have to be replaced with one of the products shown below.

Next, feel along the threshold. Air infiltration here means you need one of the bottom-of-the-door devices illustrated on the opposite page. And how's the door itself? Warping, an out-of-square frame, or deteriorated caulk around the edges give air a chance to "end-run" even the tightest weather stripping. (For more about doors and caulking, see pages 74-81, 131, and 132.) Examine storm doors, too. Some metal versions have a

bulbous gasket along their lower edges; others employ a sweep, as illustrated on the opposite page. Both should be periodically replaced.

Finally, check out any interior doors that open to an attic, garage, basement, or other unheated space. Builders often don't bother to seal these big heat-losers at all. Worse yet, some cut costs by installing hollow-core doors here. If that's the case at your house, you might be energy dollars ahead to invest in the far greater thermal efficiency of a solid- or foam-core door.

## Sealing Door Edges

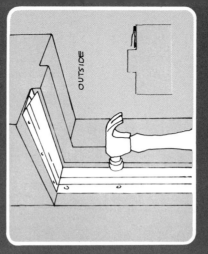

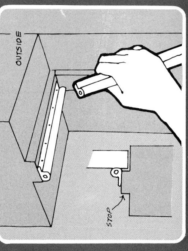

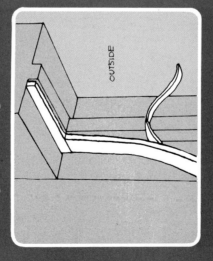

Foam tape installs easily. Just cut strips to length, peel off the backing, and press in place on the inside of the stops.

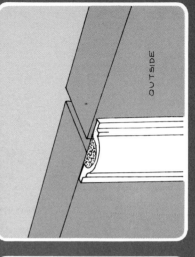

Nail spring-metal strips to the jamb inside the stop. With this type, be sure to fit carefully around the latch and any locks.

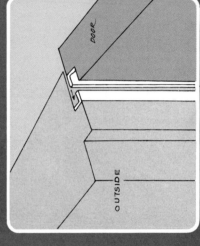

Tack rolled vinyl stripping to the stops' faces. Align so that the bulbous edge projects a bit, as shown in the inset.

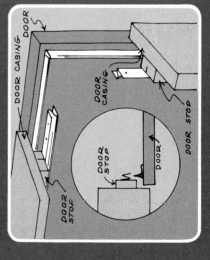

Metal "J-strips" look and seal best, but they're the most difficult to install because you must rout a channel in the door.

Use special insulated molding to seal the gap between double doors. Nail it to the face of the door that's usually closed.

Interlocking metal channels form a good seal, but are tricky to align. You must nail to both the door and the stop.

**364**

# Sealing Underneath Doors

A door's bottom edge poses two special weather-stripping problems. First, its threshold—sometimes called a *saddle*—has to withstand lots of traffic. And second, any seal you attach to the door itself must be able to clear any carpeting or unevenness on the floor within the arc the door traverses.

The devices shown here solve these difficulties with varying degrees of effectiveness. If your door has a badly worn saddle, consider replacing it with one of these or with a wood version, as shown on page 146.

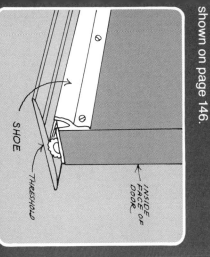

INSIDE FACE OF DOOR

SHOE

THRESHOLD

A *shoe* on the door's lower edge makes a durable seal. To install one, you'll have to remove the door and possibly plane it, too.

A *bulb threshold* works like a non-moving shoe. Bevel the door bottom as shown. You'll need to replace the bulb periodically.

INSIDE

BEVEL DOOR BOTTOM

A *sweep* works fairly well if the floor is relatively even. You simply attach it so the sweep seals against the threshold.

INSIDE OF DOOR

SWEEP

1/16"

An *automatic sweep* uses spring action to hoist itself up as you open the door, then drops down again when you close it.

OUTSIDE OF DOOR

SWEEP

PUSH ROD

PUSH ROD STRIKE PLATE

*Interlocking thresholds* make the tightest seal. Installing one calls for some tricky carpentry work and fitting, though.

INSIDE

INTERLOCK

DOOR

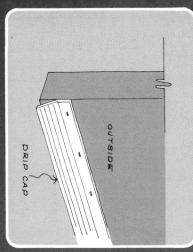

OUTSIDE

DRIP CAP

If your door lets water into the house, nail a metal *drip cap* to its outside face, as shown. Stop air with a bulb threshold.

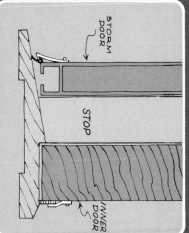

STORM DOOR

STOP

INNER DOOR

Don't forget to check stripping under storm doors, too. You can buy replacement rubber or plastic sweeps for these.

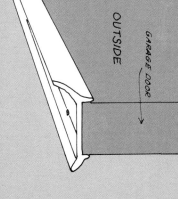

GARAGE DOOR

OUTSIDE

To weather-strip the bottom edge of a roll- or swing-up garage door, purchase a special gasket like this one.

365

# ADDING INSULATION

If your home has no insulation at all, you probably already know about the tremendous amount of heat that passes through its exterior surfaces. Proper bundling up could cut this energy drain (and your heating/cooling bills) by 50 percent or more. Most modern-day houses, though, are actually just *under*-insulated—with light doses of material in some critical places, and often none at all in others.

Would it pay to upgrade your present insulation? How can you know for sure before you buy? In most cases, the answer to the first question is yes. And you can work out the second on paper once you familiarize yourself with what *R-values* mean and do a little detective work around your house.

R-values measure how well a material resists the flow of heat. The higher the R-value, the greater the resistance and the warmer your home will be in winter. Virtually every material—wood, masonry, fiberboard sheathing, even glass—offers some resistance to heat transfer. These differ only slightly from one house to another, though, so for your purposes you need only determine what type of insulation you have and how much of it. Insulation is rated by *inches* of thickness; to compute a material's total R-value, multiply the thickness of your present insulation by its R-value per inch.

First, of course, you have to learn the kind and amount of insulation you already have. Start in the attic. Here you may find insulation stapled to rafters or laid between floor joists. Measure its depth, taking care not to compact it, then check the chart on the opposite page for its R-value per inch. Do the same on the underside of any floor over an unheated basement or crawl space.

Examining walls can be a bigger problem. Occasionally, removing the cover plate from a receptacle or switch will let you get a peek at what's in there. But generally, you'll have to make a small hole and patch it up again.

Don't poke with sharp implements, though. You could puncture a *vapor barrier.* Made of kraft paper, foil, or polyethylene, these membranes block moisture from seeping into the insulation (wet insulation has almost no R-value). If you have vapor barriers, they'll be facing the heated areas—just under floors, walls, and ceiling coverings.

Armed with R-values for your home's various elements, you're now ready to see how they stack up against the ratings shown below for each area of the country. These ratings are maximums; it may not be cost-effective to bring your home up to these standards. You'll have to weigh the costs against the increased effect.

## How Much Insulation Do You Need?

The map at right divides the continental United States into six climate zones and gives three different R-values for each. The first applies to roofs; the second to walls; the third to floors.

These standards, though widely used in new home construction, don't take into account several factors, the most important of which is the cost of energy in your area. Keep in mind that achieving R-values in excess of about 20 may well work out to be economically unattractive in terms of increased effectiveness. You may never be able to recover the amount spent.

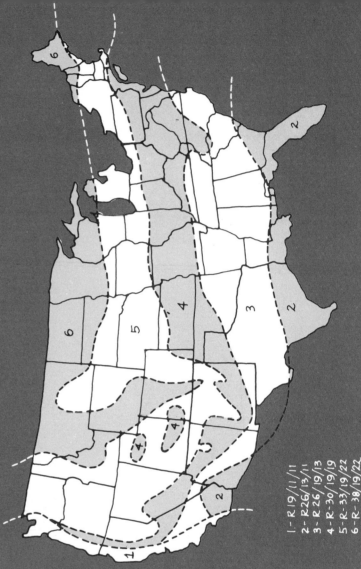

1 - R-19/11/11
2 - R26/13/11
3 - R 26/19/13
4 - R-30/19/19
5 - R- 33/19/22
6 - R- 38/19/22

# CHOOSING AND BUYING INSULATION

Insulating materials function like giant sponges, with millions of tiny air pockets that trap the heat that's trying to pass through. The more pockets per inch of thickness a material has, the higher its R-value.

You'll find an insulation's R-value and its thickness printed on the wrapper. This lets you easily compare product prices and contractors' bids. Remember, you're buying Rs, not inches.

You also need to decide what type of insulation makes the most sense for your intended use. Home insulation usually comes in one of these formats.

Batts generally consist of fluffy fiber glass or rock wool of various thickness in sections 15 to 23 inches wide (to fit joist and stud spacings) and four to eight feet long. They're moisture- and fire-resistant, and come with or without an attached vapor barrier. Though batts are easy to handle and install, you'll end up with lots of waste in irregular areas.

Blankets—also fiber glass or rock wool and sized to fit between framing—come in continuous rolls you cut. This means less waste, but also makes blankets more difficult to handle.

Loose-fill insulation can be either poured or blown into cavities. The most common are fire-retardant cellulose fiber, vermiculite, perlite, fiber glass, and rock wool. This type is especially easy to install in situations such as finished wall and floor cavities.

Foam (urea-formaldehyde and urethane) also can be used to insulate finished walls, floors, and ceilings from the outside. Foam has a higher R-value than blown-in insulation, but it's also more costly, and is subject to shrinkage.

Rigid insulation consists of boards made of molded or extruded polystyrene, polyurethane or polyisocyanurate. Polyurethane has a very high R-value. But, along with polystyrene, it's highly combustible and must be covered with at least a ½-inch thickness of drywall for fire safety.

For more about these materials and their approximate R-values, consult the chart below.

## COMPARING INSULATION MATERIALS

| Type of Insulation | R-value per Inch Thickness | Uses | Installation |
|---|---|---|---|
| **Batts** | | | |
| Fiber glass | 3.0 | Unfinished attic floors, rafters, crawl spaces, walls, ceilings. | Lay them in place or friction-fit between framing members. |
| Rock wool | 3.0 | | |
| **Blankets** | | | |
| Fiber glass | 3.1 | Unfinished floors, rafters, crawl spaces, walls, ceilings. | These usually have flanges that staple to framing. |
| Rock wool | 3.0 | | |
| **Loose-Fill—Poured** | | | |
| Fiber glass | 3.1-3.3 | Unfinished attic floors, especially those with irregular joist spacing or lots of obstructions. You can also fill walls and other cavities with these. | Very easy if you can get at the cavity. Just pour to the right depth, making sure you fill every cranny. |
| Rock wool | 3.0-3.3 | | |
| Cellulose | 3.7-4.0 | | |
| Vermiculite | 2.0-2.6 | | |
| Perlite | 2.0-2.7 | | |
| **Loose-Fill—Blown** | | | |
| Cellulose | 3.1-4.0 | Finished ceilings, walls, floors, and other closed cavities. | You can rent machinery for this fairly tricky operation. Better yet, hire a contractor. |
| Fiber glass | 2.8-3.8 | | |
| Rock wool | 2.8-3.8 | | |
| **Foam** | | | |
| Urea-formaldehyde | 4.1-5.0 | Finished ceilings, walls, floors, and other closed cavities. | Professionals inject this into cavities, then it hardens. Make sure the contractor is certified. |
| Urethane | 5.3 | | |
| **Rigid** | | | |
| Polystyrene | 4.0-5.4 | Roofs, ceilings, walls, foundations, basement walls, and other places you might need thin, high-R-value material. | Cement with adhesive, or friction-fit. Because the first two are combustible, they must be faced with drywall. |
| Polyurethane | 6.7-8.0 | | |
| Polyisocyanurate | 8.0 | | |

## INSULATING AN ATTIC FLOOR

An uninsulated or poorly insulated attic squanders energy winter and summer—sending heat right through the roof in cold weather, and serving as an enormous solar collector on hot, sunny days. Bring the R-value up to snuff here and you can reduce your heating/cooling costs considerably.

Exactly how you approach an attic insulating project depends on how you're using or planning to use the area. If it'll never be anything more than dead storage space, insulate the floor as shown here. If, however, it's finished or

you intend to finish it later, insulate the ceiling and walls, as illustrated on the opposite page.

Either way, look first for leaks that might damage insulation (see pages 110-118), check to be sure you have adequate ventilation (see page 119), and consider whether you want to cut summer heat buildup even further with an attic or whole-house exhaust fan (see pages 379 and 380).

If your attic has a floor, you'll either have to pull up sections of it and work the insulation underneath, or hire a contractor to blow in loose-fill. With unfinished floors, be sure to bring up some planks or pieces of plywood so you can get around without stepping through

the ceiling below. Ceiling materials alone won't bear your weight.

For the insulation itself, you can get batts, blankets, or loose-fill. If you already have a vapor barrier, use unfaced materials, or slash the facing so moisture can't get trapped between two barriers. Note, too, that it's important you don't cover recessed light fixtures or exhaust fans; this could cause a fire. Instead, install baffles that keep the insulation about three inches away all around.

Caution: some materials such as fiber glass and mineral wool are harmful to lungs and skin, so be sure to wear a painter's mask, gloves, and long sleeves if you'll be working with either type.

If you'll need a separate vapor barrier, staple 2-mil polyethylene between the joists. Seal all seams with tape.

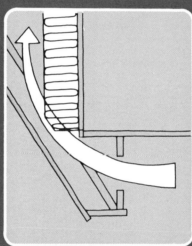

If you're placing batts or blankets, take care not to jam them against the roof—leave space at the eaves for air flow.

When you encounter diagonal-bridging or other obstacles, cut for a snug fit. Otherwise, heat will slip away through the gap.

If conditions in your area necessitate two layers of insulation, place the second layer perpendicular to the first.

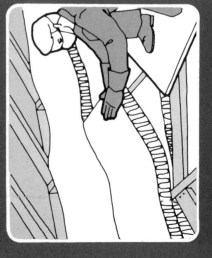

For loose-fill, nail in baffles at the eaves. Insulation should cover the top plate but not obstruct air flow needed for ventilation.

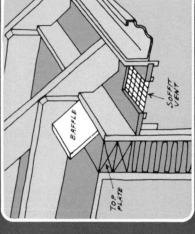

Pour the insulation between joists, then level it off with a board. Be sure you don't leave any low spots or voids.

Heating an attic that's underinsulated is a losing proposition. So if you've got big plans for that space, better budget for plenty of the "fluffy stuff."

In an unfinished attic that doesn't have the collar beams illustrated below, you might be tempted to forget about them and run insulation right up to the ridge beam. Don't! That space above the collars, coupled with vents at the ends (see page 119), gets rid of winter condensation as well as summer heat. Make the collars from 2x4s or 2x6s, depending on how heavy your future ceiling will be.

If your attic already is finished, you'll have to cut holes in knee walls and the ceiling to gain access to these areas. Fortunately, most walls and ceilings aren't difficult to patch (see pages 34-37 and page 57).

Add collar beams overhead if your attic has none. Plan the height, cut the beams to fit, then nail to the existing rafters.

Now place the new material directly over the old. Staple the flanges to the rafters, vapor barrier down, lapping as you go.

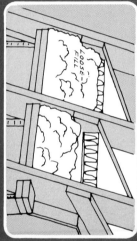

Don't insulate between the rafters in the knee-wall space. Instead, place material between the studs, vapor barrier in.

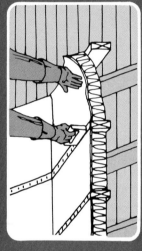

If your attic is finished, you must make openings to get at spaces above collar beams and behind knee and end walls.

Staple batts or blankets to the collar beams, vapor barrier side down. Continue on down the knee walls to the floor.

Now pour loose-fill down between the rafters in the sloping part of the ceiling. Finish off with batts above the collar beams.

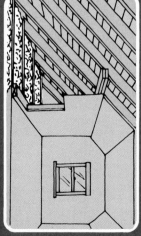

Lay loose-fill, blanket, or batt material between joists in the knee-wall space. Use a broom to poke into "unreachable" spots.

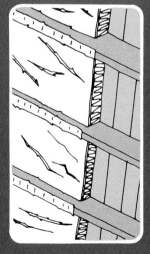

If you're beefing up old insulation, cut it and push it to the back of the cavity. Slash any vapor barrier with a sharp knife.

# INSULATING CRAWL-SPACE WALLS

After attics, unheated crawl spaces qualify as the next-most-vital places to insulate. Here you have two options: drape batts or blankets around the space's perimeter walls, or suspend material between floor joists, as explained on the opposite page.

Draping the walls generally gives better results (and warmer floors) because the crawl space becomes a sealed air chamber, adding further insulation value. With some homes, though, you have no other choice but to insulate the floor between the joists.

Wrapping up a crawl space is a dirty but not difficult chore—providing you really do have space to crawl around down there. You'll need *unfaced* batts or blankets, enough 6-mil polyethylene to cover the ground underneath, some 1x2s and nails, and a bunch of rocks or old bricks. Wear goggles and other protective gear, and watch out for insect nests while you work.

First, close off any unnecessary openings. But don't permanently seal any vents; a crawl space needs these for "breathing" in hot, muggy weather. For more about the importance of this ventilation, see page 377.

Next, examine the underside of your home's floor. You'll notice that its joists run parallel to two walls, perpendicular to the other two. The first two drawings show the slightly different treatment needed to insulate the walls that run perpendicular to the joists.

Warning: if you live in an extremely cold region, such as Alaska, Minnesota, or northern Maine, don't use the technique explained on this page; it could cause frost heaving that might damage your foundation. Check with local contractors or your community building department to learn about the techniques commonly used in your area.

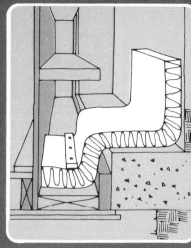

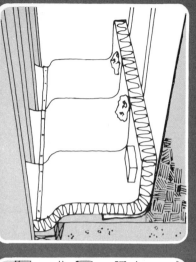

Next, insulate the walls parallel to the joists. Here you can just let material cascade down the wall, as shown.

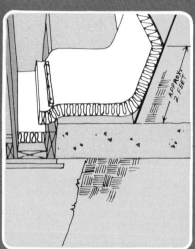

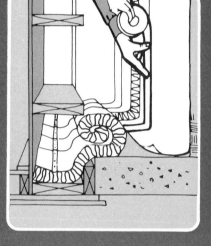

Now unroll enough insulation to overlap the header material and to cover the earth at the wall's base. Secure with 1x2s.

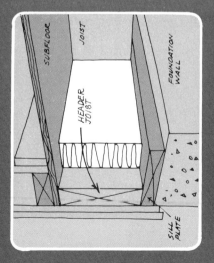

Begin by laying up pieces of insulation against the header joist. Cut them slightly oversize so you'll end up with a snug fit.

After the walls have been insulated, roll up the blankets and tuck a polyethylene vapor barrier underneath. Tape it in place.

Tape joints between strips, or lap them at least six inches. Move carefully, making sure you don't puncture the plastic.

Finally, weight the polyethylene and insulation with rocks or old bricks. Don't use wood—it could attract termites or rot.

# INSULATING A FLOOR

Floors over porches, garages, or other unheated zones require bundling up, too. Exactly how you handle these major heat-eaters depends on the situation underneath.

If the joists are covered, as with a finished garage ceiling, your best bet is to have loose-fill blown in by a contractor who has the equipment and expertise to do the job correctly. An extremely cold floor might even merit a more costly foam treatment. More about both of these on pages 374 and 375.

With open joists, install batts, blankets, or rigid planks as illustrated below.

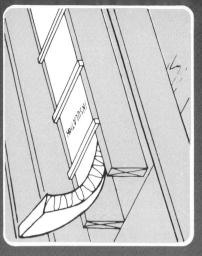

Blankets or—better yet—batts make sense if spaces between the joists aren't chopped up with lots of pipes, wiring, ducts, or bridging.

Planks let you drop below many of these obstacles, but check building codes before you decide to go this way. You'll probably have to face urethane or polystyrene insulation planks with a non-combustible material; some community codes don't permit these types at all.

Unless you're simply adding another layer to existing insulation, get faced materials and install their vapor barriers up. Foil facing works very well here because it reflects heat back into living areas. Pay special attention to achieving

good coverage at joists and headers around the floor's outside edges.

Cold slab floors present a special problem because you can't get material under them, where it would do the most good. It may help to wrap the outside of your foundation, as illustrated below, but talk to a pro first. You might end up with a higher R-value by insulating the floor itself. To do this, glue down wood sleepers with rigid planks in between, then lay new sub- and finish floorings. For information about sleeper installations, see page 19.

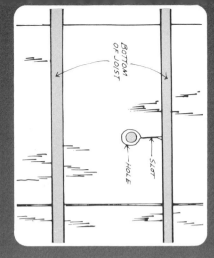

Support batts by nailing 1x2s to the undersides of joists. Space the strips about 18 inches apart, and lay the batts on top.

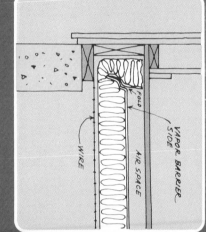

Start each strip by folding so that insulation covers header. Here, chicken wire stapled to the joists supports the batts.

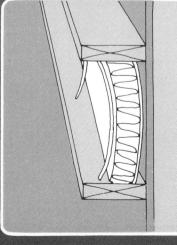

Or you can use friction-fit rods that slip between the joists. Be sure you leave some air space between insulation and floor.

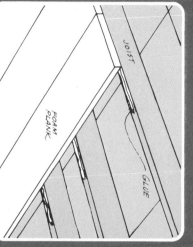

When you encounter a pipe or other obstacle, cut a slot to the opening, then fit carefully. Seal the slot with tape.

With planks, just apply adhesive to the bottoms of the joists and press the lightweight strips in place. Check fire codes first.

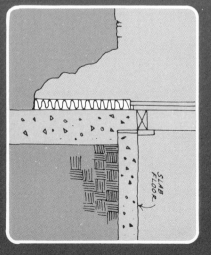

To insulate around a slab, dig a trench to the frost line, then glue up 2-inch-thick foam planks from the siding on down.

371

## INSULATING DUCTS AND PIPES

When a contractor computes a home's heating and cooling needs, he often tacks on an additional 10 or even 20 percent for losses in the system's ducts or pipes. Insulate these—especially any that run through an attic, garage, or other unheated area—and you can prevent most of this energy waste.

Unsheathed hot water pipes also allow heat to escape, which in turn forces the water heater to work much harder. Wrapping these pipes will pay big energy-saving dividends. The same can't be said for wrapping cold water lines, but doing so will eliminate dripping and sweating.

What about ducts that run through heated spaces, such as an unfinished basement? Here you have a choice. If you're using the space as a primary living area, chances are you're depending on heat losses to keep things warm down there. In this situation, you might be better off to insulate the walls as shown on the opposite page, and forget about the ducts.

If, on the other hand, your basement gets only occasional use, consider installing a couple of new basement registers (see page 338) and insulating both the ducts and the floor above. You may find you rarely need to open those registers, since temperatures below ground tend to stay constant.

Duct insulation comes in one- and two-inch thicknesses. Get the thicker stuff, especially if your ducts are rectangular; two-inch wrap cuts losses about one-third more. You'll also need several rolls of duct tape. Use this to seal all duct joints before you insulate.

If your ducts don't have dampers that let you balance the air flow, add some before you insulate. Insulation ups the temperature of air at registers and you'll want to do some fine-tuning afterward (see pages 320 and 339).

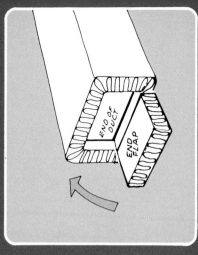

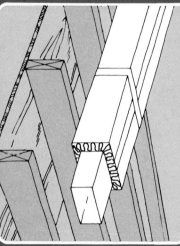

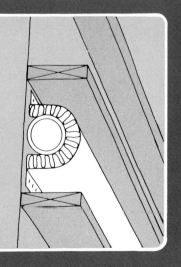

Where ducts run between joists, cut blankets and staple them as shown. Seal joints between the blankets with duct tape.

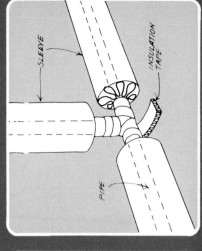

At the end of any duct, extend insulation beyond, then cut a flap. Fold up and seal all the edges with tape, package style.

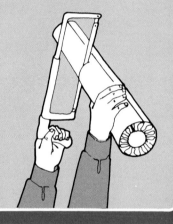

For other ductwork, wrap insulation carefully around all four sides. The vapor barrier should always be on the outside.

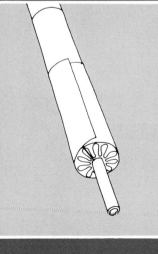

Sleeves to insulate pipes come in various lengths. A slit lets you fit the sleeve on the pipe; then you glue down the flap.

At ends or corners, cut short lengths to fit as closely as possible. Use a fine-blade hacksaw or sharp utility knife.

At pipe junctions, wrap all the uncovered areas with spongy insulation tape. Peel off the backing and wrap like a bandage.

# INSULATING BASEMENT WALLS

Thinking about finishing off a chilly basement? Rigid insulation planks and soft batts or blankets offer two different ways to go. Which you choose depends partly on where you live, and partly on how much space you're willing to give up to the installation.

If winters in your region are mild, you can get by with an R-7 rating; in colder areas, though, aim for R-11. To achieve either of these R-values with soft goods, you'll need to frame out 2x3 or 2x4 stud walls over the top of the masonry, then staple batts or blankets between the studs of your new built-out walls. The studs must be covered with drywall or paneling.

Rigid panels let you keep your new wall thickness to a minimum. With these, you simply line the walls with furring (for attaching the finished wall material), then glue up (or friction-fit) panels between the furring. But because of foam's combustibility, you must cover it with a minimum of ½-inch drywall—even if you're planning to complete the job with wood or hardboard paneling.

Solve any moisture problems before you begin. Seepage or leaks render insulating materials useless. Don't worry about mild condensation, though. Insulation and a vapor barrier will usually eliminate this. (To learn about wet-basement problems and their solutions, see pages 101-105.)

Note, too, that insulation becomes less critical as you get below ground level. To save money, you might decide to insulate only partway down—though insulating the walls' full height will provide some additional value. Either way, be sure to pay special attention to spaces above the sill, as illustrated in the drawings below.

As with crawl-space walls, these insulating techniques could cause frost-heave problems in extremely cold parts of the United States. Check local codes for approved procedures.

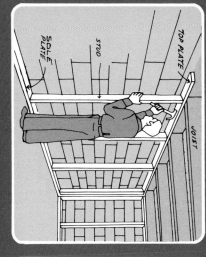

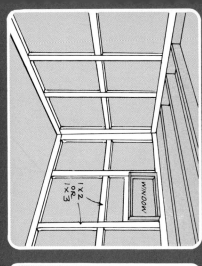

If you choose fiber glass batts or blankets, build stud walls as shown. For more about framing, see pages 48-50.

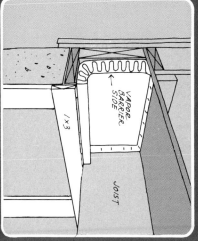

Then just staple insulation between the studs. Don't skimp on the staples. Drive one every ten or twelve inches.

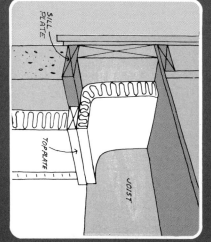
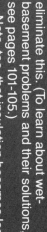

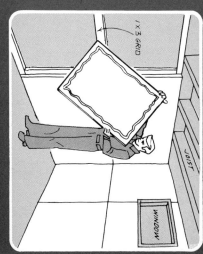

Above the sill plate, carefully fit small pieces of insulation. Secure with tape, staples, or wood strips (see page 370).

For panel insulation, make a grid of 1x2s or 1x3s, sized to fit the panels you buy. More about furring on page 45.

Here again, use pieces of batts or blankets for spaces over the top of the sill. Vapor barriers must always face inside.

Now cement panels to the furring strips. Measure and cut as you go to ensure tight butt joints. Finally, cover with drywall.

# INSULATING EXTERIOR WALLS

Everyone knows that the best time to insulate exterior walls is during construction. Problem is, most of us don't have this option available to us. And because insulating such large areas is labor intensive, the builder of your home may have been tempted to skimp here.

Even if he didn't, the 3½-inch-thick cavities between 2x4 framing can hold only so much insulation—often not enough to achieve the R-value recommended. That's why the outer walls of some modern-day homes have been framed either with 2x6s, usually spaced 24 inches apart, or with 2x4s spaced on 16-inch centers with rigid insulation panels nailed to the outside and batts in between the studs.

But don't assume that since your walls are already finished, you can't do anything about these energy-wasters. The drawings here and on the opposite page illustrate the methods commonly used to make them more efficient. Be warned, though, that none is easy or inexpensive, and that most require the services of a contractor with the specialized equipment and know-how to do the job right.

If your walls already have some insulation in them, you may well find that it doesn't make economic sense to upgrade their R-value. If there's none at all, shop carefully for a reputable installer, getting several written bids that specify R-values as well as the amounts of material needed. In a standard 2x4 wall, properly insulated, you can expect R-8 for fiber glass or rock wool, R-10 for cellulostic fiber, or R-11.5 for foam. These may not bring your home up to the standards listed on page 366, but they'll help a lot.

Unless you choose foam, you'll also need a vapor barrier to protect your new insulation against condensation. Check the bottom of the opposite page to see how you can provide one without ripping apart the walls.

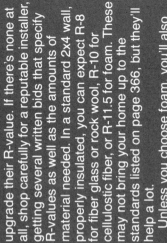
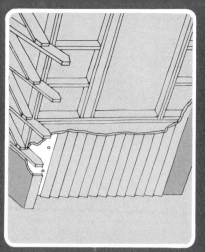

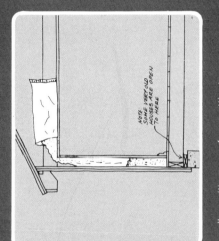
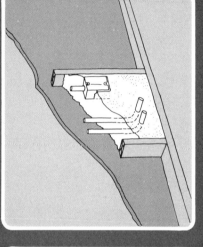

Most cavities don't run from top to bottom, so a contractor has to remove siding and bore a series of holes to gain access.

Unfinished walls are a snap to insulate. You just friction-fit batts or staple up blankets. Be sure not to compress the insulation.

If wall cavities run from attic to basement, you can pour in loose-fill. To probe yours, drop a weighted string.

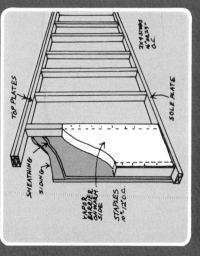
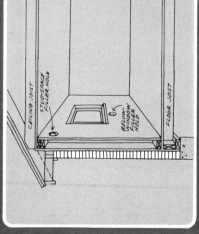

If your walls are masonry veneer, it's best to work from inside, cutting holes for each cavity in the interior wall surface.

Liquefied foam gets around pipes, wiring, and electrical boxes—and has the added advantage of providing its own vapor barrier.

# Installing Foam or Loose-Fill Insulation

Blowing or foaming insulation into finished walls calls for technical expertise and machinery that few do-it-yourselfers have. These materials must be applied to the right density, coverage, and thickness, or their insulating value will

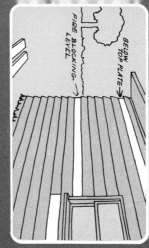

suffer—a job that requires both savvy about how houses are constructed and an understanding of specialized equipment. An amateur might miss large areas where heat could escape.

The drawings below show the steps a pro would—and should—follow. To blow in loose-fill, he'll poke into stud cavities with a big hose, like the one on a vacuum cleaner. If the contractor is using foam,

he'll pump it in through a thinner hose with an applicator. In either case, you'd be wise to make it clear to the contractor, before you sign a contract, that you want proof that the job has been done correctly. Special heat-sensing devices can pinpoint heat leaks.

First, courses of siding must come off at the top, under windows, and maybe at the four-foot level as well.

After peeling back the building paper, the installer uses a hole saw to cut openings into each separate cavity.

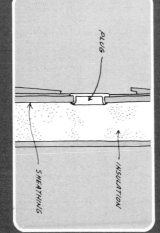

Then he probes with a steel tape to determine if there are any obstructions that might create open, uninsulated pockets.

The machine's nozzle should fill the cavity to the level of its inlet, then flip up to catch the remaining space above.

After each cavity is filled, a snap-in plug seals the hole in the sheathing. Then the building paper goes back in place.

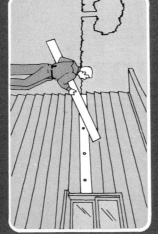

To save money, you might consider removing and replacing siding materials yourself. To learn how, see page 133.

## Providing a Vapor Barrier

Without a vapor barrier, any insulation you install (except foam) will turn into a soggy, useless mess in almost no time. The drawing at right shows why. Temperature differences between a wall's warm and cool sides cause household moisture to condense inside the stud cavities, filling up pockets that trap air.

Besides keeping insulation dry, a vapor barrier helps keep moisture in the house,

a feature you'll appreciate in the winter, when indoor air is dry.

How, though, can you get a continuous waterproof membrane into a finished wall? You can't—but you can seal the wall's interior surface for the same effect. First caulk any cracks you find at the floor, ceiling, and around doors or windows. Then apply a couple of coats of oil- or alkyd-base paint you know is waterproof (or use a paint specially formulated for this purpose).

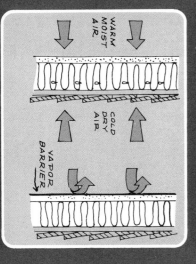

375

ADDING INSULATION

# SOLVING VENTILATION PROBLEMS

Like people, houses need to breathe—inhaling fresh or cooler outside air, and exhaling moisture, unwanted heat, and odors. So even though the idea behind weather stripping and insulation is to snug-up heated spaces, air must be allowed to pass through areas such as unheated attics and crawl spaces.

Certain other areas and equipment require venting, too. The remainder of this chapter discusses your options.

First, recognize that ventilating systems fall into two categories—static and powered. The most obvious of your home's static ventilators are its doors and windows. Opening one of these gets rid of smells and humidity in a hurry; it can also waste a lot of expensive heating or cooling energy.

Less perceptible—but just as vital to your home's well being—are the static vents that circulate fresh air through an attic, crawl space, and even the combustion chamber of a furnace or boiler. Throttling these adds to your energy bills, too—and can lead to other

moisture-related problems such as peeling paint, mildew, and rot.

Your home may already have a few powered ventilators—a hood over the range, for example, or a bathroom exhaust fan. If not, the following pages show how you can add these household pollution-removers.

Power ventilation also can reduce cooling costs by surprising amounts. A roof-mounted fan, working in tandem with static vents, removes heat buildup and takes a big load off your cooling equipment. And a larger fan in the attic floor may pull enough air through the house to cool without refrigeration.

## GETTING FRESH AIR TO A FURNACE OR BOILER

Gas and oil heating plants consume more than just fuel. Their burners also require a steady supply of air—and the flames don't care if it's warm or cool.

Chances are, your furnace or boiler draws its combustion air from the house,

then burns this air you just paid to heat and sends it up the flue. Ducting cool, outside air directly to the burner eliminates this waste—and may improve the unit's efficiency, too.

Don't confuse combustion air with that which circulates through ducts and registers. Compartments within a furnace keep the two separate, as illustrated on pages 318, 322, and 324.

Installing a fresh-air feed is a fairly easy, straightforward job, but one that should be done by a heating contractor who can properly size the duct for the amount of air your boiler or furnace needs.

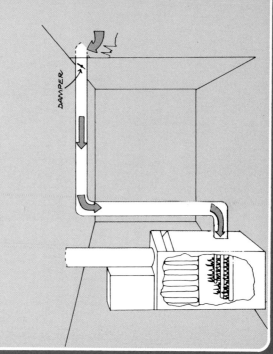

A furnace with a simple air intake like this one pulls heat from your basement or utility room, then loses it up the chimney. In a really

tight home, this situation can create a vacuum that aids air infiltration from outside.

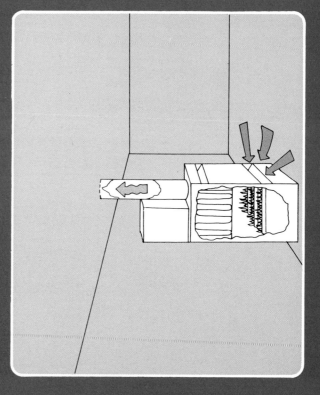

A small-diameter duct, usually the size of the flue, feeds the flames with outside air, conserving heat indoors. An automatic damper

opens only when the burner is operating. Fuel savings could offset the installation cost in a single heating season.

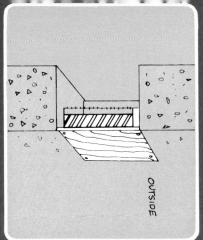

OUTSIDE

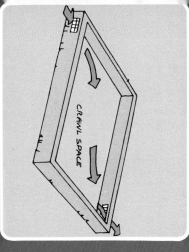

CRAWL SPACE

# ENTING A CRAWL SPACE

A crawl space that can't breathe—even a well-insulated one—turns into a giant moisture chamber in hot, humid weather. Temperature differences between its inner and outer surfaces cause water to condense on joists, subflooring, and insulation, resulting in chilly floors; dank odors, and—eventually—rot that can destroy your home's underpinnings.

That's why the builder of your house most likely installed a couple of vents in the foundation walls. These should provide one square foot of vent space for every 300 square feet of the crawl space's total area.

Check your crawl-space vents from time to time to make sure they aren't blocked by leaves or shrubbery. Shine a light inside, too, so you can look for any signs of condensation.

And realize that you need air flow through a crawl space only in the summertime. Close up vents every fall to cut heat losses, possibly making covers, as shown below.

In a few homes, the crawl space is permanently sealed so it can serve as a plenum for warm-air heating. In others, the furnace itself is located down there and depends on crawl-space air for combustion. If either of these is the case at your house, refer to the last two illustrations.

All of these recommendations presume that your crawl-space walls have been insulated, with a vapor barrier on the ground, as shown on page 370. Insulating ducts and pipes helps reduce condensation, too (see page 372).

If your home's crawl space seems to be getting adequate ventilation but you still see signs of moisture, the water may be coming from a leak or seepage through the walls. More about these on pages 100-105. And to learn about two other potential crawl-space problems —termites and rot—see pages 137, 153, and 177.

Every crawl space (picture this drawing with a house on top) needs at least two vents, located near opposite corners.

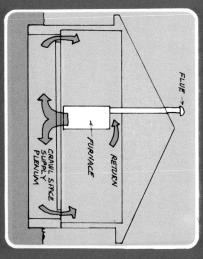

FLUE
RETURN
FURNACE
CRAWL SPACE SUPPLY PLENUM

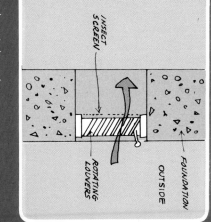

INSECT SCREEN
OUTSIDE
FOUNDATION
ROTATING LOUVERS

Good vents have louvers you can open and close. Open them wide for maximum air flow in hot, muggy periods.

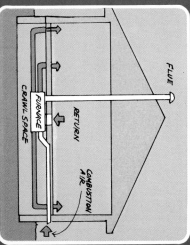

FLUE
CRAWL SPACE
FURNACE
RETURN
COMBUSTION AIR

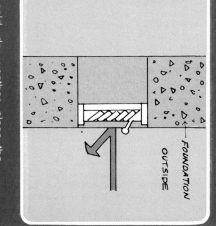

OUTSIDE
FOUNDATION

In cold, dry weather, close the louvers tightly—or leave them open just a crack if winters in your area tend to be damp.

To air out a crawl space that's part of your heating system, run the furnace blower three or four times during the summer.

If your vents aren't operable, re-place them, or seal the openings with exterior-grade plywood each winter. Secure with screws.

If your furnace is located in a crawl space, it will need a fresh-air intake (see opposite page) before you can close the vents.

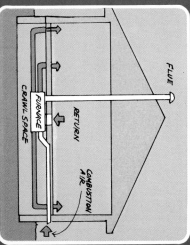

## CHOOSING AND BUYING FANS

Think of power ventilators as quick-change devices that can remove all the air within a space in just a minute or two—along with any heat, humidity, or odors the air might be carrying. As the old, stale air goes out, of course, it's replaced by fresh air from outside or somewhere else in the house.

That's why fans are sized according to the capacity of air they'll move in a minute's time. These cubic-foot-per-minute (*CFM*) ratings let you select a unit according to the space it must handle and the rate at which it will change over the air in a room.

The chart below lists a series of multipliers you can use to determine the minimum CFM ratings ventilation experts recommend for particular areas of your home. A 5x9-foot bath, for example, would need at least a 48-CFM fan. And

because units are rated in increments of 10 CFM, you'd shop for a 50-CFM model. Fans differ not only in the size and speed with which they move air, but also in the amount of noise they make. You'll find this measurement, expressed in *sones*, on the unit's rating plate. Here, the lower the rating, the quieter the fan. A 3-sone model, for instance, would be only half as noisy as the one rated at 6 sones.

Also, before you choose a power ventilator, give some thought to where the air it evacuates is going to go. Wherever possible, try to vent to the outdoors, even if that means running ductwork (see page 381).

You can get by with venting a small bathroom or laundry fan into an attic or crawl space—provided the space itself has enough ventilation to carry off any excess humidity. But don't do this with a kitchen unit; greasy air is flammable. If you can't duct outside, you'll need a ductless hood. These capture grease in

washable filters and remove cooking smells with replaceable charcoal filters. But unlike a ducted system, ductless units can't get rid of heat or moisture.

Finally, decide what kind of controls you want your new ventilator to have. For attic fans, you can choose thermostat-activated switches that automatically turn on the unit when temperatures up there reach a certain level. With a whole-house fan, a timer switch might make more sense.

In a bathroom, you might be tempted to connect a fan to an overhead light and operate them both with the same switch. Better, though, would be an independent switch or a short-duration timer. Range hoods usually come with two-speed switches or rheostat-style variable-speed controls.

## SELECTING THE RIGHT FAN FOR THE JOB

| Location | Installation | Required CFM Rating |
|---|---|---|
| **Kitchen** | | |
| Range hood | Mount directly over the cooking surface, 21 to 30 inches from the burners. Duct to the outside | (see page 381) or choose a non-ducted type to remove grease and odors only. |
| Wall/ceiling | Neither will exhaust air around the range as efficiently as a | hood unit will. Duct to the outside. |
| **Bath** | Mount in the ceiling or wall, ideally near the tub or shower. | Multiply the bath's square footage by 1.07. |
| **Laundry** | Locate as near as possible to the washer or dryer. Duct to the out- | Multiply the room's square footage by 0.8. |
| **Attic** | Install in a gable-end wall or, better yet, the roof itself. If | roofing is dark in color, you'll need a bigger unit. Multiply the attic's square footage by 0.7; add 15 percent for dark roofing. |
| **Whole-house** | Mount one of these big air-movers in the attic floor over a stair-well, central hall, or other spot where it can pull air from the en-tire house. Louver-type shutters | should close automatically when the unit is not running or if there's a fire. These can be noisy, so be sure to carefully check sone ratings before you buy any unit. Compute your home's *cubic* footage, then get a unit that size if you live in warmer climates; half that size if you live in the North. |

Granted, vents and louvers help relieve the intense heat that builds up in an attic, and insulation retards its transfer to the rooms below. But in prolonged hot spells, that's just not good enough. A well-insulated attic holds heat for several hours after the sun goes down, adding considerably to your home's overall cooling requirements.

That's why you should consider a power ventilator. Mounted on the roof near its peak and coupled with air intakes at or near the eaves, these units pull a strong, steady breeze through that attic hot box, and can reduce cooling costs by as much as 30 percent.

Note, though, that if your home does not have central cooling, and you don't plan to add it, one of the whole-house fans shown on the following page will probably do more for your comfort.

Power roof ventilators are relatively inexpensive and come pre-wired in lightweight housings that tuck under roofing materials, as shown below. Most include thermostatic switches to turn the fan on and off as needed. You also can add a humidity-activated control to automatically evacuate condensation that builds up in winter or periods of rapid temperature swings. Besides mounting the unit on the roof, a simple electrical hookup is all that's necessary to ready the unit for operation.

Before you buy, use the chart on the opposite page to compute the CFM capacity you need. You also may have to provide additional static venting at the soffits or in the lower part of the roof. Check the manufacturer's venting recommendations and page 119.

Because heat rises, you'll want to locate your ventilator as near to the roof's apex as possible, preferably in the center of a rear slope. To learn more about making an opening in your roof and flashing around it, see pages 116, 117, and 127.

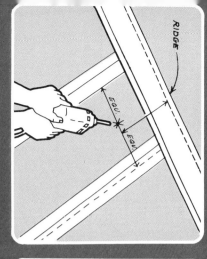

RIDGE

Measure your unit's recommended distance from the ridge down. Find the center between rafters; drill up through this point.

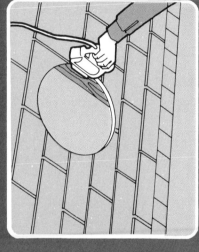

Outside, use that point as center, and scribe a circle to fit the unit you'll install. Make this cut with a saber or keyhole saw.

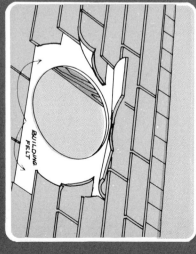

BUILDING FELT

Next, test-fit the housing, mark around its flashing, then carefully peel back shingles around the hole's top and sides.

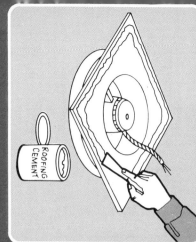

ROOFING CEMENT

Now turn the fan over and coat its edges with a good grade of roofing cement. This helps ensure a tight seal.

Slip the unit into place, with the upper part of its flashing under the rolled-back shingles. Lap the shingles below.

Nail the flashing to the roof decking; apply roof cement around flashing and to nails. Stick down all the shingles you lifted, too.

# INSTALLING A WHOLE-HOUSE FAN

Looking to lessen your dependence on air conditioning, or to do without it entirely? A powerful ventilator unit, capable of pulling big volumes of air through your home and exhausting it out through the attic, might be the answer.

A whole-house fan won't dehumidify, of course, and you'd only want to run it when the temperature is lower outside than in. But air that's moving can feel as much as ten degrees cooler—and come sundown, one of these big units begins to draw off daytime heat buildup in a matter of minutes.

You can expect a whole-house fan to cost two to three times as much as the roof ventilators shown on page 379. Its CFM capacity will be much larger (see the chart on page 378) and the unit also should include a rubber suspension system to dampen noisy vibration, as well as an automatic shutdown in case of a fire.

Installation probably will call for more carpentry work, too—especially if you decide to build the suction box illustrated below. It lets you ventilate only the attic during the day or while cooling equipment is in operation. Suction-box installations are also quieter.

Before you build a suction box, read the fan manufacturer's instructions

carefully, paying particular attention to the recommended sizes for intake and exhaust openings. Constricting these can increase the air's velocity and create wind noise.

You have lots of flexibility in operating a whole-house fan, depending on which doors and windows you open. When the outdoor temperature begins to drop, raise the lower sashes of all windows to clear the air inside; later you might want to shut some in areas that don't need ventilating. But don't close up all openings; these units can suck soot right out of your fireplace's chimney.

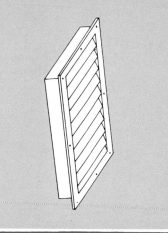

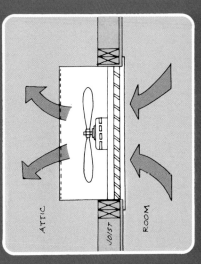

ATTIC

JOIST

ROOM

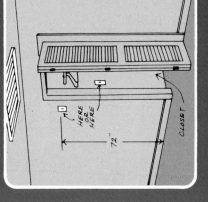

HERE OR HERE

72"

CLOSET

To cover the opening in the ceiling, choose an automatic shutter unit. Louvers open when the fan is running, close when it's off.

Locate the switch where it won't be mistaken for a light switch. Or install a timer that controls the fan automatically.

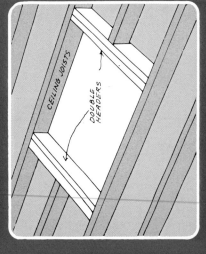

CEILING JOISTS

DOUBLE HEADERS

First cut an appropriately sized opening in the ceiling. Saw one joist and nail in double headers. More about this on page 127.

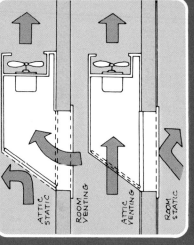

ATTIC STATIC

ROOM VENTING

ATTIC VENTING

ROOM STATIC

A horizontal mounting is easiest and effectively ventilates the house. But the fan can't be used to cool just the attic.

A trap door arrangement or automatic shutters let you exhaust the house (top) or vent the attic only (bottom).

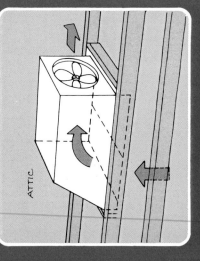

ATTIC

To cool either the attic or the house, build a sound-deadened suction box and mount the fan vertically, aimed at gable vents.

380

# INSTALLING A RANGE HOOD OR BATHROOM FAN

Tired of cracking open a window every time someone broils a steak or takes a shower? Kitchen and bath ventilating equipment clear the air faster and use a lot less energy than you lose through those open windows.

Before you set out to shop for any ventilator, refer to the chart on page 378 or the CFM capacity you'll need, making special note of the installation data listed here.

And as you survey the wide range of units available, compare their some ratings. These noise levels shouldn't

exceed 8 for range hoods, or 6.5 for bathroom fans; most units are much quieter than this.

Most also come with easy-to-follow installation instructions, but whether or not you decide to take on the job yourself probably will be governed by the carpentry work necessary to route a duct from your kitchen or bath to the outdoors.

The drawings below illustrate your major options. Choose the shortest run possible, with the least number of elbows—to a maximum of two for ducts up to five inches in diameter, three with six-inch or larger ducts. Don't plan to go more than 25 feet with any run, if at all possible.

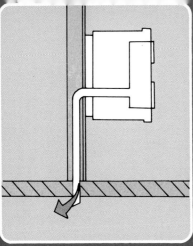

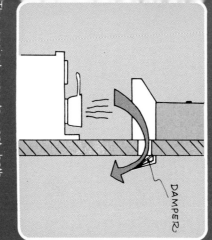

DAMPER

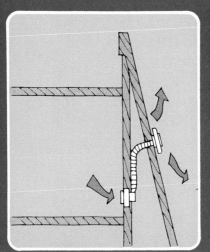

Remember, too, that a range hood handles roughly 200 pounds of airborne grease per year. Since grease is highly flammable, you should keep these ducts away from any direct heat source, and clean out the hood's filter at the intervals specified by the manufacturer. Bathroom ventilators require virtually no periodic maintenance.

You'll also need a power source, of course. Since these units draw only small amounts of current, you may be able to tap into an existing circuit, as shown on pages 237-240.

For a self-venting island range, run ducting between the floor joists. Keep the duct run to a minimum, though.

The easiest way to vent both kitchen and bath units is to go directly through an outside wall. A damper helps stop drafts.

Flexible ducting lets you exhaust a bathroom unit through the roof or a nearby wall—but don't use flexible ducts with range hoods.

Or plan a roof-mounted discharge by running a duct through the cabinet above, then through the ceiling and out the roof.

Self-venting ranges eliminate the need for a hood, but must still be ducted outside. Through the wall is easiest here, too.

# SECURITY

To be truly "at home" brings a sense of well-being that comes only with feeling secure. it's this human emotion that makes your household's security at once the simplest and the most complex of its systems.

If you haven't been thinking of security as a system, now's the time to reorient your outlook. To protect against break-ins and fire you need hardware, of course. But your own habits and procedures are as vital to security as water is to plumbing. You can, for instance, void the protection provided by even the finest lock by "hiding" its key under the welcome mat.

This chapter deals mainly with security hardware. But before you get down to locks and bolts, test your safety consciousness by reviewing the precautions outlined below, then "case" your house as explained on the opposite page.

## PROTECTING AGAINST BREAK-INS

Small-time thieves—looking for easily carried items they can sell or even use themselves—commit the great majority of household break-ins. They'll nab a purse through an open window, slit a screen door and make off with a TV set, even back a truck up to the garage and empty a house.

A surprisingly large percentage of these intruders simply walk in through a door somebody didn't bother to lock. Insist on a locked-door policy at your house—and don't confine it to nighttime hours; routine daylight comings and goings often make a better crime cover than darkness.

Also make sure everyone in your family knows the importance of identifying visitors before opening doors, and of calling the police if a character seems suspicious.

When you're not home, make it look as if you are. Program timers to turn lights on and off at different times in different rooms (see page 390). Leave a radio playing loudly enough to be heard from just outside. Ask a neighbor to park a car in the driveway while you're on vacation. All of these strategies raise doubts in a prowler's mind.

Don't put your faith in gimmicks such as bogus detective agency decals and barking dog tapes; these fool only the people who buy them. Exceptions are the Operation Identification stickers warning would-be burglars that "All items of value on these premises have been marked." This program—which includes etching an identification number on valuables with a special electric pen—has proven itself a highly effective deterrent.

If you come home to find a break-in in progress, don't panic, but don't try to apprehend the culprits, either. Get out—or don't block *their* exit. Wait until police arrive before you re-enter the house.

Properly securing your home's points of entry, as shown on the following pages, will keep out all but the most determined intruders. If you want to go further, consider the pros and cons of adding an alarm system (see pages 394 and 395). For even more protection, consult a reputable security service.

## PROTECTING AGAINST FIRE

As you browze through this book and examine the various anatomy drawings, you'll begin to notice that though houses may differ in many respects, almost all go together with highly uniform building materials, assembled in basically the same ways.

Why don't builders exercise more creativity? The answer lies in your community's building code and its principal concern—the prevention of fire. Codes rate the relative combustibility of just about all construction materials, specify where and how they shall be used, and require that each of a home's components be capable of withstanding an intense fire for a certain time period.

Familiarize yourself with local codes and building practices before you undertake any structural changes, and insist that any contractors you hire do all work "to code." Unsafe conditions jeopardize your family's lives. They may also limit or even cancel out an insurance settlement in the event of a fire-related loss.

The same goes—in spades—for any equipment that might *cause* a fire. This includes your home's electrical, gas, and heating/cooling systems, as well as any fireplaces and chimneys. For more about the hazards these present, check out the relevant chapters in this book.

Protected by modern-day building codes, you can feel secure that your home won't burn to the ground before you have time to escape. But fire safety doesn't stop with the structure itself. Too many fatalities still occur because someone has carelessly allowed a furnishing or appliance to ignite and fill a home with lethal smoke. Fumes from these fires overcome most victims long before the flames reach them. More about smoke and smoke warning devices on page 391.

Make sure that every member of your household knows—and follows—the ABCs of fire prevention promulgated by newspapers, fire departments, and the National Safety Council. And if you haven't gotten around to conducting a family fire drill, organize one now.

# SIZING UP YOUR HOME'S DEFENSES

Analyze the security at your house as if you were a prowler contemplating a break-in. Experts often do this with the zone approach illustrated here.

**Perimeter defenses** include all points easily seen from the street or a casual stroll around the property. How's your lawn? It should present a well-groomed appearance, especially when you're off on vacation. And trim back bushes near the house so intruders don't have a place to hide while they force open a window.

Get in the habit of keeping your garage door closed, whether you're home or not.

To make this practice easier, you might consider a remote-control operator (see pages 205 and 206).

Make a second check at night, with all your exterior lights ablaze. They should illuminate the drive, as well as front, side, and rear yards. Use two bulbs at entries so you'll still have light if one burns out. More about exterior lighting on pages 259 and 390.

**Points of entry** are probably the most vital zone. Survey your doors first, since nearly 90 percent of all illegal entries happen there. Check out not only front and rear doors, but also any that connect the house and garage. These are favorite targets because an intruder can work on them without being observed.

Next examine all basement and ground-floor windows—plus any others that could be reached by scaling a tree or porch. To learn about securing points of entry, see pages 384-389.

**Interior defenses** provide you with still another line of protection. An intercom not only lets you communicate with persons at the front door, it can also monitor activities in distant rooms. Alarm systems alert you to intruders and fire. And timing devices turn lights and radios on and off when you're away. More about these on pages 390-395.

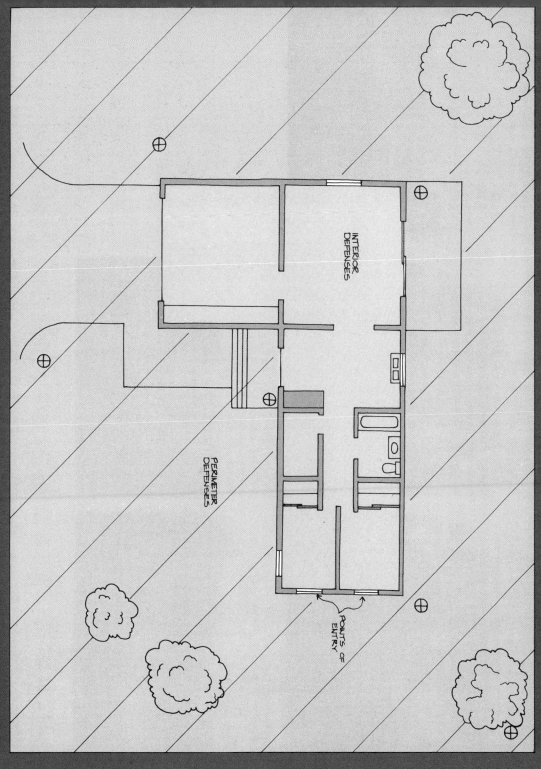

INTERIOR DEFENSES

PERIMETER DEFENSES

POINTS OF ENTRY

# SECURING POINTS OF ENTRY

Security experts agree that there's no such thing as a totally burglar-proof door, window, or even bank vault. Instead, they rate protection according to the amount of time it would take a skilled professional to get in, and these ratings usually amount to a matter of minutes—sometimes seconds.

Fortunately, talented professional thieves like to be well rewarded for their efforts and usually hit only businesses and affluent neighborhoods. Some so-called "amateurs" also can break into almost any home—but if they find yours offers the kind of resistance that takes time to penetrate or attracts attention, most will move on to easier pickings.

You can discourage these housebreakers by beefing up your home's points of entry, as shown here and on the following pages.

## MAKING DOORS SECURE

Door security begins not with a good lock—that comes third—but with the door itself and the frame it fits into. Weak door assemblies can be broken with a single kick, popped open with a jimmy bar, or even, in some cases, pried out—frame and all—from the wall.

Strong exterior doors have solid—not hollow—cores (see page 74); if they're sheathed in metal, so much the better. Unless your home is old or deteriorated, its front and rear entries probably already boast stout doors—but what about those leading to the garage or basement? Too often builders shave costs by installing flimsy units here. To learn about hanging new doors, see page 78.

Next, open each door and examine its hinges. These should be heavy-duty types, well-fastened to the door and frame. Out-swinging hinges pose a special problem because their exposed pins are easily removed. Secure these as illustrated below.

Finally, turn your attention to each door's frame and its exterior moldings. Any gaps here pose an insulation problem, as well as an open invitation to jimmy-bar artists. Replacing an exterior door/frame assembly—they usually come as a single unit—is a job best left to a professional carpenter.

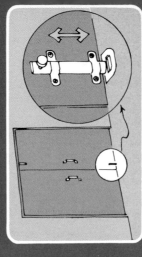

Double doors are vulnerable if both swing freely. Fix one by securing it with bar or barrel bolts top and bottom.

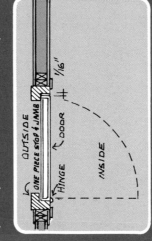

OUTSIDE
ONE PIECE STOP & JAMB
HINGE
DOOR
1/16"
INSIDE

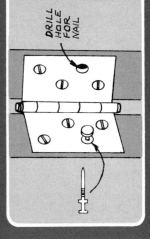

Exterior stop moldings should be part of the frame, not an easily pried-off add-on. Make sure the door fits snugly.

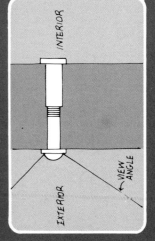

DRILL HOLE FOR NAIL

To secure a door with outside hinge pins, remove one screw from each leaf and drive a double-headed nail into the jamb.

Replace panes in a glazed door with impact-resistant acrylic—or cover its inner face with a single sheet of acrylic.

INTERIOR
EXTERIOR
VIEW ANGLE

A wide-angle peephole viewer added to any solid door allows you to safely see who's calling. Installation is quite easy.

Burglars rarely bother to pick locks. Why take the time when they can more easily slip the latch, strip out the lock innards with a screwdriver, or pry apart the door and frame?

Cheap, easily defeated locks make foolhardy economy. Check the ones on your doors against this rundown.

*Key-in-knob locks* offer about the least protection. Many have a simple, beveled spring latch that can be slipped open by inserting a credit card between the door and frame. Better key-in-knob sets include a separate tongue that can't be opened this way. But jabbing an ice pick or small screwdriver into the keyhole—or breaking off the knob—renders any of these helpless.

*Chain locks* make sense only as supplementary hardware. They let you open a door far enough to see who's there and check credentials. An improperly mounted chain lock can

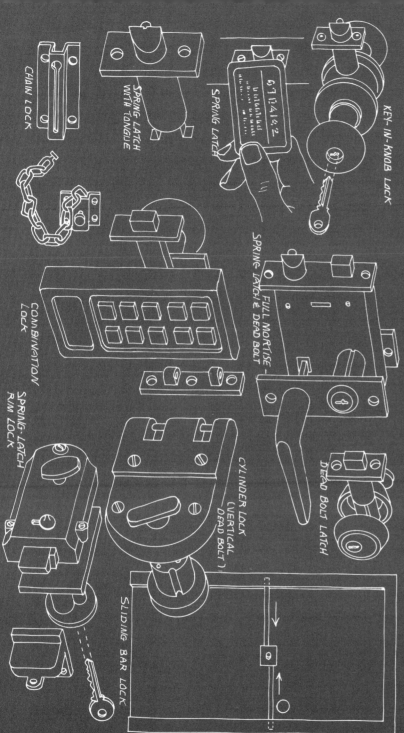

CHAIN LOCK

SPRING LATCH WITH TONGUE

SPRING LATCH

KEY-IN-KNOB LOCK

FULL MORTISE SPRING LATCH & DEAD BOLT

DEAD BOLT LATCH

COMBINATION LOCK

SPRING-LATCH RIM LOCK

CYLINDER LOCK (VERTICAL DEAD BOLT)

SLIDING BAR LOCK

promise false security, though, so see page 386 before installing one.

*Mortised locksets* combine a separate *dead bolt* with an ordinary spring latch. They're so called because you must cut a deep mortise in the door's edge. Note that breaking off the knob or handle does the intruder no good.

*Combination or keyless locks* let you forget about lost keys, and if you think someone knows the combination, you can change it in just a few minutes. Like telephones, they come in pushbutton and dial styles.

*Dead bolt latches* let you upgrade existing installations without the trouble and expense of replacing the old knob set. To be effective, any dead bolt should have at least a one-inch throw into the door jamb.

*Vertical dead bolt cylinder locks* have several things going for them. Their action makes it impossible for an intruder to gain entry by forcing a pry bar between the door and frame, then separating them far enough to disengage the lock—a tactic that works with many horizontal

dead bolt types. Also, you can surface-mount a "drop dead," a much easier job than the tricky carpentry involved in cutting in a full-mortise lockset.

A variation, the *double-cylinder vertical dead bolt* (not shown) has a second cylinder instead of an inside knob. Consider one of these for a door with panes or sidelights—even if an intruder breaks the glass and reaches inside, he can't open the door. One liability: double cylinders make it impossible for anyone without a key to get out in an emergency; some fire codes prohibit them.

*Spring-latch rim locks* mount in the center of a door. Turning the key or inside knob drives long dead bolts into each jamb. These are highly jimmy-resistant, and even with the hinge pins out, you can't get the door open. They look homely, though, and make a clanking noise when you operate them.

*Sliding bar rim locks* are surface-mounted cousins to ordinary mortised spring-latch types—and just about as effective.

## INSTALLING SURFACE-MOUNTED LOCKS

If you don't mind the utilitarian look of a surface-mounted lock, you can beef up a door's security in about half the time it takes to install a mortised dead bolt (see opposite page). Select the vertical-dead-bolt type illustrated below, and you'll get a stronger lock to boot.

All surface-mounted hardware depends upon screws for holding power; if the ones that came with your lock won't penetrate at least halfway into the door, discard them and buy a longer size. For additional strength, coat the screws with glue before driving them into pilot holes.

Double-cylinder locks require special one-way screws that you can turn in, but not out. Otherwise, an intruder could simply remove the assembly. The fittings with a double-cylinder lock generally include an extra set of conventional, slotted screws. You mount the lock and strike with these, make any adjustments, then withdraw the slotted screws and replace them with the tamper-proof versions.

Mount any surface lock about eight to ten inches higher than the existing knob set so you can see and operate it more easily. To do the job, you'll need only a screwdriver, pliers, and a drill—plus a hole saw or a spade bit big enough to bore for the cylinder. These usually

measure an inch or so in diameter. When you drill, work from one side just until the point of the bit penetrates the opposite side of the door, then switch sides to complete the hole. This prevents splintering the door's surface.

In assembling the lock, you'll note that its bolt mechanism and cylinder are actually separate components. So, if you want to re-key, all you need to do is dismantle the unit and take the cylinder to a locksmith. To get a double-cylinder lock off the door, drill out its one-way holding screws.

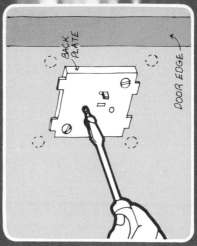

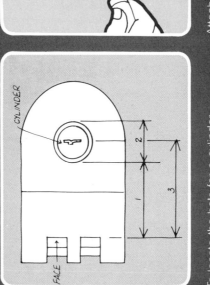

To locate the hole for a cylinder, add dimension (1) to half of diameter (2). This gives the distance from the door's edge (3).

Attach the cylinder's back plate to the inside of the door, then turn screws through the plate into the cylinder.

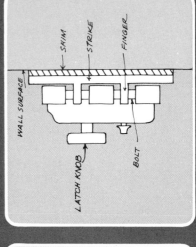

Install a chain lock as shown in this sketch. Mount the retainer with screws long enough to penetrate the jamb studs.

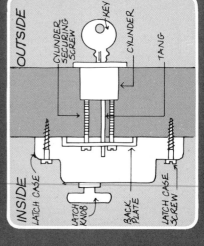

Now just slip the latch assembly over the tang, drill pilot holes, and screw it to the door. The tang gives you a little leeway.

Finally, mount the strike to the jamb. For the fingers to mesh with the bolt, you may need to shim underneath the strike.

386

# INSTALLING A MORTISED DEAD BOLT

Adding a separate dead bolt offers a relatively inexpensive way to back up a flimsy key-in-knob lock set—or provide supplementary security for any door. Though not quite as secure as a surface-mounted vertical dead bolt, a mortised unit looks like an integral part of the door itself.

With modern types, you don't need to hollow out a section of the door, as you must with full-mortise locks (see page 81). Instead, you bore holes through the door's face and edge, then cut a shallow mortise for the bolt's strike plate and a deeper one for the jamb strike, as shown in these drawings.

Measure the thickness of your door before you buy a dead bolt. Some can be adjusted to compensate for varying thicknesses; others require special spacers or a shorter cylinder.

You also can select double-cylinder mortised dead bolts (key-operated from inside as well as out), and units with special "pick-resistant" cylinders. The biggest advantage to these high-security devices is that it's very difficult for a stranger who might have temporary possession of your key to get a duplicate. Usually, you have to write to the manufacturer for extras or provide proof of ownership to a licensed locksmith.

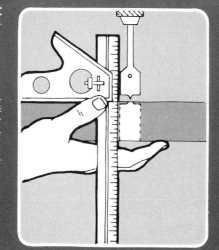

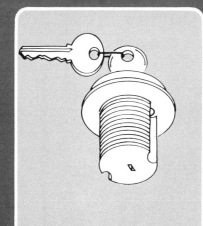

Make sure you drill holes absolutely square. And to minimize damage, drill from one side, then the other, as shown.

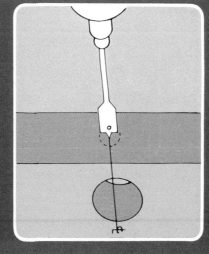

Like most lock hardware, dead bolt sets include a template that helps you accurately locate where to bore holes.

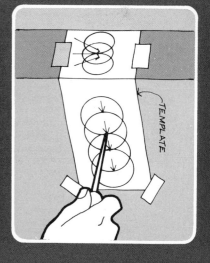

TEMPLATE

Next, bore a second hole—the one the bolt travels through—from the door's edge. Steady the door and keep everything true.

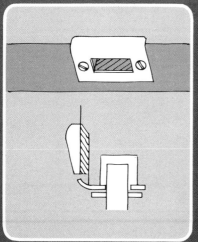

Insert the dead bolt, mark an outline for its strike plate, and cut another mortise, as explained on pages 78 and 413.

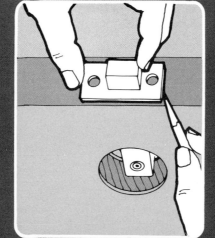

Now you're ready to assemble the components. Most mortised cylinders are threaded, with grooves for set screws that secure it.

Install the strike on the jamb as you would for any door (page 81). Often, you need simply bore a hole for the dead bolt.

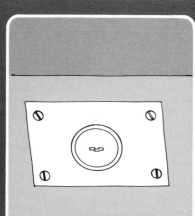

A protective plate around the cylinder makes it more difficult to get at the mechanism. Secure it with jimmy-proof screws.

# SECURING WINDOWS

Intruders usually enter homes through doors, police say. But you can't expect a house-breaker to stand on tradition—especially if you have some windows he can easily force, then climb through without being noticed.

Don't worry about large expanses of fixed glass. The clatter from smashing a picture window would rouse the entire neighborhood. More often, a burglar will concentrate on smaller, operating sashes. First, he'll try to jimmy one open. If that fails, he may use a glass cutter to make a hole big enough for his hand—or he may stick tape to a pane, break it, and quietly pull away the pieces to gain access to the latch.

The solution is to lock your windows in their open as well as their closed positions. Then no one can reach inside and enlarge the opening. The drawings here and on the opposite page show a variety of ways to go, and you may be able to devise others. Just be sure that whatever method you use doesn't block a potential fire exit.

Most homes have a lot of windows. Securing every single one of them could be costly and time-consuming, so start with all sashes—and especially sliding glass doors and basement windows—accessible from the ground. Next, analyze which upper-level windows could be reached via a balcony, garage roof, or tree. And finally, realize that enterprising second-story artists aren't above bringing along a ladder to get at the ones you think are invulnerable.

As you check out each window, make sure it's operating properly. Sashes that wobble when you crank them, that rattle in high winds, or that have to be propped open with sticks offer only token resistance. To learn about making window repairs, see pages 66-69 and 144 and 145.

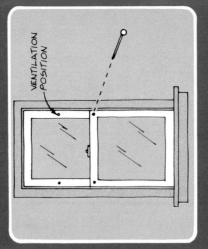

VENTILATION POSITION

You also can secure double-hung windows with holes through the bottom frame and partly into the top. Insert nails or bolts.

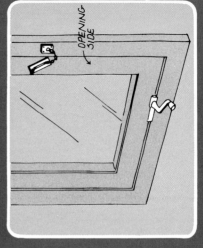

OPENING SIDE

You also can install the same type of chain lock used on doors. Fasten it down with the biggest screws the lock can take.

KEY LOCK

Key locks can't be jimmied, even if the glass is broken. Most also let you lock the window partly open for ventilation.

If a window is big enough to admit a person, leave it slightly ajar, remove the operator crank, and set it out of reach nearby.

SASH LOCK

Ordinary sash locks squeeze out drafts, but offer little security because you can open most of them easily with a knife blade.

10" MAX.

Many casement windows won't open wide enough to admit an adult. To check this, open the window fully, measure as shown.

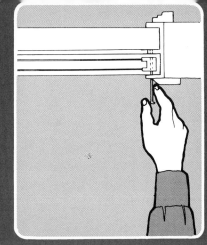

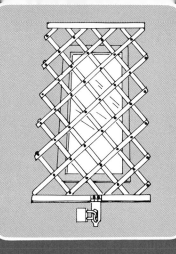

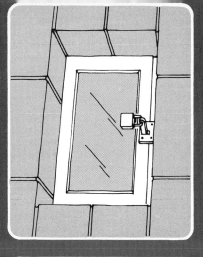

Or secure patio doors with holes that let you slip nails through both the track and the sashes' frames, as illustrated.

Scissors-type gates and hinged iron shutters can be padlocked, yet opened from inside for escape in case of emergency.

Hasps on some basement windows let you secure them with master-keyed padlocks. Keep the key somewhere that's handy.

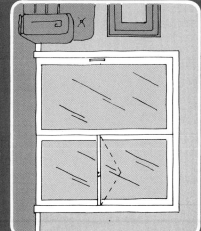

Accessory bars mount to the door frame to jam the windows. They preclude forcing the lock but don't protect against jimmying.

Thieves like sliding glass doors because many can be easily jimmied from their tracks, even when the doors are locked.

If your windows don't have hasps, try driving long screws into a stop on either side. Leave a few inches for ventilation.

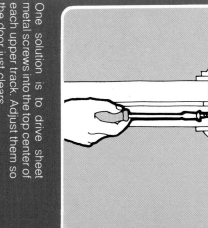

THEN IT WILL SWING FREE HERE

PRYING DOOR BELOW CAN FORCE DOOR UP IN TRACK

Toe-operated locks are the most convenient and least obtrusive. Mount the lock on the casing and drill a hole in the sash.

One solution is to drive sheet metal screws into the top center of each upper track. Adjust them so the door just clears.

Custom-made grills give basement windows a behind-bars look—but they do provide peace of mind in high-crime areas.

# SECOND LINES OF DEFENSE

Without a doubt, secure points of entry provide the primary defense for any home. But smart homeowners don't stop there. They also take care to ensure that the lighting around the perimeter of the house is sufficient to dissuade would-be intruders . . . and that they are protected from within by one or more devices

available today—electronic timers, smoke/fire detectors, fire extinguishers, intercoms, safes, and alarm systems. Incorporating any of these into your security plan will contribute significantly to the safety of everyone involved.

## LIGHTING FOR SECURITY

If you ring your home with exterior lighting and use timers to orchestrate an at-home illusion, most night prowlers will shy away from your place. Yard lights can

be expensive to operate, of course, so be sure to give yourself more control than just a couple of switches. This way, you can brighten only key areas most evenings. More about exterior lighting on page 259, and switches on page 241. Inside, you can duplicate your family's nocturnal lighting habits with one or

more timing devices. You might, for example, program them to let a living room lamp burn until bedtime, then turn on your usual night light. Switches on most timers let you override them when you wish—and one more-expensive version controls several lights on different programs.

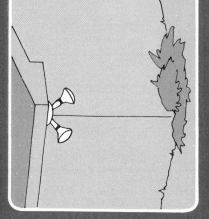

Inexpensive photoelectric cells sense darkness and turn on lights when you're away—but then leave them burning until dawn.

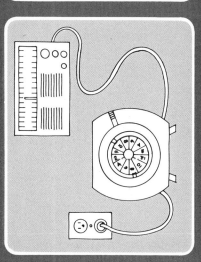

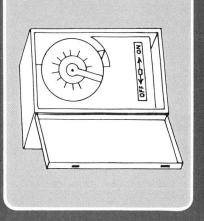

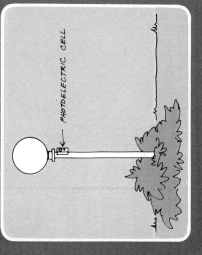

A pair of eave-mounted fixtures at one corner can illuminate two sides of your home. Use 40- or 60-watt bulbs here.

Moderately priced clock timers plug into an electric outlet. You plug a lamp into the timer. Keep the timer out of view.

To make it sound as if someone's home during the day, program another timer to turn a radio on in the morning, off at night.

Or replace a conventional wall switch with this special timer. It turns exterior lights off as well as on at preset hours.

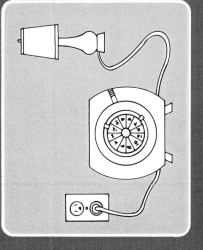

PHOTOELECTRIC CELL

Photocells offer a good way to ensure that strategic outdoor fixtures will come on whether you're home or not.

# CHOOSING AND BUYING SMOKE DETECTORS

Even a relatively small, smoldering fire can fill a house with smoke in a matter of minutes—and smoke claims many more lives than flames. That's why fire experts strongly urge that every home be equipped with at least one smoke alarm to provide the protection you need.

In shopping for smoke detectors, you'll find two types—*photoelectric* and *ionization* units. Photoelectric types include a beam of light and a photocell. When smoke enters the unit, it scatters the light, causing part of it to contact the photocell and trigger the alarm. Slow,

smoldering fires set these off more readily than fast, flaming blazes.

Ionization units employ a radioactive source that ionizes or breaks up the air inside the detector and gives it a small electrical charge. Smoke particles cut down the current flow, which sounds the warning. Ionization detectors respond more quickly than photoelectric units to fast, flaming fires.

Each type has its advantages and drawbacks. Most photoelectric models depend upon house current, which means you get no protection in a power outage or electrical fire and that you must locate them near an electric outlet. The ionization units run on house current, batteries, or both. Besides reacting more

slowly to smoldering fires, they're also more susceptible to false alarms.

For greater peace of mind, consider installing at least one of each—an ionization detector in your bedroom hallway, for example, plus a photocell unit in the main living area. A truly deluxe fire protection system might also include a series of *heat sensors* wired in tandem with each other and with smoke detectors so that all the alarms will sound if just one senses excessive heat or smoke. These require extensive wiring, of course.

# INSTALLING SMOKE DETECTORS

Most smoke detectors take only a few minutes to mount, and come with complete instructions. Knowing where to locate them, though, can help you decide how many you need, and might also have a bearing on the type you select.

Figure on attaching each unit to a ceiling, or high on a wall about eight to ten inches below ceiling level. Analyze your home's air currents and avoid "dead" corners with poor circulation. Also keep detectors away from smoky kitchen, furnace, garage, or fireplace areas.

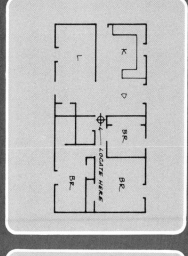

In a single-floor home with bedrooms clustered together, you probably can get by with one unit between bed and living areas.

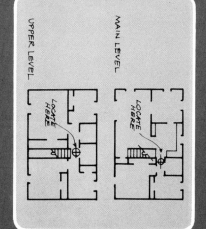

If your sleeping areas are spread out or are on different levels, you'll need at least two. Mount one at the top of the stairs.

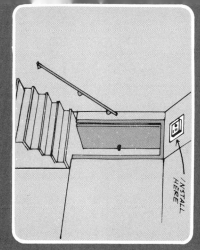

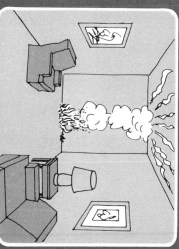

Once smoke reaches the ceiling, it spreads out horizontally. This makes the center of the room the optimum location.

Protect your basement, too. Since smoke and heat always rise, install this detector at the top of the basement stairway, if possible.

## CHOOSING AND USING FIRE EXTINGUISHERS

As you can see from the chart below, a fire in your home can involve any one of three things: combustible solids, flammable liquids, or live electricity. To protect you and your family from harm, arm yourself with a fire extinguisher, preferably one rated to handle all three types of fires (A:B:C).

When shopping for an extinguisher, look closely at its label for the number that indicates the coverage it will provide.

The larger the number, the greater the coverage.

When you get your unit home, read the use directions in front of the whole family; check to be sure the unit is charged, then put it in an easy-to-get-at location. Also check the unit periodically for charge.

### SELECTING THE RIGHT EXTINGUISHER

| Type of Fire | Extinguisher To Use |
|---|---|
| (Class-A) Combustible solids such as paper, wood, fabric, and most plastics. | Pressurized extinguishers that expel water with a gas—or an easily recharged pump type. Foam also puts out Class-A fires. |
| (Class-B) Flammable liquids—grease, oil, gasoline, and kerosene. | Foam, dry chemical, and $CO_2$ extinguishers all work against liquid fires. **Don't use water here**—it will spread the flames. |
| (Class-C) Live electricity. (With power off, these become A or B fires.) | $CO_2$ or dry chemical. **Never use foam or water on electrical fires;** you could suffer a serious shock and/or spread the fire. |

## CHOOSING AND BUYING AN INTERCOM

Of all home security devices, an internal communications system offers the most in flexibility and additional conveniences. With an intercom, you can learn who's at any door from a safe electronic distance, control a buzzer-latch on your garden gate, "look in" on a sleeping baby, and

even pipe music through each room of your house.

Intercoms vary in complexity, but all operate on low-voltage current stepped down via a transformer from your home's electrical system. This makes them relatively easy and safe for a do-it-yourselfer to string together—but you have to pay close attention to the instructions that come with the system. (More about low-voltage wiring on page 247.)

In any but a new house, you'll find the biggest challenge comes when you have to unobtrusively route or fish wires from one room to another (see below and page 238). With flush-mounted components, you also have to cut into walls, but usually you needn't alter their framing.

The master station contains circuitry that lets you call any or all of the substations. It also may include a radio.

Indoor substations often also combined speaker/microphone and switches that transfer from listen to talk modes.

Outdoor substations often also include a button that sounds the door bell or chimes. Others just beep or buzz.

Wiring consists of lightweight, multi-wire cable similar to that used for telephones. Often, you can run it along moldings.

# CHOOSING AND BUYING A SAFE

Before you shop for a home safe, consider what you want it to do. Some protect valuables in a fire, others resist burglars, and a few do both.

Good safes carry UL ratings.

*Fire-resistant* types include fireclay insulation that will keep documents up to one hour at 1,700 degrees F. (Class C), up to two hours at 1,850 degrees F. (Class B), and up to four hours at 2,000 degrees F. (Class A).

These units also must pass tough explosion and impact tests. A fire-resistant safe costs less than any other type. Keep irreplaceable papers in this one.

*Money chests,* secured to your home's structure, generally are smaller in size

and higher in price. UL rates these, too, based on their ability to withstand attacks with tools (TL), torches (TR), and explosives (TX). TR and TX ratings apply primarily to large commercial units. Many but not all home safes are classed TL.

On those that are, the TL rating is followed by a number that indicates how many minutes the safe can resist an attack by an expert who knows the safe. A TL-15 safe, for instance, will withstand 15 minutes of continuous drilling, under ideal conditions.

Note that money chests, though not always lightweight, can be pried out of a frame wall or floor, carried off, and cracked at the thief's leisure. Hiding the safe might remove it from an amateur's attention, but the pros already know to look behind pictures, under throw rugs, and just about any other place you might think of. That's why money chests are

best installed in a masonry wall or floor, or soundly bolted to framing.

*Combination types* include a burglar-resistant money chest inside a fire-resistant safe. These have thick steel walls, an even thicker door, and a combination lock with a "relocking" device. This ensures that if a lock is attacked with tools, it will lock permanently until drilled out. Bolt one of these to the floor, or better yet, set it into a foundation wall. Naturally, you can expect to pay more for a combination safe than you would for either of the other types.

# OUTFITTING A CLOSET FOR SAFE-KEEPING

No closet can offer the metal-clad security of a burglar-resistant safe. But you can beef up one and protect hobby equipment or a valued collection against the grab-it-and-run thieves who commit most household break-ins.

Treat your "safe" closet's door as if it were a point of entry to your home. This means you'll need a solid-core type, carefully fitted to its frame. An extra hinge in the center adds resistance to prying on that side, and since most closet doors swing out, you'll want to secure all hinges with double-headed nails (see page 384).

On the latch side, install a strong dead-bolt lock (page 387). Also protect against prying with a strip of heavy metal attached to the door as shown.

Finally, make room inside for your tools—especially power saws, drills, pry bars, anything an intruder might use to defeat your handiwork.

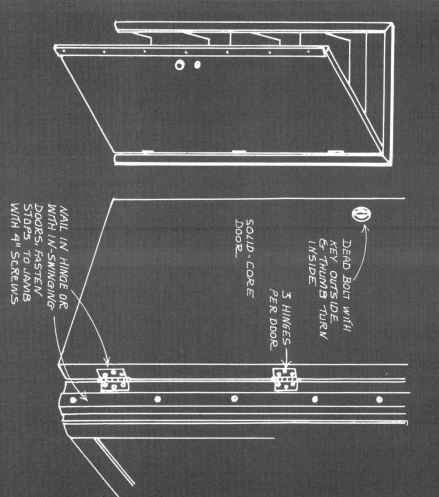

DEAD BOLT WITH KEY OUTSIDE & THUMB TURN INSIDE

SOLID-CORE DOOR

3 HINGES PER DOOR

NAIL IN HINGE OR WITH IN-SWINGING DOORS, FASTEN STOPS TO JAMB WITH 4" SCREWS

393

## CHOOSING AND BUYING AN ALARM SYSTEM

Tripping a home alarm system sets up a din that will send almost any burglar packing. This same pandemonium also can create unpleasant headaches—for your neighbors as well as yourself—if the system frequently malfunctions or if you forget to "disarm" it.

This is why you have to weigh the high deterrent value of good security equipment against its potential for nuisance. Check community ordinances, too; some limit the loudness of an alarm device or the length of time it may sound before automatically shutting off.

If you do decide to investigate electronic security gear, you'll find dozens of different ways to go. All employ a series of *sensors* in a *network* that feeds information to a *master control.* The network may consist of lightweight, low-voltage wire strung from sensor to sensor, or it may use radio beams transmitted from sensors to a receiver in the control unit.

When a sensor tells the master control that something is awry, the control center then sets off the *reporter*—an alarm bell, siren, flashing light, automatic telephone dialer, or maybe a switchboard warning at a central-station security service. Most alarm systems include a time-delay setting so you can get out of the house and back in again without sounding the alarm. More expensive ones also may offer additional circuitry for smoke and heat detectors, and even an intercom.

Different types of sensors "feel," "hear," or "see" an intruder. *Magnetic sensors* do the feeling when a door or window opens; *pressure-sensitive mats* and metal-foil *alarm tape* are also feelers. *Ultrasonic detectors* spread inaudible sound waves to learn if anyone is moving about an area. *Infrared detectors* do the same with light beams.

Sensors, especially motion-detecting devices, can be jittery, so try to get a model with some sort of sensitivity adjustment. Also keep in mind that motion detectors can be easily set off by a night-wandering child or pet, and even certain air currents.

Installing a wired security system can be a lot of work—you have to run wire from the master control to one sensor, then the next, and so on, usually looping back to the master control at the end. Wired units cost less than radio systems, though, and with most, cutting any wire sets off the alarm.

With more-expensive radio networks, you simply install a series of battery-powered transmitters and plug in the control/receiver unit. You don't have to buy a separate transmitter for every point you want to protect; one usually will handle several nearby doors or windows. In installing one of these units, though, you do add a chore to your upkeep routine because the batteries in each transmitter must be checked periodically to make sure you don't have a "dead station."

Security system control units may be powered by stepped-down house current, batteries, or both. Batteries won't let you down in a power failure, but you should have a means of testing them—and the entire system—without activating the alarm.

## ANATOMY OF A HOME ALARM SYSTEM

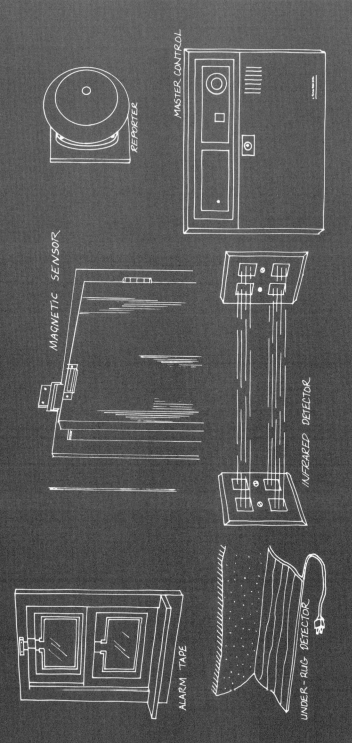

REPORTER

MASTER CONTROL

MAGNETIC SENSOR

INFRARED DETECTOR

ALARM TAPE

UNDER-RUG DETECTOR

Hooking up your own security network can be an easy, one-day job or an ongoing exercise in frustration. It all depends on the care you take in installing its components.

Most problems occur at the magnetic sensors. For these devices to work properly, their two halves must always be in perfect alignment—usually with no less than 1/8 nor more than 1/4 inch between them. To maintain this tolerance, your doors and windows must fit snugly, with virtually no play. Otherwise gusts of wind or a passing truck can set

off the alarm. (To learn about tightening up doors and windows, see pages 66-69 and 75 and 76.)

Alarm circuitry varies somewhat. Most wired systems employ a *"normally closed" circuit* that keeps current moving as long as the unit is armed. Tripping or tampering with any sensor opens the circuit and sounds the alarm.

A *"normally open" system*—typically used with wireless setups—works the other way around. Opening a door or window *closes* the circuit. Understand which type you have, and you can better track down any problems that come up during the installation or later on.

Begin by mounting the control unit in a convenient but inconspicuous location,

such as inside a closet. Next, hook up the bell or siren and test it. Then install and test each sensor before you move on to the next one. This way you know exactly where any difficulty lies.

Do-it-yourself alarm kits include only a few sensors, but you can usually add any number of additional devices. Count up all the doors and windows in your house and you'll see that full protection could require a lot of extra hardware. To save time and expense, consider permanently fixing any windows you don't usually open—such as the upper sashes in double-hung units.

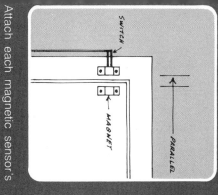

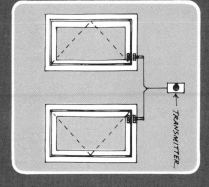

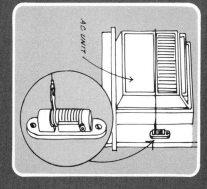

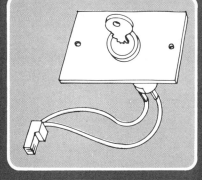

Attach each magnetic sensor's magnet to the door or window sash, its switch to the frame. These must be exactly parallel.

Another magnet on a double-hung sash lets you leave it partway open—but turn off the system when you lift the window.

Top-mounted sensors secure casement windows. These feed into a transmitter that broadcasts to a wireless master control.

Trap switches let you string a wire across several in-swinging windows—or an air conditioner a thief might try to remove.

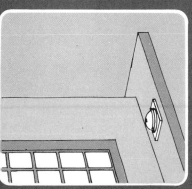

With a key switch, you can arm and disarm the system from outside. Locate this in the garage or at your back door.

Mount an interior alarm unit in a stairway, bedroom hallway, or any other location that will widely broadcast its warning.

If you decide to add an outdoor bell, place it in an inaccessible spot so an intruder can't easily silence it.

**SECTION 4**

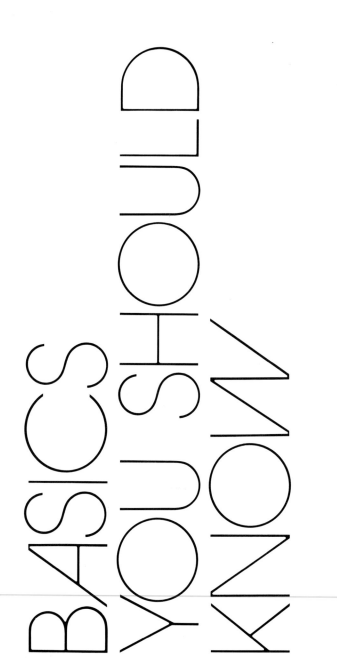

# BASICS YOU SHOULD KNOW

How can you remove a broken-off bolt? What are the true dimensions of a 2x4? Do you need to seal those new shelves before you paint them? Take on any of the around-the-house jobs illustrated in the first three sections and you may find yourself puzzling over questions like these.

For clear, concise answers, refer to the chapters that follow. They present what amounts to an encyclopedia of nuts-and-bolts information about tools, materials, and finishes—everything from how to choose the right nail size to how to paint a house the right way.

And even if you've been wielding tools and brushes for years, "Basics You Should Know" shows how to make your projects go faster and turn out better.

# TOOLS AND TECHNIQUES

"I'm just not handy", people often lament—as if others were born hitting nails squarely and sawing arrow-straight lines. Actually, each of us starts out with no manual dexterity whatsoever, then gradually develops hundreds of skills calling for hand-eye coordination—everything from grasping a rattle to driving a car.

Put aside the myth of your unhandiness and you can master any of the basic techniques shown on the 53 pages that follow. Note that the chapter presents tasks in the order in which you'd use them to complete a project: measuring first, then cutting or drilling, fastening, clamping, and finally, shaping and smoothing. Keep this organization in mind and you can quickly look up an operation when you need to know more about it.

Good craftsmanship begins with quality tools. If, like most homeowners, you already have a few items lying around, now's the time to take a critical look at them. Toss out any that are bent or broken, and those that won't hold a cutting edge—and stay away from the 99-cent bins when you shop for replacements.

What makes a quality tool? Browse through a hardware or home improvement center and you'll discover that most manufacturers offer two or even three different lines. At the bottom are those low-cost "bargains"; don't waste your money on them.

Prices jump sharply at the next level, sometimes called the "homeowner" line.

Here you'll find tools capable of performing most upkeep and improvement tasks. For just slightly more money, though, you can often go first class with professional-quality tools. Sturdily built to exacting standards, these will endure years of hard use. In fact, some companies offer lifetime guarantees.

Take your time in deciding on any tool, and try to learn what it's made of. With metal implements, you'll encounter several different alloys.

*Carbon steel*, a blend of iron and carbon, makes sense for hand tools that don't generate heat. *Low-alloy steel*, which includes some tungsten or molybdenum, is slightly more heat-resistant. For high-speed cutting tools, look for *high-alloy steel*—which has a much higher tungsten or molybdenum content—or *tungsten carbide*. Power saw blades tipped with tungsten carbide will last the average home craftsman for years.

Metal tools differ, too, in the way they're made. *Casting*, the least expensive manufacturing technique, leaves flaws in the metal that make it liable to chipping and breaking. If you'll be hitting or applying muscle to the tool, don't buy the cast type. A broken tool can cause serious injury. *Machined tools*, being much stronger, are suitable for all but the most severe duty. *Forged* or *drop-forged tools* are almost indestructible, an important quality for items such as hammers and cold chisels.

Don't overlook a tool made partly of plastic, either. For instance, fiber glass

handles on hammers and axes are as strong as steel shanks, yet they have even more resilience than old-fashioned wood handles.

Assemble your tool collection a few pieces at a time, starting with the basics, then adding specialty items and power equipment as the need arises. This way you're more likely to invest in quality, and as you gain proficiency, you'll also develop a clearer sense of what tools you'd like to purchase next.

What are the basics? With about a dozen hand tools and an electric drill, you can make most minor home repairs. The hand tools include a measuring tape, straight- and Phillips-blade screwdrivers, pliers, an 8-inch adjustable wrench, a push drill, a 16-ounce claw hammer, a combination square, a crosscut saw, a hacksaw, a nail set, and a couple of chisels.

We've included an electric drill among the basics because its extreme versatility makes it an almost universal tool. (For some of the many jobs you can do with a power drill, see page 422.)

Except for the drill—and possibly an orbital sander for big finishing jobs—confine your initial purchases to hand tools. Power tools will do the same work faster, easier, and sometimes more accurately—but in the hands of someone inexperienced with basic techniques, they can wreck expensive materials in a hurry.

When you do find yourself looking at power equipment, you'll find it falls into two categories—portable and stationary. The portables, such as a saber or circular saw, go directly to the job; with stationary equipment—table or radial arm saws, drill presses, and the like—you must bring the job to it. Use portable power equipment for any around-the-house project up to and including major construction. Usually it doesn't make sense to invest in stationary power tools unless you're planning to pursue woodworking as a hobby.

# MEASURING

Remember, too, that it's surprisingly easy to misread or miscalculate a dimension—and mistaken measurements cost time and materials. That's why modern-day carpenters still follow the old adage "*measure twice, cut once.*"

Simple linear measurements often aren't enough. In many instances, you also need to know whether a situation is *square*, *level*, and *plumb* (see page 401).

Making careful, accurate measurements takes time and concentration. Sometimes you have to climb the ladder again or wriggle into a tight space. And sometimes, especially at first, you'll goof anyway.

Almost any project you'll ever undertake will require a measurement of some sort, so you may as well develop the habit of clipping a steel tape to your belt or tucking a folding rule into your back pocket.

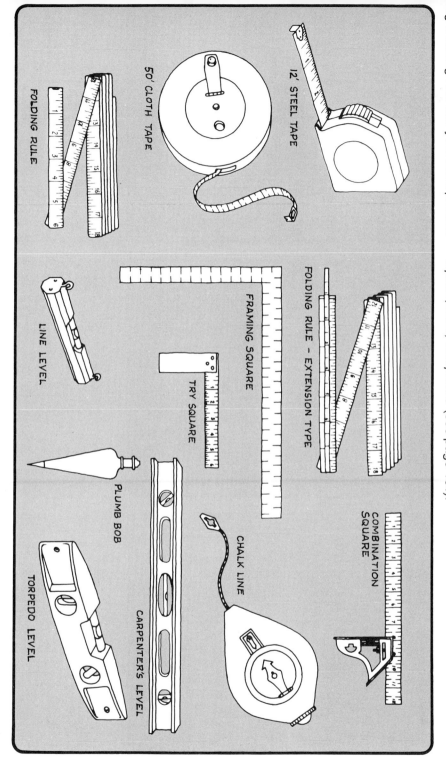

**12' STEEL TAPE**

**50' CLOTH TAPE**

**FOLDING RULE**

**FOLDING RULE – EXTENSION TYPE**

**FRAMING SQUARE**

**TRY SQUARE**

**LINE LEVEL**

**PLUMB BOB**

**CHALK LINE**

**COMBINATION SQUARE**

**TORPEDO LEVEL**

**CARPENTER'S LEVEL**

A 12-foot steel tape has lots of uses. You can make horizontal and vertical measurements, measure inside and outside curves, determine depths (as with postholes), and make round measurements. Look for one with a tape-locking feature. This device holds the tape in position while you make your mark.

If you're laying out a large project—patio, retaining wall, or deck—a 50-foot or longer *cloth tape* or a flexible steel tape with locking device saves time. A *folding rule* has multiple uses, too.

Though used mainly for marking along its edges, it also serves as a square for rough cuts or estimating. This rule, whether wood or metal, also makes short work of measuring across wide and open areas.

Depth and inside measurements are the forte of the extension-type *folding rule*. A metal blade slides out of the rule, as shown, to complete a measurement. This feature comes in especially handy in tight quarters where you can unfold only part of the rule.

A *framing square*, often called a carpenter's square, is designed for squaring almost anything. Its large size makes it ideal for squaring and marking sheet material, such as plywood and hardboard. And you can use it to mark rather than measure cuts and stringers for stairsteps.

For building walls and checking grade slopes, a *line level* is used in combination with a heavy cord. For determining or marking plumb, as when building a wall, use a *plumb bob* suspended by a cord. The *chalk line* shown here doubles as a plumb bob.

A *combination square* often substitutes for a small *try square*, which is used for squaring and marking boards and lumber for crosscuts. Most combination squares include a level in the sliding handle. The square also may be used as a marking and depth gauge and a miter square.

A short *torpedo level* will help you level foundation sills, tools on stands, and shelving. A *carpenter's level*, usually 24 to 30 inches long, provides greater accuracy over broader spans. Bubbles tell both level and plumb.

399

# MAKING ACCURATE MEASUREMENTS

Whether you're building a 50-room castle, a dog house, or just a section of fencing, there's no such measurement as "about." *Measurements must be exact.* Learning this from the outset will save you lots of time, money, and frustration.

An equally important aspect of making correct measurements is starting square. This isn't automatic, by any means—most materials aren't square, especially on ends of boards, dimension lumber, and timbers. However, almost all building materials—wood, concrete, metal, plastic, and so on—have a "factory edge." A factory edge is carpenters' vernacular for the milled edge of the material, which usually is true. Use this edge as a reference point for squaring the rest of the material.

To make truly accurate measurements, you'll need several tools, most importantly a *rule or tape.* This calibrated instrument is available in many forms, but your best bet is an 8- to 16-foot steel tape.

You'll also need a pencil with a sharp point, or better yet, a flat carpenter's pencil (these have flat rather than round lead) to transfer the mark to the material. For even more accuracy, use an awl, which looks like a short ice pick, or a scriber, which resembles a long toothpick. (Many combination squares include a scriber.)

Another important marking device, the *chalk line* has many uses. Its chief function, though, is laying down long straight lines. To use a chalk line, first make sure the line has plenty of chalk on it; don't skimp. Then, tie the line to a nail on one end, and stretch it taut. (You *must* have the line pulled tight to obtain an accurate line.) To make the mark, pinch the line between your thumb and index finger, pull the line out from the surface to be marked, and let the line snap back onto the surface. Snap the line just once.

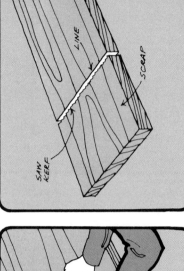

Indicate the cutoff point with the tip of a V mark. A dot is too hard to see; a short line might veer one way or the other.

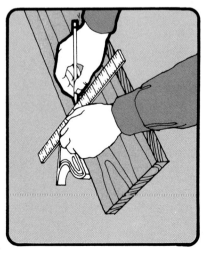

Make cuts on the scrap side of the cutoff line. Otherwise, material will end up one saw kerf shorter than the measurement you want.

Before you make any measurement, check to be sure the end or edge you're measuring from is square. If it isn't, square it up first.

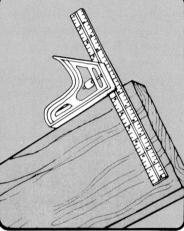

For wider stock, make two or more V marks, then use a straightedge to draw your line. Always measure from the same end.

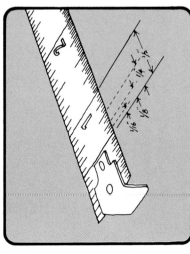

Most stee tapes are graduated in 16ths of an inch along the top edge, and 32nds for the first 6 inches along the bottom edge.

When working with fairly narrow material that has a factory edge, use a square to draw a fine line through the cutoff point.

# USING SQUARES AND LEVELS

The words "square," "level," and "plumb" are familiar to most people, but deceptively so. So before discussing how to achieve each of these desirables, let's define what they are. Square refers to an exact 90-degree relationship between two surfaces. When a material is level, it's perfectly horizontal; when it's plumb, it's at true vertical.

Never assume that any existing construction is square, level, or plumb. Chances are, it's not. To prove this to yourself, lay a level along any floor in your home, plumb a wall section in a corner, or square a door or window opening. Don't be alarmed at the results. Variation is normal in most construction, since houses usually settle slightly on their foundations, throwing square, level, and plumb out of whack. But when you make repairs or additions, you must compensate for the existing errors.

The three tools needed to establish square, level, and plumb are a framing square, a level, and a plumb bob.

A framing square has two legs, each at right angles to the other. The blade is longer and wider than the other leg, commonly known as the tongue. Usually marked in 1/8-inch increments, some squares also have scales so you can align it for rafter and other angle cuts.

A level is used to determine level and plumb. When the work is level—horizontal—or plumb—vertical—the bubbles in liquid-filled glass tubes are centered between the lines drawn on the tubes.

How can you know if a level is accurate? Lay it on a horizontal surface and shim if necessary to get a level reading. Now turn it around. If you don't get the same reading, the level needs to be adjusted or replaced. With some models, you can compensate by rotating the vial.

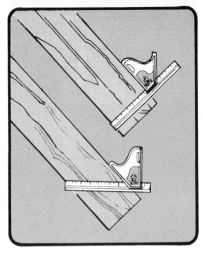

Use a combination square for marking or checking 45- and 90-degree angles and measuring depths. Blade slides in handle.

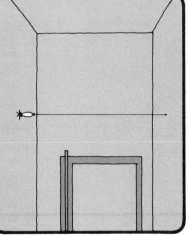

For large jobs, use a framing square—either inside- or outside-measure. When measuring, be sure to read the proper scale.

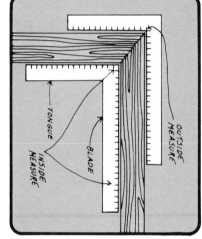

Duplicate angles with a T-bevel. Position the handle along the square edge of the item, then let the blade conform to the angle.

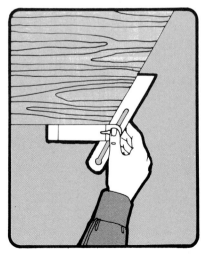

Set a level on the work and adjust the work until the bubble is centered. Some levels have a 45-degree vial.

A plumb bob helps establish plumb. Suspend it from a heavy cord with its point a fraction of an inch from the floor.

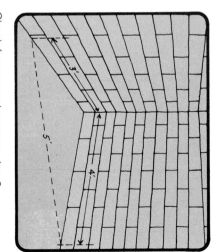

Check for square by measuring 3 feet in one direction, 4 feet in the other. The distance between points should be 5 feet.

**401**

## MAKING CURVES AND CONTOURS

The world of carpentry and home repair isn't all straight lines. You'll also encounter curves, circles, and angles that require special tools, or tools you can readily improvise.

For scribing contours, marking circles, and dividing lines, you'll need a *compass*, which has a sharp point on one leg and a pencil on the other.

Although you can't adjust a compass for large circles, it's more than adequate for marking materials that will be sawed or bored to accept pipes, electrical conduit, lighting fixtures, and so forth.

*Dividers* are used to step off a series of measurements along a scribed line, as shown below. But that's not all. You also can use them to scribe arcs, circles, and half-circles. And for pinpoint accuracy in transferring measurements from a rule to your material, or vice versa, dividers are better than a compass.

To find diameters of materials such as dowel rods, pipe, and conduit, use *outside calipers*. When used in combination with a rule, they also may be used for transferring measurements.

*Inside calipers* will help you measure the inside dimensions of pipe, conduit, or holes in most any material. Simply touch the legs of the inside calipers to the edges of the material, lock the adjusting screw, then measure from one leg to the other with a rule.

While a compass is a basic workshop necessity, dividers and calipers are classified as niceties. The reason: a compass can do the work of all three.

When you invest in a compass, dividers, and calipers, buy tools with adjusting screws rather than those that just "spread" open.

To draw curves and circles, you often can improvise with the bottoms of buckets, cans, coins—almost anything that you know is round, or fairly round.

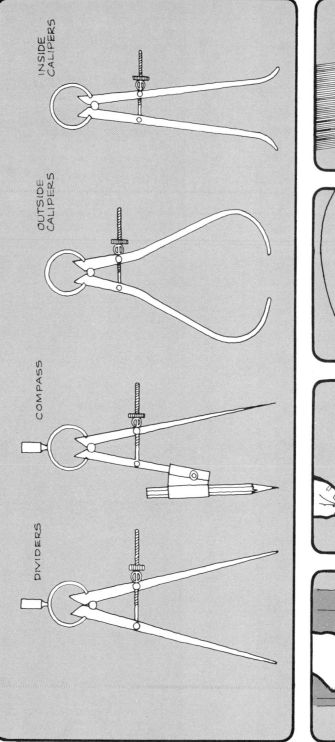

INSIDE CALIPERS

OUTSIDE CALIPERS

COMPASS

DIVIDERS

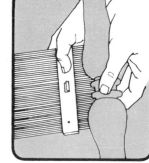

A contour gauge duplicates the profile of three-dimensional surfaces. Lock it in position and use it to mark similar contours.

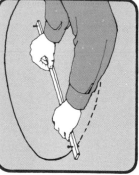

You can improvise a compass by driving nails through the ends of a yardstick or narrow board. Or use a pencil tied to a cord.

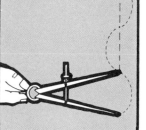

Avoid inaccurate measurements when using a divider by keeping one leg firmly planted when advancing the other.

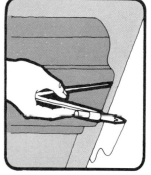

Scribe irregular surfaces by placing the compass point against the original; let the pencil mark the duplicate.

# CUTTING

Precious few repair or improvement projects don't involve cutting materials to fit. This being the case, it just makes good sense to keep the tools that perform so often in tip-top condition. Sharp, rust-free equipment not only makes

cutting easier, but safer, too. (See pages 405, 414, 417, and 423 for sharpening how-to.)

Knives, the instrument from which all other cutting tools evolved, serve do-it-yourselfers in numerous ways. Don't be caught without one in your toolbox.

Saws, actually a series of knives, are complex pieces of equipment. Each of their many teeth has to be kept sharp and in proper "set" so the saw can slice rather

than tear its way through the material you're cutting.

Chisels and planes—both knives with sharpened ends—are first cousins. Keep them sharp with a grinding wheel and/or whetstone for best cutting results.

And last but not least come wire cutters and tinsnips, best described as two knives on a common pivot.

## CHOOSING HANDSAWS

A saw actually makes two cuts, one on each side of the blade. Examine the bottom views below and you'll see that alternate teeth are set at opposing angles. Chipping away material on both sides gives the saw room to move.

The word *points* refers to the number of teeth a saw has per inch. The more points, the smoother (and slower) a saw will cut. Wood-cutting blades typically have 8 to 10 points per inch; metal-cutting blades, usually more.

In selecting a saw, first check out the blade. Quality versions use special alloys for durability; some are chemically coated to slip more easily through cuts, and have precision-ground teeth.

Next, grip the saw's handle and lift it. Does it feel awkward? You'll tire faster

with an uncomfortable tool—and tired hands make more errors.

Finally, be prepared to spend some money on a good-quality saw. A bargain-basement type can chew up its savings in materials in no time.

For most basic home repair and minor improvement projects, you can get by with an 8-point crosscut saw, a keyhole saw, and a hacksaw. As your skills and interests develop, you may want to add some of the other handsaws shown here.

A *crosscut saw* works best across the grain of wood, the most common cutting operation. You also can use a crosscut to *rip* a board with the grain, but you'll make slower headway. More about crosscuts on page 404.

A *ripsaw* cuts best with the grain. Use it for sizing boards to the widths you need, as shown on page 405.

A *coping saw* makes curves and other tight-quarter cuts. Its narrow blade

swivels in the frame so you can operate it from almost any direction (see page 406).

A *keyhole saw* has a narrow, tapered blade that also makes tight-radius cuts. Though it won't negotiate curves as sharp as a coping saw, you can use it on larger, thicker material. Its pistol-grip handle also will accommodate *compass saw* blades, which are slightly broader. More about both on page 406.

A *backsaw* is actually a small, fine-tooth crosscut saw used for cutting miters and other exacting work, as shown on page 406.

A *hacksaw* cuts almost anything—but its specialty is metals. Mount its blade so the teeth slant forward and can do their job on the push stroke (see page 407).

*Pruning* and *bow saws* make short work of limbs and logs. You can also use them to cut posts for fences.

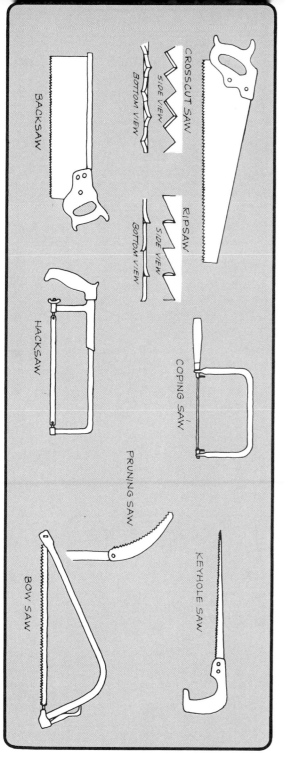

CROSSCUT SAW
SIDE VIEW
BOTTOM VIEW
BACKSAW
RIPSAW
SIDE VIEW
BOTTOM VIEW
HACKSAW
COPING SAW
PRUNING SAW
KEYHOLE SAW
BOW SAW

# USING A CROSSCUT SAW

Whenever you need to cut across the grain of wood, or cut plywood or other sheet goods, a crosscut saw is the right tool to use.

There's a special cutting rhythm in using crosscuts (and ripsaws). It's a sort of rocking stroke that starts from the shoulder and works down through the arm and hand. Very little pressure need be applied to the saw in this cutting motion. In fact, your main task is to steer the blade while it does its work. If you apply pressure to the saw with your hand and forearm, the saw will bind in its kerf, and, sometimes, wander off the cutoff line or "undercut" the wood so the cut edge is not square. These tips are illustrated below.

When cutting plywood, which has two faces, always make sure that the good side is facing you. With the good face up, the grain of the plywood will not tear or splinter as much as when the good side faces down. A piece of tape positioned over the cut line further reduces the possibility of damage. Cut solid woods with their good face up, too.

When working with wood that has lots of sap in it, keep the blade wiped clean with mineral spirits (paint thinner) to prevent the saw from binding in the saw kerf. Also, keep the blade coated with light machine oil or paste wax when not in use.

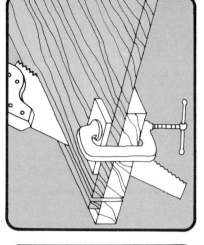

Check work for square often with a square. Put the square's blade against the saw and slide it along the wood as you cut.

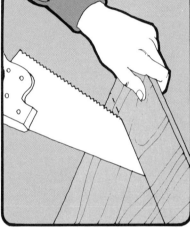

Double-cut narrow cuts by clamping a piece of scrap to the underside of the good piece and sawing through both boards.

The saw stroke rocks slightly, following an arc as your arm swings from your shoulder. Let the weight of the saw do the work.

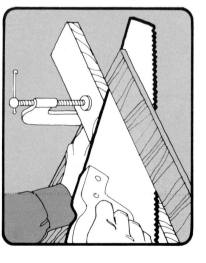

Support the scrap end of the cut. Otherwise, the scrap may splinter the wood as you make your last saw stroke.

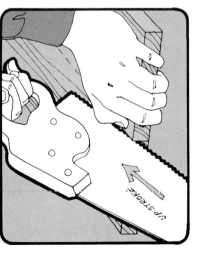

Start the saw in a piece of wood with a gentle upstroke at the heel of the saw. Use the knuckle of your thumb as a guide.

Use a saw guide on long and wide cuts. Clamp a straight board along the cutoff mark; let the edge of the guide steer the saw.

**404**

With teeth resembling small chisels, a ripsaw "rips" wood along its grain. This ripsaw usually has 5½ points per inch, set about one-third wider than the width of the blade so it slides easily, cutting only on the forward stroke.

Because of the configuration of its teeth, a ripsaw cuts fast, making short work of long boards. You'll get rougher edges than you would with a crosscut saw, but these are easily smoothed with sandpaper.

Use the same sawing techniques with a ripsaw as you would with a crosscut saw: a rocking arm motion, with the saw doing most of the work. However, the angle of cut is slightly different for a ripsaw. Hold it at about a 60-degree angle to the work as opposed to the 45-degree angle you'd use with a crosscut saw.

As with any saw, be sure to cut on the scrap side of the cutoff mark—not directly on the mark. This way, the material "fit" you want will not be short; you can remove excess wood with a plane or rasp.

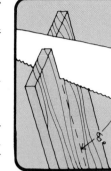

Start the ripsaw in wood at the heel of the saw. When starting the cut, use the knuckle of your thumb to guide the saw blade.

Keep the saw at approximately a 60-degree angle to the work. You'll do this automatically with experience.

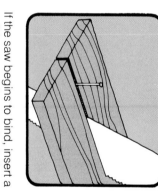

If the saw begins to bind, insert a nail to spread the saw kerf. Keep the blade clean of sap with mineral spirits.

If the saw veers away from the cutoff line, twist the saw blade slightly to steer it back to line. Do not twist too hard.

## SHARPENING A SAW

Good crosscut and ripsaws have lots of cuts in them before they need sharpening. Eventually, though, their chisel-like teeth will dull—especially if you've been working with hardwoods such as maple, oak, or walnut. Cutting through stubborn knots speeds the dulling process, too—as does accidentally hitting a nail or bolt while en route through a board.

If the saw isn't critically dull, "touching up" is what's called for. You'll need a small triangular file.

In touching up saw teeth with a file, first secure the saw in a vise, as shown below. Then, working on one side of the saw at a time, file every other tooth. Now reverse the saw and file the teeth you skipped.

Sharpening ripsaws and crosscut saws differs only in that you file a crosscut saw at a slight angle; with a ripsaw, file straight across its teeth. Be sure to count the file strokes as you sharpen each tooth so that each will be uniformly sharp.

Dreadfully dull saws require more complete sharpening, and usually it's best to turn your saw over to a professional for this. The cost is minimal, and the results miraculous.

Saw teeth also need setting occasionally, too—usually after three or four touch-ups. Setting also is best left to a pro, since a special tool is needed to bend the saw's teeth to the appropriate angle.

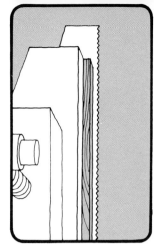

Clamp the saw in a vise between two strips of wood. Leave about ⅛ inch between the top of the strips and the saw teeth.

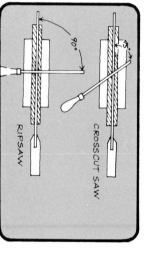

Using a triangular file, sharpen all the teeth that are set toward you. Turn the saw around and repeat for remaining teeth.

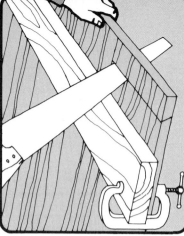

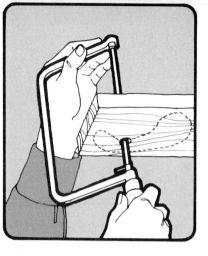

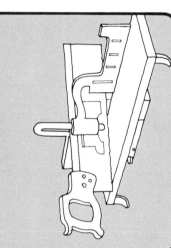

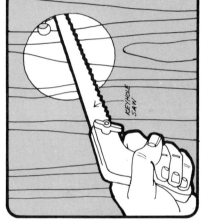

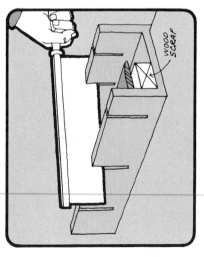

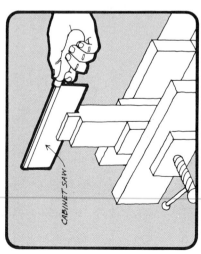

## MAKING SPECIALTY CUTS

Trimming, finishing, and cabinetmaking all call for special cuts—including miters, bevels, curves, rabbets, circles, slots, grooves, and tongues. Most of these jobs center around the simple miter, bevel, and curve cuts illustrated below.

*Miters* are angled cuts, usually made at 45 degrees, although they can be anything up to—and including—90 degrees. Usually you cut miters across the grain of wood, which requires a fine-tooth saw—an 11-point crosscut or, better yet, a *miter saw*. A miter saw, usually with 11 points to the inch, is made with a heavy spine on top of the blade to prevent the blade from bending or buckling. Generally 26 inches long, the miter saw cuts smoothly with the wood grain or across the grain.

A *backsaw*, though similar to a miter saw, usually is shorter and has 12 to 13 points to the inch. When used in a miter box, this saw will produce smooth cuts with or across the grain of wood. It's ideal for cutting special joints needed in cabinetmaking projects, too.

Also similar to a miter saw, a *cabinet* or *dovetail saw* cuts wood joints such as dovetails and mortise-and-tenons. It's smaller and finer, often with a 15-point blade, and is held differently (see below). Miter boxes come in all price ranges. Inexpensive hardwood or plastic versions

guide 45- and 90-degree cuts. With the more expensive metal boxes, you insert the saw into a slotted metal pivot, then set the blade at any angle your project requires.

Other saws you'll need for specialty cuts include a keyhole saw, a coping saw, and a compass saw, which is similar to a keyhole saw but with a somewhat wider saw blade.

For more about making specialty cuts—and the joinery techniques that go with them—see pages 458-463.

To miter wide stock, mark for the cut, make a few strokes, then clamp a strip of wood along the line to hold and guide the saw.

When using any saw in a wooden miter box, place a wood scrap beneath the material to be cut. This prevents damage to the box.

WOOD SCRAP

Metal miter boxes provide greater accuracy and let you cut almost any angle. Always use a miter saw or backsaw with this tool.

KEYHOLE SAW

To make inside cuts, first drill a hole, then insert the keyhole saw blade. A compass saw does the same job on larger circles.

CABINET SAW

Cabinet saws cut tenons, rabbets, dadoes, and similar joints. The wide blade helps you keep the saw square to the cut.

To make an inside cut with a coping saw, drill a hole, remove blade from the frame, insert blade in the hole, and reassemble.

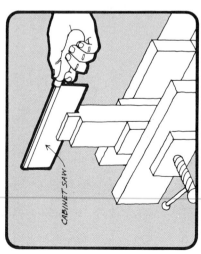

One of the most efficient tools you'll ever own, a hacksaw is a basic hand tool that, with the proper blade, can cut almost any material. It's easy to use as well as inexpensive to buy.

The blade you need for a given job depends on the type of material you're cutting. Generally, the thicker the metal being cut, the coarser the teeth should be. Most blade packages specify the material the blade is designed to cut.

Mount a hacksaw blade in the frame so the teeth slant forward. Blades usually are marked with arrows that indicate the direction the teeth must point.

The trick to using a hacksaw is to keep as many teeth on the work as possible. Apply hand/arm pressure on the forward

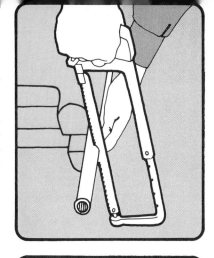

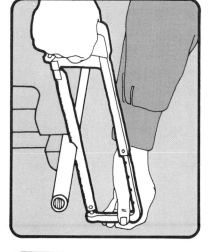

stroke, little or no pressure on the backward stroke. Make smooth, even strokes with one hand on the handle of the saw, the other on the front of the frame. This two-handed grip is necessary to apply even pressure along the length of the blade.

Make sure blades are rigid in the hacksaw frame by tightening the wing nut, but don't apply too much pressure. Also, if you break a blade while cutting, it's best not to insert a new blade in the old kerf. Instead, turn the work around and start again. A new blade may jam in an old kerf.

---

To start cuts in metal, lock the work in a vise, then make several short forward strokes, using the knuckle of your thumb as a guide.

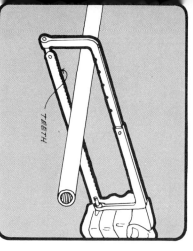

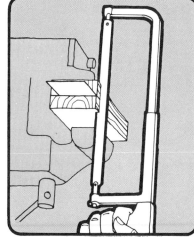

If possible, always use two hands on the saw. Do not apply pressure on the backstroke or you'll quickly dull the blade.

Keep at least two teeth on the work at all times—more if possible. The flatter the angle, the better the saw will cut.

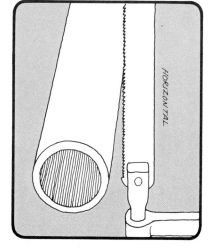

---

In tight situations, turn or reverse the blade in the frame. For angle cuts, mount the work in a vise so you can hold the saw vertically.

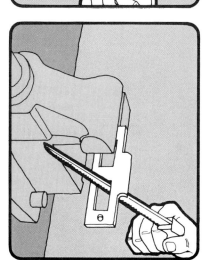

Clamp thin materials such as sheet metal between two pieces of wood. Cut all three at the same time, sawing square to the work.

A metal-cutting blade in a multi-purpose compass saw goes into places too cramped for a conventional hacksaw.

# CHOOSING PORTABLE POWER SAWS

Portable power saws will do any job that handsaws will do. And naturally, with power you can get the job done faster, easier, and more accurately. But don't make the mistake of abandoning your handsaws entirely. Rather, view portable power saws as extensions of your handsaws. There will be times in your home maintenance and improvement projects when a handsaw will be the *only* tool to use.

When trying to decide whether to buy portable power saws or stationary ones, consider the following: portable saws are much less costly. In addition, you can take them to the job site, providing there's power available. They're also easy to store. On the other hand, stationary power saws are more accurate and sometimes more versatile than their portable counterparts.

The difference really comes down to the type of work you want the equipment to do. If repairs and improvement projects are your prime concern, portable power saws are your best buy. If you

enjoy cabinet- or furniture-making, stationary saws make more sense.

Your first buy in a portable power saw should be a variable-speed *jigsaw* or *saber saw.* Follow this purchase with a *circular saw* with enough blade capacity (usually 6½ inches) to handle a 45-degree cut in two-inch-thick materials. *Reciprocating saws* and *chain saws,* though handy to own, aren't necessary for most of the repair and improvement projects you'll be doing.

## Are Power Tools Safe?

Very simply, power tools are as safe as you make them. To make your dealings with power equipment happy ones, follow these precautions.

First, dress appropriately for the job. Don't wear loose clothing, floppy shirt tails, rings, or your watch. Do wear safety glasses for protection.

Tool maintenance is part of tool safety, too. Make sure that electric power cables are in good repair, and use the grounding plug sold with the tools (purchase a plug adaptor if your outlets aren't the three-prong type). If the tool isn't self-lubricating, follow the manufacturer's

lubrication schedule. Keep blades sharp—dull ones are dangerous.

Also be sure to hold the power cord in your free hand. This keeps both cord and hand away from the blade.

Never leave any unattended power tool plugged into the power source. And lastly, when you store your power equipment, put it out of reach of children

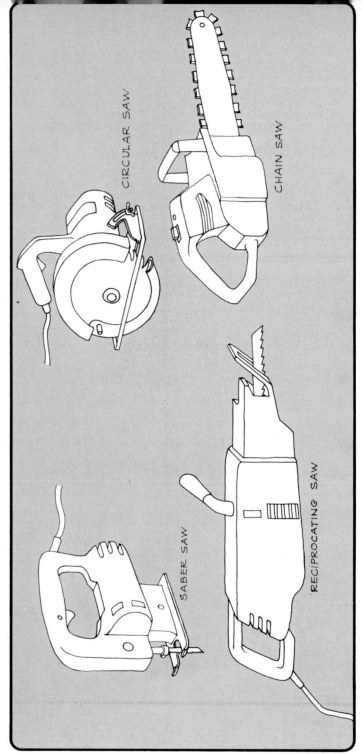

CIRCULAR SAW

CHAIN SAW

SABER SAW

RECIPROCATING SAW

Saber saws (sometimes called portable jigsaws) make straight, angle, curve, and hole cuts in boards and sheet materials.

Circular saws make straight and angle cuts, and large pocket cuts (see page 410). For most jobs, a 6½-inch blade size is sufficient.

Reciprocating saws are the heavy-duty cousins of saber saws. A variable-speed model cuts metals and lumber.

A chain saw is lawn and garden equipment, although you can use it for cutting timbers and fence posts. A gasoline model is best.

# USING A SABER SAW

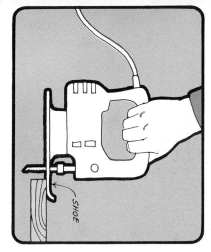

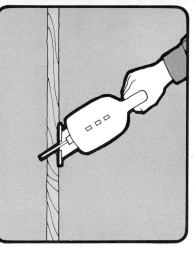

Because of its versatility, a portable electric saber saw (or jigsaw, as it's sometimes called) is an important tool for home repair and improvement jobs. Crosscut, rip, miter, bevel, and cut holes—this lightweight saw does it all in almost any material: wood, paneling, drywall, plastic laminate, hardboard, thin metal, and ceramic.

Of course, you'll need the appropriate blade for the job: coarse-tooth blades for boards and dimension lumber; fine-tooth blades for paneling and plastic materials; hacksaw blades for metal; carbide-tipped blades for ceramic tile and glass; and a knife blade for vinyl tile, leather, rubber, and soft plastic materials.

Through a gear arrangement, the rotary power from the saber saw's motor is converted into stroke power. The blade operates in an up-and-down motion, cutting on the upstroke.

Only one hand is needed to guide the saber saw through its bag of cuts, which the saw performs easily. Most cuts can be made quickly and accurately (a rip fence accessory comes in handy). A variable-speed feature lets you control the strokes-per-minute of the blade which enables you to make smooth cuts in most any material.

Before you try out a saber saw for the first time, carefully read the instructions that came with it—and keep these operating tips in mind:

● Although saber saws have powerful motors, two-inch-thick material is a big bite for the saw blade to chew. Push the blade through the stock slowly without forcing it. If you feel the motor getting hot, run it without a load for a while. After the blade cools, check its sharpness—a dull blade taxes the motor heavily.

● Always start the motor before you contact the material to be sawn. If you don't, you'll break the saw blade and probably damage the material.

● Since the saber saw cuts on the upstroke, turn the "good" face of paneling and expensive hardwoods downward when you make the cuts.

SHOE

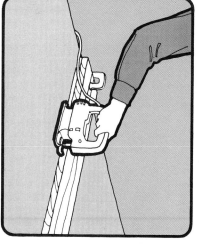

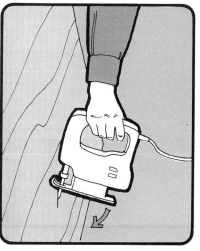

To start a cut, rest the shoe as shown, with the blade ¼ inch away from the wood. Start the saw and move it into the stock.

To ensure straight cuts, clamp a straightedge to guide the saw along the cutoff line; be sure that you saw on the line's scrap side.

A tilting base makes bevel cuts easy. Ease the blade into the cut, and don't lift the saw out of the cut until the blade has stopped.

To make a *plunge* or *pocket cut* without drilling a starter hole, tilt the saw forward, start the motor, and tilt it backward.

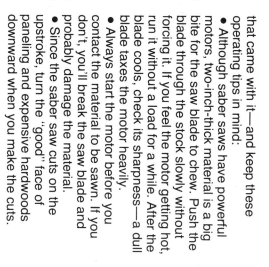

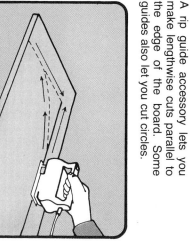

A rip guide accessory lets you make lengthwise cuts parallel to the edge of the board. Some guides also let you cut circles.

To cut corners, run the saw to the corner, back it up, then cut an arc to the other line forming the corner. Finish as shown.

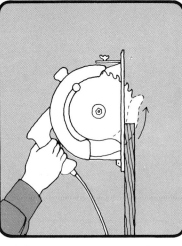

# USING A CIRCULAR SAW

Squeeze the trigger of a portable electric circular saw and you know right away that you've got a handful of powerful wood-cutting machinery. In fact, a circular saw can rip and crosscut materials just about as fast as you can move your arm.

By design, this power equipment won't do the jobs a saber saw will, but the cuts a portable circular saw makes will trim your working time to a minimum.

Ripping long boards and paneling is the job a circular saw does best. It also zips through crosscuts with accuracy, and if you want, it can make miter cuts, bevels, and pocket cuts in paneling and other sheet materials. With special blades, you can even cut metal and masonry units, such as bricks, and concrete and cinder blocks.

Circular saws come in several sizes, the largest of which is a 10-inch model. The smallest, a 4½-inch version, is called a "trim saw." The size denotes the largest blade the tool will accept.

For most around-the-house chores, you're best off buying the 6½- to 7¼-inch size. Be sure the one you buy has an automatic blade guard. This guard slips back as the saw blade enters the wood, then snaps closed after the cut is made. Other desirable saw features include a saw blade depth adjustment that allows you to make shallow cuts such as grooves; a baseplate that may be adjusted for miters and bevels; and a ripping fence accessory.

When operating a portable circular saw, keep a strong grip on the saw handle as cuts are being made. You do not have to force the saw through the work, since the motor is plenty powerful. But if you do find yourself forcing the cut, you'd better stop the saw and check the blade for sharpness. Also make sure it's the right blade for the material you're cutting.

And, for safety's sake, *never* leave an unattended saw connected to power.

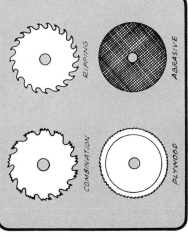

At the end of the cut, be prepared to support the saw's weight. Before you set the tool down, be sure the blade guard is over the blade.

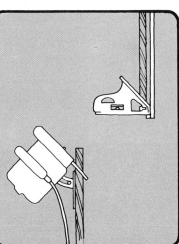

Miters are easy to cut, but always double-check them with a combination square. The gauge on your saw may not be accurate.

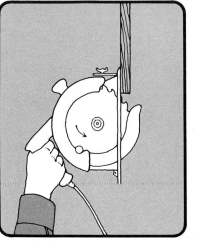

Set the saw blade just deep enough to cut through the piece. Make sure the motor is at full power before entering the work.

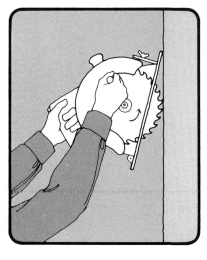

Common saw blades: a combination blade for ripping and crosscuts; a ripping blade; plywood and abrasive blades.

To make a pocket cut, set the saw to the desired depth. Retract the guard, tilt the saw forward, start the saw, and lower the blade.

# CHOOSING STATIONARY SAWS

The precision cutting that furniture and cabinetmaking projects demand is the job stationary power saws do best. This equipment is for the serious hobbyist, and is not required (although it's helpful) for most routine home improvement and repair projects.

If you're thinking about buying a stationary saw, first determine if you have enough room for one. Stationary saws require plenty of working room, since materials such as plywood have to be maneuvered around and into the saws. Access to the workshop also is important so you can get materials in and out.

In comparing work space needed, the radial arm saw needs less than a table saw because you can place it along a wall. Leave plenty of space on either side for ripping, though.

The table saw, on the other hand, needs space on all four sides. Most have locking casters so you can store the saw in an out-of-the-way place, then roll it into the center of the workshop when needed.

Band saws need space on only three sides, as do jigsaws, and like table saws, they have locking casters to permit movement.

Which type of stationary saw you choose is pretty much a matter of personal preference. Reading the following information should help you decide which one is right for you.

A radial arm saw is a truly flexible power tool. With special attachments, you can use it as a shaper, sander, planer, jointer, and drill. One feature that sets it apart from other stationary saws is that for most cuts, you pull the blade across the work. The exception to this is when ripping material. When doing this, lock the head and feed the material into the blade.

A table saw can make a variety of cuts, too, including crosscuts, rips, miters, compound miters, grooves, bevels, coves, and moldings. With special blades, you also can cut metal, plastics, masonry units, and stone. You can even convert a table saw into a disc sander and grindstone. In cutting and forming any material, you must move the material into the cutting blade.

A jigsaw, which has a reciprocating blade just like its portable counterpart, will handle almost any material—wood, metal, and plastic—with special blades. Use it for straight cuts, curves, keyhole cuts, and tight-radius cuts. For most do-it-yourselfers who do a lot of delicate work, a jigsaw is a better purchase than a bandsaw, which is more of a production-type tool for cutting thick material.

A bandsaw has a continuous blade that loops around two wheels. It will make straight cuts, miters, bevels, and radius cuts. With special blades, the saw also will cut metal and plastics. For tight-radius cuts, substitute narrow blades for wider ones.

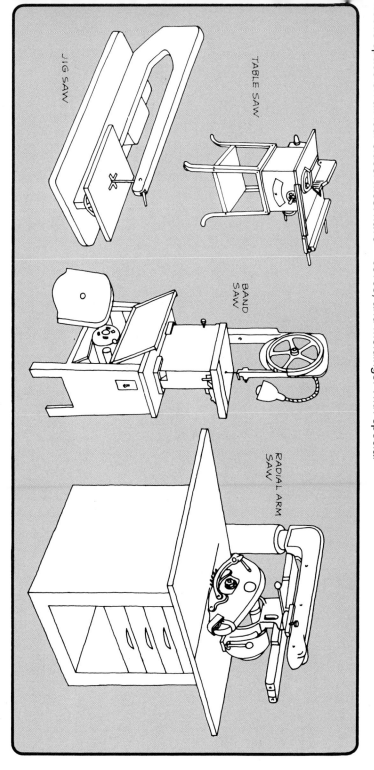

JIG SAW

TABLE SAW

BAND SAW

RADIAL ARM SAW

A table saw has a 7½- to 12-inch blade capacity. Typical is 10 inches. A variety of blades and accessories gives it flexibility.

The jigsaw you buy should have big capacity (distance from blade to support post at rear). This saw is a fairly safe tool.

A band saw slices through thick materials with ease. Most models have a tilting table and rip fence. Blades are inexpensive.

A radial arm saw has a stationary table and a moving cutting head. It's ideal for cutting miters, dadoes, rabbets, and grooves.

# CHOOSING CHISELS

Chisels get beat out of a lot of wood- and stone-working jobs these days because new tools and manufacturing techniques have replaced them. But there are some specialized projects that other tools and techniques still can't do as well, which makes these tools essential in your home workshop. Some of these jobs include shaping mortises, cutting and smoothing wood joints, removing crumbling mortar, and breaking bricks, blocks, and stones.

Don't waste your time price-shopping for chisels. You'll find these tools so inexpensive that your budget can afford top-line quality and features.

*Wood chisels* cut wood. Don't use them as screwdrivers, paint paddles, scrapers, or wire cutters. Most wood chisels manufactured today feature metal-capped handles that you can strike with a hammer or wooden mallet. If the chisels you own don't have this feature, strike them only with a wooden mallet or plastic hammer.

For your chisels to cut properly, you must keep them sharp. Not only can dull chisels ruin expensive materials, they also can slip or skip and injure you. Keeping chisels sharp is an easy job. See page 414 for sharpening how-to.

Proper storage is another must. Keep your chisels in plastic sleeves hung up on a tool board, or wrap them in cloth that's been lightly treated with household oil. Don't toss chisels into a drawer or tray with other tools; this dulls and nicks cutting edges.

*Cold chisels* cut or form metal, bricks, concrete and cinder blocks, and stone. Although plenty rugged, the chisels' cutting edges eventually will dull. When this happens, sharpen them with a grinding wheel.

Cold chisels are designed to be struck with a baby sledge—not a carpenter's hammer. When using a cold chisel, always wear safety glasses.

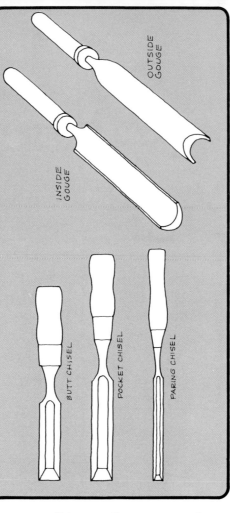

## Wood Chisels

*Butt chisels* are about six to eight inches long. Use them to remove lots of wood or to work in tight spots.

For most chiseling jobs, *pocket chisels* are a good buy. These tools are from 9½ to 10½ inches long and are balanced perfectly for hand or hammer operation.

For very fine work, you'll need *paring chisels*. These thin-bladed chisels are operated only by hand.

*Gouges*, which are rounded for outside and inside cutting, can remove a lot of wood fast, and may be used for forming.

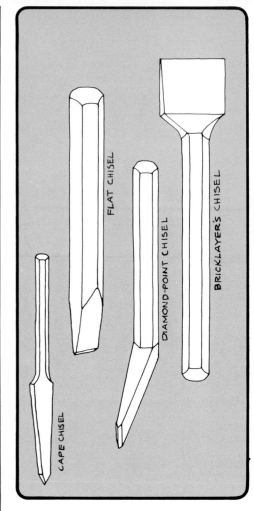

## Cold Chisels

Several whacks with a baby sledge hammer and cold chisels warm up fast to cut rusted bolts, rods, thin bar steel, bricks, blocks, and stone.

A *cape chisel* normally is used to gouge metal. A *flat chisel* may be used to cut bolts and screws; its wedge action will shear metal, too. A *diamond-point chisel* makes V-shaped cuts in metal; it also can be used to groove metal.

Use a *bricklayer's chisel* to cut and form masonry and stone materials. You can buy them in a variety of widths.

Though somewhat of a lost art these days, wood chiseling is one of those techniques that's not only useful, it's fun. With a light hand and some practice, you can learn to use wood chisels to great advantage.

You'll use a chisel more for cutting mortises than for any other repair or replacement job—see page 78. (Mortises are recesses in wood that are cut to fit pieces of hardware such as hinges.) But you can also call on these workhorses to remove excess wood from grooves and joints, shape joints, form inside and outside curves in wood, even trim wood to close-fitting tolerances.

Chisel cuts are made much like knife cuts—a paring action that produces

shavings. And whenever possible, the work is done by hand without a hammer or mallet. One hand provides the cutting force; the other hand guides the chisel and provides downward pressure.

Since both hands are used on a chisel, it's important that the work be locked tightly in a vise or clamped so it doesn't move when you apply pressure. If you're mortising a door for hinges, you can butt the top and/or bottom of the door against a wall to prevent movement.

What's the secret to using a chisel? Learning to make shallow cuts with it! To do this, the chisel must be razor sharp with no nicks or burrs along the finely honed cutting edge.

For long cuts across the grain, start out with the chisel at an angle. Then ease the handle downward as it cuts.

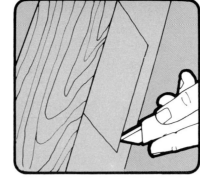

Mark, then score the outline of the mortise. Scoring prevents the wood grain from splitting at the edge of the cut.

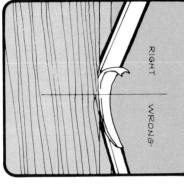

Make a series of cuts to the depth of the mortise. Hold the chisel as shown, with its bevel facing the direction of the cut.

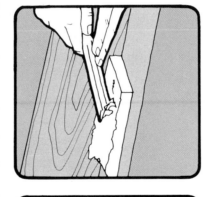

If the mortise extends to the edge of the wood, pare out chips from the edge with the bevel facing up. Use hand pressure only.

RIGHT
WRONG

When chiseling parallel to the wood's grain, cut with the grain rather than into it. Otherwise, you may dig too deep into the work.

For deep mortises, first bore a series of holes within the outline of the mortise. Then chip out the remaining wood.

Use a baby sledge to drive cold chisels. And always wear a glove to protect the chisel hand against injury. Misses hurt.

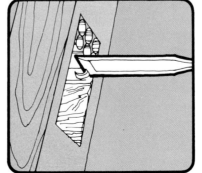

Start masonry cuts with a series of vertical blows to outline the cut. Then hold the chisel at an angle to chip out the scrap.

# KEEPING CHISELS SHARP

Squint your eyes and look down the cutting edge of a wood chisel and you can tell immediately whether or not it needs sharpening. A dull edge looks "flat" and reflects light. With a sharp edge, you won't see this reflection. If you don't trust your eyes, give a chisel the paper test for sharpness, as shown below.

You can sharpen chisels using any one of the following techniques: whetting, filing, or grinding. Whetting is done with a whetstone. Filing and grinding are done with a single-cut file or a motor-driven grinding wheel. Don't feel compelled to purchase a grinding wheel just for this job. The chisel will sharpen equally well with a whetstone or file.

Bevels on most wood chisels are at 25 degrees (15 degrees on paring chisels). But you really don't have to be too concerned about the specific angle when you sharpen chisels. Rather, follow the bevel's angle on the whetstone, grinding wheel, or file. (Notice that the bevel is a little longer than twice the thickness of the blade.)

If desired, you can buy a sharpening jig that will hold the chisel and maintain the bevel at the proper angle to the whetstone or grinding wheel. With a file, you'll have to rely on a keen eye and a steady hand to maintain the angle.

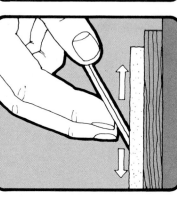

Check the edge under light. A sharp edge (A) won't reflect light. A dull edge (B) will. File or grind a nicked edge (C).

To test for chisel sharpness, shave a piece of paper at a slight angle. The blade should slide right through paper.

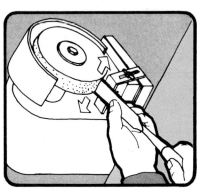

After the cutting edge is sharp, turn the chisel over and hone its flat side to remove burrs. Hone with an elliptical motion.

Whet a chisel's cutting edge by holding it at an angle slightly steeper than the bevel. Keep the stone moist with oil.

Now hold the file at the same angle as the bevel. File diagonally, working slowly and evenly. Remove burrs with a whetstone.

To regrind a bevel, set the tool at the proper angle. Now move the edge along the wheel. Go easy or you'll "burn" the edge.

To remove nicks with a power grinder, keep the chisel flat against the wheel. Move the chisel from side to side.

For badly nicked or worn edges, remove any deep nicks by filing as shown. Use a single-cut file. Clamp the chisel in a vise. Re-

# CHOOSING AND USING A ROUTER

If not the most versatile tool made, the router certainly comes close. Basically an electric chisel, the router does so many jobs it's almost scary. It planes, saws, and shapes; makes grooves, mortises, dovetails, and other joints; trims edges off plastic laminate; cuts dadoes for strong shelving; makes pocket cuts in sheet materials; and much more.

Although a router's immense power enables you to do most jobs in a jiffy, you can get along nicely without one. Chisels, saws, files, and planes can accomplish the same work.

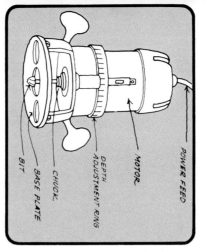

- POWER FEED
- MOTOR
- DEPTH ADJUSTMENT RING
- CHUCK
- BASE PLATE
- BIT

How much a router costs depends on the features it has and the accessories you buy for it. At the outset, you can get by with a router and the basic bits along with an edge-cutting guide or (better) a router table. Then, as your budget allows, you can add the specialty bits—those needed for fancy joints and moldings (see below for some of the bits).

The more power a router has, the more jobs it will do faster. You can buy routers with ¼ to more than 1 horsepower, and that run at 25,000 rpm to more than 30,000 rpm. The motor direct-drives a spindle to which the bit is attached. The base of the unit serves as a guide and a collar near the motor housing lets you adjust the depth of cut.

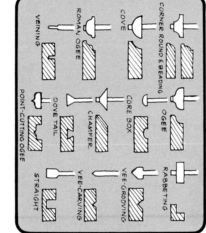

- CORNER ROUND & BEADING
- COVE
- ROMAN OGEE
- VEINING
- OGEE
- CORE BOX
- DOVE TAIL
- CHAMFER
- POINT-CUTTING OGEE
- RABBETING
- VEE-GROOVING
- VEE-CARVING
- STRAIGHT

You usually operate a router holding onto it with both hands and letting a guide do the steering. However, if you have a router table, the router remains stationary, so you simply feed material into it.

Since a router is powerful, be very careful to keep your hands away from the spinning bits. They're razor-sharp and cut fast. Also, when changing bits, remember to disconnect the power cord and lock the bits securely to the drive shaft. And, as with any power tool, never leave a router connected to its power source.

---

A router is a simple tool. The motor is connected to a chuck that holds the bit. A base plate keeps the tool square.

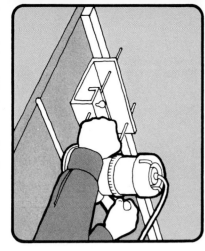

A template guide fastened to the router's base allows you to follow any shape template you've cut. Use plywood for templates.

---

Whatever shape you want to cut, there's a bit to accommodate you. Intricate cuts sometimes require two or more bits.

- FIXED POINT

A trammel point guide lets you cut perfect circles or curves. Remember to make your cuts in a counterclockwise direction.

---

When setting up any job, remember that the bit spins clockwise and cuts best if the router is fed from left to right.

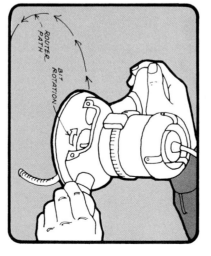

- ROUTER PATH
- BIT ROTATION

---

**415**

## THREADING WITH TAPS AND DIES

Stripping the threads in a casting or rod usually leads to one of those "what-do-I-do-now?" panics. A couple of machinists' specialties—a *tap* for cutting female threads, or a *die* for making male threads—can get you going again. You "tap out" the casting to the next larger size, or "die cut" the rod to the next smaller one, then reassemble with a new bolt or nut.

Though not indispensable in a home tool kit, taps and dies greatly extend your metal-working capabilities, letting you join metals, or join to metals, in situations

where nuts and bolts wouldn't work. And a close relative, called a *screw extractor*, offers a quick way to remove a bolt or screw when you've sheared off its head (see below).

Larger dies will also cut threads in galvanized steel, brass, or iron pipe (see page 287). You can usually rent these costly devices, along with a large handle to turn the die and a special vise to hold the pipe.

Taps come in three types—*taper* (by far the most common), *plug*, and *bottoming*. Taper taps are pointed at the end, making them easier to get started. Plug taps have less taper; bottoming taps, no taper at all. To thread a "blind" hole (one that doesn't go all the way

through the metal), you might start out with a taper tap, switch to a plug tap, then finish the job with a bottoming tap. You drive the taps by turning them with a special wrench, as shown below.

For dies, you can choose among *solid*, *adjustable*, and *hexagonal* versions. Solid dies, the least expensive, cut standard-size threads up to ½ inch. Adjustable dies include a screw you can turn to make threads slightly larger or smaller than standard. Hexagonal dies can be turned with an ordinary wrench rather than the *die stock* necessary for the other types (see below).

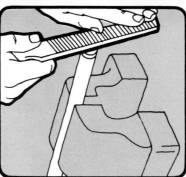

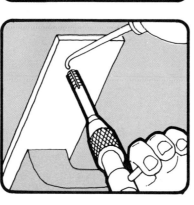

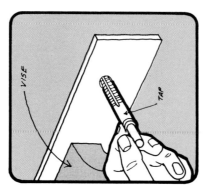

To tap a female thread, drill a hole the size specified for the tap. Then insert the tap and square it to the metal.

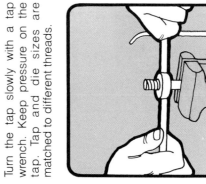

Turn the tap slowly with a tap wrench. Keep pressure on the tap. Tap and die sizes are matched to different threads.

Every two to three turns, back the tap out of the metal to clear any chips from the threads. Apply cutting oil to ease cutting.

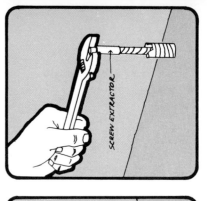

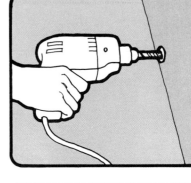

File or grind a bevel on the end of the metal before you start to cut male threads. Remove just enough metal for the die to seat.

Screw extractors tap their own threads. To remove a broken bolt or screw, first drill a hole in the center of the bolt.

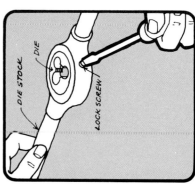

Turn the die stock to cut the threads. Remove the die often to clear away metal chips. Use plenty of oil.

Insert the proper size die in the die stock (wrench). Secure the die with the locking screw, and lightly oil the threads.

Turn the extractor counterclockwise into the drilled hole. As it seats itself, the extractor will turn out the broken bolt.

# CHOOSING KNIVES AND SHEARS

Though there are dozens of other knives and shears sold, those shown here will handle most any job you have.

A *linoleum knife* cuts sheet goods and tile. Use a *pocketknife* for scoring marks. *Tinsnips* cut sheet materials. For cutting ceiling tile and general cutting, use a *utility knife*. A *pistol grip cutter* cuts almost anything; *aviation snips,* ductwork.

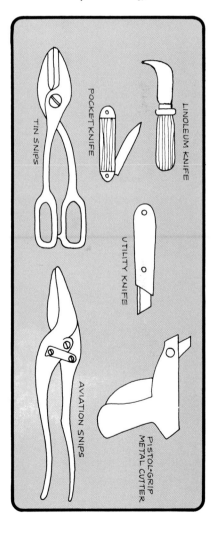

TIN SNIPS

POCKETKNIFE

LINOLEUM KNIFE

UTILITY KNIFE

AVIATION SNIPS

PISTOL-GRIP METAL CUTTER

# KEEPING EDGES SHARP

Cutting something with a dull knife is like roller-skating up a steep hill on a windy day. It's tough, frustrating work—and you risk a dangerous slip. To avoid this uphill battle, all you need to do is keep your tool sharp. It's easy to do.

Hone small tools such as knives and scissors on a whetstone. Hold the implement at the appropriate angle and stroke lightly.

To sharpen blades with inside curves, use a "slip" stone. Hold the stone so it conforms to the curve of the blade.

Depending on the type of knife you're sharpening, you'll need a whetstone, sharpening steel, or a silicon-carbide stone. To sharpen a blade with a whetstone, slide the knife along the length of the stone (working away from you), then reverse the implement and stroke the opposite side of the blade. Continue to alternate until the blade is sharp. See the sketches below for

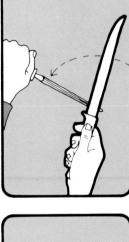

For household knives, use a sharpening steel. Pull the blade down and across the steel, alternating the sides of the blade.

Sharpen stainless steel cutlery with a silicon-carbide stone. Whet the blade with a circular motion, alternating sides.

pointers on how to sharpen other types of knives.

If the cutting edge of the blade you're sharpening is nicked, you'll need to grind it down with a grinding wheel before proceeding. Never try to sharpen knife blades having sawtooth or serrated edges; you'll ruin them.

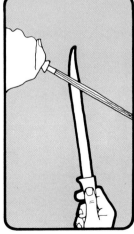

Stroke the entire length of the blade from handle to tip. Three or four strokes per side usually will restore a sharp edge.

## USING A GRINDER

If your tool collection has a full complement of planes, chisels, bits, drills, knives, and other cutting tools, start thinking "bench grinder" for your next power equipment purchase. A bench grinder not only will do a professional job of sharpening these cutting tools, it will also buff and polish a wide variety of materials.

The popular double-wheeled model usually comes packaged with eye shields, adjustable tool rests, quench trays for cooling metals, and rubber supports to reduce vibration. In addition, you can buy special attachments for sharpening drill bits and saw blades, along with special wheels for buffing—fiber and wire brushes and lamb's wool and cloth buffers. You can change the wheels with just a flick of a wrench.

For a bench grinder to operate properly, it must be firmly attached to a workbench or grinder stand with bolts. This stability is important because of the high rpm output of the grinder motor. And for safety's sake, locate it in a well-lighted spot.

To smooth soft metals such as brass, aluminum, and copper, use a coarse wheel. For hard materials, a fine wheel is best. The wheels usually are marked "coarse," "medium-coarse," "medium-fine," and "fine." Also, you'll usually find a speed limitation stamped on the wheels. Don't exceed these rpm specifications. And, before purchasing a wheel, make sure its holes fit the shaft of your grinder.

Buffing and polishing wheels come in handy for a variety of operations. Use wire wheels (coarse or fine) for removing rust, and cloth wheels for buffing and polishing metal.

To buff metal, you'll need the appropriate compound. Use *red jeweler's rouge* for gold and silver. *White rouge* is best for chrome, stainless steel, and aluminum. And for copper and brass, use *brown tripoli.*

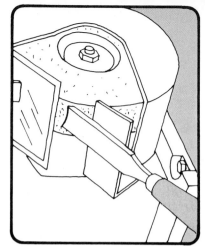

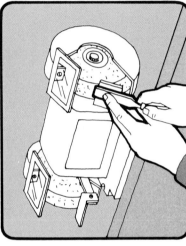

Grinding wheels produce a slightly concave or "hollow" cut. This keeps edges sharp longer and makes for better cutting.

When the edge is square, adjust the tool rest to the proper bevel angle. To do this, hold the tool on the rest and adjust the rest.

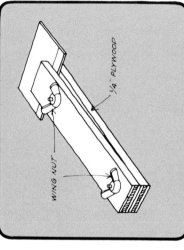

1/4" PLYWOOD

WING NUT

You can hold small tools with an improvised jig like the one shown. Use plywood for the jig; it's stronger than solid wood.

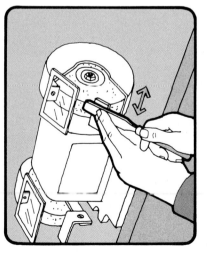

Square edges of worn or nicked tools by holding them square to the wheel. Use some pressure, but don't force the tool.

Move the tool back and forth across the wheel. Quench the tool often in water so the metal doesn't lose its "temper."

**418**

# DRILLING

Think of any drill as a specialized cutting instrument—essentially a rotary knife with two edges—and you're well on your way to understanding this essential tool. Separate in your mind, too, the distinction between a drill's blade—usually called a

bit—and its drive mechanism, which provides the rotary motion.

Once, a beginning woodworker needed several of the hand-operated drivers shown immediately below. Now, an electric drill will do all their jobs, and much more. (More about electric drills on pages 421 and 422.) Include one among your first tool purchases. Add a push drill for making small holes quickly, and you'll be adequately equipped.

Eventually, you may want to round out your tool collection with a crank-operated hand or breast drill for situations where getting power to the job takes more time than actually boring the hole. To hand-drill larger holes, you'll need a brace and an assortment of bits.

## CHOOSING DRILLS AND BITS

The standard drilling standbys are the *push drill* and the *portable electric drill.* You can use a power drill for many jobs other than drilling (see page 422). A *push drill* is excellent for drilling small holes in wood, plastic, and metal. For larger holes in these same materials, use a *brace.* A *breast drill* handles lots of pressure; you put the handle against your body for "push" and hold and crank the drill with your hands. With a *hand drill,* you hold with one hand and crank with the other.

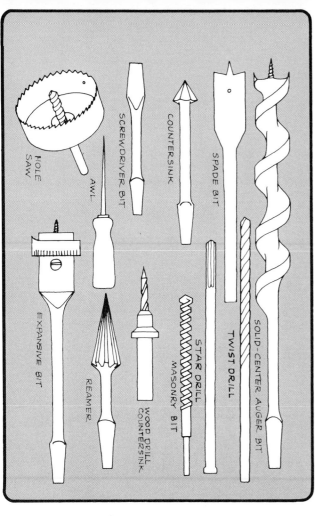

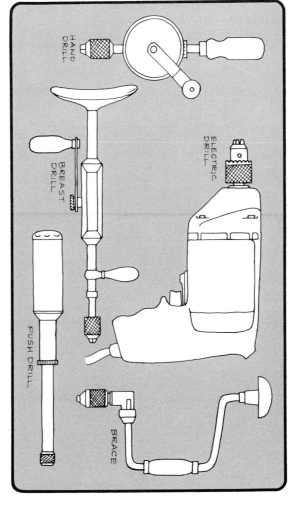

Both types of auger bits—the Jennings (or double-twist) bit and the *solid center* bit—bore holes in wood. For holes over one inch in diameter, use an *expansive bit,* which is adjustable, or a *spade bit,* which isn't. *Countersinks* enable you to set screw heads flush with or below the surface, while *reamers* are for enlarging holes in metal.

*Twist drills* cut through wood, metal, or plastic. You can buy oversized drills with ¼-inch shanks.

*Hole saws* drill oversize holes in wood. For making holes in masonry, use a carbide-tipped *masonry bit* or a *star drill,* which you drive with a hammer. *Wood drill/countersinks* are for predrilling screw holes and countersinking with power drills. *Awls* prepare the way for nails and screws in wood. *Screwdriver bits* drive and remove screws.

# USING DRILLS AND BRACES

On the business end of every drill, there is a round metal housing called a *chuck*. And inside the chuck, you'll notice two or three fitted pieces of metal called *jaws*. Bits and drills are locked into these jaws, either by turning the chuck housing with your fingers or with a chuck key. Since the chuck holds the bits or drills, it's important to buy drills with quality chucks so the bits or drills don't slide, spin, or bend when you apply the boring/drilling pressure.

An occasional cleaning and oiling keeps chucks in perfect working order. You can deter rust on other metal parts by wiping them with an oil-treated cloth.

To use a hand-operated brace or drill with success, you must keep several

things in mind. First, always turn the handle or crank slowly and evenly. Don't spin it like an egg beater. If you do, chances are good that the speed will cause the bit or drill to bind, overheat, or break. Easy does it.

Second, keep the bits and drills square to the work. For how-to, see below. And third, keep the bits and drills sharp (see page 423). Dull cutting edges take more muscle to turn, and they also risk breaking the bits or drills or burning them beyond use.

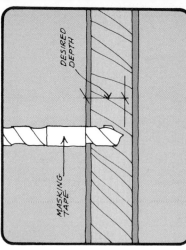

To drill a "blind" hole, wrap masking tape around the bit at the desired depth, then drill till the tape touches the material.

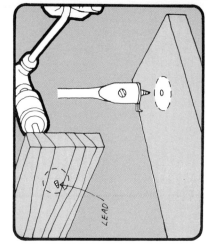

Bore an auger or expansive bit until its lead screw breaks through the other side of the material. Finish from the other side.

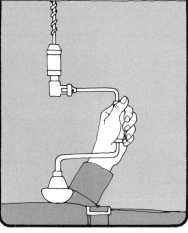

Square the drill with the work before you start. After several turns, check for square again—especially when you drill deep.

To get more pressure on a brace, hold its head against your body. Level the brace with one hand. This helps keep the bit square.

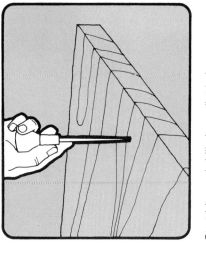

Start bits and drills in a pilot hole made with an awl. Use a center punch for metal. This will prevent the tool from "skating".

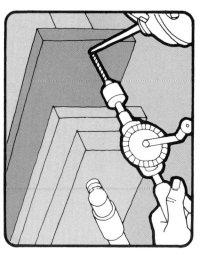

When drilling metal—especially steel—squirt light oil on the bit and the metal. This aids cutting and cools the bit.

# CHOOSING AN ELECTRIC DRILL

A motor-driven hole maker—a portable electric drill—will make you a workshop hero with little or no practice. And you won't be limited to just drilling clean, smooth, accurate holes in wood, metal, plastic, masonry, rubber, tile, and other materials, either. With special accessories, you'll be able to drive and remove screws, polish, grind, buff, sand, and saw, too.

Of all hand and power tools manufactured today, a power drill probably is the most versatile, multipurpose tool you can buy. And, because of keen competition in the marketplace, the price of power drills remains low.

For home use, you have a choice of three drill sizes: 1/4, 3/8, and 1/2 inch. These fractions refer to chuck size; motors are powered to fit different capacities. Your best choice might be the 1/4- or 3/8-inch

outfit, since you can rent a 1/2-inch drill for the few times you might need its low-speed, high-torque action.

There isn't much price difference between a 1/4- and 3/8-inch drill, so the decision usually comes down to the type of work you want it to do.

A 1/4-inch drill has plenty of rpm to bore 1/4-inch twist drills into metal and wood and 1/2-inch drills into wood. The drill performs perfectly for most grinding and buffing operations, too. Keep one thing in mind, though—this drill is not a production tool. It won't take a lot of hard, slam-bang, pressure-pushing action.

For light/heavy work, a 3/8-inch drill has lots of production guts—which comes in handy working with hardwoods, masonry, and metals in which fairly large holes are needed. You can put pounds of push on these units without seriously slowing their 1/3- to 3/8- (or more) horsepower buildup. You get a bonus in the larger 3/8-inch chuck, too, which will handle both 1/4- and 3/8-inch twist drills and special accessories.

Purchase a drill with the variable-speed feature, if possible. With it, the motor winds up from zero to full capacity rpm, depending on how hard you squeeze the trigger switch. This lets you start into the material slowly, speed up for the cutting action, then slow the drill for a non-splinter finish. You sort of "feel" your way through the material instead of just hanging onto the drill while it chews its way in and out.

Some drills have a reversible action, too, which removes screws and lets you back out sticking and binding drills without breaking them.

Most drills are permanently lubricated, double-insulated against electrical shock, and come with handle and chuck key (wrench) accessories.

For special projects, you can buy battery-powered, cordless drills and drills that convert into power hammers for brick, block, and concrete work.

Grip an electric drill with both hands to keep it steady and square to the work. Drill "wobble" can break bits fast.

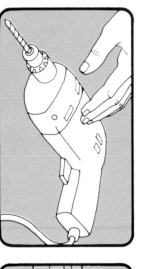

Grip an electric drill with both hands to keep it steady and square to the work. Drill "wobble" can break bits fast.

You can make pilot holes with a variable-speed drill at low speed. If the drill tip skates, use an awl or punch instead.

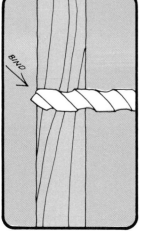

After you've operated the drill for a long period, touch the motor housing. If it's very hot, let the drill run with no load.

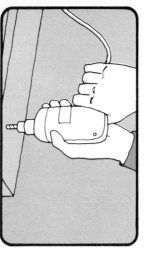

If sap- or oil-wet shavings clog the drill, remove them with the tip of a nail. Clogging can result from fast-feeding the drill.

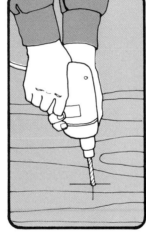

As the drill begins to break through the material, especially metal, it may bind. Simply back up the drill and start again.

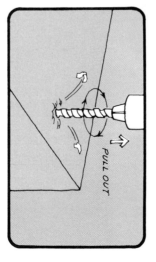

When drilling deep holes, back the drill out often, with motor still running, to clear out chips. Reinsert drill and start the motor.

# CHOOSING DRILL ACCESSORIES

Portable power drill accessories can magically convert your drill into a shop-full of wood- and metal-working equipment. Some of these changeover devices are fast to assemble; others take some patience. Overall, the many-tools-in-one concept is a good one—especially if your workshop space is limited and you don't require single-tool performance from the drill.

Keep in mind, though, that drills simply can't be expected to carry the workload of lathes or circular saws or sanders through mere conversion.

The attachments shown below do not represent the full complement of those manufactured, but they are among the most widely purchased. If you wish, you can buy such diverse items as circle cutters, hacksaw blade attachments, drilling depth gauges, and many more.

If you do plan to buy some of the accessories, be sure to invest in a 3/8-inch drill for the power source. It has the capacity to run the attachments without motor overload or damage to accessories.

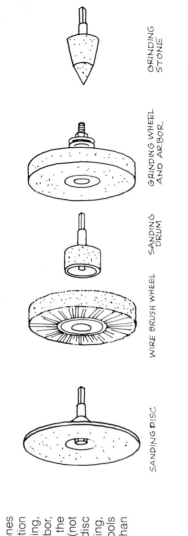

SANDING DISC

WIRE BRUSH WHEEL

SANDING DRUM

GRINDING WHEEL AND ARBOR

GRINDING STONE

Discs, brushes, drums, wheels, and stones let you use the drill chuck's rotary motion for a wide variety of sanding, cleaning, polishing, and grinding jobs. With an arbor, you can lock these attachments into the chuck fast. A lamb's wool cover (not shown), which slips over the sanding disc base and is secured with a drawstring, turns drills into buffing wheels. These tools often are sold in a package for less than you would pay for them individually.

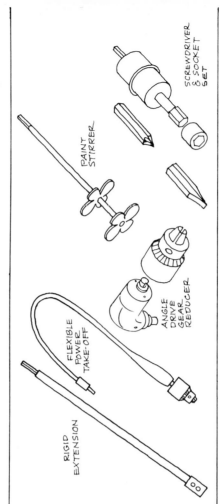

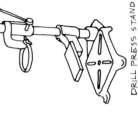

PAINT STIRRER

SCREWDRIVER & SOCKET SET

ANGLE DRIVE GEAR REDUCER

FLEXIBLE POWER TAKE-OFF

RIGID EXTENSION

In cramped quarters, one of several chuck extensions will enable you to get where you need to be to get the job done. The rigid extension makes any drill into an extension drill, while the flexible power take-off provides even more versatility. With an angle drive, you get gear reduction for slow-speed, high-torque jobs. For paint, you can buy a stirrer to make quick work of mixing. A screwdriver/socket wrench set is another top accessory for the drill. It includes standard- and Phillips-blade screwdrivers and an assortment of sockets with a drill adapter unit.

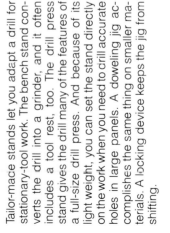

DRILL PRESS STAND

BENCH STAND

Tailor-made stands let you adapt a drill for stationary-tool work. The bench stand converts the drill into a grinder, and it often includes a tool rest, too. The drill press stand gives the drill many of the features of a full-size drill press. And because of its light weight, you can set the stand directly on the work when you need to drill accurate holes in large panels. A doweling jig accomplishes the same thing on smaller materials. A locking device keeps the jig from shifting.

# KEEPING DRILLS AND BITS SHARP

With twist drills, you have a decision to make—you can buy good ones and keep them sharpened, or you can opt for inexpensive ones and throw them away when they become dull. Cheap drills dull fast, and aren't worth the time it takes to sharpen them.

It's quite a different story with auger

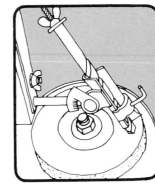

bits. Spend your money on quality. Then keep the bits sharpened and free from rust and damage.

Maintaining drills and bits is a relatively simple matter. Since twist drills often are packaged in a plastic box that may be closed, safe storage presents no problems—as long as you use it.

Auger bits sometimes come in plastic sleeves, which provide protection. However, the smart pros use a cloth pocket sleeve and keep this sleeve lightly

oiled to prevent bits from becoming rusty and dull.

The cutting edges on countersinks may be "touched up" with a file when they dull, which is seldom, since they aren't used that much. For rounded and nicked screwdriver bits, grind the tips square again and whet away any burrs along the tapers.

On twist drills, *lips* are the cutting edges, with the trailing edge behind called a *heel*. The angle shown here is for "standard" work.

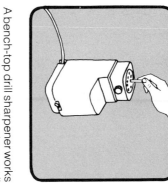

You can sharpen twist drills by "eye" if you're good. But you can get better results with a grinding jig like the one shown here.

A bench-top drill sharpener works somewhat like an electric pencil sharpener. You also can buy units powered by the drill's motor.

Sharpen auger bits with a file designed especially for filing the inside of the cutting lips. File burrs off the heels.

---

## CHOOSING A DRILL PRESS

If you're a serious woodworking buff and like to turn out fine pieces of furniture and cabinets, a stationary drill press is a "must-have" tool. Its main purpose in your life is to drill holes in any material with no-tolerance accuracy. But it can do more—use it as a drum or disc sander, router, a grinder, and a polisher.

You'll want these basic features in a drill press: a *tilting table* that adjusts up or down its pole support for wide and long materials; a *depth gauge* setting; a *light for close work*; and a *large-capacity motor*, which you usually buy separately.

Don't leave the store without a drill press vise. Buy the other accessories as you need them for specific projects. They include a fly-cutter outfit for drilling large holes, and specialty drills, such as countersinks and hole saws. Also buy a pump-type oil can, since you'll need lubrication when drilling holes in some metals.

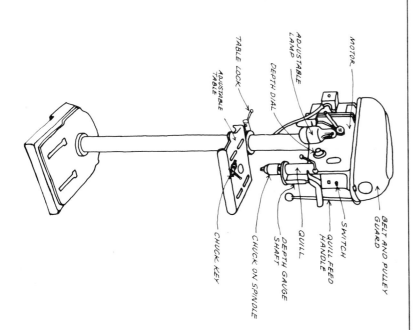

ADJUSTABLE LAMP

MOTOR

DEPTH DIAL

TABLE LOCK

ADJUSTABLE TABLE

BELT AND PULLEY GUARD

QUILL FEED HANDLE

SWITCH

QUILL

DEPTH GAUGE SHAFT

CHUCK ON SPINDLE

CHUCK KEY

# FASTENING

Once you've measured and cut or drilled materials, you usually must fasten them somehow. "Here comes the easy part of the job," you may think. "After all, anyone can pound a nail, drive a screw, or glue one piece of material to another. What's there to learn about fastening, anyway?"

You'll find out, in dramatic fashion, the first time you split a perfectly good piece of lumber, break off a screw head, or end up with a project that looks like an orange crate (but doesn't hold together nearly as well).

Actually, you don't "pound" a nail at all—you *drive* it with a few well-directed blows. And you don't drive just any old nail, either; you must select the proper size and type for the job at hand.

And before you even begin to think about which nail to use, you have to decide whether a screw wouldn't be more appropriate. Screws not only hold more tenaciously than nails, they're also easier to drive in certain situations. Again, though, you need to know the proper size and type to ask for when you venture to the hardware store.

The following pages present more than a dozen different fastening tools, devices, and techniques. Familiarize yourself with them and you'll see your repairs and improvements go together faster and stay together longer.

Besides knowing the right fastener to use, you also need to know the right joint for a given situation. For a rundown on basic joinery techniques and their applications, see pages 457-463.

Watch out, too, that you don't "over-engineer" a joint with too many fasteners. Often, an extra nail or a screw that's too large will greatly weaken a structure.

## CHOOSING HAMMERS

Don't let the array of hammers shown here intimidate you. Chances are, you'll never need to buy most of them, yet it's nice to know they're around if you need their special services.

Make a 16-ounce *curved claw hammer* your very first tool purchase. Besides driving a potpourri of fasteners, a claw hammer also pulls them. You have a selection of handles, too. *Wooden handles*, though durable, can break. *Tubular steel* and *solid steel handles* are twins; tubular steel is lighter, however. A *fiber glass handle* delivers less shock to your hand and arm. These, too, are virtually unbreakable.

*Steel* and *fiber glass handles* feature cushion grips that deter shock. The cushion also prevents damage to fine wood surfaces when you align them by tapping them with the handle.

Use a 20-ounce *ripping-claw hammer* for rough work such as removing studs. Consider, too, buying a 13-ounce claw hammer. It's easy to swing, and you get lots of hitting-the-nail-on-the-head accuracy with it.

Specialty hammers include *tack hammers* for tacks; *ball-peen hammers* for metal working; *mallets* for driving chisels and assembling wood joints; and *sledge* and *mason's hammers* for brick, block, and concrete projects.

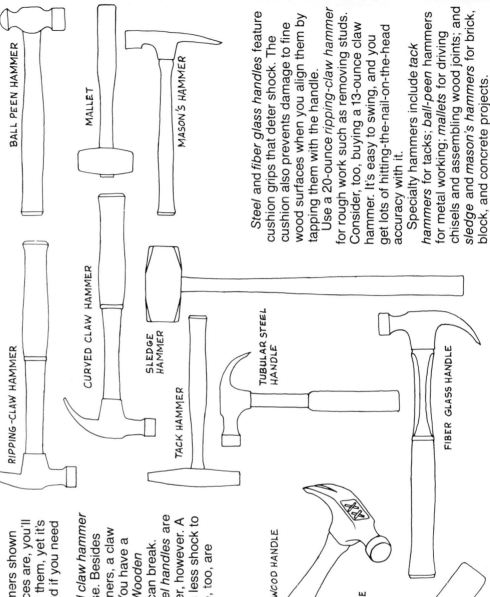

BALL PEEN HAMMER

MALLET

MASON'S HAMMER

RIPPING-CLAW HAMMER

CURVED CLAW HAMMER

SLEDGE HAMMER

TACK HAMMER

TUBULAR STEEL HANDLE

FIBER GLASS HANDLE

WOOD HANDLE

SOLID STEEL HANDLE

424

# USING HAMMERS

Ask skilled carpenters how to handle a hammer, and they'll show you their hands and tell you, "Very carefully." They've found out through painful experience that there's a right way and a wrong way to use this most basic of all tools.

For maximum leverage and control, hold onto the hammer at the end of the

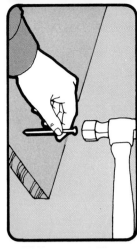

handle, not up around the neck. If you do this and concentrate on the job at hand, you'll find yourself driving nails without straining (or maiming!) your arm, wrist, or hand.

Another important rule to keep in mind is that for safety and effectiveness, you should always use a hammer whose face is at least slightly larger than the nail or tool you're striking. And if you're striking hardened metal, wear safety glasses.

Before using a hammer, always check it for a loose, bent, or split handle. Any of these maladies can turn the hammer into a lethal weapon when you swing it. Make sure, too, that no one is within striking distance should the head and handle—or your hand and the hammer—part company.

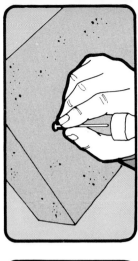

Hold the nail near its head so that if you miss, you'll hit your fingers a glancing blow rather than crush them against the wood.

Swing the hammer smoothly. To hit nails dead-on, keep your eye on the nail, never the hammer. Let the hammer do the work.

The last blow from the hammer should sink the nail's head flush with the wood's surface. Counter-sink with a nail set.

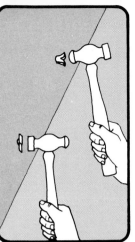

Nailing near the end of a board tends to split the wood. To help the nail punch out fibers rather than split them, blunt its tip.

For rough carpentry projects, clinching the nails you drive gives maximum holding power. Be sure to clinch with the grain.

The magnetic side of a tack hammer head holds and drives tacks. If successive blows are needed, flip the hammer over.

Spread rivets with the rounded side of a ball-peen hammer. Then smack them flat with the face of the hammer. Hit rivets squarely.

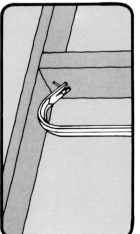

To pull a nail, work it partway out of the stock. Slip a scrap of wood under the hammer for leverage so you're pulling straight up.

Use a wrecking or pry bar to remove extra-long nails or spikes. Add a block of wood under the tool for more pulling leverage.

# CHOOSING NAILS

Few things are potentially more frustrating than walking into a hardware store and getting into a discussion with the salesperson about what type of nail is best for the job at hand. But if you read the information on this page, any confusion you have about nails should dissipate.

Once shipped in wooden kegs and sold for so many pennies per hundred, nails are available today in cardboard cartons, boxes, or individually in bins. And today they're sold by the pound. But for some reason, the terminology used to describe nail sizes hasn't changed. You

still hear a certain size nail referred to as a 16-penny or a 4-penny nail. To further complicate things, "penny" is signified by the letter "d" (representing *denarius*, Latin for "coin"). So what you see in a hardware store is a box with a label identifying the type and size nail that's inside—16d Common, for example.

As you can see by looking at the common nail in the sketch below, there's a size of nail for every job.

For small jobs, you'll want to stay with small boxes or a few pounds of nails. However, if you're installing flooring or roofing, you can buy them by the carton and usually save money. As for the number of nails you'll need, ask the personnel at the store where you buy

nails to estimate your requirements.

Just as there are many sizes of nails, there are also many types. For example, if water will come in contact with the nails, choose galvanized or aluminum types. Or, if you're installing plastic or metal roofing, specify roofing nails that have a lead or rubber washer under their heads to seal out water. You also can buy brass, copper, stainless steel, and bronze nails.

To get more holding power, select the spiral, threaded, or coated types. Coated nails have an almost transparent covering of a rosin-like substance that makes them grip the wood fibers better, without making them sticky.

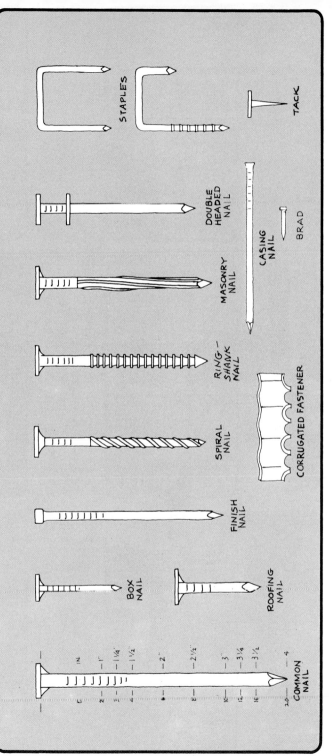

For most fastening jobs around the house, you'll need *common, box, finishing,* and *casing* nails. Keep several pound-boxes of these nails on hand, as well as an assortment of *brads.* In shape, brads are junior-sized finishing nails; use them for molding and finishing jobs. For more holding power, *spiral* and *ring-shank* nails are tops. Ring-shank nails have barbs on the shanks; spiral nails are "threaded" somewhat like screws and twist into materials.

For composition shingles, buy regular *roofing* nails. Wooden shingles require *shingle* nails. The steel used in *masonry* nails is specially hardened to withstand the heavy blows needed to drive them. Don't drive masonry nails directly into brick; rather, go through the mortar joints. You can buy stud tools and gun-powder-driven stud guns and stud-type masonry fasteners. When driving masonry nails, wear safety glasses to protect your eyes.

When you assemble concrete forms or build scaffolding, use *double-headed* nails. These fasteners are driven flush with the bottom head and pulled with the top head when the project is disassembled. Note that some of the nails illustrated above have a thicker shank. The diameter of the shank usually increases with the length of the nail. Two exceptions are flooring nails and shingle nails. Their diameters remain the same, although lengths vary.

Hammer- and machine-driven *staples* in assorted sizes are used to hold wiring, fencing, conduit, ceiling tile, pipe—almost any material or product that is thin and lightweight. *Tacks* also are for light materials; their shanks are cut or round, and lengths vary somewhat. For light fabrication jobs such as picture frames, you can use corrugated fasteners or "wiggly nails," as they are sometimes called. Several lengths are made.

Use nails long enough to go two-thirds through the width or thickness of the board you're nailing into. Nail thin to thick material.

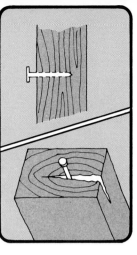

Generally, it's easy to tell the difference between nails and screws; it's knowing when to use each that takes more perception. Nails hold primarily by friction, which gives them plenty of shear strength up, down, and sideways. Unfortunately, they're easily popped by an outward thrust of any type. That's why, for example, you don't see pickets being used to corral livestock or pets—animals could push or pull slats loose.

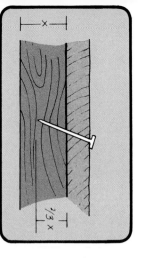

Drive nails across the grain of the wood, not with the grain. Nails in the end grain don't hold well and often split the wood.

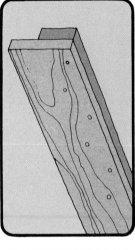

By driving nails at a slight angle, you increase their holding power. Crossing slightly staggered nails adds more strength to the joint.

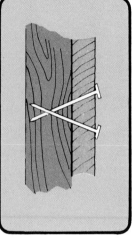

Screws, on the other hand, mechanically interlock with wood fibers or other materials, making them more suitable in situations where there's considerable outward pressure.

This is why it's so important to plan your work so that any force will be perpendicular—not parallel—to the length of the nail.

Drive masonry nails with a baby sledge. Try to plan the job so the nails go into the mortar joints instead of the masonry units.

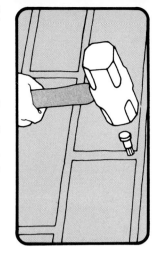

Two nails penetrating the same grain layer also can split wood, so stagger nails along length of board, angling them for strength.

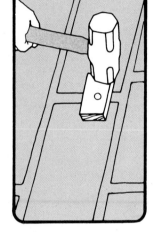

If masonry nails keep bending or breaking, drive them into a scrap of wood. Use scrap to hold and guide the nail. Split the scrap.

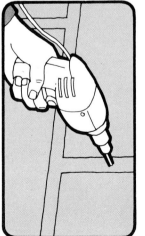

Analyze the direction of the load the nail will carry. Then drive it so the force pushes the nail deeper instead of pulling it out.

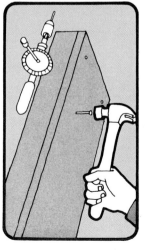

Nailing into hardwood is tough; nails bend or the wood splits. Prevent this by drilling pilot holes slightly smaller than the nails.

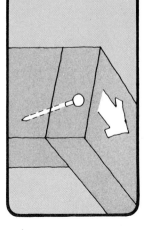

For lots of masonry nails, making pilot holes is faster than using a wood scrap. Use a carbide-tipped drill; wear safety glasses.

427

# CHOOSING SCREWDRIVERS

Yes, you can turn screws with your thumbnail, a dime, a tie clasp, the zipper tab on your windbreaker, and even a paper clip. But the right tool for the job is a screwdriver.

Though screwdrivers come in a dazzling array of sizes and designs, most have either Phillips or slotted blades—to fit the two basic types of screws. The only screws that these blades won't turn are the so-called specialty screws, most of which are driven or removed with sockets or wrenches tailored especially for them (see page 432).

But don't be misled into thinking that one Phillips and one slotted screwdriver will satisfy all of your maintenance and repair needs. The slots in screws vary in length and width, and it's important to use a screwdriver that fits the slot.

If the tip is too narrow, it will ride up out of the slot and damage the screw. If the tip is too wide, it will damage the material around the screw head when the screw is driven flush with the material.

Like any other tool you buy, quality screwdrivers are the best bargain in the long run. Their blades have been properly tempered and ground, and they will feel balanced in your hand. Buy an entire set of them if your budget will allow.

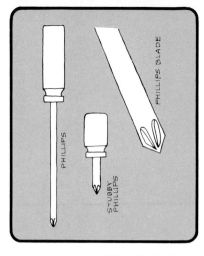

Phillips screwdrivers have multiple edges on tips for more turning power. You'll need three sizes for general-purpose work.

The basic screwdriver assortment includes these standard blade types. Sizes generally are based on length of blade.

Cabinet screwdrivers have special straight-sided tips so they can drive or remove countersunk screws without marring.

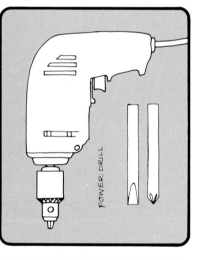

A variable-speed power drill that's also reversible is tops for driving/removing lots of screws. All standard bits are available.

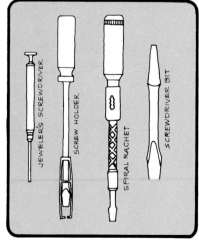

Specialty screwdrivers save time. Spiral ratchets spin screws in and out; bits are used in hand braces. A holder aids starting.

# CHOOSING SCREWS

Screws have a lot going for them. First and most important, they're tough and most important, they're tough screws often add a touch of class that customers. So tough, in fact, that they'll nails can't match.

The sketch below gives you a good provide you with all the holding power idea of what you'll find at most outlets. you could ever need.

As you can see, the slotted screws are Not only that, they're also easy to available with various types of heads— remove, making them ideal for projects flat, oval, and round. Phillips screws you may want to disassemble at some usually come with a flat head. More about them below.

future date. And for woodworking projects where fasteners will show, screws often add a touch of class that nails can't match.

The sketch below gives you a good idea of what you'll find at most outlets. As you can see, the slotted screws are available with various types of heads— flat, oval, and round. Phillips screws usually come with a flat head. More about them below.

Most of the slotted and Phillips screws are designed for use in wood. An exception is the self-tapping sheet metal screw, whose use is obvious. The others shown handle heavier loads and materials.

Most screws have a zinc coating that inhibits rust, and since you don't pay much extra for this protection, don't settle for uncoated types. Brass screws are available, too.

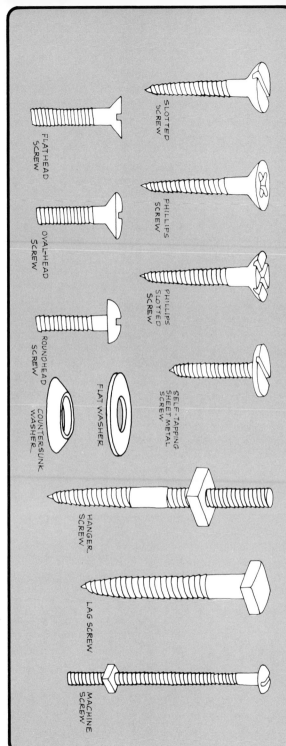

SLOTTED SCREW
FLATHEAD SCREW
PHILLIPS SCREW
OVAL-HEAD SCREW
PHILLIPS SLOTTED SCREW
ROUNDHEAD SCREW
SELF-TAPPING SHEET METAL SCREW
FLAT WASHER
COUNTERSUNK WASHER
HANGER SCREW
LAG SCREW
MACHINE SCREW

For projects where appearance is important, use flathead screws and countersink them. Others won't give that finished look.

Self-tapping sheet metal screws need pilot holes in metal. Machine screws, which are similar to bolts, must be inserted into holes.

Washers prevent the screw head from marring the surface of the material being fastened. Some washers are decorative as well.

Drive screw hangers in wood, then remove the nut and insert the object to be hung. Drive lag and hanger screws with wrenches.

## Selecting the Proper Size

Using the right size screw is critically important to the success of any fastening job. So keep these things in mind:

• The length of the screw, which is designated in inches, should be slightly shorter than the thickness of the material it will be driven into. The smooth shank of the screw should go through the top material.

• The gauge (diameter) of screws you need for a given project depends on the strength required. Designated by number, gauges range from No. 0, which has a $1/16$-inch diameter, to No. 20, which has nearly a half-inch diameter.

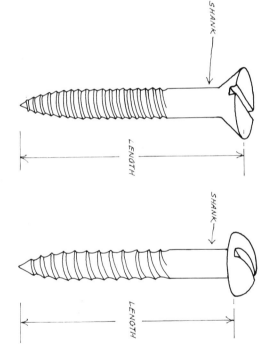

SHANK
LENGTH
SHANK
LENGTH

# DRIVING SCREWS

There aren't too many ways you can go wrong when driving screws. Just fit the screwdriver blade to the slot, using the longest blade possible, and you shouldn't have any difficulty.

If a screw seems exceptionally hard to drive, check to make sure the tip of the blade *fully* fills the screw slot. If it's narrower than the slot, it could be moving slightly, causing loss of power. Also, try using a longer screwdriver. The longer the blade, the more turning power you have at your disposal.

You can save your strength, too, if you pre-drill pilot holes for screws. Make sure these are deep enough in the stock so you're not driving the screws through solid material. And make the pilot holes slightly smaller than the diameter (gauge) of the screw.

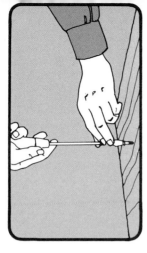

Make pilot holes for No. 8 or smaller screws with an awl. For larger sizes, drill pilot holes with a power drill.

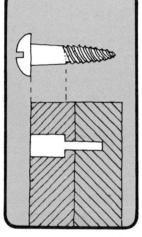

In hardwood, you need a clearance hole to accommodate the shank. Drill it first, then sink a smaller pilot hole for the threads.

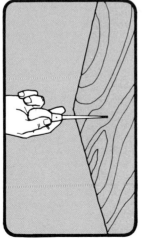

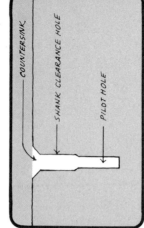

Start screws by holding the screwdriver handle with one hand, the blade with the other. Don't hold the screw.

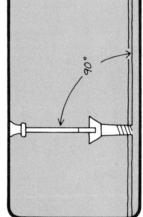

90°

Keep the screwdriver square in the slot and to the work. If it's off-center or at an angle, it may slip out and badly strip the slot.

Get more downward driving force on the screwdriver by turning it with one hand and applying top pressure with the other, as shown.

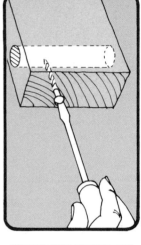

COUNTERSINK
SHANK CLEARANCE HOLE
PILOT HOLE

A countersinking bit (see page 419) drills the countersink, the hole for the shaft, and the hole for the threads in one operation.

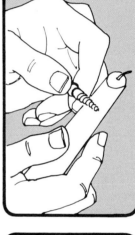

Screws drive easier when threads are lubricated with candle wax. Rub the screw against the candle and rotate.

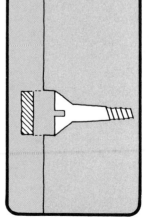

Screws don't hold well in end grain. Add strength by doweling the board and using screws long enough to penetrate the dowel.

Counterbored screws may be concealed with plugs cut from dowel material. Or, fill the holes with wood filler or water putty mix.

Removing old screws can be a real headache—especially if the screws have rusted in the material, become "frozen" through corrosion, or were stripped when they were driven. With work, though, you often can back them out. If not, you may have to turn to a screw extractor for help (see page 416). As a last resort, you can drill the screw out with a twist drill, but this will enlarge the hole and might cause trouble.

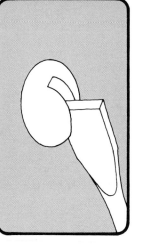

Approach a stubborn screw with care. First, test it with a screwdriver tip that fits the slot perfectly. If you encounter a lot of resistance when you try to back out the screw, stop work. Otherwise, you may damage the screw slot so it can't be used at all. Now's the time to try the other removal techniques illustrated below.

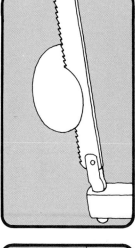

Turn screw in a quarter turn. Then work it back and forth with the screwdriver. This may be enough to break the screw free.

Remove paint, grease, or dirt from the screw slot. You can usually do this by sliding the screwdriver tip sideways in the slot.

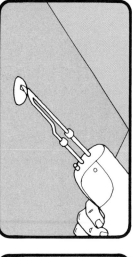

If the slot is too narrow to accept the screwdriver tip, you may be able to widen and deepen it with a hacksaw.

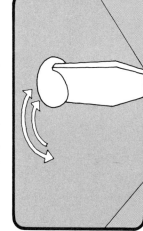

For extra leverage, use a square-shank screwdriver and wrench combination. Don't do this with round-shank drivers.

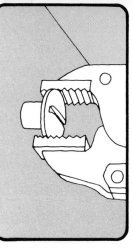

Firmly tap the handle of an old screwdriver in the slot; the shock may loosen the screw. Make sure you hit the screwhead square.

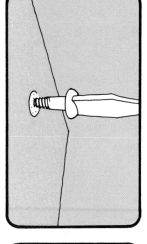

Heat applied to a screwhead with the tip of a soldering iron or gun will sometimes break it free. Test the screw often.

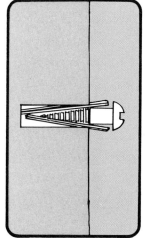

Once a screw is out a few turns, you can grip it with lock-joint pliers. Pliers will damage the screwhead, but they'll do the job.

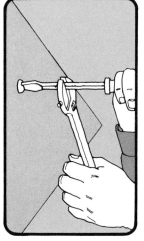

Don't replace the same screw in the same hole. Go to a longer or thicker screw. Or drill out the hole and fill it with a dowel plug.

Fill a hole with wooden matchsticks or toothpicks so screw threads have new wood to bite. Or tamp in a pinch of steel wool.

431

## CHOOSING AND USING WRENCHES

For nearly all routine home maintenance and improvement projects, you need only two types of wrenches: an *adjustable-end wrench* and an *Allen* or *hex-key* wrench. All other wrenches are specialty items that you can buy or rent as you need them.

A set of adjustable-end wrenches should be the first you buy. They range in size from 4 to 16 inches long, but if you buy the 6-, 8-, and 10-inchers, you'll be able to tackle almost any fix-it job that requires a wrench.

Allen wrenches, which generally are packaged in sets that include assorted sizes, are used to tighten set screws and screws featuring an Allen-type head.

Quality is very important in both of these tools. Since a lot of pressure is applied to tighten and loosen nuts and bolts, you want wrenches that will withstand this pressure without breaking or bending, an occurrence that can result in banged knuckles or other injuries.

For assembling pipes and round metal materials, *pipe wrenches*, sometimes called Stillson wrenches, can't be beat. You'll need to buy two of them. They can help you solve a host of plumbing problems—from repairs to new plumbing assemblies.

*Open-end*, *box-end*, *combination*, and *socket wrenches* are fixed-jaw relatives of adjustable wrenches. They can do anything an adjustable wrench can—and some things better—and they're essential for working with machinery, especially cars, washers, dryers, and so on.

*Socket wrenches* with ratchet handles have a lever adjustment that reverses the turning direction of the wrench. With these wrenches, which are built for speed, you don't have to remove the "jaws" of the sockets from the work.

If you have lots of nuts to drive or remove, you may want to rent an electric impact wrench. This handy tool is similar to a portable power drill.

Other specialty wrenches worth noting include *nut drivers* and *offset box wrenches*. A nut driver is similar to a screwdriver, but it has a tip that accepts small sockets to fit hex nuts and screws, socket-head cap screws, and metric fasteners.

When you use any wrench, pull it toward you. This way, if the wrench slips, you'll run less risk of skinning your knuckles.

With adjustable-end wrenches and pipe wrenches, you can cinch the movable jaw up tight on the work so the wrench fits snugly. Pipe wrenches have a movable jaw that tightens automatically on the pipe when you apply pressure.

Select fixed-jaw wrenches to perfectly fit the work they're to turn. If they are even slightly larger, you stand the chance of stripping the metal of the nut or bolt when you turn the wrench.

You should never force a wrench by tapping its handle with a hammer. And don't slip a piece of pipe over a wrench handle for more leverage; you may snap the wrench or the material it's tightening.

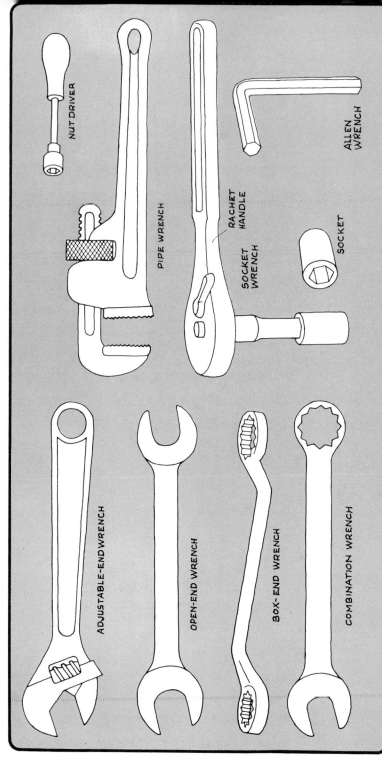

NUT DRIVER

PIPE WRENCH

RACHET HANDLE

SOCKET WRENCH

SOCKET

ALLEN WRENCH

ADJUSTABLE-END WRENCH

OPEN-END WRENCH

BOX-END WRENCH

COMBINATION WRENCH

432

# CHOOSING NUTS AND BOLTS

When you need a really strong fastener that can't pull loose yet lets you dismantle and reassemble a joint, you're literally down to nuts and bolts.

For most construction projects, look to expandable anchors, toggle bolts, and lag screws to solve your fastening problems. These "one-sided" fasteners let you work from the facing side of the material. Other bolts are "two-sided" fasteners; you have to work from both sides of the material to assemble them.

Expandable anchors and toggle bolts are made for fastening or hanging heavy objects on hollow walls and from ceilings. Although both fasteners do the same job,

each is installed differently. Slip an expandable anchor into a hole in the hollow wall, then turn the bolt. This causes the metal flanges to expand behind the wall. The flanges grip the wall, holding the anchor in position. To complete the job, remove the bolt, run it through the object you want to hang, then drive the bolt back into the anchor.

A toggle bolt also slips through a hole in the wall. Once through the thickness of the material, though, two wings on the anchor snap open. When the bolt is tightened with a screwdriver, the wings grip the back of the wall, holding the assembly in position. To use this fastener, you have to slip it through the object to be hung before pushing the bolt and wing-type anchor through the wall. If for any reason you have to remove the

bolt, the wing assembly will drop behind the wall.

Both expandable anchors and toggle bolts are made in a wide range of sizes. For attaching things to masonry, use lag screws and anchors. Drill a hole to accommodate the anchor, insert the anchor flush with the surface, then drive the screw home.

Machine, stove, and carriage bolts are utility fasteners that work well with almost any material, including metal.

The diameter of the bolt and its thread size combine to designate the size of these fasteners. For example, a bolt labeled ½x13 is ½ inch in diameter and has 13 threads to the inch. Machine bolts have both fine and coarse threads. Carriage bolts have just coarse threads.

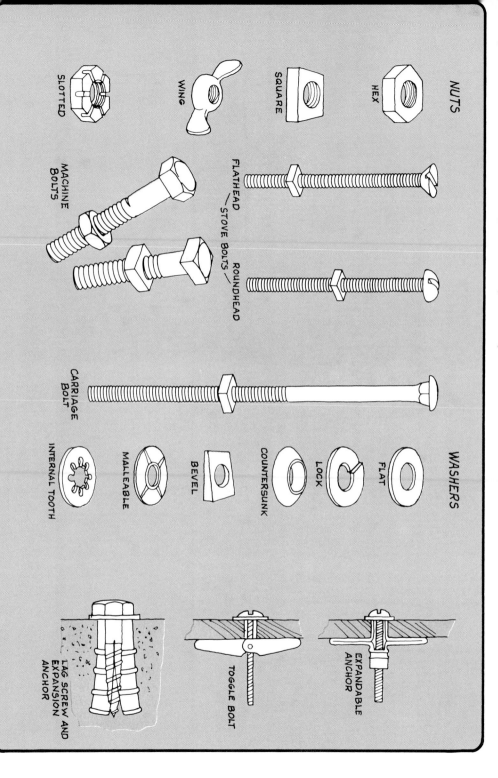

NUTS

HEX

SQUARE

WING

SLOTTED

FLATHEAD

STOVE BOLTS

ROUNDHEAD

MACHINE BOLTS

CARRIAGE BOLT

WASHERS

FLAT

LOCK

COUNTERSUNK

BEVEL

MALLEABLE

INTERNAL TOOTH

EXPANDABLE ANCHOR

TOGGLE BOLT

LAG SCREW AND EXPANSION ANCHOR

433

## CHOOSING AND USING A STAPLE TACKER

For light fabrication jobs such as installing ceiling tile, replacing window screening, and hanging insulation, no other tool can match a staple tacker for ease and efficiency.

Don't confuse this construction tool with lightweight desk-top staplers. A stapler tacker whams hefty fasteners into even hardwoods; you just set it down and squeeze the trigger. The best all-around buy is a double leverage action *"tacker"* that handles staples with leg lengths of ³/₁₆, ¹/₄, and ⁵/₁₆ inches.

For jobs such as installing roofing felt, carpet padding, and other big-sheet jobs, consider renting a *hammer stapler*. With one of these handy tools, you swing the stapler onto the work as you would hit a nail with a hammer. Or if you really want to go first-class, rent an electric stapler for large projects.

For specialty tasks, you can buy staplers for wires and cables up to ½ inch; low-profile staplers for use in tight quarters; and even an outward-clinch tacker for insulating pipes and ducts.

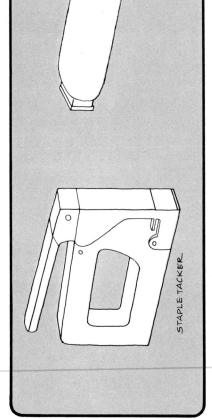

STAPLE TACKER

HAMMER STAPLER

## CHOOSING AND USING A POP RIVETER

Much maligned because they look so weak, rivets often are unjustifiably overlooked as a bonafide fastener for home use. But the fact is—they're one of the strongest. With a home riveting tool like the one shown here, you can fasten together almost any thin sheet material, including wood, metal, plastic, and leather.

Riveters handle ¹/₈-, ⁵/₃₂-, and ³/₁₆-inch-thick rivets in short, medium, and long lengths. You'll usually find the tool sold as part of a package that includes an assortment of rivets and backup plates. The plates hold the rivets securely in soft materials.

The riveting tool operates in much the same way as a tacker: you squeeze the trigger to set the rivet, which must be hand-inserted into a steel nose guide. Riveting is not limited to "pop"-type tools. You also can buy solid, tubular, and split rivets for fastening sheet materials, leather, and plastic. With these, you need a ball-peen hammer, center punch, and a solid piece of steel or a vise to back the material while you're flattening the rivets.

When assembling metal with either pop rivets or hammered rivets, don't mix metals. Use aluminum rivets with aluminum sheet, brass with brass, and so forth.

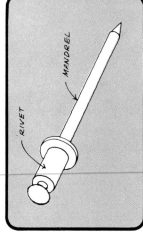

Pop rivets include a stem-like mandrel designed to break off when you squeeze the rivet tool. Little hand pressure is needed.

RIVET

MANDREL

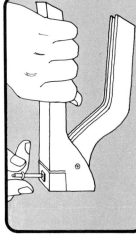

Insert the mandrel into the hole in the base of the tool. Squeeze the handle slightly to hold it while you position the tool.

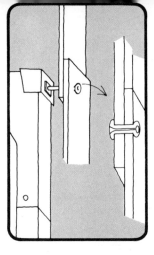

Drill a hole in the material. Then slip the rivet into the hole and squeeze. As the mandrel withdraws, the rivet will "pop."

434

# USING SOLDERING TOOLS

By itself, solder doesn't make a strong joint. You have to start with a good "mechanical" joint. For example, wires have to be twisted; sheet metal has to be crimped or folded; and connectors have to be pinched onto wire ends. Once these mechanical joints are sound, solder adds further strength and safety.

Although solder is itself a soft metal, it takes plenty of heat to fuse it to other metals. For small projects, an *electric soldering iron* or *gun* produces this necessary heat. For large projects

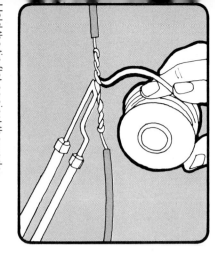

Basic soldering tools include those shown here. Both soldering guns and propane torches often are sold in kit form.

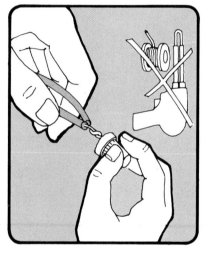

Don't solder house wiring electrical connections. Instead, twist the wires together and complete the job with wire connectors.

Hold the tip flat against the underside of the work; touch solder to top side. Solder will melt and cover the joint.

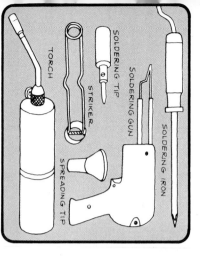

(copper pipe, gutters, and ducts) you'll need a *propane torch.*

To solder any joint with a soldering iron or gun, you must first clean the tip of the iron or gun with steel wool until it's shiny. Then heat the iron and "tin" it with solder. When the tip accepts a thin coat of the solder, it's "tinned." Also be sure the work to be soldered is absolutely clean and free of paint, grease, and fingerprints.

Apply the proper flux, and heat the metal. When the metal becomes hot enough, the solder will melt and fuse the joint (see pages 285 and 482). To solder hard materials such as steel, bronze, and silver, you need to use a propane torch; a soldering gun won't generate enough heat to do the job. Buy wire-flux or

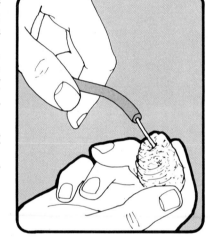

Clean the metal to be soldered with steel wool until it shines. Do not touch the cleaned surfaces; oil from skin deters fusion.

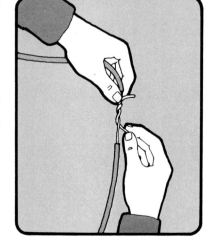

Make a mechanical joint by twisting, crimping, or lapping metals. Then apply flux, unless solder contains the proper flux core.

solid-core solder for small jobs. Choose bar solder for fabricating sheet materials: gutter runs, ducts, and so on.

Flux helps fuse the metals by ensuring that the surface is free of dirt and corrosion. For copper, brass, bronze, cadmium, and silver, use a rosin flux. Galvanized iron requires an acid flux. Soldering aluminum is extremely difficult. Stainless steel needs a flux made especially for this metal.

**Caution:** For safety reasons, do not solder house wiring electrical connections. Most electrical codes prohibit this practice.

## CHOOSING AND USING ADHESIVES

Modern-day adhesives can join almost any material known to man—often making a joint that's stronger than the original materials themselves. Use them alone or in combination with mechanical fasteners such as nails, screws, bolts, and dowels.

Quick-set formulas make the new adhesives easier to work with, too; you no longer need elaborate clamping rigs for most jobs, and some actually bond better with no clamping at all.

But prepare yourself for the mind-boggling array of adhesives from which to choose. The chart on the opposite page summarizes the properties of the ones you'll find most useful. Product names can be confusing, so read the manufacturer's fine print before you buy.

Look first for the product's *set* and *cure* times. Set refers only to an adhesive's initial drying time, which might be a matter of hours, minutes, or even seconds. The bond doesn't reach full strength, however, until it has cured—a process that usually takes several days or more. So, try not to apply stress to a glued joint until it has thoroughly cured.

Understand, too, that adhesives vary greatly in their resistance to water. With some, any moisture—even very high humidity—will destroy the bond. Others can withstand occasional light wetting, and a few remain strong even during prolonged submersion.

Good, strong glue joints don't just happen. Here's a rule-of-thumb list that will help you keep materials joined together better and longer.

• The more surface (area) you cover with adhesive, the stronger the joint.

• Avoid fastening weak joints such as butt joints and end-grain joints with glue only. You'll need a mechanical fastener, too. See pages 457 to 463 for wood joinery techniques, and page 468 for fastening plywood. Acrylic plastic can be butt-glued (see page 476).

• Unless the manufacturer specifies otherwise, use a clamp or pressure device to hold glued joints until the adhesive cures (see page 443).

• Make sure that materials to be joined are clean. Also, prefit and assemble them to ensure that they will fit tightly together when glued. If either material is uneven, the adhesive will only hold the adhesive next to it—not the material.

• Unless manufacturer's instructions specify otherwise, try to apply adhesives at temperatures above 70 degrees.

• Provide plenty of ventilation when using contact cement, rubber-based adhesive, plastic cement, and most mastic adhesives (see pages 475 and 29).

• Do not work around an open flame, heat, sparks, and so on when using any of the adhesives listed above.

• Don't glue/assemble materials on tables and benches that are sprinkled with sawdust, wood chips, metal filings, dust, dirt, oil, or grease.

• When regluing materials, be sure to clean off all old dried adhesive before applying the new.

• Never spread adhesive over a surface that is wet with water.

• Apply adhesives with the proper applicators: notched trowels for mastics; caulking guns for cartridge-packaged adhesives; and brushes for liquids.

Electric glue guns feature a heating element that allows for applying clear adhesives quickly. The gun melts special cartridges.

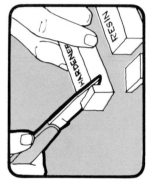

Available in cartridges for caulking-gun applications, paneling adhesives make quick work of installing bulky sheet material.

Epoxy putty comes in stick form. To mix it, cut off identical lengths of resin and hardener. Then knead together like dough.

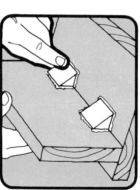

Triangular slip blocks reinforce corner joints, eliminating the need for clamps. For the best bond, slide blocks back and forth.

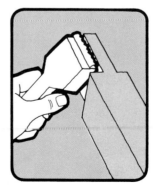

Roughen the surfaces to be glued before applying most adhesives. This adds surface area to the joint, strengthening the bond.

Spread floor and wall tile mastics with a notched trowel to control the depth of the mastic. Clean the trowel often during use.

| Type of Adhesive | Primarily Used for: | Holding Power | Water Resistance | Set Time | Cure Time | Flex of Adhesive | Type of Applicator | Vent Needed? | Flame Danger? |
|---|---|---|---|---|---|---|---|---|---|
| Contact Adhesives | Applying plastic laminate; wood veneering; veneer repair. | Good | Excellent | Must dry first, then on contact. | 30-48 hours | Soft | Brush; notched trowel; paint roller | Yes for solvent-based | Yes for solvent-based |
| Epoxy Adhesives | Bonding almost any material to any material. Must mix the parts. | Excellent | Excellent | 5-30 minutes | 1-10 hours | Medium to hard | Throw-away brush or ice cream stick | No | None |
| Latex-Based Adhesives | Bonding fabric, canvas, carpeting, paper products. | Fair | Fair | On contact to 6 hours | 10-60 hours | Soft | Built into package; brush; paint roller | No | None |
| Mastics Two types: latex (L) and rosin (R) | L: ceiling tile, floor tile, paneling. R: ceramic, plastic, wood, cork. | Good | Good | On contact to 2 hours | 2-3 days | Soft | Notched trowel or caulking gun shell | Yes for R | Yes for R |
| Paste Adhesives | Applying wall-paper and bonding other thin paper products. | Good | Poor | 30 minutes | 8-24 hours | Soft | Brush | No | None |
| Plastic Adhesives | Bonding wood, glass, plastics, pottery, china, model work. | Fair | Good | 5 minutes to 3-6 hours | 2 days | Medium to hard | Built into package; fingertip or brush | Yes | Yes |
| Polyvinyl resin or "white glue" | Bonding wood, plywood, hardboard, paper. | Good | Poor | 1-5 hours | 24-30 hours | Medium | Built into bottle; ice cream stick | No | None |
| Resorcinol, Formaldehyde | Bonding wood, plywood, hardboard; reclaimed wood products (chipboard). | Excellent | Resorcinol is excellent; Formaldehyde, poor. | 7-10 hours | 24-30 hours | Stiff | Ice cream stick; small brush | No | None |
| Rubber-based Adhesives | Bonding wood, wood to concrete, paper products, plastic, cork. | Fair to good | Good | On contact to 5 hours | 30-60 hours | Soft | Brush or notched spreader | Yes | Yes |
| Cyanoacrylates (the so-called instant-bonding adhesives) | Bonding rubber, plastics, metals, ceramics, glass. | Excellent | Fair | On contact to 2 minutes | 12-24 hours | None | Squeeze tube | Yes | Yes |

Note: Setting and curing times shown here are approximate. Times depend on temperature, humidity, and thickness of the adhesive. Carefully follow manufacturers' instructions.

# CHOOSING AND USING TAPE

What workshop product can clamp, stop leaks, prevent electrical shock and fires, seal, bird, weatherstrip, waterproof, trim, insulate, and wrap packages? You're right—tape! This workhorse can solve many of your everyday fix-it problems quickly and inexpensively.

For most jobs, have a generous supply of electrical, duct, and masking tape on hand. For specialty tasks, choose a tape that's designed to fit the need.

*Electrical tape* can do much more than insulate electrical wires. You also can use it to temporarily stop leaks in plumbing pipes, garden hoses, and auto hoses. It's great, too, for supplying extra gripping power on ball bats and hammer handles.

Because it's so flexible, this tape will conform to almost any irregular surface, except masonry materials. For more about electrical tape, see page 226.

*Duct tape*, actually a *plastic-coated cloth tape*, can repair most plastic articles, fabric, and metals. Use it, too, for sealing joints in heating, cooling, and clothes dryer ducts. It's water- and scuff-resistant, and comes in black or silver colors.

*Masking tape's* forte is protecting woodwork during painting, but it's also good for sealing packages, clamping together light materials for gluing, and as a protection for wood and metal furniture surfaces when you're moving them.

*Aluminum foil tape* patches most metals. Use it, too, as a backup material for auto body repairs, and for sealing ducts, gutters, and downspouts.

*Double-face tape* has two sticky sides Use it for holding light materials together while you saw, drill, nail, or screw them. One type is exceptionally good at holding down the edges of carpeting. Another version makes quick work of applying wall tiles.

Wrap a layer of *pipe-joint tape* around pipe threads to stop leaks. It also makes nut-and-bolt assembly easier and deters rust, too.

*Transparent weatherstrip tape* seals windows, doors, storm windows, and air conditioners. It accepts paint readily.

*Plastic decorative tape*, in a variety of colors, may be used for minor repair jobs and for decorative accents.

*Strapping tape*, a heavy-duty product, comes in handy for making temporary repairs and for reinforcing packages.

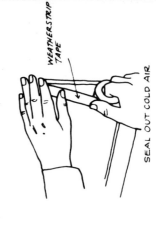

PIPE-JOINT TAPE

SEAL PIPE THREADS

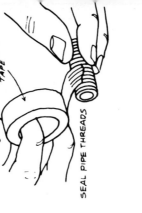

WEATHERSTRIP TAPE

SEAL OUT COLD AIR

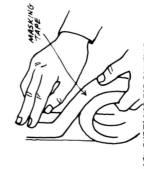

DUCT TAPE

SEAL HEATING DUCTS

MASKING TAPE

TAPE DRAWERS SHUT WHEN MOVING FURNITURE

MASKING TAPE

MASK SURFACES FOR PAINTING

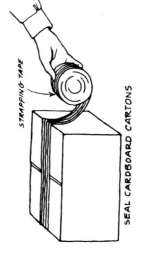

STRAPPING TAPE

SEAL CARDBOARD CARTONS

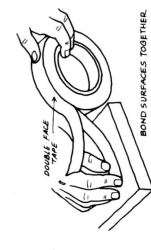

ELECTRICAL TAPE

INSULATE ELECTRICAL WIRES

DOUBLE FACE TAPE

BOND SURFACES TOGETHER

# HOLDING AND CLAMPING

## CHOOSING PLIERS

Nowhere is it more obvious that we're in the age of specialization than when choosing a pair of pliers. No matter what the task at hand, there's a type of pliers that will tackle it better than any other type.

Yet, when viewed from a distance, all types can be classified as *holders*, *turners*, or *cutters*. Holders have smooth jaws or fine serrations; turners, coarse teeth designed to turn nuts and bolts.

And cutters feature smooth jaws with cutting edges to snip wires, nails, and small bolts and screws.

Your toolbox should include at the very least pairs of slip-joint pliers, lock-joint pliers, and diagonal pliers—the big three. After these, your options are almost limitless—rib-joint, long-nose, four-position adjustable, and lineman's pliers; nippers; and so on. There are even pliers for driving and pulling staples, for forming wire loops, for retrieving small parts that have been dropped in tight quarters, and for precision work.

Pliers, clamps, and vises mechanically extend your hands and fingers—letting you get a better grip on things, increase your leverage, or apply pressure. Jury-rig a job instead of using the right holding or clamping device and you risk injuring yourself or your materials.

Include combination pliers, long-nose pliers, lock-joint pliers, and several different sizes of C-clamps among your first tool purchases. Later, you may want to add specialty pliers and clamps, plus a portable or bench-mounted vise. Note that we've also included workbench and sawhorse basics among the usual assortment of holding tools. Though mechanically quite different, they perform the same basic function; you just won't get the same good results with improvised substitutes.

Quality pliers have machine-milled jaws and are forged from high-carbon steel that has been tempered for durability. When you squeeze the handles together, joints should close smoothly and the jaws should provide a firm, even pressure on the work. Exposed metal parts should be chrome-plated to resist rust and damage. And, as with most other tools, it's best to stay away from the bargain bins when you shop for pliers.

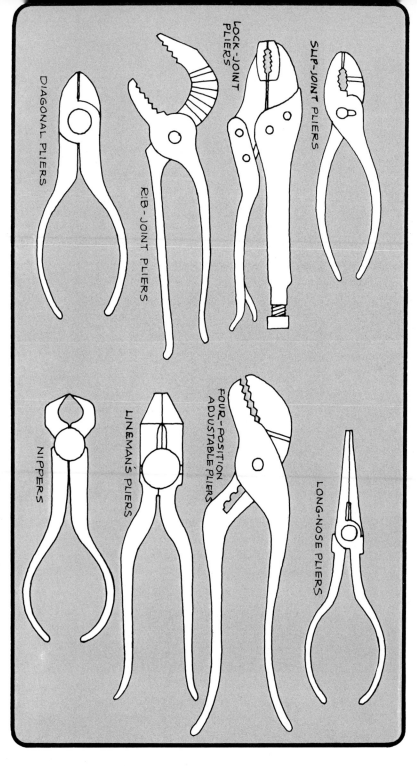

DIAGONAL PLIERS

LOCK-JOINT PLIERS

SLIP-JOINT PLIERS

RIB-JOINT PLIERS

NIPPERS

LINEMAN'S PLIERS

FOUR-POSITION ADJUSTABLE PLIERS

LONG-NOSE PLIERS

# USING PLIERS

Matching the tool to the material is the game you play when using pliers. For example, you don't use serrated lock-joint pliers to hold wood, since the pressure from the jaws would crush the fibers. Likewise, you wouldn't use long-nose pliers to tighten bolts or to hold a metal rod.

Pliers are not overachievers, either, so don't expect them to do a holding, turning, or cutting job that rightly belongs to a wrench, vise, or hacksaw. You'll ruin the material, the pliers, or both.

Pliers don't require a lot of maintenance. However, you should keep pivot bolts tight, cutters sharp, and jaws and handles free of grease and debris. An occasional buffing with fine steel wool will remove any rust and corrosion on metal parts.

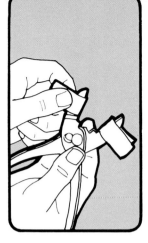

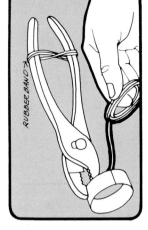

To avoid marring delicate materials such as soft woods and plastics, wrap jaws with adhesive bandages or tape.

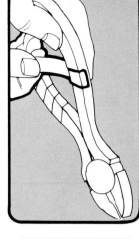

Rubber bands wrapped around the handles transform your pliers into a vise for small projects. Or, use lock-joint pliers.

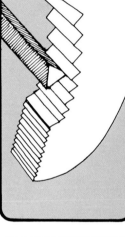

To insulate plier handles for electrical work, wrap them with electrical tape. Tape also adds padding for a comfortable grip.

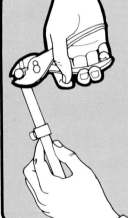

Hold pliers with your little finger inside one of the handles so you can open the jaws easily. The finger exerts outward pressure.

Use pliers to drive brads in small jobs, such as picture frames. Protect the material from the plier jaws with a paper pad.

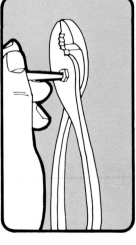

If pliers start slipping, check the jaws to be sure they're clean. If the teeth are stripped, reform them with a triangular file.

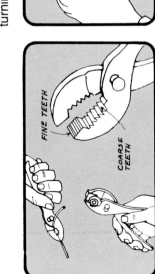

FINE TEETH

COARSE TEETH

Fine serrations grip small objects. The coarser teeth handle larger jobs. To adjust for bigger bite, slip the handles.

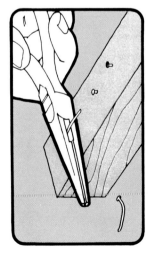

On delicate material, pull small nails with pliers instead of a hammer. For leverage, use a pulling/rolling-type motion.

To snug up a loose pivot bolt, tighten it so it doesn't wobble, then lock the bolt by tapping it with a hammer and punch.

440

# CHOOSING AND USING A VISE

Though certainly not a necessity, a vise is one of those nice-to-have-around-the-shop tools you'll eventually want to own. It acts as that extra hand so often missing when you need it most.

Ideally, it would be great to have both a bench vise and a woodworking vise at

your disposal, but unless you're strictly a woodworker, spend your money on a bench vise model. If you don't have a workbench, purchase a clamp-on vise.

When shopping for a vise, seek out one that's made from malleable iron and whose stress points are reinforced. The cheapies will give you trouble.

Mount bench and woodworking vises to workbenches with heavy bolts. If this isn't possible, use lag screws to secure

the vises. Never use nails clinched over at the heads.

Since any type of vise is subjected to sawdust, metal filings, and other material debris, it's important to keep the opening/closing screw cleaned and lightly oiled. And if the vise jaws ever wear out or get damaged, install new ones.

On some bench vises, pipe-holding jaws ride on the opening and closing screw. Regular jaws above hold smooth flat materials. A swivel base, another good feature, allows you to rotate the vise to the desired working position.

An anvil serves for peening and smoothing metals; a horn accepts ducts and tubular materials such as aluminum pipe.

Woodworking vises range in capacity from 4 to 7 inches; the 7-inch model is your best buy. Quality woodworking vises have jaw guides, and jaws that can be tightened almost with a flip of the handle.

Clamp-on vises, which you can mount on virtually any tabletop, generally have a 2½-inch capac-ity between their jaws.

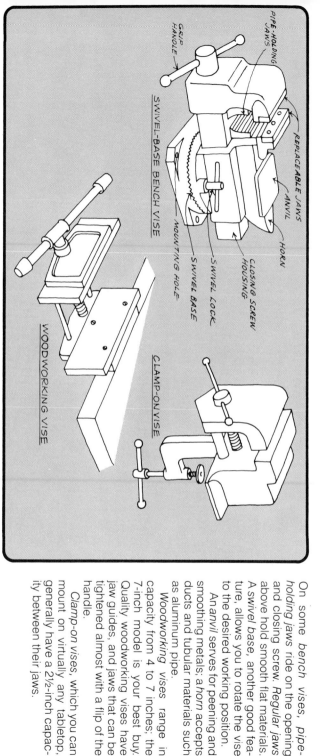

PIPE-HOLDING JAWS

GRIP HANDLE

REPLACEABLE JAWS

ANVIL

HORN

CLOSING SCREW

SWIVEL-BASE BENCH VISE

SWIVEL LOCK

SWIVEL BASE

CLOSING SCREW HOUSING

MOUNTING HOLE

WOODWORKING VISE

CLAMP-ON VISE

# MAKING SAWHORSES

Very simply, sawhorses are portable workbenches that can save you hours of time and lots of effort. So the sooner you build yourself a pair of them, the better.

Constructing sawhorses won't take long, regardless of whether you build them from scratch (see exploded view) or use either of the kit types shown.

The height for sawhorses ranges from 24 to 30 inches, although depending on your height, you may want to adjust them a few inches one way or the other. Make the length and width of the top rail any measurement you want.

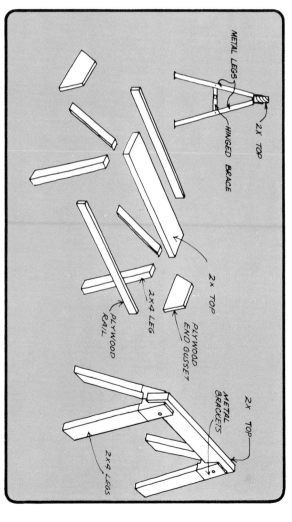

METAL LEGS

2× TOP

HINGED BRACE

2× TOP

2×4 LEG

PLYWOOD END GUSSET

PLYWOOD RAIL

2× TOP

METAL BRACKETS

2×4 LEGS

## CHOOSING OR BUILDING A WORKBENCH

If you're just setting up shop, do yourself a big favor and beg, buy, or build a workbench first thing. Without one, it's hard to operate.

Commercially made benches are worth considering. They range from simple, steel-and-particleboard arrangements to elaborate, beautifully finished versions that would satisfy even the most dedicated cabinetmaker.

Or, you can build your own workbench in a day or over a weekend—depending on how fancy you want to make it. Even if you go th s route, take a look at what's available commercially. If nothing else, you might pick up some design ideas that you can incorporate into a basic homemade bench, as shown below.

The workbench here amounts to little more than a cut-and-assemble job, yet it's plenty serviceable. You'll have to furnish your own dimensions to fit available shop space. If you're an advanced woodworker, you probably already can see refinements that you'll want to incorporate.

The height of the bench is important. To determine what's right for you, measure the distance from the floor to your hipbone—about 40 to 42 inches. The width should be 24 to 36 inches—or a comfortable reach from front to back. Length will depend on space, although 6 to 8 feet should give you plenty of working area to handle standard-length materials that don't need much cutting.

To ensure adequate support, fashion the legs from 2x4s or 4x4s; 4x4s are best, with 2x4s to support the top and the shelf. The plank top should be 2x6s. Use ¾-inch plywood for the backboard, back, and shelf. You'll need this strength to stabilize the framing.

For a tough, durable surface, screw a piece of ¼-inch tempered hardboard to the 2x6s. When the surface becomes worn and damaged, remove the screws, turn the top over, and use the other side. And when this side outlives its usefulness, you can replace the entire sheet at little cost.

Assemble the framing with carriage bolts (again, to ensure rigidity), and nail on the shelf and planking.

If you have a clamp-on vise, extend the front of the planking and top so it overhangs the frame by three inches to accept the clamp. Bolt a top-mounting vise to the top. Since a woodworking vise attaches to the front rail, provide a proper bearing surface by using a 2x8 there instead of a 2x4.

To construct the workbench, cut out the parts and test-assemble them. Then give all the parts, except the hardboard top, two coats of penetrating wood sealer. Sand the parts between coats and assemble them.

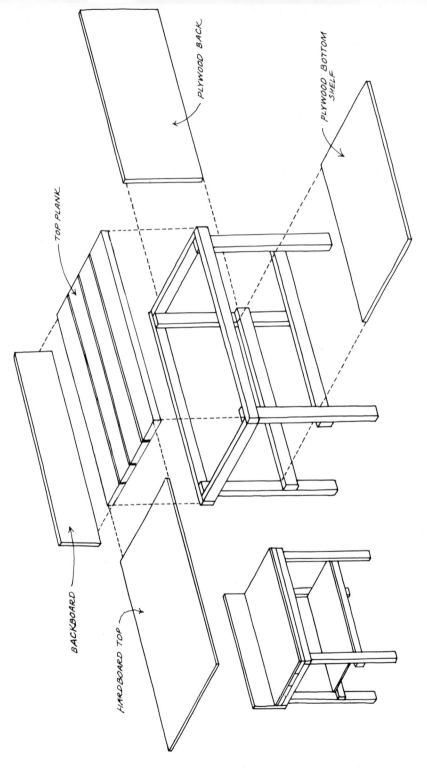

PLYWOOD BACK

PLYWOOD BOTTOM SHELF

TOP PLANK

BACKBOARD

HARDBOARD TOP

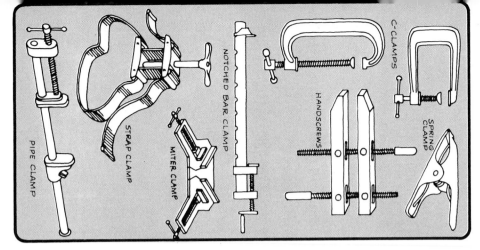

# CHOOSING AND USING CLAMPS

True, many of today's adhesives set up quickly, but you still need an assortment of clamps to help with some gluing projects—as well as for various other holding needs.

For starters, invest in four medium-size clamps. Add the specialty items—*bar, pipe, strap, miter,* and *handscrew* clamps—as you need them. The cost of most clamps is fairly moderate, with the exception of handscrews and bar clamps.

C-clamps, available either in aluminum or malleable iron, range in size from 1 to 8 inches, and with throat depths from 1 to 3¼ inches. You also can buy special deep-throat clamps.

For light fabrication, choose spring clamps; they work like big clothespins. Capacities range from 1 to 3 inches, and lengths from 4 to 9 inches.

To glue-assemble wide materials, you'll need some pipe clamps. They're sold without pipe, so you'll need galvanized steel pipe in the lengths you want. The clamp parts fit either ½- or ¾-inch pipe.

First cousins to pipe clamps, bar clamps are sold as a unit. To change the capacity of the notched model shown in the sketch, simply move the back clamp into the different notches, then tighten the screws to exert pressure.

Use miter clamps for picture frame construction and some furniture projects. Capacities range to 3 inches.

For woodworking and cabinetmaking projects, you'll need several handscrews. Since the jaws of these clamps are made from maple or selected hardwoods, you never have to add padding to protect the wood you're clamping. You can change the configuration of the clamp (up to a 10-inch capacity) by simply adjusting the screws. For most jobs, you'll need at least two handscrews; however, four are ideal if your budget allows.

Strap clamps come in handy for furniture-making projects as well as for holding together various round objects and irregular surfaces.

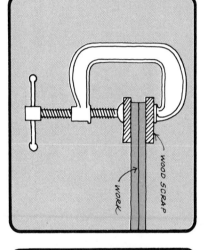

WOOD SCRAP

WORK

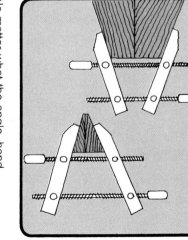

No matter what the angle, handscrews probably can hold onto the work for you. Adjust the screws as needed.

Protect the surface of the material from clamp jaws with thin wood pads. Do not overtighten any clamp; finger-tight is right.

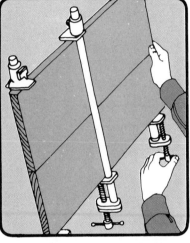

Alternate pipe clamps to equalize pressure on the material and to help prevent buckling. Pad the jaws, and *never* overtighten.

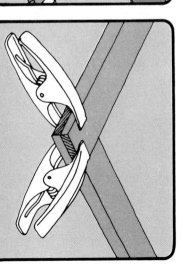

Spring clamps provide plenty of pressure. Use them for dozens of holding and hanging jobs, and while cutting or drilling.

# SHAPING AND SMOOTHING

Ever thought about why professionally done work usually looks that way? A drywall joint taper or a finish carpenter does his job in much the same way a do-it-yourselfer would. But these tradespeople know that it's how you finish off a project that really counts. And that's where smoothing and shaping come in. Most all projects benefit from it. The tools to use for these important finishing touches are files and rasps, planes, and abrasives.

Knowing what tool to use where isn't as difficult as it may seem. Choose planes to trim from ¼ to ¾ inch from wood. Files and rasps will remove ¹/₁₆ to ³/₁₆ inch of material. And abrasives remove and smooth materials from 0 to ¹/₁₆ inch.

## CHOOSING FILES AND RASPS

Files and rasps do the same thing—only to different materials. Files, in all of their many forms, remove and smooth metal and plastic; rasps, on the other hand, finish only wood.

Files take their names from their shapes: *flat, round, half-round, triangular, square, diamond,* and *crossing.* Their teeth or "cut" also give them away. A single-cut file has single teeth; a double-cut file has crossed rows of teeth; rasps feature coarse, heavy-looking teeth; and curved files, not surprisingly, have curved teeth.

When shopping for a file for a particular use, keep in mind, too, that there are many gradations of tooth coarseness from which to choose: coarse, bastard, second cut, smooth cut, and dead smooth.

Specialty items abound in this category. You can buy files for sharpening lawnmower blades; tapered round files for enlarging and smoothing holes; auger-bit files for sharpening the cutting edges of bits (see page 423); and even special files for sharpening saw blades (see page 405).

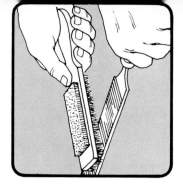

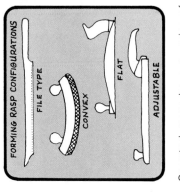

FORMING RASP CONFIGURATIONS

FILE TYPE

CONVEX

FLAT

ADJUSTABLE

Serrated rasps have a series of tiny cutting blades along a metal strip that looks like a flat file. You can buy them with file-type handles, plane handles, or combination file/plane handles. Serrated rasps cut very quickly for a usable, smooth surface. Their blades last a long time, but when one dulls, throw it away and buy a new one.

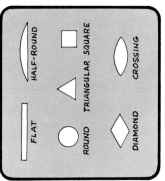

FLAT
HALF-ROUND
ROUND
TRIANGULAR
SQUARE
DIAMOND
CROSSING

File and rasp shapes often determine which file or rasp to use for what project. For example, a 6-inch triangular file is used for touching up and sharpening saws and other files; a 10-inch round bastard file is used on round openings in metal and some plastics.

SINGLE-CUT
DOUBLE-CUT
RASP
CURVED TOOTH

Single- and double-cut files come in four degrees of coarseness: coarse and bastard for rough, fast work; second cut for alloy metals and finish work; and smooth cut for fine finishing. Double-cut files remove lots of material; single-cut files are for smoothing. For removing lots of wood, use a rasp for rough shaping, then smooth with an abrasive (see page 448).

A file card has stiff metal bristles on one side for cleaning the teeth of files. The soft metal bristles on the other side are for cleaning wood and plastic debris from the teeth. To deter rust, coat metal files with light oil. Don't oil rasps; remove any rust with a wire brush. Keep all tools away from water.

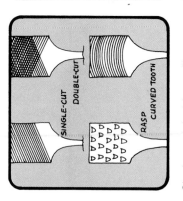

Furiously saw a file back and forth and you'll end up with an uneven edge, a dull file, and tired arms. If slow, even strokes don't do the job, you're using the wrong type of file.

For best results, first lock the work in a vise or clamp it to a firm surface. Keep the work about waist-to-elbow high so you can get the proper leverage on the tool you're using.

Grasp a rasp and all but the smallest files with both hands—one on the handle, the other on the tip. Apply pressure on the forward stroke, and lift it clear or drag it only slightly on the return. With practice, you'll gain a feel for the right amount of pressure. Too much will jamb the teeth with filings and the file

won't cut well; too little won't make any cut at all. If the pressure exerted is just right, you'll produce a pile of shavings with each stroke.

Since a rasp's job is to remove, not smooth wood, expect it to leave a rough edge. This tool cuts fast, so check your progress after every few strokes. When you're near your goal, switch to a file or an abrasive for the finishing touches.

Files and rasps are rugged tools, but you must store them in such a way that their teeth aren't dulled or damaged by knocking against other tools. Wrap them in cloth or hang them up; don't toss them unprotected into a drawer. When a file finally does dull, replace it—but keep the old one for working softer materials.

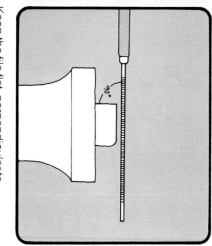

Clamp small work in a vise with the edge to be filed near the jaws (this minimizes chatter). Protect surfaces with wood scraps.

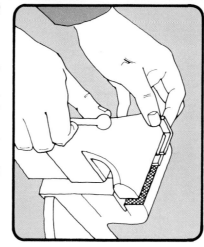

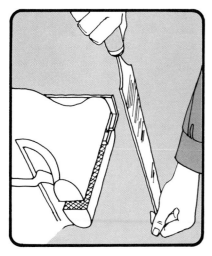

For rough cutting, grip the file at both ends to keep the pressure even and guide the file. Always use a handle on the file tang.

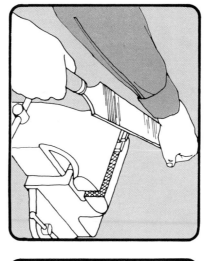

For smoothing, hold the tip of the file between your thumb and forefinger. Files cut best with lots of light strokes.

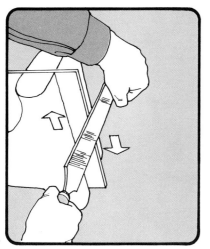

Keep the file flat, perpendicular to the edge you're filing. Avoid the tendency to rock the file; go completely across the work.

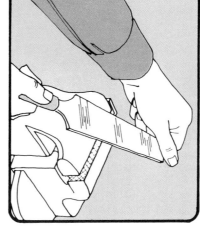

On most jobs, lift the file off work for the return stroke. If you're filing soft metal, drag it back to clear the teeth.

For finishing touches on fine work, "draw-file"—push the file across the material at right angles. Keep all work clean of filings.

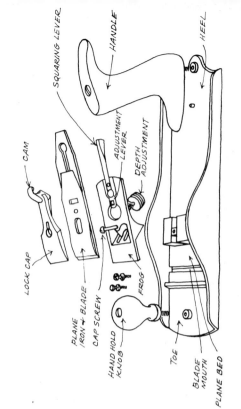

## CHOOSING A PLANE

If you've ever had to trim a door to keep it from binding, round the corners of a project you're building, or smooth a rough board or timber, you don't have to be sold on the desirability of having a plane handy. Fact is, a plane can help you do a multitude of jobs—with ease, speed, and accuracy.

Not surprisingly, the most important part of a plane is the blade. You must keep it razor-sharp so it can produce paper-thin to coarse-thick shavings without too much muscle from you. If you don't, a dull plane, just like any other dull cutting tool, will drive you to distraction.

For most home projects, you need only *smoothing* and *block planes*. The other types shown in the sketch below perform functions usually required only in furniture-making or other specialized projects.

When shopping for a plane, look for one with malleable sides and bottom. Less expensive models won't give you the accuracy and durability required of this tool.

Aside from keeping the blades sharp, planes need little maintenance. You can remove light rust and corrosion from the plane's metal parts with fine steel wool and machine oil. But be sure to clean all oil from the bottom so it doesn't foul wood surfaces.

When you lay a plane down, turn it on its side so the blade can't accidentally be dulled. And when you store one, retract the blade into the body to protect the blade's edge.

If damaged, almost any part of a plane may be replaced separately; you don't have to buy a brand-new one. For instance, you can easily replace handles and knobs, which may be wooden or plastic, by removing a couple of screws that hold them in position.

## ANATOMY OF A PLANE

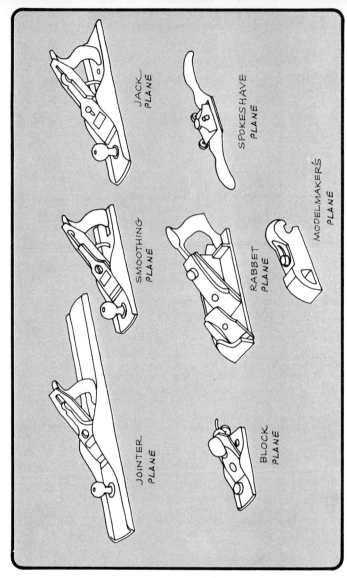

A *jointer plane* squares the edges of materials so they may be joined with adhesive or fasteners. For all-around work and sometimes to double for both a jointer and jack plane, use a *smoothing plane*. A general-use plane for both jointing and smoothing, a *jack plane* measures 12 to 15 inches long (compared to 18 and 24 inches for jointers and 7 to 10 inches for smoothers). A *block plane* is for end-grain work. A *rabbet plane* cuts rabbets for joints, while a *spokeshave* planes irregular surfaces and curves. For small planing jobs on wood and soft metal use a *model-maker's plane*.

**446**

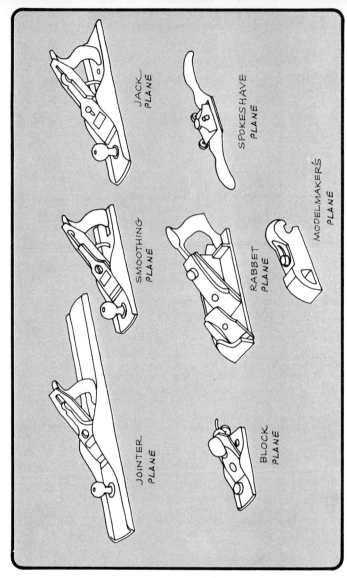
JACK PLANE

SPOKESHAVE PLANE

SMOOTHING PLANE

RABBET PLANE

MODELMAKER'S PLANE

JOINTER PLANE

BLOCK PLANE

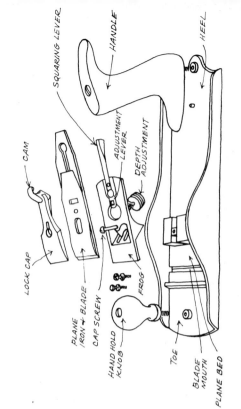
HANDLE

SQUARING LEVER

HEEL

CAM

ADJUSTMENT LEVER

DEPTH ADJUSTMENT

LOCK CAP

PLANE IRON + BLADE

CAP SCREW

FROG

HAND HOLD KNOB

TOE

BLADE MOUTH

PLANE BED

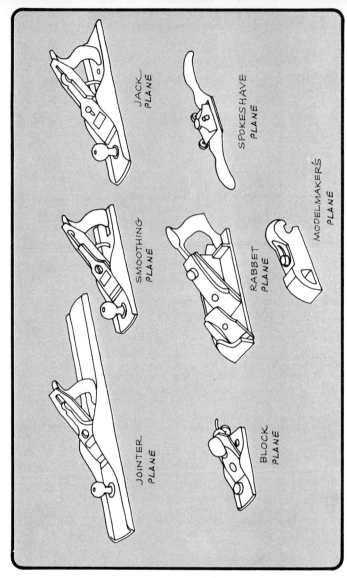

Planes cut best when the work is locked in a vise. If the work is too large for a vise, such as a door, you can wedge one end of it in a corner to hold it firm.

The trick to using a plane is balance and rhythm. You need both feet firmly planted on the floor to take smooth, even cutting strokes with the plane. The result

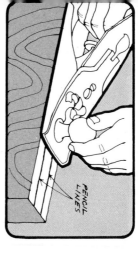

will be thin, unbroken shavings that are all the same thickness. If the shavings are thick and thin or if they crumble and break apart, you can bet that the blade isn't sharp enough, that it's improperly set, or that you're off-balance and are jabbing the work.

Planing the edges of soft metals and plastics is similar to planing wood. However, the plane blade must be set very shallow, and you must support the

material between two pieces of thin wood so the materials won't buckle under the pressure.

As a general rule, plane wood just short of the scribed line you want to match. Then finish the job with an abrasive stretched over a sandpaper block so you can keep it square to the work (see page 449).

Before you start planing, examine the wood grain to determine its direction. Then work with the grain to minimize "snagging."

Begin the stroke by applying most of the pressure to the knob end. Complete the stroke with pressure on the handle end.

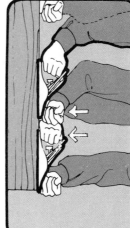

Draw several pencil lines on the edge of the piece to be planed. Use them to help you locate high spots as you work.

Using a block plane, plane end grain from either side to the middle to prevent splitting. Then smooth the hump in the middle.

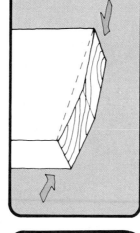

To bevel a board's edge, hold the plane at an angle. Mark the depth of the cut first, making a small bevel at the corner.

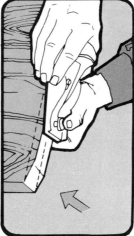

smooth complex or sharp curves with a spokeshave. Usually it's best to push this tool along the work rather than pull it.

Hold the plane at a slight angle to the work. A sharp plane, properly used, will shave off continuous ribbons.

Hone plane blades just as you would a chisel (see page 414). You can even use the same sharpening jig. Whet any burrs.

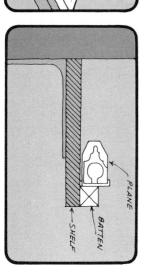

To protect the plane blades, store the plane on its side. An edge-of-shelf batten helps keep it positioned during storage.

**447**

## CHOOSING ABRASIVES

Funny thing about sandpaper: the sand isn't really sand, and chances are, the paper isn't really paper, but a composition material.

Maybe sandpaper (technically, a coated abrasive) isn't what its name implies, but it's still a smoothing and finishing tool of great import. A properly selected piece can save you plenty of time and effort on many around-the-house projects.

The chart below contains just about everything you could possibly want to know about abrasives—and most likely, a lot more than that. So consider it a connoisseur's guide.

For most jobs you'll be doing, selection is relatively easy. Most manufacturers realize the confusion that surrounds their product, so they usually label the packages with use information such as "For Metal," "For Plastics," "For Hardwoods," and so forth. They also indicate the coarseness of the sheets. For example, you might see a package labeled, "2 fine, 2 medium, 1 coarse."

### WHAT'S WHAT IN ABRASIVES

| Type of Abrasive | Coarseness Code | Uses | Color | Backing | Coating** | Durability | Cost |
|---|---|---|---|---|---|---|---|
| Aluminum oxide* | Extra-coarse, 36; coarse, 50 or 60; medium, 80 or 100; fine, 120 or 150; and extra-fine, 220 | To sand wood, metal, plastic, fiber glass | Brownish | Paper and cloth | Open/closed | Good to excellent | Moderate |
| Emery* | Fine, medium coarse, extra-coarse | To polish metals | Black | Cloth | Open/closed | Good | Moderate |
| Flint | Fine, medium, coarse | Light-duty sanding; sanding tacky surfaces | Yellowish-white | Paper | Open | Poor | Low |
| Garnet* | Extra-coarse, 36; coarse, 50 or 60; medium, 80 or 100; fine, 120 or 150; and extra-fine, 220 | For woodworking projects | Reddish | Paper | Open/closed | Good | Moderate |
| Silicon carbide* | Most popular grades—very-fine, 180, 220, or 240; extra-fine, 280 or 320; super-fine, 400; and ultra-fine, 600 | To sand floors and smooth glass, fiberglass, hard plastics, soft metals, and finishes between coats | Black | Paper | Open/closed | Good to excellent | High |
| Tungsten carbide | Coarse; medium; fine | To remove stubborn finishes | Reddish-brown | — | — | Excellent | High |
| Steel wool | No. 3, coarse; No. 2, medium coarse; No. 1, medium; No. 0, fine; No. 00, very fine; No. 000, extra fine; No. 0000, extremely fine | To remove rust or corrosion from metal; to smooth surface between finish coats | Blackish | — | — | Fair to good | Moderate |
| Pumice | Coarse to fine powder | To smooth finish coats | White | — | — | Excellent | Moderate |
| Rottenstone | Coarse to fine powder | Same as pumice | Grayish | — | — | Excellent | Moderate |

*Standard size is 9x11 inches. Precut machine and sanding block sizes also are available in many home center stores.

**Use open-coat papers on materials that are gummy and tend to clog the abrasive particles. For materials that won't clog the particles, use closed-coat papers.

Removing and smoothing material with abrasives is a heavy-light project. You start with a coarse or heavy abrasive and finish with a light one.

Although this rule isn't etched in stone, you shouldn't skip grit (abrasive) sizes as you go from heavy to light papers. Naturally, this doesn't mean you should start out with No. 12 aluminum oxide paper and hit every size up to 600. You should, however, go from very coarse to coarse, to medium, to fine, to very fine. Use your own judgment on this, too. It could be that you should start with a medium grit and work through to fine.

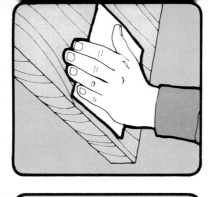

Despite what you've undoubtedly seen done or done yourself, do not cut abrasive papers with a knife or scissors. Cutting abrasives will quickly dull the edges of your tools. Instead, score the paper or cloth side wherever you want with an awl or nail. Then crease it by folding the paper over, and tear it along this creased line.

Although abrasives can remove a lot of material fast, you should first determine whether another tool will do the job better. Sometimes, you can remove old finish faster with paint remover and a scraper than with an abrasive. See pages 528 and 529 for this technique.

For general sanding purposes, stock your workshop or tool kit with very fine to very coarse aluminum oxide abrasives. Also include several tubes of very fine to medium steel wool. Purchase other abrasives as your projects demand.

Keep abrasives in a cool dry place, and lay them flat so the sheets don't curl. Use the sheets until they no longer remove or smooth materials; don't throw away abrasives just because they're slightly worn. Save them for later.

If you have lots of sanding to do, you may be able to buy abrasives by the box. More about sanding techniques on pages 530 and 531.

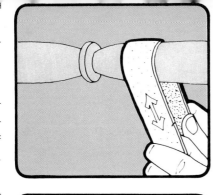

Always sand with the grain, holding the abrasive flat with the palm of your hand. Light pressure on the paper is adequate.

Or use a sanding block for more uniform pressure. Buy a wood, rubber, or plastic block, or simply staple paper to scrap wood.

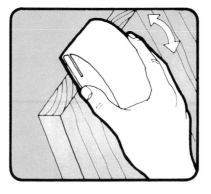

To round the corners and edges of the material you're sanding, rock the sanding block back and forth slightly as shown.

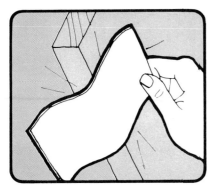

If you need a perfectly square edge, clamp the material between two pieces of scrap first. Keep the abrasive square.

To sand curves and spindles, tear one of the cloth-backed abrasives into strips and use them as you would a shoeshine cloth.

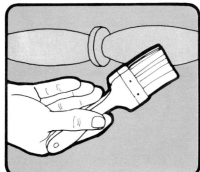

To sand crevices, crease the abrasive as shown. Use an ice cream stick or a thin piece of wood for a "block."

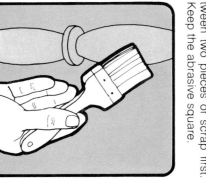

Clean clogged paper by slapping it hard. Or brush it with a file card. Keep sanding dust off the work as you sand.

For a super-smooth finish, apply a thin coat of shellac before the final sanding. Be sure to let the shellac dry thoroughly.

## CHOOSING A POWER SANDER

Portable electric sanders supply almost all the muscle you need for any sanding project—large or small; you just flip the starter switch, press down lightly, and steer. In fact, this equipment does such an efficient job of quickly removing material and smoothing, your biggest problem may be controlling the machine.

An *orbital sander*, a veritable jack of all trades, has enough spunk to remove excess material fairly quickly. Its long suit is smoothing, which it does perfectly. Make an orbital model your first sander purchase; it may satisfy all of your sanding needs.

The pads on orbital sanders, which "vibrate" in an orbital pattern, are best suited to flat areas where a lot of excess material doesn't have to be removed. With special pads, you can use them for buffing and polishing, too.

*Straight-line sanders*, sometimes called *finishing sanders*, resemble orbital types, but they vibrate with just a simple back-and-forth motion. Use these only for final finishing and smoothing work; you can't count on them to remove much material. Many orbital sanders convert to straight-line action with the flip of a lever, so you can start out in the orbital mode and switch to straight-line sanding for the last few passes.

There aren't any special tricks to using either type. Just outfit it with a sandpaper pad (either the precut type or one torn from a larger sheet), then move it with the grain, if possible. Don't apply too much downward pressure; just guide the sander and let it do the work.

A *disc sander* can serve you in several ways. The job it does best is removing excess material and rust from metal. But it's also capable of cutting across wood grain, which makes it an excellent tool for sanding end grain. Because the disc is flexible, it will go into depressions in wood and metal, and if you tilt it, it will sand curves, rounds, and contours. By changing to a wool pad, you can even buff and polish with one.

If you use this tool on wood, though, be advised that you must hold the disc perfectly square to the work surface. Otherwise, you may mar or cup the material with the edge of the disc.

Disc sanders are "iffy" tools—if you have a ¼-inch drill, you can buy a sanding disc attachment that will do the same job as the disc sander (⅜-inch drills, because they operate at lower rpm, don't make good sanders). And if you have a stationary combination belt and disc sander, you don't have any need for a disc sander, unless a particular job requires a portable tool.

For lots of heavy-duty sanding, you'll need a *belt sander*. You can rent this equipment, if you're only going to be using it from time to time. If you decide to buy one, make sure it's equipped with a dust bag attachment. This feature is worth every penny of the extra cost, since it removes a lot of the dust particles from the air and the piece on which you're working. If you use the sander for sanding floors, panels, and other large surfaces, run it with the grain of the wood, changing belts from medium-grit to fine-grit abrasive.

ORBITAL SANDER

DISC SANDER

BELT SANDER

In price, the disc and orbital sanders are comparable; belt sanders, more expensive. Since they're lightweight, disc and orbital sanders work well on both horizontal and vertical surfaces. It's difficult to control a belt sander on a vertical surface. Sometimes, belts are classified as coarse, medium, and fine abrasives rather than by number.

Important features to look for on all three sanders are locking trigger switches, quick abrasive paper changing systems, and sawdust collectors.

# CHOOSING A LATHE

If it weren't for the fact that they're pretty expensive, owning a lathe would be almost worth it just for the fun and enjoyment it can provide. Pushing a round-nose chisel into a block of spinning wood and watching the chips fly is exciting. You can see the fruits of your labors materialize in just a few short moments.

But for the serious hobbyist or craftsman who enjoys making furniture, a lathe is much, much more. It not only can turn squares into rounds with amazing speed and accuracy, a lathe also can fashion flat/round items such as dishes, trays, and lamp bases. For these operations, you'll need a *faceplate* that fastens onto the *headstock* of the lathe.

Most lathes are individual stationary tools, but some are sold as a special attachment for a radial arm saw. If you are considering a lathe, be sure you get the variable-speed motor feature. Use higher speeds for finishing cuts on small stock, slower speeds on large stock.

Pay attention to lathe capacity, too. For most woodworking projects, you'll need at least 30 inches between the head- and tailstock. Of course, this doesn't pertain to model-maker's lathes, where capacity usually isn't a factor. Your lathe also should have sufficient turning capacity for round items. This is the clearance between the headstock and tailstock

spindle and the bed of the lathe. Basic lathe tools include a round-nose chisel for shaping; a gouge for shaping rough work and cutting coves; a skew chisel for smoothing; a parting chisel for straight cuts; and a spear chisel for duplicating contours in the stock.

Another important accessory, the *tool rest* should be wide enough (12 inches or more) so you don't have to continually move it along the bed of the lathe to make the necessary cuts.

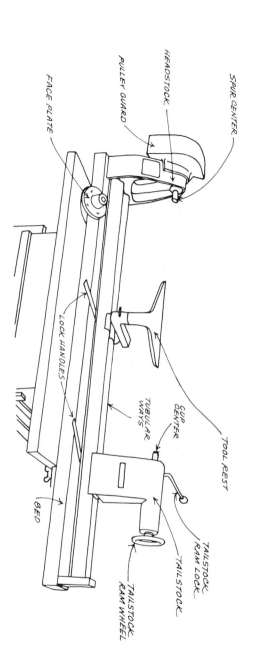

HEADSTOCK

PULLEY GUARD

FACE PLATE

SPUR CENTER

LOCK HANDLES

CUP CENTER

TOOL REST

BED

TUBULAR WAYS

TAILSTOCK RAM LOCK

TAILSTOCK

TAILSTOCK RAM WHEEL

# CHOOSING A JOINTER

Like a woodworking lathe, a jointer, sometimes called a jointer-planer, is a professional tool for the serious craftsman. You won't make much use of it for routine home maintenance.

By design, a jointer's task is to plane the edges of boards perfectly square so they can be joined with other square boards. But that's by no means all it does. It cuts rabbets, chamfers, bevels, tapers, and tenons, and if the boards are narrow enough, it can even plane their face sides.

A jointer's only working part is a steel cylinder that usually has three slots in which knives are locked. The knives do the cutting.

The front of the jointer is adjustable, enabling you to raise or lower it to set the depth of cut you want. You can adjust the fence, too, making it possible to cut angles on the edge or face of wood.

Features to look for when shopping include a well-machined table and fence, quick-adjustment levers, and the largest table capacity you can afford—most home models are about four inches. Look for high-speed ground steel knives and at least a ½-hp motor for necessary speed and power. Also nice are leveling feet for the stand and positive fence stops at 45 and 90 degrees.

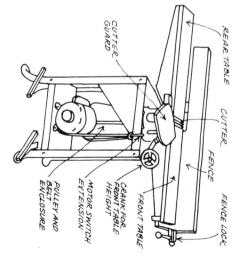

CUTTER GUARD

REAR TABLE

CUTTER

FENCE

FENCE LOCK

CRANK FOR FRONT TABLE HEIGHT

MOTOR SWITCH EXTENSION

PULLEY AND BELT ENCLOSURE

FRONT TABLE

# MATERIALS AND HOW TO USE THEM

If you've ever stepped up to the service counter at a lumberyard or home center store and ordered materials for a project you *know* that the world of materials is a complex one, full of unfamiliar terminology and an astounding array of products from which to choose. You also know that to make the best use of each dollar you spend on materials requires some knowledge of what's available and which products are best used where. Sharing that knowledge with you is the thrust of this chapter. In addition, it will show you how to work with materials after you buy them.

## CHOOSING AND BUYING LUMBER

Smart lumber buymanship begins with an understanding of a few things about lumber. First, keep in mind that lumber is either a *softwood* or a *hardwood*. Both types are discussed on pages 454 and 455.

Also realize that all pieces of lumber have a *nominal* set of dimensions and an *actual* set. For example, when you order a 2x4, you get a length of wood that actually measures 1½ inches thick and 3½ inches wide.

Why the difference? The answer lies in the way lumber is readied for market. Shrinkage is responsible for part of the loss. *Air-drying*, once the accepted means of reducing the moisture content of lumber, is a thing of the past. Largely due to ever-increasing demand, most lumber now is *kiln-dried*, a faster method that also introduces more shrinkage. Surprisingly, only thickness and width are affected. Length remains almost the same after drying.

*Milling*, the process of dressing the wood after sawing to the rough size, accounts for the remainder of the missing material. Most lumber is milled (shaved) on all four surfaces to yield a board that is smooth all around.

Also keep in mind that all lumber is graded. And as with most things, the better the quality, the more it costs. This explains the often-bewildering cost differential between two seemingly identical items.

Hardwoods are *1sts* and *2nds* (FAS), *selects*, or *No. 1 common*. Softwoods, the type you'll buy most often, break down as follows. *Select lumber* (B and Better, C, and D) has two good faces, making it ideal for "showy" projects. Use *common lumber* (#1, #2, #3, and #4) for all of your other building needs. Your lumber dealer should be able to help you determine which grade of lumber you need for a given project.

## UNDERSTANDING LINEAR AND BOARD FEET

Obviously, there's more wood in a 4-foot 2x12 than in a 2x4 the same length. That's why lumber is priced by the *board foot*. One board foot equals a piece 1 inch thick, 12 inches long, and 12 inches wide (nominal). See the sketch at right.

Actually, though, except when ordering hardwoods, you needn't worry too much about board feet. Simply tell the salesperson the number of *linear* (actual) feet you need; he will compute the cost.

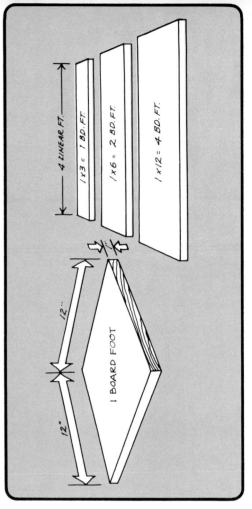

1 BOARD FOOT

1 x 3 = 1 BD. FT. — 4 LINEAR FT.

1 x 6 = 2 BD. FT.

1 x 12 = 4 BD. FT.

| WHAT TO ASK FOR | | | | |
|---|---|---|---|---|
| **What It's Called** | **Sample** | **Uses** | **Nominal Size** | **Actual Size** |
| **Strips (Furring)**<br>Wood that is less than 2 inches thick and 3 inches wide. Some unpatterned molding is classed as strips. | 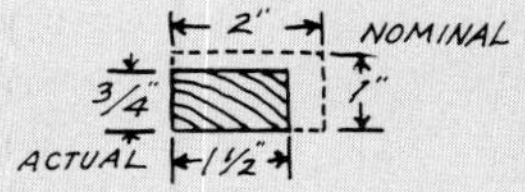 | Furring for ceiling and wall panels; trim; shims; bridging; blocking; stakes; forming; crating; battens; light framing; edging; spacers; lattice. | 1x2<br>1x3 | ¾x1½<br>¾x2½ |
| **Boards**<br>Wood that is less than 2 inches thick and more than 3 inches wide. | 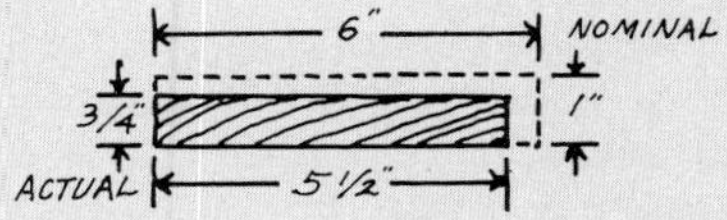 | Paneling; trim; shelving; sheathing; structural framing; structural finishing; forming; siding; fascias; soffits; flooring; decking; fencing; casing; cabinets; built-ins; tables; benches; furniture; closet lining; walks; racks; subflooring. | 1x4<br>1x6<br>1x8<br>1x10<br>1x12 | ¾x3½<br>¾x5½<br>¾x7¼<br>¾x9¼<br>¾x11¼ |
| **Dimension Lumber**<br>Two inches thick and 2 or more inches wide. Material that is 3, 4, or 6 inches wide is called a stud. "Planks" are 8 or more inches wide. Softwoods are most common, but you can buy hardwoods. | 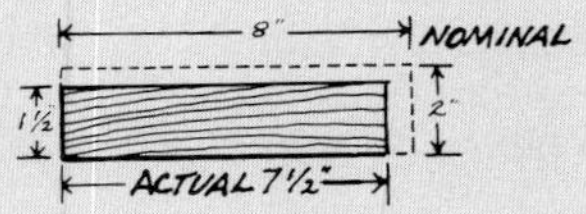 | Most often used for structural framing and finishing; forming; decking; fencing; walks; benches; screeds; steps; boxed columns. | 2x2<br>2x3<br>2x4<br>2x6<br>2x8<br>2x10<br>2x12 | 1½x1½<br>1½x2½<br>1½x3½<br>1½x5½<br>1½x7¼<br>1½x9¼<br>1½x11¼ |
| **Posts**<br>Square in cross section. | 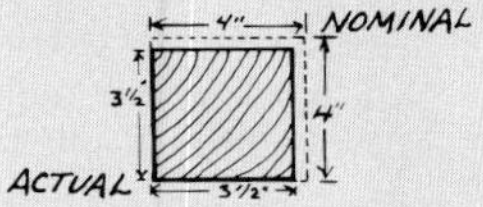 | Structural framing and supports; columns; fencing; decking; turnings for wood lathes; decorative interest. | 4x4<br>6x6 | 3½x3½<br>5½x5½ |
| **Timbers**<br>Five inches or larger in the smallest dimension. | 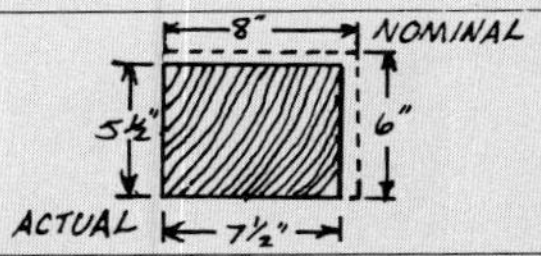 | Structural framing; columns; architectural and decorative interest. | Varies | ½ inch less than nominal size |
| **Matched Lumber**<br>Edges and/or ends are tongue and grooved. |  | Subflooring; flooring; sheathing. | Varies; see board classification. | Varies; see board classification. |
| **Shiplap**<br>The edges are rabbeted to form a strong, smooth joint. |  | Sheathing; siding; decking; underlayment; finishing. A ⅜-inch lap is common; you can buy plywood panels with shiplapped edges. | 1x4<br>1x6<br>1x8 | ¾x3⅛<br>¾x5⅛<br>¾x6⅞ |

## HOW TO ORDER LUMBER

Waiting in line at a lumberyard behind someone who doesn't know quite what he needs for his project isn't anyone's idea of fun. Nor is being the person in doubt. So before going to place your order, make a list of the items you need.

When jotting down your lumber needs, always put the number of pieces of a particular item first, then list the thickness, width, and length. If you do this, you'll be talking the salesperson's language, and will avoid confusion.

For information about ordering other materials, refer to later pages in this chapter.

## SELECTING SOFTWOODS

Actually when you order softwood lumber, there's not that much selecting to be done. Because suppliers can buy in bulk and save considerably by doing so, they usually stock relatively few varieties. So when you order so many 2x4s, for example, the salesperson may give you a couple of choices—say fir or pine.

That's not to say that you can't get most any softwood you want. You can—but it may require special ordering and/or increased cost. The chart below discusses the most commonly available species.

Softwood, which comes from cone-bearing or evergreen trees, generally is less expensive than hardwood, although some species may be very costly, depending on where you live. For example, east of the West Coast states, redwood is very expensive,

mainly because of shipping costs and restrictions on how much redwood can be logged. Its beauty and weather-resistance may be worth the price, though.

Cost also depends on the grade of the wood you purchase (see page 452). The more blemish- and knot-free the board, the more it will cost you. Anything "added" to the material, such as grooving, brushing, or a sealer, increases the cost even more.

Time was when you could go to a building material retailer and pick and choose the lumber you wanted. If you find such a retailer today, don't tell him that his competitors have a "what-you-see-is-what-you-get" policy. Even with these, though, don't hesitate to reject any piece that's useless. More about judging lumber on page 456.

Most softwoods—especially those strapped on a pallet—have extremely rough, splintered, or split ends that

should be cut off before use. Be sure to allow for this when you order.

Because of customer preference, many home center stores and building material outlets "price-stamp" lumber by the piece. This is to fulfill the needs of do-it-yourselfers who want just one board so wide, so long, and so thick. If you're in the market for lots of lumber, though, ask the retailer for a "price."

Don't overlook the bargains in used lumber, either. You may find it available at the wrecking site of an old building, or advertised in the classified section of your local newspaper. The lumber may look old and dirty, but very often underneath this coat of grime, you'll find strong, seasoned wood free of bad defects and sap pockets. And don't be surprised if you find some dirt-disguised lengths of hardwood such as walnut, oak, hickory, cherry, or maple. Builders years ago often used these fine materials for structural supports.

### SOFTWOOD SELECTOR

| Species | Outstanding Properties | Cost* | Common Uses |
|---|---|---|---|
| Cedar | Easy to work with hand and power tools; resists shrinking, swelling, warping; has natural resistance to rot. | Moderate where logged; fairly expensive elsewhere. | Trim; paneling; decks; exterior walks; fencing. |
| Redwood | Easy to work with hand and power tools; finishes well, has natural resistance to rot; weathers beautifully. Use *heartwood* for posts and near-ground structural members, *common* for decking and other elements. | Moderate to expensive where logged; very expensive elsewhere. You can save some money by asking for "garden grade." | Trim; paneling; decks; exterior walks; fencing; furniture. |
| Fir, Spruce, Pine | Excellent strength; finishes well. Pine has some natural resistance to decay; all are easy to work with hand and power tools. For below-ground applications, use treated lumber (see page 177). | Moderate; usually inexpensive where logged. | House framing; trim; paneling; decking; fencing; furniture; millwork. |
| Cypress | Good strength; finishes well; has excellent natural resistance to decay; easy to work with hand and power tools. | Moderate to expensive; may be in limited quantity in some areas. | Trim; paneling; fencing; decking; posts; some furniture; hobby use. |
| Hemlock | Lightweight and easy to work with hand and power tools; has natural resistance to decay; grain in wood is very uniform. | Moderate | Framing; paneling; decking; sheathing; subflooring; general utility lumber. |

*Prices of lumber and plywood can vary daily, since the materials are traded in the commodities market. Also, rail, truck, and boat shipping costs affect the price of materials, as do foreign imports.

454

# SELECTING HARDWOODS

For generations, people have been fascinated by the beauty of hardwood. And that fascination continues today. You can see hardwood used for interior trim; in fine furniture; veneered to the faces of doors, plywood panels, and tabletops; in strip and parquet flooring; and in a variety of decorative accents.

But today more than ever before, hardwoods are expensive and in short supply compared to softwoods. The reason: the trees that produce hardwoods (they all shed their leaves each fall) grow ever so slowly. Demand easily outstrips the available supply. That's why you see much more softwood, or hardwood veneers over softwood frames, used for projects formerly reserved solely for hardwood.

The average lumberyard or home center outlet doesn't stock much hardwood—either lumber or sheet goods. It occasionally may have a limited supply of selected fast-selling items, but your best bet, if your town has one, is a supplier who specializes in hardwoods. These dealers can get you just about any type wood you want.

While there, keep the following things in mind. When hardwood is harvested, it's cut into random lengths and widths rather than standardized units to make the best possible use of all the available wood. Thicknesses generally range from 1 inch to 2 inches.

Like softwoods, hardwood lumber also has both nominal and actual dimensions. So when you place an order, realize that a 1-inch piece of stock, for example, won't measure quite an inch thick. Likewise, a 5/4 (1¼-inch-thick) piece will be slightly less thick after milling. The same applies to widths. And if you're ordering woodwork trim, don't expect to find all of the pieces cut to the same length. You'll get what's in stock, or pay quite a premium for the yard's trouble.

## HARDWOOD SELECTOR

| Species | Outstanding Properties | Cost* | Common Uses |
|---|---|---|---|
| Ash | Strong, yet flexible; easy to work; holds nails and screws well. | Medium-priced | Furniture, especially for formed parts of chairs. |
| Oak | Extremely hard; requires very sharp hand and power tools to work. Open grain; finishes well; resists water and moisture. | Medium-priced | Flooring; furniture; decorative structural supports; trim; barrels; railings. |
| Mahogany | Easy to work with power and hand tools; has a fine grain; finishes well; has good resistance to warping, swelling, and shrinking. | Medium-priced to expensive | Furniture; cabinets; moldings; boat components; plywood inlays and veneers; facings. |
| Poplar | Holds paint and stain well. | Medium-priced | Furniture; trim; cabinets. |
| Maple, Birch | Easy to work with sharp hand and power tools. Closed grain; finishes well; has good resistance to swelling and shrinking; strong and hard. | Expensive | Furniture; flooring; moldings; cabinets; inlays; veneers; facings. |
| Walnut | Easy to work; finishes extremely well; fine grain; resists warping, swelling, and shrinking. Wood is especially strong and durable. | Very expensive | Furniture; fine cabinets; flooring and paneling veneers; molding; facings; pulls. |
| Teak | Extremely hard and durable; requires very sharp hand and power tools to work. Very resistant to rot, swelling, shrinking, warping. | Very expensive | Furniture; fine cabinets; flooring and paneling veneers; boat construction; trim. |

*Prices of hardwoods are fairly stable. Where logged, the lumber generally drops substantially in price.

# WORKING WITH LUMBER

Lumber is a wonderfully diverse material. It supports, joins, attaches, frames, and covers like nothing else—and at a cost that's not prohibitive. But it's up to you to make lumber live up to its full potential.

On the previous four pages, you've been briefed on lumber terminology, buymanship, and the properties and uses for each type of wood. On the following several pages, you'll learn about the joinery techniques you need to master as a do-it-yourselfer. One or more of these techniques will come into play whenever you undertake any kind of woodworking project—large or small.

## SIZING UP A BOARD

Don't expect perfection in the lumber you buy—you're bound to be disappointed. Lumber can have any number of ills—knots, splits, cups, twists, checks,

warps—some of them serious, others you can live with.

Hopefully, the lumberyard or home service center you deal with won't foist defective material on you. If they do, simply refuse to receive the goods. Otherwise, you'll have to cope with the

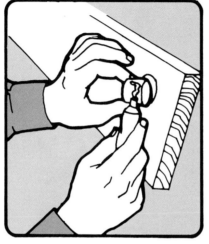

wood's problems at home—possibly for years to come.

The top left sketch below shows a board with all of the above-listed maladies. If the lumber you're considering has *serious* defects, insist on another piece.

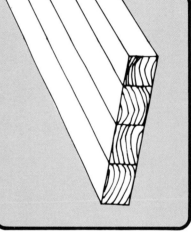

Warped lumber sometimes responds to this technique. Don't use too much weight and allow plenty of time.

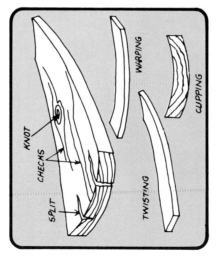

Look for these defects in the lumber you buy. Wood with major problems is best left with the building supply dealer.

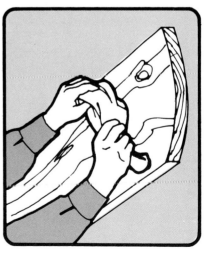

Pop out loose knots and glue them back in place. Plan your work so you won't have to cut or nail directly into or near a knot.

To minimize movement of edge-joined material, alternate grain direction. This is especially important on outdoor projects.

Cupped boards may respond to water. Wet the concave side and cover it with damp rags. Allow the water to soak in overnight.

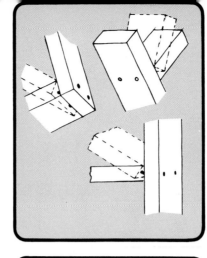

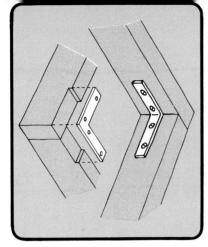

When most people think about joining one material to another, they automatically think of the butt joint. This is understandable: of all wood joinery techniques, the butt joint is the easiest to make. Unfortunately, it's also one of the weakest. So if the joint will be subjected to lots of lateral stress, be sure to reinforce it in some way.

You needn't, however, worry about beefing up butt joints that bear only vertical loads, such as the studs and plates in a frame wall. For more about framing, see pages 48-50 and 209.

When making a butt joint, first make sure that the surfaces you're joining are square. If necessary, trim lumber ends with a saw. Then apply some glue to both surfaces and nail or screw the materials together. As the glue dries, it creates more of a bond than the fastener you've used.

Wood tends to split when nails or screws are driven into it, especially near the ends. To prevent splits, drill pilot holes into the material first, then drive the nails or screws.

Generally, butt joints are face-nailed. In certain instances, though, you'll have to toenail materials together. Toenailing involves driving the nails at an angle through one of the materials into the other. For more about toenailing, see page 49.

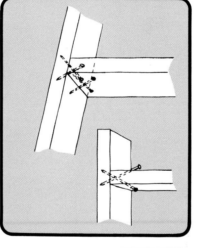

End-nailing makes the easiest butt joint—but also the weakest. Nails driven with the grain may pull out; screws are better.

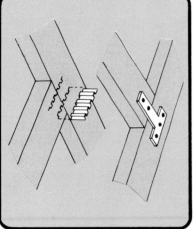

Toenailing makes a butt joint much stronger. It's also the only way to make butt joints in certain instances.

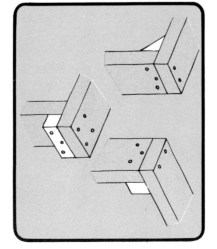

Wedges and blocks offer another way to strengthen butt joints. Use them with glue and nails or screws.

Metal angle irons or plates add strength, too. For a neat appearance, mortise them flush with the surface of the wood, as shown.

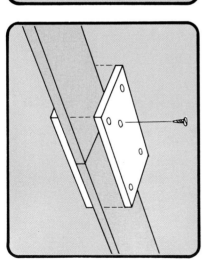

Reinforce "T" butt joints with angle irons or T-plates. Or use corrugated fasteners or wood joint staples.

For joining boards end to end, splices provide the necessary strength. Use glue and nails or screws to solidify the joint.

# MAKING LAP JOINTS

Joining the face of one material to the face of another, or a face to an edge, is what lap joints do best.

The simplest lap joint is the *plain overlap*, a good choice for framing projects where strength is necessary, yet appearance isn't critical. To make it, simply lap the end of one member over another perpendicular or parallel member, then fasten with glue and nails or screws.

Another more-difficult-to-make but stronger version, the *half-lap joint*, often sees duty in furniture- and cabinetmaking projects, where both strength and appearance count (see top right sketch below). You can cut half-lap joints with a saw and chisel, but if you have one, a

table saw with a set of dado blades makes the task much easier. Portable electric routers or radial arm saws will work, too.

*Full-lapped joints*, also a handsome furniture-making standard, are stronger than either their plain or half-lapped cousins. And since you need make only one cut with a saw and chisel, dado blades, or a router, they're much less hassle to make, too.

If you use adhesive when making lap joints (and you should), clamp the joint to ensure a good, strong bond. Don't use too much adhesive, though; you may create a situation where the adhesive bonds to itself rather than to the wood. Follow label instructions.

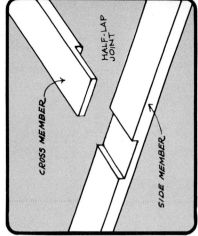

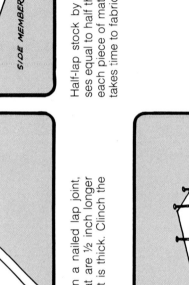

Half-lap stock by cutting recesses equal to half the thickness of each piece of material. This joint takes time to fabricate.

To strengthen a nailed lap joint, use nails that are ½ inch longer than the joint is thick. Clinch the nails.

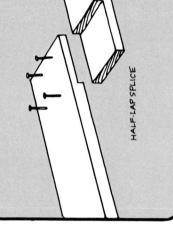

Halved splices are simply half-lap joints used to join two ends. The best way to make the cuts is with dado blades. Glue this joint.

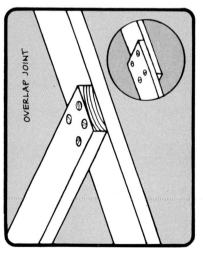

Plain overlap joints should have three or four nails or screws plus glue. Stagger the fasteners so they don't split the grain.

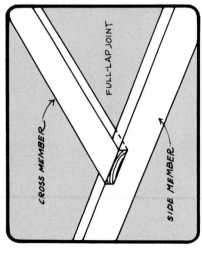

For a neat-looking, stronger joint, make a full lap by cutting a recess in one member equal to the thickness of the other.

**458**

# MAKING DADOES AND RABBETS

Used mainly to anchor bookcase and cabinet shelves, stair treads, and drawer components, a dado joint is simply a recessed cut through the face or edge of a piece of lumber. This joint's popularity stems from the fact that it's both strong and good looking.

To make a plain dado joint, make two cuts one-third of the way through the material, then chisel away what's left between them. Power equipment—a circular, table, or radial saw, or a router—cuts these joints much more easily than hand tools will.

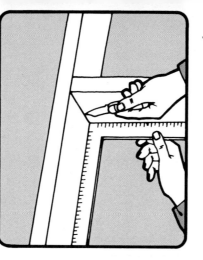

If you don't want the joint to show at all, make a stopped dado as shown below. This joint will take you some time to make, and here, especially, power tools speed progress.

Rabbet joints (recessed cuts along the edge or end of a piece of lumber) often serve to accommodate inset backs for cabinets and bookcases.

With both dado and rabbet joints, accurate measuring, marking, and cutting are a must if your projects are to have that cabinetmaker appearance. A snug fit and a smooth finish are what you're after.

Though you can secure either of these joints with only adhesive, you'll get a much better joint if you also use screws

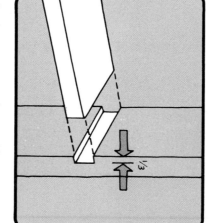

or nails. Sometimes, screws with decorative washers can enhance the appearance of a project—especially if the joint is being used for bookcase shelving or open-hutch cabinets.

If possible, clamp both dado and rabbet joints until the adhesive sets. If you can't clamp the joint, choose a fast-setting adhesive (see pages 436 and 437). And don't overfill any joint with adhesive.

For more about dadoing and rabbeting tools and techniques, see pages 403, 411-413, and 415.

---

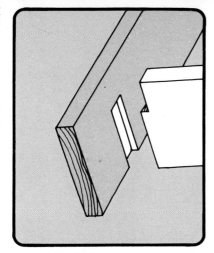

Mark for a dado cut by holding one piece exactly perpendicular to the other. Then scribe the cutting lines with a knife or awl.

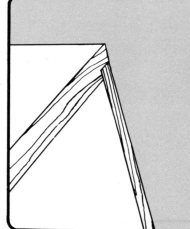

Make two cuts exactly one-third the thickness of the wood. Then chisel away the wood between these cuts. Glue and nail.

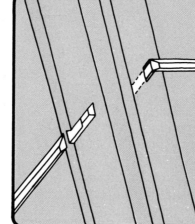

For an even neater appearance, make a stopped dado. Chisel out a small area at the stopped end to allow for the saw's movement.

DRAWER FRONT

---

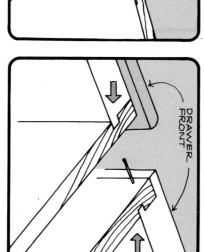

Make saw cuts and chisel out the dado to its proper depth. Then cut away one corner of the connecting board to fit the groove.

A rabbet is a partial dado. Use it for corners that won't get too much strain and for recessing the backs of cabinets and shelves.

For more strength, you can combine dado and rabbeting techniques in certain projects, such as the drawer construction here.

# MAKING MITER JOINTS

For clean good looks, few joinery techniques can outdo the miter. That's why you see them frequently used for the corners of cabinet cases, and to join crown, casing, base shoe, and picture frame moldings.

Despite their good looks, miters do have one liability—they're weak. To make them stronger, you usually need to reinforce the joint with metal angles, gussets, or mending plates. If you feel these add-ons will botch the appearance of the project, splines or dowels can more discreetly fortify the joint.

To cut miters, you'll need a miter box and backsaw, or a power saw you can adjust for 45-degree cutting. Unless you plan to do a great deal of mitering,

purchase an inexpensive miter box.

In measuring for a miter cut, keep in mind that you have to cut the angle in one direction on one piece of stock and in the other direction on the facing piece. Then, when you make the cut, split the cutoff line with the saw. If possible, cut the boards involved a hair long. When mitering long lengths of stock, be sure to support the material. If you don't, the miter cut will tear from the weight of the material.

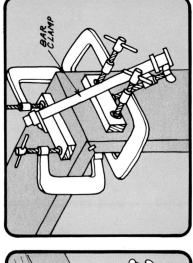

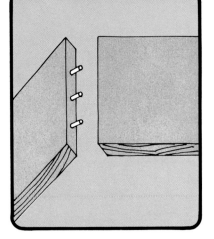

For wide stock, use clamps as shown. Wood blocks protect surfaces and give the clamps something to bite when tightened.

Doweled miters depend on accurate drilling techniques with a power or hand drill and doweling jig. See page 463 for how-to.

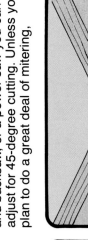

To nail a miter, improvise blocks of wood to hold the stock so you don't knock the pieces out of square. Or, buy miter clamps.

Miters also may be beefed-up with hidden, through, or cross splines. These are jobs for power tools, however.

To keep your saw from biting into your miter box, position a piece of scrap lumber between the work and the box.

For greater strength in flat stock, make a half-lap miter. In back, it's a half-lap joint; in front, it's a conventional miter.

If you see an item constructed with mortise and tenon joints, you can count on its quality. Normally, you'll find this type of joint used only for fine furniture and some window frames. And unless you're inordinately patient, forget about constructing these joints with hand tools. Even with the appropriate power tools—a saw with a combination blade, a drill press or drill press stand for a portable drill, and a chisel set—they're difficult for anyone except serious hobbyists.

Cut the mortise part of the joint first. To be on the safe side, cut a test mortise in a piece of scrap wood before you make the final cut in hardwood or the finish piece. This practice can serve as a teaching aid.

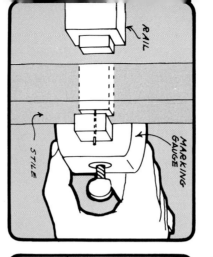

Drill the two end holes for the mortise first. Then remove the wood between the end holes with a drill. Don't overlap the holes. Drill individual holes and use a chisel to remove the wood that separates them. The two end holes must be perfectly square; the others aren't as critical.

After cutting the mortise, cut the tenon to match the mortise. The easiest way to cut tenons is with a power saw and dado blades. You can set the rip fence of the saw to the length of tenon you want, and then set the saw depth to the depth you want.

To assemble the joint, chisel and sand the tenon so it fits the mortise.

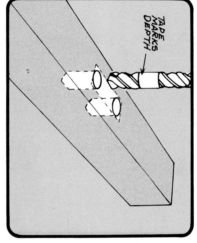

Cut the tenon to match the mortise. If the joint will be assembled with dowels, insert the tenon, then bore holes for the dowels.

---

Mark the stile for the mortise by carefully dividing it into thirds. Double-check these readings with a good rule.

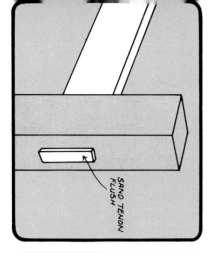

Cut out the mortise by drilling a series of holes to the depth you want. Remove scrap wood between the holes with a chisel.

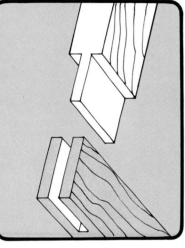

Open mortise and tenon joints are less difficult to make. Cut the mortise first, then cut and sand the tenon to fit.

---

For more strength, cut the mortise through the stock and make the tenon slightly longer. Assemble; sand off the tenon's end.

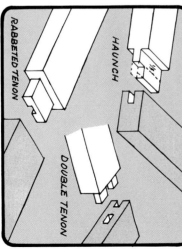

Other, more unusual mortise-and-tenon joint variations include the haunch mortise, the double tenon, and the rabbeted tenon.

## MAKING DOVETAIL AND BOX JOINTS

Dovetail and box joints are nifty. And they get top grades, too, for strength, durability, and good looks. Making them with a router is the easy way. By hand, the joints involve much tedious work.

If you own a router and have a dovetail attachment, the instruction manual will show you how to make the joints. Below, you'll find how to do the job with regular hand tools.

The wood you'll join should be the good stuff—no warps or knots. Lay out the project, squaring and matching the corners. Then mark the corners that will

be matched, i.e., A-A, B-B, C-C, and D-D. With a marking gauge, scribe a line on each end of the stock to be joined. Set the marking gauge the exact thickness of the wood, plus 1/32 inch.

Then, with a template, mark the cutting lines for the dovetails. For softwoods, use an angle ratio of 1:6; for hardwoods, a 1:8 ratio (see the first sketch below).

Use a good backsaw to make the dovetail cuts down into the wood. Saw away the excess wood with a coping saw. As you make all saw cuts, leave the scribed line, i.e., cut to the line. Smooth the cuts with a chisel.

When the dovetails on one piece of wood have been cut, use them as a template to mark the cuts on the

joining piece of wood. Make the cuts and smooth them with a chisel. Now fit the pieces together, chiseling one member or the other for a perfect fit. When this is finished, you can use the completed joint as a template for the remaining joints. If you're making box joints, clamp several pieces of stock together and make the cuts at one time.

Assemble the joints using a thin coating of adhesive. Position the joint so it's square while the glue dries. Use clamps to ensure good adhesion. For even more strength, drive nails through the dovetails.

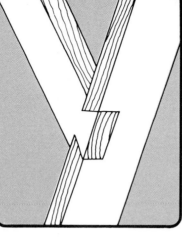

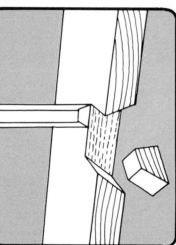

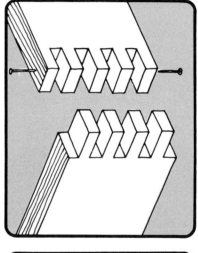

Test-fit the joint. At this point, you may have to trim away excess wood with a chisel. Go easy: trim, test, and repeat.

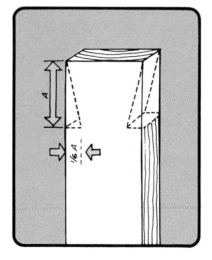

Mark the dovetails, making the ratio 1:6 for softwoods and 1:8 for hardwoods. Wide dovetails are easier to work than narrow ones.

Do all work with a backsaw and a coping saw, then smooth the cuts with a chisel. Don't make your initial cuts with a chisel.

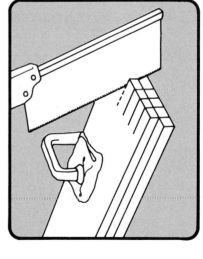

To make quick work of cutting box (finger) joints, clamp the two members together as shown and cut both at once.

You may have to do some sanding to get the members to fit snugly. Once you're satisfied with the fit, apply glue and brads.

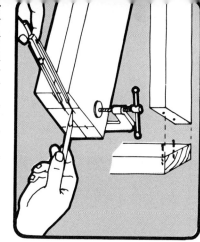

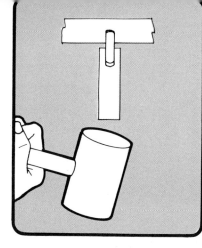

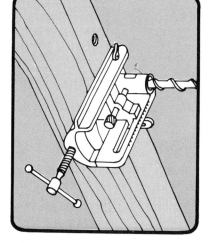

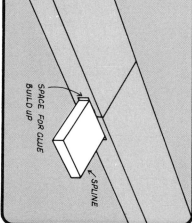

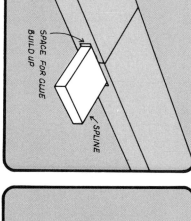

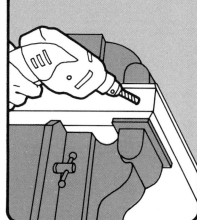

# DOWELING AND SPLINING

Strong and usually invisible, dowel and spline joints look tough and time consuming to make. Time consuming, yes; tough, no, providing your measurements are correct. Dowel joints are easier to fabricate with hand tools than are spline joints. Both can be made by hand, but power equipment will save a lot of hassle.

To make dowel joints, you should have a doweling jig—a metal clamp-on device that keeps drills and bits square to the stock—and an assortment of dowels. When cutting the dowel pins, make them slightly shorter than the holes they'll fill.

Also bevel the ends of the pins with a file or block plane, and groove the length of them with a file so the adhesive can ooze out of the dowel holes when you assemble the joint.

A spline joint consists of two grooves cut in the stock, with a spline fitted between them. This joint is ideal for joining long lengths of materials. You can make splines from hardwood, softwood, or plywood.

To end-join narrow material, you can cut grooves with a backsaw. Scribe the groove pattern on both pieces of stock so the grooves will match or align. You can cut any width of material for a spline joint with a power saw and dado

blades or a router with a groove bit. Make the width of the grooves slightly deeper than the width of the spline you'll use. And if you want a "blind" spline joint, stop the cut before you reach the end of the stock.

When you cut a groove for any spline thickness, you probably will find that the spline will fit very tightly. Don't attempt to enlarge the grooves for the spline. Instead, lightly sand the face of the spline and refit it in the grooves. If it's still too tight, take off a little more wood. The trick is to sand and test until you get it pared down for a snug fit.

Mark dowel holes by clamping together the pieces of stock you want to join, then locating holes as shown. Double-check your work.

You also can use "dowel centers," which resemble double-headed thumbtacks, for marking. Bore holes using a doweling jig.

You can make your own doweling jig by boring true holes in a piece of scrap wood. The holes must be absolutely perpendicular.

Apply glue and insert dowels into one member. Then apply glue to the other and tap the boards together with a wooden mallet.

Cut the grooves for splines about 1/16 inch deeper than the spline. Lightly coat the spline with adhesive and assemble the joint.

SPACE FOR GLUE BUILD UP

SPLINE

To dowel a miter joint, first clamp the work in a vise to secure it. Then drill the holes so the dowels will penetrate both members.

**463**

# CHOOSING AND BUYING MOLDINGS

If you've done any amount of do-it-yourselfing, you know by now that mistakes often happen that make your project less than perfect. This is especially true when working with wood. Maybe your measurements were off slightly, or your saw strayed from the cutting line. That's where moldings can help. These strips of wood can hide almost any cutting, planing, boring, and fastening mistake known to woodworking.

You also can use moldings to create decorative effects. Maybe you want to add a chair rail molding to a dining area, simulate a raised-panel look on a slab door, or personalize a room with crown molding where the ceiling and walls meet. You can do all these things and much more with moldings.

There are so many different shapes and sizes available that it would be impossible (and needless) to present them here. The sketch below shows the ones you'll probably have occasion to use. If you don't see that special pattern you want, just stroll through the molding department of any well-stocked building materials outlet. Chances are excellent that you'll find just what you need.

Moldings are sold by the piece or by the linear foot. And, naturally, those made from exotic woods or with complex patterns cost more than the others.

Depending on your needs, you can purchase moldings unfinished or prefinished. Most manufacturers of paneling also offer prefinished moldings that match their paneling. Many of these moldings are covered with a special plastic coating that resists chemicals, household detergents, water, and moisture.

If you need a molding that's no longer stocked, some outlets will mill molding to your order. You'll pay a premium for this service, but it may be the only way you can get a matching molding.

When you estimate your molding requirements, add one linear foot to every 20 feet of material you need. The extra material will allow for miter and trimming cuts.

## MOLDING SELECTOR

| Standard Pattern | Typical Use |
| --- | --- |
| Cove | To finish surfaces that adjoin at 90-degree angles; inside corners. |
| Crown | For trim around ceilings where they meet walls, fireplace mantels; pictures. |
| Base | Between flooring and sidewalls. Sometimes used for window/door casing. |
| Stool | Between a window frame and apron. See the anatomy sketch on page 64. |
| Shoe | Trim nailed to base at floor line. Often called "base shoe." |
| Corner | Outside corners; edging for shelving and some types of cabinets. |
| Seam | To hide the seam where materials join—usually paneling or wide boards. |
| Stop | For top and side jambs of doors and windows. |
| Cap | To funnel away water over windows, doors, and other openings. |
| Half-round | Hides vertical and horizontal joints in materials; rabbeted types available. |
| Screen bead | To cover fasteners and raw edges of screening on doors and windows. |

There's no quicker or better way to put the finishing touches on a project than with moldings. And once you get the hang of measuring correctly and cutting miters, it's not difficult, either.

The big trick in cutting miters is to pay attention to the direction of the cuts so the miters join properly. If you hold the uncut molding in the position in which it will be installed and mark each piece accordingly, you'll get most of them right the first time—and even pros miscut miters occasionally.

When you're fastening molding along long stretches of parallel surfaces, square the ends and cut one piece 1/16 inch longer than needed. Then bow the material, butt the ends, and nail the molding tight, starting in the middle. Or, for a neater appearance, face-miter adjoining pieces (see below).

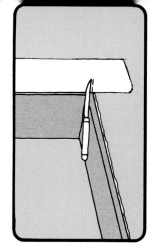

Measure door or window molding by holding the strip in position and marking the inside measurement with a sharp knife.

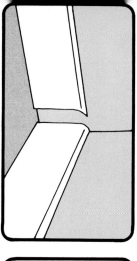

Either miter or cope inside corners. Coping involves butting one piece against the wall and cutting the other piece with a coping saw.

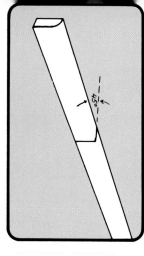

If the molding is wide and won't be painted, a face miter is the neatest way to join two pieces. Cut each at a 45-degree angle.

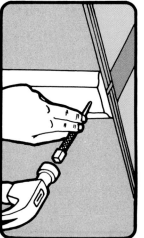

Position the molding as shown against the far side of the miter box. This way, you can hold the molding better while cutting it.

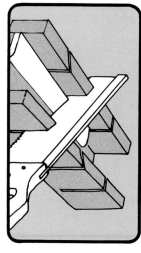

To cope a joint for an inside corner, first cut an inside miter. Then trim as shown here with a coping or saber saw.

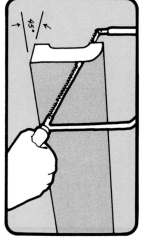

The surest way to achieve a perfect miter is to overlap and clamp the molding at 90 degrees. Cut through both pieces at once.

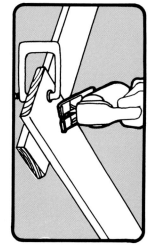

For negotiating outside corners, use miter joints. There's no need to cope even ornately designed moldings.

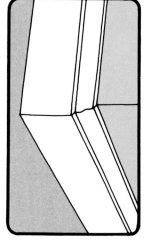

For added strength, glue molding to joints, then nail them with finishing nails. Countersink the nailheads and fill the nail holes.

# CHOOSING AND BUYING PLYWOOD

Of all the materials you'll encounter as a do-it-yourselfer, plywood stands alone as the most versatile. You can use it in dozens of ways—as shelving, subflooring, trim, and roof and wall sheathing; in furniture and cabinet construction; even as forms for concrete.

As its name implies, plywood isn't a solid wood, but rather a material composed of thin layers of wood laminated together, with the grain of each layer running perpendicular to those adjacent to it. These layers are held together by a glue bond so strong that the wood will break before the bond. The resulting product boasts superior split- and puncture-resistance as well as resistance to warping, swelling, and shrinking; good finishing qualities; and good working qualities with hand and power tool equipment.

The two types of plywood you'll most often be working with—softwood-faced plywood and hardwood-faced

plywood—are each laminated in much the same way; only the materials used differ. Softwood-faced plywood has face and back veneers (those you see) usually cut from Douglas fir, with one or more layers between. Hardwood-faced plywood features a face veneer of hardwood such as oak, walnut, cherry, birch, and so on, a back veneer of softwood or hardwood, and one or more plies between. Not surprisingly, the hardwood-veneer panels cost more.

When shopping for softwood plywood, you'll encounter two types. If you'll be using the plywood outdoors or in areas subject to high humidity, such as kitchens, bathrooms, or laundries, choose *exterior-type*. Otherwise, save some money by buying the *interior-type*.

There's one other exterior plywood worth knowing about. Called *Medium Density Overlay* (MDO), it has a smooth, resin-impregnated fiber face designed especially for flawless painted finishes. Use MDO wherever you want a really slick surface.

The face and back veneers of softwood plywood vary considerably in quality, and are graded and priced accordingly. A-veneer is smooth and ready for finishing. B-veneer has no holes or open defects, but may include tight knots or patched-in repairs. Use C- and D-veneers where looks won't matter.

Keep in mind that the face and the back veneers often have different grades. For example, if only one of the two sides will be visible in the finished project, ask for an A-D panel.

With hardwood-faced plywood, one surface will always be good, but the back veneer may have some defects.

Another choice you have to make with hardwood-faced plywood is the type of core you want: standard core (same as softwood-faced plywood), lumber core, or particleboard core. *Standard cores* have a series of laminated wood layers—with grains alternating at right angles to each other. *Lumber cores* consist of narrow, edge-glued wooden strips fitted to equalize the stress on the panel. *Particleboard cores* require no crossbanding, as they're made up of resin-coated wood particles glued and pressed together.

As for availability, most lumberyards and building products outlets maintain stocks of softwood plywood in several thicknesses—1/4, 3/8, 1/2, 5/8, 3/4, and 1 inch. Hardwood panels are not as readily available but can be had. Standard-size plywood panels measure 4 feet wide and 8 feet long, though longer lengths are available on request.

A grade stamp on plywood looks like this. Panels also have an edge mark with the same data: grade, type, and group number.

## PLYWOOD SELECTOR

| Exterior | Face | Back | Use |
|---|---|---|---|
| A-A | A | A | Exterior use where both sides will show. |
| A-B | A | B | Exterior use where both sides will show; back may be blemished. |
| A-C | A | C | One "good" side. Siding, soffits, fencing, decks. |
| B-B | B | B | Concrete forms, rough screening, temporary walks. |
| C-C | C | C | Unsanded. For backing and rough construction. |
| MDO (Medium Density Overlay) | B | B or C | Applications requiring paint or a smooth resin-coated surface on one or both sides. |
| 303 Siding | C or better | C | Siding, interior paneling, fences, storage buildings, where faces with attractive textures are desired. |

| Interior | Face | Back | Use |
|---|---|---|---|
| A-A | A | A | Cabinets, built-ins, furniture, toys, accent panels. |
| A-B | A | B | Same as A-A, except back may be blemished. |
| A-D | A | D | Same as A-B, except back will be rough. |
| B-D | B | D | Utility. Rough shelving, cabinet sides, drawer bottoms. |
| C-D | C | D | Subflooring, utility use, rough construction. |

# WORKING WITH PLYWOOD

Most people find working with plywood a joy. One reason: the panels' large size, which enables you to cover a maximum of area with a minimum of cutting and fitting problems.

Plywood has almost the same working properties as regular "solid" wood plus a desirable trait of its own. Because of the way it's made (with various plies crossbanded to each other), plywood has excellent "dimensional stability." This means that it resists warping much better than ordinary lumber.

On the minus side, plywood does tend to splinter and split. But you can overcome these deficiencies as explained below. Plywood's only other liability is its edges. They don't stand up well to sudden bumps, so handle the panels carefully.

And don't stand them on edge for long periods of time. Though highly warp-resistant, plywood isn't totally immune to this problem. That's why you should always try to lay sheets flat. If you don't have room for this, set the panels on their longest edges and as vertically as you possibly can. Also, keep interior-grade materials away from dampness, which can weaken glues and cause delamination.

## CUTTING AND DRILLING

When you're working on a plywood project requiring several different pieces and cuts, it's smart to map out the various cuts on a piece of paper. Then, transfer these to the plywood panel, allowing for saw kerfs and any damage that might be present on the edges or panel ends. Use this same mapping technique, too, when buying plywood. It will help you estimate your exact panel requirements.

If you choose to make cuts with a circular saw, a special plywood blade makes the going smoother. Otherwise, you can use the standard woodworking tools and techniques illustrated on pages 403-423.

Realize, though, that outer veneers tend to splinter where a saw blade or drill bit exits the material. The drawings below show several ways you can minimize splintering problems.

Lastly, try to avoid boring into the edges of standard- and particleboard-core plywood—the cores tend to split, and most fasteners won't hold well anyway. If you must edge-bore, be sure to drill small pilot holes first.

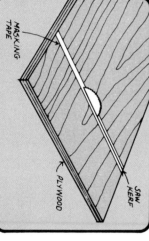

With a handsaw (use one with 12 to 15 points per inch), position the plywood good side up, and hold the saw at a low angle.

Put the good side *down* when sawing with any portable power saw. With stationary power saws, feed the plywood good side up.

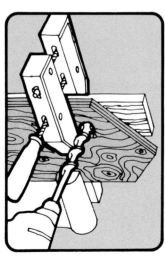

Another effective way to keep the panel from splintering along the cutoff line is to affix a strip of masking tape.

Plywood can splinter when you bore it, too. To help eliminate this, bore into a piece of scrap wood on the backside of the panel.

To cut across the grain, or to minimize splintering on either side, first score the cut with a chisel or a sharp knife.

**467**

# FASTENING PLYWOOD

Despite the obvious physical differences between lumber and plywood (one being solid; the other, laminated stock), you can use most of the same techniques to fasten both materials. So don't be afraid to make miters, rabbets, and dadoes in plywood, too. But do keep in mind that you should avoid nailing or screwing into the edges of plywood panels.

Edge-nailing generally will split the veneer or cause it to "balloon."

If you must fasten into the edges of plywood, predrill pilot holes for the fasteners, whether they be screws or nails. And use the smallest diameter fastener possible.

Using a combination of waterproof glue and a mechanical fastener results in the strongest plywood joints. Where appearance isn't important, such as when fastening sheathing and subflooring, assemble plywood with annular ring nails or spiral nails. These fasteners bite into the plywood laminations and hold them together. For finish work, use finishing or casing nails or small-diameter screws. Usually these are countersunk and the holes filled with wood putty. For thin plywood, use common brads for assembly. Or, if appearance isn't critical, you can fasten thin plywood with staples. Countersink and fill their holes, too.

To beef up miters in ¾-inch plywood, use a plywood spline. Or fasten metal angles inconspicuously.

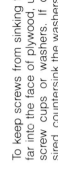

To keep screws from sinking too far into the face of plywood, use screw cups or washers. If desired, countersink the washers.

With thin panels especially, reinforce the joint with square or triangular glue blocks. Nails add more strength.

Though you can cut dadoes with a handsaw and chisel, a router or power saw with a dado blade speeds the job. Glue and clamp.

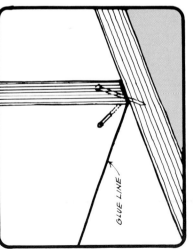

Where the stress is downward, simple butt joints are adequate for most applications of ¾-inch plywood. Keep joints square.

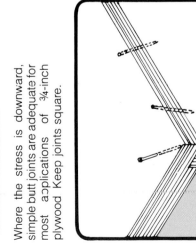

Rabbet joints work well for cabinet and drawer construction. Keep nails away from panel edges and drive them at angles.

# PLANING AND FORMING PLYWOOD

Sometimes, even when you've made smooth, accurate cuts, plywood needs planing to make it fit. When this happens, you actually have two options: sanding or planing. If only a minor adjustment is needed, use a power sander. But if it's obvious that you'd have to sand all night long to make the fit, it's time to get out your block plane.

Don't expect to shave a long, thin ribbon like the one you'd get with solid wood. The glue bond between the wood laminations produces small chips rather than long pieces.

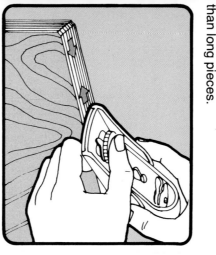

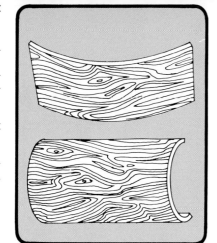

You can bend plywood in gradual curves across the grain. For tighter curves, bend the plywood parallel to the grain—don't force.

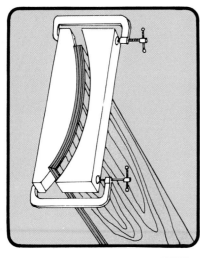

Plane plywood edges by working from both directions. Cutting a tiny bevel on each end helps prevent splintering and splits.

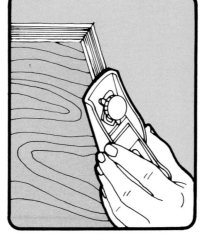

Bevel sharp edges, if you won't be applying an edge treatment. This protects the veneer from splitting.

Work the plane or smoothing tool from the edges of the material toward the center (see below). If you'll make a series of passes, bevel each end of the plywood across the edge to minimize splintering.

The same procedures apply, too, if you're working with a power sander. If you'll make several passes along the plywood edge, start sanding with a medium/coarse abrasive and then drop to a finer grit of paper (see pages 448 and 449 for information on abrasives). Always keep the sander square to the edge.

Thin plywood panels lend themselves to bending much more than does solid lumber. To bend thin plywood, make a jig with clamps and scrap wood to produce

the radius curve you want. Dampen—don't soak—both surfaces of the material with water, then make the bend and clamp it in position. When you unclamp the wood, the curve will be permanent. Then simply glue the plywood into the position you want.

To bend thicker plywood, make a series of saw kerfs across or with the grain. Make a jig, as shown below, and clamp the material in the jig. Wet the outside of the material, let it set overnight, and glue it in the desired position.

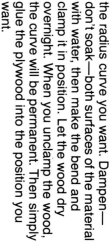

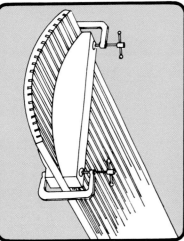

To shape thin sheets of plywood, wet the wood, clamp as shown, and let the panels set overnight. Don't soak the wood.

Or, round the edges, first with a surface-forming tool, and then sandpaper. Use the sandpaper in a shoeshine fashion.

For thicker panels, make a series of saw cuts on the back side. Dampen the panel and clamp it tight, as shown.

**469**

# BUILDING A PLYWOOD BOX

Students of design know it. Furniture- and cabinetmakers know it, and so do carpenters. But the average person probably doesn't realize just how basic the plain old box is to all sorts of home carpentry projects. Once you master the basics of box-building, you can fashion a surprising number of good-looking items for your home—cabinets, bookcases, platform bed frames, end tables, and more—and at a cost that's even more surprising.

Pictured below are two simple boxes. Though both are essentially the same,

one goes together with simple hand tools; the other, with power tools.

Plywood is an ideal material for any box design for two reasons. First, it comes in 4x8-foot sheets and in a range of thicknesses, which eliminates the special planing and milling required when using solid wood. And second, it's available in a variety of veneers.

When building a box, you first need to determine the dimensions of the sides, bottom, back, front, and any special add-ins such as shelving and drawers. From these dimensions, you can determine how many sheets of plywood you'll need for the job, plus other components such as adhesive, nails, screws, and finishing materials.

To make sure of your plywood requirements, scale-down one or more 4x8-foot sheets of plywood on graph paper, then draw in each piece within the outside borders. Pay attention to the direction of the grain as you lay out the pieces, though. The grain should run the same direction on all pieces. When you're finished, label each part "side," "bottom," "back," and so on.

Now transfer your layouts to the actual sheets of plywood, marking each part as you go. Be sure to allow room for saw kerfs and any special cuts that will require extra material to make. Double-check the cuts as explained below.

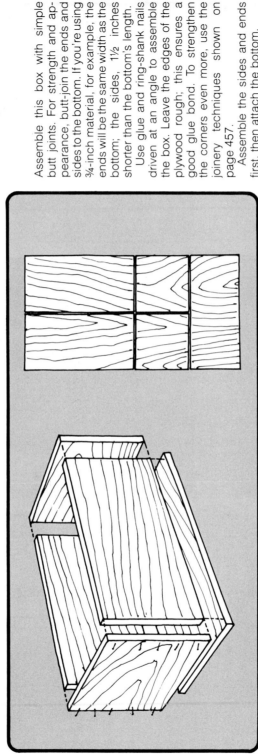

Assemble this box with simple butt joints. For strength and appearance, butt-join the ends and sides to the bottom. If you're using ¾-inch material, for example, the ends will be the same width as the bottom; the sides, 1½ inches shorter than the bottom's length.

Use glue and ring-shank nails driven at an angle to assemble the box. Leave the edges of the plywood rough; this ensures a good glue bond. To strengthen the corners even more, use the joinery techniques shown on page 457.

Assemble the sides and ends first, then attach the bottom.

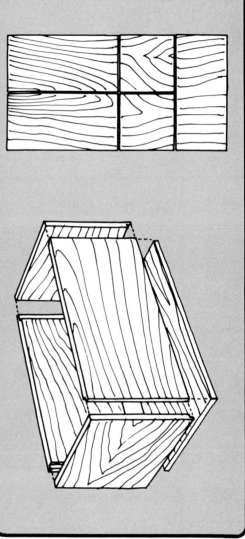

This box, assembled with the more sophisticated rabbet joint, is considerably stronger than the butted version above. Note that the ends and sides are rabbeted, but not the bottom.

Assemble the ends and the sides first, using glue and finishing nails driven at an angle. Then fit the sides and ends to the bottom. You may have to trim the rabbet cuts slightly here and there to accommodate the bottom.

Finally, countersink the nails, fill all nail holes, and apply a finish.

**470**

# BUILDING DRAWERS

Drawers are simply boxes without a lid, and depending on the joint technique you use, they can be quick and easy to construct.

First determine the measurement of the drawer—sides, back, and front. Make the drawer slightly smaller than the opening for it. And take into account that drawer guides will be attached later. The bottom can be fitted to these dimensions. Use ¾-inch plywood for the front, sides, and back of the drawer, and ⅛- or ¼-inch hardboard (or plywood) for the bottom.

If you use hand tools, construct the drawer using butt joints. Cut the sides, back, and front to width and length, and assemble them with glue and ring-shank nails. Then fit the unit into the opening to make sure it has clearance to slide when the wood or metal guides are attached. Finally, add the bottom, and attach guides to the drawer and the cabinet framework.

Flush-fitted drawers, which operate on a bottom guide, require more skill to make. Although you can use plywood for the sides, backs, and bottoms of drawers, solid wood is best for the fronts. Cut a dado around the sides, back, and front for the bottom. Don't fasten the bottom; let it "float."

To create a "lipped" drawer front, glue a slightly larger false front to the actual drawer front. This, in effect, forms a "rabbet." Then attach wooden drawer guides to the sides of the drawer and the cabinet framing with countersunk screws. The drawer simply "hangs" on these guides. Use solid wood for the guides, or buy commercial metal drawer guides. But make or buy the guides before you build the drawers so you can allow space for them.

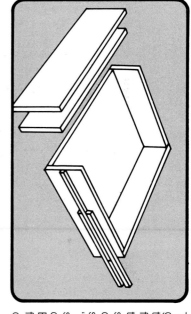

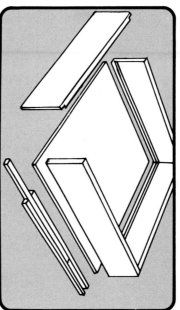

# FINISHING PLYWOOD EDGES

As you can see at right, there's no one right way to finish the edges of plywood. Adhesive and edging tape is probably the quickest way to hide plywood edges. The tape comes in a range of veneers to match the plywood that you're using.

Another simple solution is to nail on a molding—either flat or shaped. Inexpensive screen molding does an excellent job. It looks good, and accepts paint, stain, and other finishes. Mitered treatments work well, but they're fairly tricky to cut.

If you want added strength, you can spline the edging. However, you'll need a table saw or a router to make these cuts.

If you plan to paint the plywood, you can fill the edges with wood putty or edge filler. You also can use a thin mixture of spackling compound. Let the filler dry a day or so, then sand it. You may need a second application to obtain the smooth edge you want.

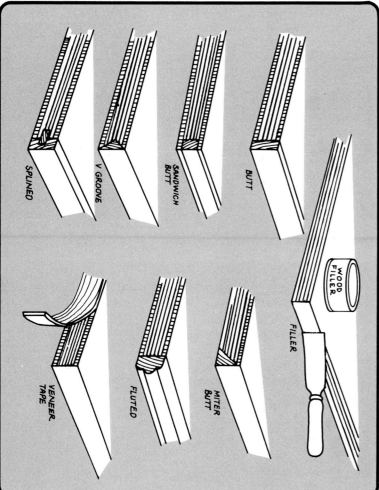

SPLINED

V GROOVE

SANDWICH BUTT

BUTT

WOOD FILLER

FILLER

VENEER TAPE

FLUTED

MITER BUTT

# CHOOSING AND BUYING HARDBOARD

A big machine with very sharp teeth grinds wood chips into fibers. Then these fibers are mixed with adhesives. When this mixture is fed into a press, the result is hardboard—one of today's basic construction materials.

Though the surface of this product can take on many different looks—grained, embossed, perforated, textured, striated, and filigreed—there are only two types of hardboard: *standard* and *tempered*. Tempered hardboard is stronger and a darker shade of brown than the standard version.

Hardboard's pressed-fiber makeup yields a dense, smooth product with several desirable characteristics. First, it accepts paint quite well, and since hardboard has no grain, the paint won't check. In addition, hardboard won't splinter or crack, yet it's flexible enough to bend for projects such as concrete forms.

*Hardboard paneling*, a stock item at most home center stores and building materials outlets, comes in solid-color panels and a wide variety of very authentic-looking wood grains. Not only is this paneling good looking, it generally costs considerably less than plywood paneling.

*Particleboard* is similar to hardboard in that it's also made from wood particles pressed into sheets. It's fairly dense, extremely heavy, and smooth on both sides. Used primarily for shelving and underlayment, and as a core material for plastic, wood, and hardboard veneers, particleboard generally must be fastened to some sort of framing material. It also tends to chip and break easily, so be sure to protect the edges.

## HARDBOARD SELECTOR

| Type | Size (panel size in feet; thickness in inches) | Fasteners | Finish | Use |
|---|---|---|---|---|
| Standard | 4x4; 4x7; 4x8; 4x10; 4x12; 4x16. $1/8$; $3/16$; $1/4$; $5/16$. | Glue; nails; bolts; screws; clips. | Smooth on one or both sides. | Interior applications such as partitions, cabinets, accent panels, work surfaces. |
| Tempered | Same as standard | Same as standard | Same as standard | Interior and exterior use; moisture-resistant. Same uses as standard hardboard. |
| Underlayment | 4x4; 4x8. $1/4$. | Glue; nails; screws. | Extra smooth and flat. | Apply over subfloors or floors as a base for carpeting, tile, resilient goods, slate. |
| Perforated; Standard/Tem-perec | 2x4; 4x4; 4x8. $1/8$; $1/4$. | Glue; nails; bolts; screws; rabbeted and dadoed frames. | Same as standard and tempered | For hanging tools, utensils, etc. Holes are drilled on $1/2$- and 1-inch centers. Special hanging hardware is available. |
| Embossed | 4x4; 4x8; 4x12; 4x16. $1/8$; $1/4$. | Same as standard | Varied | Furniture; wall paneling; decorative accents; cabinet fronts; drawer fronts. |
| Die-cut filigreed | 16"x6; 2x4; 2x6; 4x8. $1/8$. | Same as standard | Smooth both sides. | Interior applications such as room dividers, screens, cabinet fronts, furniture. |
| Concrete forming | 4"x12'; $3/16$; $1/4$ | Nails | Specially tempered for concrete forms. | Concrete forms; edging for bricks, blocks, stone, chips, and wooden rounds. |
| Siding (panels) | 4x6; 4x7; 4x8; 4x9; 4x10; 4x12; 4x16. $7/16$. | Nails | Unpainted; pre-primed. | Siding; interior accent panels. |
| Siding (lap) | 9-, 12-inch width. $1/4$ to $7/16$. | Nails | Same as panels | Same as panels. |

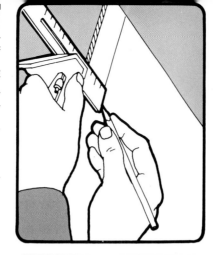

Hardboard may appear to be a weak material when you first look at it. But you'll know better the first time you try to saw or drill it. During manufacture, hardboard becomes more dense than most softwoods, hardwoods, and plywood. And because of this, you'll find that it dulls the cutting edges of tools fairly quickly, necessitating frequent whetting or sharpening.

To saw hardboard, use a 10- to 12-point crosscut saw or a crosscut blade on a power saw. And if you'll be sawing a lot of hardboard on a power saw, use a longer-wearing carbide-tipped blade for the job.

If you have to drill through hardboard, be sure to work from the smooth or finished side (some hardboard is smooth on both sides). If you don't, you risk "tearing" the material when the drill or bit penetrates the backside.

Due to its supple nature, hardboard usually requires backup support. This is particularly true if you're using ⅛-inch-thick material. But even the thicker material needs reinforcement of studs, joists, or furring strips at intervals not greater than 16 inches.

Tempered hardboard is especially well suited for use as paneling. However, if you apply it to walls that become damp from time to time, you must back it with a polyethylene vapor barrier. Hardboard panels also expand and contract with changes in temperature and humidity, so when joining panels that cover large expanses, leave a narrow gap at the joints. If this compromises the appearance of the job, cover the joints with moldings or battens. You probably can buy moldings to match the prefinished hardboard panels you're installing.

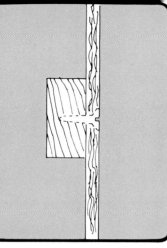

Especially with darker, tempered hardboard, you may have trouble seeing measurement lines. Use a pencil with light-colored lead.

To minimize surface damage when cutting hardboard with a power saw, set the blade so that just two or three teeth project.

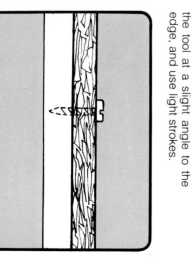

For smoothing edges, use a sharp, shallow-set plane. Hold the tool at a slight angle to the edge, and use light strokes.

Being "grainless," hardboard doesn't hold fasteners well. So always nail, screw, or bolt *through* hardboard, never into it.

If you must sand hardboard, treat it first with a wash coat of shellac. The shellac helps minimize "fuzzing" from the abrasive.

Particleboard holds nails and screws better than hardboard. For extra holding power, use sheet metal screws.

**473**

# CHOOSING AND BUYING PLASTICS

Though a relative newcomer as a building material, plastics are fast gaining respect and acceptance in this area. The reason: they've proven themselves top-notch materials for a host of tasks—covering countertops, closing-in porches, and repairing window screens, to name just a few.

Of the three basic types of plastics discussed here, you'll probably encounter *high-pressure laminates* and *fiber glass-reinforced plastics* most often. You'll find both of them for sale in most home center stores. *Acrylic*, which is clear or colored sheet plastic, is classed more as a "hobby" material. Look for it at specialty plastics outlets, picture-framing shops, and auto and marine supply outlets.

## LAMINATE

High-pressure laminate, or simply "laminate," is resin-coated paper that has been laminated under high heat and pressure. The result: a rigid sheet that's excellent for use as decorative panels as well as for covering kitchen and bathroom countertops, shower doors, furniture, and cabinets. Though laminate is extremely tough, it can be damaged by high heat and some common household cleaners that contain abrasives, peroxide, or chlorine.

Laminates are available in a staggering range of patterns and colors; some of them are even color-keyed to kitchen appliances and bathroom fixtures. You may have to special-order the laminate you want, but delivery usually doesn't take long—a day or two.

Standard laminate sheets are $1/32$ and $1/16$ inch thick and measure from 2x5 to 5x12 feet. Buy the thin sheets for vertical applications—on cabinet doors, for example—and the thicker ones for horizontal uses such as countertops.

You can use regular hand and power tools to cut, drill, trim, and form laminate. However, you should buy an inexpensive notched trowel to spread on the contact cement. This trowel creates a uniform bed of adhesive that ensures good adhesion.

Although laminate is tough, you should protect its edges and corners, as they can chip. And take care not to bend the material too much; it could snap.

## FIBER GLASS

Fiber glass sees a lot of use as patio covers, as well as a patching material for holes, dents, splits, and cracks in cars and boats.

*Fiber glass-reinforced plastic* sheets for exterior use generally look much like the corrugated sheet metal used to roof farm and ranch outbuildings. However, flat sheets also are available. You'll find these panels available in a wide range of colors, sizes, and thicknesses at most home center stores and building materials outlets.

If you plan to roof with fiber glass-reinforced plastic, be sure to buy special corrugated flashing and moldings so you end up with a professional-looking job. And install the panels with nails that have a rubber-like gasket just below the nail head. These seal the panel against moisture.

Polystyrene panels are similar to fiber glass-reinforced plastic panels, except they're best used indoors. They're available in most colors, and some are even designed to look like leaded stained glass. They make handsome room dividers, cabinet fronts, shower door panels, and window coverings. You'll generally need to support the flat polystyrene panels with framing. Fasten them with screws or clips, or glue them into position.

For auto body and boat repair, you can buy *fiber glass patching kits*. The kits contain a fiber glass cloth and a two-part resin (see page 477). Look for the patching kits at hobby shops and automobile and marine stores.

## ACRYLIC

Though not widely used for home maintenance and improvement projects, acrylic plastic still has a great deal to offer. You can cut, shape, and form it into insert panels for cabinets, panels for shower doors and stalls, and covers for indirect or recessed panel or strip lighting. You also can use it as a glass substitute in storm doors, and as shelving in open cabinets. And for specialty and hobby projects, the rigid plastic has nearly unlimited uses.

Except for its tendency to sag in medium to long runs, acrylic's only real drawback is that it scratches fairly easily. But by following the advice on page 476, you can work with it without incident.

For most projects, you should fasten acrylic to framing—wood or metal—with screws, clips, bolts, or adhesive. Once supported, the plastic is extremely strong, making it ideal for storm door and window glass replacement.

Most of the acrylic you'll see will be either $1/8$ or $1/4$ inch thick, although thicker sizes are available. And since the material is fairly expensive, you'll usually order a piece cut to size.

## LAMINATING

Plastic laminate is one of those materials that becomes more intriguing the more you work with it. And with practice, you can learn to lay it down as well as many pros. Regardless of the project, the techniques remain much the same. So let's discuss a project you may well encounter—re-covering a countertop.

First remove the old material down to the base material. If the base material is badly damaged, tear it out and replace it with particleboard or plywood. If the surface is in decent shape, sand it perfectly smooth or top it with tempered hardboard.

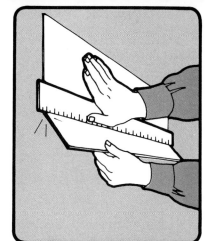

To bond high-pressure laminates to the base material, you'll need a special contact cement. Since this product adheres *on contact*, you must carefully cut and pre-fit the laminate to the base. Once in place, laminate is almost impossible to remove.

The difference between a professional-looking and a slapdash job lies in how you trim the edges. You can smooth them by hand with a file, but a router with a special laminate bit will let you zip through the job.

When applying laminates to cabinet doors and the like, first apply a balance sheet to the backside to seal out moisture, which otherwise will cause warping. Or apply laminate to both sides.

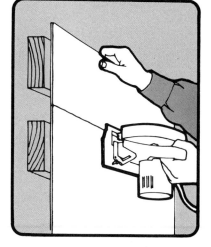

Apply contact cement to both the back of the laminate and the bonding surface. Brush it out evenly. Apply edges first.

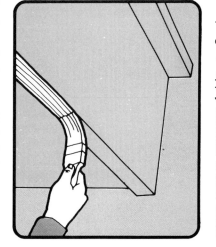

To cut laminate, score its face, then hold one side flat, grasp the other, and snap it up. Carbide-tipped blades work best.

Or saw the laminate with a fine-tooth back or circular saw. On a table saw, cut with the good face up; with a portable, face down.

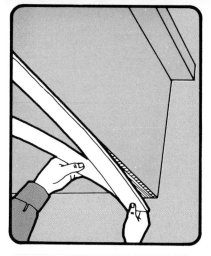

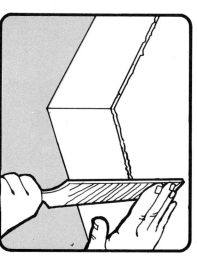

When the cement is dry to the touch, cover the surface with brown wrapping paper, position laminate, and pull out the sheet.

When all of the laminate is down, roll the entire surface with a rolling pin. Tap along the edges with a hammer and wood block.

To complete the project, rout, file, or sand off the excess material. Then file the edges gently to re-move any sharpness.

# WORKING WITH ACRYLIC

When you pick up acrylic from a plastics supplier, you'll notice there's a paper or plastic-film skin covering both sides. It's there to protect the material while you're cutting it, and to provide you with a surface on which to mark your cut lines.

You can cut acrylic in various ways. For straight cuts in thicknesses up to ¼ inch, you can get good results with the scribe-and-break method shown below. For thicker material and curved cuts, you can use either a hand or a power saw.

A fine-tooth crosscut saw works best if you're sawing by hand. Power saws equipped with a hollow-ground or plywood blade will do a much smoother job, though. To make the cut, push the material very slowly through the saw—or guide the saw slowly through the plastic. Don't force the acrylic as you would with wood. Also, saw up to, but not directly on, the cutoff line. The cut edge of the plastic will be rough, so you'll need to smooth it with wet/dry sandpaper.

If your project calls for a piece of acrylic bent to a certain shape, first measure, mark, and cut the rigid sheet to the size you want, then after peeling off the protective paper, heat the acrylic along the bend line with a "strip heater" specially designed for this purpose. When the plastic softens, bend it over a dowel rod or a piece of scrap wood. But

go easy, and bend it just a little at a time. Let the plastic cool and then apply more heat and bending pressure until you get the form you want.

You also can make holes in acrylic. Though most people simply drill through the material as shown below, in situations where appearance isn't a consideration, you also can heat a pointed metal object and push the tip of it into the plastic. If you go this route, make sure you have the hole position clearly marked, and keep the point square to the material.

Hand-drill acrylic with drill, not auger bits. With power, use bits made for plastics. Clamp the plastic; back it with wood.

Join acrylic with special solvent cement. Roughen edges with sandpaper, apply cement, and "clamp" with masking tape.

Position a dowel under the sheet at the scored line. Then, with both hands, snap the sections downward with an even thrust.

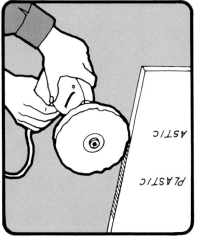

For a transparent edge, continue sanding with very-fine grit abrasive. Then buff the edge with a buffing wheel in a power drill.

After marking the cutoff line, score with a scribe, utility knife, or other pointed object, using a straightedge as a guide.

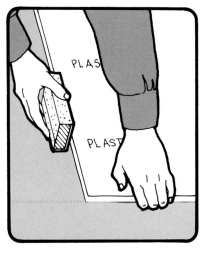

Smooth cut edges with medium-grit sandpaper. Then finish the job with a wet/dry abrasive. Use a sanding block.

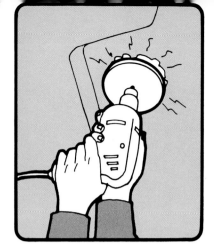

## WORKING WITH FIBER GLASS

Working with flat and corrugated *fiber glass-reinforced plastic* panels requires no special tools, but there are a few tricks to be learned. First, when sawing the material, use a fine-tooth blade and don't force the plastic into the saw or the saw into the plastic. And always drill holes for nails and other fasteners; if you don't, the panel probably will crack where the fastener penetrates the plastic. To prevent chipping, stay at least 3/8 inch away from the edge with a drilled hole.

For most construction, you should fasten the panels to framing using nails with neoprene washers or fasteners approved by the manufacturer. Instructions come with most panel materials.

Flat panels, when sandwiched between 1x2 or 1x3 wood strips, make beautiful dividers and room partitions. If the framing that supports the panels will be finished, do the finishing work before you install the panels.

If you're using fiber glass panels outdoors, be sure to weather-strip the panel joints to prevent leakage. And for fencing jobs, toenail the rails to the posts—or dado them in—so the panels will fit flush.

*Fiber glass cloth and resin,* the materials used to patch autos, boats, and so on, isn't the easiest product to use. Many people have trouble using it because if you add too much hardener to the resin, the hardening process begins immediately. Add too little, and the resin won't harden at all. So, always measure out the hardener in drops, according to the manufacturer's instructions.

Fumes from this material are extremely toxic, so be sure to work in a room that's well ventilated. Also keep in mind that the spun-glass fibers can damage your lungs, work their way into your skin, and irritate your eyes. So always work with gloves, long sleeves, and a respirator.

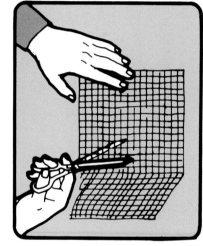

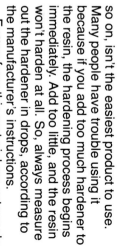

To patch with fiber glass, first grind or sand down the surrounding surfaces to bare wood or metal. Keep them clean and dry.

Cut the fiber glass cloth so that an inch or two will overlap the edges of the area to be patched. Use regular scissors for cutting.

Carefully mix the hardener with the resin according to the manufacturer's instructions. Stir well in a paper cup or metal tray.

Lay out the cloth on a piece of polyethylene and pour the mixture over it. Then, with a small brush, spread out the mixture.

Lay the saturated material over the damaged area. Work out any wrinkles or air bubbles by lightly stretching the cloth material.

After the patch hardens, sand it smooth. For an invisible patch, fill low spots with auto body putty before you paint the patch.

# CHOOSING AND BUYING METALS

You can't see most of it, but there's an estimated two tons of metal in an average 1,500- to 2,000-square-foot house. The "so what?" of this bit of trivia is that the metal you do see—gutters and downspouts, flashing, support columns, railings, windows, and doors—often needs repair or replacement.

The building metals you'll most likely encounter include aluminum, copper, galvanized steel, mild steel (nails, bolts, and screws), and wrought iron. For specialty projects, you may also need brass and bronze. See the sketch below for some shapes these metals take.

Most home center stores and building materials outlets stock aluminum sheet, aluminum gutters and flashing, and galvanized steel gutters, flashing, and sheet. You may have to special-order copper flashing, gutters, and sheet, although it's worth a call to a metal specialty shop before you do. Check the classified section of your phone directory for help in locating suppliers of the products you need. For more about flashing and gutter materials, see pages 116 and 117, and 120 and 121.

Since both aluminum and copper are "soft" metals, you can use woodworking tools when working with them. However, heavy sheet and bar stock generally call for some special metalworking equipment. Renting these tools makes sense unless you have a lot of metal-working to do, in which case it might pay to buy them. The tools include metal drills, reamers, countersinks, a ball-peen hammer, punches, a tap-and-die set, a sheet metal fly cutter, tin snips, an electric soldering iron, and a propane torch. A welder might be on your list if you plan to work extensively with metals.

## Understanding Metalwork Terminology

*Alloys* are made from two or more different types of metals. Both ferrous and nonferrous metals are alloys. *Ferrous metals* are made from iron, with traces of other metals added. Cast iron, wrought iron, carbon steel, and mild steel are ferrous metals.

*Nonferrous metals* include metals other than iron. Brass, copper, aluminum, tin, zinc, and gold are nonferrous.

*Annealing* reduces the brittleness in metal by heating, then cooling it.

*Etching* is the result of the action of acid on metal. The design to be etched is first created in a wax substance on the metal with a tool. The acid is poured over the wax surface, affecting only the scraped-away portions.

*Soldering* is a technique for joining together two pieces of metal with metal—usually lead and tin. See page 435 for soldering techniques.

*Sweating* is a technique for joining two pieces of metal by "tinning" each piece—as in sweating copper tubing. See pages 285 and 482 for techniques.

*Welding* is a technique for joining two pieces of metal by heat.

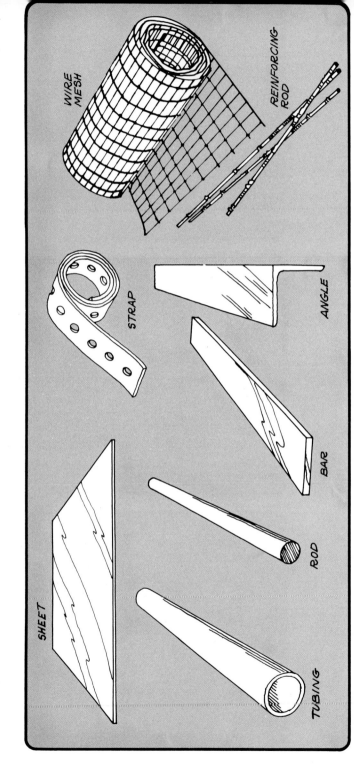

WIRE MESH

REINFORCING-ROD

STRAP

ANGLE

BAR

SHEET

ROD

TUBING

## METAL SELECTOR

| Type | Classification | Shapes Available | Special Tools Required | Cost | Uses |
|---|---|---|---|---|---|
| Aluminum | Nonferrous | Sheet, tube, rod, bar, angle, channel, embossed, special designs | Riveter | Moderate | Gutters, downspouts, flashing, patching, room dividers, furniture, cabinets, specialty hardware, hobby, crafts, fasteners |
| Copper | Nonferrous | Sheet, tube, rod | Propane torch for non-mechanical fastening | Expensive | Gutters, flashing, patching, specialty hardware, crafts, plumbing, electrical work, decorative accents, fasteners |
| Galvanized iron/steel | Ferrous | Sheet, tube, rod, bar, angle, channel, ducting | Metal drills, punches | Moderate | Flashing, roofing, ducts, patching, fasteners, braces, pipe, screening, linings, hardware |
| Mild steel | Ferrous | Sheet, rod, bar | Taps/dies, reamers, welders | Moderate | Tools, fasteners, support columns, framing |
| Brass | Nonferrous | Sheet, tube, rod | None | Expensive | Decorative accents, specialty fasteners, crafts |
| Bronze | Nonferrous | Sheet, tube, rod | None | Expensive | Specialty fasteners, decorative accents, crafts |
| Wrought iron | Ferrous | Pre-formed rod | Welding equipment for non-mechanical fastening/joining | Moderate to expensive | Railings, supports, decorative accents, crafts |
| Lead | Nonferrous | Bar, cable, sheet, rod | Heater, pot for melting | Moderate | Sheet roofing, specialty washers |
| Silver | Nonferrous | Bar, rod, particles | Pot for melting, craft equipment | Expensive | Crafts, furniture and cabinet inlays; special hardware, jewelry |
| Gold | Nonferrous | Bar, rod, particles | See silver | Expensive | Crafts, furniture and cabinet inlays, jewelry |
| Tin | Nonferrous | Sheet, rod, bar | See lead | Expensive | Generally used with lead to make solder alloys |
| Drill rod | Ferrous | Rod | Hacksaw, metal lathe | Moderate to expensive | Cutting tools, punches, small tools (taps, chisels, tool bits) |
| Cast iron | Ferrous | Bar, rod | Hacksaw | Moderate | Lavatories, tubs, and other "formed" building parts |

# WORKING WITH METALS

Chances are good that unless you took a metalwork class in school, you're a bit leery of working with metals. In fact, many people associate metalworking with something best left to professionals, so they never attempt to tackle such projects themselves.

Dispelling this notion can help you in a couple of ways. First, when you learn to work with metals, you'll become a more complete do-it-yourselfer. And second, metalworking can result in considerable savings. Suddenly, a leaky pipe or gutter isn't the catastrophe it used to be—and isn't nearly as costly to repair, either. Nor is repairing a chimney flashing or any of a number of other common repair jobs.

To be sure, there are some techniques you'll need to master. But once you get into metalworking, you'll be surprised to find that many metals are as easy to work with as wood.

Begin by reading this and the next five pages to discover just what you can do with metals—you'll be surprised.

## CUTTING

If you've ever fought with a metal, trying in vain to cut through it with the "wrong" tool, you know how important using the right tool can be.

From time to time, you'll need to cut three different classifications of metals: thin and soft metals; plate, bar, and rod metals; and thick and hard metals. For thin and soft metals, you can use a hacksaw, heavy scissors, tin snips, or a cutter designed for the material. For plate, bar, and rod stock, a hacksaw works best. And for thick and hard metals such as galvanized pipe, reinforcing rod, and girders, you'll need a hacksaw, a pipe cutter, or a gas cutting torch.

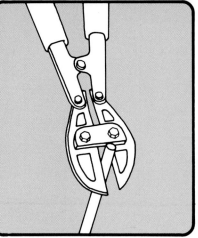

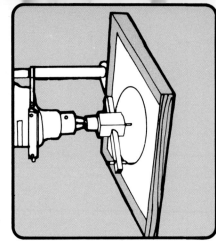

If you have lots of rods to cut, consider renting a bolt cutter. This heavy-duty performer makes easy work of it.

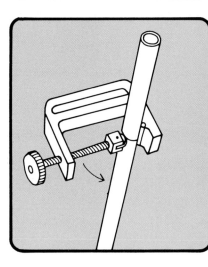

To cut copper tubing, use either a hacksaw or the special cutter shown here. For more on copper tubing, see page 285.

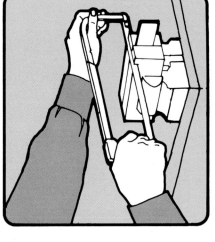

If you have a drill press or stand, you can cut holes up to eight inches in diameter in thin metal with a fly-cutter rig.

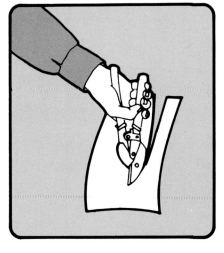

You also can use a hacksaw. If the metal chatters in the vise, sandwich it between boards and cut through all three.

Snips—especially the aviation type shown here—make fast work of sheet metal 20 gauge or lighter.

# DRILLING

For almost any hole-boring job in metal, you need a twist drill manufactured from high-speed steel. Lesser-quality drills simply can't stand up to the abuse cutting metals involves; they overheat easily and lose their temper.

If you have one, a stationary drill press or a drill press stand for a portable electric drill is the ideal equipment for

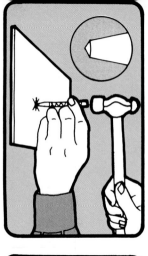

drilling metal. But you can accomplish the same goal, more slowly, with a twist drill locked in the chuck of a hand drill or brace.

Before drilling, always lock the metal in a vise or clamp it to a solid base to prevent the drill from "catching" the metal and "spinning" it out of your hand. Also wear safety glasses.

The tricks to drilling metal include keeping the drill square to the metal, applying constant, even pressure, and

keeping the metal lubricated while drilling. On tough metals such as iron and steel, use light machine oil as a lubricant coolant. For aluminum, use kerosene. Other soft and thin metals generally don't need lubrication. But if you notice the drill getting hot, use light oil.

If the work starts to smoke or the drill binds in the metal, ease up on it. You're either forcing the drill too much or working with a dull drill.

Mark the exact spot for drilling with a center punch. This tool has a pointed end that makes a niche for the tip of the drill.

If you have a variable-speed drill, start drilling at a low speed. Then increase the rpm gradually. Add lubricant; keep pressure even.

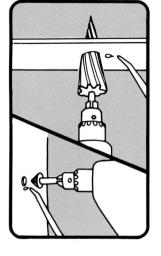

A reamer (left) enlarges holes. Never turn it backward or you'll nick the blade. A countersink (right) lets you set screw heads.

# FASTENING

Though you probably don't have access to a welding unit, that doesn't mean you can't successfully fasten metal—either to other metal or to another material. Actually, a fair number of mechanical fasteners will do the job—screws, bolts, rivets, adhesive, and nails (if you attach metal to wood or masonry). Rivets (see page 434 for more information) do the neatest and one of the strongest fastening jobs. You can buy them to

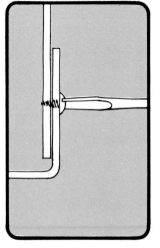

match the metal you're working with—aluminum, copper, iron, and brass.

To avoid alignment problems when joining metal, first measure, mark, and drill the holes for one fastener. Install it, then measure, mark, and drill both pieces of metal for the additional fasteners. Where you locate the fasteners isn't critical, although you should stay away from ends and edges.

Join rods and bars with this self-riveting technique. File the rod end into a tenon that fits the hole. Insert, and peen the end.

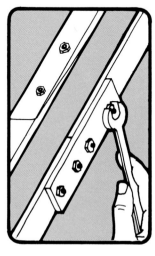

To join pieces of sheet metal, first use a center punch to start the hole, then drive sheet metal screws home.

Splice bars with a cleat of the same type of metal. You can do a neater job by grinding a taper on the ends of the splice.

## SOLDERING METAL

Another strong, safe, and easy way to join two pieces of metal is to solder them. Keep in mind, though, that you must adhere to some fairly stringent procedures to achieve good results.

First, make sure you have enough heat. Don't use a soldering iron or gun when you need a torch, such as when sweating copper pipe. Neither will generate the heat needed to melt the solder and ready the pipe.

Second, make sure the material being soldered is clean—shiny clean. Use a wire brush, sandpaper, steel wool, or a grinding wheel to remove all dust, dirt, grease, rust, corrosion, paint, and even your fingerprints.

Third, use the right solder and flux for the job. Usually, convenience dictates that you use a wire solder with a core that already contains the appropriate flux.

Use rosin flux-core solder for metals such as tin and copper, and acid flux-core solder for metals such as galvanized iron.

And, be sure to sufficiently heat the metal being joined and the solder (to its melting point). If either the solder or the metal isn't hot enough, you may get a "cold" joint that looks pitted, like unstirred sugar on the bottom of a coffee cup. The joint must be hot enough for the flux to do its cleaning job and boil away.

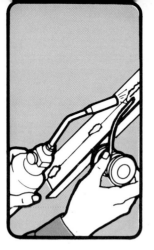

A "stovepipe seam" is the easiest way to join metal sheets. Fold the ends, interlock them, and pound them flat. Then solder one edge.

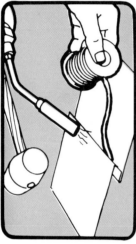

After thoroughly cleaning the surfaces to be joined, "tin" (coat) the surfaces as shown with solder. Then join them.

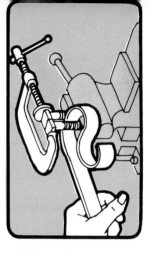

Tin and tack long joints at various intervals, then secure the joint with a continuous strip of solder "flowed" on.

## BENDING METALS

Adequate support and sometimes heat are the keys to bending metals successfully. (Heat is used most often for bending iron and steel bar and rod stock.) They minimize the weakening of the metal caused by the stretching and compressing that occurs during bending.

For most metals, you can improvise a bending jig of some sort out of scraps of wood, C-clamps, or a vise. Some thick, exceptionally hard metals, such as steel bars, defy bending. With these, your best bet is to form the bend you want in a piece of thin scrap metal and have a metalworking shop duplicate the bend for you, using the scrap piece as a template.

But thin sheet metals such as aluminum and copper are quite a different story. The only thing you have to be careful of here is not to "overbend" them. Thin metals bent and creased at right angles tend to tear almost like paper. Simply make the bend and leave alone; don't wiggle it back and forth.

When measuring the length of piece you need for a particular use, be sure to allow enough to accommodate the bend. As a general guideline, figure that right-angle bends "absorb" half the thickness of the metal.

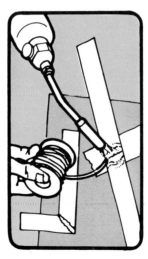

Bend corners in metal by clamping the metal in a vise and tapping it near the jaws of the vise. Use a rubber hammer for soft metals.

Bend sheet metal the same way, but extend the jaws of the vise with strips of hardwood and C-clamps. Tap a block as shown.

For complex curves, clamp bolts in a vise, slide the metal between the bolts, then make the bends in increments, moving the metal.

Files and abrasives make relatively quick work of shaping and smoothing metals. Shaping also generally requires a vise to hold the metal so it doesn't slip or vibrate. For soft metals such as aluminum and copper, use a single-cut file. For harder metals, you'll need a double-cut file.

For more information on the types of files available and their uses, see pages

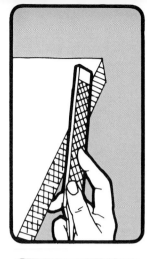

444 and 445. And see page 448 for help with choosing the proper abrasive for smoothing metal.

Filing metal is a hand-and-arm operation—without the force of your body in back of the motion. Hold the file in both hands and apply the cutting action on the forward stroke only.

For a super-smooth finish, you can draw-file the metal with a single-cut file. To do this, hold the file flat across, almost at right angles to, the metal. Then draw it

across the metal in smooth, even strokes. Using a cloth moistened with light machine oil, keep the surface of the metal free of metal chips and "dust" as you file. Also, keep the file teeth clean with a file card. Don't tap the file on a hard surface to remove debris. This usually won't dislodge much, but it will ruin some teeth.

For smooth edges, hold the file at a 30-degree angle to the work. File from left to right, then reverse the angle and cross-file.

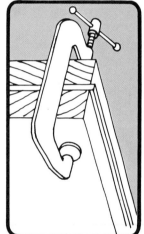

To draw-file a perfectly flat edge, clamp the work between two boards so you can't rock the file and round the edge.

For small pieces, clamp a file to a bench or tabletop and move the metal along the file. Use a round file for inside curves.

## POLISHING METALS

All metals—unless protected with a finish—rust, corrode, and/or oxidize. Silver, for example, turns black. Iron rusts and turns reddish-brown. Aluminum dulls and pits. Brass turns green. To make metals look new again, you need an abrasive suited to the metal.

*Aluminum.* Use medium to fine steel wool in a pad. Do not use a kitchen

scouring pad. You also can polish aluminum with a fine wire wheel or a flannel wheel and polishing compound.

*Copper and brass.* Use medium to fine steel wool and emery paper. Polish with a fine wire wheel or a flannel wheel and polishing compound.

*Iron and steel.* Use a coarse to medium abrasive, followed with a wire brush and a fine abrasive. If the material is extremely rough, you may have to file it with an abrasive wheel, then polish.

*Gold and silver.* Use a liquid polish manufactured especially for these metals.

*Stainless steel.* Use extra-fine steel wool and commercial metal cleaners.

Once you've polished a metal, the surface should be protected to preserve the shine. You can coat aluminum, copper, brass, bronze, iron, and steel surfaces with a clear finish. Or, paint over the surfaces with a pigmented finish. (See pages 522 and 523.)

For a satin finish, buff metal with a wire wheel powered by an electric drill. Or rub the surface with a very fine steel wool.

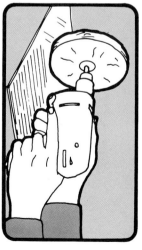

For a higher luster, rub or power-sand with increasingly finer grades of emery cloth. Reverse direction with each cut.

For a chromium-like finish on aluminum, final-buff with polishing compound. Then seal the surface with a clear finish.

**483**

# WORKING WITH ALUMINUM

It's almost impossible to walk into a building supply center that doesn't carry a good stock of aluminum materials on its shelves. You'll find sheets, rods, bars, angles, tubes, channels, track, and plain, die-cut, and embossed sheets, plus aluminum rivets, screws, bolts, and nails. This variety isn't surprising when you consider that aluminum products are ideal for many home maintenance and improvement projects.

Not only is aluminum a versatile material, it's also one of the easiest to work. Cutting it doesn't pose any special

problems. In fact, you can cut aluminum sheet with scissors or tin snips. However, both tools tend to "buckle" the material around the cut edge. So if appearance is an important consideration, use a fine-tooth handsaw or circular saw blade to make the cuts.

Though bar, rod, channel, and track aluminum are too thick to cut with scissors or tin snips, a hand- or power saw equipped with a metal-cutting blade will zip right through them.

To mark aluminum for accurate cutting, use a wax-type pencil or, better, a scratch awl or the point of a nail. Joining aluminum is almost as easy as cutting it. Screws, bolts, and rivets all work well. You even can use a staple gun to tack

aluminum sheet to wood framing, provided the sheet is thin enough.

And because aluminum is a "soft" metal, you can drill, shape, and smooth it easily, too. Just be sure to use tools designed for fabricating metals.

Sawing, drilling, sanding, and grinding aluminum produce a fine to fairly coarse metal dust or debris, so for safety's sake always wear safety glasses and gloves when you work with this material.

Aluminum won't rust, but it will corrode, leaving the metal white and pitted. To prevent this, coat it with a clear finish, or paint the surface. A special aluminum primer is required before painting. For more information on painting aluminum, see pages 522 and 523.

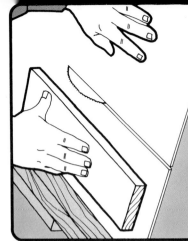

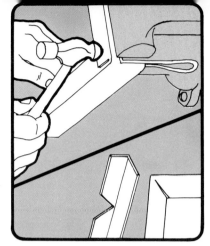

To make corners in angle stock, saw one side at 90 degrees, then bend and overlap it. Or miter it by making V-shaped cuts.

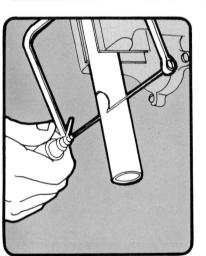

Fine-tooth power saw blades make accurate, straight cuts. Prevent the sheet from lifting up with a piece of scrap.

Fine-tooth handsaws work best on thicker material and tubing. Here a coping saw is used to cut a notch in tubing for a T-connector.

Make an angle jig for sheet by sawing a slot in a board. Planing the inside surface of the jig at an angle lets you "shape" bends.

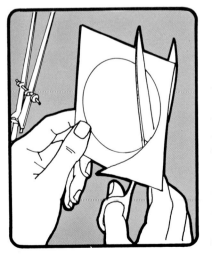

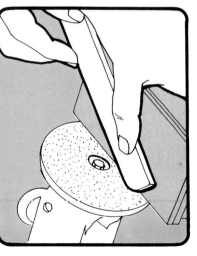

Cut thin sheets of aluminum into various shapes with sharp scissors. Mark the outline you want with an awl or wax-type pencil.

Use a disc sander to round corners and smooth cuts. Clamp an angled strip to the table and you can grind perfect miters.

Though sometimes hidden from view, metal tubing is all around us. Copper tubing carries water on its route through our homes. The aluminum type sees use as furniture legs, shelving spacers, hanger rods, and electrical conduit. And brass and steel tubing have both functional and decorative uses.

You can buy or special-order metals in both rigid and flexible tubing at most home center stores and building materials outlets. If you can't find them there, check with a nearby plumbing dealer. Tubing sizes range from $1/8$ to $1 1/4$ inches in diameter, and up to 10 feet in length. You can purchase much longer lengths of flexible tubing, which is packaged in long rolls.

By far, the slickest tool for cutting small tubing is a hand-type tube cutter. Since the blade will burr the metal, good-quality cutters incorporate an attachment that will remove the burrs.

Bending presents special problems—namely kinking. Once tubing is kinked, it's impossible to re-form it. It's best to bend tubing around a piece of wood shaped to the bend, or to use a spring-type bender (see illustrations below). Filling the tubing with sand will work, too. A bending jig or spring is most critical for small-diameter sizes, since the tubing kinks very easily when shaped with just your hands.

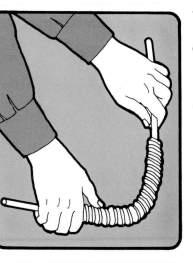

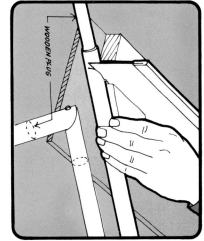

WOODEN PLUG

Bend tubing by shaping it around a wooden jig specially cut to duplicate the pattern you want. Make the bend slowly in degrees.

A commercial tube bender is best for forming small-diameter tubing. It's a spring-like device into which you insert the tubing.

Make mitered corners by driving a wooden plug into the tube, then cutting 45-degree angles. A metal screw secures the corners.

Splice tubing with wooden dowels, or saw a 1/4-inch slit in a piece of scrap tubing and slip it into the joint. Tension holds it.

Sawing a slit also provides a way to join tubing with sheet stock. Screws or bolts can then pass through both tubing and sheet.

# CHOOSING AND BUYING GLASS

Even though you probably don't live in an all-glass house or throw stones, you should know how to buy and install glass for that occasional broken window or storm door that seems to afflict us all.

Buying replacement glass may be your first problem; many home center and hardware stores don't stock it. If you can't find it in these places, check the classified section of your local phone directory under "Glass."

In case you've never shopped for glass before, you'll be surprised at how many different types are available—standard, plate, tempered, safety, wired, insulating, solar-tinted, mirror tiles, glass building block units, and more (see the chart below). If you're like most home-owners, though, standard glass will be first on your shopping list, followed by plate glass, which is generally used for shelving and tabletops.

You can purchase replacement glass in several thicknesses. Your best bet is to take a piece of the broken glass with you to the store.

Stores that stock replacement glass have it pre-cut into standard "window and door frame" sizes, so you'll need to know the exact size of the space you're fitting. Measure the sash opening, then subtract $\frac{1}{8}$ inch from this measurement on all four sides. This lets the glass "float" in the sash and helps prevent it from breaking. If the size you need is not standard, the dealer probably can cut the exact size for you. Or, you can buy a slightly larger standard size and cut it down yourself (see page 145).

When replacing broken glass in storm doors, use either tempered safety glass or acrylic sheet. Both of these products help prevent serious injuries caused by broken glass.

## GLASS SELECTOR

| Type | Break Resistance | Installation | Cost | Uses |
| --- | --- | --- | --- | --- |
| Standard (single-strength) | Poor | Easy | Inexpensive | Windows and doors; storm windows and doors; cabinet fronts; pictures |
| Standard (double-strength) | Fair | Easy | Inexpensive | Same as single-strength |
| Plate | Good | Easy | Moderate | Tabletops; shelves; high-quality mirrors |
| Tempered | Excellent | Easy | Moderate | Windows and doors; patio doors; skylights; tub and shower doors; fireplace doors |
| Safety | Excellent | Moderately difficult | Moderate to expensive | Storm doors; patio doors; skylights; tabletops |
| Wired | Excellent | Difficult | Expensive | Doors; commercial installations; basement windows; in high-crime areas |
| Insulating | Good | Have a professional install | Expensive | Windows; sliding glass doors; large glass areas |
| Solar-tinted | Good | Fairly difficult | Expensive | Prime windows and doors; large glass areas; commercial buildings; skylights |
| Frosted | Good | Moderate | Fairly expensive | Bathroom windows; shower doors and tub enclosures (if tempered) |
| Patterned | Fair | Easy | Expensive | Entrance windows; decorative accents; cabinet fronts |
| Mirror tiles | Poor | Easy | Moderate | Accent walls; bathrooms; bedrooms; cabinet liners |
| Glass blocks or bricks | Excellent | Difficult | Expensive | Basement walls in new construction and remodeling |

# WORKING WITH GLASS

Cutting, smoothing, and shaping glass are jobs that sound much more formidable than they really are. Actually, if you follow the procedures shown below and exercise a reasonable amount of caution when handling glass, you should never have any mishaps.

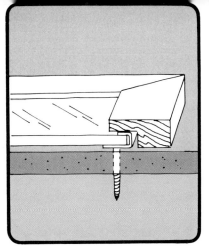

For glass work, you should invest in a *good-quality glass cutter* and a pair of glass pliers. In addition, you'll need a putty knife, a can of light machine oil, and a wooden yardstick or a thin piece of wood with a straight edge. And last but not least, you also should wear gloves and safety glasses when handling glass.

To cut glass, lay it out on a flat surface covered with several layers of newspaper or a piece of carpeting. Clean the glass with glass cleaner before you score and break it.

If you're cutting mirror glass, follow the same procedures described above, but don't cut or apply oil to the silvered side of the glass. If you're cutting "old" glass (which is harder than "new" glass) or

glass that has a pebbled or uneven surface, use a dull glass cutter and apply plenty of pressure to the cutting wheel.

Let a professional cut safety glass; he has the necessary equipment for the job.

Score and cut wired glass just like standard glass, but snip the wire with side cutters after the break is made. You may be able to bend the glass back and forth until the wire breaks.

To drill holes in glass, use a sharp tungsten-carbide bit at very slow speed and keep the tip of the bit lubricated with oil, turpentine, or kerosene.

For information on how to replace a windowpane, see page 145.

---

To make straight cuts in glass, first score the piece. Then snap it by exerting downward pressure with your hand.

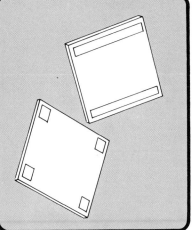

A ruler with a suction cup on one end lets you scribe curves. A glass cutter held at a certain measurement scores the glass.

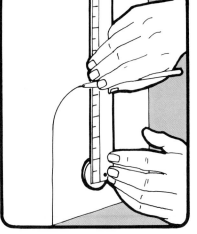

Smooth rough edges by rubbing the edges with an oilstone dipped in water. Use even strokes and keep the stone square.

---

Secure large mirrors with special steel clips sold at glass outlets and hobby and craft shops. You can cover the clips with molding.

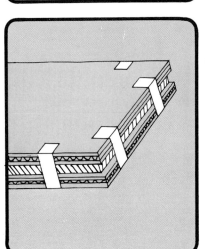

To cover a wall with mirror tiles, square them up as you would for ceramic tile (see page 29). Secure with tape or adhesive.

Store extra windowpanes by sandwiching each between two pieces of plywood and taping the package together. Set on edge.

487

# FINISHING

## INTERIOR PAINTING

Far too many home finishing projects get little more than a wish, a prayer, and a coat of something or other slapped onto a surface that's not ready for it. The result: a botched job that haunts you for years or begins to peel away a few weeks later.

The final fifty pages of this book tell the right way to paint or paper a room, revitalize your home's exterior, seal wood grain, and much more.

Note that about 90 percent of the work in a successful finishing project happens before you pop open the first can lid. No one, to be sure, really enjoys patching, scraping, and sanding chores. And priming seems to add just another product to the list of things you have to buy. But it's these no-fun procedures that spell the difference between a so-so result and a professional-looking job.

This chapter sorts out what you do and don't need to know to get good results. It starts out with interior painting, a task that almost everyone faces at sometime or other. Here the emphasis is on products and techniques that let you get the job done efficiently and with a minimum of hassles.

## CHOOSING AND BUYING INTERIOR PAINT

Shopping in a well-stocked paint store can be a bewildering experience. Latex, alkyd, acrylic, urethane, epoxy—what do all these mysterious names mean? What kind of preparation do they require, and what sort of results will they give?

Unfortunately, you can't always rely on the salesperson to straighten you out. He or she may not know much more than you do, or may be too harried for careful consideration of your needs. Product labels aren't necessarily very helpful, either—but usually a close reading will tell you a few key things.

Look first for the *thinner* specified by the manufacturer. Today's paints rarely require thinning, but you'll need the proper agent for cleaning up spatters, smears, and—after you're through for the day—your painting equipment.

Here there are only two important categories: *water-thinned* paint and *solvent-thinned* paint. Water-thinned formulations—*latex* is the most typical—can be cut with water, which means you can wipe up smears with just a damp rag, wash out brushes and rollers with soap, and scrub off your hands under a faucet. These types also dry very quickly and have almost no odor.

Solvent-thinned paints—usually *alkyd*-based—require a solvent such as mineral spirits (paint thinner) or special odorless thinners for cleanup. These are generally more durable than water-thinned paints.

The chart on the opposite page tells about the water- and solvent-thinned coatings you're most likely to use. (Note, though, that store personnel sometimes refer to alkyds as oil-base paints, since the two have many of the same characteristics.)

Next, decide on the *luster* or *gloss* you prefer. Just how shiny a surface you want depends partly on your taste, of course—but also bear in mind that the glossier a finish, the harder and more durable it will be. That's why pros generally recommend flat or low-gloss paint—variously called "satin," "eggshell," or "low-luster"—for broad expanses of walls and ceilings, semi- and high-gloss for woodwork, kitchens, baths, and other hard-wear or high-humidity areas. Flat and low-gloss paints do a better job of *hiding* whatever is underneath; you'll pay less for them, too.

After you've decided on a top coating, give careful thought to whether or not you'll need a *primer*. Designed to seal raw surfaces, these have other important uses as well. If, for example, you want to change colors or apply latex over an existing glossy surface, prime first. The right undercoat provides "tooth" to which the final finish can adhere. Selecting a primer can be slightly tricky, so consult the chart on the opposite page and double-check by asking the salesperson or reading labels before you make a final decision.

Colors present some special problems, too. First of all, they react to each other and cast reflections that may change the appearance of everything in a room. Secondly, colors look different under different lighting, and large areas may become far more intense than you might imagine while looking at relatively small chips. So if you're contemplating a drastic color change, consider buying a relatively small quantity of the hue that catches your eye and trying it out on a wall or sizable area before you invest in several gallons of paint that may not be returnable.

## COMPARING INTERIOR PAINTS

| Paint | Uses | Features/Characteristics | Thinner/Primer |
|---|---|---|---|
| Latex | The number-one choice for most home paint jobs. Don't use it over unprimed wood, metal, or wallpaper, though. | Available in glosses ranging from flat to high, it adheres to all but very slick surfaces and dries so rapidly that you can usually apply two coats in one day. Somewhat less durable and washable than alkyd-base paints. | Easy to clean up with soap and water. Prepare raw surfaces with a latex or alkyd primer. |
| Alkyd | Use this synthetic-resin formulation wherever you need a tough surface or superior hiding power. Don't apply it over unprimed drywall—this paint will roughen the surface. | Alkyds dry somewhat more slowly than latex and have a slightly stronger odor. | For thinning and cleanup, use solvents—but not water. Coat previously unfinished surfaces with alkyd primer. |
| Oil | Natural-resin oil paints have all but disappeared from the scene. | They dry slowly, give off strong, flammable fumes, and don't stand up quite as well as alkyds. | Thin with turpentine or other mineral spirits. |
| Urethane and Polyurethane | Use them over almost any porous surface or existing finish. | Basically pigmented versions of clear polyurethane "varnish" (see pages 534 and 536), these plastic-based toughies resist grease, dirt, abrasion, and alcohol. Application can be somewhat tricky. They're also expensive, so consider whether you really need extreme durability. | Most are solvent-thinned, but check the manufacturer's recommendations before you buy. The same applies for primers. |
| Epoxy | You can apply them over nonporous surfaces such as tile or glass. They won't adhere to previously painted finishes, however. | The strongest and most costly of all paints. Most require that you mix in a hardening agent just before use—a tricky procedure. | Solvent-thinned. Again, check the label for the recommended primer. |
| One-Coat | Use these only if the surface is already sealed, is almost the same color as the one you're applying, and doesn't have a lot of patchwork to be covered. | Ordinary latex or alkyd paints with additional pigment to increase their hiding power. You'll pay more, too, of course. | Thinning cuts down their hiding ability. Clean up with water or solvent, depending upon whether the paint has a latex or alkyd base. |
| Texture | Designed to cover up imperfections and give the look of stucco-finish plaster. | Some come premixed; with others, you must stir in a sand-like powder. Application is moderately difficult—usually you must paint a section at a time and "work out" the effect you want. | Again, thinning defeats their purpose, and stirring can be arduous. Check the label for compatible primers. |
| Acoustic | This one coats acoustic ceiling tiles without cutting down their sound-deadening qualities. | Apply it by spraying, or use a special roller. Color choice is limited. | Thin and clean up with water. No primer necessary. |
| Dripless | Use it on ceilings. | Considerably more expensive than ordinary paint. | Water- or solvent-thinned. Choose the appropriate primer. |
| Metal | Use over primed or bare metal surfaces. | Actually, you can coat previously painted or primed metal with almost any type of paint. Special metal paints are self-primers designed to adhere to bare surfaces. For more about these, see pages 522 and 523. | Some metal paints are water-thinned; with others you need solvent or mineral spirits. Primer depends on the metal being covered. |

## CHOOSING AND BUYING BRUSHES

The paintbrush rack at your local paint store isn't what it used to be. Stocked there is an almost unbelievable array of products. Brushes come in many sizes, styles, and different bristle types, with prices that range from under a dollar to $10 or more.

Don't let this intimidate you, though. Selecting the right brush for the job at hand isn't difficult. First off, be aware that all of those brushes hanging there fall into one of two categories: natural- (pure-) bristle brushes or synthetic-bristle brushes. Natural-bristle brushes (made with animal hairs) were formerly considered the finest type available. But some of today's synthetic (usually nylon) versions now perform just as well.

Knowing when to use each type isn't hard, either. Just keep in mind that if you're using oil-base paint, stay with a natural-bristle or a quality synthetic-bristle brush. Never use a natural-bristle brush in water-thinned finishes. If you do, the bristles will become mop-like, and the result will be bad.

Many paintbrush manufacturers label the brush package with the type of finish the brush is designed to spread. And, if the brush you're considering isn't packaged, take a look at its handle; it's probably stamped with the bristle type.

While you're browsing, also take a look at the disposable brushes that are available. These relatively new introductions to the paintbrush market come in a wide range of widths and sizes, and are suitable for many painting projects. And since they're relatively inexpensive, you can just toss them when the job's done, saving considerable cleanup time.

Should you spend the extra amount for a quality brush, or are the inexpensive ones the better buy? It depends! If you're willing to take the time to clean your brush after using it, buy a quality brush. It should serve you well for years. But if you paint only occasionally and don't like cleaning up, a less-expensive brush probably is the wiser investment.

How can you distinguish between a good-quality brush and one of lesser quality? There are several ways. One of the surest is to spread the bristles and inspect their tips. Quality natural-bristle brushes will have little "flags" on bristle ends—the more the better. On good-quality synthetic brushes, you'll see fuzzy-looking tips.

You also can give the bristles a couple of hard raps against the edge of a counter. A quality brush will lose some of its bristles, but a cheap one will lose lots. Also check out the *ferrule* of the brush. This aluminum or stainless steel band near the handle should be wrapped tightly and neatly around the brush, and solidly secured to the handle.

Let the drawing below guide your selection. Among your first buys should be a 4-inch *wall* brush, a 2-inch *trim* brush, and a 2-inch *sash-trim* brush. Later, you might want to add a 6-inch wall brush for masonry paint jobs, and a *round* brush for delicate work. A *brush spinner* speeds cleanup jobs—or choose a *foam* brush and simply throw it away when you're through.

The four handle styles shown serve different functions. A *beavertail* handle lets you grip a wider brush in the palm of your hand; *pencil* and *flat* handles allow greater fingertip control; the *kaiser* handle also offers good control, plus an easy-to-hold grip.

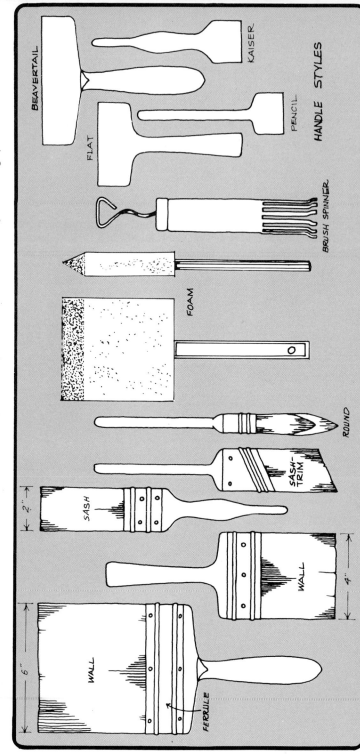

As with almost anything else, there's a right way and a wrong way to use and care for a paintbrush. The sketches and captions below will fill you in on loading, holding, and cleanup basics.

Before you use a paintbrush for the first time, first spin it by the handle between your hands. Then give it a

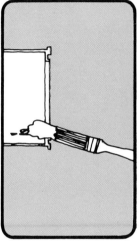

couple of hard flips against the edge of a bench or table. Both procedures help remove loose bristles.

Next, work the bristles against a rough surface such as a concrete block or brick wall. The roughness will soften the flagged or fuzzy ends of the bristles. And if yours is a natural-bristle brush, soak it 24 hours in linseed oil for conditioning.

When you start painting with a new brush, you'll notice two things: still more

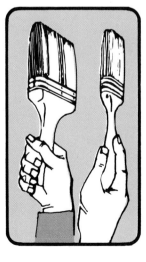

loose bristles, and stray bristles that stick out from the sides of the ferrule. You can pick up the loose bristles in fresh paint by simply dabbing the tip of the brush at the loose bristle.

For stray bristles, sandwich the blade of a putty knife between the bristle and the ferrule. Then, snap off the bristle at the ferrule.

Dip the brush into the paint to one-third the length of its bristles. Go deeper and you'll waste paint and create a mess.

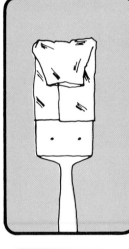

Squeeze excess paint from the bristles by pressing them lightly against the side of the container as you remove the brush.

Hold small brushes with your thumb and index finger. For larger brushes, use a palm grip or lay fingers on the ferrule.

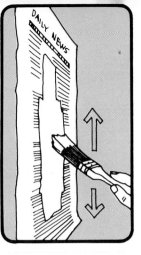

If your work is interrupted for an hour or so, leave the brush in the paint. Position it so the paint covers the bristle tips.

For longer interruptions, wrap the brush in foil or plastic and store in the freezer. Thaw when you're ready to paint again.

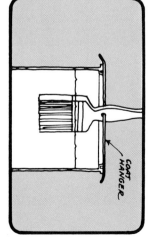

If you'll be using the brush within a day or so, immerse it in solvent or water. Drill a hole in the handle for hanging.

To clean a brush, work out remaining paint by firmly stroking the brush back and forth on newspaper. Work until the brush is "dry."

Before storing a brush for an extended period, cut away all the paint you can with appropriate thinner. Work bristles as shown.

Wash the brush in soap and water, shape the bristles and let them dry, then wrap the brush in several layers of paper toweling.

# CHOOSING AND BUYING ROLLERS

Paint rollers perform their tricks best on large, flat surfaces—you can cover about 50 percent more area in the same time it takes with a paintbrush. But you also can buy special trim rollers for small and hard-to-get-at areas, and, once you get the knack of using them, they're about as easy to control as a trim brush. Some people prefer to trim with a brush and fill in with a roller. Use the method that works best for you.

Rollers for *flat surfaces* range in width from 4 to 18 inches. They have a plastic or wooden handle (often machined to accept an extension handle) and a metal frame on which the roller cover is inserted. Of the two types of frames available—the *bird cage* type (depicted in the illustration below) and the *solid metal* versions—the bird cage frame works better if you're using fast-drying paints, as it cleans up more easily than the solid-metal type. For solvent-thinned paints, either type will work.

*Trim* rollers come in varying widths and configurations. The 3-inch-wide version shown here gets into areas too tight for a full-size roller. *Cone-shaped* types do inside corners, around door and window casings, and almost any point where two planes intersect. *Doughnut-style* rollers paint moldings and other fine work.

The type of paint you intend to use determines what type of *roller cover* you need. Luckily, most covers, which are manufactured from mohair, lamb's wool, acetate, Dynel, or polyurethane foam, are labeled with the type of paint the roller was designed to apply, helping to eliminate guesswork.

Mohair covers, for use with gloss finishes and varnishes, lay on a smooth finish because the nap is short and tightly woven. Dynel, acetate, and polyurethane foam covers may be used with all paints. Use a lamb's wool roller cover only for solvent-thinned paint.

You'll also notice on the package that roller covers vary in nap length—from 1/16 to 1 1/2 inches. Use the long naps for rough surfaces, the short ones for smooth work. The nap in turn is fastened to a cardboard or plastic sleeve. If you're using water-thinned paint, buy a plastic sleeve. For solvent-thinned paint, your best bet is a cardboard sleeve.

If you want to produce a design on the surface as you roll on the paint, buy yourself a stippling cover. When using one of these, make sure *not* to overlap previous roller strokes. Otherwise, the finished paint job will look out of "alignment."

Fairly new on the paint application scene are *pad painters*. The pads may be a carpet-like material or plastic foam inserted in a plastic mop-like applicator or a paintbrush handle. Though excellent for applying paint to almost any surface, they really earn their keep when you use them to paint shakes, fencing, screening, and shutters.

A *paint tray*, either the metal or plastic type, completes the roller painting system. If you'll be working from a stepladder, buy one with ladder "hooks" to keep the tray secure. And to save on cleanup time, purchase some plastic tray inserts, which you simply toss once the painting is done. With these, the paint never touches your tray.

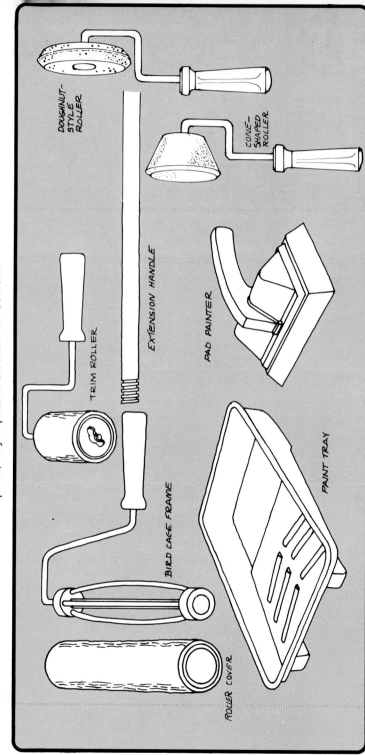

DOUGHNUT-STYLE ROLLER

CONE-SHAPED ROLLER

EXTENSION HANDLE

TRIM ROLLER

PAD PAINTER

BIRD CAGE FRAME

PAINT TRAY

ROLLER COVER

# USING ROLLERS AND PADS

Anyone who has ever painted with rollers or pads will vouch not only for their speed, but also for the ease with which they lay on paint. There's nothing to it. As long as you keep plenty of paint on the roller cover or pad, you'll get better coverage than you would with a brush.

To load a roller with paint, turn it into the edge of the paint in the tray. Even out the paint on the slant of the tray.

Rollers work well on wide, flat woodwork such as raised panel doors. Paint the recesses first, then finish the flush surfaces.

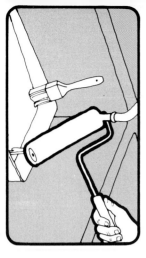

Wash out water-base paints in a sink. Let water run over the roller until clear. Squeezing the roller speeds things.

When using a roller, though, keep your eyes peeled for skid marks on the painted surface. Rollers tend to "slide" as they're moved. This sliding causes small roller tracks in the finish, which, if you're not careful, will show when the finish has dried.

Most all surfaces are irregular to some extent. So to achieve the best coverage when using rollers or pads, lay on the paint from several different directions, as

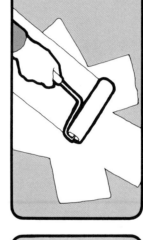

For best paint coverage, apply the paint every which way. You can minimize dripping by starting the roller on the upstroke.

To clean a roller cover, first work out all the excess paint you can on old newspaper. Keep turning to new pages as you work.

Wring the roller cover dry by squeezing it between your hands. If you're cleaning out solvent-base paint, wear rubber gloves.

shown below. This way you won't miss any shallow depressions, such as the joints between drywall panels. If you're applying glossy paint, you'll then want to finish up with vertical strokes to give the surface an even appearance. Don't worry about evening up flat paint though; roller marks fade away as the paint dries.

Don't work a roller too quickly, especially when the roller cover is loaded with paint. You'll waste paint and make a mess.

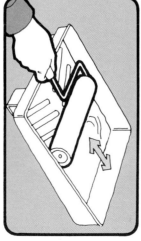

With solvent-thinned paint, pour solvent into the tray and work the roller back and forth. Repeat until the solvent remains clear.

Wrap clean, dry equipment in aluminum foil or plastic bags. Clean pad and brush painters just as you do roller covers.

# CHOOSING AND USING STEPLADDERS

If you find yourself breaking into a cold sweat every time you get above the third rung of a stepladder, you'll find a whole series of household repair and improvement projects literally over your head. To conquer these qualms, first select a ladder you can trust, then learn a few safety habits.

In buying a ladder, first decide whether you prefer wood or aluminum construction. Aluminum ladders—by far the most popular—weigh only about half as much as wood versions. Though every bit as strong and safe, metal ladders do flex somewhat as you shift your weight around.

Next, check the ladder's *rails* or sides. Here you'll usually find a rating that indicates its strength. Type III *household-grade* ladders, are rated at 200 pounds; Type II *commercial-grade*, 225 pounds; and Type I *industrial-grade*, 250 pounds. Each type has been tested at four times these loads. For security and durability, buy a Type II ladder.

Lengths range from two to 16 feet, with six-footers the norm for most indoor needs. (To learn about outdoor, extension ladders, see page 111.)

Stepladder safety involves these rules. Follow them and you needn't worry overly about accidents.

1. If possible, always lean a stepladder, unopened, against a wall. Make sure, too, that the ladder is sitting solidly on the floor.

2. If you open the ladder, double-check to make sure you've opened it fully and that you've locked the bucket tray and braces in position.

3. Work from a ladder that is long enough for the job. Don't go higher than one step below the top, and never stand on the bucket tray.

4. Never paint a wooden ladder. Paint can hide defects in the wood.

5. Never climb a stepladder that has loose or broken rungs or a split or broken side rail.

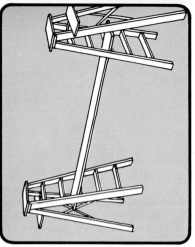

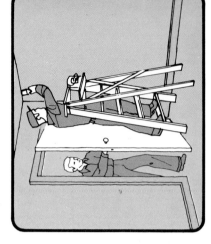

Two stepladders and a 2x12 make a convenient scaffold. But always try to work from the ladder for safety.

Try to avoid setting a ladder in front of a closed door. If you must, face the ladder's steps—not the bucket—toward the door.

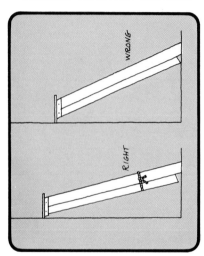

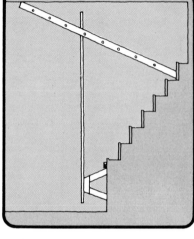

To prop a stepladder against a wall, keep the angle steep so the back legs don't catch on the floor. Or tie the legs shut.

To reach a high stairwell, use an extension ladder, a sawhorse, and planks. To protect the wall, pad the ladder rails.

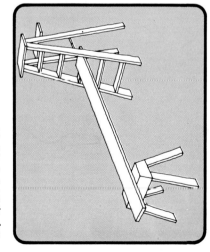

Open the ladder fully and test its stance by lifting one side and pulling toward you. Keep the braces fully open and locked.

Use a sawhorse to support one end of the plank, if you don't have a second stepladder. Or, rent scaffolding at little cost.

A fresh coat of paint can work wonders for a room's appearance—but it can't perform miracles. Paint will not, for example, heal cracked walls, smooth out rough textures, or fill any but the tiniest nail holes. In fact, you may have trouble even getting it to cling to some surfaces that haven't been properly prepped.

Now's the time—after you've cleared the room but before you pop the first paint can lid—to give every surface careful scrutiny.

Start with the walls, checking for cracks, runs, or ridges in the old paint. All of these can be easily treated with a scraper and sandpaper, plus primer for bare spots. If you encounter peeling, suspect moisture or poor preparation. Both require removing the old paint and priming the surface.

Mend superficial plaster or drywall blemishes with spackling or joint compound, as shown on pages 33 and 35. Bigger repairs (see pages 34-36) will require more time, not only for patching, but also for curing and priming. (Note: on textured walls, you may encounter difficulty making the patched area blend in completely with its surroundings.)

You can paint over clean, sound wallpaper, but in most cases you're better off to strip it, as shown on page 502. If you do decide to paint, test in a small, inconspicuous area, and wait for a few days to see if the pattern bleeds through or the paper begins to peel. Strip cracked or glopped-up paint from woodwork, too (see page 529).

After you've made repairs, give the ceiling, walls, and woodwork a thorough bath with household detergent, and rinse well. Prime all exposed spots with a primer that's compatible with both the surface and your finish coat—and you've completed at least 50 percent of your painting project.

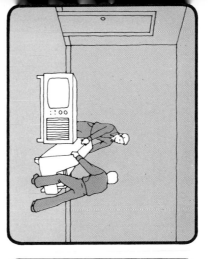

Remove all lightweight furniture from the room, group the heavy items, then carefully cover them with drop cloths.

Set up strong lights so you can see what you're painting. Aim them at angles to better highlight minor imperfections.

Even if you plan to paint switch and receptacle plates, remove them and paint separately. This prevents sticking to the wall.

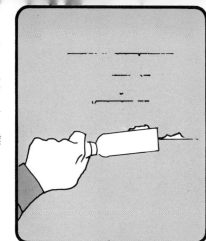

Regardless of its size, fill every hole and crack with premixed spackling paste. Sand patches lightly when dry.

Sand any rough spots smooth, and sand any runs from previous paint jobs. Liquid "sandpaper" removes the gloss from trim.

Wash or dust the ceiling and walls thoroughly, paying attention to the tops of baseboards and window and door moldings.

495

## PAINTING CEILINGS

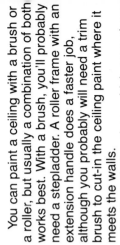

To be a big success at painting, unlike most other endeavors, you have to start at the top and work your way down. The ceiling comes first.

Except for unpainted materials, you generally can get by with just one coat of paint on the ceiling. Even stubborn stains will disappear if you first spot-prime them.

If you're planning a one-coat application, let the paint lap on the walls. If you opt for two coats on the ceiling, cut-in (trim up to the ceiling/wall line) with a trim brush. Otherwise, the paint will build up on the wall and leave a ridge.

Paint across the ceiling in the room's narrow dimension, especially if you're using a fast-drying paint. Otherwise, the paint may lose its wet edge.

You can paint a ceiling with a brush or a roller, but usually a combination of both works best. With a brush, you'll probably need a stepladder. A roller frame with an extension handle does a faster job, although you probably will need a trim brush to cut-in the ceiling paint where it meets the walls.

Unlike paintbrushes, which sometimes drip, rollers emit a fine spray of paint that settles over the room like dust. That's why it's important to cover furniture in the room as well as the floor, carpeting, and woodwork. Canvas drop cloths work best for this, but plastic drop cloths and newspapers will do the job, too. Secure plastic cloths with tape, since they slip and slide over most surfaces.

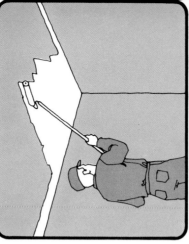

Start rolling the paint with a series of diagonal swaths. Don't worry about spreading the paint evenly; just get it on the ceiling.

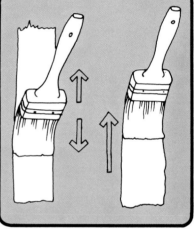

Now even out the paint and fill in any open areas by cross-rolling. Don't fret about keeping the strokes even. They won't show.

Wrap light fixtures in plastic bags. Drop fixture covers by removing the screws. To secure chandeliers, see page 254.

Start the job by cutting-in a strip as shown. If you'll be using only one coat, lap the paint onto the walls as well.

If you use a brush, apply the paint in short strokes, then level it with long, sweeping strokes, with the brush going one way.

Continue working, spreading the paint from dry areas into the wet paint. Rollers "slip" on smooth surfaces, so check for skips.

Especially when compared to the gyrations involved in getting paint up on ceilings, painting walls is a breeze.

For one thing, you can stand up straight and reach most spots without too much difficulty. For another, since you're working on a vertical surface, you can load both brushes and rollers with plenty of paint and sort of "slop" the paint on the wall—first spreading it out and then evening it. Of course, this doesn't mean you don't have to watch for drips and splatters. Load the brush or roller well, but don't saturate it. It won't take you long to get the feel for the right amount.

Begin painting walls by cutting-in the corners and around woodwork. Lap the paint only a few inches onto the wall surface.

After the walls have been properly patched and cleaned, the ceiling painted, and all switch plates removed, you're ready to paint. Do all the edging on the wall first. This includes cutting-in the ceiling and around the molding and trim. With these details out of the way, you can paint big, flat surfaces quickly.

You don't have to worry about lap marks in the paint, except with gloss and semigloss finishes. With these, take care to keep the edges wet to prevent any possible lap marks.

When painting a kitchen, bathroom, or laundry with a semi- or high-gloss finish, make the final brush strokes away from the light source in the room—windows, doors, the prime lighting fixture. This way,

For large surfaces, load the roller and apply the paint in a large "M" shape. Start the roller going up, then pull it down.

the tiny ridges that a brush leaves won't be as pronounced.

Always give the paint a brisk stirring before you start the job, even if the paint was just shaken at the store where you purchased it. And as you work, stir the paint occasionally.

Keep your eye on the paint in the roller tray, too. As long as you're filling the roller, the paint will stay properly blended. But if you leave the tray for an hour or so, stir the paint lightly with a paint paddle. When left untouched, paint skins over.

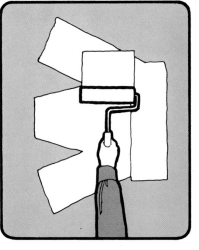

Level and fill-in the M by crossrolling. By working the paint this way, you get an even paint surface. Watch for roller skids.

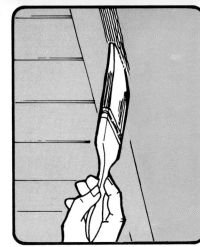

Where two colors meet, use a tapered trim brush lightly loaded with paint. Press it to 1/16 inch of the adjacent color.

Apply high-gloss or semigloss paint in short, vertical sections that measure a few feet square. Work the paint well so it's even.

# PAINTING WOODWORK

There's no denying it: painting woodwork is hard work. And next to prepping the paint job, it's also usually the most time-consuming. But if you master the tricks shown here and on the next page, you can minimize the hassle and speed your progress a great deal.

If at all possible, learn to paint freehand. With practice, anyone with a fairly steady hand and a good trim or sash brush can master the technique, and in the process save a tremendous amount of time compared to applying masking tape.

Before tackling the woodwork, check for damage. If you locate any, patch it with wood filler or water putty. Let the material dry overnight and apply a sealer before applying the finish coat.

If you will be using the same paint on the woodwork as the walls, paint the woodwork as you come to it. If it will be another color or higher gloss, do it after painting the walls.

Windows and raised-panel doors are far and away the toughest to paint. The reasons: the amount of cutting-in to be done, and the fact that you can't take a full stroke with the brush as you can on a wall or ceiling surface. Before painting windows, if you can't paint freehand, cover the glass with masking tape, or if

you'd rather, simply use special window-glass paint removal tools (razor blades and roller scrapers) to clean off any smeared paint.

If you're using a gloss finish on doors, use the cross-brush technique. To do this, first apply the paint on the door horizontally. Then make your finishing strokes vertically. Always finish a door once you've started painting it. If you don't, chances are good that the lap marks will show after the finish has dried.

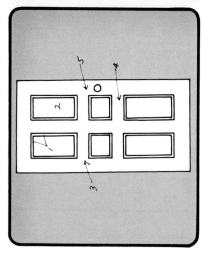

Start panel doors by painting the molded edges first. Then fill in the panels, the hinge stile, the rails, and the latch stile.

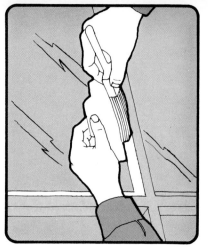

A painter's shield keeps paint off the glass, too. Wipe the paint off its edge as you work around the muntins.

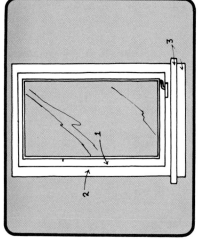

On casement windows, use the same basic sequence shown at left. Keep them slightly cracked until the paint is dry.

Masking tape can protect window panes from paint. Be sure to re-move the tape immediately after you finish the job.

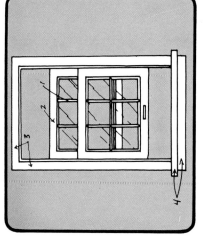

Paint double-hung windows in the sequence shown, starting with the muntins between panes, then working outward.

Flush doors are much easier and quicker to paint. Either a brush or a roller will give good—though different—results.

498

Paint the top edge of baseboards first. After this, cut-in along the floor then fill in the space between.

Clean up any overlapping edges immediately after they occur. If you don't, the paint will set up and be tougher to remove.

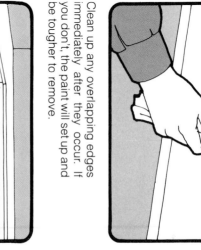

A cloth wrapped around a putty knife helps you clean up paint drippings on hardwood and resilient flooring along baseboards.

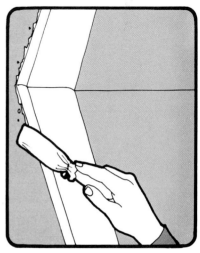

If a woodwork stain bleeds through the paint, seal the woodwork with the appropriate primer. Remove marks with steel wool.

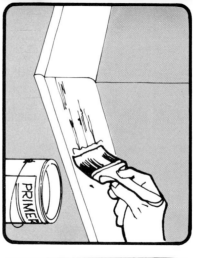

Before painting cabinets, dismantle them as far as possible. Then lay out the parts on newspaper and paint all flat surfaces first.

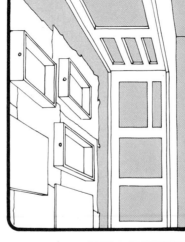

Begin painting cabinets at their least accessible points and work out. Do the inside edges first, then move onto outer surfaces.

To paint both sides and the edges of a shelf in one session, drive four small nails to serve as legs. Paint the underside, then the top.

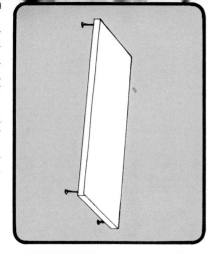

Clean any previously painted hardware by soaking it overnight in paint remover. Then buff the surfaces lightly with steel wool.

Because paint impedes the efficiency of radiators, paint only parts you can see. (More on metal paints on pages 522 and 523.)

PAINT FACES, TOPS & ENDS ONLY

499

## CLEANING UP AFTERWARD

Even professionals are messy painters. But there's one big difference between them and the average do-it-yourselfer. They're more skilled at covering up their mistakes. Their trade secret: getting after a spill or splatter immediately after it happens.

Even if you've thoroughly covered and masked the surfaces you don't want to paint, you can bet there will be some splatters here and there. For water-thinned finishes, use warm water, household detergent, and a soft cloth to remove stray paint. If the paint is

solvent-thinned, use the proper thinner (usually mineral spirits or turpentine) on a soft cloth for cleanup. When you're finished, wash the areas with water and household detergent.

If, when reorganizing a room, you happen to scuff freshly painted walls or woodwork, don't attempt to wash the scuff mark until the paint has had time to "cure"—at least thirty days. Realize, too, that though paint may be dry to the touch within hours, it doesn't fully harden until it has completely cured.

After most painting projects, there will be a small amount of paint left over. If you end up with less than a quart, pour the paint into a glass jar that you can seal tightly. The paint "keeps" better in this

small container. If it turns out that you have more than a quart of finish left, however, you can satisfactorily seal it in the original paint bucket.

Store paint in a cool, dry place where it won't be subjected to freezing and moisture, which can rust metal containers. If you don't use the paint in about a two-year period, it's best to throw it away.

Take canvas and plastic drop cloths outdoors and thoroughly shake, then fold them before storing.

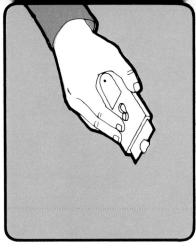

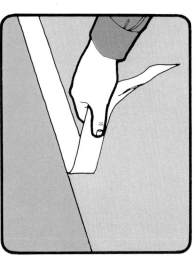

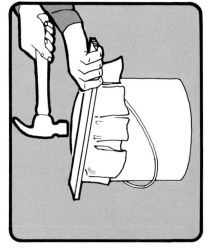

Chip off big paint droplets that already have set up with a razor-blade scraper. A putty knife will work, too.

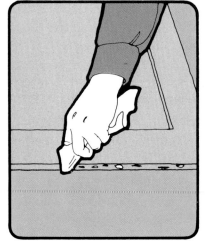

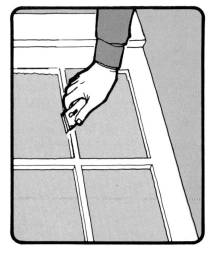

Remove masking tape as soon as you have completed a line. Otherwise, you'll end up with a ragged and crumbling edge.

Tap container lids tight with a hammer and block of wood. Store paint cans upside down to prevent a skin from forming.

Wipe away splatters with soap and water or the solvent used to thin the paint. Catch these splatters as you work, not days later.

Use a razor-blade scraper to trim around windowpanes. It's best not to break the seal between glass and paint, though.

# WALLPAPERING

Papering a room—once a messy, tricky task best left to pros—now need be no more difficult than painting the same space. Part of the credit goes to improved wall coverings that don't rip, shrink, or wrinkle nearly as easily as the old-fashioned papers. New, slower-acting adhesives help, too, by giving you time to hang the materials correctly.

This section takes you through every step of the job—from removing old paper to the advanced techniques needed for ceiling work. And because vinyl and/or pre-pasted coverings make most sense for beginners, we've also included a page devoted exclusively to hanging these time- and effort-savers.

## WALL COVERINGS AT A GLANCE

| Types | Use | Application Tips | Relative Cost |
|---|---|---|---|
| Lining paper | Forms a necessary smooth base for foils, murals, burlap, and other specialty coverings. Excellent, too, for use over rough, pitted, or cracked surfaces. | Hang with pre-sized wheat paste mixed according to package directions. If the surface is painted with a semi- or high-gloss finish, combine 1 part vinyl adhesive with 3 parts wheat paste, then mix with water. Butt the edges of the liner. | Inexpensive |
| Vinyl-coated covering | This old standard is at home in almost any situation, except in rooms with high humidity. | Paste and hang one strip at a time, then roll the seams and clean the adhesive from each seam immediately. | Wide price range |
| Paper-backed vinyl | Excellent for use in high-traffic and high-humidity areas. | Hand-printed vinyls must be trimmed; machine-printed types are pre-trimmed. When applying, make sure the backing is abundantly covered with adhesive. Do not stretch vinyl papers as they are hung. If the edges or seams curl, paste them down with vinyl-to-vinyl adhesive. Then remove excess adhesive immediately. May be stripped when redecorating. | Wide price range |
| Cloth-backed vinyl | Same uses as paper-backed vinyl. | The covering is stiff and difficult to shape to wall or ceiling surfaces. If the paper is lightweight, use a wheat paste adhesive. If it is heavy, use a vinyl adhesive. May be stripped when redecorating. | Expensive |
| Wet-look vinyl | Use in kitchens, bathrooms, laundry areas, and mud rooms. | Lining paper is required, since any imperfections on the wall or ceiling surface will show through. | Moderate |
| Flocked covering | Especially appropriate in formal areas. | Keep the adhesive off the face of the paper. If adhesive does get on the face, remove it immediately with clear water and blot, don't rub. Should the flocking matt, gently go over it with a suede brush. | Expensive |
| Foil covering | Excellent for kitchens, bathrooms, and laundry areas, since it is easy to wipe clean. | Use a liner with this paper. And don't crease the paper as you paste and hang it. Be careful when hanging foil covering around electrical switches and outlets. | Expensive |
| Burlap/grass cloth | Use this material anywhere except in hard-use areas where lots of grease, dampness, and dirt is present. | Lining paper is required. Butt the seams and roll them. Mix vinyl adhesive with ½ pint less water than instructions specify, and apply two coats of the adhesive with a mohair paint roller cover. Do not set the rolls on end; their weight will damage the edges. | Expensive |
| Cork-faced covering | Best for accents; not for hard-use areas. | The edges will curl, so roll the seams just as soon as you hang a strip. Use wheat paste with 1 part vinyl adhesive to 4 parts wheat paste. Also use a liner unless the wall is a new one. | Expensive |

# REMOVING OLD WALLPAPER

Ask anyone who has ever stripped wallpaper off of old walls and they'll tell you that if you have the option, don't do it. The reason: unless you're working with strippable-type paper, it's a messy, time-consuming task. So before you decide to take on the job, ask yourself, "Do I really need to take the old off before applying the new?" If the old wallpaper is on the wall nice and tight, leave it there. You can eradicate any small blemishes by simply cutting away the damaged section and piecing-in a patch to level the surface.

But if the old paper is in bad shape, you have no choice except to remove it. It hasn't been too many years since the only way to remove old wallpaper was to

soak it with water or with a chemical solution. This technique meant continual soaking of the paper and lots of arm-tiring reaching and scraping.

Today, if you're dealing with a type of wallpaper other than the strippable kind, your best bet is to rent a wallpaper steamer. With this work-saving device, you can now remove more old paper in an hour than you previously could in a whole day of soaking and hard work.

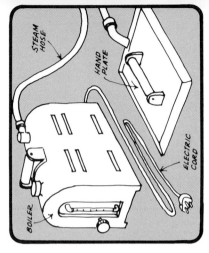

A wide-bladed wall scraper makes a good paper stripper. Work it under the paper with one hand and peel with the other.

A wallpaper steamer works well for removing lots of paper. A boiler furnishes steam to a plate that you hold against the wall.

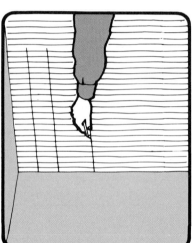

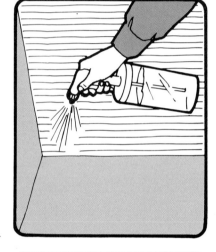

If the paper won't peel off in one strip, make a series of slits. The paper may then pop so you can peel it.

If the wall is plaster, soak the paper with mist from a plant sprayer. When wet enough, re-move the paper with a scraper.

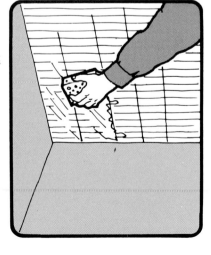

Some heavier wall coverings can be peeled off in strips—espe-cially vinyl papers. Loosen an edge with a knife and pull down.

If removing the paper without a steamer, slit it then soak the slits with a liquid wallpaper remover. Scrape off the paper.

For sheer impact, few wall treatments can rival wallpaper. Trouble is, some people rush to the paste pot too quickly and botch the job rather than taking the time to prepare the walls or ceiling. Wallpapering is one thing you just can't hurry. If you do, every nick, hole, and ridge you neglect will tell on your lack of attention.

You're in luck if the wall you want to paper is painted and in good repair. If the paint is glossy, simply dull the gloss with an abrasive so the adhesive will stick properly. Then wash down the area with a strong household detergent, let dry, and proceed wallpapering.

If the paint is peeling from the surface, remove it with a scraper and seal the surface underneath with sizing or a sealer. For walls with a sand finish, first scrape the surface. Then lightly sand the surface and cover it with lining paper.

Nicked, cracked, and crumbling walls or ceilings call for corrective action. Here you have a couple of alternatives. You can repair the surface (see pages 33-37) or use a liner, which is a plain, lightweight wallpaper without a pattern. Apply the liner with pre-sized wheat paste, butting the edges and rolling the seams. The edges needn't be butted tightly. A liner helps, but is not a cure-all for all surface problems.

Lightly sand any seam overlaps. If you don't, the seams will show through the new wallpaper. Remove grease, too.

Glue down any curled edges with wallpaper adhesive. You also may use rubber cement; coat both the paper and the wall surface.

If the old paper is loose in just a few spots and you plan to paper over it, square-off the damaged area and insert a patch.

Seal new walls or walls covered with wallpaper with sizing. The sizing keeps the surface from absorbing the adhesive.

Remove all hardware before you start hanging paper. If you don't, your trimming task will be all that much more difficult.

503

## BUYING WALL COVERINGS AND EQUIPMENT

There are so many types of wall coverings available in so many patterns that selecting the material can become almost as difficult as hanging it.

First, of course, you need to determine roughly how much material you'll need. To do this, measure the height of each wall you will paper from the baseboard to the ceiling line. Then measure the distance around the room along the baseboard. Be sure to include all door and window openings in these measurements. These figures will give you the area of the room. The wallpaper dealer will translate these figures into the number of rolls of paper you need. (One roll—regardless of its width—covers about 30 square feet.)

Next, select the type of wallpaper you want (see page 501) and ask the salesperson to recommend the right adhesive. Foils, paper-backed burlap, vinyls, backed cork, flocks, hand prints, murals, and borders require *vinyl adhesive*. For standard wallpaper and unbacked burlap, use *wheat or stainless adhesive*. And for strippable wallpaper, you'll need a *wheat or strippable adhesive*. If you plan to lap vinyl wall covering, you must use *vinyl-to-vinyl adhesive*.

As for the amount of adhesive needed, figure on about one pound of wheat paste for every six rolls of wall covering. If you're using vinyl adhesive, you'll need one gallon for every three rolls.

If you have a mildew problem in your area, buy adhesive with a mildew-resistant formula. And always use mildew-resistant paste with any coated wall covering, as the coating seals in moisture that can cause mildew.

You'll also need some equipment—some special, some everyday—for your papering job. The specialty items include a *paste brush; a water tray* for pre-pasted paper; *a seam roller;* and a *smoothing brush*. You may be able to purchase these items in kit form.

Also gather together some things you already may have on hand: a paint roller and tray (if you don't use a paste brush); a utility knife with extra blades; a tape measure; an 8-foot-long straightedge (use ³/₄-inch aluminum angle or rent a straightedge); a plumb bob and chalk line; long-bladed scissors; a stepladder; drop cloths; a wall scraper; and sponges. And unless you're hanging pre-pasted paper, you also will need a pasting table. You can either rent one or use two card tables covered with a sheet of hardboard

## HANGING WALLPAPER

The key to a visually successful papering job comes when you plot the point at which you can best live with a pattern mismatch between two adjacent strips. You can almost inevitably count on a mismatch because the last strip you put up will have to be trimmed lengthwise to butt up against the first strip.

One way to minimize a mismatch is to begin—and end—adjacent to a door or

window frame. This gives only a few inches of discord above or below the opening. Other possibilities include a floor-to-ceiling bookcase, an inconspicuous corner, or any spot that will be largely covered by draperies or furniture.

Now, you're ready to hang that all-important first strip—all-important because it "locks in position" all the strips that follow. Unless the first one is absolutely plumb, all other strips will be out of alignment, and the error will

compound itself as you apply each successive one to the wall surface.

Since wallpapering is a messy job at best, take special pains to "work clean." Wash your hands often. Use clean water and a sponge to wipe away paste after hanging each strip of paper. Also, keep the pasting table free of adhesive. And if brush handles become smeared with adhesive, clean them immediately. Remember, too, to clean the blades of scissors and utility knives as well as the roller and handle of the seam roller.

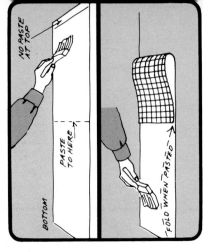

Apply adhesive to half of the strip, leaving an inch at the end so you can grasp it. Fold over and paste the other half.

Uncurl the paper by unrolling it against the edge of a table. Cut the first strip several inches longer than the wall.

Snap a plumb chalk line that measures the width of a roll of paper minus one inch. Double-check plumb with a level.

Unfold the pasted paper, the top half first. Align the paper with the plumb line. Lap the paper onto the ceiling.

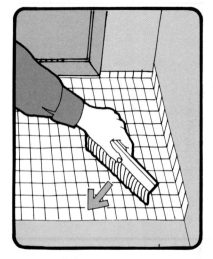

Smooth the paper onto the surface with the wall brush. Work from the center to the edges of the paper to remove any air bubbles.

Reach behind the strip and unfold the bottom half. Slip it into place against the plumb mark. You can pull and reposition it.

Smooth the lower section. With a level, check for plumb. If not plumb, start again. Smooth with vertical strokes.

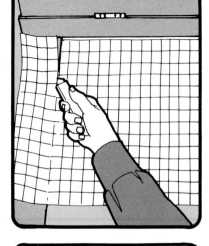

Tap the paper into corners with the end of the brush. Then trim with a utility knife. Or lift paper and trim with scissors.

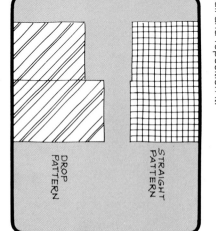

Cut several strips of paper at a time, allowing extra length for matching. Before pasting, check the matches as shown.

DROP PATTERN

STRAIGHT PATTERN

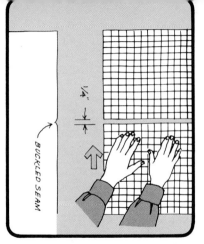

BUCKLED SEAM

¼"

Butt seams by aligning one seam about ¼ inch from the adjoining one. Then slide it over so the edges buckle slightly.

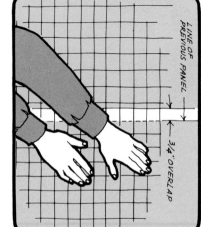

LINE OF PREVIOUS PANEL

¾" OVERLAP

Or, lap seams by overlapping the edges about ¾ inch. Slide the strip in the opposite direction until the seam measures ¼ inch.

About 15 minutes after you've hung each strip, roll the seams to ensure good adhesion. Do not roll flocked papers.

# PAPERING AROUND CORNERS

Consider yourself lucky if you find an inside or outside corner that's plumb. Most aren't! When a house settles on its foundation, every building component is thrown slightly off level and plumb. Though settling is normal, it does make papering around a corner a bit tricky.

To negotiate problem corners successfully, you need to master a technique called *double-cutting*. Though it sounds difficult to do, actually it's fairly simple. First, pattern-match and hang the strips, letting one strip overlap the other by ½ inch or so.

Then, with a sharp utility knife, cut through both layers of paper. You can do this freehand, but make sure you do it while the paste on the paper is still soft.

Next, carefully pull both selvages from the surface. Go easy; both should be cut completely through. With a smoothing brush, smooth the seam created when you removed the selvages. The seam should now fit.

At either inside or outside corners, be sure you firmly tap the paper against the surface. Then, after you've finished the corner, stick a series of thin straight pins along the edge of the corner—not in it—to "clamp" the paper until the adhesive dries. Arrange the pins carefully in the pattern so holes won't show after the pins are removed.

Snap a new plumb line on the adjacent wall, being sure to allow for an overlap onto the previously placed strip.

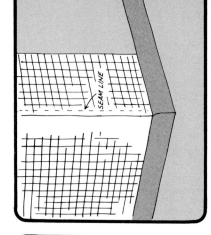

On outside corners, wrap the paper one inch or so around the corner. Then apply the next strip, overlapping it, and double-cut.

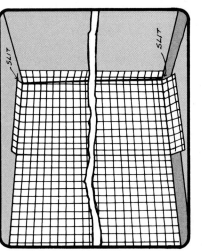

Cut, paste, and hang this strip. Tap it firmly into the corner. For a good fit, you may need to trim the margin top and bottom.

Peel off the outer layer of paper. Then lift the edge of the strip and peel off the inner layer. Smooth both edges; roll the seam.

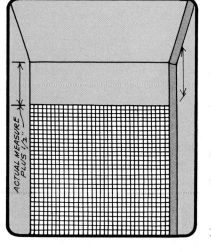

Measure the distance from the corner to the last strip of paper you applied, top and bottom. Add ½ inch to the measurements.

Hang the next strip to the plumb line. Tap the paper into the corner. Double-cut both thicknesses of wallpaper.

With the exception of negotiating corners, trimming around openings is the most demanding part of your wallpapering project. Mistakes here are embarrassingly noticeable, so take the time necessary to make good fits.

Before making your cuts around the casing (always work with a sharp-bladed knife to avoid pulling or tearing the covering), be sure that the covering is snug against it. Otherwise, you may find to your dismay that the line you've cut falls short of covering the wall. If you don't feel comfortable making the cuts freehand, try forcing a metal straightedge into the joint, then make the cut using it as a guide.

Let the strip adjoining the opening overlap the casings. Crease the covering at the molding's edge and cut it at the crease.

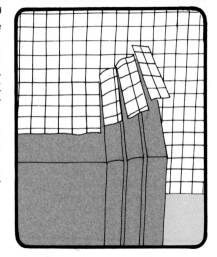

At the top of the casing, crease the paper and cut it where the molding joins the wall. Then smooth the edge of the wallpaper.

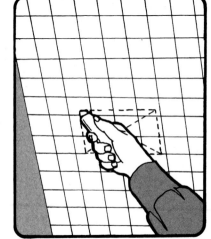

Apply paper right over switches and outlets. Then trim away the overlap. But before you cut, shut off the main power switch.

To fit around tricky corners and moldings, you may need to cut diagonal slits so the paper will lie flat. Use plenty of adhesive.

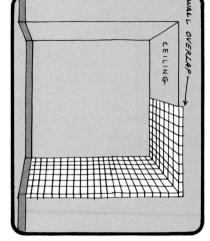

Paper recessed openings first. Lap the paper about one inch. Then overlap the strips with the strips applied to the wall.

Trim along fireplace mantels before you do the sides. This allows you to wrap the paper around the sides and make truer cuts.

**507**

# PAPERING CEILINGS

Ever wondered why more ceilings aren't wallpapered? It boils down to logistics. It's physically difficult to maneuver wallpaper strips up onto a ceiling that's eight or more feet high. The plain fact is, you might be better off painting your ceiling.

But if you're bound and determined, there are ways to do it. Note: if you paper both walls and ceiling, paper the ceiling first, then the walls.

First, prepare the ceiling as you would the walls (see page 503). Patch all cracks and cover any stains with primer. Also drop the cover plates on light fixtures, and after shutting off the power supply, disconnect the fixtures to get them out of the way.

To get up to a workable level, you'll need two stepladders and a length of scaffolding. The scaffolding must span the width of the ceiling so you can apply the wall covering without constantly moving the ladders and the scaffolding.

A helper will come in handy, too. The long lengths of wall covering are just too awkward for one person.

To start the job, snap a chalk line across the narrow dimension of the ceiling, allowing for lapping the paper onto the wall slightly. See below for the step-by-step.

If the paper is especially heavy, as some vinyls are, it's best to pin it in place until the adhesive dries.

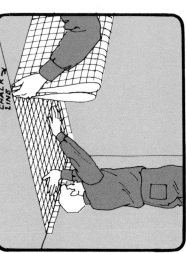

Align the first strip with the chalk line mark and pat the paper in place with your hand. The paper will overlap adjacent walls.

Apply paste and fold the paper accordion style. Don't crease the paper or touch the pattern side to the paste when you fold it.

After you've stuck down a portion of the first strip by patting it, brush it smooth. Then move on to the next section and apply it.

After applying each strip, smooth it with a smoothing brush, working out from the center. Roll the seams, too.

At the corner, cut out a notch to permit the trim edges to lie flat against the walls. Add paste, if needed.

# HANGING PRE-PASTED WALL COVERINGS

The reason for pre-pasted wall covering's popularity is no secret. It's the no-fuss, little-muss way to a beautifully papered room. There are some secrets, though—wall preparation, adhesive soaking time, and careful attention to smoothing and trimming.

The most critical of these is the soaking time. Be sure to follow the manufacturer's directions to the letter. The adhesive must be just right.

Cut the strips to length. Then loosely reroll the paper with the pattern side in. This permits the water to activate the paste.

Fill the water tank to within an inch of the top. Submerge the paper in the water, weighting it with a length of rod.

Sometimes, depending on the porosity of the wall surface you're papering, there won't be enough adhesive on the covering to hold it to the wall. If you run into this situation, mix a small amount of the proper adhesive for the paper and apply it to the edges and ends of the strips after the strips have been cut to length and soaked. Or apply the adhesive directly to the wall.

After the paper has soaked, grab it by the edges and unroll it as you climb a stepladder. Then smooth, roll, and trim the paper.

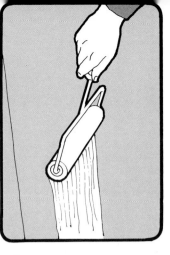

Spread the adhesive with a paint roller fitted with a mohair cover. Then fold the strip as you would a standard covering.

# HANGING VINYL WALL COVERINGS

A top-quality product, vinyl wall covering is heavier than most "standard" coverings, and you can buy it in wide widths, which reduces the number of seams to fit and roll. Also, the material usually is easy to strip from a wall or ceiling surface.

The paper acts like a top coat of plaster. The heavy vinyls have another important advantage. The strips can hide a drywall or plaster wall in poor condition.

You may use regular wallpaper adhesive to apply the lightweight vinyl papers, although for best results, special vinyl adhesive is best. Since vinyl won't stick to itself without special adhesive, all seams that are not butted should be double-cut (see page 506). If you apply

untrimmed vinyl with butted seams, be sure the adhesive is soft on both the strips. Then lap the seams about one inch. Make a freehand cut through both layers of paper, pull loose the selvages, and smooth the seam. If lapping is necessary, you can use vinyl-to-vinyl adhesive. Apply the adhesive just like regular wallpaper paste.

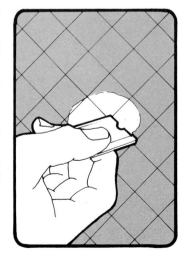

Smooth heavy vinyl strips with a straightedge, such as a strip of hardboard. Don't use steel unless the edges have been rounded.

After 20 minutes, hold a bright light against the wall and check the paper for bubbles. If you see any, puncture them.

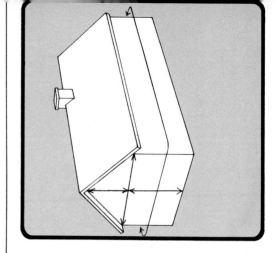

# EXTERIOR PAINTING

There's no doubt about it—painting the exterior of a house, no matter how small, is a big assignment, requiring lots of energy and persistence. And it can be an expensive one, too, especially if you have it done professionally.

At the same time, there's nothing difficult involved in basic brushwork, so it's up to you to decide which is more valuable—your free time or the extra money you'll spend to hire out the job.

## CHOOSING AND BUYING EXTERIOR PAINTS

Prices for a gallon of exterior house paint begin about where interior wall paints leave off—and you may pay more than twice as much for the best ones (some carry guarantees of up to five years). That's because exterior paints are like interior paints . . . only much more so.

First of all, they contain more *resin*, which makes them more durable and highly moisture-resistant. Secondly, most also have more *pigment*, the ingredient that gives paint its color.

Begin your selection of a new coating for your house by deciding whether a water-thinned (latex) or solvent-thinned (oil- or alkyd-base) paint makes better sense. Those with oil and alkyd bases dry slowly, making them susceptible to insects and sudden rainstorms, but once they set up, they are exceptionally durable. The latexes are easier to work with, dry quickly, and have a porous, "breathing" quality that minimizes most moisture problems. They do have a tendency to peel, though, if applied over an improperly prepared oil- or alkyd-base finish, especially if it's a "chalking" type.

*Chalking* refers to a self-cleaning quality formulated into many of today's exterior paints; they shed dirt by gradually eroding with each rainfall. Usually, you can see the "chalk" on foundation walls, shrubbery, and your coat sleeve, if you brush against a painted surface.

Once wood has been covered with either a water- or solvent-thinned product, it's best not to change types when you apply subsequent coats. You can, of course, but you may run into problems. If you're not sure what was used before, you'll probably be safest to use an alkyd-base paint.

In addition to deciding what type paint you want, you also must specify the luster—flat, semigloss, or gloss. (The word enamel often is used instead of semigloss or gloss.) Most people prefer a flat finish for large expanses, and reserve semigloss and gloss for areas subject to hard use or for trim.

What about one-coat house paints? Actually, if you plan to match or approximate the present color, almost any paint will cover in one coat. However, products sold with a one-coat guarantee—whether water- or solvent-thinned—are thicker, with more resins and pigments. Most guarantees spell out that the paint must be applied over sound existing surfaces or primed new wood. You'll pay more for a one-coat, but the extra money spent might pay off handsomely, especially in terms of time saved.

The chart on the opposite page may look formidable at first, but it will enable you to deal with the often-confusing array of products displayed in paint stores.

These fall into two broad categories: house paints—the stuff you'll be buying gallons and gallons of—and specialty coatings for a miscellany of smaller outside painting jobs. Organize your shopping list around the information presented, scrutinize labels closely, and you'll find a coating for just about any conceivable exterior use.

## Estimating Paint Needs

Exactly how much paint your house will require depends upon the type and condition of the surfaces you'll be covering, the method of application, and the paint itself. Conditions vary considerably, so your best bet is to read the manufacturer's coverage figures, then expect to get slightly less.

If your home has narrow lap siding, add another 10 percent to your estimate. For textured materials such as shingles or shakes, add 20 percent. Masonry and stucco—both porous surfaces that soak up lots of paint—can take up to 50 percent more.

Gable end walls make computing the surface area slightly tricky. First you'll need to measure from the foundation to the overhang and multiply this figure by the distance around the house. Then measure the distance from the overhang to the peak, measure the width of the wall, multiply these figures, and divide the result by two for each gable.

If you buy standard, off-the-shelf white or colored paint, you can always get more, and most stores will give credit for returns that haven't been opened. Specially mixed colors can be hard to match, though, so you might be wise to buy an extra gallon; you can use the overage for touch-ups.

# COMPARING EXTERIOR COATINGS

## HOUSE PAINTS

| Type | Characteristics/Uses | Application |
|---|---|---|
| Latex | Easy cleanup, excellent durability, and fast drying times make latex the number-one choice for amateur house painters. You can even apply it over slightly damp surfaces. Naturally mildew-proof. Note, though, that latex may be incompatible with a previous oil-base finish. | Don't try to thin latex. It's meant to be laid on with one stroke of the brush or roller. Work it out too far and you'll get thin spots in time. |
| Acrylic | Actually a type of latex, this water-thinned paint dries even faster than most and will cover just about any building material, including masonry and properly primed metal. | About the same as ordinary latex. |
| Alkyd | This solvent-thinned, synthetic-resin paint has most of the same properties as oil-base types, but it dries more rapidly. Use it over old oil- or alkyd-base coatings. Excellent hiding power. | Thicker consistency makes alkyd more tiring to apply, but it levels better than latex. |
| Oil | Slow drying times (12 to 48 hours), strong odors, and messy cleanup procedures put traditional oil-base paints at the bottom of the list. Some pros still swear by their durability, however. | Lengthy drying time makes bugs and rain a real peril. |

## SPECIALTY COATINGS

| Type | Characteristics/Uses | Application |
|---|---|---|
| Metal | Solvent- or water-thinned types in a wide variety of colors. These include rust-resisting priming ingredients so you needn't worry about small bare spots. All-bare metal should be separately primed. | You can brush, roll, or spray these for a broad range of finish effects. |
| Marine | Formulated for boats, marine paints provide a super-durable finish on wood and some metal trim. They're expensive, however, so you probably wouldn't consider them for big areas. | A gooey consistency makes them difficult to apply. |
| Masonry | Types include latex, epoxy, Portland cement, rubber, and alkyd. Some serve as their own primers. You also can seal masonry with clear silicone. For waterproofing, see pages 101-103. | Latex is easy to apply. Some others can be a lot of work. |
| Porch and deck | Choices include epoxy, alkyd, latex, polyurethane, and rubber-base types. Most work on wood or concrete floors and dry quickly. Surface preparation varies, and colors are limited. | With most, you just pour on the floor, then work out with a long-handled roller or wax applicator. |
| Primers | Seal all new wood and metal surfaces and any badly worn old ones with a primer designed for your finish coat. Generally, one coat of primer and one of finish will be more durable than two finish coats. Don't use finish as primer or vice versa. | Priming is usually easier than finishing, but porous surfaces can soak up a lot of paint. |
| Stains | Solvent- or water-thinned types provide transparent, semi-transparent, and solid finishes for natural wood siding and trim. Some include preservatives or offer a weathered look. | These you can brush, roll, or spray on almost any way you like. |
| Preser-vatives | These include rot- and insect-resistant chemicals you can apply to wood roofs, siding, posts, and other surfaces exposed to moisture. To learn more about these, see page 177. | Some can be sprayed or brushed; with others, you have to immerse the material. |

## IDENTIFYING AND SOLVING PAINT PROBLEMS

Houses typically need repainting every five to eight years. Put off the job much longer than that and you'll face a lot more preparation work; paint too soon and you could end up with a thick crust that will eventually crack and peel.

Begin with a careful analysis of the existing finish. Certain perennial problems—illustrated and discussed on the opposite page—will pop right through your new paint job. If your house suffers from any of them, you'll be time and money ahead to figure out what's causing

them, correct the condition, then scrape the surface clean and prime before you paint. If you don't, the same malady will almost certainly reappear.

Most paint difficulties can be blamed on moisture. Rain, snow, frost, and fog gradually erode even the toughest exterior coatings. But moisture can also attack from underneath—and that's where you need to take corrective action.

It's interesting that the insulation, weather-stripping, and caulking compounds being used in new construction and added to existing structures for energy conservation reasons also cause many exterior paint problems. The reason: they seal all the cracks and breaks in the walls and roof of

a house, leaving no way for this moisture to escape *except* through the walls. As this vapor penetrates the walls, it can pop the paint on the siding of the house.

The conditions created by up-to-date energy conservation practices point up more clearly than ever before the importance of adequate ventilation throughout a house (particularly in areas such as the kitchen, bathroom, and laundry where moisture abounds) and the necessity for a good vapor barrier. Ducted ventilation fans provide the best way to remove excess moisture vapor.

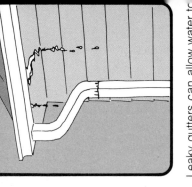

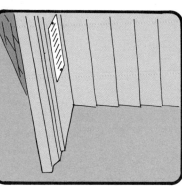

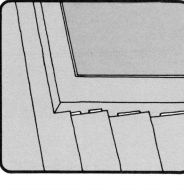

Leaky gutters can allow water to come in contact with your overhangs and siding. (For repairs, see pages 120 and 121.)

Replace loose and missing glazing compound around windows one week before you paint it. Don't replace sound putty.

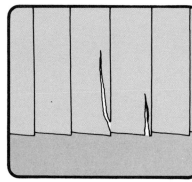

Inadequate ventilation can cause paint on soffits to peel. Correct this before you repaint by adding soffit vents (see page 119).

Replace any cracked or missing caulk. You can remove the old material with a putty knife. For more on this, see pages 131 and 132.

If your exterior walls don't have a vapor barrier (many older homes don't), consider painting the walls with non-permeable paint.

Damaged siding lets in and holds moisture, and must be repaired before you repaint. Page 133 shows you how.

Lessen the ill effects of moisture-producing areas by installing ducted ventilation fans (see page 378). Even opening windows helps.

Leaves hold moisture for many hours after a rain. Trim trees and shrubs often, especially those along the foundation.

512

# REMEDIES FOR COMMON PAINT PROBLEMS

| Problem | | Cause(s) | Remedy |
|---------|--|----------|--------|
| Peeling | | Moisture escaping from inside, or prolonged periods of contact with rain or other moisture; finish coat applied over wet surfaces. | Improve ventilation by installing siding, gable, or soffit vents (see page 119). |
| Alligatoring | | Usually a finish coat applied over a wet primer, or too much oil in the thinner. | Sand down to bare wood, apply primer, and let dry thoroughly. |
| Checking | | Shrinking and swelling of the building material over a period of time. | Bare the wood, prime the area, and let dry. |
| Blistering | | Finish coat applied over surfaces that are not thoroughly dry. | Same as for checking. |
| Bleeding | | Sap and pitch working out of the wood. | Apply sealer to all knots and pitch pockets to prepare the surface for a coat of finish. |
| Nail stains | | Using non-rust-resistant nails. | Sand the surface and seal with pigmented shellac, then repaint. |
| Mildew | | Usually a combination of moisture, high humidity, and inadequate ventilation. | Scrub off the mildew (see page 130 for particulars), let the wood dry thoroughly, then paint with a special mildew-resistant paint. |
| Chalking | | Formulation of paint used. | Before painting, wash the surface thoroughly. Chalking isn't necessarily a problem; many exterior paints have this feature. |

## REMOVING OLD PAINT

Most of the conditions illustrated on the preceding pages demand that you strip down the defective areas to bare wood and prime them before painting. Unfortunately, there's no one easy way to do this dirty, tedious job. You'll simply have to experiment with the techniques shown here and use the combination that works best for you.

Old paint comes off most readily when it's dry. Start in the worst spot, work a scraper underneath, and you may be able to lift off much of the old finish. Generally, you'll have better luck chipping from the edges rather than trying to wear through an unbroken surface.

Master the knack of using a pull scraper and you'll find you often can get down to bare wood with a single stroke. Hold the blade at a slight angle and apply firm pressure as you drag it along. When you see that a blade is no longer cutting well, either change or sharpen it.

Remove paint from metal surfaces with a wire brush attachment on an electric drill. Don't worry about baring the metal; just remove any rust, as well as the loose or caked paint, then prime as explained on pages 522 and 523.

Chemical paint strippers make sense only as a last resort. Though they do an effective job, you risk dripping the remover on sound paint, creating more problems than you're solving.

Masonry can be one of the toughest surfaces to strip. If you have large areas to do, consider hiring a pro to sandblast them. Warn your neighbors first, though; sandblasting creates lots of noise and dust. It may also cause pitting in softer brick or stone.

When you reach tight-sticking paint, feather the edges for a smooth blend, then spot-prime all bare spots, slightly overlapping the sound paint.

Power-sand large areas with an orbital sander. Don't use a belt or disc sander, as either can damage the underlying surface.

A propane torch with a spreader tip "cooks" paint fast so you can scrape it off. Be careful of fire, and have an extinguisher handy.

A sharp pull scraper shaves off damaged paint film. You must keep the blade sharp and make sure not to dig into the wood.

Chemical paint removers are best for heavy paint deposits on small areas. Follow directions to the letter. See page 529.

Remove what paint you can with a putty knife, then go over the area with a wire brush. This combination works well for small areas.

For heavy paint deposits, use an electric paint softener. Hold the tool on the paint until it "cooks," then scrape.

**514**

Consider yourself fortunate if the siding and trim on your house is in good shape when it comes time to paint. If it is, you can happily sidestep the most maddening part of an exterior paint job—removing chipped or peeling paint. But don't get out your paint clothes and brushes quite yet.

First you should go around the house and remove all screens, storm windows, and hardware that can be removed.

Then inspect the exterior and replace any damaged siding materials (see page 133); set any protruding nails.

Now give your house a bath. For this, you'll need a garden hose and a car-wash brush attachment, a scrub brush or sponge for stubborn dirt, and a

mixture of trisodium phosphate and water (to remove dirt and reduce the gloss of oil or alkyd paints).

If you're using an oil- or alkyd-base paint, wait at least a week before you paint the house. You can paint with latex the next day. While you're waiting, remove loose and cracked glazing from the windows and re-glaze them (see pages 144 and 145). Also, caulk all cracks and gaps in the siding; around porch columns; and under, over, and around windows and doors. (For caulking basics, see pages 131 and 132.)

When the siding is dry again, spot-prime all bare spots. Don't miss exposed metal surfaces on gutters, downspouts, and windows, either.

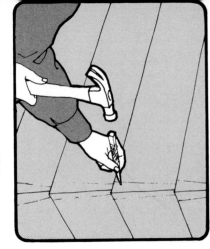

Clean and paint screens, storm windows, shutters, and other "removable" components separately to speed up the job.

Wash the house from the top down, using a mixture of trisodium phosphate and water. Rinse well and let the house dry.

For mildewed areas, scrub with household bleach and water, or use a commercial cleaner. Repaint with mildewcide paint.

With a whisk broom or paintbrush, flick off any dust you missed with the hose. Carry this brush as you paint to remove other debris.

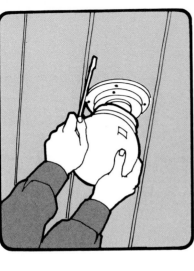

Remove fixtures, or plan to mask or cover them the day you paint. Don't forget to remove house numbers and the mailbox, too.

Set popped nails and spot-prime them with paint. Also caulk cracks, replace damaged siding, and prime any bare metal.

## GETTING A PAINT JOB STARTED

Don't plan a big evening for the end of your first day of house painting—you'll probably be too tired to enjoy it. Organize the job properly, though, and you can cut the fatigue factor.

Begin when the sun has dried off the surfaces you'll be painting—early-morning in the summer, mid-morning in the spring and fall. Always try to follow the sun so you're working in the shade; you'll save your energy, and also give the paint a chance to cure slowly and adhere better.

Just as with interior painting, there are some standard operating procedures when painting the exterior.

First, always work from the top to the bottom of the house to avoid the mess

caused by spilled or splattered paint. And in most situations, it's best to paint the siding first, then go back and paint the trim—windows, doors, railings, steps, and so forth.

There's only one exception to this. If yours is a two-story structure, you would be smart to paint the trim as you go to avoid having to lean your ladder up against freshly applied paint.

Also keep in mind that you should paint above the top of the ladder. Don't try to paint under it or you'll have ladder tracks where the rails touch the siding.

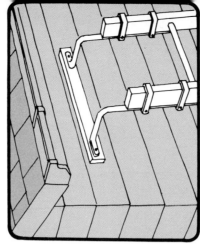

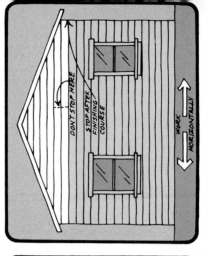

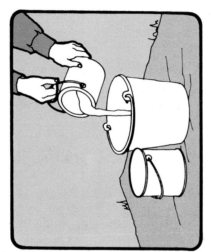

Mix the paint in a large bucket, or use two buckets for easier pouring back and forth. Stir it thoroughly, too.

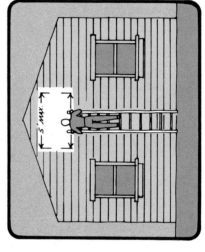

Set the ladder on sure footing. A special accessory holds it away from the sidewall for more painting "room."

For safety's sake, don't stretch more than an arm's length from either side of the ladder. Instead, move the ladder often.

Plan the work so that sundown doesn't catch you in the middle of several courses of siding. Otherwise, you'll get lap marks.

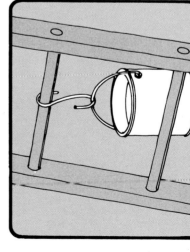

Protect shrubs, flowers, and walks with drop cloths. Use rope and canvas to tie tall bushes back out of the way.

To keep the paint bucket from spilling, attach it to the ladder with a bucket hook. Or use several lengths of coat hanger twisted.

**516**

If any part of a paint job can be deemed fun, it would have to be painting siding. Though siding often comprises the great majority of the total surface area, you'll discover that you can make a surprising amount of progress in surprisingly short periods of time.

To paint siding, first coat the undersides of three or four courses, using plenty of paint so the wood seals properly. Then level out the paint with the tip of the paintbrush.

After the undersides are covered, fill in the face of the siding courses, flowing the paint onto the surface with fairly short horizontal strokes. You needn't exert too much pressure on the brush; when the surface is covered with paint, just level and smooth it with a horizontal stroke. Make sure tiny cracks are filled.

If you're applying primer to the surface, follow the same brushing procedures you would for the finish paint. You may notice laps with the primer as it sinks into the wood or other material to seal it. Don't worry about these; they won't show after you've applied the finish coat of paint.

As you paint, keep track of the amount of paint required to cover a given area. By doing this, you can determine whether or not you'll need to buy more to complete the job. You'll probably use more primer per area covered than you will finish paint.

Start by painting the underside of the siding. If you do the faces first, you'll be touching-up continually or you'll get a "lip."

When painting next to a casing, paint the corner first and then the underside of the siding. Stab the bristles up into the corner.

Apply plenty of paint to the surface, and don't worry about lap marks yet. Just cover the surface thoroughly and seal it.

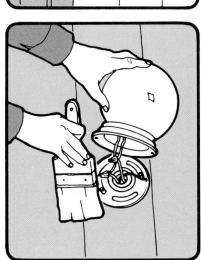

Now level the paint. Don't try to brush it thin; just even it out on the surface, using fairly long, light brush strokes.

Tip the bristles downward as you cut-in along the bottom of the last course of siding. This keeps paint off the foundation.

Pull lighting fixtures away from the siding while you paint behind and below them. Let paint dry well before replacing fixtures.

## FINISHING SHINGLES AND SHAKES

If you're about to begin finishing shingle or shake siding, you've got a couple of surprises in store. First, the job will probably take longer than you've envisioned. And second, you'll use more finish than you estimated. The reason: both shingles and shakes, being porous and full of grooves and striations, soak up finish like a blotter.

If the wood is new, you can give it a natural look simply by sealing it with a clear penetrating sealer. Since there is no pigment in the sealer, you can sort of slop it onto the wood without worrying about

lap marks. If the wood is cedar or redwood, you don't even have to finish it. It will weather into a dark silver-like finish.

Semitransparent and solid stains (see pages 511 and 533) require more care since they do contain a pigment that must be smoothed to prevent lap marks. Also, because the pigment in stain settles fairly quickly, you'll need to give the liquid a couple of whips with a paint paddle every so often to keep the finish color consistent.

Paint is the most difficult to apply. If you're planning to paint new shingles, test the paint on some not-too-prominent shingles that have dark brown stains on them. If the stains bleed through, you might as well switch to a stain finish.

Both paint and stain will dry quickly, so always work into a wet edge and finish out a course of siding before you leave for any length of time.

Regardless of the finish you apply, a 6-inch-wide brush with short bristles is the best applicator to use. As you work, keep the ferrule and handle of the brush wiped clean, though this is difficult if you're working with stain. Follow the leveling-out technique that's described on page 517.

If you use a roller or pad painter for shingles or shakes, the covers should be medium to long in nap length.

With any finish, check frequently for drips and runs. Smooth them out with a dry brush while the finish is still tacky.

For small areas, use an aerosol spray stain or paint. Use a regular spray outfit for large projects. See pages 524-526.

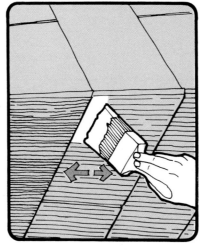

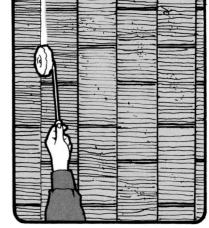

Apply paints and stains in the directions of the grain or striations—usually vertically. Check often for any missed spots.

Small corner-type rollers work well for undersides; use a medium- or long-nap roller or a wide brush for the faces.

Do the underside of shingles first, just as you would with lap siding. As you work, brush out any runs down the striations.

Special pad applicators make finishing shingles and shakes easier. Most are designed for edges as well as faces.

Most people don't react too favorably when they hear talk of painting masonry. And that's not surprising! It used to be that painting a foundation or basement floor often doomed a person to all-too-frequent repainting. Most people preferred instead to adjust to concrete's dull gray color and go on about their business.

But with today's sophisticated products and the understanding that surface preparation is the key to success, there's no reason you can't paint concrete—and be satisfied with the results.

Several types of paint will adhere to masonry. Epoxy paints, because they dry to a very hard finish, are probably the best all-around choice for floors, walls that are washed frequently, and exterior applications.

Portland cement paint, another good choice, works well on all walls except those that previously have been painted with another type of finish. Latex paint, probably the easiest to apply, adheres to foundation walls, too. Check with your paint dealer for other types suitable for specific applications.

Before you paint any masonry surface—especially basement walls and floors—be sure you correct any existing moisture problems (see pages 101-104). If you don't, no paint will adhere. Also remove peeling paint with a wire brush, and make any needed masonry repairs (see pages 134-136 and 155).

Now you're ready for the all-important prep work. First, degrease the surface with detergent and water. Next, etch it with a mixture of one part muriatic acid to three parts water. This removes and neutralizes alkaline material in the mortar joints. (Be sure to wear rubber gloves and a long-sleeved shirt to protect your skin against acid burns.) Finally, rinse everything with clear water.

Apply the finish with a wide, short-bristled brush or a roller cover with a long nap. Since the area you'll be painting is a large one—usually without obstructions—the wider the brush or roller, the faster the job will go.

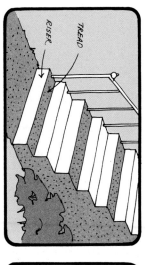

Apply a degreasing solution to oily garage or basement floors. Some types may be sprayed on; with others, use a scrub brush.

Smooth rough textures with a 1:1 cement grout mix, scrubbing it into depressions. For light textures, use an abrasive brick.

Apply paint with an old or cheap stiff-bristle brush. You'll have to push hard or even scrub it into very porous surfaces.

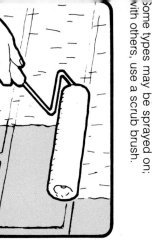

If you want a rough texture, use a long-nap roller to apply the finish. A roller works better than a brush for this type of texture.

To paint steps that are in use daily, paint the risers and every other tread. When the finish is dry, paint the treads you skipped.

To save on backaches afterward, paint patios and floors with a roller and extension handle. Paint a section at a time.

519

## PAINTING TRIM

If someone gives you your choice on whether to paint "all that siding" or the trim, do yourself a favor and take the siding. Though it doesn't consume much paint, trimming-out a house takes an inordinate amount of time. Using the same color as the siding helps some, but the job is tedious nonetheless.

Before you get out your sash brush and begin work, study the sketches on this page. They deal with some of the situations you'll encounter.

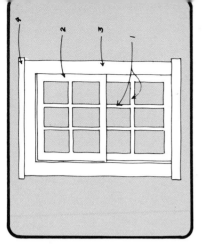

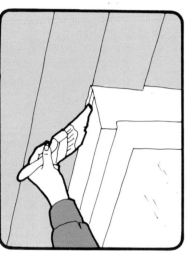

Paint the outsides of windows as you would the insides, starting with the muntins, and working outward from there.

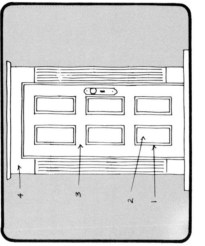

Be sure the paint forms a tight seal between the trim and siding material, especially over the tops of doors and windows.

Windowsills take a beating from the elements, so take extra care here. If they're weatherworn, give them several coats of paint.

To save time, you may want to spray-paint removable hardware such as house numbers and shutters. See page 526 for this.

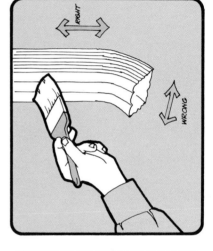

Be sure to mask or remove the knob set and other hardware before painting. Then paint the door in the order shown.

If your screens need painting or varnishing, paint screening first, then the frame. Use a special applicator pad for the screening.

Do ornamental metal and wood last. Be sure the surfaces are properly prepared first, and use the correct primer for the job.

When painting downspouts, be sure to paint parallel to the flutes. If you don't, you risk messy drips and sags.

520

Since you're spending a considerable amount of time and money painting your home, you may want to change the appearance of the house—at no extra charge. You can accomplish this simply by manipulating color—but it takes some planning.

First, draw the front of your home on sketch paper. Make the drawing fairly large. It doesn't have to be perfect; just include the different elements or components—roof, dormers, siding, porches, windows, doors, and foundation—as best you can. Or, you can take a straight-on snapshot of the house and have an enlarged print made to serve as a template. From this, you

can use tracing paper to sketch the house. Or, if your house has a fault that sticks out like a sore thumb, camouflage the offender by painting it to blend in with its surroundings.

With these guidelines in mind, get out your colored pencils and go to work. Take as much time as you need at the drawing board to come up with a color scheme that works well for you. It's far better to experiment now with colored pencils than later with expensive exterior paint.

If after all your "scheming," you're still not satisfied that you've found the right treatment, take a leisurely drive through your community and try to find some recently painted houses that are architecturally similar to yours. They may suggest some ideas worth adopting.

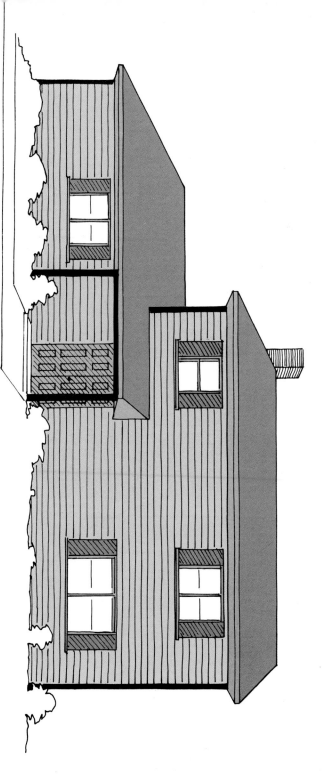

color. Or, if your house has a fault that sticks out like a sore thumb, camouflage the offender by painting it to blend in with its surroundings.

With these guidelines in mind, get out your colored pencils and go to work. Take as much time as you need at the drawing board to come up with a color scheme that works well for you. It's far better to experiment now with colored pencils than later with expensive exterior paint.

If after all your "scheming," you're still not satisfied that you've found the right treatment, take a leisurely drive through your community and try to find some recently painted houses that are architecturally similar to yours. They may suggest some ideas worth adopting.

sketches and an assortment of colored pencils, you're ready to plan your color-change strategy.

When you plan, keep in mind that dark colors make a home look smaller, while light or bright colors have the opposite effect. To scale-down a big older house, for example, paint it a dark color such as brown, red, dark green, or dark gray.

Another option to consider: you can lower a visually-too-high house by painting it to match the shingles on the roof. To "raise the roof," paint the house a contrasting color.

If your home's exterior is comprised of several different materials and looks somewhat disjointed, unify the elements by using a couple shades of the same

Equipped with one or more can use tracing paper to sketch the house. Equipped with one or more

Outline doors, windows, and even the entire house with color to call attention to the more handsome lines of the structure. Use a lighter or darker shade of the same color—or an entirely different hue.

Reverse colors for a change of pace. Paint the body of the house a darker color, and trim it in a lighter hue, or vice-versa.

A strong accent can call attention to the front door or any other

natural focal point. Don't play up more than one feature, though, or you'll create visual confusion.

Decide which house components you want to emphasize and which you'd like to "paint out." For

example, you may want to paint out a dormer on the roof. To do this, paint it the same color as the roofing material.

# PAINTING METAL

Slop any old paint over a metal surface and you're asking for trouble. The reason: all metals oxidize if not properly coated, and paint simply can't adhere to the invisible oxide coating.

To stop this process, you need to strip away grease, dirt, or existing rust, then apply a primer chemically formulated to neutralize oxidation. This primer provides a surface to which the finish can adhere.

The primer you choose will depend on the metal you're dealing with and its condition. The chart on the opposite page compares the major ones you need to know about.

Note, too, that you also can buy special "metal paints" that combine primer with a finish coating. Use these over surfaces that are still in fairly good condition. Aluminized paint, which includes aluminum dust as a pigment, also works as a combination primer-finish on painted metals not exposed to severe weathering.

As essential as a good primer is, you can't expect it to do the entire job. Virtually all of them need a finish coat or coats to protect against weather and abrasion. Here, you can use almost any paint—exterior-grade for outdoors, indoor types for inside jobs. However, don't try to apply a lacquer over anything but a lacquer-based finish paint or primer.

Even polished decorative metals such as brass, copper, and bronze need protection if you want them to keep their shine. Buff tarnished hardware items with fine steel wool, metal polish, or a felt wheel, then coat them with clear lacquer or polyurethane.

For more about working with metals, see pages 480-485.

## PREPARING METAL SURFACES

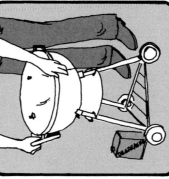

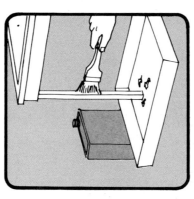

Paint remover works even better on metal than it does on wood. Use it to take off accumulated layers (see pages 528 and 529).

Hand-sand to feather the edges of sound paint around the areas you've cleared. Otherwise, the repaired area will show through.

Wire-brush rust or peeling paint right down to bare metal. A brush attachment on a power drill makes short work of this task.

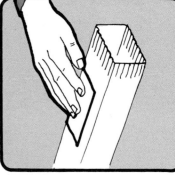

Wash away grease with a commercial degreaser, then wire-brush rust. Heat-resistant paints withstand high temperatures.

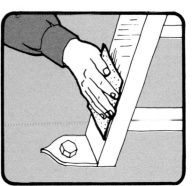

With sound existing paint, treat with liquid sander. This product provides a "tooth" that the new paint can adhere to.

Often, gutters and downspouts need only spot-sanding and priming. Clean and paint inside the gutters first, though.

For a really smooth top coat, lightly sand primed surfaces with very fine sandpaper. But don't sand through the primer.

## CHOOSING THE RIGHT PRIMER

| Metal | Condition | Preparation | Primer |
|---|---|---|---|
| Iron and steel | Lightly rusted bare metal or failing old paint. | For a medium-smooth finish, remove rust and loose paint, then feather edges. For a smoother finish, strip completely. | Zinc chromate fights rust. Protect bare metal with two or more coats. |
| | Damp, badly rusted bare metal. | Scrape and wire-brush all loose material. Wipe away surface moisture. | Red lead (this comes in other colors, too). |
| | Heavy rust and scale. | Scrape away loose material but don't try to expose bare metal. | Long-oil primers penetrate to sound metal underneath. |
| Galvanized iron and steel | Lightly rusted surfaces. | Remove rust and blistered paint. Wash new metals with detergent, let them weather, or etch them with a vinegar solution. | Zinc-oxide or other primers formulated especially for galvanized metals. |
| Aluminum | Older oxidized surfaces. | Remove oxidation, but don't sand under clear finishes. For a shiny finish, use liquid car wax. | No primer necessary, but if paint won't adhere, try a zinc-oxide primer. |
| Copper | Corroded bare metal, or blistered or peeling paint. | Clean the metal with fine steel wool or a wire brush. Newer copper may need to be etched with acid and rinsed. | No primer necessary. Finish with paint, spar varnish, or polyurethane. |
| Brass | Tarnished, corroded, or pitted. | Clean by soaking in paint remover or a vinegar-salt solution. Buff with polish or fine steel wool. Plated items may need replating. | No primer or paint needed. To maintain a shine, coat with lacquer or polyurethane. |

## APPLYING THE TOP COAT

Spray, brush, or roll on metal finishes, depending on the smoothness you want. Whichever you choose, bear in mind that several thin coats will hold up better than one or two thick layers. If you need to apply several coats, let each dry before applying the next coat. Brushed or rolled-on paint should dry at least overnight (36 hours is better) before you apply another coat.

A good job calls for patience and good light so you can correct problems before the paint dries. Try to work the paint in one direction and move from dry to wet areas. Don't lap brush strokes by letting an edge dry, then painting over it. Smooth corners, too, so they don't dry "fat."

Flow paint on with smooth, even strokes. After a few minutes, check the freshly painted areas for any drips, runs, and sags.

To make gutters really last, paint them inside with an asphalt-base paint. Besides protecting the metal, it seals tiny leaks.

To paint rusted metals, clean off what rust you can. Then prime with a long-oil-type primer, which penetrates to the sound metal.

# SPRAY-PAINTING

Spray-painting is a topic that's always sure to raise some discussion. Some people swear by it; others wouldn't get near a pressurized paint can or a painting rig if you paid them.

One thing is sure, though. Spray-painting is by far the fastest means of applying paint, stain, or other finishes. And if done carefully and knowingly, spraying on a finish yields professional-looking results that are hard to match with brush or roller.

Spray-painting does have its drawbacks, though. For one thing, it consumes much more finish than painting with a brush or roller. For another, it's a fairly messy technique. Overspray is a real problem, and one that makes spraying impractical in many situations, such as in finished rooms or outside where a neighbor's car or house will be affected. Some communities even have codes prohibiting spray-painting outside.

You'll also need plenty of ventilation if you decide to spray-paint. Inside, make sure to open any nearby windows, and if there's an exhaust fan close, turn it on. And don't begin without a painter's mask to keep airborne paint out of your nose and throat. Painting outside is somewhat less of a problem in terms of ventilation, but wear your mask nonetheless.

Following are some spray-painting pointers to keep in mind:

• Prepare all surfaces the same way you would for a brush or roller.

• *Tightly* cover anything you don't want painted. For smaller areas, use newspaper and masking tape; for large areas, use drop cloths sealed at the edges with masking tape.

• When spraying solvent-thinned paint indoors, make sure there is no open flame in the workshop area, as the evaporating solvent is flammable.

• Outside, never spray on a windy day. The air must be fairly calm.

• Paint mixtures must be specially prepared for a spray gun. If the paint is too thick, it will clog the gun. If it's too thin, the paint will run on the surface. Even with the proper mixture, you should have a paintbrush handy to catch runs and drips.

• When painting fencing with a spray gun, have a helper hold a wide piece of cardboard in back of the fence to catch the overspray.

• Don't spray gutters, corner trim, or siding material that join the foundation of your home unless you have the roof, corner, and foundation properly covered.

• Don't spray-paint windows; rather, use a sash brush. The same rule applies for other trim—doors, basement sashes, and storm windows. However, a spray gun is excellent for painting screens.

## SETTING UP A SPRAY BOOTH

Spray-painting indoors is messy business, especially if you can't control the overspray that's generated. So, if you can't take your work outside to paint it, at least take the time to set up a paint booth.

For small projects, your booth need be nothing more than newspapers taped together and positioned behind and below the item to be sprayed. If you're painting a large piece or have a lot of spraying to do, fabricate a booth from 4-mil plastic film and fasten it to the walls and floor in a corner of your workshop. How large a booth you need depends on the scale of the project being painted, of course. But be sure to give yourself plenty of working room. Overspray carries a surprising distance, and cleaning it off of masonry is a chore you want to avoid.

If, despite all your precautions, some overspray does occur, mop it up right away with a solvent-saturated rag.

Wear a spray mask and hat. If your skin is sensitive to paint thinners, wear rubber gloves and a buttoned-up long-sleeved shirt.

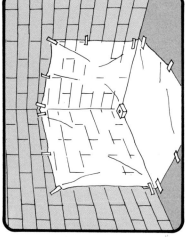

Polyethylene film positioned as shown handles big items. Keep the top of the booth open to allow paint fumes to escape.

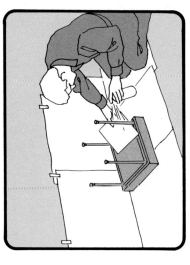

Set up small spray jobs with newspapers behind and below. A cardboard shield will absorb most of the overspray.

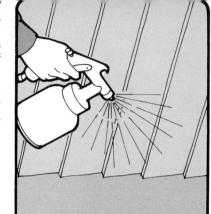

The single most important thing to learn about spray-painting with a paint gun is that you must keep your equipment clean. If you don't, you'll spend the majority of your time cleaning up spatters and runs and in the process end up with a shoddy-looking job.

Almost as crucial is the thickness of the paint being sprayed. If too thin, it will not cover well and will sag and run. And if it's too thick, you've really got trouble because it will clog your equipment and result in a rough finish. For best results, read the paint container label and follow the paint manufacturer's advice.

Your spray-gun technique also deserves special consideration. When you spray, keep a stiff wrist and hold the

gun eight to ten inches from the surface, parallel to the ground. And don't start spraying from a dead-still position. Rather, begin your movement, then pull the trigger and start spraying.

"Fan" the spray on the surface, using several light coats instead of one heavy coat. The paint will be thick at the center and feathered out at the edges. So, as you paint, overlap these edges by about a third so the thickness of the paint will be uniform.

On gutters, point the gun down away from the roof. And along foundations, paint the last two courses of siding or surface with a brush or roller. Or, carefully mask the foundation.

Before putting paint into the gun's reservoir, run it through a strainer. This rids the mixture of impurities that may clog the gun.

Experiment first on scrap material to gauge the proper distance between gun and surface. Also adjust the gun for "pattern."

Hold the gun perpendicular to the surface—don't move it in an arc. Keep your wrist stiff to deter this temptation.

For lap siding, angle the gun so you can spray the undersides. Apply a thin coating first, then let overspray fill it in.

Lap the strokes by about one-third to achieve even paint coverage. This applies to spray-can application, too.

# USING A SPRAY CAN

With aerosol painting, it's a matter of shake, rattle, and spray. You shake the can until the steel ball inside rattles for about a minute, then push the button.

Painting with spray cans is almost as expensive as it is easy. However, the time you save using them usually makes them worth it. This is especially true when dealing with such hard-to-paint items as wicker furniture, radiators, and small cabinets.

To operate the spray can, first shake the can as shown below. When you hear the rattle of the metal ball that mixes the paint, shake the can another minute. It's important that you follow this procedure.

The biggest drawback of aerosol painting is that the nozzles on spray cans tend to clog. To prevent this, invert the can and depress the button till only propellant comes out the hole, then wipe the nozzle clean after each use. When it does become clogged, you often can open it again by puncturing the paint seal over the spray hole with a needle. If this doesn't work, buy a low-cost replacement nozzle.

Aerosol paint cans are flammable, so keep them away from open flame. Likewise, don't junk an empty aerosol can in an incinerator, or puncture one.

With but one or two exceptions, the painting problems shown and discussed below apply to all types of spray-painting.

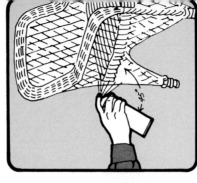

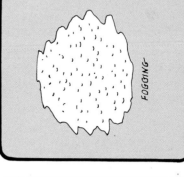

On open work, tilt the can at an angle to minimize the paint flowing through openings. Crisscross your spray pattern.

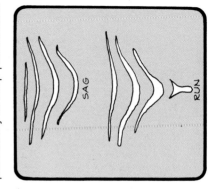

Orange-peeling results from too thick a covering of paint, or from too much air pressure. Wipe and spot-paint these.

Lap strokes by about one-third. After you've made several passes, stop and check to make sure the surface is covered.

*Fogging* is the dull, pebbled effect you get when the spray can is held too far away. Spot-in these areas as with sags.

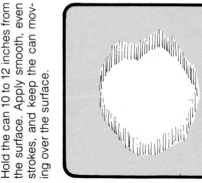

Hold the can 10 to 12 inches from the surface. Apply smooth, even strokes, and keep the can moving over the surface.

*Holidays* occur when there's not enough paint on the surface. Spot-in these areas as you would a sag or run.

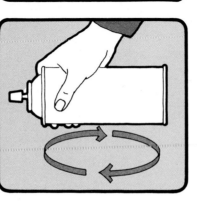

Shake the can until you hear the ball rolling freely for at least one minute. Then shake the can periodically to keep paint mixed.

*Sags* and *runs* are caused by too much paint. Wipe away the excess, then "spot" with short spray bursts to blend in the touch-up.

Though antiquing certainly won't yield a surface of the same caliber as clear wood finishes produce, this technique does have a place in the world of wood finishing. Its forte is making badly worn or outdated furniture pieces look "new" again.

Antiquing, while relatively easy to do, can be a very creative endeavor. As you can see from the sketch below, the looks you can achieve are many. One of the fun things about antiquing is that you don't have to be careful with this finish. In fact, you may want to even "distress" the surface more than it is by smacking it a few times with nails driven into a board or you get carried away, make sure that the with the claws of a hammer. But before piece of furniture you're dealing with an old finish or dirt is a real antique that's wouldn't be better refinished in some other manner. Sometimes hidden under worth plenty of money.

When antiquing an item, you have a choice. You can either strip it to bare wood or apply the base coat right over the existing surface. Most people choose the latter method. Either way, though,

make sure the surface is free of dirt and wax. Remove the drawers and hardware from the work, too. And if a mirror is involved, remove it if you can. If not, cover it with newspaper held with masking tape.

Most people buy the materials and tools needed for their project in kit form. Usually included are base and finish coats of antiquing material, brushes, and special design applicators.

The tools you'll need for the project, if the kit doesn't supply them, include a 3-inch brush, 150-grit sandpaper, a mixing bucket and paddle, thinning solvent (see the manufacturer's label), and wiping cloths.

Once you've readied the surface to your satisfaction (be sure to dull a glossy surface), brush on the base coat. (You may need two coats to hide dark surfaces.) Apply the material in even strokes. If you spot any runs or sags, catch them with the tip of the brush stroked across the grain. Look for any spots you may have missed, and if you find any, coat them now, as the base coat must completely cover the work surface.

Let the finish dry. Check the can label for drying time—usually two to four hours.

Next, sand the base coat, using 150-grit open-coat abrasive or fine steel wool. Remove all sanding residue with a vacuum cleaner or tack cloth.

Now comes the glaze. Working in a small area, brush on a thin coating; don't apply too much. Wipe the surface or apply the design you want (see the sketch below for some of the effects you can create), then move on to the next area. The glaze dries fast, so you need to work quickly.

To simulate wear, wipe corners and edges through to the base coat. Go easy over carvings and grooves to produce an antique look. On big flat surfaces, make the edges lighter than the center.

Allow the glaze to dry for 48 hours, then finish the project by applying a clear finish or hard wax to the surface.

TORTOISE-SHELL

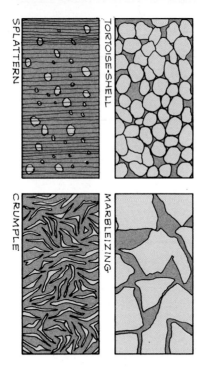

SPLATTER

MARBLEIZING

CRUMPLE

STIPPLING

DISTRESSED WOOD

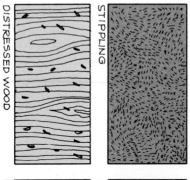

DISTRESSED PAINT

SPATTER OVER

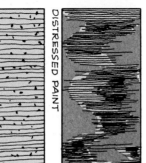

Create a *tortoise shell finish* by laying on a heavy coat of glaze, then lightly tapping the surface with the tips of your fingers. Change the angle of your hand for a more random effect.

For *marbleizing*, crumple up a plastic drop cloth, lay it in the wet

glaze, then pick it up. To make a *splattern* effect, wipe glaze coat as usual. Next, dip a small, stiff brush in mineral spirits, shake it out, and stroke the bristles to spray droplets on the wet glaze.

*Crumple* a glaze by lightly jabbing it with a wadded-up

paper or cloth towel. *Stippling* is done with a dry paintbrush jabbed straight down into wet glaze. Rotate the brush between jabs.

For a *distressed paint* look, let the glaze dry, then sand to expose the undercoat; for the illu-

sion of *distressed wood,* poke with an ice pick, then rub raw umber into scratches and dents.

*Spatter over* goes on top of other patterns. Do it like the splattern technique, but dip the brush in glaze.

527

# CLEAR-FINISHING WOOD

Flow a coat of paint over any properly prepared wood surface and you'll hide or at least mask its grain. Clear finishes do exactly the opposite—they emphasize the wood's natural beauty—or its imperfections.

That's why any clear-finishing job has to start with the wood itself. Before you get into the painstaking preparation any natural finish demands, take a close look at the wood grain. Wetting the surface slightly lets you see it better and gives a pretty good idea of what a perfectly transparent coating will do.

If you don't like a wood's *color*, you can bleach it or tint it with stain ... but no amount of staining or sanding will alter a grain's *pattern*, obliterate knots, or hide surface damage.

If you like what you see, prepare for some hard—but ultimately very satisfying—work. First you need to completely bare the wood, then sand it perfectly smooth. Some "open-grain" species—oak, walnut, and mahogany, for example—will require a *filler*. And you may also need to *seal* the surface before applying the final finish.

The following pages present the basic products and processes you'll need to know about. Master them and you can add countless variations to your repertoire of clear-finishing techniques.

## REMOVING OLD FINISHES

If the piece you're refinishing is a major one, the path of least resistance leads to a professional paint stripper. Generally for a modest price, these specialists will dip your piece in a caustic solution and have it back to you in fairly short order,

saving you lots of time and a great deal of effort.

If a paint stripper is not available in your community or the project doesn't seem to warrant sending it to one, you can find a potpourri of other paint-removing options. Consult the chart below to determine the best stripping procedure for your project.

Before you do, though, realize that some finishes that appear to need refinishing may need only cleaning. If you're in doubt about a piece, wash it with paint thinner, then give the surface three thin coats of wax. If a white haze appears after you've applied the thinner, buff it away with extra-fine (000) steel wool before waxing.

## YOUR FINISH-REMOVER ALTERNATIVES

| Method | Uses | Application Tips |
|---|---|---|
| Paint remover | For any finish, thick or thin, on wood or metal. | Available in liquid or paste; paste is best for vertical surfaces. Provide plenty of ventilation with paint remover. Apply it with a brush. Remove it and the old finish with a scraper, sandpaper, and steel wool. (Some strippers are water-soluble, which means they can be washed off.) |
| Electric paint softener/Propane torch | Either will remove old paint from wood. An electric softener is usually used on flat surfaces such as siding. | For obvious reasons use the torch with caution. The disadvantage of both methods is the danger of scorching the bare wood surfaces. Provide adequate ventilation. Both methods are tedious. |
| Abrasives (sandpaper and steel wool) | To remove very thin finishes. Don't try to sand away heavy accumulations of paint—the job will seem endless and you risk damaging the wood. | By hand, work is slow and tedious. With a power sander fitted with an open-coat abrasive, the finish comes off fast. Use a contour sander in a drill for curved and round surfaces. Be careful with any power sander. The abrasive can groove the wood or cut through veneers. |
| Scrapers | Excellent for removing old, dry paint from wood or glass surfaces. | Keep your scraper blade sharp, and maneuver it carefully to be sure you don't dig into surrounding wood as you work. |

528

Paint remover softens paint, varnish, and almost any other brush-on finish so that you can lift it off with a scraper or water pressure, depending on the type of remover you purchase. They are messy, though, so be sure to cover any work surface with several layers of newspaper

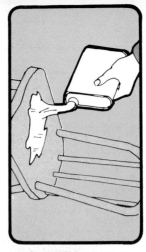

or plastic sheeting, and when the removal job has been completed, carefully dispose of the covering before the stripper dries and crumbles.

Apply paint remover with an old or inexpensive brush, then throw it away when you're finished. You'll also need a scraper, steel wool, sandpaper, and a wire brush.

Fumes from paint removers can cause eye irritation and headaches. Ideally, you

should work outside with them. If you can't, ventilate the room in which you're working, and take a fresh-air break every ten minutes or so.

Procedures—and hazards—vary somewhat from product to product, so be sure you read the label directions thoroughly before opening the container. And bear in mind that you're dealing with a combination of powerful ingredients that deserves your respect.

Apply stripper by pouring it on horizontal surfaces. Then spread it with a brush. Use plenty of remover; don't overbrush.

Brush the remover in one direction only. Don't attempt to "rub" it into the old finish—just "float" it over the surface.

After several minutes, test the surface by scraping across it with a putty knife. If you strike bare wood, start scraping.

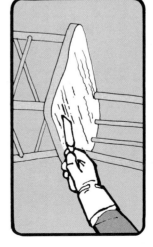

Use a wide-blade scraper or putty knife to lift off the sludge. Keep the blade at a low angle to avoid scratching the bare wood.

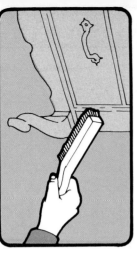

Use a medium-bristle wire or fiber brush. And don't use too much pressure—the brush can mar the surface.

For carvings, use a medium-bristle wire or fiber brush. And don't use too much pressure—the brush can mar the surface.

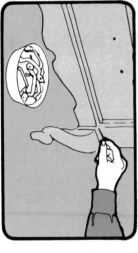

Clean off final residue with a pad of steel wool. Lift the pad often as you work, and dip it in water to remove sludge.

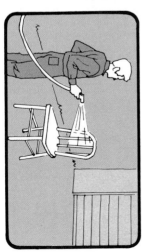

Reach into recesses with a toothbrush or toothpick. To strip hardware, soak it in remover, clean with steel wool, and wash.

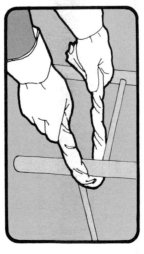

Make a burlap rope to clean round turnings. Dip it in remover and pull it back and forth like a shoe-shine rag.

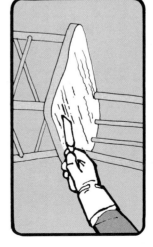

If you're using a water-soluble stripper, wash down the piece with water. Don't use on veneered surfaces or glue joints.

# SANDING

To say the sanding phase of a refinishing project is important is understating the case—no amount of finishing later on can make up for a poor effort here. So if it's a professional-looking piece you're after, here's the place to begin. (If you're working with furniture pieces, first make any needed repairs. Reglue weak joints, glue and clamp loose veneer, patch holes, and repair drawers and guides.)

The amount of sanding you'll need to do on a given piece depends, naturally, on its condition. If the surface is in decent shape, skip the first step. If it's really banged up, start out by belt-sanding it with a coarse- to medium-grit abrasive (see pages 448 and 449 and below). Be very careful, though; a belt sander cuts quickly and the edges of the abrasive can "groove" the surface of the wood or cut right through veneers. Dust away all sanding residue after this and all subsequent sandings. Then wipe the surface with a tack cloth.

For the next cut, switch to an orbital sander outfitted with medium- to fine-grit abrasive.

Though sanding with the orbital sander should yield a fairly smooth surface, don't stop yet. Unless you plan to bleach or water-stain the wood, dampen the surface of the wood to raise the grain. Then using very fine abrasive stretched

over a sanding block, finish-sand the piece by hand. Apply only enough pressure to take off the "tooth" of the grain.

Later, as you're applying the finish to the wood, be sure to sand lightly between each coat with a very-fine sandpaper. This roughens the surface enough so the next coat can adhere to the previous one.

For final-stage smoothing, you often can substitute a very-fine-grade steel wool for sandpaper. But keep in mind that it can quickly cut into sealers and undercoaters, so use light, even strokes in the direction of the grain.

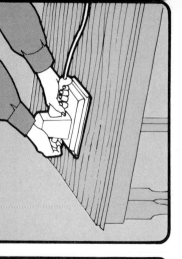

Cut down very rough solid wood with a belt sander run with the grain. Don't apply pressure—just guide the sander.

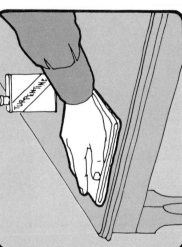

Remove all dust and other residue after each sanding. Then wipe with a cheesecloth rag dampened with mineral spirits.

If your sander doesn't have a dust pickup and the dust particles become bothersome, vacuum, then continue sanding.

Make the second cut with an orbital sander using medium or fine sandpaper. Here again, don't apply much pressure.

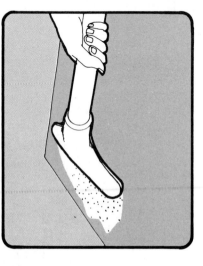

Do all final smoothing by hand. Use a fine-grit abrasive-covered sanding block to ensure a smooth, even surface.

Extra-fine (000) steel wool does an excellent finish-smoothing job. Wear gloves when using, and vacuum up metal particles.

Sanding curved surfaces calls for ingenuity. A sanding block fashioned from a piece of dowel od makes a good tool.

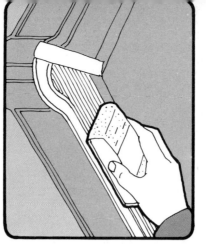

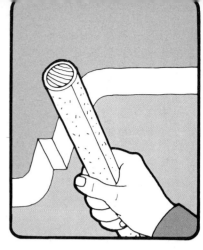

A contour sanding attachment, locked in the chuck of a power drill, smooths almost any curve. Use it for removing finish, too.

Protect edges that you don't want to sand with strips of masking tape. Make sure the edges are pressed tightly in position.

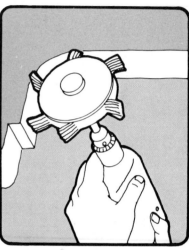

A perforated disc powered by an electric drill takes off lots of wood or old paint fast. Smooth the surface, using an orbital sander.

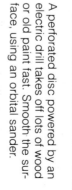
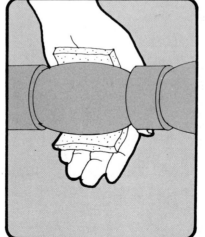

Abrasive-coated nylon pads smooth difficult items such as turnings and moldings with ease. These pads are washable.

## WOOD-FINISHING ABRASIVE SELECTOR

| Species | Sanding Recommendations |
| --- | --- |
| Pine, Fir, Hemlock, Spruce | Rough cut: 60 (coarse) for aluminum oxide, silicon carbide, or garnet; coarse for flint. Use open-coat paper on "sap-wet" or dry wood. Second cut: 80 (medium) for aluminum, silicon, and garnet papers; medium for flint. Open coat. Third cut: 120 (fine) for aluminum, silicon, and garnet papers; fine for flint. Open coat. |
| Cedar, Redwood | Rough cut: 80 (medium) for aluminum oxide, silicon carbide, or garnet; medium for flint. Open coat. Second cut: 100 (medium) for aluminum, silicon, or garnet. Closed coat. Final cut: 150 (fine) for aluminum, silicon, or garnet. Closed coat; hand-sand. |
| Oak, Birch, Gum, Maple, Beech, Ash, Hickory | Rough cut: 60 (coarse) for aluminum oxide, silicon carbide, or garnet; extra-coarse for flint. Open coat. Second cut: 80 (medium) for aluminum, silicon, or garnet; medium for flint. Open coat. Third cut: 120 (fine) for aluminum, silicon, or garnet papers. Use a closed coat. |
| Walnut, Mahogany | Rough cut: 60 (coarse) for aluminum oxide, silicon carbide, garnet; coarse for flint. Open coat. Second cut: 80 (medium) for aluminum, silicon, or garnet; medium for flint. Closed coat. Third cut: 100 (medium) for aluminum, silicon, or garnet. Closed coat. Or use 000 steel wool for final cut or smoothing. |
| All veneer woods | First cut: 150 (fine) for aluminum oxide, silicon carbide, or garnet papers. Closed coat. Finish cut: 220 (extra-fine) for aluminum, silicon, or garnet. Closed coat. Finish with 0000 steel wool. |

# FILLING AND SEALING

Some woods, such as fir and oak, have a prominent grain pattern that no amount of sanding will rub out. These—and any surfaces with nail holes or other mars —must be leveled with *filler* if you want to achieve a glassy-smooth finish.

After you've filled a wood surface, you'll probably then have to *seal* it to lock in the filler. Sealers also keep stains from bleeding up through the top coating. A few special types, applied *before* you stain, slow down the rate at which wood absorbs the pigment, giving a lighter, less grainy appearance.

Fillers and sealers differ widely, so read labels carefully before you buy. Some fillers might be called hole pluggers. These have a doughy consistency (some are mixed from a powder) that can be packed into depressions and sanded smooth. If you plan to paint the surface, the type you choose isn't critical, as long as it's compatible with the sealer or final finish you'll be using. If, on the other hand, you want to stain a piece of wood, be warned that many fillers aren't very absorbent, which means you could end up with whitish spots after you apply the stain. The solution is to buy a filler that has been tinted to match the stain you've selected, or to tint the filler yourself.

Other fillers, available in paste or liquid form, level the pores in open-grain wood. These also can be colored. For more about using both types of filler, see the illustrations below.

Sealers amount to nothing more than a clear coating that seals the filler or stain and prevents the finish coats from causing the stain or filler to bleed through or soften. Thinned shellac makes an excellent sealer, as do some varnishes. Penetrating oils (see page 537) serve as their own sealers. Just be sure that the sealer you select won't react adversely with the stain or filler you'll be using underneath, or the final finish you'll be applying over the top.

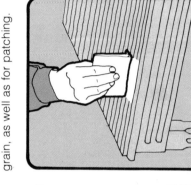

To fill end or edge grain, thin water putty to a brushing consistency. For alternative edging techniques, see page 471.

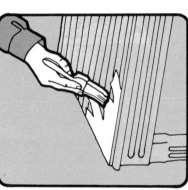

Water-mix putties work well under paint. Use them on plywood edge grain or solid wood end grain, as well as for patching.

Level the filler by dragging a piece of cardboard across the grain. When filler is nearly dry, carefully wipe with the grain.

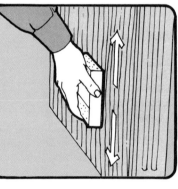

Once the filler has dried, sand it lightly with a very fine-grit abrasive paper. Be sure to sand with the grain.

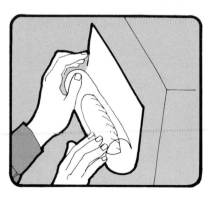

Apply pore filler by brushing it onto the surface in all directions. Work it into the grain; let it dry 10 to 15 minutes.

Tamp in wood dough and similar hole fillers with your finger, and level with a putty knife. Overfill to compensate for shrinking.

To store leftover water putty, knead it into a lump, then wrap in plastic or foil. If you don't use it within a few days, toss it.

# STAINING AND BLEACHING

If you're not satisfied with a wood's natural hue, you have a couple interesting options to pursue. One is staining; the other, bleaching. You can perform wonders with either.

Stain colors wood; bleach lightens it. Neither—except for certain varnish- or sealer-type stains—protects the surface you apply it to. For that you need a final coating of shellac, varnish, lacquer, or polyurethane.

In selecting a stain, first make sure it's compatible with whatever finish you'll be applying. Lacquer and some polyurethanes react adversely to the pigments in a few stains.

And don't let showroom samples determine your final color choice. They give only a general idea of what you'll end up with. Most dealers offer small samplers so you can make tests, as shown below. Note, too, whether the manufacturer recommends sealing the grain before or after you stain it.

Most stains dry a shade or two darker than the color you see. You control the color by the length of time you let the stain penetrate the wood. If the result is too dark, moisten a cloth with the manufacturer's recommended thinner and wipe again to dilute and wash away some of the pigment.

A few stains contain white pigment for a blond or "pickled" look, but a better way to lighten wood is to bleach it. Commercial wood bleaches call for a two-step process that usually involves an overnight wait for the chemicals to do their job.

You also can use laundry bleach or oxalic acid, but these must be neutralized after application with white vinegar or ammonia. Mix one part of either with ten parts water. And provide plenty of ventilation—bleaches and ammonia give off toxic fumes that can irritate your sinuses or eyes.

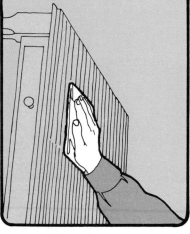

Apply stains by brushing or wiping them on in the direction of the grain. You also can spray on stain, but it's tricky.

Let the stain stand for a while, then wipe it off. The degree of darkness depends somewhat on how long you wait before wiping.

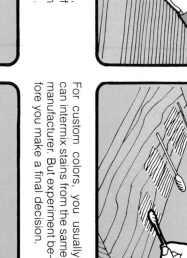

For custom colors, you usually can intermix stains from the same manufacturer. But experiment before you make a final decision.

With two-part commercial wood bleaches, start with the first solution, flowing it on freely. Or, scrub it in with steel wool.

Brush the second solution over the first after the required length of time. Then let the combination work overnight.

Neutralize the bleach as specified in the directions. Wait another 24 hours, then sand surfaces to remove the grain rise.

**533**

# CHOOSING CLEAR FINISHES

Once, the choice among natural wood top coatings could provoke hot debate among pros. Should you shellac, varnish, oil, or lacquer a particular surface? Each had its partisans and its problems.

Then the synthetics—polyurethane chiefly, but also epoxies and other plastics—arrived on the scene and settled the issue for most amateurs.

Formulated for easy brushing or spraying, polyurethane dries rapidly (a big problem with varnish), needs no rubbing or polishing (as do oils and lacquers), and makes a surface far more resistant to scratching, water, alcohol, grease, and everyday wear and tear.

In fact, the biggest dilemma with poly comes in deciding when *not* to use this versatile but relatively expensive coating. Why polyurethane a large wall, for example, when you can protect it with shellac for just a fraction of the cost?

The synthetics have a few other drawbacks, too. Most build up a thick plastic film that may not enhance a fine old piece of furniture; for a mellow, antique look, apply oil or a quality varnish. And though poly makes an excellent floor coating, you can't smoothly touch up scuffs and wear in heavy traffic areas.

The chart below summarizes the properties and characteristics of today's commonly available finishes.

## CLEAR FINISH SELECTOR

| Type | Characteristics/ Availability | Application Tips | Finish | Drying Time | Cost |
|---|---|---|---|---|---|
| Natural-resin varnish | Resists scuffs and scratches. Available in colors as well as clear. Spar varnish is recommended for outdoor use. | Best applied with a varnish brush, artist's brush, or cheesecloth pad (for furniture). Thin with recommended solvent. | Wide range— high; satin; low-gloss | 24 to 36 hours. In humid weather, let dry at least 36 hours. | Inexpensive to moderate. Some marine varnishes are expensive. |
| Polyurethane varnish | Mar resistant, durable, remains clear. | Use a natural-bristle brush with a chiseled point, roller, or spray gun. Do not apply over shellac. | Ranges from high-gloss to dull sheen | 1 to 2 hours. Let dry 12 hours between coats. | Moderate to expensive. |
| Two-part epoxy varnish | Highly resistant to scuffs and mars, making it excellent for use on floors. | Apply with brush. Check manufacturer's directions for wood filler usage. | High gloss | Let first coat dry 3 hours; let second coat dry 5 to 8 hours. | Moderate to expensive |
| Shellac | Easily damaged by water. Available clear or pigmented. Always be sure to finish a shellac-covered project with a protective coating. | Use a small brush with chiseled tips. Thin with alcohol or recommended solvent. | High gloss. Finish may be dulled by rubbing with steel wool. | About 2 hours— 30 minutes to the touch. Allow 3 to 4 hours between coats. | Inexpensive |
| Lacquer | Fast-drying. Produces a smooth finish. Used mostly for furniture. | Best sprayed. Apply many thin coats. Allow last coat to dry 48 to 60 hours, then rub smooth with very fine steel wool or hard wax. | Wide variety of finishes | Very quickly | Moderate |
| Resin oil finish | Penetrates into the wood and hardens the grain. Resists stains, scratches, burns, water, and alcohol. Easily repaired. | Usually hand-rubbed. Most often needs 2 or 3 applications. | Deep rich look | 8 to 12 hours | Moderate to expensive |

Beautiful natural-wood results can be yours with varnish, but they're by no means guaranteed. You have to make them happen. One of the most crucial steps in achieving a beautifully varnished finish is the preparation of the surface to which you plan to apply the finish.

If you're not careful, dust—varnish's mortal enemy—will collect on the newly applied finish and ruin your efforts. To keep this from happening, first shut off any forced air heating and cooling ducts in the area and begin thinking "dust free."

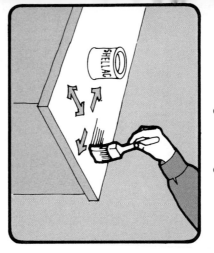

Before applying the varnish, thin it as per the instructions on the container label, using the solvent recommended by the manufacturer. Then, "float" the varnish onto the surface by first spreading it in one direction, then working across the varnish, forming a tic-tac-toe pattern. Fill in any spots you missed.

If while applying varnish you notice air bubbles on the surface of the piece, you are guilty of one of three things: shaking the can, bearing down too hard on the bristles, or wiping the brush's bristles across the rim of the can. To get rid of bubbles after they form, apply more varnish and continue to brush until you work them out.

Applying shellac isn't all that different from laying on varnish, though it generally takes more coats to complete the job. Always use a new brush when you apply a shellac finish.

Shellac is available in various cuts or thicknesses. Have your paint dealer advise you on the proper cut for the project at hand.

As a rule, you should apply from five to eight coats of shellac to a wood surface. After letting each coat dry for the time specified on the container, lightly buff the surface with very fine steel wool. Finish the job with hard paste wax, buffing the wax to a high-gloss finish. Let the wax dry 24 hours, and then wax the surface a second time, buffing it to a shine.

Apply varnish or shellac in several directions, but always finish brushing with the grain. Don't bear down on the brush.

Level the final coat of varnish or shellac with short light strokes. Using the tip of the brush results in the smoothest surface.

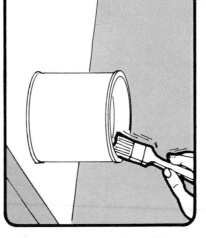

To keep bubbles to a minimum, remove excess varnish from the bristles by gently tapping them against the inside of the can.

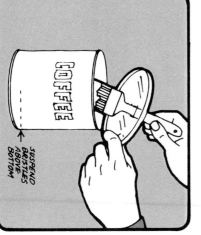

Storing brushes between coats is a breeze. Just cut a slot in the plastic lid of a coffee can and suspend the brush in thinner.

SUSPEND BRISTLES ABOVE BOTTOM

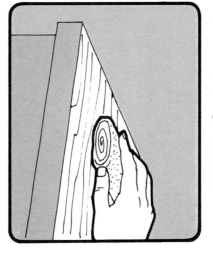

Lightly sand or steel-wool the finish between coats. Doing this roughens the surface enough to allow the next coat to adhere.

## USING POLYURETHANE VARNISH

When you apply polyurethane to a surface, you're actually sealing it in plastic—a plastic so tough that hardly anything can penetrate it. In addition to its extraordinary durability, you'll find polyurethane easy to apply, fairly fast-drying (this helps solve the dust problem), super-resistant to chemicals and water, and available in low-gloss, satin, and high-gloss finishes.

As with most other finishes, you can apply polyurethane over any sound surface after completing the preparation steps discussed in this section. If you've applied a stain or wood filler, make sure the surface is absolutely dry before applying the polyurethane.

Apply polyurethane finish with a brush, roller, or spray gun. If you spray it, you may have to thin the finish somewhat. Since there are several different manufacturers of this product, thinning and application procedures may vary somewhat. So be sure to check the manufacturer's recommendations on the container before you buy the material or start working with it.

You'll usually need two coats of polyurethane on any wood. The first coat serves as a primer and sealer; the second, as a finish coat. Sanding is desirable if dust or lint get into the wet finish. It also makes it easier to see where you've been on the following coat.

When you apply the finish—both coats—keep the work between you and a light. This way, you can see any missed spots as the finish is applied. These spots, often caused by inadequate application or penetration into the wood, leave little dimples in the finished surface, and they're almost impossible to spot-in after the material has dried.

Not all polyurethanes are clear. Some are colored to resemble pigmented shellac. With these, you'll usually need to apply several coats of the finish to reach the color tone you want. Each coat of finish will produce a deeper tone, so you should test on scrap before you use it. If you reach the color tone before achieving the sheen you want, let the surface thoroughly dry and then apply clear polyurethane finish to complete the project. The clear finish will not change the color underneath it.

If you apply the clear finish over a colored paint, for example, the first finish should be in perfect condition. Don't expect the polyurethane to hide any defects—it won't!

Note, too, that low- and satin-gloss polyurethanes cost more than high-gloss types—and are also less durable. Use these as top coats only; they'll cut the shine off high-gloss undercoatings.

As with other varnish and shellac finishes, dust and dirt control is critical with polyurethane. Work in a "still" room with no puffs of hot or cold air from heating and cooling ducts. And don't do anything that will cause dust to become airborne—especially sweeping the floor just before the finish is applied. Instead, use a tack cloth to remove dust from the work.

## USING LACQUER

Lacquer is the kind of finish that has lots of advantages and disadvantages, and the decision to use it or not boils down to playing the pluses against the minuses.

First, the advantages. Lacquer produces a very smooth, quality finish. It dries super-fast, making it a dust-dodger to some extent. And after it dries, you can rub away dust and brush marks from its surface. It's also inexpensive and available in clear and a variety of colors.

Lacquer's drying time also is one of its disadvantages, however. It dries so quickly that you must correct mistakes fast. Lacquer may sag and run (many thin coats with a spray gun are best).

Lastly, you can't apply lacquer over any painted finish. The lacquer's solvent will lift off a paint finish underneath it. If, when applying lacquer, you spot a sag or run, let it dry, then remove the defect using wet or dry sandpaper. Or wipe the run or sag immediately with lacquer thinner on a soft, lint-free cloth. Go over the problem area right down to the bare wood or metal. Then spot-fill and continue on with the work. The blemish will show after the lacquer has dried, but it won't be noticeable after the surface has been properly rubbed with steel wool or rubbing compound and wax.

Prepare the surface as you would for any other clear wood finish (see pages 528-533).

Generally, for lacquer to look and perform its best, you'll need to apply at least three coats. But, unlike most other clear finishes, you don't have to sand or steel-wool the surface between coats, since the material sort of "dissolves" and blends into the preceding coats. Work quickly; lacquer dries rapidly and nozzles clog and dry if they aren't kept wet.

After the lacquer has dried for 48 to 60 hours, finish the surface by rubbing it with very-fine steel wool and hard wax. Or buy a lacquer rubbing compound.

As you apply the wax or rubbing compound, work in a small area. Complete rubbing out this area before you move on. Otherwise, the compound will dry and be hard to remove.

That deep, rich patina you see on old gunstocks and some antique furniture probably consists of nothing more than boiled linseed oil and turpentine—coat upon coat, laboriously rubbed into the wood's grain.

You can do the same yourself. Just combine two parts of the oil with one part turpentine, pour it on, rub off the excess, and let dry completely. Then repeat and repeat and repeat . . . until you've totally saturated the grain—a process that may take six to ten applications and dozens of hours of tiresome rubbing.

But achieving this lustrous effect needn't be that difficult. Using a commercial *resin-oil finish* will ease the workload considerably. Like ordinary oil, these penetrate into the wood for a surface that's more than skin deep. But they also include a synthetic or natural resin that hardens inside the grain. The result: a finish that actually toughens the wood, yet doesn't call for nearly as much rubbing.

Usually you need only two or three applications of resin oil to get a deep, lasting finish. Unlike linseed oil, it dries overnight, doesn't gum up in warm temperatures, and rarely needs to be renewed. Yet it's just as resistant to stains, scratches, minor burns, water,

and alcohol—and if damage does occur, you can just rub it out with sandpaper or steel wool and apply more penetrating oil. Unlike polyurethane, oil lends itself to spot repairs.

Penetrating resin oils vary somewhat. Some include varnish, others plastics, and still others are combined with wax. A few also come in different weights to suit open- or closed-pore woods, and you can tint most of them for staining effects.

Read the manufacturer's instructions before applying a resin oil. Most go on with the easy steps illustrated in the drawings below.

Flood the surface with oil, then spread it with a brush, making sure to cover all surfaces. The first coat will soak in quickly.

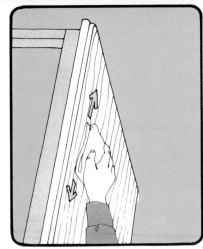

Apply each subsequent coat with the grain, rubbing hard. Let the surface dry for 24 to 48 hours between coats.

Wait a few minutes, then test the surface. If it feels dry, apply more oil. Wait a few minutes and wipe off the excess.

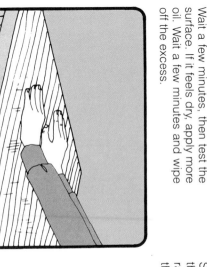

Apply the final coat with the palms of your hands; your hands supply the needed heat. If desired, finish with hard wax.

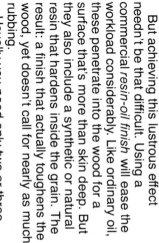

Sand the surface lightly before the second coat to remove the raised grain from the wood. After this, don't sand the work again.

CLEAR-FINISHING WOOD

# MAKING SENSE OF METRICS

When the United States and Canada replace the customary feet, pounds, and gallons with the meters, kilograms, and liters used by all other industrialized countries, most of us will need to learn how to measure in two different languages.

Perhaps you've already discovered how easy it is to change from one metric unit to another or to compare prices of metrically sized articles.

Unfortunately, however, converting from customary to metric measurements—or vice versa—calls for the kind of math best done on a pocket calculator. The table below gives the equivalents you'll need to know to make the various conversions.

Don't let the "new terminology" bother you. Just remember that the metric system is based on the number 10 and all of the strange-sounding prefixes merely tell you how much of a particular measurement you're dealing with. For example, milli- means 1/1,000, centi-, 1/100, and kilo-, 1,000.

## U.S. UNITS TO METRIC EQUIVALENTS

| | To Convert From | Multiply By | To Get |
|---|---|---|---|
| **LENGTH** | Inches | 25.4 | Millimeters (mm) |
| | Inches | 2.54 | Centimeters (cm) |
| | Feet | 30.48 | Centimeters (cm) |
| | Feet | 0.3048 | Meters (m) |
| | Yards | 0.9144 | Meters (m) |
| | Miles | 1.6093 | Kilometers (km) |
| **AREA** | Square inches | 6.4516 | Square centimeters (sq cm) |
| | Square feet | 0.0929 | Square meters (sq m) |
| | Square yards | 0.8361 | Square meters (sq m) |
| | Acres | 0.4047 | Hectares (ha) |
| | Square miles | 2.5899 | Square kilometers (sq km) |
| **VOLUME** | Cubic inches | 16.387 | Cubic centimeters (cu cm) |
| | Cubic feet | 0.0283 | Cubic meters (cu m) |
| | Cubic feet | 28.316 | Liters (l) |
| | Cubic yards | 0.7646 | Cubic meters (cu m) |
| | Cubic yards | 764.55 | Liters (l) |
| **LIQUID MEASURE** | Fluid ounces | 29.574 | Milliliters (ml) |
| | Cups | 0.2366 | Liters (l) |
| | Pints | 0.4732 | Liters (l) |
| | Quarts | 0.9464 | Liters (l) |
| | Gallons | 3.7854 | Liters (l) |
| **DRY MEASURE** | Pints | 0.5506 | Liters (l) |
| | Quarts | 1.1012 | Liters (l) |
| | Pecks | 8.8098 | Liters (l) |
| | Bushels | 35.239 | Liters (l) |
| | Bushels | 3.5239 | Dekaliters (dkl) |
| **WEIGHT** | Drams | 1.7718 | Grams (g) |
| | Ounces | 28.350 | Grams (g) |
| | Pounds | 0.4536 | Kilograms (kg) |

To convert from degrees Fahrenheit (F.) to degrees Celsius (C), first subtract 32, then multiply by 5/9.

## METRIC UNITS TO U.S. EQUIVALENTS

| | To Convert From | Multiply By | To Get |
|---|---|---|---|
| **LENGTH** | Millimeters | 0.0394 | Inches |
| | Centimeters | 0.3937 | Inches |
| | Centimeters | 0.0328 | Feet |
| | Meters | 3.2808 | Feet |
| | Meters | 1.0936 | Yards |
| | Kilometers | 0.6214 | Miles |
| **AREA** | Square centimeters | 0.1550 | Square inches |
| | Square meters | 10.764 | Square feet |
| | Square meters | 1.1960 | Square yards |
| | Hectares | 2.4711 | Acres |
| | Square kilometers | 0.3861 | Square miles |
| **VOLUME** | Cubic centimeters (or milliliters) | 0.0610 | Cubic inches |
| | Cubic meters | 35.315 | Cubic feet |
| | Liters | 0.0353 | Cubic feet |
| | Cubic meters | 1.3080 | Cubic yards |
| | Liters | 0.0013 | Cubic yards |
| **LIQUID MEASURE** | Milliliters | 0.0338 | Fluid ounces |
| | Liters | 4.2268 | Cups |
| | Liters | 2.1134 | Pints |
| | Liters | 1.0567 | Quarts |
| | Liters | 0.2642 | Gallons |
| **DRY MEASURE** | Liters | 1.8162 | Pints |
| | Liters | 0.9081 | Quarts |
| | Liters | 0.1135 | Pecks |
| | Liters | 0.0284 | Bushels |
| | Dekaliters | 0.2838 | Bushels |
| **WEIGHT** | Grams | 0.5644 | Drams |
| | Grams | 0.0353 | Ounces |
| | Kilograms | 2.2046 | Pounds |

To convert from degrees Celsius to degrees Fahrenheit, multiply by 9/5, then add 32.

*Here are definitions of some important words you may not be familiar with. For words not included here—or for more about those that are—consult the Index beginning on page 543.*

**Amp** (A). A measure of the amount of electrical current going through a circuit at any given time. Also see *volt* and *watt*.

**Back-up system.** Auxiliary heating equipment that kicks in when the main unit—usually a heat pump or solar setup—can't handle the full load.

**Balancing.** Fine-tuning the air flow of a heating/cooling system to even up the delivery through a home.

**Balusters.** Spindles that help support a staircase handrail.

**Bat.** A half-brick.

**Batt.** A section of fiber-glass or rock-wool insulation measuring 15 or 23 inches wide by four to eight feet long.

**Batten.** A narrow strip used to cover joints between boards or panels.

**Beam.** A horizontal support member. Also see *post and post-and-beam*.

**Bearing wall.** An interior or exterior wall that helps support the roof or the floor joists above.

**Blankets.** Fiber-glass or rock-wool insulation that comes in long rolls 15 or 23 inches wide.

**Bond.** The pattern in which bricks or other masonry units are laid. Also, the cementing action of an adhesive.

**BTU** (British thermal unit). The amount of heat needed to raise one pound of water one degree Fahrenheit. Heating and cooling equipment commonly is rated by the BTUs it can deliver or absorb. Also see *heat gain* and *heat loss*.

**Building codes.** Community ordinances governing the manner in which a home may be constructed or modified. Most codes primarily concern themselves with fire and health, with separate sections relating to electrical, plumbing, and structural work. Also see *zoning*.

**Butt.** To place materials end-to-end or end-to-edge without overlapping.

**Butt hinge.** The most common type. One leaf attaches to the door's edge, the other to its *jamb*.

**Cantilever.** A beam or beams projecting beyond a support member.

**Casing.** Trimwork around a door, window, or other opening.

**Caulk.** Any of a variety of different compounds used to seal seams and joints against infiltration of water and air.

**Cement.** A powder that serves as the binding element in concrete and mortar. Also, any adhesive.

**CFM** (cubic feet per minute). A rating that expresses the amount of air a blower or fan can move.

**Chalking.** The tendency of some exterior paints to gradually erode away over a period of time.

**Circuit breaker.** A protective switch that automatically shuts off current in the event of a short or overload. Also see *fuse, short circuit*.

**Compressor.** The part of a cooling unit or heat pump that compresses refrigerant gas so it can absorb heat.

**Concrete.** A basic building and paving material made by mixing water with sand, gravel, and cement. Also see *mortar and cement*.

**Condensing unit.** The outdoor segment of a cooling system. It includes a *compressor* and *condensing coil* designed to give off heat. Also see *evaporator coil*.

**Continuous air circulation.** Setting the blower unit in a heating/cooling system so that air moves constantly throughout the house, regardless of whether or not the burners or cooling unit are operating.

**Convection.** Currents created by heating air, which then rises and pulls cooler air behind it. Also see *radiation*.

**COP** (coefficient of performance). A measure of the efficiency of any heating unit—arrived at by dividing its output in BTUs by its input in BTUs.

**Coping.** A cap at the top of a wall that's rounded or beveled to shed water. Also, a curved cut made so that one contoured molding can join neatly with another.

**Corner bead.** Lightweight, perforated metal angle used to reinforce outside corners in drywall construction.

**Courses.** Parallel layers of building materials such as bricks, shingles, or siding laid up horizontally.

**Cove.** A concave curve where vertical and horizontal surfaces join.

**Cripples.** Short studs above or below a door or window opening.

**Crown.** Paving slightly humped so that water will run off. Also a contoured molding sometimes installed at the junctures of walls and ceilings.

**Cupping.** A type of *warping* that causes boards to curl up at their edges.

**Damper.** A valve inside a duct or flue that can be used to slow or stop the flow of air or smoke.

**Dead bolt.** A locking device that can be activated only with a key or thumb turn. Unlike a *latch*, which has a beveled tongue, dead bolts have square ends.

**Double cylinder.** A type of lock that must be operated with a key from inside as well as outside.

*continued*

**Dry wall.** A masonry wall laid up without mortar.

**Drywall.** A basic interior building material consisting of big sheets of pressed gypsum faced with heavy paper on both sides. Also known as *gypsum board*, *plasterboard*, and *Sheetrock* (a trade name).

**DWV** (drain-waste-vent). The section of a plumbing system that carries water and sewer gases out of a home.

**EER** (energy efficiency ratio). A measure of cooling efficiency computed by dividing a cooling unit's output in BTUs by its input in watts.

**Efflorescence.** A whitish powder sometimes exuded by the mortar joints in masonry work. It's caused by salts rising to the surface.

**Elbow** (ell). A plumbing or electrical fitting that lets you change directions in runs of pipe or conduit.

**Evaporator coil.** The part of a cooling system that absorbs heat from air in your home. Also see *condensing unit*.

**Expansion joint.** Flexible material between two surfaces that enables joints to ride out differing rates of expansion and contraction.

**Fascia board.** Horizontal trim attached to the outside ends of rafters or to the top of an exterior wall.

**Female.** Any part, such as a nut or fitting, into which another (male) part can be inserted. Internal threads are female.

**Fire blocking.** Short horizontal members sometimes nailed between studs, usually about halfway up a wall.

**Firebrick.** Highly heat-resistant brick for lining fireplaces and boilers.

**Flashing.** Metal or composition strips used to seal junctions between roofing and other surfaces, or in the valleys between different slopes.

**Floating.** The next-to-last stage in concrete work, when you smooth off the job and bring water to the surface.

**Flue.** A pipe or other channel that carries off smoke and combustion gases to the outside air.

**Fluorescent lamp.** A light source that, instead of "burning," as incandescent bulbs do, uses an ionization process to produce ultraviolet radiation. This turns into visible light when it hits a coating on the tube's inner surface.

**Footing.** The base on which a masonry wall rests. It spreads out the load.

**Frost line.** The depth to which the ground freezes below the surface. This varies from region to region, and determines how deep *footings* must be.

**Furring.** Lightweight wood or metal strips that even up a wall or ceiling for paneling or drywall. On masonry, furring provides a surface on which to nail.

**Fuse.** A safety device designed to burn out if a circuit shorts or overloads. This protects against fire. Also see *circuit breaker*, *short circuit*.

**Gate valve.** A valve that lets you completely stop—but not modulate—the flow within a pipe. Also see *globe valve*.

**GFCI** (ground fault circuit interrupter). An electrical safety device that instantly shuts down a circuit if a leakage occurs. Codes commonly require them on bathroom and outdoor circuits.

**Glazing.** The process of installing glass, which commonly is secured with *glazier's points* and *glazing compound*.

**Globe valve.** A valve that lets you adjust the flow of water to any rate between fully on and fully off. Also see *gate valve*.

**Grade.** Ground level, or the elevation at any given point.

**Grain.** The direction of fibers in lumber or other materials.

**Ground.** Refers to electricity's habit of seeking the shortest route to earth. Neutral wires carry it there in all circuits. An additional grounding wire—or the sheathing of metal-clad cable or conduit—protects against shock if the neutral leg is interrupted.

**Grout.** Thin mortar that fills the joints between tiles or other masonry.

**Gypsum board.** See *drywall*.

**Hardboard.** A manufactured building material made by pressing wood fibers into sheet goods.

**Header.** Heavier framing—usually doubled and laid on edge—at the top of a window, door, or other opening. In masonry, a *header course* of bricks or stones laid on edge provides strength.

**Heat gain.** Heat coming into a home from sources other than its heating/cooling system. Most gains come from the sun.

**Heat loss.** Heat escaping from a home, usually to outside air. Heat gains and losses are expressed in BTUs per hour.

**Heat pump.** A reversible air conditioner that can extract heat from outside as well as inside air.

**HID** (high intensity discharge) **lamp.** A lamp that operates in the same way as a fluorescent tube, but that has a bulb like incandescent lamps.

**Hot wire.** The wire that carries electrical energy *to* a receptacle or other device—in contrast to a *neutral*, which carries electricity away again. Also see *ground*.

**Incandescent lamp.** A lamp employing an electrically charged metal filament that glows at white heat.

**Inside corner.** The point at which two walls form an internal angle, as in the corner of a room.

**Jambs.** The top and sides of a door, window, or other opening. Includes studs as well as the frame and trim.

**Joint compound.** A synthetic-based formula used in combination with paper tape to conceal joints between drywall panels. Also see *taping.*

**Joists.** Horizontal framing members that support a floor and/or ceiling.

**Kilowatt** (kw). One thousand watts. A *kilowatt hour* is the base unit used in measuring electrical consumption. Also see *watts.*

**Latch.** A beveled metal tongue operated by a spring-loaded knob or lever. The tongue's bevel lets you close the door and engage the locking mechanism, if any, without using a key. Contrasts with *dead bolt.*

**Laminating.** Bonding together two or more layers of materials.

**Lath.** Strips of wood, expanded metal mesh, or a special drywall that serve as a base for plaster or stucco.

**Level.** True horizontal. Also a tool used to determine level.

**Limit switch.** A safety control that automatically shuts off a furnace if it gets too hot. Most also control blower cycles.

**Lintel.** A load-bearing beam over an opening in masonry, such as a door or fireplace.

**Male.** Any part, such as a bolt, designed to fit into another (female) part. External threads are male.

**Miter.** A joint formed by beveling the edges or ends of two pieces at 45-degree angles, then fitting them together to make a 90-degree angle.

**Mortar.** The bonding agent between bricks, blocks, or other masonry units. Consists of water, sand, and cement —but not gravel. Also see *concrete.*

**Mortise.** A hole, slot, groove, or other recess into which another element fits. Most hinges, for example, are mortised so they lie flush.

**NEC** (National Electrical Code). A set of rules governing safe wiring methods. Local codes—which are backed by law—may differ from the NEC in some ways.

**Neutral wire.** Usually color-coded white, this carries electricity *from* an outlet back to ground. Also see *hot wire* and *ground.*

**Newel post.** A post at the bottom, landing, or top of a staircase to which the handrail is secured.

**No-hub.** A clamp-and-sleeve system for joining together cast-iron drainage pipes. Older hub-type pipes had to be leaded at all joints.

**OC** (on-center). The distance from the center of one regularly spaced framing member to the next. Studs and joists are commonly 16 or 24 inches OC.

**Outside corner.** The point at which two walls form an external angle, one you usually can walk around.

**Panel.** Wood, glass, plastic, or other material set into a frame, such as in a door. Also, a large, flat, rectangular building material such as plywood, hardboard, or drywall.

**Partition.** An interior dividing wall. Partitions may or may not be *bearing.*

**Paving.** Materials—commonly masonry—laid down to make a firm, even surface.

**Payback.** The length of time before the money you save with new equipment, insulation, etc. will equal your original investment. Commonly used in evaluating energy-related items.

**Pier.** A masonry post. Piers often serve as *footings* for wood or steel posts.

**Pilot hole.** A small-diameter hole that guides a nail or screw.

**Pilot light.** A small, continuous flame that ignites gas or oil burners when needed.

**Plenum.** The main hot-air supply duct leading from a furnace.

**Plumb.** True vertical. Also see *level.*

**Plywood.** A building panel made by gluing together thin layers of wood. Alternating grain directions from one layer to the next adds strength.

**Post.** Any vertical support member.

**Post-and-beam.** A basic building method that uses just a few hefty *posts* and *beams* to support an entire structure. Contrasts with *stud framing.*

**Pressure-treated wood.** Lumber that has been saturated with a preservative.

**Primer.** A first coating formulated to seal raw surfaces and hold succeeding finish coats.

**PVC** (polyvinyl chloride). A type of plastic pipe that's suitable for cold water, but not hot.

**Radiation.** Energy transmitted from a heat source to the air around it. So-called "radiators" actually depend more on *convection* than radiation.

**Rafters.** Parallel framing members that support a roof.

**Rail.** Any relatively lightweight horizontal element, especially those found in fences. Also the horizontal pieces between panels in a panel door.

**Retaining wall.** A structure that holds back a slope and prevents erosion.

**Ridgeboard.** The topmost beam at the peak of a roof to which rafters tie.

**Rise.** The vertical distance from one point to another above it; a measurement you need in planning a stairway or ramp. Also see *run.*

**Riser.** The upright piece between two stairsteps. Also see *tread.*

*continued*

**Roofing cement.** A pliable asphalt- or plastic-based compound used as an adhesive and to seal flashings, minor leaks, etc.

**Roughing-in.** The initial stage of a plumbing, electrical, carpentry, or other project, when all components that won't be seen after the second *finishing* phase are assembled.

**Run.** The horizontal distance a ramp or stairway traverses. Also see *rise*.

**R-value.** A measure of the resistance an insulating material offers to heat transfer. The higher the R-value, the more effective the insulation.

**Saddle.** The plate at the bottom of some—usually exterior—door openings. Sometimes called a *threshold*.

**Sash.** The openable part of a window, consisting of a frame and one or more panes of glass.

**Setback.** The distance a home must be built from property lines (this is dictated by local zoning ordinances). Also a temporary change in a thermostat's setting.

**Settlement.** Shifts in a structure, usually caused by freeze-thaw cycles underground.

**Sheathing.** The first covering on a roof or exterior wall, usually fastened directly to rafters or studs.

**Shim.** Thin material inserted to make adjustments in level or plumb. Tapered wood shingles make excellent shims in carpentry work.

**Shoe molding.** Strips of quarter round commonly used where a baseboard meets the floor. Also sometimes known as *base shoe*.

**Short circuit.** A situation that occurs when hot and neutral wires come in contact with each other. *Fuses* and *circuit breakers* protect against fire that could result from a short.

**Sill.** The lowest horizontal piece of a window, door, or wall framework.

**Sleepers.** Boards laid directly over a masonry floor to serve as nailers for plywood, or strip or plank flooring.

**Soffit.** Covering attached to the underside of eaves or a staircase.

**Soil pipe.** A large pipe that carries liquid and solid wastes to a sewer or septic tank.

**Sole plate.** The bottommost horizontal part of a stud partition. When a plate rests on a foundation, it's called a *sill plate*.

**Square.** A situation that exists when two elements are at right angles to each other. Also a tool for checking this.

**Stile.** The vertical upright on either side (and sometimes the center) of a panel door.

**Stops.** Moldings along the inner edges of a door or window frame. Also valves used to shut off water to a fixture.

**Strike.** The plate on a door frame that engages a *latch* or *dead bolt*.

**Stud framing.** A building method that distributes structural loads to each of a series of relatively lightweight studs. Contrasts with *post-and-beam*.

**Studs.** Vertical 2x3, 2x4, or 2x6 framing members spaced at regular intervals within a wall.

**Taping.** The process of covering drywall joints with paper tape and *joint compound*.

**Tee.** A T-shaped plumbing fitting.

**Three-four-five triangle.** An easy, mathematical way to check whether a large angle is square. Measure three feet along one side, four feet along the other; if the corner is square, the diagonal distance between those two points will equal five feet.

**Threshold.** See *saddle*.

**Throat.** The opening at the top of a fireplace through which smoke passes enroute to the flue.

**Ton.** A measure of cooling power. One ton equals 12,000 BTUs.

**Top plate.** The topmost horizontal element of a stud-frame wall.

**Trap.** A plumbing fitting that holds water to prevent air, gas, and vermin from backing up into a fixture.

**Treads.** The level parts of a staircase. Also see *risers*.

**Trimmers.** Studs at either side of a door, window, or other opening that are used to support the *header*.

**UL** (Underwriters' Laboratories). An independent testing agency that checks electrical and other components for possible safety hazards.

**Union.** A plumbing fitting that joins pipes end-to-end so they can be dismantled.

**Valley.** The intersection of two roof slopes.

**Vapor barrier.** A waterproof membrane in a floor, wall, or ceiling that blocks the transfer of condensation.

**Volt** (V). A measure of electrical pressure. Volts × amps = watts.

**Warping.** Any distortion in a material.

**Watt** (W). A measure of the power an electrical device consumes. *Watt hours* (WH) express the quantity of energy consumed. Also see *volt*, *amp*, and *kilowatt*.

**Y** (wye). A Y-shaped plumbing fitting.

**Zoning.** Ordinances regulating the ways in which a property may be used in any given neighborhood. Zoning laws may limit where you can locate a structure. Also see *building codes*.

# HUNDREDS OF OTHER IDEAS YOU'LL ENJOY

## ALL FROM BETTER HOMES AND GARDENS®

Here are more than a dozen other books from Better Homes and Gardens® containing hundreds of bright ideas.

## PROJECTS YOU CAN BUILD SERIES

Imagine the thrill of standing back and admiring something that looks as if it were custom built by a professional...

only you made it yourself, from start to finish! Armed with some basic tools and these project books, you can give your home a whole new look. Here are projects for the family room, the bath and bedroom, the kitchen, and the yard to help you create practical furniture, space-saving storage ideas, and ways to save energy. Each colorful, hard-cover book is filled with problem-solving home-improvement projects you can build, complete with materials lists and detailed instructions.

## YOU CAN GROW SERIES

Transform your home with armfuls of cut flowers... that didn't come from a flower shop. Cram your freezer with just-picked vegetables that never saw a store. Stroll through the scented air of a garden heavy with fragrance and alive with vibrant color. These six 96-page hard-cover "You Can Grow" books bring it all within reach of almost everyone. Choose from *Annuals, Perennials, Vegetables &*

*Herbs, Easiest Plants, Container Plants,* and those all-time favorites, *Roses.*

## COMPLETE GUIDE TO GARDENING

You'd have to be a professional gardener before you'd want something more comprehensive than this big, 552-page hard-cover book. In it you'll learn how to deal with the problems that beset beginner and expert gardeners alike, such as how to win against weeds and pests; how to feed, prune, and propagate; and when to plant and pic. You won't find a collection of more useful facts, tips, and ideas than those contained in this book's 16 chapters, 550 drawings, 520 color photos, and many comparison charts. The *Complete Guide to Gardening* is for everyone who wants the thrill of a successful garden.

These and half-a-hundred other Better Homes and Gardens® titles are available wherever books are sold.